"Value-packed, comprehensive...

"Unbeatable..."

—The Washington Post

Let's Go
GERMANY & SWITZERLAND

is the best book for anyone traveling on a budget. Here's why:

■ No other guidebook has as many budget listings.

Take Munich, for example. We list 15 places to stay for under $25. We tell you how to get there the cheapest way, whether by bus, plane, or bike, and where to get an inexpensive and satisfying meal once you've arrived. We give hundreds of money-saving tips that anyone can use, plus invaluable advice on discounts and deals for students, children, families, and senior travelers.

■ Let's Go researchers have to make it on their own.

Our Harvard-Radcliffe researcher-writers travel on budgets as tight as your own—no expense accounts, no free hotel rooms.

■ Let's Go is completely revised each year.

We don't just update the prices, we go back to the place. If a charming café has become an overpriced tourist trap, we'll replace the listing with a new and better one.

■ No other guidebook includes all this:

Honest, engaging coverage of both the cities and the countryside; up-to-the-minute prices, directions, addresses, phone numbers, and opening hours; in-depth essays on local culture, history, and politics; comprehensive listings on transportation between and within regions and cities; straight advice on work and study, budget accommodations, sights, nightlife, and food; detailed city and regional maps; and much more.

■ Let's Go is for anyone who wants to see Germany and Switzerland on a budget.

Books by Let's Go, Inc.

EUROPE

Let's Go: *Europe*

Let's Go: *Austria*

Let's Go: *Britain & Ireland*

Let's Go: *France*

Let's Go: *Germany & Switzerland*

Let's Go: *Greece & Turkey*

Let's Go: *Ireland*

Let's Go: *Italy*

Let's Go: *London*

Let's Go: *Paris*

Let's Go: *Rome*

Let's Go: *Spain & Portugal*

NORTH & CENTRAL AMERICA

Let's Go: *USA & Canada*

Let's Go: *Alaska & The Pacific Northwest*

Let's Go: *California & Hawaii*

Let's Go: *New York City*

Let's Go: *Washington, D.C.*

Let's Go: *Mexico*

MIDDLE EAST & ASIA

Let's Go: *Israel & Egypt*

Let's Go: *Thailand*

Let's Go

The Budget Guide to

GERMANY & SWITZERLAND
1994

Amy Sarah Davidson
Editor

Miriam Naomi Schultz
Assistant Editor

Written by
Let's Go, Inc.
A subsidiary of
Harvard Student Agencies, Inc.

M
Macmillan Reference

HELPING LET'S GO

If you have suggestions or corrections, or just want to share your discoveries, drop us a line. We read every piece of correspondence, whether a 10-page letter, a velveteen Elvis postcard, or, as in one case, a collage. All suggestions are passed along to our researcher-writers. Please note that mail received after May 5, 1994 will probably be too late for the 1995 book, but will be retained for the following edition. Address mail to:

> **Let's Go: Germany & Switzerland**
> **Let's Go, Inc.**
> **1 Story Street**
> **Cambridge, MA 02138**
> **USA**

In addition to the invaluable travel advice our readers share with us, many are kind enough to offer their services as researchers or editors. Unfortunately, the charter of Let's Go, Inc. and Harvard Student Agencies, Inc. enables us to employ only currently enrolled Harvard students.

Published in Great Britain 1994 by Pan Macmillan Ltd., Cavaye Place, London SW10 9PG.

10 9 8 7 6 5 4 3 2 1

Maps by David Lindroth, copyright © 1994, 1993, 1992 by St. Martin's Press, Inc.

Published in the United States of America by St. Martin's Press, Inc.

ISBN: 0333-61156-X

Let's Go: Germany & Switzerland is written by the Publishing Division of Let's Go, Inc., 1 Story Street, Cambridge, MA 02138.

Let's Go® is a registered trademark of Let's Go, Inc.
Printed in the U.S.A. on recycled paper with biodegradable soy ink.

Acknowledgments

From Germany, **Tanya Bezreh** did more than write, research and explore. She saved our sanity with her wit, resilience, and powerful aesthetic sense. All that we could wish for her, and for us, is that she keeps on writing and drawing. **Declan Fox** was ready for Hamburg and Berlin, wove his own cosmopolitan spirit into fine prose, and took on Lower Saxony and Schleswig-Holstein with a sense of adventure. **Christopher Capozzola** brought with him a wealth of experience in the world of the travel guide, and deployed it effectively. Then he came back and helped us proofread. **Beate Krieger** has all of our admiration for her professionalism, her sensitivity, and her understanding of the new Germany. She earned our trust, as well as our gratitude. Someday, **Moses Hohman** will make a brilliant absent minded professor. He was a fine researcher as well, with flashes of wit that almost dizzied us. On her own in Switzerland, the lovely **Karin Braverman** sent us meticulous copy and the prettiest picture postcards. She faced landscapes ranging from sun-drenched vineyards to Alpine towns, with an unflappable sense of style. Austria researcher **Sucharita Mulpuru's** foray across the border yielded high-quality copy.

In the office, Peter Keith manage edited every word of the book you now hold in your hands, while dealing with his AE and editors' foul moods. Where'd he get that funk from? Publishing director Mark Templeton was always approachable and willing to listen. Thanks to Ed Owen, who answered unanswerable questions, and Sue Krause, who was kind, all-knowing, and made Amy happy by driving to Walden pond. Justin and Marc shared our windowless office corner; we offered them Munich, but they inexplicably turned us down. The UGH men made this office a better place by unleashing their humor upon us unrelentlessly. Thanks to Liz Stein and Sujatha Baliga, our Eurofriends, for their interest and responsiveness. We always turned to Adina Astor not because her desk was right outside our office, but because of her sense of humor and her solid judgement. We were worried about finishing the book until Jane Yeh arrived. Thank you Mark G. and Anna just for representing a sunny Mediterranean country and not rubbing it in, Mike for churning out prose at a moment's notice and Peter for bringing wisdom from the Oberland. Natasha, Dan S., Lynne and other late nighters. Eve, Maia, Ben P. and our hero Dov helped us out in the final hours, and may all good things come to them. Thanks go to all of our favorite travel officials, here and abroad, for their kindness to us and to our researchers: Christa Willibad, Hilde Brenner-Khan, and Hedy Wuerz, all at the GNTO in NYC and Erika Lieben at the SNTO; their 13-page faxes and quick responses and saved us. Elizabeth Derbes and Geoff Rodkey, '93 editors, left us a fine inheritance.

A.S.D. thanks: Eliza, who is pretty much perfect; Miranda, whose absence I felt deeply this summer; Alexandra, a witty and constant companion; Rebecca Spang and JennyD., true friends. This was a good job because I came to know and adore Natasha, Tracey, and Mira. JT, who is shockingly wonderful; Peter L., who made my head spin. BenW. listened to all my whining, and Mike told me stories. Helgard, Katerina and Inge helped me see Germany. To my childhood friends Blake, Ben D., Kevin, and my sister Laurie, none of whom I see often enough. Also to my roommates this spring and summer. Above all to Mimi, with much affection, for her spirit and sharp sense of irony.

M.N.S. thanks the women: JT, I told you you'd be here. You were a phone call away all summer and it made all the difference. To Al & Z, my cohorts in collegiate decadence—so often this year you've both been physically absent, but you're always *there* and that's what's important to me. I thank and admire Samantha-you-floated-into-my-life-Harvey for her strength of body and mind. Purple Jen, you're my favorite girl group. Thanks to Greg for his lines from Nice & Florence, the other Mimi for her jet-setting and faxing, Ben-if-you-will-waterpark-it-is-no-dream Wizner, and my new friends Alexis, Dov, Ben P., Andrew, and Alexandra (sights!), who kept me sane. Amy D., after a long summer, I feel like I finally know you. And I like it. Many thanks, always, to my parents, who know more than anyone what a summer it's been, and to Tucson, the Tasty, and Fresh Brother Michael who wants to stay young forever.

About Let's Go

Back in 1960, a few students at Harvard got together to produce a 20-page pamphlet offering a collection of tips on budget travel in Europe. For three years, Harvard Student Agencies, a student-run nonprofit corporation, had been doing a brisk business booking charter flights to Europe; this modest, mimeographed packet was offered to passengers as an extra. The following year, students traveling to Europe researched the first full-fledged edition of *Let's Go: Europe*, a pocket-sized book featuring advice on shoestring travel, irreverent write-ups of sights, and a decidedly youthful slant.

Throughout the 60s, the guides reflected the times: one section of the 1968 *Let's Go: Europe* talked about "Street Singing in Europe on No Dollars a Day." During the 70s, *Let's Go* gradually became a large-scale operation, adding regional European guides and expanding coverage into North Africa and Asia. The 80s saw the arrival of *Let's Go: USA & Canada* and *Let's Go: Mexico*, as well as regional North American guides; in the 90s we introduced five in-depth city guides to Paris, London, Rome, New York, and Washington, DC.

This year we're proud to announce three new guides: *Let's Go: Austria* (including Prague and Budapest), *Let's Go: Ireland*, and *Let's Go: Thailand* (including Honolulu, Tokyo, and Singapore), bringing our total number of titles up to twenty.

We've seen a lot in thirty-four years. *Let's Go: Europe* is now the world's #1 best selling international guide, translated into seven languages. And our guides are still researched, written, and produced entirely by students who know first-hand how to see the world on the cheap.

Every spring, we recruit nearly 100 researchers and an editorial team of 50 to write our books anew. Come summertime, after several months of training, researchers hit the road for seven weeks of exploration, from Bangkok to Budapest, Anchorage to Ankara. With pen and notebook in hand, a few changes of underwear stuffed in our backpacks, and a budget as tight as yours, we visit every *pensione*, *palapa*, pizzeria, café, club, campground, or castle we can find to make sure you'll get the most out of *your* trip.

We've put the best of our discoveries into the book you're now holding. A brand-new edition of each guide hits the shelves every year, only months after it was researched, so you know you're getting the most reliable, up-to-date, and comprehensive information available. And even as you read this, work on next year's editions is well underway.

At *Let's Go*, we think of budget travel not only as a means of cutting down on costs, but as a way of breaking down a few walls as well. Living cheap and simple on the road brings you closer to the real people and places you've been saving up to visit. This book will ease your anxieties and answer your questions about the basics—to help *you* get off the beaten track and explore. We encourage you to put *Let's Go* away now and then and strike out on your own. As any seasoned traveler will tell you, the best discoveries are often those you make yourself. If you find something worth sharing, drop us a line and let us know. We're at Let's Go, Inc., 1 Story Street, Cambridge, MA, 02138, USA.

Happy travels!

WITH OUR RAIL PASSES YOU'LL HAVE UP TO 70% MORE MONEY TO WASTE.

With savings of up to 70% off the price of point-to-point tickets, you'll be laughing all the way to the souvenir stand. Rail passes are available for travel throughout Germany, Austria, Switzerland or the country of your choice—we can also book air travel, rental cars, and hotel reservations. So all you'll have to do is leave some extra room in your suitcase. For more information just call **1-800-4-EURAIL**.

Contents

Good cheese doesn't have to be expensive.

In fact, our price for a few servings is a real steal, considering:

You also get a round-trip ticket from the U.S. to Zurich.

You'll enjoy Swiss service (no small consideration) and our brand new fleet of jets.

Prefer business class? Our "Relax Class" costs less than many airlines coach seats. And that should help you relax too.

For more information call us at: 1-800-322-5247

The leisure line of Swissair. **balair** ✚ **cta**

Maps

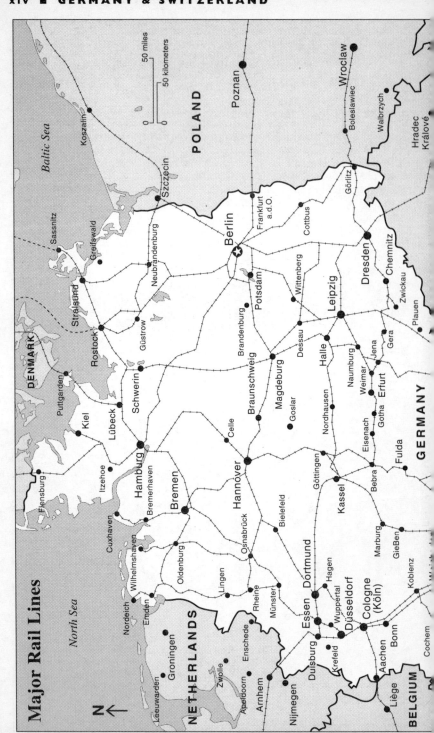

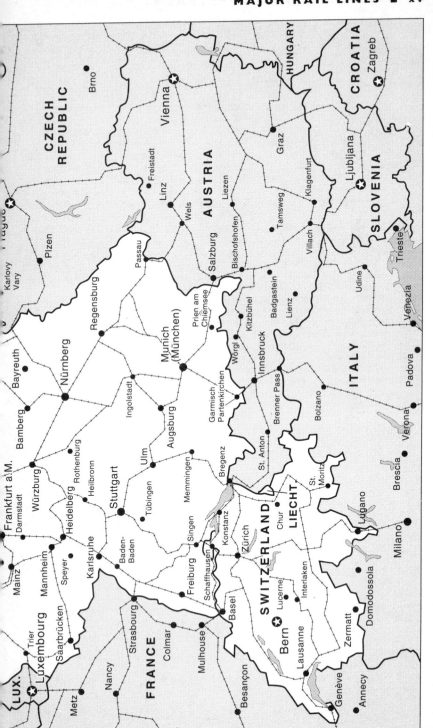

How To Use This Book

The more you know before you get where you're going, the more time you'll have for spontaneity once you get there. We have split the book into three main parts. First comes **Essentials**, of which all the information will be helpful *before* you leave on your trip. All material in Essentials should be skimmed while you're still in your home country; sub-categories like**Documents and Formalities** and **Getting There** will provide you with helpful addresses, publications, suggestions, and budget travel tips to get you on your way to Germany and/or Switzerland. This is also where you'll find information on getting a hostel membership (in Accommodations) or Eurailpass (in Transportation) before heading off. Following Essentials comes the two countries you're trying to see: **Germany**, followed by **Switzerland (including Liechtenstein).** Each country's **Once There** section includes crucial information you'll need once you've arrived. The sub-categories Getting Around, Accommodations, and Keeping in Touch, for example, will help you to orient yourself in your new surroundings. We offer special tips for students, seniors, families, women, gay and lesbian travelers, and others. Following Once There in both Germany and Switzerland you'll find **Life and Times,** which fills you in on German or Swiss history, politics, art, architecture, film, and literary life. In addition, Life and Times includes cultural information on **Food and Drink, Media,** and more.

Once you've passed Life and Times, you'll enter into the real meat of the book: our coverage of the many **regions, cities,** and **towns** in Germany and Switzerland. Germany is divided into three major sections: **Eastern Germany, Western Germany,** and **Berlin-Brandenburg.** These three categories are all divided into *Länder* (Federal States). **Practical Information** directs you to resources, facilities, and transport connections. Under **Food** and **Accommodations,** we direct you to districts rich in these goods and list specific establishments in order of *value*; the one we list first may not be the cheapest, but it should give you the most for your Mark or Swiss Franc. We cover **Sights, Entertainment,** and **Nightlife** in every city with a heartbeat. Switzerland is divided into six distinctive geographical regions (Central Switzerland, Swiss Jura and Fribourg, Lake Geneva, Valais, Bern and the Berner Oberland, Italian Switzerland, and the Graubünden). Check out our **Appendices** for phone assistance, useful phrases, and more at-your-fingertips reference information.

How *not* to use this book: budget travel should be enjoyed. Don't succumb to "budget obsession," the terrible compulsion to spend as much and move as fast as humanly possible. You're on a vacation, not a crusade. And remember the words of Noel Coward: "Don't let's be beastly to the Germans," at least not to the over-worked ticket seller who may not speak English. Learn a little German, and don't be afraid of trying it out. Try to meet the Germans and the Swiss , and listen to them.

A NOTE TO OUR READERS

The information for this book is gathered by *Let's Go*'s researchers during the late spring and summer months. Each listing is derived from the assigned researcher's opinion based upon his or her visit at a particular time. The opinions are expressed in a candid and forthright manner. Other travelers might disagree. Those traveling at a different time may have different experiences since prices, dates, hours, and conditions are always subject to change. You are urged to check beforehand to avoid inconvenience and surprises. Travel always involves a certain degree of risk, especially in low-cost areas. When traveling, especially on a budget, you should always take particular care to ensure your safety.

■ Essentials

■■■ PLANNING YOUR TRIP

A trip to Germany or Switzerland, like anywhere else in Europe, requires some prep-aration. Fortunately, there are big industries devoted to helping travelers tackle it. The many organizations listed below, especially national tourist offices, will send you a daunting mound of literature. Dive in and plan a trip tailored to your specific interests. Resist the urge to see everything—a madcap schedule will only detract from your enjoyment. If you try to see Berlin, Munich, Cologne, and Zurich in a week, you'll come away from your vacation with nothing but vague memories of train stations and youth hostels. Choose your traveling companions carefully. Be aware that traveling with a group of friends from home may effectively insulate you from local culture; on the other hand, they will share in food and lodging costs, pro-vide extra safety in numbers, and often be an invaluable source of energy and com-fort. Going solo can be both the best way to travel and the worst. Freedom of movement is counterbalanced by the danger of severe loneliness. You are sure to meet many other travelers along the way who will soon become close friends—many believe that a lone traveler is never truly alone.

■■■ WHEN TO GO

In July and August, airfares, temperatures, and tempers rise right along with the number of tourists. In the winter months, some hostels close and museum hours may be abbreviated. May and June are perhaps the best of both worlds. Winter sports gear up in November and continue even into May, depending on the loca-tion. High season for skiing is mid-December to mid-January and February to March. High season for glacier skiing is July and August. Germans head to vacation spots en masse with the onset of school vacations; airports and train stations become jammed and the traffic on the *Autobahn* can be measured in meters per hour. The policy of staggering vacation periods among the federal states has alleviated the crunch somewhat, but you should still avoid taking a trip across Germany on the day after school lets out. May, June, and September are considered the best months to travel through Switzerland, especially if you're going by bicycle or by foot.

■■■ USEFUL ADDRESSES

■ Tourist Offices

These outposts can be a passel of help in planning your trip; have them mail you their brochures before you leave. The **German National Tourist Offices,** for exam-ple, distribute useful publications such as *Travel Tips, Camping in Germany,* and *Youth Hostels.*

German National Tourist Offices

U.S.: New York, 122 East 42nd St., New York, NY 10168-0072 (tel. (212) 661-7200, fax (212) 661-7174). **Los Angeles,** 11766 Wilshire Blvd., Suite 750, Los Angeles, CA 90025 (tel. (310) 575-9799, fax (310) 575-1565). The **German Infor-mation Center,** 950 Third Ave., New York, NY 10022 (tel. (212) 888-9840), will send you a useful, updated guide of basic historical and cultural information about Germany.

Canada: 175 Bloor St. E., E. North Tower, 6th floor, Toronto, Ont. M4W 3R8 (tel. (416) 968-1570, fax (416) 968-1986).

U.K.: Nightingale House, 65 Curzon St., London W1Y 7PE (tel. (071) 495 39 90, fax (071) 495 61 29).

Australia: Lufthansa House, 9th floor, 143 Macquarie St., Sydney 2000 (tel. (02) 367 38 90, fax (02) 367 38 95).

Swiss National Tourist Offices

U.S.: New York, 608 Fifth Ave., New York, NY 10020 (tel. (212) 757-5944, fax (212) 262-6116); **Los Angeles,** 222 N. Sepulveda Blvd. #1570, El Segundo, CA 90245 (tel. (310) 335-5980, fax (310) 335-5982). **Chicago,** 150 N. Michigan Ave. #2930, Chicago, IL 60601 (tel. (312) 630-5840, fax (312) 630-5848); **San Francisco,** 260 Stockton St., San Francisco, CA 94108 (tel. (415) 362-2260, fax (415) 391-1508).

Canada: 154 University St. #610, Toronto, Ont. M5H 3Y9 (tel. (416) 971-9734, fax (416) 971-6452).

U.K.: Swiss Centre, 1 New Coventry St., London W1V 8EE (tel. (071) 734 19 21, fax (071) 437 45 77).

■ Useful Travel Organizations

Council on International Educational Exchange (CIEE/Council Travel): In the United States provides low-cost travel arrangements and airline tickets, arranges homestays, sells international student ID cards, travel literature, travel insurance, and hostel cards. CIEE also helps students secure work visas and find employment through its work-exchange programs. Operates 43 offices throughout the U.S. including those listed below and branches in Providence, RI; Amherst and Cambridge, MA; Berkeley, La Jolla, Long Beach, CA, and one more SF office. **Boston:** 729 Boylston St. #201, MA 02116 (tel. (617) 266-1926). **Chicago:** 1153 N. Dearborn St., IL 60610 (tel. (312) 951-0585).**Dallas:** 6923 Snider Plaza B, TX 75205 (tel. (214) 363-9941). **Los Angeles:** 1093 Broxton Ave. #220, CA 90024 (tel. (310) 208-3551).**New York:** 205 E. 42nd St., NY 10017 (tel. (212) 661-1450); 2 other NYC offices.**Portland:** 715 S.W. Morrison #600, OR 97205 (tel. (503) 228-1900).**San Diego:** 953 Garnet Ave., CA 94108 (tel. (619) 270-6401).**San Francisco:** 919 Irving St. #102, CA 94122 (tel. (415) 566-6222).**Seattle:** 1314 N.E. 43rd St. #210, WA 98105 (tel. (206) 632-2448).

Council on International Educational Exchange (CIEE) international affiliates: Offer budget travel services similar to U.S. offices above. If you can't locate an office in your country, contact **CIEE Main Office,** 205 E. 42nd St., New York, NY 10017 (tel. (212) 661-1450; 800-223-7402 for charter flights only), or the **International Student Travel Confederation,** Store Kongensgade 40H, 1264 Copenhagen K, Denmark (tel. (045) 33 93 93 03).**Australia: SSA/STA Swap Program:** P.O. Box 399 (1st Floor), 220 Faraday St., Carlton South, Melbourne, Victoria 3053 (tel. 03 347 69 11).**United Kingdom: London Student Travel,** 52 Grosvenor Gardens, London WC1 (tel. (071) 730 34 02).**Canada: Travel CUTS (Canadian University Travel Services Ltd.):** 187 College St., Toronto, Ont. M5T 1P7 (tel. (416) 979-2406).

STA Travel, 17 E. 45th St., New York, NY 10017 (tel. (800) 777-0112 or (212) 986-9470) operates 10 offices in the U.S. and over 100 offices around the world. Youth and student fares, railpasses, accommodations, tours, insurance, and ISICs. **Boston:** 273 Newbury St., MA 02116 (tel. (617) 266-6014).**Los Angeles:** 7202 Melrose Ave., CA 90046 (tel. (213) 934-8722). **New York:** 48 E. 11th St., NY 10003 (tel. (212) 477-7166). **Philadelphia:** University City Travel, 3730 Walnut St., PA 19104 (tel. (215) 382-2928). **San Francisco:** 51 Grant Ave., CA 94108 (tel. (415) 391-8407). **U.K.:** STA's main office is at 86 Old Brompton Rd., London SW7 3LQ and 117 Euston Rd., London NW1 2SX (tel. (071) 937 99 21 for European travel; (071) 937 99 71 for North American; (071) 937 99 62 for Long Haul Travel; (071) 937 17 33 for Round the World Travel). **New Zealand:** 10 High St., Auckland (tel. (09) 309 9995).

Campus Travel, offering youth fares, travel insurance, and IDs. Office at 52 Grosvenor Gardens, London SW1W 0AG (tel. (071) 730 88 32, fax (071) 730 57 39).

Educational Travel Centre (ETC), 438 North Frances St., Madison, WI 53703 (tel. (608) 256-5551). Flight information, HI/AYH cards, rail passes. Write for their free pamphlet *Taking Off.*

International Student Exchange Flights (ISE), 5010 East Shea Blvd., #A104, Scottsdale, AZ 85254 (tel. (602) 951-1177). Student flights, rail passes, traveler's checks, and travel guides, including *Let's Go.* Free catalog.

Let's Go Travel, Harvard Student Agencies, Thayer Hall-B, Harvard University, Cambridge, MA 02138 (tel. (617) 495-9649 or (800) 553-8746).

London Student Travel, 52 Grosvenor Gardens, London WC1 (tel. (071) 730 34 02); in **Ireland, USIT Ltd.,** Aston Quay, O'Connell Bridge, Dublin 2 (tel. (01) 679 88 33, fax (01) 677 88 43).

■ Useful Publications

The publications we list here are useful for preparation for your trip. If you're interested in books on culture or history, see Life and Times: Literature.

Maps and Guides

European Association of Music Festivals, 122, rue de Lausanne, 1202 Geneva, Switzerland (tel. (022) 732 28 03, fax (022) 738 40 12) publishes the booklet *Festivals,* listing dates and programs for major European music and theater festivals. Student rates and standing room are often available.

Forsyth Travel Library, P.O. Box 2975, Shawnee Mission, KS 66201 (tel. (800) 367-7984). Catalog of maps, guidebooks, railpasses, and timetables.

Hippocrene Books, Inc., 171 Madison Ave., New York, NY 10016 (tel. (212) 685-4371; orders (718) 454-2360, fax (718) 454-1391). Free catalog of travel reference books, travel guides, maps, and foreign-language dictionaries.

Michelin Maps and Guides, P.O. Box 565, Harrow, Middlesex, HAI 2UP, England (tel. +44 (081) 861 2121). Their famous Green Guides for Western Europe offer great historical and cultural background. A good bookstore, or in the U.S., contact P.O. Box 3305, Spartanburg, SC 29304 (tel. (800) 423-0485 or (803) 599-0850).

Travelling Books, P.O. Box 77114, Seattle, WA 98177, publishes a catalogue of travel guides which will make the armchair traveler weep with wanderlust.

Wide World Books and Maps, 1911 N. 45th St., Seattle, WA 98103 (tel. (206) 634-3453). Write them for hard-to-find maps. Open Mon.-Fri. 10am-7pm, Sat. 10am-6pm, Sun. noon-5pm.

Atlantik-Brücke, Adenauerallee 131, 53113 Bonn (tel. (0228) 21 41 60; fax (0228) 21 46 59). An organization devoted to promoting mutual understanding between Germans and Americans (hence "Atlantic Bridge") publishes the amazingly helpful little book *These Strange German Ways*—a must for anyone planning on living in Germany—as well as *Meet United Germany, German Holidays and Folk Customs, Meeting German Business,* and *German Place Names.*

By Train, Timetables

Ariel Publications, 14417 SE 19 Place, Bellevue, WA 98007 (tel. (800) 367-7984 or (206) 641-0518), publishes *Camp Europe by Train,* by Lenore Baken (US$17). This excellent book covers nearly all aspects of train travel and includes sections on railpasses, packing, and the specifics of rail travel in each country.

Thomas Cook European Timetable (US$24, postage US$4) covers all major and many minor train routes in Europe (but is awfully large to carry around). Updated monthly. Available from Forsyth Travel Library (see Useful Publications).

The Eurail Guide (US$15, postage $3), published by Eurail Guide Annual, 27540 Pacific Coast Highway, Malibu, CA 90265, lists train schedules and brief cultural information for almost every country on earth.

Guides for the Alps

100 Hikes in the Alps. Details various tried and true trails (US$15). Write to *The Mountaineers* Books, 306 2nd Ave. W., Seattle WA 98119 (tel. (206) 223-6303, fax 223-6306).

Downhill Walking in Switzerland, by Richard and Linda Williams, gives hope to those who can't deal with the uphill thing. Details on how to arrive at the top and then GET DOWN (US$12). Old World Travel Books Inc., P.O. Box 700863, Tulsa OK 74170 (tel. (918) 493-2642).

Swiss-Bernese Oberland, a new book for the independent mountain wanderer. Covers Interlaken, Grindelwald, Wengen, Mürren, and Kandersteg. Color pictures and maps (US$17 plus US$2 handling). Write to Intercon Publishing, P.O. Box 18500-N, Irvine, CA 92713 (tel. (714) 955-2344).

■■■ DOCUMENTS AND FORMALITIES

Be sure to file all applications several weeks or months in advance of your planned departure date. Remember, government agencies will take time to complete these transactions; many a trip has been put off because of a bureaucratic snarl. Your application may contain errors, so you should be sure to leave enough leeway time to resubmit it. Most offices suggest that you apply in the winter off-season (between August and December) for speedier service.

When you travel, *always carry on your person two or more forms of identification, including at least one photo ID.* A passport combined with a driver's license or birth certificate usually serves as adequate proof of your identity and citizenship. Many establishments, especially banks, require several IDs before cashing traveler's checks. Never carry your passport, travel ticket, identification documents, money, traveler's checks, insurance, and credit cards all together, or you risk being left entirely without ID or funds in case of theft or loss. Carry a half-dozen extra passport-size photos to attach to the IDs and transit passes you will eventually acquire.

For general information about documents and formalities and prudent travel abroad, procure the booklet *Your Trip Abroad* from the U.S. Department of State, Bureau of Consular Affairs, Public Affairs, Room 5807, Washington, DC 20520-4818 or from a State Department office.

■ Entrance Requirements

Citizens of the U.S., Canada, the U.K., Ireland, Australia, New Zealand, and South Africa all need valid passports to enter Germany and Switzerland. Be advised that some countries will not allow entrance if the holder's passport will expire in less than six months, and returning to the U.S. with an expired passport may result in a fine. If your travels extend beyond Germany or Switzerland, remember that some countries in Europe require a visa. When you enter Germany or Switzerland, carry proof of your **financial independence,** such as a visa to the next country on your itinerary, an air ticket, enough money to cover the cost of your living expenses, etc. The standard period of admission is 3 months. To stay longer, you must show that you will be able to support yourself for an extended period of time, and authorities often require a medical examination. Admission as a visitor does not include the right to work, which requires a work permit (see Alternatives to Tourism below).

Passports

As a precaution in case your passport is lost or stolen, be sure *before you leave* to photocopy the page of your passport that contains your photograph and identifying information. Especially important is your passport number. Carry this photocopy in a safe place apart from your passport, perhaps with a traveling companion, and leave another copy at home. Better yet, carry a photocopy of all the pages of the passport, including all visa stamps, apart from your actual passport, and leave a duplicate copy with a relative or friend. These measures will help prove your citizenship and facilitate the issuing of a new passport. Consulates also recommend that you carry an expired passport or an *official* copy of your birth certificate (not necessarily the one issued at birth, of course) in a part of your baggage separate from other documents. You can request a duplicate birth certificate from the **Bureau of Vital Records and Statistics** in your state or province of birth.

Losing your passport can be a nightmare. It may take weeks to process a replacement, and your new passport may be valid only for a limited time. In addition, any visas stamped in your old passport will be irretrievably lost. If it is lost or stolen, however, immediately notify the local police and the nearest embassy or consulate of your home government. To expedite the replacement of your passport, you will need to know *all the information that you had previously recorded and photocopied* and to show identification and proof of citizenship. Some consulates can issue new passports within two days if you give them proof of citizenship. In an emergency, ask for immediate temporary traveling papers that will permit you to return to your home country. Remember that your passport is a public document that belongs to your nation's government. You may have to surrender your passport to a foreign government official; if you don't get it back in a reasonable time, inform the nearest mission of your home country.

Applying for a passport is complicated. Passport offices often have information desks; use them. Every passport application requires certain documents (birth certificates, photos, etc.) so be sure to call the passport office (or write) and find out exactly what you need. This way, you won't get turned away after waiting in line for a long, precious amount of time.

U.S. citizens may apply for a passport, valid for 10 years (5 yr. if under 18) at any federal or state **courthouses** or **post offices** authorized to accept passport applications, or at a **U.S. Passport Agency** in Boston, Chicago, Honolulu, Houston, Los Angeles, Miami, New Orleans, New York, Philadelphia, San Francisco, Seattle, Stamford, CT, and Washington, DC. Refer to the "U.S. Government, State Department" section of the telephone book or call your local post office for addresses. A passport will cost US$65 (under 18 $40). You can **renew** your passport by mail (or in person) for $55. Processing usually takes three to four weeks. *File your application as early as possible.* Passport agencies offer **rush service:** if you have proof that you are departing within five working days, a Passport Agency will issue a passport while you wait. For **more information,** contact the U.S. Passport Information's helpful 24-hour recorded message (tel. (202) 647-0518).

Canadian application forms in English and French are available at all **passport offices, post offices,** and most travel agencies. Citizens may apply in person at any one of 29 regional **Passport Offices** across Canada. You can apply by mail by sending a completed application form with appropriate documentation and the $35 fee to Passport Office, External Affairs, Ottawa, Ont., K1A 0G3. The processing time is approximately five business days for in-person applications and three weeks for mailed ones. For **additional information,** call the 24-hr. number (tel. (800) 567-6868; in Metro Toronto, 973-3251; in Montreal, 283-2151). Refer to the booklet *Bon Voyage, But...* for further help and a list of Canadian embassies and consulates abroad, available free of charge from any passport office or from Info-Export (BPTE), External Affairs, Ottawa, Ont., K1A 0G2, Canada.

British citizens can obtain either a full passport or a more restricted Visitor's Passport. For a **full passport** valid for 10 years (5 yr. if under 16), apply in person or by mail to the London **Passport Office** or by mail to a Passport Office located in Liverpool, Newport, Peterborough, Glasgow, and Belfast. The London office offers same-day walk-in rush service; arrive early. For a **Visitor's Passport,** valid for one year in Western Europe only, the fee is around £9.

Irish citizens can apply for a passport by mail to one of the following two passport offices: in **Dublin,** Department of Foreign Affairs, Passport Office, Setanta Centre, Molesworth St., Dublin 2 (tel. (01) 671 16 33); in **Cork,** Passport Office, 1A South Mall, Cork (tel. (021) 27 25 25). You can obtain an application at a Garda station or request one from a passport office. Passports cost £45, valid for 10 years.

Australian citizens must apply for a passport in person at a local **post office** or **passport office,** or an Australian diplomatic mission overseas. Passport offices are located in Adelaide, Brisbane, Canberra, Darwin, Hobart, Melbourne, Newcastle, Perth, and Sydney. Application fees are *adjusted every three months;* call the toll-free **information line** for details (tel. 13 12 32).

New Zealand citizens must contact their local Link Centre, travel agent, or New Zealand Representative for an application form, which they must complete and **mail** to the **New Zealand Passport Office,** Documents of National Identity Division, Department of Internal Affairs, Box 10-526, Wellington (tel. (04) 474 81 00). The application fee is NZ$56.25 (under 16, NZ$25.30) for an application lodged in New Zealand and NZ$110 for one lodged overseas (under 16, NZ$49.50). Overseas citizens should send the passport application to the nearest embassy, high commission, or consulate that is authorized to issue passports.

Visas

A visa is an endorsement that a foreign government stamps into a passport; it allows the bearer to stay in that country for a specified purpose and period of time. Most visas cost US$10-30 and allow you to spend about a month in a country, within six months to a year from the date of issue.

U.S., Canadian, British, Irish, Australian, and **New Zealand citizens** do not need to obtain a visa ahead of time. These citizens need to carry only a valid passport in order to remain in Germany or Switzerland for three months. Holders of passports of countries not listed above should inquire at the nearest German or Swiss Consulate General for more information.

If you want to stay for longer, apply for a visa at the German or Swiss embassy or consulate in your home country well before your departure. Unless you are a student, extending your stay once you are abroad is more difficult. You must contact the country's immigration officials or local police well before your time is up and you must show sound proof of financial resources (see Entrance Requirements,).

For more information, send for the U.S. government pamphlet *Foreign Visa Requirements.* Mail a check for 50¢ to Consumer Information Center, Dept. 454V, Pueblo, CO 81009 (tel. (719) 948-3334). Or contact the private organization **Visa Center, Inc.,** 507 Fifth Ave., Suite 904, New York, NY 10017 (tel. (212) 986 0924). This company secures visas for travel to and from all possible countries. The service charge varies, but the average cost for a U.S. citizen is US$15-20 per visa.

■ Customs

Unless you plan to import a BMW or a barnyard beast, you will probably pass right over the customs barrier with minimal ado. The many rules and regulations of customs and duties hardly pose a threat to the budget traveler. Most countries prohibit or restrict the importation of firearms, explosives, ammunition, fireworks, controlled drugs, most plants and animals, lottery tickets, and obscene literature and films. To avoid problems when you transport **prescription drugs,** ensure that the bottles are clearly marked, and carry a copy of the prescription to show the customs officer. When dealing with customs officers, always be polite and look responsible.

Upon returning home, you must declare all articles you acquired abroad and pay a duty on the value of those articles that exceeds the allowance established by your country's customs service. Holding onto receipts for purchases made abroad will help establish values when you return. *Make a list,* including serial numbers, of any valuables that you carry from home; if you register this list with customs before your departure and have an official stamp it, you will ensure an easy passage upon your return. Be especially careful to document items manufactured abroad. If you have country-specific questions, contact one of the agencies in the Returning Home section, below. Goods and gifts purchased at duty-free shops abroad are *not* exempt from duty or sales tax at your point of return; you must declare these items. "Duty-free" merely means that you avoid taxes in the country of purchase.

Entering Germany and Switzerland

Citizens of EC member countries can bring up to 300 **cigarettes** into Germany and 200 cigarettes into Switzerland. Travelers from outside the EC can carry 200 cigarettes into Germany and 400 cigarettes into Switzerland. Germany allows 1.5 liters of **alcoholic beverage** above 44 proof for EC members, 1 liter for travelers outside the EC. Switzerland allows 1 liter over 15 proof (applies to all travelers). No one under age 17 is entitled to the aforementioned allowances. Neither Germany nor Switzerland have strict regulations on the import or export of currency.

   Gifts and commodities for personal use are allowed into both Germany and Switzerland with the following regulations: In Germany, the total value of goods imported from the EC cannot exceed DM780, while goods from outside the EEC cannot exceed DM115. For Switzerland, up to 100SFr worth of goods can be brought in duty-free. You can obtain more details from the German or Swiss Consulate General in your own country. Generally, a budget traveler need not worry about these regulations; you'll want to bring only the bare necessities (see Packing).

Returning Home

United States citizens should consult the brochure *Know Before You Go,* available from R. Woods, Consumer Information Center, Pueblo, CO 81009 (item 477Y). Direct other questions to the U.S. Customs Service, P.O. Box 7407, Washington, DC 20044 (tel. (202) 927-6724). Foreign nationals living in the U.S. are subject to different regulations; refer to the leaflet *Customs Hints for Visitors.*
Canadian citizens: Write to External Affairs, Communications Branch, Mackenzie Ave., Ottawa, Ont., K1A 0L5 (tel. (613) 957 0275).
EC nationals who travel between EC countries no longer need to declare the goods they purchase abroad.
British citizens contact Her Majesty's Customs and Excise, Custom House, Heathrow Airport North, Hounslow, Middlesex, TW6 2LA (tel. (081) 750 16 03, fax 081 750 1549). *HM Customs & Excise Notice 1* explains the allowances for people traveling to the U.K. both from within and without the European Community.
Irish citizens should contact The Revenue Commissioners, Dublin Castle (tel. (01) 679 27 77, fax (01) 671 20 21).
Australian citizens should address questions to a consulate.
New Zealand citizens should consult the *New Zealand Customs Guide for Travelers,* available from customs offices, or contact New Zealand Customs, 50 Anzac Avenue, Box 29, Auckland (tel. (09) 377 35 20, fax 309 29 78).

■ Youth and Student Identification

In the world of budget travel, youth has its privileges. Two main forms of student and youth identification are accepted worldwide; they are extremely useful, especially for the insurance packages that accompany them. The **International Student Identity Card (ISIC)** is the most widely accepted form of student identification. Some one million plus students flash it every year, garnering discounts for sights, theaters, museums, accommodations, train, ferry, and plane travel, and other services throughout Germany and Switzerland. Ask about discounts even when none are advertised. It also provides accident insurance of up to US$3000 as well as US$100 per day of in-hospital care for up to 60 days. Cardholders have access to a toll-free Traveler's Assistance hotline whose multilingual staff can help in medical, legal, and financial emergencies overseas. In many cases, establishments will also honor an ordinary student ID from your college or university for student discounts.

   To apply, supply in person or by mail: (1) current, dated proof of your degree-seeking student status (a letter signed and sealed by the registrar, a photocopied grade report, or a Bursar's receipt with school seal that indicates full payment for fall 1993, spring 1994, or summer 1994 sessions); (2) a 1½" x 2" photo (vending machine-size) with your name printed and signed on the back; (3) proof of your birthdate and nationality; and (4) the name, address, and phone number of a beneficiary; in the event of the insured's death, payment will be made to the beneficiary. Mail these items to CIEE (see Useful Travel Organizations, above). You must be at least 12 years old and must be a student at a secondary or post-secondary school. (1994 card is valid Sept. 1993-Dec. 1994. US$15.)

Many student travel offices issue ISICs, including Council Travel, STA, and International Student Travel Confederation (ISTC) affiliates (see Useful Addresses: Travel Services). When you apply for the card, procure a copy of the *International Student Identity Card Handbook,* which lists by country some of the available discounts. You can also write to CIEE for a copy. The new US$16 **International Teacher Identity Card (ITIC)** offers identical discounts, in theory, but because of its recent introduction many establishments are reluctant to honor it. The application process is the same as for an ISIC. Because of the proliferation of phony and improperly issued ISIC cards, many airlines and some other services now require double proof of student identity. It is wise to carry your school ID card.

Federation of International Youth Travel Organizations (FIYTO) issues its own discount card to travelers who are not students but are under 26. Also known as the **International Youth Discount Travel Card** or the **GO 25 Card,** this one-year card offers many of the same benefits as the ISIC, and most organizations that sell the ISIC also sell the Go 25 Card. A brochure that lists discounts is free when you purchase the card. For more information, contact FIYTO at Bredgage 25H, DK-1260, Copenhagen K, Denmark (tel. (+45) 33 33 96 00, fax (+45) 33 93 96 76).

∎∎∎ MONEY

If you stay in hostels and prepare your own food, expect to spend anywhere from US$20-50 per day, depending on local cost of living and your needs. Transportation will increase these figures. Don't sacrifice your health or safety for a cheaper tab; if you end up with pneumonia after pitching a tent on that cliff in northern Schleswig-Holstein, ain't no one to blame but yourself, baby. No matter how low your budget, if you plan to travel for more than a couple of days, you will need to keep handy a much larger amount of cash than usual. Carrying it around with you, even in a money belt, is risky; personal checks from home may not be accepted no matter how many forms of ID you have (even banks shy away from accepting checks). Inevitably you will have to rely on some combination of innovations of the modern financial world, but keep their shortcomings in mind.

∎ Currency and Exchange

Remember that it is usually more expensive to buy foreign currency at home than it is once there; however, purchasing a small amount of German or Swiss currency before you go will allow you to breeze through the airport while others languish in exchange counter lines. This is also a good practice in case you find yourself stuck with no money after banking hours or on a holiday, or if your flight arrives late in the evening. Observe commission rates closely when abroad; check newspapers to get the standard rate of exchange. Bank rates are generally preferable to those of travel agencies, tourist offices, restaurants, and hotels. In Germany, post offices generally offer the best exchange rates. Since you lose money with every transaction, it's wise to convert in large sums (provided the exchange rate is either staying constant or deteriorating), but not more than you will need. For details on either the German *Deutschmark* or the Swiss *franc,* see the Once There: Money section for each.

∎ Traveler's Checks

Traveler's checks are the safest way to carry large sums of money. They are refundable if lost or stolen, and many issuing agencies offer additional services such as refund hotlines, message relaying, travel insurance, and emergency assistance. Most tourist establishments will accept traveler's checks and almost any bank will cash

Always travel with a friend.

Get the International
Student Identity Card,
recognized worldwide.

For information call toll-free **1-800-GET-AN-ID**.
or contact any Council Travel office. (See inside front cover.)

 Council on International Educational Exchange
205 East 42nd Street, New York, NY 10017

them. Most banks sell traveler's checks for a 1-2% commission, although your own bank may waive the surcharge. Buying checks in small denominations ($20 rather than $50 or higher) is safer and more convenient—otherwise, after a small purchase, you'll be carrying around a large amount of cash. Be prepared to convert at least US$100 into traveler's checks; many places will not exchange less. For more information on different sorts of checks, contact one of the organizations listed below. Refunds on lost or stolen checks can be time-consuming. To avoid red tape, *keep check receipts and a record of which checks you've cashed in a separate place from the checks themselves.* Leave a photocopy of check serial numbers with someone at home as back-up in case you lose your copy. Sign your checks once when you get them; never countersign checks until you're prepared to cash them.

American Express: Call (800) 221-7282 in the U.S. and Canada; (0800) 52 13 13 in the U.K.; (02) 886 0689 in Australia, New Zealand, and the South Pacific with questions or to report lost or stolen Cheques. Elsewhere, call U.S. collect (801) 964-6665. AmEx Travelers Cheques are the most widely recognized worldwide and easiest to replace if lost or stolen—just call the information number or the AmEx Travel office nearest you. Ask for AmEx's booklet *Traveler's Companion* which gives office addresses and stolen Cheque hotlines for each European country. AmEx offices cash their own cheques commission-free (except where prohibited by national government) and sell "Cheques for Two," which can be signed by either of 2 people traveling together. Cheques available in 7 currencies. **AAA** members can obtain AmEx Travelers Cheques commission-free at AAA offices.

Barclays Bank: Sells Visa traveler's checks. For lost or stolen checks, call Visa (tel. (800) 645-6556); for Barclays information specifically, call (800) 221-2426 in the U.S. and Canada, (202) 67 12 12 in the U.K.; from elsewhere call New York collect (212) 858-8500. Many branches throughout Britain. Commission on purchase of checks varies from branch to branch (usually 1-3%). Checks in z4 currencies. Barclays branches cash Barclays-Visa and any other Visa traveler's checks for free.

Citicorp: Sells Visa traveler's checks. Call (800) 645-6556 in the U.S. and Canada, in London (071) 982 4040; from abroad call collect (813) 623-1709. Commission 1-2% on check purchases. Check holders automatically enrolled in **Travel Assist Hotline** (tel. (800) 523-1199) for 45 days after checks are bought; this service provides travelers with lists of English-speaking doctors, lawyers, and interpreters as well as traveler's check refund assistance. Citicorp has a **World Courier Service,** which guarantees delivery of traveler's checks anywhere in the world.

Mastercard International: Call (800) 223-9920 in the U.S. and Canada, from abroad call collect (609) 987-7300. Commission varies from 1-2% for purchases depending on the bank. Issued in US$ only.

Thomas Cook: Thomas Cook and Mastercard International have formed a "global alliance" by which Thomas Cook distributes traveler's checks with both company logos. In contrast to MC International, Thomas Cook handles the distribution of checks in US$ as well as checks in 10 other currencies. Call (800) 223-7373 for refunds in U.S., (800) 223-4030 for orders. From elsewhere call collect (212) 974-5696. Some Thomas Cook Currency Services offices (located in major cities around the globe) do not charge commission for purchase of checks while others charge 1-2%. You can buy Mastercard travelers checks from Thomas Cook at any bank displaying a Mastercard sign.

Visa: (tel. (800) 227-6811 in the U.S. and Canada; from abroad, call New York collect (212) 858-8500 or London (071) 937-8091). Similar to the Thomas Cook/Mastercard alliance, Visa and Barclay's Bank have formed a team by which Visa checks can be cashed for free at any Barclay's bank.

■ Credit Cards

Credit cards are not always useful to the budget traveler—many smaller establishments will not accept them, and those enticing, pricier establishments accept them all too willingly—but they can prove invaluable in an emergency. Visa and Mastercard are the most common, followed by American Express and Diner's Club. Note

Don't forget to write.

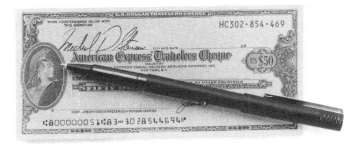

Now that you've said, "Let's go," it's time to say
"Let's get American Express® Travelers Cheques." If they are lost or
stolen, you can get a fast and full refund virtually anywhere you
travel. So before you leave be sure and write.

that the British "Barclaycard" and "Access" are equivalent to Visa and Mastercard, respectively. You can often reduce conversion fees by charging a purchase instead of changing traveler's checks. With credit cards such as **American Express, Visa,** and **Mastercard**, associated banks will give you an instant cash advance in the local currency as large as your remaining credit line. Unfortunately, in most cases you will pay mortifying rates of interest for such an advance.

American Express (tel. (800) 528-4800) has a hefty annual fee (US$55) but offers a number of services to cardholders. AmEx offices abroad can cash personal checks at AmEx offices abroad (up to US$1000, Goldcard $US5000). **Global Assist**, a 24-hour hotline offering information and legal assistance in emergencies, is also available to cardholders (tel. (800) 333-2639 in U.S. and Canada; from abroad call collect (tel. (202) 554-2639). Card holders can take advantage of the American Express Travel Service; benefits include assistance in changing airline, hotel, and car rental reservations, sending mailgrams and international cables, and holding your mail at more than 1500 AmEx offices around the world. In addition, there's a Purchase Protection Plan for cardholders that will refund or replace deficient products you buy with the card (certain restrictions apply). **Mastercard** (tel. (800) 999-0454) and **Visa** (tel. (800) 336-8472) credit cards are sold by individual banks, and each bank offers different services in conjunction with the card.

■ Electronic Banking

Automatic Teller Machines (frequently abbreviated as ATMs; operated by bank cards) offer 24-hour service in banks, groceries, gas stations, and even in telephone booths across the U.S. ATMs in continental Europe are not quite as prevalent as in North America, but you will find that most banks in the larger cities are connected to an international money network, usually **Plus** (tel. 800-THE-PLUS (843-7587)) or **Cirrus** (tel. 800-4-CIRRUS (424-7787)). Depending on the system that your bank at home uses, you will probably be able to access your own personal bank account. ATM machines get the wholesale exchange rate which is generally 5% better than the retail rate most banks use. Most charge a withdrawal fee ($2-5); ask your bank.

American Express card holders can sign up for AmEx's free Express Cash service through which you can access cash from your account at any ATM with the AmEx trademark, but each transaction costs a minimum US$2.50 (max. US$10) plus conversion fees and interest. For a list of ATMs where you can use your card, call AmEx at 800-CASH-NOW (227-4669) and they'll send you a list of participating machines wherever you're going. Make sure to set up your Express Cash account a few weeks before you plan to travel. **Visa** cards can access ATM networks in 40 countries around the world (usually Cirrus, but it varies according to the issuing bank). Be sure to contact your issuer before you travel in order to get a **PIN** (personal identification number) essential for ATM use. **Mastercard** functions in the same way as Visa. As a final note, don't rely too heavily on automation. There is often a limit on the amount of money you can withdraw per day, and computer failures are not uncommon.

■ Sending Money

Sending money overseas is a complicated, expensive, and often extremely frustrating adventure. It is less fun than dental work. Do your best to avoid it; carry a credit card or a separate stash of emergency traveler's checks. The easiest way to obtain money from home is to bring an **American Express Card.** AmEx allows green-card holders to draw cash from their checking accounts (checkbook welcomed but not required) at any of its major offices and many of its representatives' offices (up to US$1000 every 7 days, no service charge, no interest). With someone feeding money into your account back home, you'll be set. You can also wire money through **Western Union** (tel. (800) 225-5227) or **American Express** (tel. (800) 543-4080; in Canada (800) 933-3278). The sender visits one of their offices or calls and charges it to a credit card; the sender can pick up cash at any overseas office within minutes (fee US$22-50 to send US$250, US$50-75 to send US$1000). American Express serves more countries than Western Union, but Western Union maybe a bit cheaper, especially in Western Europe. To pick up the money, you'll need either a picture ID or the answer to a test question.

Finally, if you find yourself in an **emergency,** you can usually have money sent through your government's diplomatic mission in the country in which you're traveling. Citizens of the United States who are very desperate should turn to a U.S. Consular section of the U.S. Embassy or Consulate, which will assist by contacting friends or family in the U.S. and arranging for them to send money. Senders at home should contact the **State Department's Citizens Emergency Center** (tel. (202) 647-5225, after-hours and holiday emergencies, tel. (202) 647-4000). This service provides, among other things, repatriation loans to pay for destitute Americans' direct return to the U.S. More information can be found in the pamphlet *The Citizens Emergency Center,* available from the Bureau of Consular Affairs, Public Affairs Staff, U.S. Dept. of State, Washington, DC 20570-4818. Citizens of other countries might check if their own government provides a similar service.

■■■ HEALTH

Staying Healthy and First Aid Common sense is the simplest prescription for good health while you travel: eat well, drink enough (water, not beer), get enough sleep, and don't overexert yourself. S You will need plenty of protein (for sustained energy) and fluids (to prevent dehydration and constipation, two of the most common health problems for travelers). Remember to treat your most valuable resource well: lavish your feet with attention. For minor health problems on the road, a compact **first-aid kit** should suffice. Some hardware stores carry ready-made kits, but it's just as easy to assemble your own. Items you might want to include are bandages, aspirin, antiseptic soap or antibiotic cream, a thermometer, a Swiss Army knife with tweezers, moleskin, a decongestant, sunscreen, insect repellent, burn ointment, and an elastic bandage.

Travelers in **high altitudes** should allow their body a couple of days to adjust to the lower atmospheric oxygen levels before engaging in any strenuous activity. This particularly applies to those intent on setting out on long alpine hikes. Those new to high-altitude areas may feel drowsy, and one alcoholic beverage may have the same effect as three at a lower altitude. Extreme cold, something you might be likely to encounter even on a summer day in the Alps, is no less dangerous—it brings risks of hypothermia and frostbite. **Hypothermia** is a result of exposure to cold and can occur even in the middle of the summer, especially in rainy or windy conditions. The signs are easy to detect: body temperature drops rapidly, resulting in the failure to produce body heat. Other possible symptoms are uncontrollable shivering, poor coordination, and exhaustion followed by slurred speech, sleepiness, hallucinations, combativeness, and amnesia. *Do not* let victims fall asleep if they are in advanced stages—if they lose consciousness, they might die. To avoid hypothermia, always keep dry. **Wear wool,** *especially* in soggy weather—it retains its insulating properties even when wet. Dress in layers, and stay out of the wind, which carries heat away from the body. Remember that most loss of body heat is through your head, so always carry a wool hat with you. **Frostbite** occurs in freezing temperatures. The affected skin will turn white, then waxy and cold. The victim should drink warm beverages, stay or get dry, and gently and slowly warm the frostbitten area in dry fabric or with steady body contact. NEVER *rub* frostbite—the skin is easily damaged. Take cases to a doctor or medic as soon as possible.

When traveling in the summer, protect yourself against the dangers of the sun and heat, especially to the dangers of **heatstroke.** Heatstroke can begin without direct exposure to the sun; it results from continuous heat stress, lack of fitness, or over-activity following heat exhaustion. In the early stages of heatstroke, sweating stops, body temperature rises, and an intense headache develops, soon followed by confusion. Those who suffer from heatstroke are generally cooled off immediately with fruit juice or salted water, wet towels, and shade, and rushed to a hospital.

Special Medical Concerns Travelers with chronic medical conditions should consult with their physicians before leaving. Always go prepared with any medication you may need while away as well as a copy of the prescription and/or a statement from your doctor, especially if you will be bringing insulin, syringes, or narcotics into the country. Be aware that matching prescriptions with foreign equivalents may be difficult. To get a prescription filled in Germany or Switzerland you must go to an *Apotheke*; a shop called a *Drogerie* sells only toilet articles.

All travelers should be concerned about **Acquired Immune Deficiency Syndrome (AIDS),** transmitted through the exchange of body fluids with an infected individual (HIV-positive). Remember that there is no assurance that someone is not infected; do not have unprotected sex or share intravenous needles with anyone. Note that the state of Bavaria requires foreigners seeking a residency permit for more than 6 months to be HIV negative, and they don't accept the results of tests taken abroad. Those travelers who are HIV-positive or have AIDS should thoroughly check on other possible immigration restrictions. The Center for Disease Control's **AIDS Hotline** provides information on AIDS in the U.S. and can refer you to other organizations with information on Germany and Switzerland (tel. (800) 342-2437; Spanish (800) 344-7432). Call the U.S. State Department for country-specific restrictions for HIV-positive travelers (tel. (202) 647-1488). The World Health Organization provides written material on AIDS internationally (tel. (202) 861-4346). Reliable **contraception** may be difficult to come by while traveling. Women on the pill should bring enough to allow for possible loss or extended stays. In Germany and Switzerland, condoms are widely available. For information on **abortion laws** in Germany and Switzerland, see the Once There section for each.

International Association for Medical Assistance to Travelers (IAMAT). IAMAT provides several brochures on health for travelers, an ID card, and a worldwide directory of English-speaking physicians. Membership to the organization is free and doctors are on call 24 hours a day for members. In the **U.S.,** 417 Center St., Lewiston, NY, 14092 (tel. (716) 754-4883); in **Canada,** 40 Regal Rd. Guelph, Ont., N1K 1B5 (tel. (519) 836-0102) and 1287 St. Clair Ave. West, Toronto, Ont., M6E 1B8 (tel. (416) 652-0137); in **New Zealand,** P.O. Box 5049, 438 Pananui Rd., Christchurch 5 (tel. (03) 352 90 53; fax (03) 352 46 30).

Superintendent of Documents, U.S. Government Printing Office, Washington DC 20402 (tel. (202) 783-3238). US$5 will get you their publication *Health Information for International Travel* detailing immunization requirements and other health precautions for travelers.

American Red Cross. *First-Aid and Safety Handbook* (US$15), available from your local office or American Red Cross, 99 Brookline Ave., Boston, MA 02215.

■■■ INSURANCE

Beware of unnecessary coverage—your current policies might well extend to many travel-related accidents. **Medical insurance** (especially university policies) often cover costs incurred abroad. **Medicare's** foreign travel coverage is limited and is valid only in Canada and Mexico. Canadians are protected by their home province's health insurance plan: check with the provincial Ministry of Health or Health Plan Headquarters. Your **homeowners' insurance** (or your family's coverage) often covers theft during travel. Homeowners are generally covered against loss of travel documents (passport, plane ticket, railpass, etc.) up to about US$500.

Buying an **ISIC** or International Teacher ID in the U.S. provides US$3000 worth of accident and illness insurance and US$100 per day up to 60 days of hospitalization while the card is valid. **CIEE** offers and inexpensive Trip-Safe plan with options covering medical treatment and hospitalization, accidents, baggage loss, and even charter flights missed due to illness; **STA** offers a more expensive, more comprehensive plan. American Express cardholders receive automatic car-rental and flight insurance on purchases made with the card. (For addresses, see Useful Travel Organizations). Remember that insurance companies usually require a copy of the police report for thefts, or evidence of having paid medical expenses (doctor's statements, receipts) before they will honor a claim and may have time limits on filing for reimbursement. Have all documents written in English to avoid possible translating fees. Always carry policy numbers and proof of insurance. Note that some of the plans listed below offer cash advances or guaranteed bills. Check with each insurance carrier for specific restrictions. If your coverage doesn't include on-the-spot payments or cash transferals, budget for emergencies.

Access America, Inc., 6600 West Broad St., P.O. Box 11188, Richmond, VA 23230 (tel. (800) 284-8300). Covers trip cancellation/interruption, on-the-spot hospital admittance costs, emergency medical evacuation. 24hr. hotline.

ARM Coverage, Inc./Carefree Travel Insurance, P.O. Box 310, Mineola, NY 11501 (tel. (800) 323-3149 or (516) 294-0220). Offers 2 comprehensive packages including coverage for trip delay, accident and sickness, medical, baggage loss, bag delay, accidental death and dismemberment, travel supplier insolvency. Trip cancellation/interruption may be purchased separately at a rate of US$5.50 per US$100 of coverage. 24hr. hotline.

Globalcare Travel Insurance, 220 Broadway, Lynnfield, MA 01940 (tel. (800) 821-2488; fax (617) 592-7720). Complete medical, legal, emergency, and travel-related services. On-the-spot payments and special student programs.

Travelers Aid International, 918 16th St. NW, Washington, DC 20006 (tel. (202) 659-9468; fax (202) 659-2910), provides help for theft, car failure, illness, and other "mobility-related problems." No fee, but you are expected to reimburse the organization for expenses.

Travel Assistance International, 1133 15th St. NW, Washington, DC 20005 (tel. (202) 821-2828; fax (202) 331-1609). 'Round the corner from Travelers Aid—perfect for comparison shopping. Provides on-the-spot medical coverage ranging (US$15,000-90,000) and unlimited medical evacuation insurance, 24hr. emergency multilingual assistance hotline and worldwide local presence. Optional coverages such as trip cancellation/interruption, baggage and accidental death and dismemberment insurance are also offered. Short-term and long-term plans.

Travel Guard Internationale, 1145 Clark St., Stevens Point, WI 54481 (tel. (800) 826-1300 or (715) 345-0505; fax (715) 345-0525). Offers "Travel Guard Gold" packages: Basic (US$19), Deluxe (US$39), and Comprehensive (8% of total trip cost) for medical expenses, baggage and travel documents, baggage delay, emergency assistance, and delay/cancellation/interruption. 24hr. emergency hotline.

The Traveler's Insurance Company, 1 Tower Sq., Hartford, CT 06183-5040 (tel. (800) 243-3174). Insurance against accident, baggage loss, sickness, trip cancellation/interruption, and company default. Covers emergency medical evacuation.

■■■ SAFETY AND SECURITY

■ Staying Safe

Violent crime is less common in Germany than in most countries, but it still exists, especially in big cities like Frankfurt, Hanover, and Hamburg. Switzerland is safer still, though by no means free of crime. Neo-Nazi skinheads in the large cities of former East Germany have been known to attack foreigners, especially non-whites. Tourists are particularly vulnerable to crime for two reasons: they often carry large amounts of cash and they are not as savvy as locals. Time spent learning local style will be well worth it. Walking purposefully into a café or shop and checking your map there is better than letting on that you feel scared. Walking with nervous, over-the-shoulder glances can be a tip that you have something valuable to protect. Carry all your valuables (including your passport, railpass, traveler's checks, and airline ticket) either in a **money belt** or **neckpouch** stashed securely inside your clothing. These will protect you from skilled thieves who use razors to slash backpacks and fanny packs (particular favorites of skilled bag-snatchers). Making **photocopies** of important documents will allow you to recover them in case they are filched or lost. Carry one copy separately and leave another copy at home. When exploring a new city, extra vigilance may be wise, but don't go overboard and let fear cut you off from experiencing another culture. When walking at night, you should turn daytime precautions into mandates. Stay near crowded and well-lit areas and do not attempt to cross through parks, parking lots or any other large, deserted areas.

Trains are other notoriously easy spots for thieving. Professionals wait for tourists to fall asleep and then carry off everything they can. When traveling in pairs, sleep in alternating shifts; when alone, use good judgement in selecting a train compartment: never stay in an empty one. *Always* padlock your pack to a permanent fixture in your compartment. If you must sleep in your car, it is best to do so in a well-lit area as close to a police station or 24-hour service station as possible. Sleeping outside can be even more dangerous—camp only in official supervised campsites.

There is no sure-fire set of precautions that will protect you from all situations you might encounter when you travel. A good self-defense course will give you more concrete ways to react to different types of aggression, but it might cost you more money than your trip. **Model Mugging,** a national U.S. organization with offices in several major cities, teaches a very effective, comprehensive course on self-defense (course prices vary from $400-500). Women's and men's courses are offered. Call Model Mugging (tel. East Coast (617) 232-2900; Midwest (312) 338-4545; West Coast (415) 592-7300). For official Department of State travel advisories on Germany and Switzerland, including crime and security, call their 24-hour hotline at (202) 647-5225. More complete information on safety while traveling may be found in *Travel Safety: Security and Safeguards at Home and Abroad*, from Hippocrene Books, Inc. (see Useful Publications).

■ Drugs

Every year thousands of travelers are arrested for trafficking or possession of drugs, or for simply being in the company of a suspected user. Marijuana, hashish, cocaine, and narcotics are illegal in Germany and Switzerland, and the penalties for illegal possession of drugs range from severe to horrific. It is not uncommon for a dealer to increase profits by first selling drugs to tourists and then turning them in to the authorities for a reward. Even reputedly liberal cities such as Zürich and Frankfurt take a dim view of strung-out tourists. The worst thing you can possibly do is carry drugs across an international border; not only could you end up in prison, you could be blessed with a "Drug Trafficker" stamp on your passport for the rest of your life. If you are arrested, all your home country's consulate can do is visit, provide a list of attorneys, and inform family and friends. The London-based organization **Release** (tel. +44 (071) 377 5905 or 603 8654) advises people who have been arrested on drug charges, but is hardly a life raft; abroad you are subject to local laws. If you think extradition is the worst possible fate of a convicted traveler, try a foreign jail. Make sure you get a statement and prescription from your doctor if you'll be carrying insulin, syringes, or any narcotic medications. Leave all medicines in their original labeled containers. What is legal at home may not necessarily be legal abroad; check with the appropriate foreign consulate before leaving to avoid surprises. Politely refuse to carry even a nun's excess luggage onto a plane; you're more likely to wind up in jail for possession of drugs than in heaven for your goodwill.

■■■ GETTING THERE FROM AFAR

The first challenge in European budget travel is getting there. The airline industry manipulates their computerized reservation systems to squeeze every dollar from customers; finding a cheap airfare in this deliberate confusion will be easier if you understand the airlines' machinations better than they think you do. Call every toll-free number and don't be afraid to ask about discounts. Have a knowledgeable travel agent guide you through the options; better yet, have several travel agents guide you. Remember that travel agents might not want to do the legwork to find the cheapest fares (for which they receive the lowest commissions). Students and people under 26 should never need to pay full price for a ticket. Seniors can also get mint bargains; many airlines offer senior traveler club deals or airline passes and discounts for seniors' companions. Travel sections in Sunday newspapers often list bargain fares from the local airport. Outfox airline reps with the phone-book-sized *Official Airline Guide* (at large libraries); this monthly guide lists every scheduled flight in the world (including prices). George Brown's *The Airline Passenger's Guerilla Handbook* (US$15; last published in 1990) is a more renegade resource.

Most airlines maintain a fare structure that peaks between mid-June and early September. Midweek (Mon.-Thurs.) flights run about US$30 cheaper each way than on weekends. Leaving from a travel hub such as New York, Atlanta, Dallas, Chicago, Los Angeles, San Francisco, Vancouver, Toronto, Melbourne, or Sydney will win you a more competitive fare than from smaller cities; the gains are not as great when departing from hubs monopolized by one airline, so call around. Flying to London is usually the cheapest way across the Atlantic, though special fares to other cities—Amsterdam or Brussels—can cost even less. It's often cheaper to fly to a nearby city and take a train or ferry to your final stop. Check fares for these alternate routes carefully; since train tickets are often expensive themselves and might not be worth the aggravation. An average fare to a German or Swiss city such as Berlin, Munich, Geneva, or Zurich (round-trip from New York City) can range from US$650-750.

Return-date flexibility is usually not an option for the budget traveler; except on youth fares purchased through the airlines, traveling with an "open return" ticket can be pricier than fixing a return date and paying to change it. Often, you can change the return date for a not-too-exorbitant fee; inquire when you buy. Avoid one way tickets, too: the flight to Europe may be economical, but the return fares can be outrageous. Whenever flying internationally, pick up your ticket in advance of the departure date and arrive at the airport several hours before your flight.

Commercial Airlines Even if you pay an airline's lowest published fare, you may be spending hundreds of dollars. The commercial airlines' lowest regular offer is the **APEX** (Advance Purchase Excursion Fare); specials advertised in newspapers may be cheaper, but have correspondingly more restrictions and fewer available seats. APEX fares provide you with confirmed reservations and allow "open-jaw" tickets (landing in and returning from different cities). Reservations must usually be made at least 21 days in advance, with 7- to 14-day minimum and 60- to 90-day maximum stay limitations, and hefty cancellation and change-of-reservation penalties. For summer travel, book APEX fares early; by May you will have difficulty getting the departure date you want. The national airlines of Germany and Switzerland—**Deutsche Lufthansa** (tel. (800) 645-3880) and **Swissair** (tel. (800) 221-4750), respectively—serve the most cities, but their fares tend to be high.

Most airlines no longer offer standby fares, once a staple of the budget traveler. Standby has given way to the **three-day-advance-purchase youth fare,** a cousin of the one-day variety prevalent in Europe. It's available only to those under 25 (sometimes 24) and only within three days of departure—a gamble that often pays off, but could backfire if the airline's all booked up. Return dates are open, but you must come back within a year, and once again can book your return seat no more than three days ahead. Youth fares in summer aren't really cheaper than APEX, but off-

season prices drop deliciously. **Icelandair** (tel. (800) 223-5500) is one of the few airlines which still offer this three-day fare. Check with a travel agent for details.

A few airlines offer other miscellaneous discounts. Look into flights to relatively less popular destinations or smaller carriers. Call **Icelandair** or **Virgin Atlantic Airways** (tel. (800) 862-8621) for information on their last-minute offers. Icelandair offers a "get-up-and-go" fare from New York to Luxembourg, which is convenient to Cologne and the Rhinelands (June-Sept. US$299 weekdays, US$329 weekends; Oct.-May US$268 weekdays, US$288 weekends). Reservations can be made no more than three days before departure. After arrival, Icelandair offers discounts on trains and buses from Luxembourg. Virgin Atlantic offers their Instant Purchase Plan (New York to London round trip US$432), in which reservations can be made no more than 10 days before departure.

Student Travel Agencies Students and people under 26 with proper ID qualify for deliciously reduced airfares. These are rarely available from airlines or travel agents, but instead from student travel agencies like CIEE's **Council Travel** or **STA** (see Useful Travel Organizations). These agencies negotiate special reduced-rate bulk purchases with the airlines, then resell them to the youth market; in 1993, peak season round-trip rates from the East Coast of North America to even the offbeat corners of Europe rarely topped US$700, and off-season fares were considerably lower. Return date change fees also tend to be low (around US$50). Most of their flights are on major scheduled airlines, though in peak season some seats may be on less reliable chartered aircraft. Student travel agencies can also help non-students and people over 26, but may not be able to get the same low fares.

Charter Flights And Ticket Consolidators Ticket consolidators resell unsold tickets on commercial and charter airlines that might otherwise have gone begging. Look for their tiny ads in weekend papers (in the U.S., the Sunday *New York Times* travel section is best), and start calling them all. There is rarely a maximum age; tickets are also heavily discounted, and may offer extra flexibility or bypass advance purchase requirements, since you are not tangled in airline bureaucracy. But unlike tickets bought through an airline, you won't be able to use your tickets on another flight if you miss yours, and you will have to go back to the consolidator—not the airline—to get a refund. Phone around and pay with a credit card; you can't stop a cash payment if you never receive your tickets. Don't be tempted solely by the low prices; find out all you can about the agency you're considering, and get their refund policy *in writing*. Ask also about accommodations and car rental discounts; some consolidators have fingers in many pies. *Insist* on a **receipt** that gives full details about the tickets, refunds and restrictions, and if they don't want to give you one or just generally seem clueless, use a different company.

It's best to buy from a major organization that has experience in placing individuals on charter flights. One of the most reputable is the CIEE-affiliated **Council Charter,** 205 E. 42nd St., New York, NY 10017 (tel. (800) 800-8222); their flights can also be booked through Council Travel offices. Another good organization is **Unitravel** (tel. (800) 325-2222); they offer discounted airfares on major scheduled airlines from the U.S. to over 50 cities in Europe and will hold all payments in a bank escrow until completion of your trip. Other companies book charter flights: **Access International** (tel. (800) 825-3633); **Interworld** (tel. (800) 331-4456, and in Florida (305) 443-4929); **Rebel** (tel. (800) 227-3235); and **Travac** (tel. (800) 872-8800)—don't be afraid to hunt for the best deal.

Consolidators sell a mixture of tickets; some are on scheduled airlines, some on **charter flights.** Once an entire system of its own, the charter business has shriveled and effectively merged with the ticket consolidator network. The theory behind a charter is that a tour operator contracts with an airline (usually a fairly obscure one that specializes in charters) to use their planes to fly extra loads of passengers to peak-season destinations. Charter flights thus fly less frequently than major airlines and have correspondingly more restrictions. They are also almost always fully booked, schedules and itineraries may change at the last moment, and flights may be traumatically cancelled. Shoot for a scheduled air ticket if you can, and pay with a credit card. You might also consider traveler's insurance against trip interruption.

Airhitch, 2790 Broadway #100, New York, NY 10025 (tel. (212) 864-2000) advertises a similar service: you choose a five-day date range in which to travel and a list of preferred European destinations, and they try to place you in a vacant spot in a flight in your date range to one of those destinations. Absolute flexibility—on both sides of the Atlantic—is necessary, but the savings might be worth it: flights cost US$169 each way when departing from the East Coast of the U.S., US$269 from the West Coast, and US$229 from most places in between. Airhitch usually gets you where you want to go, but they only guarantee that you'll end up in Europe. Check all flight times and departure sites directly with the airline carrier, and read *all* the fine print they send you and compare it to what people tell you. The Better Business Bureau of New York received complaints about Airhitch a few years ago; they still don't recommend them, but they don't discourage you from using them, either. Icelandair's **Supergrouper** plan puts travelers on round-trip flights to Luxembourg, but does not require a specific return date (must return within 1 year; tickets US$669).

Last minute **discount clubs** and **fare brokers** offer members savings on European travel, including charter flights and tour packages. Research your options carefully. **Last Minute Travel Club,** 1249 Boylston St., Boston, MA 02215 (tel. (800) 527-8646 or (617) 267-9800) is one of the few travel clubs that doesn't require a membership fee. Others include **Discount Travel International** (tel. (800) 324-9294), **Moment's Notice** (tel. (212) 486-0503; US$25 annual fee), **Traveler's Advantage** (tel. (800) 835-8747; US$49 annual fee), and **Worldwide Discount Travel Club** (tel. (305) 534-2082; US$50 annual fee). For US$25, **Travel Avenue** will search for the lowest international airfare available and then discount it 5-17% (tel. (800) 333-3335). The often labyrinthine contracts for all these organizations deserve close study—you may prefer not to stop over in Luxembourg for eleven hours.

Courier Flights Those who travel light should consider flying to Europe as a courier. The company hiring you will use your checked luggage space for freight; you're left with the carry-on allowance. Restrictions to watch for: most flights are round-trip only with fixed-length stays (usually short), you may not be able to travel with a companion (single tickets only) and most flights are from New York (including a scenic visit to the courier office in the 'burbs). Round-trip fares to Western Europe from the U.S. range from US$199-349 (off-season) to US$399-549 (summer). **Now Voyager,** 74 Varick St., #307, New York, NY 10013 (tel. (212) 431-1616), acts as an agent for many courier flights worldwide from New York, although some flights are available from Houston. They also offer special last-minute deals to such cities as London, Paris, Rome and Frankfurt which go for as little as US$299 round-trip. **Halbart Express,** 147-05 176th St., Jamaica, NY 11434 (tel. (718) 656-8279), and **Courier Travel Service,** 530 Central Avenue, Cedarhurst, NY 11516 (tel. (516) 374-2299), are other courier agents to try. And if you have travel time to spare, Ford's Travel Guides, 19448 Londelius St., Northridge, CA 91324 (tel. (818) 701-7414), lists **freighter companies** that will take passengers for trans-Atlantic crossings. Ask for their *Freighter Travel Guide and Waterways of the World* (US$15).

You can also go directly through courier companies in New York, or check your bookstore or library for handbooks such as *The Insider's Guide to Air Courier Bargains* (US$15). The *Courier Air Travel Handbook* (US$10.70), which explains the procedure for traveling as an air courier and contains names, telephone numbers, and contact points of courier companies, can be ordered directly from Thunderbird Press, 5930-10 W. Greenway Rd., Suite 112, Glendale, AZ 85306, or by calling (800) 345-0096. **Travel Unlimited,** P.O. Box 1058, Allston, MA 02134-1058 (no phone), publishes a comprehensive, monthly newsletter that details all possible options for courier travel. A one-year subscription is US$25 (abroad US$35).

■■■ TRANSPORTATION: PLANNING YOUR TRIP

■ By Train

The railway systems of Germany and Switzerland are indisputably the best in Europe. Second-class travel is pleasant, and compartments, which seat six, are excellent places to meet folks of all ages and nationalities. Trains are in no way theft-proof; lock the door of your compartment if you can, and keep your valuables on your person at all times. Many train stations have different counters for domestic tickets, international tickets, seat reservations, and information; check before lining up. On major lines, reservations are always advisable, and often required, even if you have a railpass; make them at least a few hours in advance at the train station.

You may be tempted to save on accommodations by taking an overnight train in a regular coach seat, but there are problems; *if* you get to sleep you are sure to wake up exhausted and aching, security problems are rampant, and if you spread yourself over several seats in an empty compartment, someone is sure to come in at 2am and claim one of them. A sleeping berth in a bunkbedded couchette car, with linen provided, is a somewhat affordable luxury (about US$24; reserve at the station at least several days in advance). Very few countries give students or young people discounts on regular domestic rail tickets, but many will sell a student or youth card valid for one-half or one-third off all fares for an entire year (see Essentials: Rail Passes, or refer to Germany or Switzerland's Once There: Getting Around section).

Buying a **railpass** is both a popular and sensible option in many circumstances. But railpasses don't always pay off. Find a travel agent with a copy of the *Eurailtariff* manual (or call **Rail Europe** in the U.S. at (800) 438-7245 and ask for the latest edition of the *Rail Europe Traveler's Guide*), add up the second-class fares for the major routes you plan to cover, deduct 5% (the listed price includes a commission), deduct a rough 35% if you're under 26 and eligible for BIJ (see below) and compare. If the total cost of all your trips comes close to the price of the pass, the convenience of avoiding ticket lines may be worth the difference. Avoid an obsession with making the pass pay for itself; you may come home only with blurred memories of train stations.

The Eurailpass

The various **Eurailpasses** are ideal for extensive international travel. Ideally conceived, a railpass allows you to jump on any train in Europe, go wherever you want, whenever you want, and change your plans at will. The handbook that comes with your railpass tells you everything you need to know and includes a timetable for major routes, a map and details on ferry discounts. In practice, of course, it's not so simple. You still must stand in line to pay for seat reservations (the only guarantee you have against standing up), for supplements, for couchette reservations, and to have your pass validated when you first use it. The Eurailpass is one of the best options in European rail passes for Americans. CIEE, STA, and many travel agents sell them (see Useful Travel Organizations above). Some rail stations in Europe sell them too, but you'll probably find it much easier to purchase your Eurailpass *before you arrive* in Europe. A few major train stations in Europe sell them too (though American agents usually deny this). If you're stuck in Europe and unable to find someone to sell you a Eurailpass, make a transatlantic call to an American railpass agent, which should be able to send a pass to you by express mail. The passes are valid in all Western European countries (except in England) and in Hungary. They entitle you to travel on all trains except privately run lines. They do not cover the fee to guarantee a seat on a train (US$2-10). The pass also allows free transit on many ferries. In addition, Eurailpass offers the free booklet *Through Europe by Train*, with timetables for the most convenient intercity rail hubs in the 17 European countries whose railroads honor Eurailpasses. Write to Eurailpass, P.O. Box 325, Old Greenwich, CT 06870.

The first-class Eurailpass is very rarely profitable (15 days unlimited travel US$498, 21 days US$648, 1 month US$798, 2 months US$1098 and 3 months US$1398). If you are traveling in a group, you might prefer the **Eurail Saverpass,** which allows unlimited first-class travel for 15 days for US$430 per person for two or more people traveling together (3 or more April-Sept.). There are also 21-day (US$550 per person) and one-month (US$678 per person) Saverpasses. Travelers (under 26 by the 1st day of travel) can buy the **Eurail Youthpass,** good for 15 days (US$398), one month (US$578), or two months (US$768) of second-class unlimited travel. The one-month pass is tough to make pay off; the two-month pass is better. The first-class **Eurail Flexipass** allows limited travel within a longer period. Three packages are offered: five days of travel within a two-month period for US$348, 10 days of travel within a two-month period for US$560, or 15 days of travel in a two-month period for US$740. **Youth Flexipasses** (under 26) are also available (5 days within 2 months US$255, 10 days within 2 months US$398, and 15 days within 2 months US$540). To get a Eurailpass replaced in case of loss, you must purchase **insurance** on it from Eurail after buying the pass. *All prices listed above are for 1994;* you may be able to purchase a pass for a better price if you buy *before* January '94. Eurailpasses are not refundable once validated; you will be able to get a replacement *only* if you have purchased insurance on the pass from Eurail—something that cannot be done through a travel agent. Ask a travel agent for specifics, and be sure you know how it all works before you get to Europe. The **EurailDrive Pass** combines the Eurail Flexipass with a specified period of unlimited mileage car rental from Hertz. Prices vary based on the size of the group and the class of car. You must be at least 21 (23 for Hertz) and possess a major credit card and a driver's license at least one year old.

If you are planning on extensive travel in **Germany,** know that Eurailpass holders get free passage on the S-Bahn (commuter rail) and on DB bus lines (marked *Bahn*) throughout the country. Passholders also get free rides and discounts on the Romantic Road buses and some Rhine steamers, and railpasses are valid for the ferries from Puttgarden, Warnemünde, and Saßnitz to Denmark and Sweden (most trains drive right onto the ferry anyway). For more country-specific information, see Germany: Once There: Getting Around.

National Rail Passes

If you plan to focus your travels in one country, consider a national railpass. Both Germany and Switzerland have **regional railpass** options; *Let's Go* those which are sold outside of Germany and Switzerland here and, if you're likely to buy the pass once you've arrived at your travel destination, in the Once There: Getting Around section for each country. Some of these passes can be purchased *only* in Europe, and some only outside of Europe, such as the **German Railpass.** Check with a railpass agent or with national tourist offices. Those country passes that can be bought in Europe are usually *cheaper* in Europe; travel agents rarely tell you this.

The **German Railpass** can only be purchased in the U.S. or Canada before you leave on your trip. The **GermanRail Flexipass** (in its adult and **Junior** variety) entitles you to unlimited travel in all parts of the country (2nd class; any 5 days in 1 month US$170, under 26 US$130; any 10 days US$268, under 26 US$178; any 15 days US$348, under 26 US$218; usually a US$7.50 "special handling fee" tagged on; 1st-class passes also available). They also offer a **Saver Pass,** by which one person pays full fare and the second gets a reduced fare (2nd class; any 5 days in 1 month US$130; any 10 days US$200; any 15 days US$250; 1st class passes also available).

Deutsche Bundesbahn-authorized travel companies in the U.S. and Canada sell both the German Railpass and the Eurail Pass: GermanRail Flexipasses, Junior Flexipasses, SaverPasses, Eurailpasses and EurailDrive passes. Passes can be purchased in person or by mail. Offices are located in: **Atlanta,** 3400 Peachtree Rd., NE, Atlanta, GA 30326 (tel. (404) 266-9555); **Boston,** 20 Park Plaza, Boston, MA 02116 (tel. (617)

542-0577); **Chicago,** 9575 W. Higgins Road, Rosemont, IL 60018 (tel. (708) 692-4141); **Dallas,** 222 W. Las Colinas, Irving, TX 75039 (tel. (214) 402-8377); **Los Angeles,** 11933 Wilshire Boulevard, Los Angeles, CA 90025 (tel. (310) 479-2772); **New York,** 122 E. 42nd St., Suite 1904, New York, NY 10168 (tel. (212) 308-3100); **Toronto,** 904 The East Mall, Etobicoke, Ont. M9B 6K2 (tel. (416) 695-1211).

Keep in mind that there are passes similar to the GermanRail Pass that can be bought *only* in Germany (the *Tramper-Monats* and the *Bahncard);* if you're not willing to commit to buying a pass while still in your home country, wait until you arrive and decide then (see Germany: Getting Around by Train, for details). The railways of Switzerland also offer a similar pass called the **Swiss Pass;** we detail this in the Switzerland: Once There: Getting Around section.

Youth Fares

For those under 26, **BIJ** tickets (Billets Internationals de Jeunesse, sold under the **Wasteels, Eurotrain** and **Route 26** names) are an excellent alternative to railpasses. Available for international trips within Europe, they save an average of 30-45% off regular second-class fares. Tickets are sold from point to point, with free and unlimited stopovers along the way. However, you cannot take longer than two months to complete your trip, and you can stop only at points along the specific direct route of your ticket. In 1993, for instance, Wasteels offered round-trip tickets from London to Berlin for approximately £90, and a London-Amsterdam-Berlin-Prague-Budapest-Vienna-Zurich-Brussels-London ticket for £190—significantly less than the cost of a 2-month youth railpass. You can always buy BIJ tickets at Wasteels or Eurotrain offices (usually in or near train stations). In some countries (including Germany and Switzerland), BIJ tickets are also available from regular ticket counters. Some travel agencies also sell BIJ. In the U.S., contact Wasteels at (407) 351-2537, in London call (071) 834 7066.

■ By Car and Van

See both Germany and Switzerland: Once There: Getting Around for driving tips in those countries. Cars offer great speed, great freedom, access to the countryside, and an escape from the town-to-town mentality of trains. Unfortunately, they also insulate you from the *esprit de corps* of European rail travelers. Although a single traveler won't save by renting a car, four usually will; groups of two or three may find renting cheaper than a railpass (although gas in Europe costs US$3-4 per gallon). If you can't decide between train and car travel, you may relish a combination of the two; rail and car packages offered by Avis and Hertz are often effective for two or more people traveling together, and Rail Europe and other railpass vendors (see By Train: Rail Passes) offer economical "Euraildrive" passes. At most agencies in Europe, all that's required to rent a car is a U.S. license and proof that you've had it for a year. Permits such as the **International Driver's Permit** are available if needed, but check with the car rental agency in Europe before you purchase one—they may not require it (see below for more details). The **International Insurance Certificate,** sometimes called the "green card," is standard auto insurance. Get it from an insurance company or rental agency. Again, check with the European car rental agency you're planning to use before buying additional insurance to see what they offer in the cost of rental and what they require from you. If you have a collision while in Europe, the accident will show up on your domestic records. Theft insurance is not paid by the rental agency in some countries; in any case, you will be required to pay for insurance when the agency does not.

Renting and Leasing

You can **rent** a car from either a U.S.-based multinational firm (Avis, Budget, or Hertz) with its own European offices, from a European-based company with local representatives (National and American International represent Europcar and Ansa respectively), or from a tour operator (Europe by Car, Auto Europe, Foremost,

Kemwel and Wheels International), which will arrange a rental for you from a European company at its own rates. Not surprisingly, the multinationals offer greater flexibility, but the tour operators often strike good deals and may have lower rates. Rentals vary considerably by company, season of rental, and pick-up point; expect to pay at least US$140 a week, plus tax, for a teensy car. Reserve well before leaving for Europe and pay in advance if you can; rates within Europe are harsh. Always check if prices quoted include tax and collision insurance; some credit card companies will cover this automatically. This may be a substantial savings, but ask if a credit hold will be put on your account and, if so, how much. Ask about student and other discounts and be flexible in your itinerary; picking up your car in Brussels or Luxembourg is usually cheaper than renting from Paris. Ask your airline about special packages; sometimes you can get up to a week of free rental. Minimum age restrictions vary by country; rarely, if ever, is it below 21. Try **Auto Europe** (tel. (800) 223-5555); **Avis Rent a Car** (tel. (800) 331-1084); **Budget Rent a Car** (tel. (800) 472-3325); **Connex** (tel. (800) 333-3949); **Europe by Car,** Rockefeller Plaza, New York, NY 10020 (tel.(800) 223-1516 or (212) 581-3040); **Foremost Euro-Car** (tel. (800) 272-3299; (800) 253-3876 in Canada); **France Auto Vacances** (tel. (800) 234-1426); **Hertz Rent a Car** (tel. (800) 654-3001); **The Kemwel Group** (tel. (800) 678-0678), or **Payless Car Rental** (tel. (800) PAY-LESS).

For longer than three weeks, **leasing** can be cheaper than renting; it is sometimes the only option for those aged 18-20. The cheapest leases are actually agreements where you buy the car, drive it, and then sell it back to the car manufacturer at a pre-agreed price. As far as you're concerned, though, it's a simple lease and doesn't entail galactic financial transactions. Leases include full insurance coverage and are not taxed. The most affordable leases usually originate in Belgium and France and start at around US$500 for 23 days and US$1000 for 60 days. Contact **Foremost**, **Europe by Car** or **Auto Europe.** You will need to make arrangements in advance.

If you're brave or know what you're doing, **buying** a used car or van in Europe and selling it just before you leave can provide the cheapest wheels on the Continent. Check with consulates for different countries' import-export laws concerning used vehicles, registration, and safety and emission standards. David Shore and Patty Campbell's *Europe By Van And Motorhome* (US$14 postpaid, US$6 for overseas airmail) guides you through the entire process, from buy-back agreements to insurance and dealer listings. To order, write to 1842 Santa Margarita Dr., Fallbrook, CA 92028 (tel. (619) 723-6184). *How to Buy and Sell a Used Car in Europe* (U.S. $6 plus 75¢ postage) contains useful tips; write to Gil Friedman, P.O. Box 1063, Arcata, CA 95521 (tel. (707) 822-5001).

Caravanning, usually involving a campervan or motorhome, gives the advantages of car rental without the hassle of finding lodgings or cramming six friends into a Renault. You'll need those six friends to split the gasoline bills, however, although many European vehicles use diesel or propane, which are much cheaper than ordinary gasoline. Prices vary even more than for cars, but for the outdoor-oriented group trip, caravanning can be a dream. Contact the car rental firms listed above for more information. Shore and Campbell's book also has tips.

International Driver's License

Although visitors to Germany and Switzerland from the United States and Canada may drive in both Germany and Switzerland for one year with a national license, an **International Driving Permit (IDP)** smooths out difficulties with foreign police officers, especially if you do not speak the language. If you choose to drive with only a national license, it must be accompanied by a translation issued from one of the following offices: (1) German diplomatic offices, (2) International motor vehicle offices in the country where the license was issued, or (3) German automobile club (ADAC; see address in Germany Getting Around: By Car). Most car rental agencies do not require the IDP; thus, some drivers risk driving without one. Also, a valid driver's license from your home country must always accompany the IDP. Your IDP must be issued in your own country before you depart. Applicants in the U.S. or Canada must be over 18. U.S. license holders can obtain an International Driving Permit (US$10), valid for one year, at any **American Automobile Association (AAA)** office or by writing to its main office, AAA Florida, Travel Agency Services Department, 1000 AAA Drive, Heathrow, FL 32746-5080 (tel. (800) 222-4357 or (407) 444-7883, fax (407) 444-7380). You may also procure an IDP from the **American Automobile Touring Alliance,** Bayside Plaza, 188 The Embarcadero, San Francisco, CA 94105. **Canadian** license holders can obtain an IDP (CDN$10) through any **Canadian Automobile Association (CAA)** branch office in Canada, or by writing to CAA Toronto, 60 Commerce Valley Dr. East, Markham, Ont., L3T 7P9 (tel. (416) 771-3170). Most credit cards cover standard **insurance.** If you drive your own car or rent or borrow one, you will need a **green card,** or **International Insurance Certificate,** to prove that you have liability insurance. The application forms are available at any AAA or CAA office. Or, you can get one through the car rental agency; most of them include coverage in their prices. If you lease a car, you can obtain a green card from the dealer. Some travel agents offer the card, and it may be available at the border. Verify whether your auto insurance applies abroad; even if it does, you will still need a green card to certify this to foreign officials.

■ By Airplane

Unless you're under 25, flying across Europe on regularly scheduled flights will eat through your budget; nearly all airlines cater to business travelers and set prices accordingly. If you are 24 or under, special fares on most European airlines requiring ticket purchase either the day before or the day of departure are a happy exception to this rule. These are often cheaper than the corresponding regular train fare, though not always as cheap as student rail tickets or railpasses. Student travel agencies in Europe and America also sell cheap tickets. Budget fares are also frequently available in the spring and summer on high-volume routes between northern Europe and resort areas in Spain, Italy and Greece. Consult budget travel agents and local newspapers and magazines.

■ By Boat

Travel by boat is a bewitching alternative much favored by Europeans but overlooked by most foreigners. Most European ferries are straightforward, comfortable and well-equipped; the cheapest fare class sometimes includes use of a reclining chair or couchette where you can sleep the trip away. You should check in at least two hours early for a prime spot and allow plenty of time for late trains and getting to the port. It's a good idea to bring your own food and avoid the mushy, astronomically priced cafeteria cuisine. Fares jump sharply in July and August. Always ask for discounts; ISIC holders can often get student fares and Eurail passholders get many reductions and free trips (check the brochure that comes with your railpass). You'll occasionally have to pay a small port tax (under US$10). Advance planning and reserved ticket purchases through a travel agency can spare you several tedious days of waiting in dreary ports for the next sailing. The best American source for information on Scandinavian ferries and visa-free cruises to Russia is **EuroCruises,** 303 W. 13th St., New York, NY 10014 (tel. (212) 691-2099 or (800) 688-3876).

Riverboats acquaint you with many towns that trains can only wink at. The Moselle, Rhine and Danube steamers have been overrun by gaudy tourists; less commercial-looking lines can be more seductive. *Let's Go* details many ferry schedules in the appropriate towns in Germany and Switzerland.

■ By Bicycle

Today, biking is one of the key elements of the classic budget Eurovoyage. Everyone else in the youth hostel is doing it, and with the proliferation of mountain bikes, you can do some serious natural sightseeing. For information about touring routes, consult national tourist offices or any of the numerous books available.

Europe By Bike, by Karen and Terry Whitehill (US$15), is a great source of specific area tours. *Cycling Europe: Budget Bike Touring in the Old World,* by N. Slavinski (US$13), may also be a helpful addition to your library. Michelin road maps are clear and detailed guides. Take some reasonably challenging day-long rides before you leave to prepare. Have your bike tuned up. Learn the international signals for turns and use them. Although you may not be able to build a frame, learn how to fix a modern derailleur-equipped mount and change a tire before leaving, and practice on your own bike before you have to do it overseas. A few tools and a good bike manual will be invaluable. You might want to consider an organized **bicycle tour;** they are arranged for a wide range of cycling abilities. **College Bicycle Tours** offers co-ed bicycle tours through seven countries in Europe that are exclusively for the college-aged; contact them at (800) 736-BIKE in U.S. and Canada for details. Most airlines will count your bicycle as your second free piece of luggage (you're usually allowed two pieces of checked baggage and a carry-on piece). As an additional piece, it costs about US$85 each way. Policies on charters and budget flights vary; check with the airline. The safest way to send your bike is in a box, with the handlebars, pedals and front wheel detached. Within Europe, most ferries let you take bikes on for free. You can always ship your bike on trains, though the cost varies from a small fixed fee to a substantial fraction of the ticket price.

Riding a bike with a frame pack strapped on it or on your back is about as safe as pedaling blindfolded over a sheet of ice; panniers are essential. The first thing to buy is a suitable **bike helmet.** At about US$50-100, they're better than head injury or death. A **U**-shaped **Citadel** or **Kryptonite** lock is expensive (about US$20-49), but the companies insure their locks against theft of your bike for one or two years.

Renting a bike is preferable to bringing your own if your touring will be confined to one or two regions. A sturdy if unexciting one-speed model will cost US$8-12 per day; be prepared to lay down a sizable deposit. *Let's Go* lists bike rental shops in most cities and towns. Some youth hostels rent bicycles for low prices. In many countries (including Germany and Switzerland), train stations rent bikes and often allow you to drop them off elsewhere in the country without charge. See Once There for more details about getting around by bicycle in Germany and Switzerland.

■ By Moped and Motorcycle

Motorized bikes have long spiced southern European roads with their flashy colors and perpetual buzz. They offer an enjoyable, relatively inexpensive way to tour coastal areas and countryside, particularly when there are few cars. They don't use much gas, can be put on trains and ferries, and are a good compromise between the high cost of car travel and the limited range of bicycles. However, long distances become never-ending when sitting upright and cruising at only 40km per hour. Mopeds are also dangerous in the rain and unpredictable on rough roads or gravel. Always wear a helmet and never ride wearing a backpack. If you've never been on a moped before, a twisting Alpine road is not the place to start. In general expect to pay US$15-35 per day; try auto repair shops and remember to bargain. Motorcycles are faster and more expensive; they normally require a license. Before renting, ask if the quoted price includes tax and insurance or you may be hit for an unexpected additional fee. Avoid handing your passport over as a deposit; if you have an accident or mechanical failure you may not get it back until you cover all repairs. Pay ahead of time instead.

■ By Thumb

> *Let's Go* strongly urges you to seriously consider the risks before you choose
> to hitch. We do not recommend hitching as a safe means of transportation and
> none of the information presented here is intended to do so.

No one should hitch without careful consideration of the risks involved. Not
everyone can be an airplane pilot, but most every bozo can drive a car, and hitching
means entrusting your life to a randomly selected person who happens to stop
beside you on the road, risking theft, assault, sexual harrassment and unsafe driving.
In spite of this, the gains are many: favorable hitching experiences allow you to
meet local people and get where you're going. The choice, however, remains yours.
Consider this section akin to handing out condoms to high school students: we
don't endorse it, but if you're going to do it anyway, we'll tell you some ways to
make it safer. If you do decide to hitch, read what *Let's Go* has to say about hitching
in the Once There: Getting Around section for either Germany or Switzerland.

Depending on the circumstances and the norms of the country, men and women
traveling in groups and men traveling alone might consider hitching (called
"autostop" in much of Europe) to locations beyond the scope of bus or train routes.
If you're a woman traveling alone, *don't hitch.* It's just too dangerous. A man and a
woman are a safer combination, two men will have a harder time finding a ride and
three will go nowhere. Hitching (or even standing) on super-highways is generally
illegal: you may only thumb at rest stops, or at the entrance ramps to highways—*in
front* of the cute blue and white superhighway pictograph (a bridge over a road). In
the Practical Information section of many cities, we list the tram or bus lines that
will take travelers to strategic points for hitching out.

Your success will depend on *what you look like.* Successful hitchers travel light
and stack their belongings in a compact but visible cluster. Most Europeans signal
with an open hand, rather than a thumb; many write their destination on a sign in
large, bold letters and draw a smiley-face under it. Drivers like hitchers who are neat
and wholesome, yet dynamic. No one stops for a grump, or for anyone wearing sun-
glasses. Safety issues are always imperative, even when you're traveling with
another person. Avoid getting in the back of a two-door car, and never let go of your
backpack. *Hitchhiking at night can be particularly dangerous;* think hard about
whether it's worth it. Stand in a well-lit place and expect drivers to be leery of noc-
turnal thumbers. When you get into a car, make sure you know how to get out again
in a hurry. Couples may avoid hassles with male drivers if the woman sits in the
back or next to the door. If you ever feel threatened, insist on being let off, regard-
less of where you are. If the driver refuses to stop, try acting as though you're going
to open the car door or vomit on the upholstery.*Europe: A Manual for Hitchhikers*
gives directions for hitching out of hundreds of cities, rates rest areas and entrance
ramps and deciphers national highway and license plate systems. It's available from
Vacation Work Publications (complete address in the Work section).

Most Western European countries offer a ride service, a cross between hitchhiking and the ride boards common at many university campuses. Organizations pair
drivers with riders, with a fee to both agency (about US$25) and driver (per km).
Eurostop International (called **Verband der Deutschen Mitfahrzentralen** in Germany) is one of the largest in Europe. Look them up in any big city. Not all of these
organizations screen drivers and riders; ask in advance.

■ ■ ■ ACCOMMODATIONS

Let's Go is not an exhaustive guide to budget accommodations—although we try,
we really do try. Most local tourist offices distribute extensive listings free of charge
and will also reserve a room for a small fee. National Tourist Offices (listed in Essentials) and travel agencies (Useful Travel Organizations, also early in the book) will

supply more complete lists of campsites and hotels. For information on the particular accommodation culture of either Germany or Switzerland, see Once There: Accommodations for each country.

■ Hotels

Hotels are quite expensive in Germany and Switzerland: rock bottom for singles is US$17-20, for doubles US$22-24, and the price is never subject to haggling. Inexpensive European hotels might come as a rude shock to pampered North American travelers. A bathroom of your own is a rarity and costs extra when provided. Hot showers may also cost extra. *Pension* (guesthouse) owners run smaller establishments and will often direct you to points of interest in the town and countryside. Unmarried couples will generally have no trouble getting a room together, although couples under 21 may occasionally encounter resistance.

If you wish to make reservations (at hotels or hostels), you can ensure a prompt reply by enclosing two International Postal Reply Coupons (available at any post office). Indicate your night of arrival and the number of nights you plan to stay. The hotel will send you a confirmation and may request payment for the first night. Not all hotels accept reservations, and few accept checks in U.S. currency. The **Deutscher Hotel-und Gaststättenverban e.V.** (German Hotel Association or DEHOGA), Kronprinzenstr. 46, Postfach 20 04 55, 53173 Bonn (tel. (0228) 82 00 80, fax (0228) 820 08 46).

■ Hostels

The Basics

Hostels are the hubs of the gigantic backpacker subculture that overtakes Europe every summer, providing innumerable opportunities to meet travelers from all over the world. You can find new traveling partners, trade stories, and learn about places to visit. Most guests are ages 17 to 25, but hostels are rapidly becoming a resource for all ages. Many German and Swiss hostels are open to families. Hostel prices are extraordinarily low—US$8-14 a night for shared rooms. Only camping is cheaper. Meals are frequently available, though they are rarely delicious. For those who wish to cook for themselves, many hostels have fully equipped kitchen facilities. Some hostels are set in strikingly beautiful castles, others in run-down barracks far from the town center. The most common disadvantage is an early curfew—fine if you're climbing a mountain the next morning, but a distinct cramp in your style if you plan to rage in Berlin, Munich, or Zurich. Many are out of the way, conditions are sometimes spartan and cramped, there's little privacy, rooms are usually segregated by sex, and you may run into more screaming pre-teen tour groups than you care to remember. Finally, there is often a lockout from morning to mid-afternoon. Sheet sleeping sacks are required at many of these hostels. Sleeping bags are usually prohibited (for sanitary reasons), but most hostels provide free blankets. You can make your own sheet sack by folding a sheet and sewing it shut on two sides, or order one (about US$14) from Let's Go Travel or AYH (see Useful Travel Organizations above).

The most extensive group of hostels is organized by **Hostelling International (HI),** the new and universal trademark name adopted by the International Youth Hostel Federation (IYHF). The 6,000 official youth hostels worldwide will normally display the new HI logo (a blue triangle) alongside the symbol of one of the 70 national hostel associations. For information on HI membership, see below. The guide *Budget Accommodation Vol. 1: Europe and the Mediterranean* (US$14 including postage and handling) lists up-to-date information on HI hostels. They contain English, French, German, and Spanish translations and are available from any hostel association. HI has recently instituted an **International Booking Network.** To reserve space in high season, obtain an International Booking Voucher from any national youth hostel association and send it to a participating hostel (4-8

weeks in advance, US$2 in local currency). You can contact some hostels, indicated in the guide, by fax. If your plans are firm enough, pre-booking is wise. For more country-specific information, or for the *Jugendherbergen in Deutschland* guide, contact **Deutsches Jugenherbergeswerk (DJH)** Bismarckstr. 8, Postfach 1455, 32756 Detmold (tel. (05231) 7401-0, fax (05231) 7401-49, -66, or -67). There are a few private hostels in Germany and Switzerland. No membership is required, and you won't always have to contend with early curfews or daytime lockouts. HI hostels in Bavaria do not admit guests over age 26.For more details on youth hostels, see Germany or Switzerland: Once There: Accommodations.

Hostel Membership

In a few countries you must be a member to be eligible to stay in **Hostelling International (HI)** hostels; in others, non-members pay a supplement. A **one-year membership** permits you to stay at youth hostels all over Germany and Switzerland at unbeatable prices. And, despite the name, you need not be a youth; travelers over 25 pay only a bit more. It's best to procure a membership card *before* you leave home; some hostels do not sell them on the spot. One-year hostel membership cards are available from some travel agencies, including Council Travel, Let's Go Travel, and STA Travel (see Useful Addresses), and from HI affiliates:

International Youth Hostel Federation (IYHF), headquarters, 9 Guessens Rd., Welwyn Garden City, Hertfordshire AL8 6QW, England (tel. (0707) 33 24 87).

American Youth Hostels (AYH), 733 15th St. NW, Suite 840, Washington, DC, 20005 (tel. (202) 783-6161, fax (202) 783-6171); also dozens of regional offices across the U.S. (call above number for information). Fee US$25, under 18 US$10, over 54 US$15. Contact AYH for ISICs, student and charter flights, travel equipment, and literature on budget travel.

Hostelling International Canada (HI-C), National Office, 1600 James Naismith Dr., #608, Gloucester, Ont. K1B 5N4, Canada (tel. (613) 748-5638). 1-year membership fee CDN$26.75, under 18 CDN$12.84; 2-year CDN$37.45.

Youth Hostels Association of England and Wales (YHA), Trevelyan House, 8 St. Stephen's Hill, St. Albans, Herts AL1 2DY, England (tel. (0727) 85 52 15).

An Oíge (Irish Youth Hostel Association), 61 Mountjoy Sq., Dublin 7, Ireland (tel. (01) 30 45 55, fax (01) 30 58 08). Fee £9, under 18 £3.

Australian Youth Hostels Association (AYHA), Level 3, 10 Mallett St., Camperdown, New South Wales, 2050 Australia (tel. (02) 565 16 99).

Youth Hostels Association of New Zealand, P.O. Box 436, corner of Manchester and Gloucester St., Christchurch 1, New Zealand (tel. 79 99 70). Fee NZ$24.

■ Alternative Accommodations

Ask at tourist offices in university/college towns whether student dormitories are available to travelers when school is not in session. When they are available, they are rented to visitors for a nominal fee, usually comparable to youth hostel prices. You usually won't have to share a room with strangers or endure stringent curfew and eviction regulations. Most rooms are reserved for students looking for apartments. **Mitwohnzentrale** match people who want to lease apartments from a few days to a couple of months. A number of host networks will help you find accommodations with families throughout Europe. **Servas** is an organization devoted to promoting world peace and understanding by providing opportunities for more personal contacts among people of diverse cultures. Travelers are invited to share life in host's homes in over 100 countries. You are asked to contact hosts in advance, and you must be willing to fit into the household routine. Prospective travelers must submit an application with references, have an interview, and pay a membership fee of US$55, plus a US$25 deposit for up to five host lists. The host lists provide short self-descriptions of each host member. Write to U.S. Servas, Inc., 11 John St., #407, New York, NY 10038 (tel. (212) 267-0252). Sleeping in European train stations is a time-honored tradition. However, the romance of being "down and out" is overshadowed by reality. While it *is* free and often tolerated by local authorities, it is *neither* comfortable *nor* safe. Spending the night is even less safe.

■ Camping and the Outdoors

Camping: The Basics Organized campgrounds exist in almost every German city and many Swiss cities, most accessible by foot or by public transportation. Often however, they resemble battlegrounds, with weary travelers and screaming children stacked next to each other. Money and time expended in getting to the campsite may eat away at your budget and your patience. Camping in the countryside is far more attractive (often in breathtaking and deliciously empty sites), but considerably less convenient if you have no car. Showers, bathrooms, and a small restaurant or store are common; some sites have more elaborate facilities. Prices range from US$1-10 per person with an additional charge for a tent and vehicle.

Europa Camping and Caravanning, an annually updated catalog of campsites in Europe, is available through Recreational Equipment, Inc. for US$20 (see below for address). The excellent *Camp Europe by Train* (US$17, including postage; published by Ariel Publications, 14417 SE 19th Place, Bellevue, WA 98007 (tel. (206) 641-0518), also available from Forsyth Travel Library (see Useful Addresses), contains general camping tips and suggestions for camping areas along Eurail lines. Finally, the **Automobile Association**, Fanum House, Basingstoke, Hampshire RG21 2EA, England (tel. (0256) 491 510), publishes *Camping and Caravanning in Europe*. An **International Camping Carnet** (membership card) is required by some European campgrounds but can usually be bought on the spot. The card entitles you to a discount at some campgrounds, and often may be substituted for your passport as a security deposit. In the U.S., it's available for US$30 through the **National Campers and Hikers Association,** Inc., 4804 Transit Rd., Bldg. #2, Depew, NY 14043 (tel. (716) 668-6242). Their magazine *Camping Today* is distributed to all members (Carnet price includes a membership fee).

Equipment Prospective campers will need to invest in good camping equipment. Spend some time skimming catalogs and questioning knowledgeable salespeople before buying anything. Use the reputable mail-order firms to gauge prices; order from them if you can't do as well locally. In the fall, last year's merchandise may be reduced by as much as 50%. Purchase your equipment before you leave. See Packing, above, for information on **backpacks.** Most of the better **sleeping bags,** down (lightweight and warm) or synthetic (cheaper, heavier, more durable, and warmer when wet)—have ratings for specific minimum temperatures. The lower the mercury, the higher the price. Anticipate the most severe conditions you may encounter, subtract a few degrees, and then buy a bag. The warmest bag will keep you *warm,* so don't overpurchase if you need a bag just for the summer. Expect to pay at least US$60 for a synthetic bag and up to US$250 for a down bagfor use in sub-freezing temperatures. **Sleeping bag pads** range from US$12-80, while air mattresses go for about US$30-60 (the cheapest foam varieties are plenty comfortable: buy one that's at least three-quarters body length). The best **tents** are free-standing, with frames and suspension systems, set up quickly and require no staking. Make sure you have and use the tent's protective rain fly (dew can be quite soggy). Backpackers and cyclists will require especially small, lightweight models. **Sierra Design,** 2039 4th St., Berkeley, CA, 94710, sells a two-person tent that weighs less than 1.4 kg (3 lbs.) Expect to pay at least US$100 for a good two-person tent.

Other camping basics include a battery-operated **lantern** (*never* gas) for use inside the tent and a simple plastic **groundcloth** to protect the tent floor. Large, collapsible **water sacks** weigh practically nothing when empty. **Campstoves** come in all sizes, weights, and fuel types, but none is truly cheap (US$30-120) or light. Consider GAZ, a form of bottled propane gas that is easy to use and widely available in Europe. Bring some **waterproof matches. Cooking equipment** can prove more of an albatross than a convenience–consider your eating requirements and preferences carefully. A **canteen, Swiss army knife,** and **insect repellent** are small, essential items to throw in with your gear. For further information about camping equipment and other camping concerns, contact **Wilderness Press,** 2440 Bancroft Way, Berkeley, CA 94704-1676, tel. (800) 443-7227 or (510) 543-8080, which publishes *Backpacking Basics* (US$9, ppd.) and *Backpacking with Babies and Small Children* (US$10, ppd.).

Wilderness Concerns The first thing to preserve in the wilderness is you—health, safety, and food should be your primary concerns when you camp. See Health for information about basic medical concerns and first-aid. A comprehensive guide to outdoor survival is *How to Stay Alive in the Woods,* by Bradford Angier (Macmillan, $8). *Never go camping or hiking by yourself for any significant time or distance* unless you are extremely confident in your ability to get along in the wilderness and have years of outdoor survival experience behind you. If you're going into an area that is not well-traveled or well-marked, let someone know where you're hiking and how long you intend to be out. If you fail to return on schedule or if you need to be reached for some reason, searchers will at least know where to look for you. The second thing to protect while you are outdoors is the wilderness itself. Because firewood is scarce in popular parks, using a campstove is the more cautious way to cook. Check ahead to see if the park prohibits campfires altogether. *Biosafe* soap or detergents may be used in streams or lakes. Otherwise, don't use soaps in or near bodies of water. Always pack up your trash in a plastic bag and carry it with you until you reach the next trash can; burning and burying pollute the environment. Ancient Appalachian Trail wisdom suggests that the only thing you should leave behind when you camp are your footprints. In more populated camping areas, it's important to respect fellow campers. Keep light and noise to a minimum.

■■■ ALTERNATIVES TO TOURISM

■ Study

Foreign study seems a fail-proof good time; be aware that programs vary tremendously in expense, academic quality, living conditions, degree of contact with local students, and exposure to the local culture and language. Most American undergraduates enroll in programs sponsored by domestic universities, and many colleges staff offices to give advice and information on study abroad. Take advantage of these counselors and put in some hours in their libraries. Ask for the names of recent participants in the programs, and impose on them. If you have extensive language ability, consider enrolling directly in a European university; German universities are far cheaper than those in North America.

Goethe Institute runs numerous language programs in Germany and abroad. For information on these and on their many cultural offerings, contact your local Goethe Institute (American branches in New York, Washington, DC, Boston, Atlanta, San Francisco, Los Angeles, and Seattle) or write to Goethe House New York, 1014 Fifth Ave., New York, NY 10028.

ABI (Aktion Bildungsinformation e.V.), Alte Poststr. 5, 53111 Bonn-Bad Godesberg, has published various leaflets with information on travel for the purpose of studying a language, e.g. *Learning a Foreign Language in Germany.*

American Field Service (AFS), 313 E. 43rd St., New York, NY 10017 (tel. (800) 237-4636 or (212) 949-4242). High school, summer, and year-long homestay exchange programs. Financial aid available. Includes Germany and Switzerland.

American Institute for Foreign Study/American Council for International Studies, 102 Greenwich Ave., Greenwich, CT 06830 (tel. (800) 727-2437; high school students, call Boston office at (617) 421-9575). Organizes study in various European universities for high school and college. Offers programs in Berlin.

Central Bureau for Educational Visits and Exchanges, Seymour Mews House, Seymour Mews, London W1H 9PE, England (tel. (071) 486 5101). Publishes *Study Holidays* (£7.75) which gives basic facts on over 600 language study programs in 25 European countries. Distributed in North America by IIE (see below).

Council on International Educational Exchange (CIEE) publishes booklets about studying abroad. See Useful Travel Organizations for address.

Deutscher Akademischer Austauschdienst (DAAD), 950 3rd Ave., New York NY 10022 (tel. (212) 758 3223); in Germany, Kennedyallee 50, 53175 Bonn-Bad Godesberg. Information on language instruction, and exchanges. The place to contact if you want to enroll in a German university; distributes application forms and the valuable *Academic Study in the Federal Republic of Germany.*

Institute of International Education Books (IIE Books), 809 United Nations Plaza, New York, NY 10017-3580 (tel. (212) 984-5412, fax 984-5358). Several annual reference books on study abroad. They also run the **International Education Information Center** at the UN Plaza, open Tues.-Fri. 11am-4pm.

Unipub Co., 4611-F Assembly Dr., Lanham, MD 20706-4391 (tel. (800) 274-4888). Distributes International Agency publications including UNESCO's *Study Abroad* (US$24, postage $2.50). International scholarships and courses for students of various ages. Unwieldy but excellent book.

■ Work

There is no better way to submerge yourself in a foreign culture than to become part of its economy. The bad news is that unless you have connections, it will rarely be glamorous and may not even pay for your plane ticket over. Getting permission to work in Germany or Switzerland is a challenge. If you hold EC citizenship, you may work in Germany (but not in Switzerland) without any special permission, though you must register with local police to take up residence. The organizations and publications listed below can help point you toward employment abroad; you should, however, speak with former clients before paying any registration fees.

With unemployment on the rise even before unification, Germany's days as a mecca for unskilled foreign workers are over. The German government maintains a series of federally run employment offices, the **Bundesanstalt für Arbeit,** throughout the country. Foreign applications are directed to the central office at Feuerbachstr. 42-6, 60325 Frankfurt am Main. The office tends to treat EC citizens with specific skills more favorably than those from other countries. The youth division is a bit more welcoming for foreign students ages 18 to 30 seeking summer employment; jobs frequently involve manual labor. If you don't know anyone in a foreign country, don't have the flexibility to work casual labor, and are a full-time student at a U.S. or Canadian university, then consider applying for a **temporary student work visa** through the **Council on International Educational Exchange (CIEE).** For a US$125 application fee, CIEE can procure temporary work permits for American university students in Germany and several other countries. For an application and more information, contact CIEE, Work Abroad, 205 E. 42nd St., New York, NY 10017 (see Useful Travel Organizations for more addresses).

The best tips on jobs for foreigners come from other travelers, so be alert and inquisitive. Many travelers follow the grape harvest in the fall—mostly in France, but also in Switzerland and Germany's Mosel Valley. More or less menial jobs can be found anywhere in Europe; for instance, Swiss ski resorts leave much of the grunt-work to foreigners. Ask at pubs, cafés, restaurants, and hotels. *Be sure* to be aware of your rights as an employee; should a crafty national try to refuse payment at the end of the season, it'll help if you have a written confirmation of your agreement. Youth hostels frequently provide room and board to travelers willing to stay a while and help run the place. Consider a job **teaching English.** Post a sign in markets or learning centers stating that you are a native speaker, and scan the classifieds of local newspapers . Teaching English may be your only option in Eastern Germany; various organizations in the U.S. will place you in a (low-paying) teaching job, finding one will require patience and legwork. Professional English-teaching positions are harder to get; most European schools require at least a bachelor's degree and most often training in teaching English as a foreign language.

Start with CIEE's free booklet *Work Abroad,* then graduate to the excellent publications put out by **Vacation Work,** 9 Park End St., Oxford OX1 1HJ, England (tel. +44 (0865) 24 19 78). Many of their books are also available in bookstores in the United States, through Travel CUTS or from **Peterson's Guides,** 202 Carnegie Center, P.O. Box 2123, Princeton NJ 08543 (tel. (800) 338-3282 or (609) 243-9111). **InterExchange Program**, 161 Sixth Ave., New York, NY 10013 (tel. (212) 924-0446), provides information in pamphlet form on international work programs and *au pair* positions. **World Trade Academy Press,** 50 East 42nd St. Suite 509, New York, NY 10017 (tel. (212) 697-4999) publishes *Looking for Employment in Foreign Countries* (US$16.50) which gives information on federal, commercial and volunteer jobs abroad and advice on resumes and interviews. Remember that many of the organizations listed in books like these have very few jobs available and have very specific requirements (like a degree in forestry or fluency in Finnish). The **Zentralstelle für Arbeitsvermittlung (ZAV),** Feuerbachstr. 42-46, 60325 Frankfurt am Main, will provide information on work and *au pair* opportunities in Germany.

■ Volunteering

Volunteer jobs are readily available almost everywhere; in some countries, they're your only hope. You may receive room and board in exchange for your labor, and the work can be fascinating. In Germany and Switzerland, opportunities include community and workcamp projects. The following organizations and publications can help you to explore the range of possibilities. Keep in mind: the organizations that arrange placement sometimes charge high application fees in addition to the workcamps' charges for room and board. You can *sometimes* avoid this extra fee by contacting the individual workcamps directly; check with the organization. Listings

in Vacation Work's *International Directory of Voluntary Work* (£9; see Work above) can be helpful.

> **Volunteers for Peace,** 43 Tiffany Rd., Belmont, VT 05730 (tel. (802) 259-2759). Arranges placement in over 800 workcamps in 37 countries, primarily in Europe. Gives its most complete and up-to-date listings in the annual *International Workcamp Directory* (US$10 ppd.). Registration fee US$125.

Service Civil International/International Voluntary Service-USA, Rte. 2, Box 506, Crozet, VA 22932 (tel. (804) 823-1826). Arranges placement in workcamps in Europe, U.S., Russia, Turkey, Greenland, Asia, and Africa. You must be 16 to work in U.S. camps, 18 in European camps. Registration fees for the placement service in 1993 were US$40-200 depending on the camp location.

Willing Workers on Organic Farms (WWOOF), Speerstr. 7, CH-8305 Dietlikon (tel. (01) 834 02 34), distributes a list of names of organic farmers who offer room and board in exchange for help on the farm. Wwith a wwittle wwillingness, wwone can wwork wwonders.

■■■ SPECIFIC CONCERNS

■ Women and Travel

Women exploring any area on their own inevitably face additional safety concerns. In all situations it is best to trust your instincts: if you'd feel better somewhere else, don't hesitate to move on. You may want to consider staying in hostels which offer single rooms that lock from the inside or religious organizations that offer rooms for women only. Stick to centrally-located accommodations and avoid late-night treks or metro rides. Remember that hitching is *never* safe for lone women, or even for two women traveling together. Choose train compartments occupied by other women or couples. In some parts of the world women (foreign or local) are frequently beset by unwanted and tenacious followers. Exercise reasonable caution without feeling that you must avoid all local men. To escape unwanted attention, follow the example of local women; in many cases—the less you look like a tourist, the better off you'll be. In general, dress conservatively, especially in more rural areas. If you spend time in cities, you may be harassed no matter how you're dressed. Look as if you know where you're going (even when you don't) and ask women or couples for directions if you're lost or if you feel uncomfortable. Your best answer to verbal harassment is no answer at all, but unlike in some parts of southern Europe, catcalls and whistling are not acceptable behavior in Germany and Switzerland; you can feel comfortable rebuking your harasser. Loudly saying *"Laß mich in Ruhe!"* ("Leave me alone!" pronounced LAHSS MEEKH EEN ROOH-eh) should suffice. Wearing a conspicuous wedding band may help prevent such incidents. Don't hesitate to seek out a police officer or a passerby if you are being harassed. Memorize the emergency numbers in the countries you visit, and always carry change for the phone and extra money for a bus or taxi. Carry a whistle on your keychain, and don't hesitate to use it in an emergency. All of these warnings and suggestions should not discourage women from traveling alone. Don't take unnecessary risks, but don't lose your spirit of adventure either.

A series of recent travelogues by women outline their sojourns; check for these and other books: *Nothing to Declare: Memoirs of a Woman Traveling Alone* (Penguin Books; US$9) and *Wall to Wall: From Beijing to Berlin by Rail* (Penguin Books; US$10) by Mary Morris; *One Dry Season* (Knopf) by Caroline Alexander; *Tracks* (Pantheon) by Robin Davidson; *The Road Through Miyama* (Random House/Vintage) by Leila Philips. For additional tips and suggestions, consult *The Handbook for Women Travelers* (£8) by Maggie and Gemma Moss, published by Piatkus Books, 5 Windmill St., London W1P 1HF England (tel. +44 (071) 6310710).

Women Going Places, a new women's travel and resource guide emphasizing women-owned enterprises. Geared towards lesbians, but offers advice appropriate for all women. US$14. Available from Inland Book Company, P.O. Box 120261, East Haven, CT 06512 (tel. (203) 467-4257).

Wander Women, a travel and adventure networking organization for women over 40, publishes a quarterly newsletter *Journal 'n Footnotes*, an informational source for the various aspects of travel, as well as a forum for women to share their travel experiences. The 12-page newsletter is designed to inspire adventure and the sharing of travel experiences. Membership in the organization, US$29 per year, entitles women to receive the membership directory, the newsletter, and travel discounts. For a sample copy of the newsletter send US$1 to Wander Women, 136 N. Grand Ave. #237, West Covina, CA 91791.

■ Older Travelers and Senior Citizens

AARP (American Association of Retired Persons), 601 E St. NW, Washington, DC 20049 (tel. (202) 434-2277 or (800) 927-0111). U.S. residents over 50 and their spouses receive benefits which include travel programs and discounts for groups and individuals, as well as discounts on lodging, car and RV rental, air arrangements and sightseeing. US$8 annual fee.

Elderhostel, 75 Federal St., 3rd floor, Boston, MA 02110. You must be 60 or over, and may bring a spouse who is over 50. Programs at colleges and universities in over 40 countries focus on varied subjects and generally last 1 week.

Gateway Books, P.O. Box 10244, San Rafael, CA 94912 (orders tel. (800) 669-0773). Publishes *Get Up and Go: A Guide for the Mature Traveler* (US$11, postage US$2). Offers recommendations and hints for budget-conscious seniors.

National Council of Senior Citizens, 1331 F St. NW, Washington, DC 20004 (tel. (202) 347-8800). For US$12 a year or US$150 (lifetime) an individual or couple of any age receive hotel and auto rental discounts, a senior citizen newspaper, use of a discount travel agency and supplemental Medicare insurance (over 65 only).

Pilot Books, 103 Cooper St., Babylon, NY 11702 (tel. (516) 422-2225). Publishes *The International Health Guide for Senior Citizens* (US$5, postage US$1) and *The Senior Citizens' Guide to Budget Travel in Europe* (US$6 ppd.).

■ Travelers with Children

Lonely Planet Publications, Embarcadero West, 112 Linden St., Oakland, CA 94607 (tel. (510) 893-8555 or (800) 275-8555); also P.O. Box 617, Hawthorn, Victoria 3122, Australia. Publishes Maureen Wheeler's *Travel with Children* (US$11, postage US$1.50 in the U.S.).

■ Travelers with Disabilities

By and large, Germany and Switzerland are two of the more accessible countries for travelers with disabilities (*Behinderte* or *Schwerbehinderte*). Rail is probably the most convenient form of travel. Trains have a few seats or an integrated compartment reserved for passengers with disabilities. Almost all EuroCity (EC) trains in and out of Germany and Switzerland have wheelchair facilities. For more information, check individual country introductions or contact **Rail Europe** in the U.S. at (800) 345-1990, fax (914) 682-2821. Some museums and sights have access as well. Recently renovated sites try to be accessible, but often fail in practice. Many hostels and train platforms can be hard to reach; alternative platforms sometimes exist.

Most countries require a six-month quarantine for all animals, including guide dogs. To obtain an import license, owners must supply current certification of the animal's rabies, distemper and contagious hepatitis inoculations and a veterinarian's letter attesting to its health. The **American Foundation for the Blind,** 15 W. 16th St., New York, NY 10011 (tel. (212) 620-2147) has ID cards (US$10); write for an application, or call the Product Center at (800) 829-0500. Also call this number to order AFB catalogs in Braille, print, or on cassette or disk. See individual country

Special Concerns for further details on travelers with disabilities in Germany and Switzerland.

Directions Unlimited, 720 North Bedford Rd., Bedford Hills, NY 10507 (tel. (800) 533-5343 or (914) 241-1700). Specializes in arranging individual and group vacations, tours and cruises for those with disabilities. Organizes tours for individuals rather than for groups.

Disability Press, Ltd., Applemarket House, 17 Union St., Kingston-upon-Thames, Surrey KT1 1RP, England (tel.+44 (081) 549 6399). Publishes the *Disabled Traveler's International Phrasebook,* including French, German, Italian, Spanish, Portuguese, Swedish, and Dutch phrases (£1.75). Supplements in Norwegian, Hungarian and Serbo-Croatian (60p each).

Evergreen Travel Service, 4114 198th St. SW, Suite #13, Lynnwood, WA 98036 (tel. (800) 435-2288 or (206) 776-1184). Arranges wheelchair-accessible tours and individual travel worldwide. Other services include tours for people who are blind, or deaf, and tours for those not wanting a fast-paced itinerary.

The Guided Tour, Inc. Elkins Park House, Suite 114B, 7900 Old York Road, Elkins Park, PA 19117-2348 (tel. (215) 782-1370 or (800) 738-5843). Year-round travel programs for persons with developmental and physical challenges as well as those geared to the needs of persons requiring renal dialysis. Trips and vacations planned both domestically and internationally. Call or write for a free brochure.

Mobility International, USA (MIUSA), P.O. Box 3551, Eugene, OR 97403 (tel. (503) 343-1284 voice and TDD). International headquarters: 228 Borough High St., London SE1 1JX (tel. +44 (071) 403 5688). Contacts in 30 countries. Information on travel programs, international workcamps, accommodations, access guides, and organized tours. Membership US$20 per year, newsletter US$10. Sells updated and expanded *A World of Options: A Guide to International Educational Exchange, Community Service, and Travel for Persons with Disabilities* (US$14 for members, US$16 for non-members, ppd.).

Moss Rehabilitation Hospital Travel Information Service, 1200 W. Tabor Rd., Philadelphia, PA 19141 (tel. (215) 456-9603). Information on international travel accessibility.

Society for the Advancement of Travel for the Handicapped (SATH), 347 Fifth Ave., Suite 610, New York, NY 10016 (tel. (212) 447-7284), fax (212) 725-8253). Publishes quarterly travel newsletter *SATH News* and information booklets (free for members, US$3 each for nonmembers). Advice on trip planning for people with disabilities. Annual membership is US$45, students and seniors US$25.

Twin Peaks Press, P.O. Box 129, Vancouver, WA 98666 (tel. (206) 694-2462, orders only (800) 637-2256). *Travel for the Disabled* lists tips and resources (US$20). *Directory for Travel Agencies of the Disabled* (US$20) and *Wheelchair Vagabond* (US$15). Postage US$2 for first book, $1 per additional book.

■ Bisexual, Gay, and Lesbian Travelers

Germany is fairly tolerant of homosexuality, Switzerland a little less so.*Let's Go* provides information on local bisexual, gay, and lesbian culture in Practical Information listings and Entertainment sections of city descriptions. See Once There: Special Concerns for detailed information on bisexual, gay, and lesbian life in Germany and Switzerland.

Are You Two Together?, published by Random House; available at bookstores (US$18). A new gay and lesbian guide to spots in Europe. Written by a lesbian couple; covers Western European capitals and gay resorts.

Ferrari Publications, P.O. Box 37887, Phoenix, AZ 85069 (tel. (602) 863-2408). Publishes *Ferrari's Places of Interest* (US$15), *Ferrari's Places for Men* (US$14), *Ferrari's Places for Women* (US$12), and *Inn Places: USA and Worldwide Gay Accommodations* (US$15). Also available from Giovanni's Room (see below).

Gay's the Word, 66 Marchmont St., London WC1N 1AB, England (tel. (071) 278 7654). Tube: Russel Sq. Information for gay and lesbian travelers. Mail order service available. Open Mon.-Fri. 11am-7pm, Sat. 10-6, Sun. and holidays 2-6pm.

Giovanni's Room, 345 S. 12th St., Philadelphia, PA 19107 (tel. (215) 923-2960, fax (215) 923-0813). International feminist, lesbian and gay bookstore with mail-order service.

Spartacus International Gay Guide, (US$30). Order from 100 East Biddle St., Baltimore, MD 21202 (tel. (410) 727-5677) or c/o Bruno-Lützow-Str., P.O. Box 301345, D-1000 Berlin 30, Germany (tel. +49 (30) 25 49 82 00); also available from Giovanni's Room (see above) and from Renaissance House, P.O. Box 292 Village Station, New York, NY 10014 (tel. (212) 674-0120). Extensive list of gay bars, restaurants, hotels, bookstores and hotlines throughout the world. Very specifically for men.

Women Going Places: see above listing under Women Travelers.

■ Kosher and Vegetarian Travelers

For historic and political reasons, few Jews choose to live in Germany, and the kosher offerings are correspondingly small. Although both Germany and Switzerland are unapologetically carnivorous, vegetarian restaurants have proliferated along with the blooming "alternative scene" in larger cities. *Let's Go* makes an effort to identify restaurants that offer a variety of vegetarian choices. Dairy products are excellent, especially in Switzerland, and fish is widely available on the North Sea coast and in lakeside towns. National tourist offices often publish lists of kosher and vegetarian restaurants.

Jewish Chronicle Publications, London EC4A 1JT, England. Publishes the *Jewish Travel Guide* (US$12, postage $1.75). Available in the U.S. from Sepher-Hermon Press, 1265 46th St., Brooklyn, NY 11219 (tel. (718) 972-9010). In the U.K., order from Jewish Chronicle Publications, 25 Furnival St., London EC4A England. Lists synagogues, kosher restaurants and institutions in over 80 countries.

North American Vegetarian Society, P.O. Box 72, Dolgeville, NY 13329 (tel. (518) 568-7970). Ask about their publications.

■■■ PACKING

Your backpack or suitcase may be light as a feather when you buy it or drag it out of storage and as buoyant as your enthusiasm all the way to the airport, but as soon as the plane lands it will become a ponderous, hot, uncomfortable nuisance. Before you leave, pack your bag and take it for a walk. Try to convince yourself that you're in Berlin or on the Matterhorn already. At the slightest sign of heaviness, curb vanity and hedonism and unpack something. A good general rule is to pack only what you absolutely need, then take half the clothes and twice the money.

If you plan to cover a lot of ground by foot, a sturdy **backpack** with several external compartments is hard to beat. **Backpacks** come with either an external or an internal frame. Internals stand up to airline baggage handlers and can often be converted to shoulder bags; externals distribute weight more evenly and lift the pack off your back. If your load is not extraordinarily heavy and you plan to use the pack mainly as a suitcase, choose an internal-frame model; it's more manageable. Make sure your pack has a strong, padded hip belt, which transfers much of the pack's weight from shoulders to legs. A good pack costs US$100-300. Avoid extremely low-range prices—you get what you pay for. If checking a backpack on your flight, tape down loose straps, which can catch in the conveyer belt. Take a light **suitcase** or a large **shoulder bag** if you will not be doing much walking. A plastic bag or lightweight duffel packed inside your luggage will be useful for dirty laundry, while a small **daypack** is also great for flights, sightseeing, carrying a camera, or keeping valuables with you.

With **Raingear**, shoot for a system that will cover you *and* your pack. Gore-Tex, a miracle fabric that's both waterproof and breathable, is also expensive. If you plan on doing Alpine hiking, bite the bullet and buy Gore-Tex. A waterproof Gore-Tex jacket plus a backpack cover does nicely, while a rain **poncho** can serve as an impromptu ground-cover for campers. Comfortable **shoes** are crucial. In warm weather, sturdy leather sandals or other light shoes serve well. For hiking, lace-up walking boots are necessary. Leather-reinforced nylon hiking boots are particularly good for hiking and for walking: they're lightweight, rugged and dry quickly. Double socks—cotton inside and wool outside—will cushion and help prevent blisters. In cold weather, replace the cotton inner sock with a "stay-dry" fabric such as **polypropelene.** Bring light flip-flops for protection against the fungal floors.

Bare shoulders and shorts above the knee are occasionally forbidden in European places of worship. A long, easily thrown-on **wrap-around skirt** is an easy way to cover up (for men or women). Otherwise, carry along a pair of pants. Men should bring a pair of pants for when they want to dress like Europeans. Also consider taking a pocketknife, tweezers, a flashlight, needle and thread, a plastic water bottle, clothespins lines, a pencil with electrical tape wound around it, a small notebook, a travel clock, rubber bands, sturdy plastic containers (for soap and detergent), ziplock bags, a squash ball (to use as a sink plug) and a padlock to secure your pack.

In Germany and Switzerland, as in most European countries, **electricity** is 220V AC, enough to fry any 110V North American appliance. Visit a hardware store for an adapter (which changes the shape of the plug) and a converter (which changes the voltage). Do not make the mistake of using only an adapter, or you'll melt your radio. Travelers who heat-disinfect their contact lenses should consider switching temporarily to a chemical disinfection system. Contact **Franzus**, Murtha Industrial Park, P.O. Box 142, Railroad Ave., Beacon Falls, CT 06403 (tel. (203) 723-6664) for their free pamphlet, *Foreign Electricity is No Deep Dark Secret.*

■■■ KEEPING IN TOUCH

■ By Mail

Mail can be sent internationally through **Poste Restante** (the international phrase for General Delivery) to any city or town. It is well worth using and more reliable than one might think. People can mail you letters, and the post office will hold them for a limited number of days until you pick them up. See Germany and Switzerland: Once There for instructions on addressing *Poste Restante* mail. As a rule, it is best to use the largest post office in the area (*Let's Go* lists main post offices and codes in Practical Information sections). Bring your passport or other ID with you when you pick up your mail. Sending mail care of **American Express** offices is quite reliable; offices will hold your mail for free if you have American Express traveler's checks or a card. Even if you buy another brand of traveler's checks, you may want to buy some American Express checks in order to use this service. Mail will automatically be held 30 days; to have it held longer, just write "Hold for x days" on the envelope. The sender should underline and capitalize your last name, marking the envelope "Client Letter Service." There are offices in most large cities. A complete list is available for free; call (800) 528-4800 and ask for the booklet *Traveler's Companion.*

Postcards and letters, when mailed from the U.S. to Europe, cost 40¢ and 50¢ respectively. It is safer, quicker, and more reliable to send mail express or registered. Many U.S. city post offices offer **International Express Mail** service, which sends packages (under 8 oz. to major overseas cities in 40-72hr. for US$11.50-14). Private mail services provide fast and perhaps the most reliable service between the U.S. and Europe. **Federal Express** (tel. (800) 238-5355 in the U.S. and Canada; +44 (81) 844 23 44 in London; +61 (2) 317 66 66 in Sydney; +64 (9) 256 83 00 in Aukland; +010 (353) 1 847 34 73 in Dublin) takes an express letter from North America to Western Europe (US$25-28, 2-3 days). **DHL** (tel. (800) 225-5345 in the U.S. and

Canada,; +44 (81) 890 9393 in London; +61 (2) 317 8300 in Sydney; +64 (9) 636 5000 in Auckland; +010 (353) 1 844 47 44 in Dublin) gets mail to Western Europe.

Between the U.S. and Europe, airmail averages one week to ten days. Surface mail is by far the cheapest and slowest way to send mail. It takes one to three months to cross the Atlantic and is only appropriate for sending large quantities of items you know you won't need for a while. It is vital to distinguish your airmail from surface mail by labelling it "air mail" in the appropriate language (in German, *Luftpost*; in French, *Por Avion*; in Italian *Via Aerea*).When ordering books and materials from another country, include an **International Reply Coupon (IRC),** available at the post office. IRCs provide the recipient of your order with postage to cover delivery.

■ By Telephone

Phoning home from Europe can be a rustrating experience. Phones are often scarce,or otherwise unmanageable, and most emit a range of unintelligible sounds. Never dial from a hotel and pay later; you'll be charged sky-high international rates plus a fat commission tacked on. Collect calls are not possible from German phone booths. **EurAide** offers a helpful answering service called **Overseas Access** for travelers in Europe. Correspondents call a "home base" in Europe and leave a short message. Your call to "home base" is much cheaper than an overseas call. For more information, contact EurAide, P.O. Box 2375, Naperville, IL 60567 (tel. (708) 420-2343).To **call Germany,** first dial the international access code (in the United States, 011), then the **country code** (49), then the city code *minus the first zero,* then the telephone number. The **country code** for **Switzerland** is 41. For information on international calls (including calling card calls) from Germany or Switzerland, for basic information on how to make phone calls from cities within Germany or Switzerland, our for more country code information, see our Appendix.

GERMANY (Deutschland)

US$1 = 1.47 *Deutschmark* (DM)   1DM= US$0.68
CDN$1 = 1.24DM   1DM = CDN$0.81
UK£1 = 2.82DM   1DM = UK£0.35
IR£ = 2.36DM   1DM = IR£0.42
AUS$1 = 1.08DM   1DM = AUS$0.92
NZ$1 = 0.80DM   1DM = NZ$1.26

It seems somehow appropriate that as the world reinvents itself, Germany once again stands at the center of it all. While the historical truths underlying popular stereotypes do provide some insight into what it means to be German, the nation that has finally emerged from the horrors of World War II and the surreal bipolarism of the Cold War is decidedly non-stereotypical. There are, to be sure, certain "German" characteristics—industriousness, efficiency, and a mystifying refusal to cross the street against the light, even in the absence of traffic—but the broad social and political range that comprises the nation defies easy categorization.

Despite its long history of reactionary governments, Germany has always been a wellspring of revolutionaries—for better and for worse. One of the first heroes of German history, Karl der Große (Charlemagne), was the first to unify post-Roman Europe under enlightened rule. An obscure German monk, Martin Luther, stands as one of the most influential figures in Western history for the revolutionary forces unleashed by the Protestant Reformation. Lessing, Bach, and Beethoven turned the worlds of drama and music upside down. Socialist pioneers Karl Marx and Friedrich Engels equipped the revolutionary groundswell of 19th-century Europe with an ideology and a goal whose power has only been blunted and re-directed, never defused. Adolf Hitler, the most loathsome figure in Western history, organized in his country the capacity to perform deeds—the seizure of power, the conquest of Europe, the Holocaust—that simply defy explanation. This last image, of course, indelibly colors all subsequent German history. Germans must grapple with the wrenching fact that the cradle of Goethe and Beethoven also nurtured Auschwitz and Treblinka. Eternally burdened by the crimes of the Third Reich, Germany is also blessed with a cultural tradition without compare. No major European artistic movement of the last 500 years is entirely without debt to Germans, and quite a few would be unthinkable without German influence.

Not that you'll hear all of this from the Germans themselves, who these days are busy typecasting each other as they go about the painful process of reconciling their recently divergent pasts. The Wall had barely come down when West Berlin dilettantes started cracking jokes about putting it back up, and some forty-odd years of socialism won't be erased within the next decade, or probably even within the next generation. Yet at precisely the same moment the Germans are turning inward, their position is becoming increasingly relevant in a global sense. In the wake of Europe's most recent wave of revolution, the newly reunited Germany's position at the border of East and West is even more important than it was during the Cold War, and as the only country ever to come face to face collectively with the moral bankruptcy of its nationalism, Germany brings a unique perspective—and motivation—to the project of building an integrated Europe, and recent nationalist conflicts.

It's worth remembering all of this as you pass through the country—that the legacy represented by the wealth of artistic, historical, and cultural treasures that Germany has managed to accumulate throughout centuries of war and division not only defines a healthy chunk of Western civilization's collective past, but may conceal more than just a glimpse into the future.

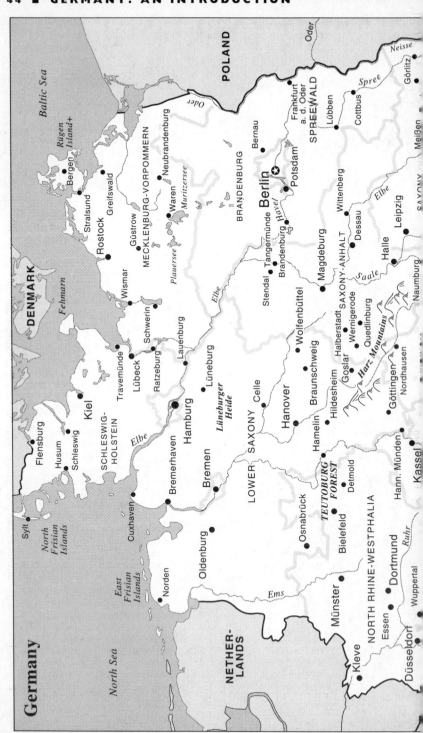

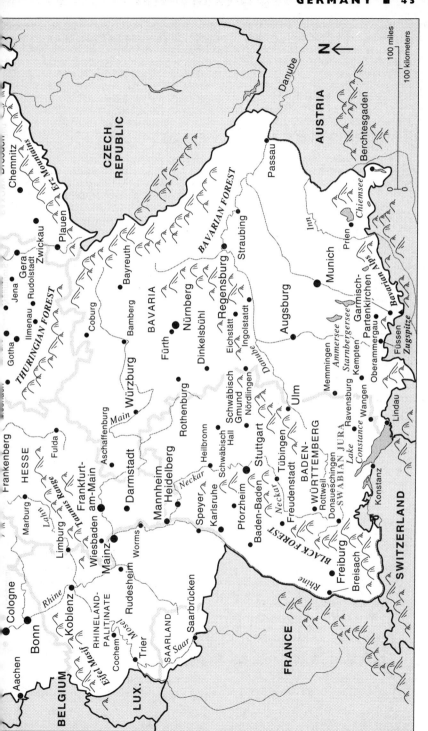

■ Germany: An Introduction

ONCE THERE

■■■ TOURIST OFFICES

Every German town of any touristic importance whatsoever is served by a local tourist office. These go by a bewildering variety of names—*Verkerhsamt, Fremden-verkehrsbüro, Verkehrsverein, Fremdenverkehsverein, Tourist-Information, Gemeindeamt,* and (in spa towns) *Kurverwaltung* or *Kurverein.* To simplify things, all are marked by a standard thick lowercase "i" sign. Tourist offices are usually located in the town square or by the main train station—sometimes both. Exploit these offices for city maps (often free), cycling routes and rental options, information on sights and museums, and lists of accommodations. Many offices will track down a vacant room for you and make a reservation, sometimes for free, otherwise for DM1-5. *Let's Go* lists tourist offices in the Practical Information section.

■■■ EMBASSIES AND CONSULATES

If you're seriously ill or in trouble, your embassy can provide a list of doctors or pertinent legal advice, and can also contact your relatives. In *extreme* cases, they can offer emergency financial assistance. Embassies are located in Bonn; consulates can be found in other major cities. For the addresses of consulates not listed here, check the Practical Information sections of individual cities.

United States: Embassy (*Botschaft von Vereinigte Staaten von Amerika*): **Bonn,** Deichmanns Aue 29, 53179 (tel. (0228) 339 20 53, fax 339 26 63). **Consulates: Frankfurt Am Main,** Siesmayerstr. 21, 60323 (tel. (069) 753 50); **Leipzig,** Wilhelm-Seyfferth-Str. 4, 04107. Other consulates located in **Hamburg, Munich,** and **Stuttgart.**

Canada: Embassy (*Botschaft von Kanada*): **Bonn,** Friedrich-Wilhelm-Str. 16, 53113, and Godesberger Allee 119, 53175 (tel. (0228) 81 00 60, fax 23 08 57). **Consulates: Berlin,** Europa-Center, 12 Stock, 10789 (tel. (030) 261 11 61 62); **Düsseldorf,** Immarmannstr. 65d, 40210 (tel. (0211) 35 34 71). There's another consulate in **Munich.**

U.K.: Embassy (*Botschaft von Vereinigte Königreich*): **Bonn,** Friedrich-Ebert-Allee 77, 53113 (tel. (0228) 23 40 61). **Consulates: Frankfurt Am Main,** Generalkonsultat, Bookenheimer Landstr. 42, 60323 (tel. (069) 170 00 20). Also consulates in **Düsseldorf, Hamburg, Hanover, Munich,** and **Stuttgart.**

Australia: Embassy (*Australische Botschaft*): Godesberger Allee 105-107, 53175 Bonn (tel. (0228) 810 30). **Consulates: Berlin,** Palast-Hotel, Karl-Liebknecht-Str. 5, 10178. There is another consulate in **Frankfurt.**

Ireland: Embassy (*Botschaft von Irland*): **Bonn,** Godesberger Allee 119, 53175 (tel. (0228) 37 69 37 or -39). **Consulate: Munich,** Mauerkircherstr. 1a, 81679 (tel. (089) 98 57 23).

New Zealand: Embassy (*Botschaft von Neuseland*): **Bonn,** Bundeskanzlerplatz 2-10, 53113 (tel. (0228) 22 80 70, fax 22 16 87).

■■■ LAW AND ORDER

Everything you've heard about the compulsive law-abidance of Germans is true. The first time you see a German standing at an intersection in the pouring rain, with no cars in sight yet still waiting for the "Walk" signal, you'll know what we mean. Jay-walking is only one of the petty offenses that will mark you as a foreigner (and subject you to fines); littering is another. The younger generation tends such matters a bit less seriously. Although police are polite and businesslike, they aren't to be messed with. If you fail to treat police officers with proper respect (for instance, addressing them in the familiar "*du*"), they can slap you with on-the-spot fines. Few police officers speak more than a bit of English. The **drinking age** is 16; driving under the influence is a severe offense. See Getting Around: By Car for traffic rules.

■■■ GETTING AROUND

■ By Train

"The trains run on time." It's a cliche, almost a joke, and not infallibly true. At the same time, it points out an important truth about getting around in Germany—if the trains aren't perfect, they do go almost everywhere a traveler would want to be, with the exception of some very rural areas. In fact, the train system's obligation to run line to inaccessible areas, even at a loss, is written into Germany's basic law. In the midst of integrating the western **Deutsche Bundesbahn (DB)** and old eastern **Deutsche Reichsbahn (DR),** Germany is also on the verge of privatizing the entire federal rail system. The plan is to replace both companies with one, the **Deutsche Bahn.** Signs of this process may already be visible, but *"Ein Land, zwei Bahnen,"* (one country, two railroads) is still the motto to travel by. Moving from west to east there are significant differences in quality and service. Averaging faster than 120kph including stops, the DB network is one of Europe's best and most expensive. The *Reichsbahn* is getting better, but is still not up to par. One problem is connections; on an indirect route, allow about twice as much time as you would in the west.

Commuter trains, marked "City-Bahn" (CB), "S-Bahn" or "Nahverkehrszug" (N), are fairly slow; "D" and "E" (Eilzug) trains are slightly faster and "FD" trains are faster still. "InterRegio" (IR) trains, between neighboring cities, are speedy and comfortable. From metropolis to metropolis, "IC" (InterCity) trains fairly zoom along between major cities. Unless you have a full-fare railpass (such as the Tramper-Monats Ticket; see below), you must purchase a supplementary "IC Zuschlag" to ride an "IC" or "EC" train (DM6 when bought in the station, DM8 on the train). Even the IC yields to the new super-sleek InterCity Express (ICE), which approaches the luxury and speed of an airplane: it does the Hamburg to Munich run in six hours flat.

Most German cities have a main train station; in German, the *Hauptbahnhof.* (This is the point referred to when *Let's Go* gives directions "from the station".) In train stations, yellow signs indicate departures (*Abfahrt*), white signs indicate arrivals (*Ankuft*). The number next to *"Gleis"* is the track number.

For those intending on a long stay in Germany, or for those who decide to purchase a railpass once in Germany, there are some passes that can *only* be purchased once you've arrived. For anyone under age 23, and students under age 27, the best deal going is the **Tramper-Monats Ticket,** good for one month of unlimited second-class travel on all DB trains (except the ICE), the railroad-run buses (*Bahnbusse*), and the local S-Bahn (DM300; combined DB/DR ticket DM350; with ICE DM465). Bring proof of age and a student ID. International train stations (Frankfurt's, for example) may not sell the Tramper-Monats Ticket to foreigners over 23 who are not students at a German university; go to a nearby, smaller station and try again. The **Bahncard**, available to travelers ages 18 to 22 and students under 27 (DM110), is valid for one year and gets you a 50% discount on all rail tickets, DB and DR alike (DM110). The Bahncard has the same deal for everyone between 12 and 17 (DM50), and anyone over age 60 (DM110). Passes are only available at major train stations throughout Germany, and all require a small photo. If you're interested in purchasing railpasses for Germany before you depart, different passes are available in your home country (see Essentials: Getting Around: Planning Your Trip by Train).

■ By Bus

Germany does have regions inaccessible by train, and some bus lines fill the gap. Bus service between cities and to small, outlying towns usually run from the *Zentral Omnibus Bahnhof (ZOB),* which is often near the main train station. Buses are usually slightly more expensive than the train for comparable distances. Check the bulletin boards in university buildings or the classified pages of local magazines for occasional deals. Rail passes are not valid on any buses other than those (relatively few) run by the national rail company (DB). Most lines are run either by regional or local public transit authorities, or by private companies.

■ By Car

Yes, Virginia, there really is no speed limit on the *Autobahn.* Germans drive *fast;* before venturing on the road, be *very* familiar with traffic rules and especially signs and symbols. Germans drive on the right side of the road. It is dreadfully illegal to pass on the right, *even on superhighways.* When not otherwise indicated, the speed limit in Western Germany is 100kph (62 mph) for passenger cars, 50kph (31 mph) in cities and towns. The recommended speed on the *Autobahn* is 130kph (81 mph), but if you drive that slowly in the left lane you'll see cars looming large in your rear-view mirror with lights flashing. Passenger cars with trailers are limited to 80kph (50 mph). In Eastern Germany, the speed limit for cars on the highway is 100kph in rural areas, 80kph in urban ones. Drivers might want to know that dotting the *Autobahn* along its 6000 toll-free mi. are 169 restaurants and 268 service stations open 24 hours a day.

German law requires that front seat passengers wear **seatbelts;** motorcycle drivers and riders must wear **helmets.** Children under 12 may not sit in the front seat unless special seats have been installed. Studded snow tires are also *verboten.* The maximum permissible blood alcohol content is 0.08%—if you even *think* of alcohol, you're probably over the limit. Other rules and regulations apply; for more information, contact **Allgemeiner Deutscher Automobil Club (ADAC)** by mail at Redaktion ADAC motorwelt, 81360 München, or visit the office once in Germany at Am Westpark 8, Munich-Sendling (tel. (089) 767 60, fax (089) 76 76 25 00). Or contact **Automobil Club von Deutschland (AvD),** Lyoner-Str. 16, 60528 Frankfurt-Neiderrad (tel. (069) 66 03 60). ADAC maintains **Straßenwachthilfe** which patrol the roads and assist disabled vehicles. ADAC will provide **road assistance** free of charge if the damage can be repaired within half an hour; if not, you'll pay repair and towing fees. Orange emergency telephones indicated by blue *Notruf* (emergency call) signs summon the free service. A critically important word is *Stau,* meaning "traffic jam." Tune into local radio stations for traffic reports.

■ By Air

More than 90 international airlines serve Germany, but flying across the country is generally expensive and unnecessary. The headquarters for **Lufthansa German Airlines,** the national carrier (tel. (0221) 82 60), are at Deutsche Lufthansa AG, Von-Gablenz-Str. 2-6, 50679 Cologne. Lufthansa's air hub is located in Frankfurt am Main; from there, all Lufthansa destinations can be reached in an average of 50 minutes. *Let's Go* lists airports and flight information telephone numbers in the Practical Information sections of major cities. Usually, S-Bahn or bus shuttles run between the airport and the nearest city's main train station.

■ By Boat

River boat and motor boat services abound on many inland waters in Germany. In addition to connecting towns within Germany, many passenger and car ferries make connections to offshore islands (the Frisian Islands, for example) in the North and Baltic Seas. On the Danube, Elbe, Main, Moselle, Neckar, Rhine, Oder, Saale, and Weser rivers you can hop a ferry and enjoy seeing Germany from a new perspective. Be sure to ask about discounts if you're holding any kind of railpass or ISIC. You may qualify for a discounted fare up to 50%—a true score for budget travelers.

■ By Bicycle

Bikes are sight-seeing power tools; Germany makes it easy with its wealth of trails and bike tours, including some organized through hostels and through the rail system. In urban areas, a bicycle can be one of the most efficient ways to get around, and cycling is treated as a basic mode of transportation rather than as a recreational sport. German cities and towns usually have designated bike lanes, sometimes in the street, and sometimes laid out in the sidewalk itself. Pedestrians should look out for tell-tale bike icons or changes in pavement color; it may look like those bikers are on the sidewalk, but they move fast, they have right-of-way, and with all the conviction of self-righteous biking zeal, they expect you to be the one to get out of the way, and quickly. Bike rentals are available at approximately 250 train stations throughout the country where German Rail's *Fahrrad am Bahnhof* ("Bikes at the Station") program has rentals at DM6-10 per day. Usually bikes can be rented from one station and returned at another with a deposit of some kind; just ask for details at the station. For information about bike routes, regulations, and maps, contact **Allgemeiner Deutscher Fahrrad-Club**, Postfach 10 77 44, 2800 Bremen, or the **Bund Deutscher Radfahrer** (Association of German Cyclists), Otto-Fleck-Schneise 4, 60528 Frankfurt. A bike tour guidebook, including extensive maps, is available from **Deutsches Jugendherbergswerk (DJH);** see address in Accommodations: Hostels.

■ By Thumb

Let's Go cannot recommend hitchhiking as a method of travel due to the many dangers associated with it; however, many travelers have done very well by it. Hitchhiking is admittedly glamorous, and may be the way to go if you are traveling to Germany to gather stories to tell your grandchildren or to include in your first novel. It is illegal to hitch on the *Autobahnen* (expressways). Hitchers must stand in front of the "*Autobahn*" signs at on-ramps, or at **Raststätten** (rest stops) and **Tankstellen** (gas stations). *Autobahn* hitchers will need a good map to navigate the tangled interchanges in the Rhine-Ruhr area, and should pay attention to license plates; B=Berlin, M=Munich, F=Frankfurt, HH=Hamburg. There's also plentiful hitching on the heavily traveled *Bundesstraßen*, scenic secondary roads marked by signs with a yellow diamond. Several **Mitfahrzentralen** (ride-share centers) pair drivers with riders, with a fee to both agency (about US$20) and driver (per km). Some offices belong to nation-wide chains (**CityNetz Mitfahrzentrale** branches have computerized listings), others are local store-front operations. *Let's Go* lists *Mitfahrzentralen* under practical information; if we can't give you a lead, check the white and yellow pages under "Mitfahrzentrale."

■ Public Transportation

Urban public transit is excellent in the west and fair to middling in the east. You'll see four types in German cities: **Straßenbahn** (streetcars), **S-Bahn** (commuter rail), **U-Bahn** (subways), and regular **buses**. Eurailpass holders get free passage only on the S-Bahn (commuter rail). Berlin, Cologne, Düsseldorf, Frankfurt, Hamburg, Munich, and Stuttgart have U-Bahn systems. Consider purchasing a day card (*Tagesnetzkarte*) or multiple-ride ticket (*Mehrfahrkarte* or *Sammelkarte*), which usually pay for themselves by the third ride. Most German public transit systems operate on an "honor system." The usual procedure is to buy your ticket from a kiosk or an automat and then **validate** it in a little box marked with an **"E."** On subways, you must do this *before* getting in the car or, if the validation box is inside the car, *as soon as* you enter and before the subway begins to move. Once the doors are sealed up and the train gets underway, plainclothes inspectors will appear to thrust an orange badge in your face that says *"Kontrollier."* If you cannot produce a valid ticket that has been properly cancelled, you will be subject to large fines and immense humiliation. The inspectors don't take excuses and they don't take American Express; if you can't pay up on the spot, a police officer will meet you at the next stop to take you to jail. English-speaking backpackers have a very bad reputation for *Schwarzfahren* ("black riding," or riding without a ticket), so don't expect any sympathy. If you try the "I didn't understand, I don't speak German," excuse, the inspector will brusquely point out the explanatory signs in English. "I thought my Eurailpass was valid," never works, either. Don't assume that everyone else is riding illegally because you don't see them canceling tickets; when the inspector appears, you'll discover that they're all carrying monthly passes.

■■■ MONEY

The *Deutsche Mark* or *Deutschmark* (abbreviated DM, DEM, or simply M) is the primary unit of currency in Germany. One DM equals 100 Pfennig (Pf). Coins come in 1, 2, 5, 10, and 50Pf, and DM1, 2, and 5 amounts. Bills come in DM5, 10, 20, 50, 100, 200, 500, and 1000 denominations. Though some (especially Americans) may think of minted metal disks as inconsequential pieces of aluminum that simply gather dust, remember that a DM5 coin can easily buy you a meal at a supermarket. Also keep in mind that fewer **credit card** and **ATM** opportunities exist in Germany than in most western countries; locals tend to carry large wads of hard cash in their pockets. All this means is that you should *not* rely on your plastic; carry **traveler's checks.** Finally, a new barrage of bills has recently been unleashed upon the people of Germany; don't be disconcerted if you find yourself with two very different-looking bills worth the same amount (the new ones have a silver stripe). Old issue bills are still very much is use, but automats will only accept the new breed. *Deutschmark*s and foreign currency may be freely exported and imported. Old East German currency lost all but sentimental value in July 1990. For more information on traveler's checks and credit cards, see Essentials: Money, above.

■■■ ACCOMMODATIONS

Much of our accommodations wisdom is applicable to both Germany and Switzerland; for this reason, be sure to check out the Essentials: Accommodations section at the beginning of the book.

■ Hotels

The cheapest hotel-style accommodations are places with *Gasthof, Gästehaus,* or *Hotel-Garni* in the name. Continental breakfast (*Frühstuck*), almost always included, consists of a roll, butter, jam, coffee or tea, and usually some sausage and cheese slices. Rooms in private homes (*Privatzimmer*) or guest houses are widely available and are less expensive than hotels or *Pensionen,* though most require a minimum stay of two or more nights. Bookings are usually handled by local tourist offices, either for free or for a DM2-5 fee; in less urban areas, look for signs saying *Zimmer frei* (room available). Finding affordable hotel rooms, or any at all, in the new Federal States to the east is generally a challenge. During the week most are booked solid, as the available pool was not ready to meet the new tide of tourists and westerners working on reconstructing the former GDR. The best bet in the east is often a private room. Costs generally run DM20-30 per person, less than for comparable private rooms in the west. Travelers over 26 who would otherwise pay senior prices at youth hostels will probably find these rooms well within budget range.

■ Hostels

In 1908, a German named Richard Schirmann, believing that life in industrial cities was harmful to the physical and moral development of youth, built in Altena the world's first youth hostel—a budget dormitory that would bring travel within the means of poor youth. Germany has been a leader in hosteling ever since, and Schirmann is something of a mythic figure. Construction of hostels *(Jugendherbergen)* in Germany exploded as neo-Romantic folk groups fled the cities for the rejuvenation of the wilds. The Nazis found hostels especially useful as a resource for Hitler Youth wilderness trips. **Deutsches Jugendherbergswerk (DJH)** (tel. (05231) 7401-0, fax (05231) 7401-49, -66, -67) oversees German hostels. The DJH has, in recent years, initiated a growing number of *Jugendgästehäuser* (youth guest-houses), the more adult face of the HI system. These generally are more expensive, have more facilities, and attract slightly older guests. All German hostels are rated according to a six-category scale. The most basic fall in category I, the modern *Jugendgästehäuser* in category VI. Prices correspond roughly to these categories. The nightly charge builds from the odd category I hostel in Eastern Germany asking DM12 per night, to the demand for DM32 for a bed in a four-person room from a brand-new *Jugendgästehaus*. However, because the prices are set locally and not nationally, this system is not uniform; a category III hostel might be less expensive than a category II spot elsewhere. The DJH has absorbed hundreds of hostels in Eastern Germany with remarkable efficiency—although somewhere in the process of unification, prices leapt upwards. Many of the better eastern hostels have been converted into costly hotels, or closed outright while bureaucrats try to decipher ownership, since new laws allow the original owners of property nationalized under GDR to re-claim their assets. Still, Germany currently has more than 650 hostels—more than any other nation on earth—and the state hostel associations comprise the well-maintained infrastructure of a youth culture that has no equal anywhere.

DJH publishes *Deutsches Jugendherbergsverzeichnis* (DM6), a guidebook to all federated German hostels that is readily available at German bookstores and major train station newsstands; or write to DJH-Hauptverband, Bismarckstr. 8, Postfach 1455, 32756 Detmold, Germany. For information on how to obtain a **Hostelling International (HI) membership,** or for information on books and hostelling guides available in your home country, see the Documents section of *Let's Go* Essentials.

HI hostels in Bavaria do not accept guest over the age of 26.

■ Camping

There exist something like 2600 campsites in Germany, about 400 of which are open in the winter. If you're prepared to go rustic, camping is the best option. If you're not carrying a tent, some sites will lend one to you for a small fee. Blue signs with a black tent on a white background indicate official sites. **Deutscher Camping-Club e.v. (DCC),** Mandlstr. 28, 80802 München (tel. (089) 33 40 21), and **Allgemeiner Deutscher Automobil-Club (ADAC)** (see Getting Around: By Car, above) have specific information on German campgrounds, and the German National Tourist Office distributes a free map, *Camping in Germany,* with a full list of campgrounds. For more information on camping and how to obtain an **International Camping Carnet** (membership card) to get reduced rates at some campgrounds, see Essentials: Camping and the Outdoors.

■■■ KEEPING IN TOUCH

■ Telephones

If you spend a week or more in Germany, invest in a *Telefonkarte* (telephone card), the most sensible way to make calls from public phones. The cards come in DM12,

DM20, and DM50 denominations. In February 1993, the two German phone systems were completely merged, although the availability of private phone lines is still a problem in the East (many businesses get by with mobile phones). Still, except in some very small towns, you should have no trouble finding a public card phone. Germany's **country code** is 049.

For information on the twists and turns of making phone calls in Germany, and details on how to conduct international calls, see the Appendix at the very end of the book.

■ Mail

Notice: With a glorious fanfare and an endearing mascot in the shape of the number five, the German postal system, in July 1993, introduced a **new five-digit postal code system** in order to completely integrate east and west. The new system is similar to the one in the United States; codes are based on geographic zones and most cities are divided into many postal code zones. Large companies and industries even have their own postal codes. All codes listed in this *Let's Go* are updated according to the just-published *Postleitzahlenbuch* (Postal Code directory) distributed by *Deutsche Bundespost* (German Postal Service). Shun the old four-digit numbers (not in *our* guide, of course) with "W" or "O" (*West* and *Ost*) prefixes; they're outdated. Ask for new postal codes (*neue Postleitzahl*) at any post office. Due to the aforementioned changes, rather than printing a single postal code for each city or town as we have in past years, we have instead listed individual codes for important addresses, for example, the main post office in each city, large hostels in major cities, or for addresses that you'll have to write to months in advance, such as festival ticket offices. While we will, for example, refer to Cologne by its English name in our text, we give the German spelling, "Köln," when listing a mailing address.

Airmail between North America and Germany takes 10 to 14 days. Allow at least two and a half weeks for Australia and New Zealand. Mail moves significantly faster within the west than within the east, and crossovers are even slower. **Postcards** to any European destination from Germany cost DM0.80, and to any non-European country DM2. **Letters** (up to 20g) cost DM1 to Europe, DM3 (airmail) beyond. Despite postal unity, it's still slower to mail letters from eastern Germany.

The main post office in a town (frequently in the main train station) generally has the longest hours. You can have your mail sent to you through **Postlagernde Briefe** (the German phrase for General Delivery or *Post Restante*) in any city or town. Mark the envelope "BITTE HALTEN" (please hold) and address it, for example, "Mimi SCHULTZ, Postlagernde Briefe, 50668 Köln, Germany." The last name should be underlined and capitalized. Unless you specify a specific post office by street address or postal code, it will wind up at the *Hauptpostamt* (main post office). When picking up your mail, bring your passport or other ID with you. If the clerk insists that there is nothing for you, try checking under your first name as well. For information on how to send mail care of **American Express** or how to contact express mail services such as **Federal Express** or **DHL,** see Essentials: Keeping in Touch: Mail, above.

■ Fax and More

As in many other European countries, most of western Germany's businesses (including banks, hostels, and tourist offices) have fax machines, and they are spreading slowly through Eastern Germany. These marvels of technology can be just what you need if you're in a bind. If your visas aren't in order before you leave for Europe, note the fax number of the appropriate embassy or consulate. To send a fax, head to an office or computer shop. Check out "e-mail", the electronic mail system, if you plan to spend time on a university campus. You can beam messages across the seas for free with a minimum of computer knowledge. It really works.

■■■ SPECIFIC CONCERNS

Women travelers should exercise caution and good judgement, particularly when traveling alone. Wearing shoes (even at night) that allow you to run if necessary are also a smart bet. Technically, you must be over 18 to purchase and use various pocket-sized containers of mace (DM12-18), available in many knife and scissor stores. Yes, knife and scissor stores. Catcalls and whistling should be granted no response or attention whatsoever; a bold *"Laß mich in Ruhe!"* (leave me alone) should be somewhat effective. Various English obscenities are internationally understood, but their invocation brings unwanted conversation to an even baser level. Budget traveling doesn't mean taking every risk possible. Hitchhiking alone is extremely dangerous. **Abortion** is a complicated legal issue in Germany. It is only available within the first trimester, and not on demand; a woman must indicate a reason, and only certain reasons are accepted. If you find yourself with an unwanted pregnancy in Germany and choose to seek an abortion, be aware of the bureaucracy and limits involved, which are stricter in certain states—notably Bavaria—than in others. Hope that you are not in Bavaria, and if you are, remember it's only a few hours by train out of there. Or, you might choose to do what many German women do, and go to Holland, where laws are much more liberal. If you have questions, consider going to your embassy, depending on your own country's policies. See Germany Life and Times: History for more background and specifics on abortion laws. The German word for abortion is *Abtreibung;* the word for abortion rights is *Abtreibungsrecht.* The "morning after" pill is not available in Germany.

Gay, Lesbian, and Bisexual Travelers Some basic vocabulary—the German word for gay is *Schwul,* for lesbian *Lesben.* In general, the larger the city and the farther north you travel, the more tolerant the attitudes towards bisexual, gay, and lesbian travelers. The major centers of gay life are Berlin, Hamburg, Frankfurt and Munich; there is also a scene in Cologne. Women should look for *Frauencafes* and *Frauenkneipen,* woman-only cafés and bars. The local *Frauenbuchladung* (women's bookstore) is a good resource. In 1994, lesbian and gay travelers should look for special events celebrating the anniversary of the repeal of the legal code which imposed penalties on homosexual activity.

Seniors receive discounts at many museums and sights. It's absolutely ordinary for Germany's senior citizens to be out and about, especially with excellent public transportation systems that make everything easily accessible. This also goes for **travelers with disabilities;** many public transport systems are wheelchair accessible. The international **wheelchair** icon or a large letter "B" indicates access. Major cities have audible crossing signals for the blind.

Minority Concerns Germany has a significant minority population composed mainly of ethnic Turks. In addition, there are refugees from Eastern and Southern Europe and, facing increasing hostility, a number of Romany-Sinti people (also known as Gypsies). Eastern Germany also has a number of Vietnamese residents. All the same, conspicuously non-German foreigners may stand out. Muslim visitors should see Religious Life, above, for a list of resources.

In certain regions, tourists of color or members of certain religious groups may feel threatened by local residents. Neo-Nazi skinheads in the large cities of former East Germany, as well as in Western Germany, have been known to attack foreigners, especially non-whites. In these areas, common sense will serve you best. Either historical or newly-developed discrimination against established minority residents may surface against travelers who are members of those minority groups. Let's Go researchers are instructed not to include establishments which discriminate in our guides.

■■■ RELIGIOUS LIFE

It is impossible to discuss religion in present-day Germany without hearing the many voices of past and present: the voices of Holocaust survivors, the voices of young neo-Nazis, the voice of the modern Basic Law which states that "freedom of faith and conscience as well as freedom of religious or other belief shall be inviolable. The undisturbed practice of religion shall be guaranteed" (article 4). Despite having had Europe's most liberal immigration policies for asylum-seekers (some of these policies have been rescinded in the recent anti-foreigner climate), Germany remains an overwhelmingly Christian nation. The total Jewish population in Germany today is approximately 40-50 thousand. The largest Jewish congregations are in Berlin and Frankfurt Am Main, which together are home to over 10,000 Jews. A great increase in foreign workers has brought along with it a strong Islamic population; today, almost 2 million Muslims, mostly from Turkey, live in the Federal Republic of Germany. For information, contact any of the following organizations. Aside from major Jewish community centers there are few **kosher** restaurants in Germany. A call to any one of the headquarters listed below can provide resources, from **vegetarian** restaurants to private homes.

> **Protestant:** Kirchenamt der Evangelischen Kirche in Deutschland, Herrenhauser-Str. 12, 30419 Hanover.
> **Catholic:** Sekretariat der Bischofskonferenz, Kaiserstr. 163, 53113 Bonn.
> **Muslim:** Islamische Gemeinschaft. **Munich:** Bergmannstr. 13, (tel. (400) 502 55 25) or **Berlin:** Einemstr. 8 Berlin (tel. (030) 262 54 69).
> **Jewish:** There are Jewish community centers in each of the following cities. **Berlin:** Fasanenstr. 79-80 (tel. (030) 884 20 30); **Bonn:** Tempelstr. 2-4 (tel. (0228) 21 35 60); **Cologne:** Roonstr. 50 (tel. (0221) 23 56 26 or -27); **Düsseldorf:** Zietenstr. 50 (tel. (0211) 48 03 13); **Frankfurt:** Altkonigstr. 27 (tel. (069) 72 38 03).

■■■ BUSINESS HOURS

Store hours in Germany are maddeningly brief, thanks to the *Ladenschlussgesetzt* (store closing law) which applies to most businesses. The hours listed below are only approximate. **Store hours** are Monday-Friday 8am-6:30pm, Saturday 7am-2pm. Some stores remain open until 8:30pm on Thursday and some are open until 6:30pm on the first Saturday of each month. Flower shops are allowed to open briefly on Sunday mornings—convenient, huh? Avoid trying to buy anything 5-6:30pm, when working wives try to cram all of their shopping in. To avoid starvation after hours and on Sunday, try shops inside train stations in larger cities, which are allowed to remain open longer. Many smaller shops and restaurants take a midday break (*Mittagspause*), usually noon-2pm. **Bank hours** are Monday-Wednesday and Friday 9am-12:30pm and 2:30-4pm, Thursday 9am-12:30pm and 2:30-5:30pm.

■■■ CLIMATE

Climate varies across Germany, but is comparable to New England in the U.S. Summers are rarely unbearably hot-90F is about tops. The Alps are perpetually cool, while everything north of Hamburg is rainy. Figures below are degrees Fahrenheit.

	July	October	January	April
Berlin	58-76	43-56	27-36	40-56
Dresden	56-76	41-56	25-36	40-58
Dusseldorf	56-74	47-59	32-40	41-58
Frankfurt	59-77	45-58	29-38	43-61
Freiburg	58-76	43-58	29-40	41-59
Hamburg	56-72	43-56	29-36	38-56
Munich	56-74	40-56	23-34	38-58

LIFE AND TIMES

■■■ HISTORY

All history involves conflict, but in Germany, the interpretation of history is especially contested ground. Witness the *Historikerstreit* (Historians' Dispute) of the early 1980s, when a disagreement among historians as how to best locate the Third Reich in the context of European history erupted into a major, highly public, political brawl, which divided politicians and excited the tabloid press. There is less controversy attached to the earlier history of Germanic peoples in the area which would eventually become the German nation, from scuffles with the Roman empire to the Frankish Carolingian dynasty, the age of Charlemagne, and the rise and division of the Holy Roman Empire. That is where we pick up the story.

Under the Habsburg Empire

Late in the 12th century, **Emperor Friedrich Barbarossa** of the Swabian house of Hohenstaufen feudalized and federalized the Holy Roman Empire. He created a new class of imperial princes below the emperor and above the other nobles, winning the support of strong territorial lords for his plans by promoting them to these positions. His designs were undermined by his own grandson, **Friedrich II.** In exchange for support from princes and the pope for his Italian military expeditions, Friedrich II ceded significant legal, administrative, and judicial authority to them, further fragmenting Germany. Squabbles between the princes after Friedrich's death in 1250 left the empire without clear leadership. As a compromise between warring factions, the **Golden Bull of 1356** declared that electors from seven major territories—three archbishops and four secular leaders—would approve the selection of each emperor. Aspirants to the imperial throne bribed the Electors with territorial and political concessions, gradually diluting the power of the emperor. On the other hand, the electors made a financial killing every time an emperor died. Under these daunting conditions, members of the well-heeled **House of Habsburg** maneuvered their way to the top, occupying the throne for the next five centuries with the support of their Austrian domains. Meanwhile, settlers left their homes in western Germany and moved to eastern Germany, Bohemia, and Austria; the phrase describing this movement, *Drang nach Osten* (drive to the East), was resurrected by Nazi ideologists centuries later. Around the same time, in 1358 several towns organized the **Hanseatic League,** designed to help its members protect their trading interests.

The Reformation and the Thirty Years War

On Halloween Day 1517, **Martin Luther,** a monk and professor of Biblical studies at Wittenberg University in Saxony, posted his **95 Theses** on the door of the castle church. The reverberations of the **Reformation** he unleashed are still felt today. Luther attacked the Roman Catholic Church for both the extravagant lifestyle of the papal court in Rome and for its practice of selling indulgences—essentially gift certificates for the soul which promised to reduce the number of years that the owner would spend in purgatory. In their place, Luther propounded the doctrine that salvation comes only through God's grace. Luther found immediate support for his views with Friedrich the Wise, elector of Saxony, who had not permitted the sale of papal indulgences in Saxony. Other princes soon adopted Lutheranism, captivated by the idea of being able to seize church assets without going to hell for it. Armed conflicts soon erupted. Serfs rebelled during the **Peasants' Wars** in 1525-6. The chaos was too much for Luther, who called upon the princes to crush the bands of peasants. As Lutheranism spread throughout Europe, **Emperor Karl V** declared his intention to uproot the subversive doctrine and destroy those who professed it. But in the **Peace of Augsburg** in 1555, Karl was compelled to suspend the **Counter Reformation** and concede to individual princes the right to determine the religion practiced in their territory, a system that led to a number of overnight conversions among the nobility. The **Thirty Years War** (1618-48) was a catastrophe for Germany: casualties were atrociously high, towns were laid to waste, and famine stalked the population. The **Peace of Westphalia,** which ended the war, granted 300 princes the right to participate as Electors of the emperor. The Habsburgs retained the right to interfere in intra-state squabbles, but the imperial administration had effectively been dismantled. Moreover, the principle of rulers determining the religion of their subjects remained in place.

The Rise of Brandenburg-Prussia

The war indirectly benefited the leaders of **Brandenburg-Prussia.** Elector Friedrich Wilhelm of the **House of Hohenzollern** concluded a peace agreement with Sweden that did not estrange him from the Habsburgs. He enlisted the support of the landed nobility, the **Junkers,** by making them officers in the army. His son, Friedrich— known as **Friedrich the Great**—further consolidated what would someday become infamous as the Prussian-led **German Empire.** Friedrich the Great is revered in German history as an enlightened ruler, notable for his administrative and military skill as well as his patronage of the arts. Friedrich also happened to be gay, a trait which did not sit well with his father.The skirmishes inaugurated by Friedrich the Great paled in comparison to the havoc wreaked by the French army in the wake of the French Revolution. **Napoleon** conquered Central Europe, disbanded the Holy Roman Empire, and fused hundreds of territories into the **Confederation of the Rhine** in 1806. But Napoleon's armies bogged down in Russia, and a general rebellion in Germany known as the **War of Liberation** ejected Napoleon from German territory. The **Congress of Vienna** in 1815 attempted to restore the pre-war German state system by creating the Austrian-led **German Confederation.** The conference awarded Prussia portions of Rhineland-Westphalia, which would become Germany's industrial heartland.

In 1848, revolution broke out again in France, and the discontent spread rapidly to other parts of Europe. The German Confederation agreed to let an elected assembly decide the future of the confederation. This **National Assembly** met in Frankfurt, drafted a liberal constitution, and invited King Friedrich Wilhelm IV of Prussia to serve as emperor. In a victory of absolutism over democracy, he spurned their offer, saying that he would not accept a crown created by the rabble. The Assembly disbanded, and the ensuing revolt in Frankfurt was crushed by the Prussian army.

Bismarck and the Second Reich

In 1862, Prussian King Wilhelm I appointed a worldly *Junker* aristocrat named **Otto von Bismarck** as Chancellor. History's greatest practitioner of *Realpolitik,* Bismarck's incomparable career was marked by a remarkably complex series of alliances and compromises that were more than occasionally dissolved in favor of more violent tactics—*"Blut und Eisen"* (Blood and Iron), Bismarck liked to point out, were really all that mattered in the long run. Like his fellow *Junker* conservatives, Bismarck despised liberals and parliamentarians. Unlike his fellow *Junker* conservatives, he believed in the cause of German unity, and was prepared to go to war to achieve it. This is he did well and often, fighting Denmark, Austria, and France in rapid succession. So well-planned were Bismarck's ventures that in 1871, Wilhelm I was crowned **Emperor (Kaiser) of the German Reich** in the Hall of Mirrors at the Palace of Versailles, while Paris lay under siege a few miles away. With France thus disposed of, Bismarck was free to **unify Germany** on his own terms, and the lesser German states were unable to resist him. In one of the world's great instances of political Machiavellianism, he engaged in a long series of initiatives that revolved around reforms and repression (known as the **Kulturkampf**). Taking a "carrot and stick" approach, he banned the Social Democratic Party but increased social welfare programs for the working class. By 1890, Bismarck had created such a politically stable state that Kaiser Wilhelm II fired him. Breakneck industrialization, brazen forays into colonial imperialism, unenlightened autocracy, a self-consciously bureaucratic bureaucracy, and crass diplomacy were Germany's most salient characteristics from the late 19th century until 1914, after which things got rapidly worse.

World War I and the Failed Revolution

On the eve of World War I, Europe was entangled in a complex system of alliances in which minor disputes could easily escalate into a full-blown continental war. That crisis broke out in 1914, when a Serbian nationalist assassinated the Habsburg heir to the Austrian throne, **Archduke Franz-Ferdinand,** in Sarajevo, and culminated in a massive war in which Germany, allied with Austria-Hungary, went to war with most of the rest of the continent. Almost the entire Reichstag, including the Social Democratic delegates, got on the bandwagon and voted for the war. Four years of agonizing **trench warfare** followed. Eventually, the destruction of the German navy, coupled with economic distress and the entry of the United States on the allied side, led to Germany's defeat. In late 1918, with the German army on the brink of collapse, riots and mutinies broke out on the homefront. On November 9, 1918, Social Democratic leader **Phillip Scheidemann** declared a republic in Berlin. **Friedrich Ebert** became the first president. The Kaiser and his flunkies fled.

A negotiated peace followed. France insisted on imposing a harsh peace on Germany in the **Treaty of Versailles,** which included demands for staggering reparations payments and a clause ascribing the blame for the war to Germany. Because the war had never reached German soil and the propaganda had promised a smashing victory right up to the end, Germans were unprepared for defeat. The Republican government had no choice but to accept the treaty. From 1918-20, Germany was consumed by abortive revolutions and coups. The newly formed **Communist Party** (Kommunistische Partei Deutschlands—KPD) led a revolt in Berlin and attempted to establish a government of workers' councils, with a certain amount of popular support. The Republic crushed the revolution by appealing to bands of right-wing army veterans called **Freikorps.** In a fit of reactionary fervor, the **Freikorps** turned against the government, while the army stood idly by. **Wolfgang Kapp** lead a coup to overthrow the Republic from the right; The workers, staunchly supporting the new Republic, responded with a general strike; ironically, the left also helped save the day, by organizing a force of 50-80,000 against the coup in the Ruhr industrial area. The coup failed, and the Republic emerged bruised but intact.

The Weimar Republic and the Great Depression

The leaders of the new Republic met to draw up a constitution in the city of **Weimar.** Weimar was chosen for its historical legacy as the birthplace of the German Enlightenment, and gave its name to a period of intense cultural activity coupled with economic and political uncertainty (for at look at the artistic side, see Life and Times: Culture, below). Outstanding war debts and the burden of reparations produced the staggering **hyperinflation** of 1922-23, during which time the German *Reichsmark* sunk from four to one U.S. dollar to 4.2 trillion to the dollar. Eventually, the Republic achieved a degree of stability, but the seeds of authoritarianism never grew sterile. The old, reactionary order still clung to power in many segments of society: the army, police, big business, civil service, and judiciary. When an Austrian corporal named **Adolf Hitler** was arrested for treason after his abortive 1923 **Beer Hall Putsch,** he was not deported on the grounds that he "believed he was German" and was sentenced to the minimum term of five years, of which he served only 10 months. During his time in jail, Hitler wrote a book—*Mein Kampf*—and decided that his party, the National Socialist German Workers Party (*Nationalsozialistische Deutsche Arbeiter Partei*—NSDAP), also known as the **Nazis,** would have to seize power through constitutional means. Two aspects of the Weimar constitution— pure proportional representation, which proliferated political parties, and the infamous **Article 48,** which provided for rule by decree in emergency—expedited this.

The Nazis were still a fringe party when the **Great Depression** struck in 1929, and 25% of the population was left unemployed within months. Membership in the NSDAP exploded—the **SA** (*Sturmabteilung*), the party's paramilitary arm, grew as large as the German army. The Nazis' slogan was "Germany, awake!" a call to root out Jewish, Bolshevist, and other supposed "foreign influences" that had allegedly poisoned Germany's national spirit and led it into disgrace. Hitler's own powerful oratory and the brilliant propaganda apparatus of Josef Goebbels amplified the message. Hitler failed in a presidential bid against the nearly senile war-hero Hindenburg in 1932, but the parliamentary elections in July of the same year yielded the Nazis' highest vote total (37%) and made them the largest party in the *Reichstag*. President von Hindenburg appointed Hitler as Chancellor on January 30, 1933.

The Third Reich

The Nazi Seizure of Power

The conservatives who backed the Hitler government had always been hostile to the Republic, and they naïvely believed they could control Hitler and establish an authoritarian regime ruled by the traditional elites. When Hitler's government was formed in January 1933, the Nazis controlled only one other cabinet ministry and one minister-without-portfolio. During the next two months, Hitler persuaded President Hindenburg to dissolve the *Reichstag* and call new elections; this gave Hitler seven weeks to **rule by decree.** During this time, he curtailed freedom of the press, authorized the SA and SS as auxiliary police, and brutalized opponents. A week before the elections, the mysterious **Reichstag fire** gave Hitler an occasion to declare a state of emergency and begin rounding up communists, socialists, and other political opponents, many of whom were relocated to newly commissioned **concentration camps.** In the elections of March 5, 1933, the Nazis fell well short of a majority. Nonetheless, they arrested and browbeat enough opposing legislators to pass an **Enabling Act** making Hitler the **legal dictator** of Germany—authorized to ban all opposition and rule by decree. The Nazis quickly established party control over the country—not just the government, but universities, professional associations, indeed every imaginable aspect of civil society was strictly regulated.

In the early years of the Third Reich a massive program of industrialization in preparation for rearmament restored full employment, and the economic status of many improved. Initially, the only people who didn't benefit from the Third Reich were Jews, minorities, democrats, communists, artists, the disabled, free-thinking human beings, and a lot of people in Czech Bohemia, which Hitler annexed in 1938. Austria was also annexed, a move which was welcomed by many Austrians.

World War II: Blitzkrieg to D-Day

On September 1, 1939, German tanks rolled into Poland. England and France, which were bound by treaty to defend Poland, immediately declared war on Germany, but did not take the offensive. In four weeks, Poland was vanquished, and Hitler and Stalin divided up Poland under the terms of a secret agreement. For almost a year, the French and English remained hunkered down behind the Maginot Line. On April 9, 1940, Hitler relieved the tedium by rolling over Denmark and Norway. A month later, the *Blitzkrieg* roared through Luxembourg, Belgium, the Netherlands, and France. However, the Nazis failed to subdue England in the **Battle of Britain.** The German **invasion of the USSR** in June 1941 ended the Hitler-Stalin pact. The invasion came close to success and the Soviets suffered extremely high casualties, but the *Blitzkrieg* faltered in the Russian winter and Hitler sacrificed thousands of German soldiers in his adamant refusal to retreat. Hitler committed a second fateful error when he declared war on the United States. Soon Germany was retreating on all fronts. The American-British-Canadian landing in Normandy on **D-Day** (June 6, 1944) preceded an arduous, bloody Allied advance across Europe. In March, 1945, the Western Allies crossed the Rhine. In April 1945, with Red Army troops overhead, Hitler married Eva Braun just prior to killing himself.

The Holocaust

Hitler made no secret of his desire to exterminate world Jewry, and the Nazis' **"Final Solution to the Jewish problem"** can be seen as the extension of the persecution, deprivation, and deportation to which Jews had been subjected since the first days of the Third Reich. One of the government's first acts was to institute a boycott of Jewish businesses and to expel Jews from professions and the civil service. In 1935, the first of the anti-Semitic **Racial Purity Laws** (also known as the **Nuremberg Laws,** after the city in which they were conceived) were enacted, depriving Jews of German citizenship and prohibiting intercourse between "Aryan" and Jew. The anti-Semitic agenda reached a new level of violence in 1938 with the Nazi pogrom of *Reichskristallnacht,* referred to euphemistically by the Nazis as **Kristallnacht** (Night of Broken Glass). On November 9 of that year, Nazis destroyed thousands of Jewish businesses, burned synagogues, killed scores of Jews, and sent at least 20,000 to concentration camps. The mass gassing of Jews in specially constructed **extermination camps** began in 1942, though **SS Sonderkommmmando** (special commands) which followed the *Wehrmacht* through Russia had earlier staged mass executions. Full-fledged extermination camps, **Auschwitz, Buchenwald, Chelmno, Treblinka, Majdanek, Sobibor, and Belzec,** plus dozens of other labor camps, were operating before war's end. Some six million Jews, representing every Nazi-occupied country but mostly from Poland and the USSR, had been gassed, shot, starved, worked to death, or killed by exposure. All together, more than 4,950 cities and towns saw their Jewish populations destroyed. Five million or more other victims—Soviet prisoners of war, Slavs, Gypsies, homosexuals, the mentally retarded, and various political opponents of the regime—also died in Nazi camps, but only Jews were targeted for total genocide. What occurred during the years of Nazi tyranny reaches beyond the scope of tragedy to a horror so great that it is, for most, inconceivable.

The Living Archives

Today, while Holocaust survivors and their families still grapple with questions of faith and loss, scores of just-published scholarly works confront "revisionist" theories that claim the Holocaust never happened. As the living memory of the Holocaust slowly fades, the aging remains of **concentration camps** become the most crucial, tangible testimony available to any audience willing to see and listen.

Robert Musil wrote "there is nothing in this world as invisible as a monument," and just as a monument can lose its power to shock by becoming all-too-familiar to the passer-by, so can the very existence of "museums" and guided tours on the grounds of Dachau seem to only trivialize what occurred there. The very fact that concentration camps are noted as points of interest in many travel guides (including this one), must be recognized as somewhat troubling in itself. The buildings do have the power to teach, but other concerns exist. In this book we cover four major camps: **Buchenwald, Bergen-Belsen, Dachau,** and **Sachsenhausen;** if you choose to visit one, keep in mind that while some treat these grounds as "just another stop" on a list of things to see, coming in ignorance and leaving unaffected, many visitors come with a knowledge of the camp's past or perhaps a personal memory of a loved one who perished within its walls. Be aware of the pain involved, and make an effort not to treat the grounds with disrespect. In addition, know that the exhibits here do not tell the whole story; no single medium can embrace such a narrative. Read up before you come. Better yet, a discussion with a survivor will inevitably shed more light on the dark history of these camps than any exhibit ever will.

Occupation and Division

Germans call their defeat in the Second World War **Nullpunkt**—"Point Zero"—the moment at which everything began again. Germany's battlefield defeat was total, unmistakable, and indisputable. The Allies occupied and partitioned the country: the East under the Soviets, the West under the British and Americans, and Berlin under joint control. The economy was in shambles. Virtually every city had been bombed into ruin. More than five million German soldiers and civilians had been killed in the war, and millions remained in POW camps. Ten to 12 million ethnic Germans were expelled from Poland and Czechoslovakia. Every institution and every existing authority in Germany was discredited by involvement with the Nazi regime. The Allied program for the **Occupation**—demilitarization, democratization, and de-Nazification—proceeded apace, but growing animosity between the Soviets and the Western allies made joint control of Germany increasingly difficult.

In 1947, the Western Allies merged their occupation zones into a single economic unit known as **Bizonia** (later Trizonia, after a French occupation zone was carved out of the British and American zones). The Western Allies began to rebuild their zone along the lines of a market economy with the aid of huge cash infusions from America's **Marshall Plan.** The Soviets, who had suffered immeasurably more in the war than either America or Britain, had neither the desire nor the spare cash to help the East rebuild at once. The Western Allies in 1948 effectively severed the East's economy from the West's by introducing a new currency to Bizonia, the **Deutschmark.** The dispute over currency reform was the proximate cause of the **Berlin Blockade** (see Berlin History) and the ultimate **division of Germany** in 1949. The Allies were desperate to staff key positions with competent Germans. They were not always as rigorous in de-Nazifying Germany as they should perhaps have been.

Germany Since the War

The Federal Republic of Germany

The Federal Republic of Germany (*Bundesrepublik Deutschland*) was established as a provisional government of the Western states on May 24, 1949. The Allies retained the right to ultimately veto any measure by the German government. A **Basic Law** (*Grundgesetz*), drawn up by German academics and politicians under the direction of the Western Allies, which safeguarded individual rights, and established a system of Federal States. One of the most visionary paragraphs of the Basic Law was the one which established a Right of Asylum, guaranteeing refuge to any person fleeing persecution. Germany joined **NATO** and became a charter member of the **EEC,** later the **European Community.** The Allies ended the state of war and, in 1955, recognized the Federal Republic's sovereignty.

Electoral Politics: Parties and Chancellors

The **Social Democratic Party** (SPD) seemed poised to dominate post-war German politics under the leadership of the popular **Kurt Schumacher,** a fierce anti-communist and anti-fascist. However, Germany's historically fragmented conservatives and centrists managed to unite around a new party, the **Christian Democratic Union** (*Christliche Demokratische Union*—CDU), which had its roots in the old Catholic Center Party. With **Konrad Adenauer** at the helm, the CDU won a small plurality of *Bundestag* seats in the first elections. Another new party, the **Free Democratic Party** (*Freidemokratische Partei*—FDP), assembled bourgeois liberals and professionals together with a disconcertingly high number of former Nazis. Although the FDP remaiñed small, it acquired power as a coalition partner. The Communists did notably poorly in the West. Various marginal right-wing and neo-Nazi parties have sprung up on occasion. The aging chancellor stepped down in 1963. He was replaced by Ludwig Erhard, who proved to be uncharismatic and abrasive as chancellor. At this point, the SPD found a dynamic leader in **Willy Brandt,** the charismatic former Berlin mayor who had worked in the anti-Nazi Resistance. The 1969 *Bundestag* elections catapulted the SPD into power. After Brandt resigned in 1974, **Helmut Schmidt,** Brandt's economics minister, assumed the chancellorship.

In 1982, the FDP and the CDU formed a government under **Helmut Kohl.** Kohl's government pursued a policy of welfare state retrenchment, tight monetary policy, and military cooperation with the U.S. Around the same time, a new political force emerged in Germany: the Green Party (*die Grünen*), which fought for disarmament and environmentalism, won a surprisingly large following by rejecting the traditional coalition politics of the Left. The Greens were divided between the unstructured idealism of the *fundis* and the pragmatism of the *realos*. This schism hurt their standing, as did the fact that they were the only major party not to stand jointly with their Eastern affiliates in the post-reunification elections.

The New Germany: Economy and Society

By the mid-1950s, Germany's post-war **Economic Miracle** (*Wirtschaftswunder*) was in full swing, and the CDU's dominance of German politics seemed unshakeable. Germany achieved full employment by the late 1950s and soon began recruiting what would become millions of **foreign workers** (*Gastarbeiter*). The FRG under Schmidt racked up an economic record that was the envy of the industrial world; nevertheless, persistent structural problems in heavy industry contributed to **mounting unemployment** and dissatisfaction with the SPD in the late 1970s. Brandt's **Ostpolitik** (Eastern Policy) government extended recognition to East Germany. The goal of this was to take "small steps" towards bringing the Germanys together. The late 1960s and early 70s also saw the emergence of a radical **youth rebellion,** informed by the ideas of Herbert Marcuse and Jürgen Habermas and aimed primarily against the American war in Vietnam, as well as against the stifling intellectual conformity of 1950s West Germany. Although most of this protest took the same peaceful form as American campus demonstrations, radical groups such as the **Baader-Meinhof** gang and their more violent offshoot, the **Red Army Faction (RAF).** Launched a wave of violent terrorist attacks. The government responded with an extremely controversial set of emergency laws that placed restrictions on civil liberties. In 1984, Richard von Weizsäcker of the CDU was elected to the largely symbolic post of Federal President, from which he urged Germans to shoulder fully their moral responsibility for the Third Reich—an implicit rebuke of politicians like Kohl who spoke of "the grace of late birth."

The German Democratic Republic

When the Red Army occupied Eastern Germany, a cadre of German communists who had spent the war in exile in Moscow came close on their heels. Even before the surrender was signed, these party functionaries had begun setting up a communist-dominated administrative apparatus to run the Soviet occupation zone. The first party licensed to operate in the Soviet Sector was the communist KPD under **Wilhelm Pieck** and **Walter Ulbricht,** but versions of the Western parties were established shortly afterwards. At first, the German communists pledged to establish a parliamentary democracy and a distinctively "German path to socialism." However, their dependence on Moscow became apparent.

In Berlin, the one area where the SPD was permitted to operate freely, independent Social Democrats soundly defeated the SED at the ballot box. The Soviets responded by not holding any more freely contested elections; future elections required voters to approve or reject a **"unity list"** of candidates that ensured the dominance of the SED. On October 7, 1949, a People's Congress selected by such methods declared the establishment of the **German Democratic Republic** (*Deutsche Demokratische Republik*), with the national capital in Berlin. After the death of Josef Stalin, political conditions relaxed a bit in the GDR, though the nationalization of industry proceeded without hesitation. Impossibly high work goals led to a **workers' revolt** across the GDR on June 17, 1953, which was ruthlessly crushed (see Berlin History). The GDR became a party to the **Warsaw Pact** in 1955.

In 1961, the GDR decided to remedy the exodus of skilled young workers to the Federal Republic (about three million since 1945). Although borders to the West had been sealed off, escape through Berlin remained a possibility. On the night of August 12-13, the first, primitive barriers of the **Berlin Wall** were laid (see Berlin History). The regime called it an "anti-fascist protective wall," but Berliners knew which way the guns were pointed. Stanching the flow of refugees to the West gave

Ulbricht room to launch his hard-line **New Economic System** in 1968. This document diluted most constitutional rights. After Ulbricht died in 1973, his replacement, **Erich Honecker,** eliminated reformist experiments. German-German relations improved remarkably during the era of Willy Brandt's **Ostpolitik.** Meanwhile, the hated secret police, the **Stasi,** maintained a network of hundreds of thousands of agents and paid informants that strove to envelop every citizen. Despite the scars of the war and the inefficiency of central planning, East Germans enjoyed by the late 1970s the highest standard of living in the Eastern Bloc.

With the ascension of the *glasnost*-minded **Mikhail Gorbachev** to the leadership of the USSR in 1985, reform began to spread throughout the Eastern Bloc—except the GDR, which adhered to a rigid, Brezhnev-style orthodoxy. In May 1989, Hungary began dismantling the barbed-wire border with Austria, giving some 55,000 East Germans a route to the West. By October, police in Czechoslovakia (to which East Germans could travel without a visa) were tolerating a flood of GDR citizens into the West German embassy; thousands were permitted to emigrate. On October 6, while on a state visit to celebrate the GDR's fortieth birthday, Gorbachev publicly reprimanded Honecker and announced that the Soviet Union would not interfere in the GDR's domestic affairs. With the weakness of the regime thus exposed, clandestine dissident groups (supported and protected by the Lutheran church) such as **New Forum** began to operate more freely, and massive **anti-government demonstrations** broke out in the streets of Leipzig, Dresden, Berlin, and other cities, demanding free elections, freedom of the press, and freedom to travel. Honecker soon resigned. His successor, **Egon Krenz,** promised reforms. Meanwhile, tens of thousands of GDR citizens—largely young professionals—continued to flee via Czechoslovakia, which had completely opened its border with West Germany. The entire GDR Politburo resigned on November 8, and a day later, a spokesperson for the Central Committee announced the **opening of all borders to the West,** including the Berlin Wall.

Reunification

The End of the GDR and the Route to Unity

The opening of the Wall did not immediately herald the death of the GDR or the communist regime. The party remained in power and the Stasi continued to operate. Throughout December, popular demonstrations continued unabated. Honecker was whisked away to the Soviet Union and the SED renamed itself the **Party of Democratic Socialism (PDS).** In the East, opposition parties took shape as the West's political parties frantically scrambled to assert their influence. Buoyed by Kohl's success at getting Moscow to assent to unification, the CDU-backed **Alliance for Germany** emerged as the strongest party. Following the election, the new government authorized **economic and social union** with the Federal Republic, which occurred on July 2, 1990. The wartime Allies still had to agree to permit the **complete political reunification** of Germany; the last remaining obstacle, the USSR's insistence that United Germany remain outside NATO, was overcome when Kohl traded promises of substantial economic aid and a pledge not to station NATO troops in the East for Gorbachev's approval of unification.

Despite catch-phrases such as *Wiedervereinigung* (reunification), East and West Germany did not unify to create a new nation-state. Rather, East Germany was absorbed into the Federal Republic, accepting the institutions and structures of the West. When the FRG was founded in 1949, the Basic Law (*Grundgesetz*) was intended to be a provisional constitution until eventual unification, when a new constitution would be drawn up for a sovereign Germany. This ideal was embodied in paragraph 146. However, under the Basic Law's paragraph 23, any territory had the power to accede, or simply declare themselves ready to be annexed by, the Federal Republic, and adhere to its norms and structures. This was a faster route to unity, and after a great deal of debate, it was the one Germany took. On **October 3, 1990,** the Allies forfeited their occupation rights, the GDR ceased to exist, and Germany became one united, sovereign nation for the first time in 45 years. Germans now distinguish between East and West with the labels "**New Federal States**" and "**Old Federal States.**"

Germany Lately

At first, nationalistic euphoria blurred the state of things for Germans on both sides of the wall. Rapidly the problems became blatantly apparent. Kohl's popularity has plummeted to the point where Eastern voters pelted him with rotten fruit during a recent visit and his party failed to carry his own state in state elections. The inefficient industries and institutions in the East led to massive unemployment and the Federal Republic's worst-ever recession. Westerners resent the inflation and taxes brought on by the cost of rebuilding the new federal states; Easterners have had to give up the generous social benefits Communism had afforded them. A rightward-moving political climate in the West pulled the East with it, restricting social programs not only in welfare but also in areas such as abortion.

Recently, the anger has spread to an intense distrust of **foreigners,** especially immigrants from Eastern Europe and the *Gastarbeiter* (see above), some of whom have been living in Germany for decades now. German Law does not automatically grant citizenship to children born in Germany; parentage is considered the paramount factor. This has become more and more of a troubling point as the children of immigrants grow up in Germany, speak only German, know no other home, but are defined as life-long outsiders. Violent attacks on foreigners, sometimes resulting in murder, have become more frequent throughout Germany. In 1992, particularly wide-scale assaults resulting in multiple deaths were launched against immigrants in Mölln and Rostock; in June 1993, an arson attack on the home of a Turkish family in the western town of Solingen claimed several lives, including those of a number of young children. Although the general reaction in Germany has been outrage, there have been statements of "understanding" for the attackers motives, including an implicit one from the government itself: soon after Solingen, Germany's liberal **Asylum law** was repealed. Nazi graffiti is most apparent in the new federal states, although neo-Nazis are also active, if not as visible, in the west.

Abortion laws have changed abruptly a number of times in the years since Reunification. Paragraph 218 of the Basic Law vaguely refers to a "right to life," but prior to reunification, abortion was technically legal in Germany, but not available on demand. Germany works according to an "indication" model—a woman must show that the reason she is seeking an abortion is acceptable to the state. These include medical (woman's life is in danger) and legal (the pregnancy is a result of rape). There is one loose category, a "social indication," meaning that the pregnancy would unacceptably disrupt the woman's life. The problem was that whether or not a woman met this standard was determined on a state-by-state basis. Officials in cities like Berlin were usually willing to concede to the woman's judgment, while those in Catholic Bavaria almost never did. The state also mandated counseling, which in Bavaria was carried out by the Catholic church. In the GDR, abortion was legal and fully available on demand. When the GDR collapsed, many women in Eastern Germany were concerned that they would be worse off in this corner of their life, while many pro-choice West German women saw it all as an opportunity to press for a liberalization. In summer 1992, the Bundestag voted to do away with the indications model, but still mandated counseling and a lengthy process of bureaucratic maneuvering. Woman in the East were a bit worse off, women in the West a bit better off, and nobody was completely happy. Least of all the State of Bavaria, which promptly sued the federal government in the Constitutional Court. In May 1993, the court decided against liberalization, and actually set limits which were stricter for *everyone* than they were before reunification.

It is hard to end an essay on German history, because it is a narrative which reaches greedily in many directions across time. There are always new dreams and bursts of change which seem to have no precedent. At the same time there are

CULTURE

moments when one seems to be hearing the same story again, to hear the same turns of phrase deployed in different settings, the same insistence and the same denial. It is easy to be caught and lost in what Bertolt Brecht called "this Babylonian confusion of words," the narrative of Germany.

Further Reading

Gordon A. Craig's *Germany 1866-1945* provides a definitive history of those years. For a more in-depth look at post-war German history, pick up Henry Ashby Turner's *The Two Germanies Since 1945,* or Peter J. Katzenstein's *Policy and Politics in Western Germany.* For more on contemporary German society, try John Ardagh's *Germany and the Germans,* published by Harper and Row. Also, read anything and everything that novelist Günter Grass has written on the subject of Reunification. He criticizes the rapidity of the process and the forgetfulness and abandonment of the historic lessons Germany might have learned in the years since the war. Grass has emerged as a powerful moral voice in contemporary Germany, one worth attention and respect. His novels are also excellent (see Literature, below.)

■■■ CULTURE

Germany, the Germans like to say, is the land of the *"Dichter und Denker"*—the poet and the philosopher. Poet Bertolt Brecht, in a bitter moment, claimed that a truer epithet was land of the *"Richter und Henker"*—the judge and the hangman. But Brecht's own literary life is but one of many that belie his statement. What is striking about Germany is not the absence of a cultural spirit, but the ways in which a peculiarly German sense of the role culture plays in everyday life might intersect with the "peculiarities" of German history. Germany's cultural legacy is rich, indeed richer than that of almost any nation in Europe. This international inheritance extends to the visual arts, architecture, music, literature, and film.

■ Visual Art

Art in Germany extends back to Celtic and Roman artifacts and tribal folk decorations. With the rise of Christianity, the artistic impulse in medieval Germany focused on religious themes. Distinctively German painting flourished in the Renaissance. The **School of the Danube,** a group of South German painters, advanced the idea of the Cologne school still farther into the secular world, giving the landscape or architectural environment primary importance over human subjects. **Lucas Cranach** was particularly taken with the idea of combining the beauty of nature with the sublimity of divine subjects. Cranach produced paintings like a man possessed; his work can be seen all over Europe. **Hans Holbein the Younger** is renowned for his portraits, executed at both the German and English courts; his *Henry VIII* is an eerie, detached portrait of the noble with the standard *memento mori.* **Matthias Grünewald** clung to medieval forms for his haunting, highly symbolic religious works. His medium of choice was the altar dip- or triptych. **Albrecht Dürer,** one of Germany's most renowned Renaissance artists, worked in painting, drafting, and woodcuts; his work in all three is dark in psychological atmosphere and vigorous in line. His work attempted to rejuvenate the tradition of German art independent of Italian influences. After the Thirty Years War virtually halted construction and laid Germany to waste, the **Baroque** era invigorated staid Renaissance architecture with bold, flamboyant decoration. The outstanding figure of this period was **Tillman Riemschneider,** a woodcarver who produced statuary for churches and palaces.

The cool, stark simplicity of Neoclassicism softened into **Romanticism,** harking back to German national idioms and to local Gothic and Romanesque architectural styles. The Wars of Liberation (as Germans call the Napoleonic Wars) infused paintings with highly **national themes** of German landscape and legend, some frolicksome and pastoral, others mystical and serious. The intriguing master of the latter type was **Kaspar David Friedrich,** with his brilliant, haunting works obsessed with man's solitude and insignificance in the universe. Many of his works capture dramattic, uninhabitable landscapes such as icy oceans and wind-blown cemeteries. If you squint your eyes, you can see the world the way **Max Liebermann** did—he began as a master Impressionist (*Munich Beer Garden*) and from there went on to lead the Berlin faction of the **Secession movement** in the 1890s: in two adjectives, decadence and eroticism. This trend became **Jugendstil** (literally, "youth-style"), which rose to popularity in Vienna, Berlin, and Budapest in the early 20th century.

The years of the **Weimar Republic** saw an extraordinary density of artistic genius. The symbolist tendencies of *Jugendstil* intensified into the larger **Expressionist** movement, with a deliberately anti-naturalist aesthetic that distorted objects and colors in order to identify them with an abstract idea. A series of city-based groups created consortia of Expressionist effort. **Die Brücke** (The Bridge) was the earliest of these, founded at Dresden in 1905 with the explicit aim of heightening the intensity of expression in art. The **blaue Reiter** (Blue Rider) group, founded in Munich in 1909 by the Russian emigré **Wassily Kandinsky** and named after one of his paintings, included Kandinsky, **Franz Marc,** and **Paul Klee. Max Beckmann** left a large body of Expressionist works (although he shunned the label) focused on the anxieties of a dehumanized culture. The smaller **Realist** movement devoted itself to bleak, critical works such as **Käthe Kollwitz's** posters for social reform.

The rise of Nazism drove most artists of the Weimar era into exile. They were either the "wrong" race or religion, or their works were branded "decadent and subversive" and banished from view. Wartime art was extremely limited and colored by Nazi ideology. Visual arts in Nazi Germany were dominated by themes of **Blut und Boden** (Blood and Soil), depicting the mythical union of *völkisch* blood and German soil through idealized images of workers, farmers, and soldiers.

Postwar artistic effort has not spawned any unified movement. Some of the old Expressionist masters were still alive and working in the 50s and 60s, but the fragmentation of "postmodern" culture has splintered newer artists into a host of different styles that borrow and reshape the idioms and icons of German culture for the contemporary spirit. The **Zero Group** produced abstractions in Düsseldorf during the first decades after the war. A neo-expressionist group called the **Junge Wilde** (Young Savages) surfaced in Berlin in the late 70s using vivid colors and strong movement. **Josef Beuys** was a charismatic, controversial figure who worked with deliberately low-brow juxtapositions.

Art in the GDR has a more nuanced history than the western stereotyp of a socialist cultural desert would imply. After an initial flirtation with liberal tolerance, the ruling Socialist Unity Party (SED) "Stalinized" the arts. The regime-sponsored orthodox style was known as **Socialist Realism,** exemplified by paintings such as **Lea Grundig's** *Coal and Steel for Peace* and **Otto Nagel's** *Jungpionere* (Young Pioneers). The painters **Hans Grundig, Rudolf Bergander,** and **Eva Schulze-Knabe** and the sculptor **Fritz Cremer** (who designed the Buchenwald Memorial) were also leading figures in the movement. Ambiguity had no place in Socialist Realism: the GDR and the Socialist Unity Party (SED) were to be depicted as glorious, and "bourgeois influence" was to be rooted out. East German artists managed a remarkable amount of innovation and experimentation despite the repression.

■ Architecture and Design

In the medieval period, violent, highly stylized images and masterworks of carving and glasswork ornamented the quiet, somber lines of the cathedrals. The **Romanesque** period followed, spanning the years 1000-1300, with a style of architecture that emerged in direct imitation of antique ruins. Outstanding Romanesque cathedrals can be found at Speyer, Trier, and Mainz. The **Gothic** style gradually replaced the Romanesque from 1300 to 1500. The 14th century was a transitional period that spawned the **Cologne Cathedral.** Stained glass filled the windows of Gothic cathedrals with ever more elaborate patterns of divine light.

During the Renaissance, though churches were still being built, although the Lutheran reforms of the 1550s put a damper on the unrestrained extravagance of cathedrals, and effort was instead channelled into such secular buildings as the **Augsburg Rathaus** (town hall) and **Heidelberg Castle.** Early Baroque shows itself in the **Rathaus** in Leipzig and that in Bremen, as well as the **Würzburg Residenz.** Baroque developed quickly into the extravagant ornamentation of **Rococo**; Munich's **Amalienburg Palace** and **Residenztheater** are typical of the hyper-ornate flamboyance of that movement. The French Revolution snuffed out the courtliness that fueled Baroque and Rococo, replacing them with ideals of "noble simplicity" (*Einfalt*). These ideals spawned a Greek revival of clean lined classical forms.

Wertheim's Department Store in Berlin and the **Exhibition** buildings at Darmstadt are two architectural manifestations of *Jugendstil*, the early 20th-century movement of decorative, stylized design (discussed in detail in Visual Art section, above). **Erich Mendelsohn** later brought the Expressionist aesthetic to architecture, creating curvaceous structures like the **Einstein Tower** at Potsdam, a structure Einstein himself approved with a single word: "Organic." The ideas behind **Neue Sachlichkeit** (New Objectivity) revolutionized design. **Peter Behrens** pioneered these ideas; he designed objects to suit the efficient new materials of industry, concentrating on unornamented geometric harmonies. **Walter Gropius,** the major figure of the Bauhaus, designed several sensational buildings with clean forms, flat roofs, and broad windows, all made possible by new concrete-and-steel construction techniques. In 1919 Gropius founded the **Bauhaus,** a school of design that incorporated theoretical training in the new principles of design efficiency with exposure to the realities of mass production. The school moved to **Dessau** in 1925, where Gropius designed the school's new facility, which became the symbol of the modern style.

Hitler disapproved of the new buildings; he named a design school reject, **Albert Speer,** as his minister of architecture, and commissioned buildings of a ponderous Neoclassical style, intended to last the "Thousand-Year Reich." Many were intended for public rallies, such as the **Congress Hall** and **Stadium** at Nuremburg.

The architecture in the GDR was decidedly un-Bauhaus: a pseudo-Classical, grotesquely ornamented "wedding cake" style. The overblown buildings lining **Karl-Marx-Allee** in Eastern Berlin represent the apogee, such as it is, of **Socialist Realist** architecture. The East's most noted architect, **Hermann Henselmann,** was a former Bauhaus member who apparently forgot everything he had learned. As Chief of Architecture for the development projects in Berlin from 1953 to 1959, he designed several of the sterile edifices on **Alexanderplatz** in Berlin and conceived the plan for the television tower. The hideous building at the heart of the former **Karl Marx Universität** in Leipzig bears his mark as well.

■ Literature

The history of German literature can be traced back to the early Middle Ages. 13th century heroic lyrics had developed into full-fledged **epics.** The most famous and popular of these is the **Nibelungenlied,** the story of Prince Sigfried. But a self-consciously German canon emerged in the 18th century.

The dramatist **Gotthold Ephraim Lessing** produced a series of plays that diverged sharply from contemporary French-influenced drama. Lessing broke the ground for the overtly critical and emotional works to come in the series of sub-movements that form the Romantic era. The writers of the well-known **Sturm und Drang** (Storm and Stress) movement ventured further into the depths of human emotion. The works of this era emphasize the primacy of individual conscience, intuition, and emotion over reason. **Johann Wolfgang von Goethe** was the first major success of this movement, and remains a monumental figure in German literature as a whole. His hugely popular *Die Leiden des jungen Werthers* (The Sorrows of Young Werther) spawned a wave of what can only be called a fad. This and other early works virtually ignored the principle of dramatic simplicity. Instead they were powerful, psychological works with vigorous, complex characters and an unrestrained natural form that had been fostered by the teaching of the elder figure of the *Sturm und Drang,* **Johann Gottfried Herder.** Herder's insistence on originality of image and on a distinctly national style characterized his literary criticism. **Friedrich von Schiller** also catapulted to continental fame. By the 1790s the *Sturm und Drang* had begun to metamorphose into a quieter movement balancing feeling and reason, a tendency that gave the period its **Classical** label. Schiller and Goethe composed masterworks in this mature, innovative period just before the full flowering of Romanticism. At Weimar, Goethe completed *Faust* and *Wilhelm Meister,* which became the favorite of the later Romantics. The **brothers Grimm** composed their famous collections of German fairy tales, providing a foundation for German philology. **Heinrich Wilhelm von Kleist** wove pessimistic tales; the best known is *Die Marquise von O.* Many writers, even during the height of Romanticism, were members of the politicized, anti-mystical, anti-Goethe **Young Germany** school banned as subversive by the *Bundesrat* in 1835. **Heinrich Heine** professed allegiance to this Young German movement. He was an active cynic, who composed lyric poems and songs, usually strongly ironic. **Georg Büchner** was Heine's counterpart in drama; his *Woyzeck* introduced the first lower-class tragic hero in German literature.

The turn of the century saw a progression into the **Naturalistic** mode, inspired by the work of Zola. In Germany the movement was based around finding beauty and value in the objects and patterns of everyday life. **Gerhart Hauptmann** was the foremost author of Naturalist drama. Naturalism was opposed by the **Symbolist** movement in the 20th-century years before the war. **Stefan George** utterly rejected Naturalism in favor of fleeting, sonorous image-poems, and gathered around him a passionate circle of like-minded, well-dressed artists. The truly brilliant works of these years were written by Rilke, Hesse, and Mann. **Rainer Maria Rilke** composed supple rhymes and haunting images that captured fragments of experience. He constantly sought to express the difficulty of grasping one's own spiritual nature. **Hermann Hesse** had a similar interest in spirituality; his *Steppenwolf* considers the plight of modernity and the breakdown of the bourgeois identity. **Thomas Mann** carried Symbolism to its purest form with the *Der Zauberberg* (The Magic Mountain). His brother **Heinrich,** also a novelist, wrote passionate novels including *Der Untertan* (The Subject), an attack on the subservience of the Germans.

The **Weimar era** marked an intense and magnificent outpouring of artistic expression, producing more masterpieces in less time than any other period in German history. Germany's version of the Lost Generation articulated its disillusionment in the **Neue Sachlichkeit** (New Objectivity) movement. The most famous was **Erich Maria Remarque,** who wrote *Im Westen nichts Neues* (All Quiet on the Western Front), an account of the horror of war. Inspired by the ferment of Viennese art nouveau and nonrepresentational art, **Expressionism** picked up the torch of Symbolism after the First World War. **Alfred Döblin's** *Berlin Alexanderplatz* traces shifts in consciousness in the metropolis. **Bertolt Brecht's** dramas and poems present humankind in all its grotesque absurdity, and sought to awake the consciousness of his audience. His *Dreigroschenoper* (Three-Penny Opera) was set to music by Kurt Weill. The years of the Third Reich yielded little of artistic note. Some 2500 authors went into exile, and others underwent "internal emigration" and ceased to write. Many of Brecht's plays were written while he was in wartime exile.

The experience of war, defeat, and genocide inspired a greater social conscience in many Germans. Many authors of the **Social Realism** movement came together formally in 1947 to reform German writing. The resulting coalition, known as **Gruppe 47,** maintained heavy influence on the state of German literature well into the 1970s. A major issue for these postwar German authors was how to reclaim their language after its corruption under fascist rule. *Gruppe 47's* ranks include most of the largest names in contemporary German literature. **Heinrich Böll,** one of the founding members, won the Nobel Prize for Literature in 1972. **Günter Grass** has written a stunning series of novels relating to recent German history, including *Der Blechtrommel* (The Tin Drum). **Peter Handke** is the on-the-road type of modern writer; his *Der kurze Brief zum langen Abschied* is set entirely in America. A new school of drama developed, through playwrights like **Rolf Hochhuth** *(Die Soldaten)* and **Peter Weiss** *(Marat/Sade)*.

The state of letters in the **GDR** followed the same pattern of waxing and waning government control that affected the visual arts (see above). Many expatriate writers, particularly those with Marxist leanings from before the war, returned to the East with great hopes. Brecht made his home in the GDR after the war. But the communist leadership was not interested in eliciting free artistic expression. The combination of personal danger and the burden of censorship led many immensely talented writers to leave, including **Ernst Bloch, Uwe Johnson,** and **Heiner Kipphardt.** Disillusionment drove many others to emigrate. In the 1970s and 80s, some East German writers were able to publish in the West, though not at home, and took that option as a middle ground. **Christa Wolf,** one of the most prominent German women writers, voluntarily remained in the GDR. Another prominent dissident author was **Stefan Heym.** Radical-left GDR playwright **Heiner Müller** shocked Western audiences throughout the 70s with the disgusted protagonists and stripped-down scenarios of Beckett-esque plays such as *Hämletmachine*. Since reunification, there has been a period of artistic anxiety and occasional malaise; in the new Federal States (the former GDR) many authors are caught up in controversies over co-workers who may have worked with the Stasi. Others, both East and West, have found that just thinking about the future of their country and what it means to be a German today, consumes their emotional and creative energies.

■ Philosophy

Luther Kant Leibniz Fichte Hegel Feuerbach Marx Schopenhauer Nietzsche von Hartmann Fischer Husserl Cassirer Paulsen Simmel Weber Benjamin Bloch Horkheimer Adorno Marcuse Mannheim Lowenthal Heidegger Jaspers Arendt Habermas.

■ Film

The newborn medium of film was used brilliantly by directors in the **Weimar era.** Simply put, these early **German Expressionist** films, along with a few American silents, form the basis of all serious study of film today. *Das Kabinett des Dr. Caligari* (The Cabinet of Dr. Caligari), an early horror film, plays out a melodrama of autonomy and control against brilliantly expressive sets of painted shadows and tilted walls. **Fritz Lang** produced a remarkable succession of classic films, including *M., Dr. Mabuse der Spieler*, and *Metropolis,* a dark and brutal vision of the technofascist city of the future. **Ernst Lubitsch, F. W. Murnau,** and **Josef von Sternberg** rounded out the field in the 1920s with their silent classics, while **Carl Zuckmayer** extended the tradition into sound with his satiric and pathetic *Der blaue Engel* (The Blue Angel), starring the immortal Marlene Dietrich as a cabaret singer.

Understanding Hitler's prediction that "without motor-cars, sound films, and wireless, [there can be] no victory for National Socialism," propaganda minister **Joseph Goebbels** became a masterful manipulator. Most **Nazi film** fell into two categories: political propaganda and escapism. *Der Ewige Jude* (The Eternal Jew) and *Jud Süss* glorified anti-Semitism. The masterful propaganda films of **Leni Riefenstahl**, including *Triumph des Willens* (Triumph of the Will), which depicted a Nuremberg Party Rally, and *Olympiad*, found a wide audience.

Film has been perhaps the most vigorous artistic medium in **post-war** Germany. The late 60s and the 70s saw the greatest flood of cinematic excellence. **Rainer Werner Fassbinder** made fatalistic films about individuals corrupted or defeated by society, including a mammoth screen production of Alfred Döblin's mammoth novel *Berlin Alexanderplatz*. Fassbinder's film *Die Ehe der Maria Braun* (The Marriage of Maria Braun) and **Volker Schlöndorf's** *Der Blechtrommel* (The Tin Drum, based on the novel by Günther Grass) were the films that brought the new German wave to the wider, international audience. **Werner Herzog's** *Nosferatu,* a characteristically fantastic, bizarre vampire film starring the demented Klaus Kinski, won the 1976 Critic's Prize at the Cannes Film Festival. **Wolfgang Petersen** directed the epic *Das Boot* (The Boat), in fact one of the largest German feature projects to date. **Wim Wenders's** restless, romantic quest films, particularly his "road films" like *Paris, Texas*, an express his fascination with America. Also in 1984, **Edgar Reitz,** a director of the 60s generation, created the 15-hour epic *Heimat* (Home); Reitz's film captured the full range of detail and experience involved, from the depths of war to the epiphanies of love, in following a German family from 1919 to 1982.

East German film was subject to more constraints than other artistic media, owing to the difficulty of producing films without large-scale financial backing–which only the state could provide. Just after the war, directors in the Soviet Zone produced several internationally acclaimed films, among them **Wolfgang Staudte's** *Die Mörder sind unter uns* (The Murderers are Among Us), about a Nazi war criminal who evades detection and goes on to lead the good life; **Kurt Maetzig's** *Ehe im Schatten (Marriage in the Shadows)*, and **Erich Engel's** *Affaire Blum* (The Blum Affair). After the establishment of the GDR, the ministry of culture operated its own studios, the German Film Corporation (DEFA). **Slatan Dudow** produced the first of DEFA's films, *Unser tägliches Brot* (Our Daily Bread), a paean to the nationalization of industry, and went on to make one of the best East German films, *Stärker als die Nacht* (Stronger than the Night), which tells the story of a communist couple persecuted by the Nazis. After a brief post-Stalinist thaw, few East German films departed from the standard format of socialist heroism or love stories. **Egon Günther's** *Lots Weib* (Lot's Wife), an explicitly feminist exploration of marital breakdown and divorce, was one notable exception. The next year, 1966, saw three major films, Maetzig's *Das Kaninchen bin ich* (The Rabbit is Me), **Frank Vogel's** *Denk bloß nicht, ich heule* (Just Don't Think I'm Crying), and **Frank Beyer's** *Spur der Steine* (Track of Stones). Beyer later made the critically acclaimed *Jakob der Lügner* (Jacob the Liar), which was nominated for an Oscar. Another promising director stifled by the GDR, **Konrad Wolf,** produced such films as *Ich war neunzehn* (I was Nineteen), *Goya*, and *Sonnensucher* (Sun Seekers), the last of which was not permitted to be released until 14 years after its completion. The GDR devoted a healthy portion of its filmmaking resources to the **documentary** genre.

■ Music

Documented German music goes back to the medieval songs of the **Minnesänger,** the German troubadours, whose tradition of sung poetry passed gradually to the **Meistersänger,** commoners who had passed through five ranks from apprentice to *Meister* (Master). Singers remained in local guilds; their instrumental incarnation was the **town-piper,** whose own guilds were the forerunners of modern orchestras. Lutheran hymns applied new polyphonic techniques to folk song forms. The 16th century saw both the *cantata* and the passion, a work thematizing a saint's transcendence. **Michael Praetorius** and **Johann Pachelbel** (best known for his *Canon*) worked in these modes. **Georg Friedrich Händel's** passion *Messiah* is familiar Christmastime music throughout the Western world. **Johann Sebastian Bach** was the stand-out in a long line of musically successful Bachs. His early compositions were God-glorifying music for the organ, clavichord, and harpsichord. In mid-career he produced more secular works; the *Brandenburg Concerti* are famous for their exploration of the happy tensions between solo instruments and chamber orchestra. After moving to Leipzig in 1723 he returned to the somber Lutheran sound; his *St. Matthew Passion* used Biblical texts with the arias and choruses.

The 19th century was a time of German musical hegemony. **Ludwig van Beethoven's** works bridged Classicism and Romanticism. His imposing *Ninth Symphony* and masterful late string quartets were written in the 1820s. Influenced by German Romantic literature, including lyric poetry and songs, **Robert Schumann** composed settings for the poetry of Goethe, Byron, Scott, and particularly Heinrich

FOOD AND DRINK

Heine. The ethereal work of **Felix Mendelssohn-Bartholdy** is well-represented by his overture to *A Midsummer Night's Dream.*

The second generation of Romantic composers included **Johannes Brahms,** a protégé of Schumann, whose talent for variation many popular German *Lieder* (songs). **Richard Wagner** embodied both the artistic strengths and ideological weaknesses of late 19th-century Romanticism. He composed many of the world's best-known operas—*Tannhäuser, Die Meistersinger, Der Ring des Nibelungen*—in an attempt to revolutionize the form with topics chosen specially for musical suitability, simple characters, and a mythic plot filled with divinity and the supernatural. He envisioned a stream of "endless melody" distinguishing itself through changes in mood or key, or through the reappearance of a *Leitmotif.* Wagner's plots are highly nationalistic in their simplicity and celebration of Germanic legend, and were easily exploited by German-Aryan supremacists. Wagner himself wrote a vociferously anti-Semitic tract *Jewishness in Music.* The center of musical genius shifted to **Vienna** in the late 19th and early 20th centuries as Romanticism over-ripened into decadence.

The unstable economy of the Weimar Republic and the anti-Romantic backlash encouraged smaller, cheaper musical forms. A new movement of *Gebrauchsmusik* (utilitarian music) engendered music for amateur players and film scores. Schönberg's disciples, **Anton Webern** and **Alban Berg** were masters of atonality. Berg's opera *Wozzeck* described squalor and tragedy through a progression of forms. **Paul Hindemith** headed a group of neoclassicists influenced by the *Neue Sachlichkeit* (New Objectivity) and the emphasis on craftsmanship introduced by the *Werkbund* and Bauhaus. They embraced the older, variational forms (such as the sonata) most suited to the abstract aesthetic of the time. **Carl Orff** is most noted for his Neoclassical *Carmina Burana,* a resurrection of 13th-century traditional lyrics with a bombastic score. The work was later reinterpreted as a well loved ballet, though Orff's legacy is tainted by his work under the Third Reich. Lighter music-hall works were popular through the Second World War, breeding satiric operettas and songs of the political avant-garde. **Kurt Weill's** partnership with Bertolt Brecht produced such masterpieces of the genre as *Die Dreigroschenoper* (Three-Penny Opera).

The 1960s produced groups like **Neu, Can,** and the **Silver Apples,** featuring fragmented electronic sounds and collage. The electronic motif was extended in the 70s by **Kraftwerk,** who began robotically and gradually shifted to the disco-inflected. Theatrical, hard rock **Nina Hagen** screamed from the 70s to 80s . **Einstürzende Neubauten** combine noise-collage with punk rock. The **Scorpions** have been churning out garden-variety heavy metal for more than two decades, and joined Roger Waters at his historic concert atop the Berlin Wall.

■■■ FOOD AND DRINK

German cuisine is not the best in Europe. In fact, German cuisine isn't always the best in Germany, a fact to which a variety of good ethnic restaurants in the larger cities can attest. But if your tastes run more toward meat and potatoes than tofu, you'll find the food in Germany hearty and satisfying. Be careful when ordering from a German menu if you don't speak the language; ingredients such as eel, blood sausage, and brains are not uncommon, and may represent an acquired taste. Don't let this deter you from taking risks—brains are probably a lot tastier than you think.

The typical German **breakfast** (*Frühstuck*) is coffee or tea with rolls (*Brötchen*), butter, marmalade, slices of bread, sausage (*Wurst*), and cheese (*Käse*). **Lunch** (*Mittagessen*) is usually the main meal of the day, consisting of soup, broiled sausage or roasted meat, potatoes or dumplings, and a salad or some vegetables. **Supper** (*Abendessen* or *Abendbrot*) is a re-enactment of breakfast, only beer replaces coffee and the selection of meat and cheese is wider. **Bread** (*Brot*) is the staff of life in Germany; the quality and variety are astounding. *Vollkornbrot* is whole-wheat (which has a completely different meaning in Germany) and *Roggenbrot* is rye bread. *Schwarzbrot* (black bread) is a dense, dark loaf that's slighly acidic and most delicious when it's fresh. Go to a bakery (*Bäckerei*) and point to whatever looks good. Generally they sell you the whole loaf; for half, ask for *ein halbes*. **Dessert** after meals isn't all that common, but many Germans indulge in a daily ritual of **Kaffee und Kuchen** (coffee and cake), a fourth meal consisting of pastry and coffee, about 3-4pm. Beer and wine are the meal-time **beverages** (see Beer and Wine below). Fruit juice (*Saft*), plain or mixed with sparkling water (*Gespritzt*), is an alternative. Germans rarely drink tap water; if they drink water with a meal, it's mineral water. If you ask for *Wasser* in a restaurant, you get mineral water (which costs); for tap water, ask for *Leitungswasser*, and be prepared for funny looks.

Unpretentious **restaurants** (that's most of them) expect you to seat yourself. If there are no tables free, feel free to ask someone for permission to take a free seat (ask *"Darf ich Platz nehmen?"*, pronounced "dahrf eekh plahts nay-men,"). In traditional restaurants, Address waiters "Herr Ober," and waitresses (but no one else) as "Fräulein." In a hip *Kneipe*, just say *hallo*. When you're finished, you pay at the table. Ask the server *Zahlen, bitte,* (pronounced "TSAH-len, BIT-ah,"). Taxes (*Mehrwertsteuer*) and service is usually included in the price, but it is customary to leave a little something extra, usually by rounding up the bill by a mark or two. Eating in restaurants at every meal will quickly drain your budget. One strategy is to stick to the daily *prix-fixé* option, called the *Tagesmenu*. A cheaper option is to buy food in grocery stores, which *Let's Go* lists in major cities. German university students eat at cafeterias called **Mensa**. Most *Mensen* require an ISIC card (or charge higher prices for non-students), and some are open only to local students, though this can often be evaded by casually strolling in as if you belonged. In smaller towns, the best budget option is to stop by a local bakery (*Bäckerei*) for bread and garnish it with sausage purchased from a butcher shop (*Fleischerei* or *Metzgerei*).

In addition to bread, the staples of the German diet are *Wurst* (sausage, in myriad varieties), *Schweinfleisch* (pork), *Rindfleisch* (beef), *Kalbsfleisch* (veal), *Kartoffeln* (potatoes), and *Eier* (eggs). Dairy products, including *Käse* (cheese) and *Butter*—but especially *Schlagsahne* (whipped cream)—are favorites. To sample the various **local specialties** as you travel around Germany is to appreciate the diversity and particularism of the German tradition. Everyone knows *Sauerbraten* (pickled beef) and *Sauerkraut* (pickled cabbage), but there's much more to German cuisine than that. In **Bavaria,** *Knödel* (potato and flour dumplings, sometimes filled with meat) are ubiquitous. *Leberknödel* are filled with liver. *Weißwurst* is also a Bayern specialty; it is a sausage made with milk. It spoils so quickly that it has to be eaten the day it's made. The preferred vehicles for starch in **Baden** and **Swabia** are *Spätzle* (noodles) and *Maultaschen* (pasta pockets). *Pfanenkuchen* (pancake) are much heavier and bigger than the flap-jacks back home, and are served with toppings. *Kaiserschmarren* is chopped-up pancake with powdered sugar. **Hessians** do amazing things with potatoes, including smothering them in delectable *grüne Soße* (green sauce).

■ Beer

Germans have brewed up frothy malt beverages since the 8th century BC, and they've been consuming and exporting them in prodigious quantities ever since. Germans drink more than 140 liters of beer per person, per year—the most of any people on Earth. According to legend, the German king Gambrinus invented the modern beer recipe when he threw some hops into the fermenting malt. Brewers still honor him. During the Middle Ages, monastic orders refined the art of brewing, imbibing to stave off starvation during long fasts. It wasn't long before the monks' lucrative trade caught the eye of secular lords, who established of court breweries (*Hofbraüereien*). In 1516, Duke Wilhelm IV of Bavaria decreed that beer could contain only water, barley, and hops. This Purity Law (*Reinheitsgebot*) remains in force today, to the great chagrin of foreign brewers who are excluded from the market.

The variety of beers in Germany boggles the mind. Most beer is *Vollbier,* containing 4% alcohol. *Export* (5%) and *Bockbier* (6.25%) are also popular. *Doppelbock* (double bock) is an eye-popping concoction understandably reserved for special occasions. Ordering "*ein Helles*" will get you a standard light-colored beer, while "*Dunkles*" can look like anything from Coca-Cola to molasses. Among specialty beers, *Pils* is most popular in the north. Its characteristic clarity and bitter taste come from the addition of extra hops. From the south, especially Bavaria, comes *Weißbier*, a smooth, potent brew. Despite the name, *Weißbier* is not white, but a rich brown. (The name is a corruption of *Weizenbier*, meaning wheat beer.) The term *Weizenbier* now generally refers to a darker wheat beer, while *Hefe-Weizen* is wheat beer with a layer of yeast in the bottom. *Faßbier* simply means beer from a barrel. Sampling local brews numbers among the finest of Germany's pleasures. In Cologne, one drinks *Kölsch*, a light-colored, top-fermented beer; a Düsseldorf specialty is *Altbier*, a darker top-fermented beer. Older Berliners are partial to *Berliner Weiße*, a mixture of beer and lime-flavored syrup (or *Berliner Rote* with raspberry syrup). On hot summer days, lightweight drinkers prefer *Radler*, a Bavarian mix containing half beer and half lemon-lime soda. *Diesel* is a mix of *Bier* with cola.

The variety of places to drink beer is almost as staggering as the variety of brews. The traditional *Biergarten* consists of outdoor tables under chestnut trees. The broad leaves of the trees originally kept beer barrels cool in the days before refrigeration, until one enterprising brewer figured out that they could do the same thing for beer drinkers. The *Bierkeller* is an indoor version of the *Biergarten,* where local breweries dispense their product. During the summer, breweries sponsor carnivals with rides and beer under a tent. To order "*Ein bier,*" hold up your thumb, not your index finger. Raise your glass to a "*Prosit,*" and drink. (For more on Beer Halls, see Munich: Beer, below). Another option for beer drinking is the *Gaststätte*, a simple, local restaurant. It's considered bad form to order only drinks at a *Gaststätte* during mealtimes, but any other time, friends can linger at a table for hours over beers. Many *Gaststätten* have a *Stammtisch* (locals' table), marked by a flag, where interlopers should not sit. The same group of friends may meet at the *Stammtisch* every week for decades, doing nothing but drinking, playing cards, and shooting the breeze. *Kneipen* are small bars where young people gather.

■ Wine and Spirits

Though overshadowed by Germany's more famous export beverage, German wines win over connoisseurs and casual drinkers alike. Virtually all German wines are white, though they vary widely in sweetness and alcohol content. The cheapest wines are classified as *Tafelwein* (table wine), while *Qualitätswein* (quality wine) is slightly better and *Qualitätswein mit Prädikat* (quality wine with distinction) is better yet. *Prädikat* wines are further subdivided according to the ripeness of the grapes when harvested: *Kabinett, Spätlese, Auslese, Beerenauslese,* or *Trockenbeerenauslesen.* The grapes that produce *Trockenbeerenauslesen* are left on the vine until they have shriveled up into raisins and begun to rot—no kidding. The label *Qualitätswein bestimmter Anbaugebiete* designates quality wine from a particular cultivation region. The major concentrations of viniculture lie along the Rhine and Mosel valleys, along the Main River in Franconia, and in Baden. Rhine wines are bottled in brown glass, all others in green. Of the dozens of varieties in Germany, the most famous are *Riesling, Müller-Thurgau,* and *Traminer* (source of *Gewürztraminer*). But don't miss the equally delicious wines made from the *Lemberger, Spätburgunder,* and *Trollinger* varieties. In wine-producing towns, thirsty travelers can stop by a *Weinstube* to sample the local produce. In Hessen, the beverage of choice is *Äppelwoi* (apple wine), a hard cider similar in potency to beer. After a meal, many Germans aid their digestion by throwing back a shot of *Schnaps*, distilled from fruits. *Kirschwasser*, a cherry liqueur from the Black Forest, is the best known and probably the easiest to stomach, but adventurous sorts can experiment with *Zwetschgenwasser* (made from plums, also known as *Schliwowitz*), *Aprikosenlikör* (from apricots), and *Himbeergeist* (from raspberries). Each year, unsuspecting tourists are seduced into buying little green bottles of *Jägermeister,* an herb liqueur slightly more palatable then raw eggs flavored with soap.

■■■ CUSTOMS AND ETIQUETTE

The byzantine rules surrounding German etiquette make Emily Post look like a gas station attendant. Of course, it varies dramatically depending on who it is you're trying to impress, but it's generally true that Germans (and Swiss) are much more formal than Americans and Australians, and incredibly big on punctuality (especially to meals). Among the older generations, be careful not to use the informal "*du*" or a first name without being invited to do so. "*Du*" is appropriate when addressing fellow students and friends at a youth hostel, or when addressing children. Only waitresses in traditional restaurants are addressed as "*Fräulein*;" address other women as *Frau* (followed by a name). At the table, Germans eat with the fork in the left hand and the knife in the right. A hand not in use is kept on the table, not in your lap. An invitation to a German home is a major courtesy; you should bring along flowers for the hostess. As anywhere, you should write a thank-you note.

■■■ MEDIA

British dailies, such as the *Times, Financial Times, Observer,* and *Guardian* are widely available at train stations and kiosks in major cities. The *International Herald Tribune* and the European edition of the *Wall Street Journal* (approximately DM3) are the most common U.S. papers. *The Economist* and the international editions (better than the domestic editions) of *Time* and *Newsweek* are easy to come by. American and British armed forces maintain English-language radio stations. German-speakers can keep track of things with *Der Spiegel,* one of the world's leading weekly newsmagazines with a circulation of over one million, or *Die Zeit,* the witty, left-leaning weekly journal of opinion. *Stern,* the primary competitor of *Der Spiegel* (modeled after Time magazine), has lost respect since it published the bogus Hitler Diaries, but you'll appreciate its ample color photography if your German is weak. *Frankfurter Allgemeine* is a stodgy, conservative-leaning newspaper comparable to the *New York Times.* Munich's *Süddeutsche Zeitung* is Germany's best daily paper, though the racy, trashy, semi-rag *Bild Zeitung* is far more popular. For perspective on *Bild,* read Heinrich Böll's *Lost Honor of Katerina Blum,* an open attack on the tabloid and its distinctive style. Coming at you from Berlin are the properly liberal *Berliner Tagespiegel* and the iconoclastic, left leaning *Tageszeitung (TAZ).*

Western Germany

NORTH RHINE-WESTPHALIA (NORDRHEIN-WESTFALEN)

The Federal Republic's most populous *Land*, North Rhine-Westphalia (*Nordrhein-Westfalen*) has always gotten something of a bad rap. True enough, it's home to an unattractive and phenomenally large industrial sprawl in the Rhine-Ruhr area—Europe's densest concentration of highways, rail lines, and people. But this festival of cities also embraces the towering majesty of Cologne's cathedral, the cultural treasures of Bonn and Düsseldorf, and the tranquil forests of the Teutoburg and Eifel. Social democracy, trade unionism and revolutionary communism took deep roots throughout the region during the industrial boom of the late 19th century—the popular moniker "Red Ruhr" certainly didn't refer to the color of the water. As the industrial heart of the Nazi war machine, the region took an especially hard beating at the hands of Allied bombers, and several cities were rebuilt in a dull, modern style, though many smaller cities remain beautifully preserved. In order not to split up the economic nucleus of the country, the Allies forced a merger of the traditionally distinct regions of Westphalia, Lippe, and the Rhinelands into a single *Land,* which quickly became the most prosperous in the country. Despite structural downturns in heavy industry and persistently high unemployment, the great industrial wealth of the region continues to support a striking multitude of cultural offerings for the 17 million citizens of North Rhine-Westphalia's busy towns and achingly beautiful river valleys.

■■■ COLOGNE (Köln)

Cologne is no recent accident of a metropolis; it draws its life from a rich urban culture 2000 years old. Petrarch called it his "city of dreams" when the rest of Germany was still a wilderness. The city began as a Roman colony (Colonia, hence Köln) in AD 48, and made its money as a center for medieval intrigue and trade. Its economic power was matched by the brilliance of its scholarship. In 1389 the city opportunistically recruited professors fleeing from the plague in Heidelberg to teach at the first municipally founded German university; Thomas Aquinas studied and taught here.

Cologne is well appointed, with an admirable stock of museums, bustling commerce and traffic on the Rhine. Towering above them all is Cologne's one absolute—the spectacular Gothic *Dom*. Struck by at least 14 bombs during World War II, the cathedral miraculously remained standing in 1945, and it became the nation's most powerful icon in the years that followed. The rest of the city was not so lucky. On May 31, 1942, Cologne was the target of the Allies' first experimental 1000-bomber air-raid; 90% of the inner city was in ruins by war's end. The city pulled itself up by its bootstraps after the war and began a miraculous recovery. This is the modern city of Nobel Prize-winning novelist Heinrich Böll, who set *The Lost Honor of Katharina Blum* and the scandalous *Clown* here. Both concern the corruption of rumors, appropriate to Germany's media capital; Cologne is home base to a host of national media and TV networks, and Karl Marx got his revolutionary start as the 1848 editor of one of the local newspapers. Cologne's citizens conduct their own communications in the impenetrable "Kölsch" dialect, not to be confused with the delectable Kölsch beer that further loosens the tongue.

ORIENTATION AND PRACTICAL INFORMATION

Eight bridges spread Cologne over the Rhine, just north of Bonn. Germany's fourth-largest city, well-connected Cologne is 25 minutes from Düsseldorf by frequent trains, with direct lines to Frankfurt (2½hr.), Munich, Hamburg, and Berlin.

Tourist Office: Verkehrsamt, Unter Fettenhennen 19 (tel. 221 33 45, fax 221 33 20), across from the main entrance to the cathedral. Will provide you with a free city map (you must pay for most other brochures), book you a room (DM3-5 fee), and try to sell you a poster. Be kind to the extremely helpful, multilingual staff—they're overworked and underpaid. Like us. Be sure to pick up the *Monatsvorschau*, a booklet with essential information and a complete monthly schedule of events. Open Mon.-Sat. 8am-10:30pm, Sun. 9am-10:30pm; mid-Oct. to April Mon.-Sat. 8am-9pm, Sun. 9:30am-7pm.

Currency Exchange: There's an office at the **train station** (open daily 7am-9pm), but the service charges are lower at the post office.

American Express: Burgmauerstr. 14 (tel. 257 74 84), near the *Dom*. ATM. Client letter service only with AmEx card. Open Mon.-Fri. 9am-5:30pm, Sat. 9am-noon; cashier closed noon-2pm.

Post Office: Main office at An den Dominikanern, 50668 Köln, straight out from the train station and to the right of the *Dom*. However, the office in the station is open longer, Mon.-Fri. 7am-10pm, Sat. 11am-8pm, Sun. 10am-10pm.

Telephones: City code: 0221.

Flights: Flights depart **Köln-Bonn Flughafen** for 40 destinations non-stop, plus a Berlin shuttle 20 times per day and many other national and international cities. Call (02203) 40 40 01 or 40 40 02 for more information. Bus #170 leaves the *Hauptbahnhof* at 5:40am, 6am, and 6:30am, every 15min. 7am-8pm, and every ½hr. 8-11pm; it arrives at Köln-Deutz 5min. later, and then proceeds directly to the airport (15min.; DM3.60, children DM2.40).

Public Transportation: Any **VRS** (Verkehrsverbund Rhein-Seig) office will have a plan of the S- and U-Bahn lines throughout the Cologne-Bonn area, as well as a map of city bus and streetcar lines. Major convergence points include the *Hauptbahnhof*, Köln-Deutz, Appellhofplatz, and Barbarossaplatz. Tickets are priced by distance; the short-ride single cards (DM1.70), 4-ride cards (DM6), and day-cards (DM8) are available at automats and designated stations.

Ferries: Köln-Düsseldorfer (tel. 20 88 318 or 319) sails to 40 landings on the Rhine between Cologne and Mainz, including Königswinter (roundtrip DM37). Connections to Mosel River ferries. Departures Tues.-Sun. 9, 9:30 and 11am, Mon. 9:30 and 11am; April-June and Sept.-late Oct. Tues.-Sun. 9 and 9:30am, Mon. 9:30am. Mon. and Fri. seniors ½-price.

Gondola: Rheinseilbahn, Europe's only river-crossing **gondola lift,** spans the Rhine north of the city, between the zoo on the west bank and the Rheinpark on the east. Open April-Oct. 10:30am-dark. DM5, round-trip DM8, children ½-price.

Taxi: Funk-zentrale (tel. 28 82). Get funky.

Mitfahrzentrale: Citynetz Mitfahrzentrale, Saarstr. 22 (tel. 194 44). Open Mon.-Sat. 9am-7pm. Smaller **Mitfahrzentrale,** Maximinstr. 2 (tel. 12 20 21), near the *Hauptbahnhof*, also lists rides. Open Mon.-Fri. 8:30am-5pm, Sat. 8:30am-noon.

Car Rental: Avis, Hertz, interRent Europcar, and **Sixt-Budget** all have bureaus in the airport.

Hitchhiking: Let's Go does not recommend hitchhiking as a safe mode of transportation. Hitchers who seek to reach Aachen, and thence Holland or Belgium, take the train toward Aachen 3 stops to Groß Königsdorf, exit left from the station, take the first left, cross the bridge, and turn right onto the access road leading to the Autobahn rest stop.

English Agency: Amerika Haus, Aposteinkloster 13-15 (tel. 20 90 10, fax 24 45 43), by St. Aposteln church, is a valuable resource for cultural activities and potential job placement for Americans wishing to teach in Germany. Has a full English-language library open Tues.-Fri. 1-6pm. **The British Council,** around the corner at Hahnenstr. 6 (tel. 20 64 40), has much the same purpose with a British

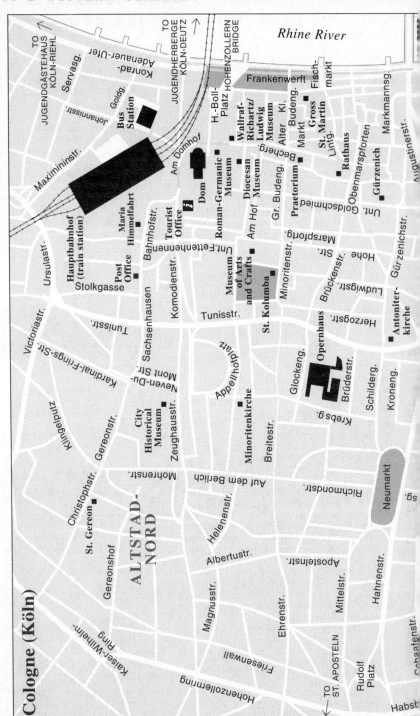

Cologne (Köln)

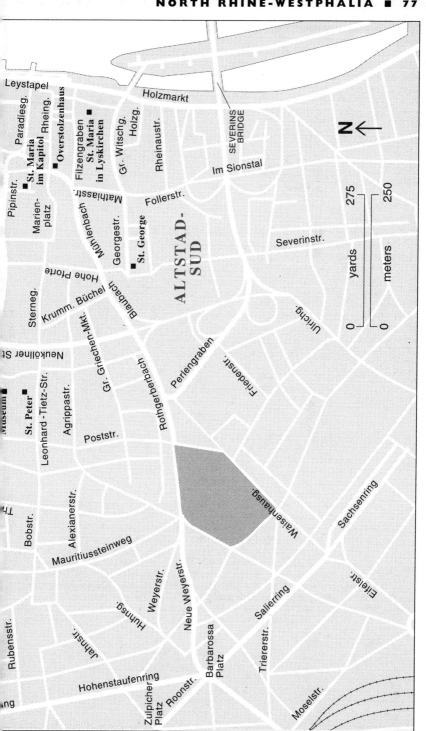

Leystapel

Paradiesg.

Pipinstr.

St. Maria
im Kapitol

Overstolzenhaus

Rheing.

St. Maria
in Lyskirchen

Filzengraben

Gr. Witschg.

Holzg.

Rheinaustr.

Holzmarkt

SEVERINS
BRIDGE

Im Sionstal

Marien-
platz

Mathiasstr.

Follerstr.

Mühlenbach

Georgestr.

St. George

ALTSTADT-
SUD

Severinstr.

N

275 yards

250 meters

Sterneg.

Hohe Pforte

Krumm. Büchel

Blaubach

Neukölner St

Gr. Griechen-Mkt.

Rothgerberbach

Perlengraben

Friedenstr.

Ulrichg.

Museum

St. Peter

Leonhard-Tietz-Str.

Agrippastr.

Poststr.

Th

Bobstr.

Alexianerstr.

Mauritiussteinweg

Walsenhausg

Sachsenring

Rubensstr.

Jahnstr.

Huhnsg.

Weyerstr.

Neue Weyerstr.

Barbarossa
Platz

Sallerring

Triererstr.

Eifelstr.

ng

Hohenstaufenring

Zulpicher
Platz

Roonstr.

Moselstr.

slant. Their library is open Mon. and Thurs.-Fri. 11am-5pm, Tues.-Wed. 11am-7pm.

Women's Agency: The municipal **Frauenamt,** at Markmansgasse 7, fields questions. Open Mon.-Fri. 8am-noon.

Student Agency: AsTA, Kölner Studentenwerk at Universitätsstr. 16, 2nd floor, will do their best to help with the commonplace difficulties of student life.

English Bookstore: Herder, Komodienstr. 11 (tel. 257 75 44), has a small selection of classic paperbacks, but boasts a disproportionately large display of P.D. James, Sara Paretsky, and Barbara Vine. Don't get your hopes up; no *Let's Go.* Open Mon.-Fri. 9:30am-6:30pm, Sat. 9:30am-2pm.

Laundry: Öko-Express, Neue Weyerstr. 1. Wash DM6, dry DM1 per 15min. Soap included. Open Mon.-Sat. 6am-11pm. Laundry also available at the Köln-Deutz hostel.

Pharmacy: Dom Apotheke, Komodienstr. 5, near the station. Their *Pharmacie-Internationale* gives advice in English. A list of after-hours pharmacies is posted outside.

Police: 110.

ACCOMMODATIONS AND CAMPING

Cologne does a brisk convention and tour business with its wealth of rooms; the trick is pinning one down. Hotels fill up (and often raise prices) in the spring and fall when trade winds blow conventioneers this way; summer is high season for Cologne's two hostels, which are both filled to the beams from June to September. Hotel-central is on the less interesting side of the Bahnhof, concentrated mostly on Brandenburgerstr. An alternative is a visit to the **Mitwohnzentrale,** An der Bottmuhle 16 (tel. 32 70 84), which hooks up visitors with apartments for longer stays. Looking for a last-minute room during Karneval is utterly futile. When all else fails, try schlepping down to the hostel in Bonn.

If you stay at a Köln hotel, be sure to pick up the **Köln Bonbon,** a packet of 12 vouchers for free goods that is only available through the hotel system. The vouchers enable the holder to receive a great print of the 1531 town panorama woodcut, discounts on various Rhine cruises, reduced admission to area attractions, and a three-day pass good for free entry into all the city's nine museums (DM15, Bonbon: with discount voucher for 2hr. **city bus tour** DM26).

Jugendherberge Köln-Deutz (HI), Siegesstr. 5a (tel. 81 47 11, fax 88 44 25), just over the Hohenzollern Bridge. S-Bahn 6, 11, or 12 (from the *Hauptbahnhof*): Köln-Deutz (1 stop), cross Ottoplatz and you're there (2min.). Cramped rooms, but a hard-to-beat location with numerous common rooms, a pink neon jukebox, free laundry, and not 1 but 2 pinball machines. The hostel's 374 beds fill up quickly; the best time to check in is 6-9am. Reception is more risky, but open noon-10pm. Curfew 12:30am. DM23, over 26 DM27. Sheets and breakfast included. Visa, AmEx, MC.

Jugendgästehaus Köln-Riehl (HI), An der Schanz 14 (tel. 76 70 81, fax 76 15 55), on the Rhine north of the zoo. S-Bahn 5 (from the *Hauptbahnhof*, Mon.-Fri. until 7pm), or U-Bahn 16 or 18 (direction "Ebertplatz/Mülheim"): Boltensternstr., or walk 40min. along the Rhine on Konrad-Adenauer-Uferstr., which becomes Niederländer-Ufer and finally An der Schanz. More luxurious but less convenient than Köln-Deutz, and also fairly crowded. Great crowd—probably because the anal-compulsive people arrive early and get into Köln-Deutz. Reception open 24hrs. No curfew. DM 28.50. Doubles available for married couples. Sheets and breakfast included. The **Köln-Treff Café** on the first floor sells beer, baguettes, and fries. Open daily 8pm-12:30am.

Hotel Hubertus Hof, Mühlenbach 30 (tel. 21 73 86), south of the center. U-Bahn: Heumart, or walk all the way down the Hohe-Str. shopping zone until it becomes Hohe Pforte, and turn left onto Mühlenbach. Wallpaper vines climb the walls, echoing the floral prints in the rooms. You won't be complaining that there's too much space, but the price is perfect. Reception open Mon.-Sat. 7am-10pm. Singles DM50. Doubles DM70-75. Breakfast included.

Hotel Rossner, Jakordenstr. 19 (tel. 12 27 03). Walk out the back of the *Haupt-bahnhof* (2min.); Jakordenstr. is the 4th left off of Johannisstr. A good value and more convenient. The marble entry hall is decked out with pictures of local power mongers. Classic noble German rooms, but the foliage-patterned wallpaper trend has to stop. Singles DM55, with shower DM75. Doubles DM80, with shower DM110. Triples also available. Breakfast included.

Hotel Im Kupferkessel, Probstgasse 6 (tel. 13 53 38, fax 12 51 21). Walk out of the train station, bear right, and follow that street as it changes from Dompropost-Ketzer-Str. to An den Dominikern to Unter Sachsenhausen to Gereonstr. and finally to Christophstr., then turn right on Probsteigasse. The newly renovated building somehow remains quaint inside. Reception open daily 7am-8pm, or call. Singles DM55, with shower, phone, and TV DM65. Doubles DM88, with all the toys DM 105. Visa, AmEx, MC.

das kleine Stapelhäuschen, Fischmarkt 1-3 (tel. 21 30 43). A fantastic mazelike conglomerate of 3 tiny houses in the shadow of the Groß St. Martin church, one block from the Rhine. The luxurious, history-filled quarters sit over an excellent restaurant (pricey meals DM29 and up; kitchen open 11:30am-11:30pm). If you enjoy having huge medieval oaken mill wheels suspended above your bed, ask for the *historisches Turmzimmer* (historical tower-room; no extra charge). Singles DM65-75, with shower DM100, with shower and toilet DM98. Doubles DM97-100, with shower DM158, with shower and toilet DM185-195. Breakfast buffet included.

Hotel Berg, Brandenburger Str. 6 (tel. 12 11 24). Bear left onto Johannisstr. from the back exit of the *Hauptbahnhof*, and take the 3rd left onto Brandenburger Str. On a small street with about 12 hotels. Double doors to ensure quiet rooms. Clock radios and telephones in most rooms. Singles DM60, with shower DM80. Doubles DM90, with shower DM120. Breakfast included. Visa, AmEx, MC.

Hotel Brandenburger Hof, Brandenburger Str. 2-4 (tel. 12 28 89). Rooms are newish and just fine, with a tiny outdoor Biergarten and a shaggy throw-rug in every room. Singles DM65, with shower and toilet DM75. Doubles DM85, with shower and toilet DM125. 3- and 4-bed rooms also available. Breakfast included.

Hotel Flintsch, Moselstr. 16-20 (tel. 23 21 42, fax 21 21 17). U-Bahn 12, 16, or 18: Barbarossa Platz, then head down Luxemburgerstr. and take a left onto Moselstr. A block from the Köln-Sud train station and thus a bit noisy, but also near all the student fun. The yellow bathroom-tile decor of the entry fades to pink linen and hunting prints. Singles with shower DM65. Doubles with shower DM90. Visa, AmEx, MC.

Camping:

Campingplatz Poll (tel. 83 19 66), southeast of the Altstadt at Weidenweg on the Rhine. U-Bahn 16 (from the station): Marienburg, and cross the Rodden-kirchener Bridge. The more convenient Cologne spot. Reception open 8-11am and 4-8pm. DM3-7.50 per tent, DM5.50 per person.

Campingplatz Berge, Uferstr. (tel. 39 24 21)U-Bahn 16: Marienburg, change to bus # 130: Uferstr. Farther downstream and harder to get to. DM5 per person, DM8 per lot.

FOOD

If Kölners aren't eating, it's probably because they're drinking. You shouldn't pass through Cologne without sampling the city's eponymous and extraordinarily smooth beer, Kölsch, served in relatively tiny glasses (0.2L). Local brews include Sion, Küppers, Früh, and the devout Dom. Inexpensive food—and just about anything else—is available along **Schildergasse** and **Hohe Straße,** the main pedestrian shopping thoroughfares by the cathedral. Stands between the station and the cathedral offer *Rievekochen* (dialect for "potato pancakes") with *Apfelmuß* late into the night. The basement of the Karstadt department store on Hohestr. offers groceries. Off **Zulpicherplatz,** supermarket **Plus** gives the deepest price cuts. The most interesting area for inexpensive food is on Weidengasse, in the Turkish district. Restaurants, *Imbiß* and specialty stores compose the street, though at night they edge on the red-light district. The **neuform Reformhaus Lesske** (tel. 81 22 80), at the Heumarkt Passage, and **Dahmen,** on Zülpicher Platz, sell health-food everything, from grains and jams to herbal tea to medicinal supplements (open Mon.-Fri. 9am-6:30pm and Sat. 9am-2pm). An open-air **Markt,** on Wilhelmsplatz in the northern Nippes neighborhood, offers farm-fresh items (open Mon.-Sat. 7-11:30am).

Universität Mensa, off Zülpicher Str. in the university complex, offers palatable meals. Pick up an English newspaper at the newsstand downstairs to digest daily events while you eat. The announcement board at any of the several stations will list where each menu choice is served. Student meals DM1.50-3.90, guests DM3.80-6.90. Lunch 11:30am-2pm. Dinner 5:30-7:30pm. Open all year.

Vanille, Zülpicherstr. 25, comes up with a different breakfast special every day from an eclectic international cookbook. Dinner (noodles with Gorgonzola sauce, DM8.50) precedes a nighttime drinking crowd. Open Mon.-Sat. 10am-1am, Sun. 11am-1am.

Café Waschsalon, Friesenstr. 80, is filled with washers that might actually be made operational, but for now, no spin cycle will spill your drink. Breakfast (DM 5.50 and up) is served until 1am, and you can sit outside. Open Sun.-Thurs. 10am-1am, Fri. and Sat. 10am-3am.

Rendevous, Zülpicherstr. Packed with students putting away pizzas and pastas for under DM10. Breakfast spreads served all day. Open Sun.-Thurs. 8am-1am, Fri.-Sat. 8am-3am.

Mexican Food House, Luxemburger-Str. 42 (tel. 21 96 93). If your Tex-Mex blood level is dropping desperately low, this tiny bistro may save you; however, the spicy good food can only be described as Kölsch-Mex: really good, but not all that South-of-the-Border.

SIGHTS

The Dom

As soon as you exit Cologne's *Bahnhof* you are faced with the smoke-colored beauty of the colossal *Dom* (cathedral). Visually overwhelming in intricacy and scale, the edifice took six centuries to build. For 500 years a giant wooden crane, now kept inside, was as much Cologne's trademark as the two massive towers are now. Giving the *Dom* stained-glass windows was a favorite royal charity from the Renaissance on (now the favorite charity is the *Dom* itself). The final result is an intensely moving and fragile play of colored light over the interior.

Inside stands the **Dombild triptych,** a gilded altarpiece from the 15th-century Cologne School of Painting; at the other rests the **Shrine of the Magi,** a reliquary of the Three Kings in blinding gold. The Three Kings, brought to Cologne in 1164, are the town's holy patrons; they float above the Cathedral in a magnificent 1531 wood-cut of the town by Anton Woensam, and their three crowns grace Cologne's official heraldic shield. Tapestries of Ruben's *Triumph of the Eucharist* line the central nave. While in the *Dom,* be sure to find the **Gero Crucifix** as well; it's the oldest intact sculpture of the Crucifixion in the world (976). (Cathedral open daily 7am-7pm. Tours Mon.-Fri. 10, 11am, 2:30, and 3:30pm, Sat. 10 and 11am, Sun. 2:30pm. Free organ concerts mid-June to Sept. Tues. 8pm.)

Five hundred and nine steps are all it takes to reach the top of the **Südturm** (south tower) and peer down at the river below. Catch your breath at the *Glockenstübe* (400 steps high), chamber for the tower's nine bells. Four of the *Glocken* date to the Middle Ages, but the upstart 19th-century bell known affectionately as **Der große Peter** (at 24 tons, the world's heaviest swinging bell) rings the loudest. Hailed as "Germany's bell on the Rhine," it bears an engraved call for national unity (tower open 9am-5:30pm; March-April and Oct. 9am-4:30pm; Nov.-Feb. 9am-3:30pm; admission DM2, students DM1). The **Domschtazkammer** in a corner of the cathedral holds the requisite clerical artworks; including thorn, cross, and nail bits as well as pieces of 18 saints. (Open Mon.-Sat. 9am-5pm, Sun 1-4pm; Nov.-March Mon.-Sat. 9am-4pm, Sun. 1-4pm. Admission DM3, under 18 DM1.50.) More ecclesiastical favors are in the **Diözesan Museum,** at Roncalliplatz 2, just outside the south portal (open Fri.-Wed. 10am-5pm; free).

The cathedral is colorfully illuminated daily from dark until midnight. The darkened monument draws more interesting hair colors and music types to the expansive **Domvorplatz** plaza. Time, pollution and acid rain have corroded much of the cathedral's original detail, though it would take much more to dull its impact. Gradually, each single piece is being reproduced and replaced, in new and treated stone. To help speed up this hellish project, you can play the *Dom* lottery at posts around the plaza and save a statue's fingernail (DM1 or DM2).

Across the Domvorplatz, the Alt-Köln building sounds its **Glockenspiel** daily at 10, 11:45am, 6, and 8pm.

Central City

In the shadow of the cathedral, the **Hohenzollern Brücke** crosses the Rhine. The majestic bridge empties out onto a promenade, guarded by equestrian statues of the imperial family. A monumental flight of stairs leads to the **Heinrich Böll Cultural Center** (see Museums, below), a piece of modern architecture which actually complements, rather than insults, the *Dom*. Farther on, the squares and crooked streets of the old **Fischmarkt** district open onto paths along the Rhine.

The **Rathaus** (Town Hall) was partially bombed to the ground, but it's been reconstructed in the original style (or styles). Its Gothic **tower** stands guard over the Baroque cherubs flying around a perfectly ornate Renaissance arcade, the 1570 *loggia*, the only section to survive the war. On the *Rathaus* façade, a **Glockenspiel** rings out at noon and 5pm daily (open Mon.-Fri. 7:30am-4:45pm; tours Mon., Wed., and Sat. 3pm). For Cologne Italian-style, the **Römisches Praetorium und Kanal,** Kleine Budengasse, in the basement of the *Rathaus,* is the excavated ruins of the former Roman military headquarters. Looking like the abandoned set from a gladiator movie, the council chamber leads to the 100m canal (open Tues.-Sun. 10am-5pm; admission DM3, students DM1.50). The square behind the *Rathaus* contains something else the city's scientists dug up: the **Mikwe,** a 12th-century Jewish ritual bath that tunnels 15m down to groundwater (the key is available inside the town hall Mon.-Sat. 8am-4pm).

Goethe, whose success with the opposite sex was legendary, noted "how grateful the women are for the fragrance of Eau de Cologne." This magic water, once prescribed as an imbibable panacea, made the town, or at least the town's oft-mimicked export, a household name. Make sure your tourist bottle says *"Echt kölnisch Wasser"* (real Cologne water) if you're after the authentic article, or look for the world-renowned "4711" label. The name stems from the Mühlens family house (where cologne has been produced since 1792), which was labeled **house #4711** with the Napoleonic system that gave everything in Cologne a number and took away street's names. The house is on Glockengasse; from Hohestr., turn right on Brückenstr., which becomes Glockengasse. As a special treat, the **Glockenspiel** on the house chimes on the hour daily from 9am to 8pm.

Churches

Samuel Taylor Coleridge once scorned, "In Köln, a town of monks and bones/ And pavements fanged with murderous stones/ And rags, and hags, and hideous wenches…." Monks, bones and the like fit in with Cologne's dozen churches, surrounding the inner city. Beautiful even in comparison to the *Dom,* they attest to both the religious glory and the trading frenzy of the Renaissance archbishopric.

The exterior of the 12th-century **Groß St. Martin,** once on an island surrounded by the then-Rhine-flooded pedestrian zone, is more striking despite extensive wartime damage. The interior of the four-spired riverside landmark is big and empty, lending the new renovations a strange, old flavor. Crypts downstairs house ancient Roman tombs. The courtyard outside holds the **Schmitz-Säule,** a column of Roman stones. In **St. Peter's** church, a tiny little construction just south of St. Cäcilien, there's the rare opportunity to see a masterwork in its original position; Rubens' **The Crucifixion of St. Peter** hangs, as it always has, above a side altar (church open Mon.-Sat. 11am-5pm, Sun. noon-5pm). **Basilika St. Gereon,** in the west part of the inner city, is capped by an extremely unusual decagon. Its main hall is breathtaking, with a tremendous canopied altar topped by an angel-supported crown (open Mon.-Sat. 9am-noon and 3-6pm, Sun. 3-6pm).

The entrance to **St. Maria im Kapitol** is on Kasinostr.; this church, defiantly built in 1030 on the grounds of a Roman temple, started the European cloverleaf architectural fad. The building was severely damaged in the war, and it shows. The floor mosaic and smatterings of wall frescoes are still visible, but the roof and outer wall are entirely reconstructed. Thankfully, the sole remaining wooden altar door from the Middle Ages survived the war; its masterfully carved 11th-century panels relate the life of Christ. St. Albertus Magnus's final resting place is in the crypts of **St. Andreas,** off of Komödienstr. (open Mon.-Fri. 8am-8pm, Sat.-Sun. 8:30am-7pm). **St. Maria in der Kupfergasse,** near the Stadtmuseum, features a blatantly Baroque wood-carved altarpiece in an otherwise unassuming church. Don't miss the "black" bejeweled Madonna in the small center chapel.

The **St. Ursula** church, north of the *Dom,* commemorates Ursula's desperate struggle for celibacy despite her betrothal, which ended with her and 11 virgins under her tutelage being mistaken for Roman legionnaires and burning at sea. The Latin record noted 11M, meaning 11 blasted martyrs, but was misread as 11 thousand virgins. The walls of the **Goldene Kammer** inside are lined with over 300 human skulls and innumerable reliquaries; it's more attractive then you would think. (Church open Mon.-Fri. 9:30am-noon and 12:30-4:30pm, Sat. 10am-5pm. Goldene Kammer open Mon. and Thurs. 11am-noon, Wed. and Fri. 3-4pm, Sat. 4-5pm. Admission to chamber DM1.50, students DM1, under 16 DM0.50.) In the courtyard of the bombed ruins of **Alt St. Alban** church, parents mourn the children of war in a statue by Käthe Kollwitz.

MUSEUMS

Museums in Cologne are healthily funded and hold impressive collections. The principal museums are free with the **Köln Bonbon** (see introduction to Accommodations, above). In any major city, the less generic, quirky museums have that intriguing fanaticism of specialization on their side; this is especially true here. Some of these are sprinkled around the student district, and many are free to all visitors.

Near the Cathedral

Heinrich-Böll-Platz, Bischofsgartenstr. 1, next to the *Dom.* 1 unusual building, designed to provide a maximum of natural light, houses 3 separate museums. Open Tues.-Thurs. 10am-8pm, Fri.-Sun. 10am-6pm. Comprehensive admission DM8, students DM4. Special exhibits extra. Free with the *Bonbon.*

Museum Ludwig (tel. 221 23 82) travels from Impressionism through Picasso, Dalí, Klee, and Roy Lichtenstein to art where the glue and paint is not quite dry. Tours Wed. 6:30pm, Sat. and Sun. 11am. Free.

Agfa Foto-Historama (tel. 221 24 11). Chemical art of the last 150 years, including the biggest Hugo Erfurt collection as well as old-timer cameras and facilities.

Wallraf-Richartz Museum (tel. 221 23 82) Shares space with the Ludwig, so it's only a few steps from the sublime to the ridiculous. Features those crackly-paint masterpieces of the 13th to 19th century, right up to Renoir, Manet, and all of that crowd.

Römische-Germanisches Museum, Roncalliplatz 4 (tel. 221 44 38), other side of the *Dom* from Heinrich-Böll-Platz. Artifacts dating as far back as AD 50. Imperial mementos include the **Dionysos-Mosaik** (a nearly complete, neatly risqué tile floor), the back-lit tomb of a Roman officer, and shard upon shard of pottery. Open Tues.-Sun. 10am-5pm. Tours Sun. 11:30am. Admission DM5, students DM2.50.

Elsewhere in Cologne

Kölnisches Stadtmusuem, Zeughausstr.1/3, (tel. 221 23 52). U-Bahn: Appellhofplatz/Zeughaus. Within the 16th-century red-and-white shuttered Armory, aerial photos and 3-D maps show the progress from Roman ruins to post-war rubble and back again. "The city's memory." Open Tues.-Sun. 10am-5pm. Tours Sat. 3pm and Sun. 11am. Admission DM5, students DM2.50, free with the *Bonbon.*

Schnütgen Musuem, Cäcilienstr. 29, in the St. Cecilia Church. U-Bahn or S-Bahn: Neumarkt. Ecclesiastical art from the Middle Ages to the Baroque, particularly tapestry, liturgy and priestly fashion industry displays, plus some 6th-century crosses. The church is only used for services twice a year during Christmas mass. Open Tues.-Sun. 10am-5pm. Tours Sun. 11am, Wed. 3pm. Admission DM5, students DM2.50; free 1st Thurs. of the month 5-8pm, or with the *Bonbon.*

Museum für Andgewandte Kunst (Museum of Applied Art), An der Rechtschule, near the Dom. A giant arts and crafts fair spanning 7 centuries with a fabulous 20th-century design display, but no tie-dye stand. Open Tues.-Sun. 10am-5pm. Tours Sat. 2:30pm, Sun. 11:30am. Admission DM5, students DM2.50. Free with the *Bonbon.*

Kölner Karnevalsorden Museum, Unter Käster 12 (tel. 25 36 00), near Heumarkt. Paraphernalia from years of Karneval crazes soberly document the drunken revelry. Open Mon.-Sat. 3-8pm, Sun. 11am-4pm. Admission DM5.

Käthe-Kollwitz-Musuem, Neumarkt 18-24 (tel. 227 23 63), in the Neumarkt-Passage. Displays the world's largest collection of sketches, sculptures and prints by the brilliant turn-of-the-century artist. Open Tues.-Wed. and Fri.-Sun. 10am-5pm, Thurs. 10am-8pm. Tours Sun. 11am. Free.

EL-DE-Haus, Am Appellhofplatz 23/25. A sobering monument to the victims of the secret police; in the basement of this formerly Gestapo-owned house, there are 10 cells with over 1200 wall inscriptions from political prisoners. Open Tues.-Sun. 10am-5pm.

Besteckmuseum Bodo Glaub (Eating Utensil Museum—we're not even kidding), Burgmauer 68, past the fork at the tourist office which cuts into Burgmauer and Komödienstr. 2000 years of confusing place settings. Open Tues.-Fri. 3-6pm, Sat. 11am-2pm.

Beatles Museum, Heinsbergstr. 13, off Zülpicherstr. Absolutely crammed with Fab Four memorabilia. They're talking about a renovation, but hey, you know, they don't want to change the price. Open Sept.-July Wed.-Sat. 10am-7pm. Admission DM3.

ENTERTAINMENT

Cologne becomes a living spectacle during the **Karneval,** a week-long pre-Lenten festival. Celebrated in the hedonistic spirit of the city's Roman past, Karneval is made up of fifty major and minor neighborhood processions in the weeks before Ash Wednesday. **Weiberfastnacht,** on the Thursday before Ash Wednesday (Feb. 10 in 1994), is the first major to-do, when the mayor mounts the platform at Alter Markt and abdicates leadership of the city to a trio of fools. For the rest of the day, the city's *Weiber* (an archaic and not at all politically correct term for women) are given the rule of the roost. In the afternoon, the first of the big parades begins at Severinstor. The weekend builds up to the out-of-control, dancing-in-the-streets parade on **Rosenmontag,** the last Monday before Lent (Feb. 14 in 1994). Everyone's in costume and everyone gets a couple dozen *Bützchen*—that's Kölnisch for a kiss on a stranger's cheek. Arrive early, get a map of the route, and don't pick a standing place anywhere near the station or cathedral—you'll be pulverized by the crowds. While most of the revelers nurse their hangovers on Shrove Tuesday, pubs and restaurants set fire to the straw scarecrows that have been hanging out of their windows—wander around and watch them burn. For more information on the festival and tickets to events, inquire at the **Festkomitee des Kölner Karnevals,** Antwerperstr. 55. Also pick up the *Köln, Karneval* booklet at the tourist office, crammed with helpful hints to enjoy the celebration.

The **Cinemanthek** entrance is on the ground floor of the three-museum building in Heinrich-Böll-Platz; the Cinemanthek shows current movies almost daily, with most films in the original English. Pick up a schedule at the information kiosk inside for movie times. "V.O." denotes an original version with German subtitles (call 211 36 for more movie information). If that's not enough, the 200-seat **Philharmonic Hall** is located in the basement of the same building; check the tourist office for concert information. The brand new 3000 seat **Cinedom** with 13 different screens is part of **Media Park**, a converted train station which opened in 1992.

From April to October, catch the **flea market** and **craft market** every third Saturday of the month in the *Altstadt*.

NIGHTLIFE

Cologne does everything, including nightlife, on a large scale, but the closer you venture to the Rhine and the *Dom,* the more that scale directly applies to your wallet—unless you choose to take part in a popular beer-on-the-Rhine-bank picnic with the lit *Dom* as majestic backdrop. The nightly jazz (from 8:30) at **Papa Joe's Jazzlokal,** Buttermarkt 37 (tel. 21 79 50), near Fischmarkt and the Rhine, is as good as jazz gets in these parts, but with a somewhat upscale crowd. Check out the *Jazzfrühschoppen*—morning drinking with a Dixieland band—every Saturday at 11am (open daily 7:30pm-3am; no cover). **Papa Joe's Biersalon,** Alter Markt 52 (tel. 21 67 59), is the sister ship to the Jazzlokal, but this incarnantion is more a staightahead piano-playing saloon (open daily 11am-1am).

Students congregate in the **Quartier Lateng,** a.k.a. the *Bermuda Dreieck* (triangle), the area bounded by Zülpicherstr., Zülpicher Platz, Roonstr. and Luxemburgstr. The center of gay nightlife runs up Matthiasstr. to Möhlenbach, Hohe Pforte, Marienplatz, and up to Heumarkt in the area by the Deutzer Brücke. Radiating westward from Friesenplatz, the **Belgisches Viertel** is spotted with slightly more sophisticated and expensive bars and cafés, which are consequently slightly more beautiful.

The tradition of getting plastered is most respected by the various *Brauhäuser*, where the original Kölsch is brewed and served in house. Here the Köbes will bring one beer after the other until you fall under the table, or lay your coaster across your glass. "*Ich bin nicht zum spaß hier*" ("I'm not here to fool around") informs the Köbes of your serious intentions, just watch out that the lines on your coaster correspond to the number of beers you actually drank—they have been caught counting on the fact that you won't be able to count.

Museum, Zylpicherplatz 9 (tel. 23 20 98). No temple of science is complete without a 2-story dinosaur looking out over blood alcohol level experiments. Popular Köln University field trip, naturally. Open Sun.-Tues. 4pm-1am, Wed.-Thurs. 4pm-2am, Fri.-Sat. 4pm-3am.

Päffgen Brauhaus, Friesenstr. 64-66 (tel. 13 54 61). Legendary Kölsch is brewed on the premises and consumed in big halls or the Biergarten (0.2L shot DM2). Follow Brauhaus rules as enumerated above. Open 10am-midnight. Hearty, inexpensive meals served 11am-10:30pm. **Päffgen in der Altstadt,** Heumarkt 62 (tel. 257 77 65) is the same thing. Less authentic, but also less crowded during main drinking hours. Open Tues.-Sun. noon-1am.

Filmdose, Zülpicherstr. 39 (tel. 23 96 43). Café-bar with a creative performance space. The sophisticated, liberal crowd can be enjoyed with no cover after the theatricals are over. Performances Tues.-Thurs. and Sun. 8pm, Fri.-Sat. 7:30pm. *Kneipe* open Tues.-Thurs. and Sun. to 1am, Fri.-Sat. to 3am.

Gloria, Apostelnstr. 11 (tel. 25 44 33). Crowded gay and lesbian café is foreground to a popular disco (DM7) housed in a converted porno theater. Café open Sun.-Thurs. 9am-1am, Fri.-Sat. 9am-3am. Disco open nightly, every other Sun. men only; every other Thurs. women only.

Luxor, Luxemburgstr. 40 (tel. 21 95 03). Bug out to 70s rock with a little bit of funk. Gotta have that funk. Open daily 8pm-3am.

42 D.P. ("Don't Panic"), Hohenstaufenring 25 (tel. 24 79 71). Mainstream music menu: Tues. techno, Wed. soul/funk, Thurs. house, Fri. reggae/hiphop (however those fit together), Sat. mix. Don't Panik if the schedule changes. Open Tues.-Sat. 11pm-4:30am. Cover Tues.-Thurs. DM6, includes a DM5 drink; Fri.-Sat. DM12, includes two DM5 drinks.

Moulin Rouge, Maastrichterstr. 6-8. (tel. 25 20 61). Red velvet ex-brothel draws in the sexy and the freaky for roaring good times; gets going around 1am. Belly dancing or poetry performances (3 per week) can cost DM15-20, but Fri.and Sat. cost DM5 whether it's just the café or a transvestite diva singing TV's greatest theme songs, and there's no cover most weeknights. Open daily 11pm-4:30am. Call for current schedule.

Hallmackenreuther, Hallmackenreuther 9 (tel. 52 41 41). Thoroughly 50s *Kneipe*, where if you're not feeling too inhibited, you can get a refill for your PEZ dispenser from the vending machine. For camp fanatics. Open daily 11pm-1am.

■ Near Cologne

As Cologne gained world-class status, the city sprouted suburbs, some of which claim outstanding attractions of their own. The **Rheinseilbahn** (gondola, see above) has a terminus in Köln-Riehl's **zoo** (open daily 9am-5pm), **aquarium** (open daily 9:30am-6pm), and **botanical garden** (open daily 8am-dusk) complex. Köln-Bayenthal, south of the city center, hosts the **Historische Braustätte der Küppers-Kölsch-Brauerei,** Alteburgerstr. 157, the brewery where *Küppers* is still made as it has been for a century (open Sat. 11am-4pm).

Cities on the Rhine somehow demand Fairy-Tale Castles (FTCs). **Zons,** misty and fortified, is 25km north of Cologne on the banks of the Rhine, and it has a fine FTC. Reach it by the Köln-Düsseldorfer ferry line (see Cologne Practical Information) or by taking the *Bundesbahn* to the parent town of **Dormagen,** then a short ride on hourly bus #875 to the castle at Zons. Walk between the ramparts of the castle complex and under the two towers. The ruins, especially those of the **Schloß Friedestrom** section, are hopelessly romantic. Local tall tales are dragged out in the museum at the **Herrenhaus,** at the eastern end of the complex, complemented by a suitably fabulous *fin-de-siècle* art-object collection (open Tues.-Fri. 2-7pm, Sat.-Sun. 10am-12:30pm and 2-6pm; free). Plays are staged at the **Freilichtbühne Zons** within the fortress walls. Call (02133) 422 74 for open-air show information; tickets cost DM7, under 14 DM5. Zons started life as a river customs checkpoint, a sort of medieval passport control center. Latter-day civil servants at the **tourist office,** behind the Juddeturm tower in the central square (tel. (02106) 423 88), help book rooms. Should you arrive at Zons on a Tuesday, the **market** that rages from 8am to noon. Get two castles for the price of…well, two, with a ferry across the Rhine from Zons to Düsseldorf's **Schloß Benrath** and back. Call **Personenschiffahrt Zons** (tel. (02133) 421 49) for more information. (Departures Mon-Sat. every hour, Sun. more frequently. DM3, under 12 DM2.50; round-trip DM5, under 12 DM4.)

■■■ AACHEN

Charlemagne tramped across 8th-century Europe, but fell for Aachen and made it the capital of the rising Frankish Empire. For the thousands of students at Aachen's universities, it is a less permanent but equally appealing home. Long ago the capital of the kingdom of Germania, it has carried much of its medieval internationalism into the present.

PRACTICAL INFORMATION

At the crossroads between Germany, Belgium, and the Netherlands, Aachen is also a departure point for trains to France (Aachen-Paris Twen-Tours fare DM56) and England (Aachen-London Twen-Tours fare DM110). Cologne is less than an hour away by train. Lots of people make the 15-minute bike ride to Holland to buy coffee.

Tourist Office: Aachen's central tourist office, **Atrium Elisenbrunnen,** on Friedrich-Wilhelm Platz (tel. 180 29 60, fax 180 29 31), dispenses literature and room advice; they tack a DM3 charge onto any hotel reservations they make. The **branch office,** Bahnhofplatz 4 (tel. 180 29 65), opposite the train station, performs the same functions for the same fees. Both open Mon.-Fri. 9am-6:30pm, Sat. 9am-1pm. Check either tourist office for city tours, like the DM2 guided stroll through the *Rathaus.*

Currency Exchange: At the station. Open Mon.-Fri. 8:30am-12:30pm and 1:30-4:30pm, Sat. 9am-1:30pm. Also at any bank, or post office.

Post Office: The *Hauptpostamt,* Kapuzinergraße, 52068 Aachen, is to the left of the station, down Franzstr., and then right on Kapuzinergraße.

Telephones: City Code: 0241.

Public Transportation: Many hotels offer DM7 tickets good for 2 days unlimited travel; if your lodging doesn't stock this special, try the *Tagesnetzkarte* (day ticket) for 5 people traveling anywhere in Aachen (DM6). The day-ticket becomes a DM5 "Happy-Day-Ticket" on Saturday, when Aachen's auto-free *Fußgängerzone* (pedestrian zone) magically swells to absorb all of the area inside the *Alleenring* composed of Ludwigsallee, Monheimsallee, Heinrichsallee, Lagerhausstr., Boxgraben, and Junkerstr.

Mitfahrzentrale: Röermonderstr. 4 (tel. 15 20 11). Matches riders and drivers. Open Mon.-Thurs. 10am-7pm, Fri. 9am-7pm, Sat. 10am-4pm.

Car Rental: Flach has an office at Bahnhofplatz 4 (tel. 240 25), adjacent to the tourist office.

Bike Rental: Hobbit Fahrradverleih, Beeckstr. 1 (tel. 434 75). From the station head up Bahnhofstr., turn right at Gottfriedstr., then head onto Beeckstr. Open Mon.-Wed. and Fri. 10am-1pm and 3-6:30pm, Sat. 10am-1pm.

Bookstore: Mayersche Buchhandlung (tel. 477 70), at Ursulinerstr. and Buchkremerstr. A 3-building colossus with a very hefty selection of English paperbacks, including Cliff Notes and children's books. Open Mon.-Wed. and Fri. 9:30am-6:30pm, Thurs. 9:30am-8:30pm, Sat. 9:30am-2pm.

Laundromat: Miele Wäscherei, Sandkaulstr. 39. The staff will wash your clothes or point you to machines in the back. Self-service wash and dry DM11; soap included. Open Mon.-Fri. 8am-6:30pm, Sat. 9am-1pm.

Rape Crisis Hotline: tel. 344 11.

ACCOMMODATIONS AND CAMPING

Aachen has too much history for a town of its size, and the loads of visitors push the lodging prices up; it helps to call ahead. The **Mitwohnzentrale,** Süsterfeldstr. 24 (tel. 87 53 46), will set you up with lodging for longer stays. Take bus #7 (direction "Siedlung Schönau") or #33 (direction "Vaals"): Westbahnhof. (Open Mon.-Tues. and Fri. 4-7pm, Wed. 10am-1pm and 4-7pm, Thurs. 10am-1pm and 6-8pm, Sat. 10am-1pm.)

Jugendherberge (HI), Maria-Theresia-Allee 260 (tel. 711 01) From the station, walk left on Lagerhausstr. until it intersects Karmeliterstr. and Mozartstr. at the Finanzamt; from there, bus #2 (direction "Preusswald"): Ronheide or bus #12 (direction "Diepenbendem"): Colynshof. Walk uphill to the stone courtyard of the old whitewashed brick building, on the fringes of a forest south of the city. Inside, charcoal drawings adorn the walls outside the standard rooms, giving a preview or recap of area sights. Reception open until 10pm. Curfew 11:30pm. DM17.30, over 26 DM20.80. Breakfast included.

Hotel Weiss, Adalbertsteinweg 67 (tel. 50 50 07). Bus #3 or 13: Kaiserplatz and turn onto Adalbertsteinweg, or bus #56, 68, or 166: Scheibenstr.; on foot, walk over Bahnhofplatz, turn right on Römerstr. and left on Wilhelmstr., and bear right at Kaiserplatz onto Adalbertsteinweg. A thoroughly average establishment in a well-traveled part of town; you may have to sacrifice silence for some of the lowest prices in Aachen. Showers on the hall. Singles DM58. Doubles DM88.

Hotel Cortis, Krefelder-Str. 52 (tel. 15 60 11), is just as loud as Rütten, its neighbor, but somehow a bit more cozy. Reception open Mon. and Wed.-Sun. 8am-midnight. Singles DM57. Doubles DM89, with shower and toilet DM102. Breakfast included.

Hotel Rösener, Theaterstr. 62 (tel. 40 72 15). Very spartan, with bare walls and the city's traffic outside, but extraordinarily near to the train station and the *Altstadt.* Take Bahnhofstr. straight and turn left on Theaterstr. Walk up the stairs to reception, but don't pull the chain in the stairwell for service; it's attached to a fire alarm. Singles DM50. Doubles DM80.

Hotel Marx, Hubertusstr. 33-35 (tel. 375 41; fax 267 05). Surprisingly quiet considering the distance from the station; simply walk left on Lagerhausstr., which becomes Boxgraben, turn right on Stephanstr., and left on Hubertusstr. Singles DM60, with shower and toilet DM85. Doubles DM80-100, with shower and toilet DM130-160. Breakfast included.

Camping: Campingplatz Aachen, Paßstr. 79 (tel. 15 85 02). Centrally located behind the city garden near the Ludwig Forum and the Sports Arena. Follow the directions for Hotel Rütten, above, but get off of bus #51 at Ungarplatz instead. Reception open 7am-1pm and 3-10pm. DM4 per person, DM4 per tent, DM3.50 per car. Open May-Sept.

FOOD

From the edge of the pedestrian zone to medieval Pont Tor, **Pontstraße** is lined with restaurants and student pubs, but beware—this region is also the prowling ground of the *Bahkauv.* This fearsome mythical blend of dog, puma, and dragon, which inexplicably derives its name from *"Bachkalb"* (stream calf), pounces on the necks of drunken revelers, thereby inducing the hangovers that Aachen students know all too well. The *Bahkauv*'s commemorative fountain is over on Buchkremerstr., one of many water-augmented sculptures near the open-air cafés of the Markt. Most bakeries sell the city's special *Aachner Printen,* nut-studded ginger cookies.

Katakomben Studentenzentrum, Pontstr. 74-76, encloses **Café Chico Mendes,** a co-op café of the Catholic College. The inexpensive food is appropriately wholesome: the smaller daily dinners *(Tagesgericht)* run DM5.50, while the more generous portions are only DM8.50. Occasional live music brightens the somewhat slow atmosphere. Open Mon.-Fri. 4pm-1am, Sat. 6pm-1am.

zur golden Kette, Markt 1-3, with a full vegetarian menu and plenty o' pancakes, from blueberry to beef stroganoff (DM4.90-15.90). Sip a soup or snack on a salad in the *Biergarten*/terrace in the back. Open Mon.-Fri. 11am-1am, Sat.-Sun. 11am-3am.

Van Den Daele, Büchel 18 (tel. 357 24), just off the *Markt.* Could be your grandmother's old house except that every room is the dining room, passionately decorated. *Kaffee-und-Kuchen* heaven. Open Mon.-Fri. 10am-6:30pm, Sat. 10am-6pm, Sun. 2-6pm.

SIGHTS

In 765, the Frankish King Pepin took a dip in the hot springs north of the present city center. When his son, Charlemagne (known locally as *Karl der Große*), assumed power, the family's former vacation spot became the capital of the rapidly expanding empire. The emperor's presence still dominates the city. His unique **Dom** in the center of the city circle is one of the world's best-known cathedrals. The 8th-century octagonal, neo-Byzantine dome at its center, atop three tiers of marble arches separating gilded roof from mosaic floor, joins Western practice with the forms of the Eastern Orthodox church. Inside, his throne is a simple chair of marble slabs, perched high above the main apse. Stained glass panels ring the 15th-century Gothic choir; beneath the chancel lie the bones of the big guy himself. Their place is marked by the gold-and-gem *Karlschreine* with a blinking doll-sized effigy. (Cathedral open daily 7am-7pm; the gateway to throne and shrine is only open daily 1-2pm and for tours 5-6pm.)

Old Charlie cuts more of a figure in the **Schatzkammer,** around the corner to the right from the *Dom* exit, tucked into the Klostergasse. The most famous likeness of the emperor, a solid gold bust *(der Karlsbüste)*, shines here in this exceptionally rich treasury. He's actually kind of good-looking. Among the other golden bits of Karl, you'll find Christ's belt and scourge rope and the Imperial Crown Jewels. Groupies shouldn't miss Charlemagne's wall-size "Missionary Man" tour map. (Open Mon. 10am-2pm, Tues.-Sat. 10am-6pm, Sun. 10:30am-5pm.; late-Oct. to early-April Mon. 10am-2pm, Tues.-Sat. 10am-5pm, Sun. 10:30am-5pm. Last entrance 30min. before closing. Admission DM3, students DM2.) With swarms of tourists squeezing through the single *Dom* entrance, it may be easier to join one of the **tours** leaving from the *Schatzkammer*, in order to push your way in with a large, "official" mass. Don't let the guide shepherd you in without relating the legend of the immense bronze doors in front; supposedly the devil, chased out when the Cathedral was completed, slammed the doors in fury—catching his thumb in the process. Keep your eyes open; the bronzed "thumb" and rage-induced crack in the door still exist. (Tours Mon. 11am and noon, Tues.-Fri. 11am, noon, 2:30, and 3:30pm, Sat. 2:30 and 3:30pm, Sun. 12:30, 2, 3, and 4pm. DM2.)

The 14th-century stone **Rathaus,** built on the ruins of Charlemagne's palace, looms over the wide *Marktplatz* beside the cathedral. Seventeenth-century citizens who couldn't stop decorating added Baroque flourishes to the façade. On the northern face stand 50 statues of former German sovereigns, 31 of whom were crowned in Aachen (open Mon.-Fri. 8am-1pm and 2-5pm, Sat.-Sun. 10am-1pm and 2-5pm). A copy of the famed Charlemagne statue, in the fountain on the square, draws a picnicking multicolored-hair crowd; the genuine statue is inside the *Rathaus,* along with a copy of the Imperial Crown Jewels. East of the **Katschhof** between the *Dom* and *Rathaus,* Tuesday and Thursday markets add to the raucous atmosphere.

All you horse-fans out there—Aachen annually hosts the **World Equestrian Festival** from the end of June to the beginning of July. If you want more information on specific events and scheduling, check at the tourist office.

MUSEUMS

Suermondt-Ludwig Museum, Komphhausbadstr. 19 (tel. 432 44 20). Surveys the pre-18th-century artistic landscape. Open Tues.-Sat. 10am-5pm, Sun. 10am-1pm. Admission DM2, students DM1.

Ludwig Forum für Internationale Künst, Jülicherstr. 97-109 (tel. 180 70). More daring newborn cousin of the Suermondt-Ludwig (above), the "Forum" scorns the title "museum"; a converted Bauhaus umbrella factory provides the setting for all the modern musts, from stodgy Andy Warhol to ultra-hip Barbara Kruger. The Forum opened in 1991 and the timing couldn't have been better—there was enough space to invest in a stunning, hot-off-the-press Eastern European collection. Open Tues.-Wed. and Fri.-Sun. 11am-7pm, Thurs. 11am-10pm. Admission DM6, students DM3. Free tours Thurs. 8pm and Sun. 11:30am.

Couven Museum (tel. 432 44 21), on Hühnermarkt near the Rathaus. Exhibits cover anything and everything about domestic culture since the death of Karl der Große. Open Tues.-Fri. and Sun. 10am-5pm, Sat. 10am-1pm. Admission DM2, students DM0.50.

Internationales Zeitungsmuseum (International Newspaper Museum; tel. 432 45 08), just up from the *Markt* at Pontstr. 13. Newsworthy: houses over 120,000 different newspapers from around the world, including chatty Enlightenment broadsheets, 1930s rags, and some distinctly non-Western newsprints. Open Tues.-Fri. 9:30am-1pm and 2:30-5pm, Sat. 9:30am-1pm. Last entry ½hr. before closing. Free.

■■■ EIFEL MASSIF

The wooded hills of the Eifel Massif rise just north of the Mosel Valley and stretch as far as Aachen to the north and well into Belgium and Luxembourg to the west. On the Belgian side of the border, the Eifel becomes the Ardennes, historically memorable as the site of Hitler's last offensive, the Battle of the Bulge. The German half of the forest functions as something of a refuge for vacationing Germans looking to avoid the mass tourism that has tainted most of Germany's better-known resort locales. As such, Eifel Massif is more peaceful and relaxed than regions like the Black Forest or the Harz. On the other hand, there's not as much to see or do. Transportation to the area is also sketchy; nearly all of the local rail lines are no longer in use, and the existing bus lines are tryingly slow. The most heavily traveled—and most easily accessible—part of the Eifel is the **Ahrtal** (Ahr Valley), south of Bonn, which is at its most scenic around the tiny town of **Altenahr.** The **Hohe Eifel** (High Eifel) in the center of the Massif is notable for the crater lakes and odd-looking rock formations that now-dormant volcanoes produced as recently as 10,000 years ago. The **Nordeifel** (North Eifel) is home to the Seven Lakes—all of them artificial but nonetheless popular venues for fishing and water sports. The Eifel is famous for its *Schinken* (ham), a specialty from the Roman occupation, older than its lakes.

MONSCHAU

The sleepy village of **Monschau**—relatively metropolitan by Eifel standards—lies in a narrow, secluded valley cut through by the swift-flowing Ruhr about 30km south of Aachen. The town itself is a visual compendium of gray slate roofs, gray cobblestone streets, gray brickwork, and a prodigious amount of gray-toned paint; somehow, it is both monochromatic and attractive. Head up to the **Burg,** a well-preserved set of castle ruins on the hill above town. A steep set of stairs leads directly to the Burg from the middle of town. Nearby, a rare break in the color scheme is provided by the **Rotes Haus** (Red House), Laufenstr. 10. Built by a local cloth merchant in 1760 to house his factory and his family, the building now contains a museum of period pieces (tours Tues.-Sun. 10, 11am, 2, 3, and 4pm; admission DM3, students DM1.50). There's also a **Glassworks Museum** *(Glashutte),* Burgau 15. (Open Tues.-Sun. 10am-6pm. Glass-blowing demonstrations every hour on the ½hr. 10:30am-4:30pm. Admission DM2.50, students DM1.50.) On the opposite end of town is an authentic 19th-century **Mustard Mill,** Laufenstr. 118, because, as everyone knows, Monschau is famous for its mustard (open for demonstrations March-Oct. Wed. 11am and 2pm; admission DM2.50, students DM1.50).

Hourly bus service connects Monschau to Aachen (bus #166; departs from *Bushof,* the Aachen central bus terminal; DM7.90). The **tourist office,** Stadtstr. 1 (tel. (02472) 33 00) is just across the street from the stairs that lead to the *Burg* (open Mon.-Fri. 9am-noon and 1-4pm, Sat. 11am-3pm, Sun. 11am-2pm; in winter, Mon.-Fri. 9am-noon and 1-4pm). The **Jugendherberge (HI),** Auf dem Schloß 4 (tel. (02472) 23 14), is inside the *Burg* ruins. The rooms are slightly cramped, but some offer excellent views, provided you can fit your head into the porthole-sized windows. (Members only. Curfew 10pm. DM17.30, over 25 DM20.80.) There's a larger, more modern **Jugendherberge (HI),** Hargardsgasse 5 (tel. (02472) 21 80, fax 45 27), just outside of town; a bus runs direct from the station. (Curfew 10pm. DM18.30, over 25 DM22.30.) **Alt Montjoie,** Stadtstr. 18 (tel. (02472) 32 89), has pleasant rooms and serves up a mean lunch and dinner in its downstairs restaurant (rooms DM33 per person, with shower DM35). **Camp at Perlenau** (tel. (02472) 636), 1.5km from town. (Reception open 8:30am-11pm. DM5 per person, DM3 per car, DM4.50 per tent. Open Easter-Oct.)

ALTENAHR

In addition to its gorgeous location on the **Ahr,** with hiking options winding through hills and golden flowers, Altenahr has **Burg Are.** Slowly crumbling into its hilltop perch, the castle still raises the urge to search for long-lost treasure. The *Sommerrodelbahn,* 3km out of town toward Bonn, is a 500m-long slide that hurls you through the hills. There is no bus connection, but it makes for a good hike (slide DM2.50, DM1.90 per person if several ride together).

The **tourist office** (tel. (02643) 84 48) is located in the train station. The **Jugendherberge Altenahr,** Langfigtal 8 (tel. (02643) 18 80), was gently placed into a nature reserve. A 30-minute walk from the station; follow the signs. (Reception open 5-6pm, and briefly at 9:45pm, with possible exceptions if you call first. Curfew 10pm. DM16.50, over 26 DM20.50.) On the bank of the Ahr, one lone **campground** (tel. (02643) 85 03) offers its bosom to your tired body. Turn right in front of the station and walk five minutes; it's on the other side of the tracks. (Reception 8am-10pm. Adults DM4.50, children DM1.50. Tiny tent DM2.50, regular tent DM6. Open April-Oct.)

■■■ DÜSSELDORF

As Germany's modish fashion and advertising center, multinational corporate base, and capital of the densely populated province of North Rhine-Westphalia, Düsseldorf runneth over with German patricians and wannabe-aristocrats. Set on the majestic Rhine, Germany's *"Hautstadt"* (a pun on *Hauptstadt* and *haute couture*) is a stately, rather than gritty, modern metropolis. Residents have a maxim that Düsseldorf is not on the Rhine, but the **Königsallee** (the central promenade, a.k.a. "the Kö"), a kilometer-long fashion runway that runs down either side of the old town moat. At night, the scene shifts back to the historic *Altstadt*, which overflows with more than 500 pubs. Düsseldorf's glassy-eyed materialism has been the source of both relish and anger among young Germans, but established citizens are unequivocally proud of the city's beauty. The adage, "if you look good, you'll feel good," gets Düsseldorf through the night.

PRACTICAL INFORMATION

Tourist Office: Main office, Konrad-Adenauer Platz (tel. 35 05 05). Walk up and to the right from the station and look for the towering Immermanhof building. Their free monthly *Düsseldorf Monatsprogram* is just one of many extremely helpful brochures packed with information. Open for ticket sales (fee 10%) and general services Mon.-Fri. 8:30am-6pm, Sat. 9am-12:30pm; for hotel reservations (DM5) Mon.-Sat. 8am-10pm, Sun. 4-10pm. The **branch office,** Heinrich Heine Allee 24 (tel. 899 23 46) specializes in cultural listings. Open Mon.-Fri. 9am-5pm; Oct.-March Mon.-Thurs. 9am-5pm, Fri. 9am-1pm.

Consulates: Canada, Immermannstr. 40 (tel. 02 28 96 80). Open Mon.-Fri. 1-3pm. **United Kingdom,** Yorckstr. 19 (tel. 944 80).

Currency Exchange: Deutsche Verkehrs Credit Bank in the *Hauptbahnhof.* Open daily 7:30am-8pm; or at the airport, open daily 6am-10pm. Better rates with no service charge are available at AmEx (see below).

American Express: Heinrich Heine Allee 14 (tel. 802 22). Mail held (DM3 if you're not a cardholder). All financial services. Open Mon.-Fri. 9am-5:30pm, Sat. 9am-noon.

Post Office: Hauptpostamt, Konrad-Adenauer-Platz, 40210 Düsseldorf, to the right of the tourist office. Open Mon.-Fri. 8am-6pm, Sat. 10am-2pm, Sun. noon-1pm, but open for reduced after-hours service Mon.-Fri. 6-8pm, Sat.-Sun. noon-8pm. **Branch office** in the *Hauptbahnhof.*

Telephones: At main post office, and at the *Hauptbahnhof.* **City code:** 0211.

Airport: Frequent S-Bahns and a Lufthansa shuttle travel from the station to the international **Flughafen Düsseldorf.** Call for flight information (tel. 421 22 23) 6am-midnight.

Trains: All trains arrive at **Düsseldorf Hauptbahnhof.** Information: tel. 194 19.

Public Transportation: The *Rheinbahn* includes subways, streetcars, buses, and the S-Bahn. **Single tickets** cost DM1.60-10 depending on distance traveled. The DM7.70 *Tagesticket* (higher prices for longer distances) is the best value around—groups of up to 5 people can travel all day on any line. Tickets sold mostly by automat; pick up the *Fahrausweis* brochure in the tourist office (see above) for step-by-step instructions. Düsseldorf's S-Bahn is integrated into the sprawling **VRR** (Verkehrsverbund Rein-Ruhr) system, which connects Bochum, Dortmund, Duisburg, Essen, Hagen, Krefeld, Mönchengladbach, Mühlheim,

Oberhausen, Recklinghausen, Solingen, and Wuppertal. **Schedule information:** tel. 582 28.

Taxi: tel. 333 33 or 194 10.

Car Rental: Hertz, Immermannstr. 65 (tel. 35 70 25).

Bike Rental: Ackerstr. 143 (tel. 66 21 34). Call ahead to check availability. Bikes range DM15-30 per day. ID required. Open daily 9:30am-6:30pm.

Mitfahrzentrale: Konrad-Adenauer Platz 13 (tel. 37 60 81), to the left as you exit the station, and upstairs over a tiny travel office. Open Mon.-Fri. 10am-6:30pm, Sat. 10am-1pm. **City-Netz Mitfahrzentrale,** Kurfürstenstr. 30 (tel. (0211) 194 44), is a more professional chain but slightly higher fees. Open Mon.-Fri. 10am-6pm, Sat. 10am-1pm.

Women's Agency: Concerns can be directed to the **Frauenbüro,** Mühlenstr. 29 (tel. 899 36 01), a municipal office. Walk-in times Thurs. 10am-noon and 3-6pm.

Bookstore: Stern-Verlag, Friedrichstr. 24-26. A huge selection of English paperbacks. Open Mon.-Fri. 9am-6:30pm, Sat. 9am-2pm.

Laundromat: Wasch Center, Friedrichstr. 92. Wash DM6, dry DM1 per 15min. Soap included. Open daily 6am-11pm. Last load 10pm.

Pharmacy: In the *Hauptbahnhof.* Closed pharmacies post a list indicating the nearest open ones. **Emergency pharmacy:** tel. 115 00.

Emergencies: Police: tel. 110. **Ambulance:** tel. 38 89 89. **Fire:** tel. 112.

ACCOMMODATIONS

Düsseldorf is a convention city, and during fairs, crowds make rooms scarce and costly; it's not unusual for hotels to double their prices during a convention. If you're considering a budget hotel stay, call the tourist office for trade fair *(Messe)* dates and show up during a lull. Most spots go for at least DM40 per person even in the off-season. Check the area around the train station or consider taking a room in nearby Mönchengladbach or Neuss, each about 20 minutes away by S-Bahn. The hostel in Duisburg (12min. by S-Bahn) is another option. If you plan to stay for a longer period of time, the **Mitwohnzentrale** at Witzelstr. 32 (tel. 31 20 53), or **Marion Biel,** an independent agent (tel. 691 15 21), may be able to help with a sublet; settle fees *first,* or the commission percentage may skyrocket.

Jugendherberge und Jugendgästehaus Düsseldorf (HI), Düsseldorfer Str. 1 (tel. 57 40 41, fax 57 25 13), conveniently located in the Oberkassel part of town, just over the Rheinkniebrücke bridge from the *Altstadt.* Bus #835 (from the station): Jugendherberge, or U-Bahn 70, 705, or 117: Luegplatz, then walk 500m down Kaiser-Wilhelm-Ring. Choose between the cheaper but above-average **Jugendherberge** (DM20, over 26 DM24; breakfast included) or the possibility of a private single in the adjacent **Jugendgästehaus** (single DM34.50, double DM63, quads DM114). For both, reception open 7-9:30am, 12:30-5:30pm, and 6-10:30pm. Curfew for both 1am, but open briefly for stragglers at 2, 3, 4, and 5am. Both open early Jan. to mid-Dec.

Jugendherberge Duisburg-Wedau, Kalkweg 148E (tel. (0203) 72 41 64, fax 72 08 34). S-Bahn 1 or 21 (from either Düsseldorf or Duisburg *Hauptbahnhof*): Duisburg Schlenk, and follow the *Jugendherberge* and *Sportpark Wedau* signs (10 min.). In a green spot on the southern edge of the city center. DM18.30, over 26 DM22.30. Open mid-Jan. to mid-Dec.

CVJM-Hotel, Graf-Adolf-Str. 102 (tel. 36 07 64, fax 361 31 60). Down the street to the left of the train station, just past 4 peep shows. The *Christliche Verein Junger Menschen* (German version of the YMCA/YWCA) has Bible literature for its guests, but otherwise it's a standard hotel. Very brown. Couples can stay here. Rooms have hot and cold water but no showers. Singles DM55. Doubles DM90. Streetside rooms DM2 cheaper, due to the noise. Breakfast DM8.

Hotel Manhattan, Graf-Adolf-Str. 39 (tel. 37 02 44, fax 37 02 47), straight up from the station. The fun mirror-plated lobby (with a subtle touch of neon) shines of 1970s dance fever, but the clean, desk-equipped rooms are surprisingly non-metropolitan in their charm. Students, backpackers, and disco-freaks welcome. Singles DM60-135. Doubles DM95-180, all depending on ritzy scale of furnishings

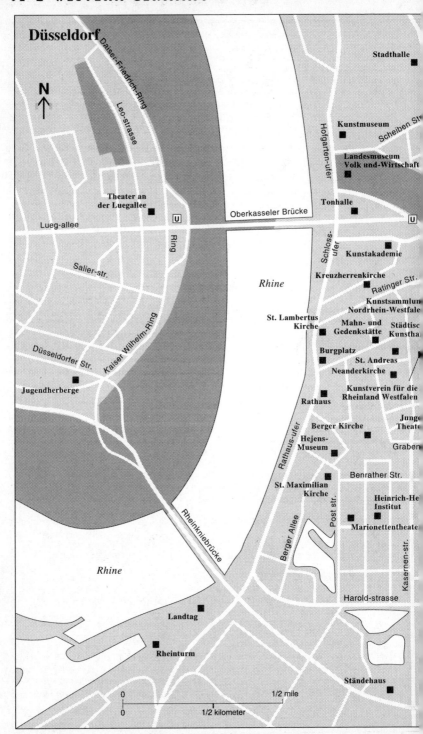

Düsseldorf

N

Stadthalle

Daiser-Friedrich-Ring

Leo-strasse

Hofgarten-ufer

Kunstmuseum

Scheiben Str

Landesmuseum
Volk und-Wirtschaft

Theater an
der Luegallee

Oberkasseler Brücke

Tonhalle

Lueg-allee

Ring

U

U

Salier-str.

Schloss-ufer

Kunstakademie

Kreuzherrenkirche

Ratinger Str.

Rhine

Kunstsammlun
Nordrhein-Westfale

St. Lambertus
Kirche

Mahn- und
Gedenkstätte

Städtisc
Kunstha

Kaiser Wilhelm-Ring

Düsseldorfer Str.

Burgplatz

St. Andreas
Neanderkirche

Jugendherberge

Kunstverein für die
Rheinland Westfalen

Rathaus

Junge
Theate

Berger Kirche

Graben

Rathaus-ufer

Hejens-
Museum

Benrather Str.

St. Maximilian
Kirche

Berger Allee

Post str.

Heinrich-He
Institut

Marionettentheate

Kasernen-str.

Rheinkniebrücke

Harold-strasse

Rhine

Landtag

Rheinturm

Ständehaus

0   1/2 mile

0   1/2 kilometer

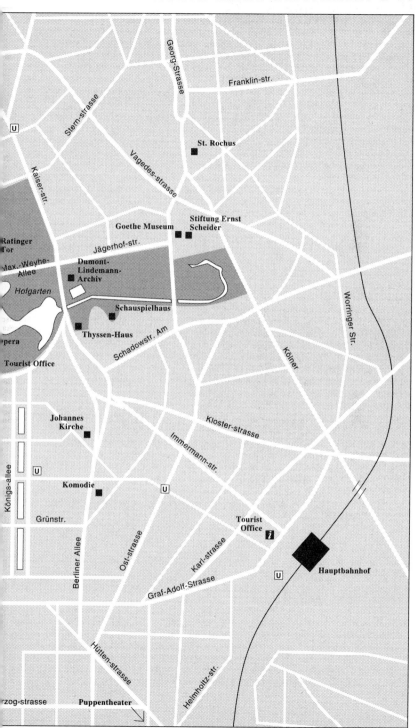

Georg-Strasse

Franklin-str.

Stern-strasse

U

St. Rochus

Vagedes-strasse

Kaiser-str.

Stiftung Ernst
Scheider

Goethe Museum

Ratinger
Tor

Jägerhof-str.

Max.-Weyhe-
Allee

Dumont-
Lindemann-
Archiv

Hofgarten

Schauspielhaus

pera

Thyssen-Haus

Schadowstr. Am

Kölner

Worringer Str.

Tourist Office

Kloster-strasse

Johannes
Kirche

Immermann-str.

Königs-allee

U

Komodie

U

Grünstr.

Berliner Allee

Ost-strasse

Tourist
Office

i

Karl-strasse

Graf-Adolf-Strasse

U

Hauptbahnhof

Hütten-strasse

Helmholtz-str.

rzog-strasse

Puppentheater

DÜSSELDORF

and whether it's convention time. The owner freely admits he'll bargain if you're friendly and destitute. Breakfast buffet included. Call far in advance, if possible.

Hotel Diana, Jahnstr. 31 (tel. 37 50 71, fax 36 49 43). From the station, head left down Graf-Adolf-Str. and turn left onto Jahnstr. where Hülten-Str. bends left (5 blocks). Rooms are aging, but clean and relatively cheap. Singles DM55-80. Doubles DM80-115. Breakfast included.

Hotel Amsterdam, Stressemannstr. 20 (tel. 84 05 89), between Oststr. and Berliner Allee. From the station start up Graf-Adolf-Str., and turn right at Stressemannplatz. Pale blue Baroque-style rooms, princess-style furniture. Fills up during conventions. Reception open daily 7am-midnight. Singles from DM70, with shower DM80. Doubles with shower and toilet DM150. Call ahead.

Hotel Bristol, Aderstr. 8 (tel. 37 07 50, fax 37 37 54), 1 block south of Graf-Adolf-Str. at the bottom tip of the Königsallee. A well-situated, well-furnished, friendly place to retire to after a stroll on the Kö. Call ahead; it's packed during conventions. Singles with shower and TV DM80, with shower, toilet, and TV DM100. Doubles with shower and TV DM90, with shower, toilet, and TV DM120. Breakfast included.

Camping: Kleiner Torfbruch (tel. 899 20 38). S-Bahn: Düsseldorf Geresheim, change to bus #737 (direction "Stamesberg"): Seestr. Or, S-Bahn: Düsseldorf Eller, change to bus #735: Unterbach. Reception open daily. DM27.50 per site for up to 3 people, DM7 per additional person, DM24 per family. **Meerbusch Langst** (tel. (02150) 25 02), or **Neus Grimlinghausen** (tel. (02101) 398 68), are somewhat less convenient options.

FOOD

For a boring lunch, try the food stands in the basement of the department store in the **Carschhaus,** Heinrich Heine Platz, off the Heinrich Heine Allee. The **Markt** on Karlsplatz offers all sorts of produce and foods, including *Sauerbraten* (pickled beef) with greens on the side (open Mon.-Sat. 8am-2pm). **Breweries** sell cheap meals in addition to their house concoctions; **Hausbrauerei "zum Schlüssel"** and **Schumacher Bräu "Im Goldenen Kessel",** at Bolkerstr. 45 and 44 respectively, are two fine examples (see Nightlife, below, for places open late).

Marché, in the Kö-Galerie mall at Königsallee 60. Vegetarians can enjoy the *Gemüsebuffet* (vegetable buffet) and fancy-dancy juice bar. Hearty breakfasts for under DM6 and regular meals for DM8.90-12.50. Open Mon.-Thurs. and Sun. 8am-11pm, Fri.-Sat. 8am-11:30pm.

Burghof, in Kaiserwerth next to Friedrich's ruins on the Rhine. Take U-Bahn #79: Klemensplatz. A big *Biergarten* packed with Düsseldorfers eating sausages in good weather.

Heine Geburtshaus, Bolderstr. 53. Dine in the birthplace of Heinrich Heine, Düsseldorf's legendary poet. While you're waiting, peruse the dozens of literary newspapers or magazines gathered here, or perhaps, get crazy and read one of Heine's works. Open daily noon-1am.

Asia Grill, Hunsrückenstr. 20, perpendicular to Bolkerstr. in the heart of beer-life. Plastic dragon-lamps. Good selection of filling meals, the most expensive of which is duck for DM10.50. Open 10am-6am.

Arlecchino, on Andreasstr. 1 block up and parallel to Bolkerstr., has personal pizzas with any topping for DM4.

SIGHTS

A visit to Düsseldorf must include a walk down the ever-so-posh **Kö** boulevard, properly called the Königsallee, 10min. by foot down Graf-Adolf-Str. from the station. The Belle-Epoque beauty was laid out over a century ago, with small stone bridges over the moat and a grassy central strip ending in an utterly decadent statue of the sea god Triton. Cafés—the see-and-be-seen-in type—fill the east side of the Allee all day and then some, even after the shops have closed. Three shopping guides for the Kö alone are printed by the tourist office, and innumerable other private chains along the alley vend their wares via glitzy brochures. The **Kö-Galerie** mall, midway up, is, in Nietzschean terms, an *Übermall*. Using *Let's Go* and shopping on Kö are really not compatible; prices *start* at US$100. At the upper end of the Kö, the **Hofgarten** park adds an oasis of green and culture to urban Düsseldorf. **Schloß Jägerhof,** at the western end of the garden, is painfully ornate. The Hofgarten meets the Rhine at Ehrenhof, a plaza of museums (see Museums, below). The **opera house** is here, as well as the neoclassical **Ratinger Tor,** a Napoleonic edifice.

Düsseldorf has had mixed luck with its cultural heroes. Resident Robert Schumann tried to end it all in the Rhine by jumping off a town bridge—he was miserable here. Nationally beloved Heinrich Heine is a much more popular son. His birthplace and homestead are marked by plaques, and every third restaurant and fast-food stand on his Bolkerstr. block bears the Heine name. The author's dignity is maintained a bit better at the **Heinrich Heine Institut,** Bilkerstr. 12-14 (tel. 899 55 71), with its collection of manuscripts and a discomfiting death mask cast from Heinrich's still-warm features. (Open Tues.-Sun. 11am-5pm. Library open Tues.-Fri. 10am-4pm. Admission DM3, students DM1.50.) **Burgplatz** used to be the site of a glorious castle, but tired citizens have only saved a single tower; given the structure's history, you can't blame them. The castle was built in 1324, burnt in 1490, rebuilt in 1559, razed in 1794, rebuilt in 1851, and flattened in 1872, at which point the townsfolk gave up—only the tower was reconstructed in 1900, and that was bombed into rubble during the Second World War. Pessimistic citizens then waited until 1984 to rebuild.

North along the Rhine, the **Nordpark** provides attractive grounds for the **Löbbeck Museum/Aquazoo** (see Museums, above). Even farther north on the Rhine, but still in Düsseldorf, are the well-preserved **ruins** of Emperor Friedrich's palace in the tiny town of **Kaiserwerth.** Built in 1184, the palace was destroyed in 1702 during the War of Spanish Secession, but the romantic Kaiserpfalz frame remains. Take U-Bahn 79: Klemensplatz, and follow Kaiserwerther Markt to the Rhine and walk left another 150m (open Mon.-Fri. 3-7pm, Sat.-Sun. 10am-7pm; free). Finally, just in case you're curious, the **confusing tower** with the blinking lights, visible at night from the Rhine, is actually a clock called the *Rheinturm*. From the bottom to the top, the dots represent 1 second, 10 seconds, 1 minute, 10 minutes, 1 hour, and 10 hours. You won't miss any curfews if you check it periodically.

MUSEUMS

This is a city of museums; most are clustered around the Hofgarten, with internationally important holdings in the string of museums on Grabbeplatz and Ehrenhof.

Grabbeplatz

Kunstsammlung Nordrhein-Westfalen, Grabbeplatz 5 (tel. 838 10), is the black-reflecting-glass thing west of the Hofgarten. U-Bahn 70, 76, 78, 79, 705, or 717: Heinrich-Heine-Allee and walk north 2 blocks, or bus #725: Grabbeplatz. An exceptional modern art museum. Skylights flood sunshine onto the exhibits—Matisse, Picasso, Surrealists and Expressionists. The Paul Klee collection is one of the most extensive in the world. Open Tues.-Sun. 10am-6pm. Admission DM10, students DM5. Tours Sun. 11am.

Städtische Kunsthalle, Grabbeplatz 4, across the square from the Kunstsammlung Nordrhein-Westfalen. Holds visiting exhibits only—but good ones. Open Tues.-Sun. 11am-6pm. Admission DM7, students DM3.50.

Ehrenhof—Hofgarten

Kunstmuseum Düsseldorf, Ehrenhof 5, ringing the fountain. A spectacular collection of sculpture, painting, weaving, and crafts spanning 2 stories and 11 centuries. Don't miss the stunning glassware (especially if you have a machine gun along) or the 80,000 prints and drawings drawing heavily on the Baroque and Renaissance periods—both assortments are on the ground floor. Open Tues.-Sun. 11am-6pm. Admission DM5, students DM2.50.

Landesmuseum Volk und Wirtschaft, Ehrenhof 2. Unpacks every nut and bolt of the region's trade development, with a little social history of local workers on the side. Open Mon.-Tues. and Thurs.-Fri. 9am-5pm, Wed. 9am-8pm, Sun. 1am-6pm. Admission DM1, students DM0.50.

Kunstpalast, on the far left end of Ehrenhof. A museum dedicated, like the Kunsthalle, to the display of continually rotating contemporary collections. Open Tues.-Sun. 11am-6pm. Admission varies.

Dumont-Lindemann Archiv, Jägerhofstr. 1, sits at the end of a tree-lined promenade in the middle of the *Hofgarten,* in the chief gardener's old house. This tiny **Theater Museum** manages to cram in costumes, puppets, marionettes, playbills, and paper stages celebrating the art of local thespians. Open Tues.-Sun. 11am-5pm. Admission DM3, students DM1.50.

Goethe Museum, Jakobistr. 2 (tel. 899 62 62), in Schloß Jägerhoff, at the east end of the garden. Streetcar #707 or bus #722: Schloß Jägerho. Lacks a hometown advantage (Goethe was not from these parts), but makes up for it in the sheer extent of its collections—30,000 souvenirs of the poet and all his friends. Everything in the mini-palace is furnished as Goethe would have expected, to evoke the era of the genius. Open Tues.-Fri. and Sun. 11am-5pm, Sat. 1-5pm. Library open Tues.-Fri. 10am-noon and 2-4pm. Admission DM3, students DM1.50.

Elsewhere in Düsseldorf

Stadtmuseum, at Berger Alleez by the Rheinkniebrücke. The 3-year-old building clashes a bit with its turn-of-the-century surroundings, but the opulent exhibits inside match Düsseldorf's lavish consumer history perfectly. Open Tues., Thurs-Fri., and Sun. 11am-5pm, Wed. 11am-8pm, Sat. 1-5pm. Admission DM3, students DM1.50; special exhibits DM10, students DM5.

Mahn-und Gedenkstätte, Mühlenstr. 29. Museum and document collection which commemorates, in strong terms, those who stood against the Third Reich. Open Tues.-Fri. 11am-6pm, Sat. 1-5pm, Sun. 10am-6pm. Free.

Düsseldorf Schiffahrt-Museum, housed in the tower in the Burgplatz. With models and paintings recreating 3000 years of the town's Rhine dominance. Open Tues.-Sun. 10am-5pm. Admission DM3, students DM1.50.

Neanderthal Museum, Thekhauser Quall (tel. (02104) 311 49), in the suburb of Erkrath. Exhibits on the history and significance of our 60,000-year-old predecessors. The cows you'll see if you walk through the wooded hills outside the museum represent efforts to reverse evolution and inbreed the cattle back to their prehistoric woolliness. Open Tues.-Sat. 10am-5pm, Sun. 11am-6pm. Admission DM2, students DM1.

ENTERTAINMENT AND NIGHTLIFE

Folklore holds that Düsseldorf's 500 pubs make up "die längste Theke der Welt" (the longest bar in the world). Bolkerstr. is jam-packed nightly with street performers. *Prinz* magazine (DM4) is Düsseldorf's fashion cop and scene detective; it's often available free at the youth hostel. *Coolibri* and *Biograph* are free cultural guides, less complete but still more than you'll ever need to keep it (your thang, that is) shakin' all night long. **Das Kommödchen** (tel. 32 94 43) is a tiny, extraordinarily popular theater behind the Kunsthalle at Grabbeplatz. (Box office open Mon.-Fri. 11am-2pm and 4-8pm, Sat. 2pm until performance time.) Ballet and opera tickets are best bought (without service charge) at the **Opernhaus** (tel. (0211) 890 82 11), on Heinrich Heine Allee. (Box office open Mon.-Fri. 11am-6:30pm, Sat. 11am-1pm, and 1hr. before performances. Tickets can be purchased by phone (Mon.-Fri. 9am-5pm). **Black Box,** Schulstr. 4 (tel. 899 24 90), off Rathaus-Ufer along the Rhine, services the art film aficionado with languages unadulterated. (Admission DM7, students DM5. Seminars DM2.)

Zum Goldenen Einhorn and Brauerei zum Uel, Rattinger 16-18, in the *Altstadt.* Papered with listings for musical happenings. Requisite *Schlösser Alt* (0.2L DM2). On good nights the crowds of students block traffic on Rattingstr. On bad nights they drink their beer indoors. Open Mon.-Sat. 11am-1am.

Rheinstraße, Hofgartenufer 7 (tel. 49 40 43). *Biergarten* which fabulously fills its 1000-person capacity. Open Mon.-Sat. 5-11pm, Sun. 11am-11pm.

Die Kneipe, Liefergasse 1-3. Rolls out the barrel in a vaulted cellar downstairs from an average student bar. Open Sun.-Thurs. 6pm-1am, Fri.-Sat. 6pm-3am.

Rheingold (tel. 16 26 26), just to the right of the main train station, shakes the atmosphere with a spacious ensemble of bars, cafés, balconies, and a fun dance floor. Fri. is freak/grunge night (i.e. white guys with dreadlocks) 10pm-morning, Sat. is soul/funk/house night starting at 10pm, and Thurs. hears hip-hop/soul from 10pm. Every second Sun. is Greek night. Admission DM7.

Purple Haze, Liefergasse 7 (tel. 32 82 20). Has atmosphere (cough, cough). Open Wed. 10pm-2am, Fri.-Sat. 10pm-5am, Sun. 9pm-2am.

Galerie Burghof, Burgallee 1-3 (tel. 40 14 23). U-Bahn 79: Klemensplatz. In Kaiserwerth, next to Friedrich's ruins on the Rhine. Golden *Biergarten*, glowing restaurant (pancakes DM12.50), and glitzy clientele. Open Mon.-Sat. 5pm-midnight, Sun. noon-midnight.

McLaughlin's Irish Pub, Kurzestr. 11, loads up on live bands and Americans loading up. **Engelchen,** next door, is sweetly punk.

Tor 3, Ronsdorferstr. 143 (tel. 32 91 91). S-Bahn 707: Rondorfer-Str. Facing away from downtown (where the streetcar came from) turn right onto Ronsdorferstr. Prepare for alternate transport home from this factory-turned-disco for the fashion elite—the S-Bahn will have stopped running by the time you're ready to leave. Alternative music Fri., techno Sat. Open Fri.-Sat. 10pm-5am. Cover DM10-12.

ZAKK (Zentrum für Aktion, Kultur und Kommunikation), Fichtenstr. 40 (tel. 973 00 10), is in the same corner of town as Tor 3. S-Bahn 705, 706, 707, 717, or bus #732 or 736. Disco, concerts, shows, movies, debates, readings, and *Merengue*. Cover nights cost DM7. Every Thurs. is a women-only disco, 9pm-3am. Call or get hold of a schedule.

∎ Near Düsseldorf: Mönchengladbach

Mönchengladbach, 30km west of Düsseldorf, makes for a pleasant excursion; the majestic **Schloß Rheydt** looms over the east side of town. This Renaissance castle has an actual moat in addition to its near-perfect gables. The castle houses two museums; the one with all the paintings is closed for renovation until 1995, while the one with weaving and carpentry exhibits is still open. You can't have it all. (Open Tues.-Sun. 10am-6pm; Nov.-Feb. Wed. and Sat.-Sun. 11am-5pm; admission DM2.) Mönchengladbach's suburban Hardterwald section is blessed with a **Jugendherberge (HI),** Brahmstr. 156 (tel. (02161) 55 95 12), another escape from Düsseldorf housing. From the Mönchengladbach station, take bus #13 or 23: Hardtmarkt, and follow the signs. (DM17.30, over 26 DM20.80. Breakfast included.) The **tourist office,** Bismarckstr. 23-27 (tel. (02161) 220 01), near the station, finds rooms (open Mon.-Fri. 9:30am-6pm, Sat. 9:30am-12:30pm).

∎∎∎ RUHR REGION (Ruhrgebiet)

Düsseldorf owes a good deal of its modern prosperity to the industry of the Ruhr Valley, a sprawling conglomeration of cities along the river that continues on to Essen, Bochum, Duisburg and Dortmund (see below). Solingen and Wuppertal, between the Ruhr and the Wupper, belong to this region as well. The area is steeped in a brand of German history quite distant from the classical, rarified world of Goethe. This is where work gets done, where steel is milled, and where, over the past century, industrial disputes have been slugged out. The Allies bombed many of the towns in their drive to cripple the war machine. Some, in rebuilding, have accepted the loss of historic districts and put their assets in a brace of excellent museums. An integrated S-Bahn, streetcar, bus, and U-Bahn system, run by the Verkehrsverbund Rhein-Ruhr (VRR), links many of the cities. The Ruhr region is veiled in the most dense concentration of rail lines anyhere in the world. But not all is dark here, and there is something dizzyingly pleasurable about jumping on frequent, fast trains, stopping off to catch a glance of the modest but significant flashes of light in each.

ESSEN

Essen has a bad reputation. The "black town" on the Ruhr once outsmoked Birmingham, England, burning up the same rich coal deposits that powered the Prussian war machine. But the skies here are now as clear as they get in Germany, and the university and museums are full—not that Essen doesn't still work for its keep. In recent decades, Essen, the sixth-largest city in Germany, has replaced its notorious smokestack factories with a curious variety of light industries. A cross-section of local outfits offer **factory tours,** including pipeworks, breweries, and the local Coca-Cola bottler. The tourist office has a master list and a scheduling guide.

Infamous 19th-century arms and railroad mogul Alfred Krupp perfected steel-casting in industrial Essen. The **Villa Hügel,** for decades the Krupp family home, was given to the city in the 1950s in order to brighten the company's image, tarnished by unsavory wartime activities (Krupp profited from an SS-run slave-labor camp). The house itself reflects Krupp's gaudy arrogance; exhibits and concerts take advantage of the mahogany halls. (S-Bahn 6: Essen-Hügel. Grounds open daily 8am-8pm. Villa open Tues.-Sun. 10am-6pm. Special exhibits open Mon. and Wed.-Sun. 10am-7pm, Tues. 10am-9pm. Admission DM1.50; special exhibits DM10.) The two most evocative spots in Essen itself are both houses of God. Essen's **Münster,** on Burgplatz, is ancient and cloistered, a string of courtyards, crypts, and altars. The doll-like *Goldene Madonna* stands beside the nave (open daily 7:30am-6:30pm). Built in 1913, Essen's massive **Alte Synagoge,** Steelerstr. 29, grew old early. Nazis gutted the temple in 1938, but it remained standing as the largest synagogue this side of the Alps. The **Dokumentationsforum** inside is a moving monument to the Jews of Essen. (U-Bahn: Porscheplatz. Open Tues.-Sun. 10am-6pm; free; tours Wed. 3pm.)

Museum Folkwang, in the *Museumzentrum* at Goethestr. 41 (tel. (0201) 88 84 84), drops all the big names in modern art. In the same complex, the Folkwang's **Fotographische Sammlung** takes on camerawork from the early days. (Streetcar #101, 107, or 127, or U-Bahn 11: Rütten-Scheider Stern. Both open Tues.-Wed. and Fri.-Sun. 10am-6pm, Thurs. 10am-9pm. Combined admission DM5, students DM2.) Exhibits at the **Design Zentrum Nordrhein Westfalen,** Hindenburgstr. 25-27 (tel. (0201) 82 02 10), document the effects of cultural fads on product design. (U-Bahn 17 or 18: Bismarckplatz. Open Tues.-Fri. 10am-6pm, Sat. 10am-2pm. Free.) The **Deutsches Plakat Museum** (German Poster Museum), Rathenausstr. 2 (tel. (0201) 88 41 14), also concerns the fate of art in the "age of mechanical reproduction." Posters from Toulouse-Lautrec's dance halls to politics. Germans know good propaganda when they see it. (5min. walk from the *Bahnhof*, past Horten, then left by the Sparkasse. Open Tues.-Sun. noon-8pm. Admission DM2, students free.)

The **tourist office,** at the south entrance of the main station—look for the "Freiheit" signs and turn right at the exit (tel. (0201) 23 54 27)—finds rooms for free. Hit them up for a city map (open Mon.-Fri. 9am-6pm, Sat. 10am-2pm). More in-depth information, but no room reservations, can be found at the towering Bauhaus *Rathaus* (tel. 88 35 64). (U-Bahn: Porscheplatz, Open Mon.-Tues. and Thurs.-Fri. 8:30am-12:30pm and 2-3pm, Wed. 8:30am-12:30pm.) **U-Bahn** and **streetcar** lines dart around at DM2 per ride. The **Mitfahrzentrale** pairs riders with drivers at Heinickestr. 33 (tel. (0201) 22 10 31; open Mon.-Fri. 9am-6pm, Sat. 9am-2pm).

Essen's **Jugendherberge (HI),** Pastoratsberg 2 (tel. (0201) 49 11 63), is in a park in the Werden district, also home to the 8th-century **Abteikirche** and the **Luciuskirche,** the oldest parish church north of the Alps. (S-Bahn 6: Bahnhof Werden, cross the Rhine bridge, take the 2nd right onto Bungerstr., and follow Kemensborn uphill as it winds all over the map to a sharp right on Pastoratsberg.) The grounds contain a grass basketball court (we don't understand it, either). (Reception open 2-5pm and 8-10pm. Curfew 11:30pm. DM18.30, over 26 DM22.30. Breakfast included.) The basic, comfortable **Hotel Kessing,** Hachestr. 30 (tel. (0201) 23

99 88), is close to the train station; turn left on Hachestr. (Singles DM55, with shower and toilet DM79. Doubles DM98, with bath DM128. Breakfast included.) Camp at **"Stadt-Camping" Essen-Werden,** Im Löwental 67 (tel. (0201) 49 29 78), on the west bank of the Ruhr. (S-Bahn: Essen-Werden, and then continue south along the river. Reception open daily 9am-1pm and 3-10pm.DM12 per tent, DM5.50 per person.) **Porscheplatz,** near the *Rathaus,* is cheap-food central—stop by the **Spar** cafeteria, or any of the fresh food vending stands. There's also a university **Mensa** (U-Bahn: Universität, and follow the signs to the green-rimmed building).

DORTMUND

Dortmund produces beer, and lots of it. This city of 600,000 men, women, and children produces 600 million liters of beer annually—you do the math—making it the second-largest beer-producing city in the world after Milwaukee. As part of Germany's industrial machine, Dortmund was a tempting target for Allied bombers, and 93% of the inner city was leveled in World War II. Largely industrial, it's not a terribly attractive place, but as bar bills add up, so do the city's cultural assets; the emphasis is definitely on museums. **Museum am Ostwall,** Ostwall 7, was built in 1947 over the ruins of the *Altstadt* in order to make room for modern art of the — especially that suppressed by the Third Reich. The German Expressionists assembled here make up a definitive collection of the *Blauer Reiter* and *die Brucke* schools. The collection concludes with a 1970s explosion (open Tues.-Sun. 10am-6pm; free). The spiralling (Guggenheim-style) **Museum fur Kunst und Kulturgeschichte,** Hansastr. 3 (5min. from the station) is full of period rooms, decorative pieces, and occasionally daring special exhibits (open Tues.-Sun. 10am-6pm; free).

Dortmund also has a museum for beer. The **Brauerei-Museum,** Markischestr. 85, in the Kronen Beer Works southeast of the city center, shows just how Dortmunders have achieved beverage excellence. Unfortunately, there are no samples. (U-Bahn 41, 45, 47, or 49: Markgrafenstr., and walk through the park. Open Tues.-Sun. 10am-6pm. Free.) Another beer landmark is the massive **U** icon on a tower to the right of the station, symbol of the Dortmund Union Brewery. Conrad von Soest's master-triptych in the **Marienkirche,** Kampfstr. (up from the station and left), captures the medieval skyline (open Tues.-Fri. 10am-noon and 2-4pm, Sat. 10am-1pm).

The main **tourist office** *(Informationsamt),* Friedensplatz 3 (tel. 54 22 56 66), is in the Stadtgarten near the round U-Bahn station. Rooms booked for DM3, maps and museum lists distributed (open Mon.-Wed. 8am-3:30pm, Thurs. 8am-5pm, Fri. 8am-noon). The **Information-Pavillion,** Konigwall 20 (tel. 54 22 21 64), across from the station, helps out with the same services (open Mon.-Fri. 9am-1pm and 2-6pm, Sat. 9am-1pm). The **telephone city code** is 0231. Dortmund is on the eastern edge of the tangle of cities in the Ruhr River area. The S-Bahn (1,2,4, and 21) connects it to Essen and Düsseldorf, 30 minutes away. Hotel prices in Dortmund are staggering, and there is no hostel or campground; hostelers can jump the train to nearby Essen (see above). Close to the station, **Hotel-garni Carlton,** Lutge-Brucke-Str. 5-7 (tel. 52 80 30, fax 52 50 20), has nice big rooms. (Singles from DM45 to a royal suite at DM140. Doubles DM90-190. Breakfast included.) Head up the wide steps from the station to the well-stocked pedestrian zone. **Restaurant Marche,** Ostenhellweg 3, has *Musli,* salad, and pasta bars (open Mon.-Sat. 8am-11pm, Sun. 10am-11pm). Many establishments near the university allow access to student life.

WUPPERTAL

Wuppertal is a new German city made necessary by the weight of industry. Not one mill town but many incorporated in 1929 to form Wuppertal; today, the two districts of Elberfeld and Barmen form twin inner-cities. This is a region that takes work and transport seriously, but compared to the somber black spiderweb of rail lines, Wuppertal has a sense of humor. Its hallmark suspension-railway, the **Schwebebahn,** was likened to a flying millipede when its turn-of-the-century tracks were laid down, and it's not a bad description. Orange cars dangle from a green iron skeleton, with claws on either side of the Wupper River. Watching the smooth route over the water can be more fun than actually riding.

A statue group of writhing stone proletariats sits in front of the gray-slate **Engelshaus,** Engelstr. 10, birthplace of Marx's co-author and pamphleteer Friedrich Engels. Stubborn citizens have stood by their favorite son through thick and thin. The guest book here is filled with all sorts of multilingual devotions. The **Museum für Frühindustrialisierung** (early industrialization), in an old textile mill to the rear of the house, explains some of Fred's political ire, documenting overcrowding and inhumane work conditions. Guides operate the old machinery, explaining every whirr. (Open Tues.-Sun. 10am-1pm and 3-5pm. Free, but alienated from itself. Ring the doorbells to enter.) This **Historisches Zentrum** (the house and mill) is easily accessible from the *Schwebebahn* Adlerbrücke stop, the Wuppertal-Barmen train station (down Flügelstr. and right past the Opera), and the #610 bus. **Friedrich-straße,** lined with bars, pubs, and cafés ends at the copper tower of the Elberfeld *Rathaus* and a huge, flamboyant fountain of Neptune.

Get a hotel reservation at the **tourist office,** Döppersberg Pavillion at the foot of the "Elberfeld Bahnhof" *Schwebebahn* stop (tel. (0202) 563 62 31). Take the tunnel from the Elberfeld station to the pedestrian zone, and turn right upon exiting. (Open Mon.-Fri. 9am-6pm, Sat. 9am-1pm.) Wuppertal's workaday **Jugendherberge (HI),** Obere Lichtenplatzerstr. 70 (tel. (0202) 55 23 72, fax 55 73 54), is in a park in Barmen, south of the center. From the Barmen station, take bus #610 or 640 to Jugendherberge, or walk right on Winklerstr., turn right on Fischertal, walk up the hill and make a right on Amalienstraße, and then turn left on the path opposite Fischerstr.; look for the hostel up the dirt path and to your right. (Reception until 10pm. Curfew 11:30pm. DM18.30, over 26 DM22.30. Breakfast included.) From the "Elberfeld" station, go past the end of Poststraße, continue on up Friedrichstr.past innumerable cafés, and on to **Café-Kneipe Agathe,** Albrechtstr. 5. This crepe club (DM4-8 per crepe) of sorts is a popular hangout, with local magazines and event schedules lining the walls. (Open Mon.-Fri. 5pm-1am, Sat.-Sun. 10am-1am.) Only women are welcome at bookshop-café **Dröppel-Femina,** Am Brögel 1, the gathering place for Wuppertal's feminist and lesbian community. (Open Mon.-Fri. 10am-11pm, Sun. 3-8pm.)

SOLINGEN

Medieval **Solingen** was renowned for its swordmaking, and for 600 years the town has been the scissor and flatware capital of Europe. In the last year, Solingen has taken on an entirely different historical role. In June, 1993, the home a Turkish family was set on fire by unknown attackers believed to be associated with neo-Nazi organizations (a swastika was found scratched in the children's sand-box). Five people died, a grandmother, a young woman, and three small children. The family had lived in Germany for over twenty years, and the younger victims had been born in Germany, although press reports (and German law) still referred to them as "foreigners." (See Germany: Life and Times, above, for some background on immigration, citizenship, and recent right-wing violence.) Although much of the public was outraged, many were struck by the fact that Chancellor Kohl failed to pay a quick visit to the sight, and surprised that many German politicians regarded the attack as an argument for tighter restrictions on immigration, rather than as a call to come face to face with the threat of racism and xenophobia. In the week following the attack, a wave of violence spread across Germany. It included more attacks on foreigners, as though a dam had broken, and rioting in the streets by rightists, leftists, and Turks. People from around Germany converged on Solingen, where a good part of the rioting took place.

That week in June changed Solingen indelibly. On the surface, Solingen looks like many other towns in these hills—green shutters, gray slate roofs—indeed like many other towns in Germany. It has a decent castle and is surrounded by the proverbial rolling green hills. *Let's Go* has listed it for years. Solingen was also the birthplace of

Adolf Eichmann, one of the Gestapo's chief officials, a fact about which the town has maintained a stony silence, even as his shadow has fallen here again. By chance, a *Let's Go's* researcher was scheduled to visit Solingen only days after the arson attack, in the midst of the violent disorder. We chose to cancel that stop on her itinerary. For that reason, we do not feel that we can properly account for the towns two hostels (which did receive high marks in past years). If you are staying in the Ruhr region and choose to look for housing here, feel free to contact the hostels directly. They are: **Jugendherberge Solingen-Oberburg (HI),** An der Jugendherberge 11 (tel. (0212) 410 25, fax 49 449), and **Jugendherberge Solingen-Gräfrath (HI),** Flockertsholzerweg 10 (tel. (0212) 59 11 98).

■■■ TEUTOBURG FOREST (Teutoburger Wald)

This is the forest where the Germanic tribes first stood up to the Roman legions and, in the eyes of 19th-century Romantics, first learned to be German. West of the *Weser,* the thickly wooded stretch of the Teutoburg Forest protects legends that predate both fairy tales and Christianity. Ideally the area should be biked or hiked, with short stops in the towns scattered through the woods. Direct rail connections to the Teutoburger Wald are through Bielefeld, Detmold, and Alterbeker.

The most visible sign of the mythologized German past stands outside of the regional seat Detmold—the 50m-high **Hermanns Denkmal.** In 9 AD, the Teutonic chief Armenius Hermann took on three Roman legions and annihilated them so completely that no one came to bury the dead for six years. Over-enthusiastic nationalists placed Hermann's monolithic likeness on an old encampment in 1875, and Kaiser Wilhelm I came to cut the ribbon. The statue itself, complete with a winged helmet, wields a 7m sword with the disconcerting inscription, "German unity is my power, my power is Germany's might." The memorial is also Germany's confusion, as research continually relocates the battle onto other Teutoburg hills. The only fact agreed upon is that the colossus does *not* mark the spot. From it, however, radiate spiraling hiking paths into the surrounding forest and to the nearby **Hünenringe,** trails which wind among the ruins of medieval ramparts.

An **Eagle Watch** (*Adlerwarte*), just south of Detmold (tel. (05231) 471 71), strikes a militant note, with 80 glowering birds of prey. To get there from the Detmold train station, follow Paulinenstr., turn right on Allee, and bear left onto Paderbornerstr. until you reach the small town of **Berlebeck.** Or, do as the Deutschen do and hike it, on Hermannsweg south from the *Denkmal.* Though the eagles are captive for most of the day, they fly free for a few hours around lunchtime. (Open daily 8:30am-6pm, Nov.-March 10am-dusk; free flying 11am-3pm, Nov.-March 11am-2:30pm. Admission DM5, children DM2, reduced rates for groups.) Cannon are still poised in the courtyard of the **Fürstliches Residenzschloß,** a Renaissance castle in the town's central park. Its **roter Saal** is as red and as decadent as can be, down the hall from the **Jagdwaffen** (tel. (05231) 225 07), an array of 400-year-old hunting equipment. (Tours given daily at 10, 11am, noon, 2, 4, and 5pm. English translations available to read along. Admission DM4, children DM2, groups DM3.).

Detmold's true pride is access to the greater Teutoburg Forest. There's no substitute for the excellent network of bike and hiking routes emanating from the Denkmal. Get information on the big wide woods at the **tourist office,** Rathaus 1 (tel. (05231) 97 73 28 or 97 73 27), which also books rooms. (Open Mon.-Thurs. 9am-noon and 1-5pm, Fri. 9am-4pm, Sat. 9am-noon; Nov.-March Mon.-Thurs. 9am-noon and 1-5pm, Fri. 9am-noon.) From the station head left on Bahnhofstr., right on Paulinenstr., and left on Bruchstr. into the pedestrian zone. Detmold's **Jugendherberge (HI)** is at Schirrmanstr. 49 (tel. (05231) 247 39, fax 289 27). To reach it, take the bus to "Hidessen" and follow the huntsmen on the multi-colored signs. (Reception open 5-10pm. DM16.90, over 26 DM20.40. Breakfast included.) **Käseglocke,** on Langestr., vends wine, cheese, fruit, and salads (open Mon.-Thurs. 8:30am-1pm and

3-5:30pm, Fri. 8:30am-6:30pm, Sat. 8am-1pm). Surround your sandwich with a *Brötchen* from any one of the nearby bakeries.

A 11km hiking trail begins in front of the Detmold station and ends at Lemgo, a flawless Weser Renaissance town, with a **Weserrenaissance-Museum** (tel. (05261) 20 75) right inside **Schloß Brake,** the central castle (museum open Tues.-Sun. 9am-6pm; admission DM4, students DM2). Down the road stands the **Hexenbürger-meisterhaus Lemgo** (tel. (05261) 21 32 76), a collection of historical odds and ends with a special focus on the witch-trial era (open Tues.-Fri. and Sun. 9am-1pm and 2-5pm, Sat. 10am-1pm). For more attractions, try the **Lemgo tourist office** (tel. (05261) 21 33 47).

Horn, in southern Teutoburger Wald (1 stop before Detmold on the train from Alterbeker), is the seat of the **Externsteine,** a bizarre hollow of sculpted limestone. Christians displaced pagan rituals here by reworking the landscape in the 11th century and creating a Jerusalem of the mind. Priests hewed one hill into a likeness of Calvary, according to biblical specifications. Their success is questionable; one formation looks a bit like a five-story fist, and the surrounding forest gives the whole business a pre-Christian feel. Information on rooms and rituals is available from the **tourist office** at Rathausplatz 2 (tel. (05234) 20 12 62), near the town hall (open Mon.-Wed. and Fri. 8:30am-noon, Thurs. 8:30am-noon and 2-5:30pm).

The 40-minute hike from the station to the **Jugendherberge (HI),** Jahnstr. 36 (tel. (05234) 25 34, fax 691 99), brings you near the Externsteine. Buses run from Detmold; take the Horn line to Jahnstr., then follow the signs. (Reception open 5-9pm; building closes at 10pm. DM16.90, over 26 DM20.40. Breakfast included.) The wooded **Campingplatz Horn-Bad Meinburg,** Kempenerstr. 33 (tel. (0255) 236), has only 30 sites; call ahead.

The first night of Easter is the best time to visit the nearby hamlet of **Lügde.** In another pagan feast, flaming giant **Catherine wheels** *(Osterräder)* tumble downhill. The rest of the time, Lügde reverts to a nice old Christian town with a 13th-century church and ivy-covered towers. The Lügde **tourist office,** Mittlerestr. 3 (tel. (05281) 780 29), at the end of the main street, offers brochures (open Mon.-Fri. 10am-noon). Lügde is on the **train line** from Hanover to Alterbeker.

■■■ MÜNSTER

German author Helmut Domke once noted that Münster was a city "without a triumphal arch…without base ambitions." Its long history has been eventful, sometimes rough, nonetheless. *Münster* is German for monastery, named for the church founded here by one of Charlemagne's evangelists in 805. The conversion took all too well; religious conflicts in the 16th century almost burned the city to the ground. As the capital of the old Kingdom of Westphalia, Münster presided over the 1648 Peace which brought the Thirty Years War to an end, defining the borders of scores of German statelets for the next few hundred years. Modern Münster's 270,000 citizens lead a comparably placid existence, their contentment marred only by the occasional party cooked up by the 55,000 students enrolled at Wilhelms Universität, the second-largest university in Germany.

PRACTICAL INFORMATION

Münster is located at the confluence of the lower channels of the Ems River, in the midst of the Münsterland plain. Frequent trains run from Düsseldorf and Cologne to the southwest, and from Bremen to the northeast.

Tourist Office: Berlinerplatz 22 (tel. 492 27 10), across Bahnhofstr. from the train station. Offers room booking, tours, theater tickets, and souvenirs. Open Mon.-Fri. 10am-6pm, Sat. 10am-1pm, Sun. 10am-1pm.

Post Office: Berlinerstr. 37, 48143 Münster, directly to the left of the train station. Open Mon.-Fri. 8am-6pm, Sat. 8am-1pm, Sun. 9-10am. For limited services open Mon.-Fri. 7:30am-10pm, Sat. 7:30am-6pm, Sun. 10am-1pm.
Telephones: City code: 0251.
Flights: Flights daily to Berlin, Frankfurt, Munich, and Zürich; Sun.-Fri. to London, Mon.-Fri. to Paris and Amsterdam from **Flughafen Münster-Osnabrück,** located to the northeast of the city. Buses shuttle between the train station and the airport; bus schedule posted in the station. **Flight information:** tel. 50 31 23.
Mitfahrzentrale: ASTA runs a ride-share office, Schloßplatz 1 (tel. 83 56 43). **Flottweg Mitfahrzentrale,** Hamburgerstr. 8, is closer to the station (tel. 601 41).
Car Rental: Hertz, Hammerstr. 186 (tel. 773 78).
Bike Rental: The largest train-station bike rental service in Europe; 300 bikes up for grabs. DM10 per day, DM6 per day with a train ticket. Reserve wheels by phone (tel. 69 13 20). Open daily 7am-10pm.
Boat Rental: The only way to see the middle of the Aasee Lake. **Segelschule** (tel. 803 03), offers rentals and basic lessons, as well as **water tours** for the passive.
Bookstore: Bücher bei Baader, Am Drubbel 19 (tel. 445 71), next to St. Lambert's, sells English-language books. Open Mon.-Wed. and Fri. 9am-6:30pm, Thurs. 9am-8:30pm.
Laundromat: Wasch Center, Moltkestr. 5-7. Wash DM6. Open Mon.-Fri. 6am-11pm.

ACCOMMODATIONS AND CAMPING

Some travelers hit up students for a place to sleep, because this thriving little town is not cheap. The brand new *Jugendgästehaus* is no steal, and hotels can fill up quickly, so be sure to call ahead. In a pinch, there's a hostel in Nottuln, 25km out of town and a 50-minute ride away (bus #560: Nottuln-Steinstr.). For **camping,** try **Wersewinkel,** Dorbaumstr. 35 (tel. 32 93 12) or **Campingplatz Münster,** Laerer Werseufer/Wolbeckerstr. (tel. 31 19 82).

Jugendgästehaus Aasee, Bismarckallee 31 (tel. (0251) 53 24 70, fax 52 12 71). Bus #13: Hoppendamm. Huge, new hostel sits right on the shore of the Aasee. 4-bed room DM32 per person, 2-bed room DM38 per person; cheaper if you stay longer than 4 days stay. Breakfast buffet included.
Haus vom Guten Hirten, Mauritz-Lindenweg 61 (tel. 360 48, fax 933 05 14). To the right of the train station, right onto Wolbeckerstr., left onto Hohenzollern-Ring, right onto Manfred-von-Richthofen-Str., then left on Andreas-Hofer-Str. to Mauritz-Lindenweg. A considerable distance from both the station and the *Altstadt.* Run by a church group, but mixed-up couples who've lost sight of God are still welcome; they can take the doubles and enjoy the well-stocked bookshelves. Scenic park and cemetery a block away (open 8am-6pm). Singles DM48. Doubles DM88. Triples DM126.
Hotel Conti, Berlinerplatz 2a (tel. 404 44). Walk right across Bahnhofstr. from the station; reception is on the 5th floor (take the elevator). *The* most convenient spot for late-night travelers. Enjoy the cuisine; there's a Ritter-Sport chocolate on every pillow and Frosted Flakes in the breakfast buffet. Singles with sink DM69; with shower, telephone, and TV DM149. Doubles DM98, with shower DM135.
Hotel-Restaurant Martinihof, Hörsterstr. 25-26 (tel. 41 86 20, fax 547 43). The main feature here is the restaurant. Reception open 24hrs. except Sun. 3-6pm. Singles with sink and telephone DM55-61. Doubles with sink and telephone DM98. Breakfast buffet included.

FOOD AND NIGHTLIFE

On Wednesdays and Saturdays, a Farmer's Market takes over the plaza in front of the *Dom* with stands vending fresh produce and sausages (open 6:30am-3:30pm). The entire **Kuhviertel** (the old student quarter) is lined with late-night *Kneipen* and inexpensive eateries.

MÜNSTER

Blechtrommel, Hansaring 26, features live music at least twice a month and a menu that changes weekly. For Günter Grass fans: the name means "tin drum." Large pizzas DM10-14, small DM7-9. Open daily 6pm-1am; kitchen open 7-11:30pm.

Café Malik, Frauenstr. 14. Fabulous zebra-striped bohemian coffeehouse where a foil-wrapped chocolate and a large selection of international newspapers accompany each cup (DM2.20). Brilliantly original soup with bread (DM5.50), many salads (DM5.80-14), and other meals (DM10-14). Try the apple pancakes with ice cream (DM9.20) and peruse the poetry (with angst!) on the menu. Open daily 9am-1am.

Cavete Akademische Bieranstalt, Kreuzstr. 38. Founded by students for students in 1959, with hordes of noodles (DM7-8.50) and one heck of a beer selection. Open Mon.-Sat. 7pm-1am.

Cuba-Kneipe, Achtermannstr. 10. Soothe yourself with reggae as you enjoy the wonderful Sun. brunch (10am-2pm, DM15). Also an impressive selection of other meals (DM9-18). Open Sun.-Fri. 10am-1am, Sat. 6pm-1am; meals served daily 6pm-midnight.

Diesel, Harsewinkelgasse 1-4, by the intersection of Windhorststr., Stubengasse and Loerstr.; just look for the 6m pedestal surmounted by 2m cherries. Play pool or darts for a while, then relax with one of the many magazines while munching on a baguette (DM7.80). Breakfast served daily 11am-4pm; dinner 7-11pm.

Gaststätte Pinkus Müller, Kreuzstr. 7. Overpriced meals (DM10-35), but the beer's brewed right upstairs. Sample a *Pinkus Alt* for just DM3. Open Mon.-Sat. 11:30am-2pm and 5pm-midnight.

SIGHTS

When Goethe's carriage turned onto the tree-lined **Promenade** encircling the *Altstadt,* he would slow it and smell the seasonal flowers and fruits. It's an inexpensive literary habit worth imitating. Continue through the Baroque façade of the **Schloß,** now the administrative center of **Wilhelms Universität,** to **Dom St. Paulus,** the largest cathedral in Westphalia.

The *Dom* was nearly destroyed in World War II, but it has since been beautifully restored. A stone from the similarly bombed Cathedral of Coventry stands in the entranceway, surrounded by photographs of local destruction and carrying a wish for mutual forgiveness between the combatants. From his pulpit within, Bishop Clemens von Galen delivered a courageous sermon against the Nazi program of euthanasia for so-called "incurables." Bishop von Galen began the address with the powerful indictment "Have you, have I, the right to live only as long as we are productive, as long as it is known that we will be productive?" After the sermon was distributed widely, pressure from the church prompted a rare partial retreat on Hitler's part. The speech can be found in its entirety, along with other paraphernalia, in the **Domkammer** (open Tues.-Sat. 10am-noon and 2-6pm, Sun. 2-6pm; admission DM1). A barefooted statue of St. Christopher points its massive toes to the ornate 16th-century **Astronomical Clock,** which recreates the movements of the planets; 16th-century horoscopes are, sadly, not provided. (*Dom* open Mon.-Sat. 6am-6pm, Sun. 6:30am-7:30pm.) Around the corner from the Domplatz is the **Prinzipalmarkt,** with glamourous window displays and correspondingly unapproachable prices.

The cages on the front face of **St. Lambert's church,** just off the Prinzipalmarkt, make it a place of more prurient than religious interest. In the 16th century, rebel Anabaptists took over town, led by the self-styled Prophet Jan van Leiden. He had 16 wives, and anyone who criticized polygamy or the absolution of private property was killed. After a bloodbath of bishopric reconquest, the three leader's bodies were left to decompose in the cages. The authorities finally cleaned the cages out, but left them hanging as a "reminder." Also suspended at the church is Germany's only free-hanging organ. Next door to the church is the **Friedensaal** (Hall of Peace) which apparently kept at least one prolific wood-carver very, very busy for a very, very long time. The treaty that ended the Thirty Years War was signed here. (Open

Mon.-Fri. 9am-5pm, Sat. 9am-4pm, Sun. 10am-1pm. Admission DM1.50, children DM0.80; call 83 25 80 for group rates.)

MUSEUMS

Other items of historical interest can be found in Münster's many museums. For those still unsated, there remain a **Railway Museum,** a **Carnival Museum,** and a **Museum of Organs** (unrelated to the Leprosy Museum), but all are located far off in the suburbs. Ask for more info at the tourist office.

Landesmuseum für Kunst und Kultur, Domplatz 10 (tel. 59 07 01). Modern sculpture and ancient paintings arranged on 3 floors around a central courtyard-style atrium. Open Tues.-Sun. 10am-6pm. Free.

Mühlenhof-Freilichtmuseum, Sentruperstr. 225 (tel. 820 74), an acres-large hodgepodge of restored buildings from the past 4 centuries. Open daily 9am-5pm; Nov.-March Mon.-Sat. 1:30-4pm, Sun. 11am-4pm. Admission DM4, students DM2.50.

Museum of Leprosy, Kinderhaus 15 (tel. (0251) 21 10), to the northeast of the *Altstadt,* is a little far away, but you should definitely drop by. The exhibits are strictly hands-off. Open Sun. 11am-1pm and 3-5pm. Call for an appointment on other days. Free.

■■■ LOWER RHINE

Composer Richard Wagner saw the grandiose essence of Germany's soul reflected in the legends of the lower Rhineland, but the old towns of the region avoid such operatic thundering. Moreover, their spirit these days is palpably Dutch, following the shore of the river to the Netherlands, northwest of the Ruhr Valley. For years **Xanten** had two dubious distinctions—it is the only German town beginning with "X" and the only one flattened by Canadians in WWII. The town, whose *nom de ville* is a contraction of *Ad Sanctos* (to the saints), is just a hop and a skip from Holland. Xanten's woods figure heavily in Wagner's *Nibelungen* cycle—Siegfried was born here. The medieval castle is equally mythic—so mythic, in fact, that it's no longer standing, but the fringe of ruins is sufficiently operatic to satisfy any Wagnerian pilgrim. Ironically, the recently unearthed **Roman ruins** are better preserved. Some have been pieced back together like a jigsaw puzzle, recreating the imperial outpost Xanten once was, complete with amphitheater. (Archaeological park open daily 9am-6pm. Admission DM3.)

Much to the intial horror of his neighbors, the eccentric owner of a private mansion out past the soccer stadium has set a mammoth red **pistol sculpture** in his front yard, making an unwilling Xanten into a pop-art shrine. On holier artistic grounds the 12th-century **Victoridom** is the architectural pride of the valley, with better altarpieces than your average cathedral. The 16th-century chapel is pure *Altrhein,* a curiosity shop of Gothic statuary—the best specimen is the *Tree of Jesse* rendered in ornate relief. (Open April to mid-Oct. 10am-noon and 2-6pm; Nov.-March 10am-noon and 2-5pm.) Xanten's **tourist office** (tel. (02821) 372 38) directs visitors to hotels from their office in the *Rathaus* on the *Markt.* Head up Bahnhofstr. from the station. (Open mid-March to mid-Oct. 10am-4:30pm, Sat.-Sun. 10am-1pm and 2:30-4pm; mid-Oct. to mid-March daily 11am-2pm.)

The town of **Kleve** is called Cleves in English, as in **Anne of Cleves,** the local princess whom Henry VIII *didn't* make the happiest woman in the world. Henry's third wife had just died (the only one he didn't dump in one way or another), so he sent Hans Holbein out to paint lots of princesses so that he could choose a new one. Holbein stayed at Anne's parents' castle, so his portrait of her was very flattering. Henry picked her out, but when she showed up in England Henry thought she looked like a horse, told her so to her face, and insulted her until she went home. He also banished Holbein from court. The town itself is smack up against the Dutch border; regular buses cross the border to museum-rich Arnhem (see *Let's Go: Europe*). Cleves hugs the hill around the 11th-century **Schwanenburg** (Swan's Castle), the castle romanticized in Wagner's *Lohengrin*, a sort of *Swan Lake* in drag. The long-necked **tower** affords climbers a bird's-eye-view of the valley. (Tower open daily 11am-5pm; Nov.-March Sat.-Sun. 11am-5pm. Admission DM2, children DM1.) Anne's relatives are buried in the **St. Mariae Himmelfahrt** church, but the main ecclesiastical treasures are assembled in **Haus Köekkoek**, on central Kavariner-Str. The museum boasts illuminated manuscripts and Dutch Renaissance statuary. (Open Tues.-Sun. 10am-1pm and 2-5pm. Free.) Cleves is accessible by **rail,** or more conveniently, by **bus** from Xanten. The **tourist office**, in the *Rathaus* on Kavariner-Str. (tel. (02821) 842 54), gives out city maps and gossip about Anne and Henry. They also handle hotel reservations. (Open Mon. and Wed. 8:30am-5pm, Tues. and Thurs. 8:30am-4pm, Fri. 8:30am-1pm.) Perch at the **Jugendherberge Kleve (HI),** St. Annaberg 2 (tel. (02821) 236 71) at the west end of town (from the station, bus #57: Jugendherberge). This is the main hostel option in this corner of the Rhineland—the next stopover is the Arnhem hostel in Holland. (Reception open daily 4:30-8pm. DM17.30. Curfew 10pm.) The **Reichswald nature preserve** is close by the hostel for hiking or just relaxing.

■■■ BONN

"A small town in Germany" was spymaster John Le Carré's codename for Bonn; to Germans, it is better known as the *"Hauptdorf"* (capital village). Founded by the Romans and a historical nonentity for most of its 2000 years, the unassuming Rhenish town of Bonn made it big by chance; Konrad Adenauer, the Federal Republic's first chancellor, already owned a house in the suburbs, so the ever-considerate occupying powers made Bonn the "provisional capital" of the Western Occupation Zone, and then the *Hauptstadt* (capital) of the fledgling Republic. "Chaos in Bonn" read the headlines in the summer of 1991, as Berlin fought for the right to relocate the seat of government in a political catfight that divided every party from the CDU to the Greens. By the narrowest of margins, Berlin won, and the *Bundestag* will pack up and move within a decade or so. Easy come, easy go. The bureaucrats are working in their mysterious ways to keep as many offices here as possible. Berliners joke that Bonn is "half the size of a Chicago cemetery and twice as dead," but with more than its share of museums and a respectable university, Bonn is a worthwhile destination even without the political clout.

PRACTICAL INFORMATION

Tourist Office: Münsterstr. 20 (tel. 77 34 66), tucked in a passageway at the edge of the pedestrian zone. Take the "Stadtmitte" exit from the station, walk 60m up Poststr., turn left at Münsterstr. and left again. The staff will make hotel reservations, but only for the same day, not for advance bookings (DM3-5 fee). Pick up information on the 12 guided tours they offer. Open Mon.-Sat. 8am-9pm, Sun. 9:30am-12:30pm; Oct.-Feb. 8am-7pm, Sun. 9:30am-12:30pm.

Consulates: If there's one thing Bonn's got, it's consulates. The 4-page alphabetical list (at the tourist office) runs from *Ägypten* (Egypt) to *Zypern* (Cyprus). Highlights: **U.S.,** Deichman Ave. 29 (tel. 339 20 53); U-Bahn 16 or 63: Rhineallee, then bus #613: Meisengarten. Open Mon.-Fri. 8:30-11:30am. **Australia,** Godesberger Allee 105 (tel. 810 30); U-Bahn 16 or 63: Max-Löbner. Open Mon.-Fri. 9am-noon. **Canada,** Godesberger Allee 119 (tel. 81 00 60). Open Mon.-Fri. 8am-noon. **New Zealand,** Bundeskanzlerplatz 2-10 (tel. 22 80 70); U-Bahn 16 or 63: Heussallee. Open 9am-1pm. **U.K.** citizens go to the consulate in Düsseldorf.

Post Office: Münsterplatz 17, 53111 Bonn; just walk down Poststr. from the station. Open Mon.-Wed. and Fri. 8am-6pm, Thurs. 8am-8:30pm, Sat. 8am-1pm. For limited services, like changing money in small amounts, open daily 6am-midnight.

Telephones: City Code: 0228.

Flights: International departures from the **Köln-Bonn Flughafen.** Bus #670 shuttles from the *Hauptbahnhof* to the airport 5:40-7:10am and 8:10-9:40pm every ½hr., 7:10am-8:10pm every 20min. DM7.20, children DM3.60.

Public Transportation: Bonn is linked to Cologne and other riverside cities through the massive **VRR** (Verkehrsverbund Rhein-Sieg) S-, U-, and Bundesbahn network. Areas are divided into **Tarifzonen;** the farther you go, the more you pay. Single tickets (DM1.70), 4-ride tickets (DM6.40), and day tickets (DM9) are available at automats and designated vending stations; prices higher for longer distances. Stop by the **Vorverkaufsstelle VRS** under the *Hauptbahnhof* for network maps and more ticket information. With the *Minigruppenkarte* (DM9), 5 people can ride Mon.-Fri. from 9am on, and Sat.-Sun. all day.

Taxi: Funk-Zentrale (tel. 55 55 55) sends out the cars.

Mitfahrzentrale: Herwarthstr. 11 (tel. 194 44), pairs drivers with riders. Open Mon.-Fri. 10am-6:30pm, Sat. 10am-2pm, Sun. 11am-2pm.

Car Rental: Hertz, Avis, interRent Europcar, and **Sixt-Budget** all have offices at the airport.

Bike Rental: Kurscheid, Römerstr. 4 (tel. 63 14 33), charges DM15 per day but has a DM20 per weekend special. Cars rented here as well. ID required as deposit. Open daily 7am-7pm.

Bookstore: The mammoth **Bouvier,** Am Hof 18 (tel. 729 01 64), across from the University *Schloß*, has a wide range of foreign books on the top floor. Concert tickets also sold. Open Mon.-Fri. 9am-6:30pm, Sat. 9am-2pm.

Laundromat: Wasch Center on the corner of Breite-Str. and Kölnstr. Wash DM9, dry DM1 per 6min. Soap included. Open Mon-Sat 7am-11pm.

Women's Agencies: The **Frauenberatungstelle** (tel. 65 95 00), near Wilhlempl. in an alley off of Kölnstr., will answer questions, provide help, and direct women to other appropriate agencies. Open Mon. 5-8pm, Wed.-Fri. 10am-noon. **24hr. Hotline:** tel. 63 53 69.

Emergencies: Police: tel. 110. **Rape Crisis:** tel. 63 55 24.

ACCOMMODATIONS AND CAMPING

National capitals attract transients, and come what may, Bonn has built up a nice stock of hotels to make them welcome; government bigwigs have hefty bankrolls, though, and most hotel prices are more suited to those supported by a large taxpayer base. With two *Jugendgästehäuser* but no *Jugendherberge,* even hosteling is expensive.

Jugendgästehaus Bonn-Venusberg (HI), Haager Weg 42 (tel. 28 12 00, fax 289 97 14), far from the center of town. Bus #621 (direction "Ippendorf Altenheim"): Jugendherberge. Renovations were finished in late 1991; the modern touch makes the place first-rate. Curfew 1am. DM28.50. Sheets and breakfast included. Wheelchair access.

Jugendgästehaus Bonn-Bad Godesburg (HI), Horionstr. 60 (tel. 31 75 16, fax 31 45 37). Closer to town, but by no means close. U-Bahn 16 or 63 (from Bonn's main station): Rheinallee or the DB train: Bonn-Bad Godesberg Bahnhof, then bus #615 (direction "Stadtwald/Evangelische Krankenhaus"): Venner-Str.; look for the sign on the opposite side of the street. Fastidiously neat, with 4 species of herbal tea at breakfast. Curfew 1am. DM28.50. Sheets and breakfast included.

Hotel Deutsches Haus, Kasernenstr. 19-21 (tel. 63 37 77). Same directions as Bergmann. Near Beethovenhalle and Beethovenhaus. The restaurant downstairs is the home base for the Bonner Schubert Choir; if you like looking at pictures of people's grandkids, ask to see the choir mementos. Singles DM55, with shower DM65, with shower and toilet DM75. Doubles DM95, with shower DM90, with shower and toilet DM110. Reception open daily 5am-11:30pm.

Hotel Virneburg, Sandkaule 3a (tel. 63 63 66). U-Bahn 62, 64, or 66: Bertha-von-Suttner-Platz *or* walk up Postr., bear right on Acherstr. at the north end of Münsterpl., turn left on Rathausgasse, and left again on Belderberg, which runs into Sandkaule. Very bare and barely furnished, but cheap and convenient. Singles DM45, with shower DM65. Doubles DM70, with shower DM90.

Hotel Weiland, Breite Str. 98a (tel. 65 28 24, fax 63 49 41). Streetcar #61: Wilhelmplatz, then walk one block down Kölnstr. to Breite Str.; to walk to Wilhelmplatz, head up Poststr. over Münsterplatz, left on Dreieck, right on Kasernenstr.; at the end, left on Kölnstr. Whew. Some spacious rooms have small balconies. Reception open daily 6am-1:30am. Singles with shower and toilet DM95. Doubles with shower and toilet DM130. Breakfast included. Visa, AmEx, MC.

Hotel Mozart, Mozartstr. 1 (tel. 65 90 71, fax 65 90 75). Walk out the south exit of the station, right onto Herwarthstr., left on Bachstr., and right on Mozartstr. Around the corner from Beethovenplatz. Close to the station, but you're more likely to hear the strains of a concert than the screech of a train in this quiet area. Singles DM60-65, with shower DM80-150. Doubles DM95-185. Visa, MC.

With the rise of Christianity, the artistic impulse in medieval Germany focused on religious themes. **Campingplatz Genienaue,** Im Frankenkeller 49 (tel. 34 49 49). U-Bahn 16 or 63: Rheinallee and change for bus #613 (direction "Giselherstr."): Gunterstr. Rhine-side camping in the Mehlem suburb. Open year-round.

FOOD

Münsterplatz hosts several fast-food counters and numerous small cafés as well as an open-air market; Monday through Saturday from 8am to 6pm, fruit, vegetable, and meat vendors are embroiled in Bonn's most torrid negotiations. Come at the end of the day, when voices rise and prices fall. Further from the *Altstadt,* ethnic restaurants retain high quality and low prices.

University Mensa, Nassestr. 11, a 15min. walk from the train station along Kaiserstr. Young Bonners make the best of inexpensive but barely palatable meals (DM2.20-3.40; DM1 extra for non-students), with a ridiculously cheap salad bar upstairs (DM5 per kg). The compound is often open when no meals are being served; hang out, check listings of special events on the walls. Open Mon.-Fri. 8am-4pm, lunch served 11:30am-2pm; late Sept. to mid-July open Mon.-Sat. 8am-8pm, lunch served Mon.-Thurs. 11:30am-2:15pm and 5:30-8pm, Fri. 11:30am-2pm, Sat. noon-1:45pm. For **Mensa Poppelsdorf,** turn right from the Quantiusstr. exit of the main station, go down Colmanstr., over Beethovenplatz to the end of Endericher Allee. Open late Aug. to mid-July.

Cassius Garten, Maximilianstr. 28d, at the edge of the *Altstadt* facing the station, with a back entrance in the round court of the tourist-office complex. The buffet-style realization of a vegetarian's wildest fantasies. Warm and cold, colorful pasta, 50 kinds of salad, 30 teas and juices, and a *vollkorn* bake shop upstairs. Pay by weight (DM2.12 per 100g) and sit down in rainbow-tinted pale wood booths. We love it. Open Mon.-Wed. and Fri. 11am-8pm, Thurs. 11am-9pm, Sat. 11am-3pm.

Rosa Lu, Vorgebirgsstr. 80 (tel. 63 77 30). From Berliner Platz, follow Max-Str. until it becomes Vorgebirgsstr. Real good inexpensive food in a hopping student spot. Open Mon.-Fri. noon-1am, Sat. 6pm-1am, Sun. 10am-1am.

SIGHTS

Bonn's old town center winds into a busy pedestrian zone studded with historic corners. Before there was the *Bundestag,* Bonn had Beethoven. Ludwig wailed his first notes in what is now called **Beethovens Geburtshaus** (Birthplace), Bonngasse 20 (tel. 63 51 88). Ludwig's mom's house in Koblenz is nothing compared to this. Among the silhouettes, busts and portraits, there are various manuscripts, mementos, and musical instruments, as well as the trumpets Beethoven stuck in his ears to improve his hearing. (S-Bahn 62, 64, or 66: Bertha von Suttner Platz, or follow the signs through the pedestrian zone. Open Mon.-Sat. 10am-5pm, Sun. 10am-1pm; Oct.-March Mon.-Sat. 10am-4pm, Sun. 10am-1pm. Last entry 30min. before close. Admission DM5, students DM1.50. Call ahead for English tours.) The symphonic ghost grips Bonn every two or three years for the summer-long **Beethoven Festival.** The first fête, organized by Franz Liszt in 1845 was a regular riot, with Liszt brawling with French nationalist Berlioz and King Ludwig's mistress Lola Montez's unscheduled dancing on the tables. Despite upset plates and scandalized Bonners, the festival was in town to stay. Call the tourist office for information.

From the Beethovenhaus, walk down Bonngasse toward the **Altstadt** and the **Namen-Jesu Kirche.** The essentially Gothic structure houses magnificently Baroque innards, including a swirling marble altar capped by radiating cherubs. Down the street, the 18th-century pink-and-blue pastel **Rathaus** presides over the Marktplatz; in the similarly colorful 1960s, de Gaulle, Kennedy, and Elizabeth II all made the building their photo-op backdrop. Take Remigiusstr. toward the station to find Bonn's center, the open expanse of **Münsterplatz.** The towers of the **Münster** basilica, completed as the Cologne Cathedral was begun, dominate this gathering place. Inside, three stories of arches within arches within arches yield finally to a gold-leaf mosaic; a 12th-century cloister laced with crossways and passages branches off to the side. (*Münster* open daily 7am-7pm. Cloister open daily 9:30am-5:30pm.)

The castles, palaces, and museums (see listings, below) that give the area cultural meaning are just outside the inner city. 40,000 students grace the **Kurfürstliches Schloß,** an 18th-century palace later converted into the central building of Bonn's Friedrichs-Wilhelms Universität. The *Schloß* is gateway to the refreshing **Hofgarten** and **Stadtgarten,** filled with students and punks. To find Bonn's "other" palace, stroll or bike down the Poppelsdorfer Allee promenade to the 18th-century **Poppelsdorfer Schloß.** The eclectic castle has a French façade and an Italian courtyard, backed by the manicured **Botanic Gardens.** The *Schloß* itself is filled with university offices. (Gardens open Mon.-Fri. 9am-6pm, Sun. 9am-1pm; Oct.-April Mon-Fri. 9am-4pm. Greenhouses open Mon.-Fri. 10:30am-noon and 2-4pm; Oct.-March Mon.-Fri. 10:30am-noon and 2-4pm. Free on weekdays, DM1 on Sundays. Oct.-April free.)

From the bank of the Rhine, you can view the **Bundeshaus,** Germany's Parliament, on Görresstr., and several other monuments to national government. Although it may escape the visitor, Bonn is still the seat of government, and the area south of the center along the Rhine is full of federal fun spots. Nasty diplomats have largely taken over the historic **Südstadt** neighborhood (between Poppeldorfer Allee and Reuterstr.). The vaguely Bauhaus **Bundestag** itself. (Bundeshaus, Eingang V; tel. 16 21 52. U-Bahn 16, 63, or 66: Heussallee/Bundeshaus, or bus #610 from the main station: Bundeshaus.) This edifice has earned the coveted title of "Least Prepossessing Parliament Building" in the whole wide world. If raw political power (or a sense of nostalgia) is enough for you, take the tour. (Open Mon.-Fri. 9am-4pm, Sat.-Sun. 10am-4pm; Jan. to mid-March Mon.-Fri. 9am-4pm. Closed holidays. Obligatory tours begin on the hour at Hermann-Ehlers-Str. 29, opposite the Hochhaus; bring your passport.) The architectural mandate to turn a small town into a world-class city has had quirky results. One of the campier examples is the old **Post Ministry** at Zweite Fahrgasse on the river. The Rhine-side face sports the interpretive relief *Tier Symbole der Fünf Kontinente* (Animal Symbols of the Five Continents), with a megalithic eagle (America), bull (Europe), elephant (Africa), kangaroo (Australia), and a big friendly wildcat for Asia. This is what happens when you give people money and tell them to go build a national capital. The **Postwertzeichen** museum inside celebrates the stamps of those nations privileged enough to belong to the world postal union. (Open Wed. 10am-3pm, Sun. 9am-12:30pm.)

As you walk down Adenauerallee, south of the city center, you'll pass the **Villa Hammerschmidt** and **Palais Schaumburg,** home to the German chancellor and president, respectively. One of Germany and Bonn's most prominent figures is ex-Chancellor Konrad Adenauer; his current **Denkmal** (monument), though, is somewhat less than majestic. Nicknamed *"der Alte"* (the old guy), the first post-war chancellor was Bonn's guiding soul; the 10-foot hollow-cheeked bust at Adenauerallee 135-141 looks more like a cross between an allegory of old age and a skull lifted from a pirate flag; see it and believe it. Engraved in his cranium are allegorical figures including various animals, a pair of bound hands, and two French cathedrals.

MUSEUMS

Bonn has enjoyed 44 years of federal funding, and much of the public wealth was channeled into the renovation or creation of the town's museums. Bonn's "museum mile" begins at the **Museum Alexander Koenig** (U-Bahn 16, 63, or 66).

Museum Mile

Kunstmuseum Bonn, Friedrich-Ebert Allee. U-Bahn 16, 63, or 66: Heussallee. One of the most recent cultural children of the state, a superb assembly of Expressionist and contemporary German art transplanted from the old city museum. An especially striking new feature is the stock of electronic media, comprised of experimental videos and performance-art tapes. Open Tues.-Sun. 10am-7pm. Admission DM5, students DM3.

Kunst-und Ausstellungshalle der BRD. U-Bahn 16, 63, or 66: Heussallee gets you to utopia; the 16 landmark columns flanking the *Ausstellungshalle* represent the new *Bundesländer*. Inside, art so new you can smell the glue from the changing exhibits. Open same hours as Kunstmuseum. Admission DM8, students DM4.

Museum Alexander Koenig (tel. 912 22 11), south of the city. U-Bahn 16, 63, or 66: Museum Koenig. The building, which was the site of the first Parliamentary Council meeting in 1948, now houses an amazing assortment of creatures; more models of mounted mammals than you thought possible. Open Tues.-Fri. 9am-5pm, Sat. 9am-12:30pm, Sun. 9:30am-5pm. Admission DM4, students DM2.

Haus der Geschichte (tel. 26 09 90), one block from the Kunstmuseum Bonn. This new, futuristic museum, dedicated to "interactive" German history from after World War II, should be ready to open some eyes in early 1994.

Elsewhere in Bonn

Bundeskanzler-Adenauer-Haus, Konrad Adenauer Str. 8c (tel. (02224) 67 31). S-Bahn 66: Bad Honnef. For Chancellor fans: the notorious country spot itself. Adenauer, then mayor of Cologne, retired here in 1937, driven from office by local Nazis. Exhibits tell the story of Adenauer's personal and political survival. Open Tues.-Sun. 10am-4:30pm. Last entry 4pm.

Rheinisches Landesmuseum Bonn, Colmantstr. 14-16; take the back exit out of the train station. History, the Romans, and local artists from the Middle Ages on. Visiting exhibits are more adventurous. Open Tues. and Thurs. 9am-5pm, Wed. 9am-8pm, Fri. 9am-4pm, Sat.-Sun. 11am-5pm. Admission DM4, students DM2.

Akademisches Kunstmuseum (tel. 73 77 38), on the far side of the Hofgarten. Boasts the largest collection of plaster casts of ancient sculpture in Germany, including the Venus de Milo, the Colossus of Samos, and Läocoon. Hilarious. Open Sun.-Wed. and Fri. 10am-1pm, Thurs. 10am-1pm and 4-6pm. Admission DM0.50, students free.

Frauen Museum, Im Krausfeld 10 (tel. 69 13 44), north of the Altstadt, is the first museum by, for, and about women with regular performances and readings by WOMEN. Open Tues.-Wed. and Fri.-Sat. 2-5pm, Thurs. 2-8pm, Sun. 11am-5pm. Admission DM5, students DM3.

NIGHTLIFE

Sure, Bonn has a nightlife; you just have to look to find it. Of Bonn's several cultural monthly glossies, *Schnüss* is a must for who, what, when, and where; the *Bonner Gästeführer* and *Szene Bonn* are both free but notoriously incomplete. Even though 70% of Bonn's citizens are civil servants, the town is still a lot of fun—thanks largely to the thousands of students, journalists, and foreign visitors who make up the difference. **Brauhaus Bönnsch,** Sterntorbrücke 4, pours its own smooth-tasting 0.2-liter beers (DM2). You can buy the glasses, which are creatively contoured to your hand for easy imbibing, for DM5 apiece. (Open Mon.-Thurs. and Sun. 11am-1am, Fri.-Sat. 11am-3am.) **The Jazz Galerie,** Oxfordstr. 24, is a concert hub almost every night, except for the occasional salsa party break. (Open 9pm-3am, on concert night opens 8pm, concerts start about 9:15pm.)

RHINELAND-PALATINATE (RHEINLAND-PFALZ)

Disheartening as it is to do exactly the most touristy thing, a trip to the Rhineland-Palatinate—to see the castles and wine towns along the Rhine—will not go unrewarded. If you are in love and need more wine to quench your desire, the Mosel River curls from the Rhine gorge to a softer bed of castle-backed hills. Trier is a multi-millenial collage of sights; the medieval towns of Worms and Speyer are demure homes to glorious cathedrals. The Land is parent to one particularly prominent son, Helmut Kohl, the thick-skinned conservative Chancellor of Germany.

■■■ KOBLENZ

At the north end of the Rhine Gorge stands Koblenz, whose strategic location at the confluence of the Rhine and the Mosel has kept it in the limelight since its founding by the Romans. The Europeans were a covetous bunch; Koblenz's beauty has been in Roman, Frankish, French, Prussian, and German possession over the past 2000 years. The pyrotechnics are now more decorative than destructive: Koblenz sparks the annual **Rhein in Flammen** (Rhine in Flames) fireworks festival (2nd weekend in Aug.). Even when brilliant explosives aren't illuminating the castles and bridges over their banks, the Rhine and the Mosel are deservedly popular.

ORIENTATION AND PRACTICAL INFORMATION

Bus line #1 connects the train station to the main docks at the Rheinfahre stop (DM1.60); on foot, it's a 25-minute walk from the station down Markenbildchen Weg, followed by a left along the river. Cruises depart frequently from the docks.

> **Tourist Offices: Main office:** across the street from the train station (tel. 313 04). Provides boat schedules and city maps, with hotel, restaurant, and pub listings. They'll also find you a room for a DM2 fee (using the same list they gave you). Open Mon.-Sat. 8:30am-8:15pm, Sun. 2-7pm; Nov-April Mon.-Fri. 8:30am-1pm and 2-5pm. **Konrad-Adenauer-Ufer:** next to the docks, has more on ferry schedules but won't book accommodations. Open June-Sept. Tues.-Sat. noon-6:25pm. **Rheinland-Pfalz information office:** Lohrstr. 103-105, 3rd floor of the office building. Gather information on the area south of Koblenz. Open Mon.-Fri. 8am-4pm.
>
> **Telephones: City Code:** 0261.
>
> **Post Office: Hauptpostamt,** to your right as you exit the Bahnhof. Open Mon.-Fri. 6am-9pm, Sat. 8am-noon, Sun. 11am-noon. In addition, limited services rendered, Sat. 6-8am and noon-6pm, Sun. 10am-11am and noon-6pm.
>
> **Car Rental: Avis,** Friedrich-Ebert-Ring 50 (tel. 379 10).
>
> **Bike Rental:** see the tourist office pamphlet *Rund ums Rad*. **Radschlag Fahrrad,** run through the PRO-JU organization, is the cheapest and most personable option; their selection ranges from 1-gear cycles (DM6 per day) to mountain bikes (DM15 per day) and tandems (DM30 per day). For a DM15 surcharge, you can drop the bikes off in Bingen or Trier. Open Mon.-Fri. 8:30am-6pm, Sat. 9am-1pm.
>
> **Bookstore: Reuffel,** Lohrstr. 92, has an impressive assortment of English materials including children's books, newspapers, books on tape, and hordes of thriller paperbacks. Open Mon.-Fri. 9:30am-6:30pm, Sat. 9am-2pm.
>
> **Laundromat: Wasch Center,** at the corner of Rizzastr. and Lohrstr. Wash DM6, dry DM1 per 15min. Open Mon-Sat. 6am-midnight.
>
> **Police:** tel. 110.

ACCOMMODATIONS AND CAMPING

Koblenz's youth hostel is blessed by one of the most scenic locations of any hostel in Germany, but cursed by the grueling walk up. Call ahead; other people know

KOBLENZ

about it too, and it will most likely be swamped. Don't expect your walk to elicit sympathy; if the hostel is full, you will be turned away. Some of the hotels nearer the station offer inexpensive rooms, but they go quickly, so call ahead.

Jugendherberge Koblenz (HI) (tel. 737 37, fax 70 27 07), in the castle. Mailing address: Festung Ehrenbreitstein, W-5400 Koblenz. **Getting There: Option 1:** Bus #7, 8, 9, or 10 (from the main station): Charlottenstr. (DM2.40), continue up the river, and turn right onto the "main road" leading to the castle (follow the signs). **Option 2:** Bus #9 or 10: Obertal (DM2.40), and continue down Obertal to the *Sesselbahn* (chair lift), which runs to the top May-Oct. 9am-4:45pm (DM4); by far the least grueling option, if you can spare the cash. **Option 3:** Bus #9: Neudorf/Bergstr. (DM2.40), and hike up Bergstr., the "back road" to the castle. **Option 4:** if you must walk from the train station (your budget must be really tight), walk past the information office onto Markenbilchenweg, turn left onto Mainzer Str., right on Rizzastr., and cross the Pfaffendorfer Brücke; bear left on Bruckenstr. and keep to your left until you find the pedestrian path along the right side of the Rhine, and when the path veers right for the second time, cross under the train tracks to Hofstr., which brings you to Charlottenstr. (see option 1; 1hr.). Reception hours change; call ahead. Curfew 11:30pm, but where are you going to go? DM18.20, over 26 DM22.20. Breakfast buffet included.

Hotel Jan-van-Werth, Van-Werth-Str. 9 (tel. 365 00). This classy family-run establishment is the best value in Koblenz. From the station, walk through Bahnhofsplatz to Emil-Schuller-Str. up to your left; at the end take a left onto Hohenzollernstr. and then walk left (5min.) onto Van-Werth-Str. Reception open 7-10pm, or call ahead. Singles DM30, with shower and toilet DM55. Doubles DM75, with shower and toilet DM110. Breakfast included.

Hotel National, Roonstr. 47 (tel. 141 94). 200m left of the station. Fine rooms have a couch and telephone in the hall. Often full, so call ahead. The trains next door may be a bit loud. Singles DM48-68. Doubles DM85-98. Breakfast included.

Campingplatz Rhein-Mosel, (tel. 80 24 89), across the Mosel from the Deutsches Eck; a ferry makes the journey across the river during the day. Reception open 8am-noon and 2pm-8pm, but you can arrive later if you call. DM5 per person, DM4 per tent. Open April to mid-Oct.

FOOD

Balkan Restaurant, Hohenzollernstr. 116, near the end of Schutzenstr., serves heaping helpings of quality Central and East European cuisine, but you have to listen to the painfully mellow piped-in music. Stick to the tasty *Tagesmenu* (DM8-13) to avoid getting gouged. Open daily noon-3pm and 5:30pm-midnight.

Altes Brauhaus, Braugasse 4 (tel. 150 01). Big, traditional German dishes with many options for under DM10. Home brew between meals. Open Mon.-Sat. 10:30am-11pm. Kitchen open 11:30am-2:30pm and 5:30-11pm.

Café Bistro, in the Rathauspassage pedestrian zone. Redundantly named, but popular. Small dishes up to DM9; come for the atmosphere, not filling portions. Open Mon.-Thurs. 8:30am-10pm, Fri.-Sat. 8:30am-2am.

SIGHTS

The focal point of the city is the **Deutsches Eck** (German Corner), the peninsula at the confluence of the Rhine and Mosel that supposedly saw the birth of the German nation when the Teutonic Order of Knights settled here in 1216. On it stands the tremendous **Mahnmal der Deutschen Einheit** (Monument to German Unity), a massive structure commemorating a rather different sort of union. The stones were erected in 1897 in tribute to Kaiser Wilhelm I for forcibly reconciling the differences within the German empire (though the Kaiser actually played second fiddle to the politically sharp Chancellor Otto von Bismarck). The 14m-high equestrian statue of the Kaiser that once topped the monument was destroyed in 1945, but—in a move that raised questions about German aesthetic sensibilities, not to mention resurgent nationalism—was replaced by a duplicate on September 2, 1993. The base, with its 100-odd steps, augments the Mahnmal's grandeur.

Most of the nearby **Altstadt** was leveled during World War II, but several important buildings have been carefully restored. Koblenz's churches are exceptional in their bursts of vibrant color, from the bold yellow stripes of the **Florinskirche** towers (open daily 11am-5pm; free) to the snaking green vines on the ceiling of the southerly **St.-Josef-Kirche** (open daily 8am-noon and 3-6:15pm; free). The word for the **Herz-Jesu-Kirche,** on the corner of Moselring and Lohrstr., is round—the dome fades into arches and rosette windows duplicated on every conceivable scale. The **Liebfrauenkirche** is in the north end of the city's pedestrian zone; its oval Baroque towers, emerald and sapphire stained glass, deep gray and ruby arches, and intricate ceiling latticework are stunning. The **rose garden** on the Rhine side of the **St.-Kastor-Kirche** is just a minor highlight of this history-filled edifice; in 842, the treaty of Verdun dividing Charlemagne's lands was prepared in this church. The **fountain** in front was erected by Napoleon to commemorate the "certain impending victory" in the Russian campaign. The Russians, after routing the French army, added the mocking inscription "seen and approved." The only reason to see the **Jesuitenkirche,** in the **Rathausplatz,** is the blazing rosette window; walk in and turn around before your eyes adjust to the dark (open daily 6am-12:30pm and 1:30-6pm).

From one of the many boat docks on the Rhine, a ferry (DM1.20) crosses the river to **Festung Ehrenbreitstein,** a fortress that in Prussian days was the largest in Europe. (Ferries run Mon.-Fri. 7am-7pm, Sat. 8am-7pm, Sun. 8:30am-7pm. Boats leave when they're "full.") The 25-minute climb uphill to the battlements is worth it for the view (or the hostel). A chairlift *(Sesselbahn)* also makes the trip; from the dock, cross under the train tracks, turn left on Hofstr. and right on Charlottenstr., then follow the signs onto Obertal. (Chair runs May-Oct. 9am to about 5pm; DM4, round-trip DM7. For more on reaching the castle, see Jugendherberge Koblenz, above.) In the valley below the fortress, just off Hofstr., there's a typically German example of cultural obsession; a museum in the house where **Beethoven's mother** was born, Wambachstr. 204. All but the most ardent Ludwig van aficionados will most likely be disappointed by the few letters on display (open Tues.-Sat. 10am-1pm and 3-5pm, Sun. 10am-1pm; Oct.-April Wed. and Sat. 2-5pm).

Avoid the barricades between Regierungstr. and Konrad-Adenauer-Ufer; rumor has it that the fence-and-barbed-wire fortress encloses the offices of some *Bundeswehr* higher-ups. Anyone who knows for sure isn't about to let the secret out. The **Kurfurstliches Schloß** next door is more showy but less interesting; the curved taupe and crimson wings only flank a medium-sized administrative building. **Theater** information and tickets are available at the *Rathaus* box office (tel. (0261) 129 28 40; open Tues.-Fri. 11am-1pm and 2-4pm, Sat. 11am-1pm).

MUSEUMS

Museum Ludwig im Deutschherrenhaus, Danziger Freiheit 1. Brand new galleries show brand new art gathered by the famous collector, with a special focus on contemporary French artists. Open Wed., Fri., and Sat. noon-7pm, Thurs. noon-9pm, Sun. 11am-6pm; admission DM5, students DM3.

Wehrtechnische Studiensammlung, Meyener-Str. 85-87, across the Balduinbrucke on the opposite side of the Mosel. A collection of military equipment that ranges from Panzer tanks to Kalashnikov assault rifles. Open daily 9:30am-4:30pm. Admission DM2, free for soldiers in uniform.

Rhein Museum, Florinsmarkt 15-17, in the Altes Kaufhaus. An extensive collection of German art and antiques, highlighted by German Baroque master Januarius Zick. Open Tues. and Thurs.-Sun. 10am-4:30pm, Wed. 10am-9pm. Free.

Mittelrheinisches Postmuseum, Friedrich-Ebert-Ring 14-20, in the Oberpostdirektion building (enter through the Friedrichstr. door). Exhibits cover postal scandals and postage stamps. Open through rain, hail, sleet, and snow Mon.-Thurs. 10am-1pm and 2-4:30pm, Sun. noon-5:30pm. Free.

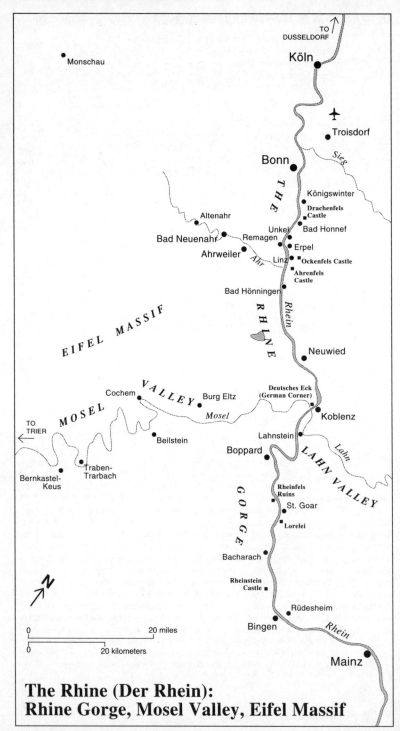

The Rhine (Der Rhein):
Rhine Gorge, Mosel Valley, Eifel Massif

■■■ THE RHINE GORGE

At present, the sun and moon alone cast their light upon these old buildings famed in story and gnawed by time, whose walls are falling stone by stone into the Rhine, and whose history is fast fading into oblivion. O noble tower! O poor, paralyzed giants! A steamboat packed with travelers now spews its smoke in your faces!

—Victor Hugo

Though the Rhine River runs all the way from Switzerland to the North Sea, the Rhine of the imagination exists only in the 80km of the Gorge that stretch north of Mainz to Bonn. As the river rolls to the sea, treacherous whirlpools and craggy banks surround the castles of erstwhile aristocratic clans. This is the Rhine that has figured so profoundly in sailors' nightmares, in poetic songs, and at times in the rhetorical storms of nationalism. From the famed Lorelei Cliffs, sirens once lured passing sailors to their deaths on the sharp rocks below. Heinrich Heine immortalized the spot in his 1823 poem *Die Lorelei*, but he can hardly take sole credit for the literary resonances felt everywhere along this river. The renowned Rhine wines that issue forth from the hillside vineyards have engendered many a lesser illusion. Two different train lines, one on each bank, traverse this fabled stretch; the line on the west bank that runs between Koblenz and Mainz sticks closer to the water and provides superior views. The best way to see the sights is undoubtedly by **boat**. The **Köln-Düsseldorfer (KD) Line** makes the complete Mainz-Koblenz run three times per day during the summer, with more frequent excursions along shorter stretches (fewer trips in the off-season; DM72.60, discounts on round-trip fares, free with Eurailpass). English copies of the schedule are available at local tourist offices or along the docks; for more information, call (0221) 208 83 18 or 208 83 19.

RÜDESHEIM

The shameless little tourist trap of Rüdesheim lies on the Hessian side of the Rhine along the Koblenz-Wiesbaden train line, in the heart of the Rheingau wine-producing region. As many as three million visitors shuttle through this "little town with a great name" (maybe they know something we don't) every year to feast their eyes on about an afternoon's worth of sights. The definitive guide to the town is a free *Welcome to Rüdesheim* newspaper available in several languages at the tourist office (see below). The 12th-century **Brömserburg** fortress, like the rest of Rüdesheim, has succumbed to Bacchanalian excess; it's now **a wine museum** (tel. (06722) 23 48), just five minutes from the train station along Rheinstr. (Open mid-March to mid-Nov. daily 9am-6pm. Admission DM3, students DM2; tour with wine tasting DM6. Call ahead for the tour package.) Servings are available along the nearby **Drosselgasse**, a tiny alley lined with nothing but wine pubs packed with nothing but tourists. The souvenir shops that spring up between every other café hawk items in four currencies. Up Drosselgasse and to the left, you'll find signs for **Siegfrieds Mechanisches Musikkabinett,** Oberstr. 29, the *first* German museum for automatic musical instruments and one of the largest collections of music boxes and player pianos in the world (open mid-March to mid-Nov. 10am-10pm). Next door is the **Kleine Museum Russischer Zaren** (Small Museum of the Russian Tsars), Oberstr. 25, with Peter the Great's perambulator, Rasputin's dinner bell, and other tidbits. (Open daily 10am-6pm; Oct.-April Mon.-Fri. 1-6pm, Sat.-Sun. 10am-6pm. Admission DM4, students DM2.) The **Niederwalddenkmal,** a 38m monument crowned by the unnervingly nationalistic figure of *Germania* wielding a 1400kg sword, looms above the treeline high above the town. Built to commemorate the establishment of the ill-fated Second Reich in 1871, the central frieze features huge winged emblems of war and peace flanking legions of life-sized troops pledging their loyalty to the Kaiser. The bronze piece of allegorical extremism is best reached by a **chairlift** *(Seilbahn)* from the top of Christofelstr., the first right after the tourist office (10min.; DM5, round-trip DM7).

The **tourist office** *(Verkehrsamt),* Rheinstr. 16 (tel. (06722) 29 62), is located right along the river (open Mon.-Fri. 8:30am-12:30pm and 2-6pm, Sat.-Sun. 2-6pm). Rüdesheim's **Jugendherberge (HI),** am Kreuzberg (tel. (06722) 27 11), is in the vineyards high above the town—the view is great, but the 25-minute uphill walk may do you in. From the train station, walk down Rheinstr. and take a left on any street that catches your fancy up to and including Löhrstr.; at Oberstr., turn right and bear left at the fork onto Germaniastr., and follow that to Kuhweg and the "Jugendherberge" signs. You should still be alive when you reach the hostel. (Reception open 5-9pm. Curfew 11:30pm. Members only. DM18, over 26 DM21.50. Breakfast included.) **Campingplatz am Rhein** (tel. (06722) 25 28) has prime riverside real estate for those with portable roofs. From the train station, walk toward and past town hugging the Rhine, and you'll run right into the campsite. (DM5.30 per person, children DM3.50, DM5-8 per tent, DM4.50 per car. Open May-Oct.)

BINGEN

Downstream from Rüdesheim on an island near the village of Bingen, the **Mäuseturm** (Mouse Tower) leans over the Rhine. According to legend, Archbishop Hatto of Mainz was challenged by starving peasants who demanded the food he was hoarding in the midst of a famine, so he locked them up in a barn and set it on fire. Hearing their shrieks of pain, the sadistic Hatto cackled, "Listen to my mice squeaking." Suddenly, a horde of mice rushed out of the barn, chased the class enemy into the tower, and gave the archbishop what he had coming: he was eaten alive. Bingen's **Burg Klopp** (tel. (06721) 149 86) protects the region's past in the Heimatmuseum. **Jugendherberge Bingen-Bingerbrück,** Herterstr. 51 (tel. (06721) 321 63), is an uphill walk (10min.) from the train station, (DM16.50, over 26 DM20.50).

BACHARACH

Some 20km to the north on the opposite shore lies Bacharach, a wine-growing village that's much less touristed and much more hip than Rüdesheim. Bacharach's namesake is Bacchus, the Roman god of wine and revelry, and the town is brimming with **Weinkeller** (wine cellars) and **Weinstuben** (wine pubs) determined to honor the deity's hedonism. The tourist office (below) has a detailed listing of the offerings; pick up a copy or simply head down the street to **Weinstube Jost,** Oberstr. 14 (open Wed.-Sun. 9am-10pm). From the Gothic **Peterskirche** in the center of town, a set of stairs leads up to the **Wernerkapelle,** a red sandstone frame of a chapel that took 140 years to build (1294-1434) and only a few hours to destroy during the War of Palatine Succession in 1689. The **tourist office** in the *Rathaus,* Overstr. 1 (tel. (06743) 12 97), a three-minute walk up to the right from the station, has maps of hiking trails (open Mon.-Fri. 8:30am-12:30pm and 1:30-5pm). A 15-minute walk farther uphill from the *Wernerkapelle* ends at **Jugendherberge Stahleck (HI)** (tel. (06743) 12 66, fax 26 84), a gorgeously old castle that has 30,000 overnight visitors a year and a fabulous view of the Rhine Gorge. The manager rarely turns guests away once they make the ascent. If he has to, he might even put guests on the floor of the dining hall, where moonlight filters through stained-glass windows onto sleeping faces. (Curfew 10pm. DM16.50, over 26 DM20.50.) South of town (10min.) is **Campingplatz Bacharach** (tel. 17 52; DM6 per person, DM5 per tent).

LORELEI CLIFFS AND CASTLES

"Art is a temptation, a seduction, a *Lorelei,*" wrote H.L. Mencken. The mythic past of the Rhine comes to a head under the **Cliffs of the Lorelei.** This section of the river, with its switchbacks, big rocks, and springs was so disastrously navigated that a legend developed of a siren (Lorelei) who distracted sailors with her intoxicating song. It's probably safe now, but look around. How many Germans are on this boat with you? Heinrich Heine's lyric *Lorelei* is so much of a part of German cultural history that, although works by Heine, a converted Jew, were banned under the Third Reich, the poem was still published under the sobriquet "Anonymous." The aspect of the cliffs which most lives up to the romance surrounding them is the view from the top; climb up the marked path which begins in the village of **St. Goarshausen,** below. If you have no pride, you can see the Lorelei saga as a musical revue (May to Oct. Wed.-Sun. at 11:30am, 2, and 4:30pm at the open-air stage in St. Goarshausen; DM22, under 14 DM11; tel. (06771) 28 80).

Under the cliffs in **Oberwesel,** follow the signs up, and then farther up, to the ruins of Burg Schonburg, a phalanx of three castles ringed together by a crumbling set of fortifications. To reach the better-kept **Jugendgästehaus (HI),** Auf dem Schön-burg (tel. (06744) 70 45, fax 74 46), aim for the castle; the youth hostel is next door. It has singles, doubles, and four-bed rooms, and even an indoor pool. (DM21.50-27, over 26 DM25.50-31. Breakfast included. Wheelchair access.)

Past the Lorelei, **Burg Katz** (cat) and **Burg Maus** (mouse) feud across the river from **St. Goar,** home to the area's first bear-and-doll museum and a standard **Jugendherberge (HI),** 10minutes from the train station at Bismarckweg 17 (tel. (06741) 388). (DM 17, over 26 DM21. Breakfast included.)

REMAGEN

After Koblenz, the castles stop appearing around every other corner and the landscape mellows out a bit. Just upstream from the confluence of the Rhine and the Ahr River you pass Remagen. In March, 1945, Nazi engineers were busily demolishing bridges across the Rhine to slow the Allied advance when American troops found the bridge at Remagen intact except for a small crater. Under heavy fire, a company of American troops crossed the bridge—even though it was laden with high explosives—and held off a German counterattack until the crossing could be secured. The event inspired Ken Hechler's popular novel *The Bridge at Remagen,* and the town remains famous even though the bridge collapsed soon after. The restored bridge towers are today a memorial to peace, with exhibits depicting the bridge's history and various dove-like treatises from local celebrities (open March-Nov. daily 10am-5pm; admission DM2, students DM1). To reach the former bridge, walk east (to the right if you're facing the Rhine) all the way down Rheinpromenade. West of both the *Bahnhof* and the ferry landing point is the town center, with a small **Römisches Museum** (Roman Museum), Kirchstr. 9. (Open March-Oct. Wed.-Sun. 3-5pm. Admission DM2, students DM1, under 14 free.) From the museum, walk down Neipengasse away from the Rhine, over Drususplatz and all the way up Bergstr. to find Remagen's beautiful mountainside **Apollinariskirche;** you'll see its distinctive Gothic spires both from the Rhine and from the city center. The **tourist office,** Backstr. 2, is in the *Rathaus* (tel. (02642) 20 10); from the train station, bear left on Bahnhofstr. to Josefstr., turn left on Marktstr., cross the Marktplatz; from the ferry landing, right on Rheinpromenade, left on Ackermannsgasse, and right on Marktstr. (open Mon.-Fri. 8am-12:30pm and 2-4pm). The **Campingplatz Goldene Meile** (tel. (026422) 222 22) is just east of the remnants of the bridge.

NONNENWERTH AND DRACHENFELS

The **Rolandsbogen** castle, now a ruin on the hill, overlooks **Nonnenwerth Island** several kilometers upstream from Remagen. Named for the convent that once stood there *(Nonnen* means nuns), the island now holds a hotel. (Singles DM30. Doubles DM56. Prices drop by DM3 per person after the 3rd night. You must make a reservation; call (02228) 600 90 for information.) According to legend, Roland's wife, believing that her husband had been killed at Roncevalles, took a vow of chastity at the convent. Moments later, Roland miraculously showed up. Crushed, he constructed the Rolandsbogen, so that he could catch occasional glimpses of her.

The last major sight in the Gorge before Bad Godesberg and Bonn is the ruined **Castle Drachenfels.** "The castled crag of Drachenfels frowns o'er the wide and winding Rhine," wrote George Gordon, Lord Byron, in *Childe Harold's Pilgrimage.*

In the *Nibelungenlied*, Siegfried slew a dragon *(Drachen)* here and bathed in its blood, thus making himself invincible.

■■■ MAINZ

Ah, this is a place like a poet's dream!

—Heinrich von Kleist

Ah, von Kleist…a man given over to slight but unmistakable hyperbole. Mainz has grown big and modern as the capital of the Rhineland-Palatinate. ZDF, Channel 2, is centered here and the inter-ad entertainers are called *Mainzelmänchen*. They're very famous (in Germany).

Practical Information The **tourist office,** Bahnhofstr. 15 (tel. (06131) 28 62 10), down the street opposite the train station, has maps and reserves rooms for DM5. Unfortunately, the town has few inexpensive ones (open Mon.-Fri. 9am-6pm, Sat. 9am-1pm). The **telephone city code** is 06131. **Köln-Düsseldorfer ferries** depart from the docks across from the ultramodern façade of the *Rathaus* (see Rhine Gorge listing below for more info on tours). Mainz is the starting point for a cruise up the Rhine, though going downstream from Koblenz makes more environmental and psychological sense. **Gutenberg Buchhandlung,** Große Bleiche 29, has a good selection of English-language books (open Mon.-Fri. 9am-6pm, Sat. 9am-2pm).

Accommodations Mainz's **Jugendgästehaus (HI),** Otto-Brunfels-Schneise 4 (tel. (06131) 853 32), is in the Volkspark in Weisenau (bus #1: Jugendgästehaus or #22: Viktorstift); an efficient, well-run place. (Reception open 5-10pm. Curfew 11:30pm. DM17, over 26 DM20.50. Singles DM39.75, over 26 DM43.25. Doubles DM56.40, over 26 DM63.40.) **Hotel Stadt Coblenz,** Rheinstr. 49 (tel. 22 76 02; bus #13, 17, or 19: Rheingoldhalle), has the cheapest rooms near the city center. (Singles DM60. Doubles DM99, with shower and toilet DM135. Breakfast included.) **Campingplatz Maaraue** (tel. 43 83), lies close to the Theodor-Heuss bridge; cross it and turn right. Or take bus #13 (from the train station) to Brückenkopf-Kastel. (Reception open 7am-1pm and 3-10pm. DM5.50 per person, DM4.50 per tent, DM4 per car. Open April-Sept.)

Food And Entertainment One swell eating option is **União Desportiva Portuguesa de Mainz,** Schießgartenstr. 9A, 2nd fl. From the Landesmuseum on Große Bleiche, go down Schießgartenstr. past Metzgerei Frankenberg and turn left through the gate labeled 9A; stay left of the stairs, then turn right into the apartment building. It's a bizarrely obscure eatery, run by the Portuguese sports club (open Tues.-Sun. 6pm-midnight). **KUZ (Kulturzentrum),** Dagobertstr. 20b (tel. (06131) 28 68 60), rakes together cultural events and hip crowds. (Open for disco Wed. 9pm-3am and Fri. 9pm-4am; Sept.-June also Sat. 9pm-4am.)

In late June, after the city holiday of *Johannistag,* Mainz celebrates *Johannisnacht,* three days of good old-fashioned revelry dedicated to the grand Gutenberg himself. In addition, Mainz has created a huge pre-Lenten celebration for itself, but it is much more commercial and modern than comparable festivities in more traditional towns.

Sights To make the maze of Mainz more maneuverable, streets running parallel to the Rhine have blue nameplates, and streets running perpendicular to the river have red nameplates. Across Liebfrauenplatz stands the colossal 11th-century red sandstone **Martinsdom,** one of the most impressive cathedrals in Germany and the final resting place of the archbishops of Mainz, whose extravagant tombs line the walls (open Mon.-Fri. 9am-6:30pm, Sat. 9am-4pm, Sun. 1-2:45pm and 4-6:30pm; Oct.-

March Mon.-Fri. 9am-5pm, Sat. 9am-4pm, Sun. 1-5pm). The adjacent **Dom Museum** houses a variety of sculpture artifacts dating from the beginning of the Holy Roman Empire (open Mon.-Wed. and Fri. 10am-4pm, Thurs. 10am-8pm, Sat. 10am-2pm; free).

Behind the *Dom*, the *Altstadt* stretches for a few blocks in and around Augustinerstr. On a hill several blocks to the south in the opposite direction from the river is the **Stephanskirche,** notable for the stunning set of stained-glass windows created by the Russian artist-in-exile **Marc Chagall** in the eight years prior to his death in 1984 (open daily 10am-noon and 2-5pm). The **Gutenberg Museum** on Liebfrauenplatz is one of the best museums of its kind in the world. Favorite son Johannes Gutenberg, the father of movable type, is immortalized here along with his most important creations; the museum contains woodcuts, lithographs, a variety of early printing presses, and some of the earliest printed books in the world, including— surprise, surprise—several Gutenberg bibles. (Open Tues.-Sat. 10am-6pm, Sun. 10am-1pm. Movie shown at 11:15am. Free.) Located close to the museum, the **Experimental Print Shop** (tel. (06131) 12 26 86) is also worth a visit. The shop is pedagogically oriented; visitors can try their luck with Gutenberg's craft by setting and printing words and images, lettering, and other materials of their own design. Go get creative (open Mon.-Fri. 10am-5pm).

Along the river near the Theodor-Heuss-Brücke is the **Kurfürstliches Schloß,** former palace of the archbishopric and now home to the **Römisch-Germanisches Museum,** a middle-league collection of Roman-era miscellany (open Tues.-Sun. 10am-6pm; free). A slightly more interesting collection of art and archeology is presented in the **Landesmuseum,** up the street at Große Bleiche 49-51 (open Tues.-Thurs. and Sat.-Sun. 10am-5pm, Fri. 10am-4pm; free).

■■■ WORMS

Once frequented by such Middle Age heavyweights as Charlemagne and Friedrich Barbarossa, not much of historical importance has happened in Worms (VUHRMS) since 1521, when Emperor Charles V summoned the Imperial Diet to the city. This so-called Diet of Worms (not a joke) sent Martin Luther into exile for refusing to renounce his religious beliefs, thereby igniting centuries of Catholic-Protestant enmity in Germany. For the next three centuries, the pious citizens of Worms set themselves to work constructing no fewer than seven churches, all of which lie within a stone's throw of one another in and around the *Altstadt.* Worms is also remembered as the site of the Huns' crushing of the Burgundians in 436 in the battle that inspired the blood-and-guts saga of the *Nibelungenlied.*

Practical Information and Accommodations Across the street from the Dom St. Peter, to the east, is the **tourist office** *(Verkehrsverein),* Neumarkt 14 (tel. (06241) 250 45; open Mon.-Fri. 9am-noon and 2-5pm, Sat. 9am-noon). Guided **walking tours** in German meet at the south portal of the *Dom* (Sat. 10am and Sun. 3pm, 2hrs.; DM2, students DM1). The Worms **telephone code** is 06421. To walk to the **Jugendgästehaus (HI),** Dechaneigasse 1 (tel. 257 80), from the main train station, follow Bahnhofstr. to Andreasstr. and proceed to the south side of the *Dom.* With two-, four -, and six-bed rooms, it is large, rarely full, and convenient. (Strict curfew 11:30pm. DM22.50-29, over 26 DM26.50-33.) **Hotel zum Lortze Eck,** Färbergasse 10 (tel. (06241) 245 61), above an inviting restaurant (meals start at DM12.50), has big rooms with TVs. (Reception open 10am-10pm. Singles DM45. Doubles DM75, with shower DM85.)

Food and Fun The Worms University **Mensa** is currently under construction, but cheap meals are served amid the clatter (open Sept.-July Mon.-Fri. 11:30am-2pm). To reach the university walk down Friedrich Ebertstr. (through an attractive old part of town), across the bridge by the station, and left down Erenburgerstr. On campus, **Taverna** is a groovy *Studenten Kneipe* (bar) with disco on Thurs. night. En route, at Friedrich Ebertstr. 20, is an intimate **Frauen Café** (women's café; open Mon.-Thurs. 3-about 10pm, Lesbian Table Mon. at 8pm). To the right of the train station, the great café **Ohne Gleich,** Kriemhildenstr. 11 (tel. 231 01), looks like the embodiment of a Magritte. This is not a café. (Banana juice DM3.80. Open Mon.-Thurs. 9am-1am, Fri.-Sat. 9am-2am, Sun. 10am-1am). The farmer's produce **Markt** eliminates the middle man on, of course, the Marktplatz (Mon., Thurs., and Sat. mornings). The **Backfischfest** brings the party to Worms for nine days beginning with the last weekend in August.

Sights At the north end of the *Altstadt* is the **Heylshofgarten,** marking the site where Luther appeared before the Diet and stunned its stodgy membership by declaring, "Here I stand, I can do no other" (open 9am-dusk). Inside the garden is the **Kunsthaus Heylshof,** an art museum housing a powerful collection of late Gothic and Renaissance art including Peter Paul Rubens's *Madonna with Child.* (Open Tues.-Sun. 10am-noon and 2-5pm; Oct.-Apr. Tues.-Sat. 2-4pm, Sun. 10am-noon and 2-4pm. Admission DM2, students DM1.) On the edge of the pedestrian zone are **Lutherplatz** where students congregate, and the **Lutherdenkmal** (Luther Memorial), a series of larger-than-life statues erected in 1868 to commemorate Luther's stand before the Diet.

Chief among Worms's architectural treasures is the **Dom St. Peter,** a magnificent Romanesque cathedral with a chilling crypt, perfect for vampire fantasies. According to the *Nibelungenlied,* Siegfried's wife Kriemhilde had a spat with her sister-in-law Brunhilde in the square in front of the cathedral. Then the two of them went on to racier scenes in the Ring cycle saga. (Open daily 8am-5:45pm. Free, but usurious DM50, students DM20 donation requested. Truly.) Worms's other six churches pale in comparison to the majesty of the *Dom;* of them, only the late Gothic **Liebfrauenkirche,** several blocks to the north of the *Altstadt* off Mainzer Str., is particularly noteworthy. The vineyards surrounding the church produce cloying *Liebfraumilch,* best-known in its export variety as "Blue Nun" wine. Across from the *Dom* to the south (and behind the youth hostel) is the tiny **Magnuskirche,** the oldest Protestant church in Germany and the starting point for the Reformation in Worms.

The area around the **Judengasse,** at the north end of the pedestrian zone, stands as witness to the thousand-year legacy of Worms's Jewish community, which thrived during the Middle Ages but was wiped out in the Holocaust. The 900-year old **Heiliger Sand** (Holy Sand), the oldest Jewish cemetery in Europe, is the resting place for rabbis, martyrs, and leaders. The cemetery can be entered through a gate on Andreasring south of the main train station. On the opposite end of the *Altstadt,* just off Judengasse, is the **synagogue** which houses the yeshiva of the famous Talmudic commentator Rabbi Shlomo Ben-Yitzhak, known as Rashi. (Synagogue open daily 10am-noon and 2-5pm, Nov.-Apr. 10am-noon and 2-4pm.) Behind the synagogue is the **Rashi-Haus Museum** with a modest collection tracing the history of Worms's Jewish community. (Open Tues.-Sun. 10am-noon and 2-5pm. Admission DM1, students DM0.50, free 1st Sun. of each month.)

■■■ MANNHEIM

Founded in 1606 as a military outpost at the confluence of the Rhine and Neckar rivers, Mannheim became the capital of the Rhineland Palatinate in 1720, only to have the court pack up and move to Munich 57 years later. The street plan that the Palatinate Electors designed for Mannheim survives to this day as one of the earliest and most creative examples of urban planning. The buildings that the nobility left behind should keep modern-day tourists amused for an afternoon or so, and frequent trains from Frankfurt and Heidelberg make such a jaunt quick and easy.

Orientation The peninsula on which Mannheim sits is partitioned by **Kaiser-ringstraße** (directly in front of the Hauptbahnhof) into two parts. To the west lies the **Innenstadt** (inner city); to the east lies the rest of the city. The *Innenstadt* is divided into a grid of 144 blocks along a central axis, the **Kurpfalzerstraße**, which runs from the center of the Residenzschloß northward to the Kurpfalzerbrücke on the Neckar River. Each block is designated by a letter and a number. Streets to the west of Kurpfalzerstr. are designated by the letters **A** through **K** from south to north; streets to the east are lettered **L** through **U**. The blocks located on the central axis receive the number 1, and the number of the block increases as one moves away from Kurpfalzerstr. The entire grid is bounded by Bismarkstr. to the south, Parkring to the west, Luisenring to the north, and Friedrichsring and Kaiserring to the east. East of Kaiserringstr., streets have regular street names. Maybe the Palatinate electors ran out of letters. Mannheim is only 20 minutes from Heidelberg by frequent trains, and 1½ hours by rail from both Frankfurt and Stuttgart. This Orientation section was brought to you by the letter **T**.

Practical Information The **tourist office,** Kaiserring 10-16 (tel. (0621) 10 10 11), a block and a half directly in front of the main train station, distributes maps and information on accommodations and tickets to upcoming events (open Mon.-Fri. 8am-6pm, Sat. 9am-noon). The **post office** is one block due east of the main train station, easily within sight. **Postlagernde Sendungen** (Poste Restante) can be received here at counters 10 and 11 (open Mon.-Fri. 7am-10pm, Sat. 7am-noon, Sun. 10am-6pm). The **Mitfahrzentrale** is opposite the station at L 14, 11, down Kaiserstr. on the left (tel. (06221) 194 44; open Mon.-Fri. 9am-6pm, Sat. 10am-2pm, Sun. 11am-2pm). **Friedrich Penn GmbH,** Waldhofstr. 20 (tel. 33 13 24), **rents bikes.** (DM10 per day, DM20 Fri.-Mon. morning stretch. Deposit DM100 and ID required. Open Mon.-Fri. 9am-12:30pm and 2:30-6pm, Sat. 9am-1pm.) Free 24-hour bike rental for a DM5 deposit is available at ten stations in the east of town. The main *Tag & Nacht* brochure has a map of the stations.

Accommodations Mannheim's **Jugendherberge (HI)** (tel. (0621) 82 27 18) is a 10-minute walk from the train station; take the underground passage to the back entrance of the station, follow Joseph-Keller-Str. to Rennershofstr., and turn left. The hostel is ahead on the right (150m), just inside the park. A little bit dark, but very friendly. (Reception open 8:30-9:30am, 5-7 pm, and 10-11:30pm. Curfew 11:30pm. Members only. DM16.70; over 26 DM21.70. Breakfast included.) The best value is the spotless and conveniently located **Pension Arabella,** M2, 12 (tel. 230 50), two blocks north of the *Schloß.* (Singles DM40. Doubles DM70. Breakfast DM5.) **Goldene Gans,** Tattersallstr. 19 (tel. 10 52 77), two blocks northwest of the train station, offers pleasant service and clean rooms marred only by the sound of traffic in quarters facing the street. (Reception open Mon.-Sat. 6am-midnight, Sun. 7am-1pm. Singles from DM48. Doubles from DM85.)

Food and Nightlife For students only, the cheapest meal in town is at the government-subsidized **Studentenwerk Mannheim Mensa** (open Mon.-Fri. 11:30am-2pm; DM2.80) and the slightly more expensive adjacent cafeteria (open Mon.-Thurs. 8:30am-4pm, Fri. 8:30am-3:45pm). The Mensa is located behind the *Residenzschloß* in the southwest corner. An old piano, lots of theater posters, and antiques fill up **Harlekin,** Kaiserring 40. It has an extensive menu with meals almost all under DM10. (Open daily 11am-1am. Kitchen open daily 11:30am-2pm and 6-11:30pm. **Rick's Café,** N5, 2, serves simple meals but its specialty is nightlife, with a cover-free **disco**. (Café open Mon.-Thurs. 9am-1am, Fri.-Sat. 9am-2am, Sun. 10am-1am. Disco Tues.-Sat.)

Sights To reach the city's emblematic masterpiece, the **Wasserturm** (water tower) and the surrounding gardens of **Friedrichsplatz,** from the train station, walk

10 minutes north on Kaiserring. Rebuilt in its original form in 1956, the elegant sandstone tower lives up to its billing as "the most beautiful water tower in the world," especially considering the competition. One block south of the manicured foliage and magnificent fountains of Friedrichsplatz is the **Kunsthalle,** an art museum containing a reasonably complete survey of art since the mid-19th century, with an emphasis on the very modern. (Open Tues.-Wed. and Fri.-Sun. 10am-5pm, Thurs. noon-8pm. Admission DM4, students DM2.)

Along with the bizarre street-naming scheme, the Palatinate left behind the giant *Residenzschloß,* the largest palace of the Baroque period, which now houses the **Universität Mannheim.** In the oddly gaudy **Schloßkirche,** the sleek coffer in the crypt holds Karl Phillip's third wife, Violante von Thurn und Taxis. Many scandals here; it's all true. The **Reiß Museum** consists of three separate buildings located around C5, northwest of the *Schloß.* The buildings contain exhibits on archeology and ethnology, the history of art and theater, and natural science respectively. (Open Tues.-Wed. and Fri.-Sun. 10am-5pm, Thurs. 1-8pm. Admission DM4, students DM2, free on Thurs.) Between the museum and the *Schloß* at block A4, the **Jesuit Church**—built as a symbol of the Palatinate court's reconversion to Catholicism—is quite grand. The poet Friedrich Hölderlin called the church "the most splendid building I have encountered during my travels," leaving future generations to decide whether he was exaggerating or just didn't leave home very often.

On the other side of the *Innenstadt,* several blocks to the northeast of the *Wasserturm,* is the 100-acre **Luisenpark,** whose greenhouses, flower gardens, aviary, zoo, water sports, mini-golf, and frequent afternoon concerts purport to offer something for everyone. (Open daily 9am-9pm. Admission DM3.50, students DM3; after 6pm DM1.50, students DM1.) South of Luisenpark and due east of Friedrichsplatz on the Augustanlage lies the **Landesmuseum der Technik und Arbeit** (State Museum of Technology and Work), which allows visitors to pass through "250 years of technical and social change and industrialization in Southwest Germany." (Open Tues. and Thurs.-Sun. 10am-5pm, Wed. 10am-8pm. Admission DM4, students DM2, families DM6.)

■■■ SPEYER

Spared during World War II and well off the beaten path, Speyer is an intriguing anachronism. The town rose to importance during the reign of the Salian emperors, when it served as a principal meeting place for the Imperial Diets. As the emperors' power waned, Speyer declined in significance, although the Supreme Court of the Empire officiated here until the Palatinate War of Succession in 1689, when the entire city was burned to the ground. Today, the steep roofs and detailed façades on the buildings lining **Maximilianstraße** preserve for the town the spacious 18th-century ambiance that many German cities lost forever somewhere around 1944.

Since its construction in the 12th century, the **Kaiserdom** (Imperial Cathedral) has served as a visual symbol of the town. The largest structure of the Romanesque period, the imposing cathedral is noted for its statue-flanked main portals, its high-vaulted ceiling, and the crypt under its east end which keeps hold of the remains of eight Holy Roman Emperors (open daily 9am-7pm except during Sunday services; Nov.-March daily 9am-5pm). Just south of the *Dom* is the **Historisches Museum der Pfalz** (Historical Museum of the Palatinate) whose adjacent **Dommuseum** (tel. (06232) 132 50) harbors what is purported to be the **oldest bottle of wine in the world,** a leftover from some wild Roman blowout in the 3rd century AD. (The museums are connected and open Tues.-Wed. and Thurs.-Sun. 10am-6pm, Wed. 10am-8pm. Due to renovations, parts of the complex will be closed until May 1994, except for special exhibits. Admission DM2, students DM1.) Leaving the museum, a left turn down Große Pfaffengasse followed by a quick right down the Judengasse alley leads to the **Judenbad,** a Jewish ritual bathhouse (*mikwe;* pronounced mikvuh) dating from the 12th century. (Open daily April-Oct. 10am-noon and 2-5pm. Admission DM1.50.)

Returning to the *Dom*, Maximilianstr., Speyer's main thoroughfare, culminates in the medieval **Altpörtel**, a former city gateway that can be scaled for DM1 (open April-Oct. Mon.-Fri. 10am-noon and 2-4pm, Sat.-Sun. 10am-5pm). From the **Altpörtel**, traveling south on Gilgenstr. brings one to the **Church of St. Joseph** and its partner across the street, the **Gedächtniskirche.** Of the two, only the Gothic *Gedächtniskirche*, with its beautiful stained glass windows, is particularly striking—especially if you've reached the "one-too-many-churches" stage of sight-seeing (open Mon.-Sat. 10am-noon and 2-6pm, Sun. 2-6pm). All of these sights can be exhaustively visited in the course of an afternoon.

Speyer is easily reached by rail from Mannheim (30min.) or by bus #7007 from Heidelberg (1½hrs.), which deposits passengers at the steps of the cathedral. The **tourist office,** Maximilianstr. 11 (tel. (06232) 143 92 or 143 95), lies two blocks ahead of the cathedral's main entrance; from the train station, take the city shuttle: Maximilianstr. (open Mon.-Fri. 9am-5pm, Sat. 10am-noon). **Tours** of the city depart in front of the tourist office (April-Sept. Sat.-Sun. 11am; DM7). The **shuttle bus** runs (every 10min.) from one end of the city to the other (1-day ticket DM1).

Speyer's **Jugendherberge (HI),** Geibstr. 5 (tel. (06232) 753 80), would be gravely overcrowded if filled to capacity, but rarely is. The hostel is about 300m southeast of town next to the municipal swimming pool; the city shuttle stops just outside its gate. Single travelers are put in 18- and occasionally six-bed rooms. (Reception open 5-7:30pm and 9:45-10pm. Curfew 10pm. Members only. DM16.50; over 26 DM20.50.) To the south of Maximilianstr., the **Gasthaus zum Deutschen Kaiser** (tel. 756 30), Allerheiligenstr. 37, offers simple rooms. (Singles DM35. Doubles DM65. Breakfast included. Call ahead.)

The small side streets of Korngasse and Große Himmelsgasse, north of Maximilianstr., are home to a number of excellent small restaurants. Cheap sit-down meals are available on the third floor of the **Kaufhof** on Maximilianstr. near the *Altpörtel.* (Full meals DM6-11. Open Fri.-Wed. 8am-6pm, Thurs. 8am-8:30pm. AmEx, Visa.)

The second weekend in July, stretching from Friday to Tuesday, Speyer celebrates its **Bretzelfest** (pretzel festival), which involves all sorts of music, parades, games, and special events. Of course, pretzels baked five times daily at any bakery in this town are going to be fresher than the supply needed to satisfy the hungry celebrants, but hey, it's as good an excuse as any for a party.

■■■ TRIER

At the western end of the German-held stretch of the Mosel Valley lies Trier, the oldest city in Germany. Now just a shade over 2000 years old, Trier was founded by the Romans during the reign of Augustus and reached the height of its prominence in the early 4th century as the capital of the Western Empire and the residence of Constantine. From there, it was a long, slow, 1600-year decline to its current status as a regional economic center and popular tourist destination. The fall was a relatively graceful one; the city retains a variety of Roman ruins in excellent condition and an *Altstadt* that is as attractive and well-preserved as they come. Birthplace and boyhood home of Karl Marx, Trier may eventually be the only city left in united Germany with a "Karl-Marx-Straße."

ORIENTATION AND PRACTICAL INFORMATION

Trier lies on the Mosel River less than 50km from the Luxembourg border. Most of the city's sights lie in and around the compact *Altstadt.* The gate to the *Altstadt* is the *Porta Nigra*, a ten-minute walk down Theodor Heuss Allee or Christophstr. from the train station. Though most everything is within walking distance, the bus system will carry you any old place (get it? old? oldest city in Germany?) for DM2.40.

Tourist Office: Tourist-Information, in the shadow of the Porta Nigra (tel. 97 80 80). **Tours** (DM8) in English May-Oct. daily 2pm (DM8). Open Mon.-Sat. 9am-6pm and Sun. 9am-3:30pm; Nov.-March Mon.-Sat. 9am-6pm and Sun. 9am-1pm.

Post Office: Most convenient is the branch office on Bahnhofplatz, 45492 Trier, right next to the train station. Open Mon.-Fri. 8am-6pm, Sat. 8am-noon. Pick up **Poste Restante** *(Postlagernde Briefe)* at counter 9.

Telephones: at the post office by the train station. Open Mon.-Fri. 6:30am-8pm, Sat. 6:30am-4pm, Sun. 10am-noon. **City code:** 0651.

Trains: Frequent trains to Koblenz (1½hr.) and rosy Luxembourg (10 per day; 35min.; day excursion DM10.90).

Ferries: Personen-Schiffahrt (tel. 263 17), sails the Mosel to Bernkastel-Kues; May-Oct. departure daily 9:15am. Round-trip DM41.

Mitfahzentrale: Mi(e)twohn- und Mitfahrzentrale, Kaiserstr. 24 (tel. 474 47, fax 492 32). Ride- and apartment shares hooked up in one office.

English Bookstore: Akademische Buchhandlung, Fleischstr. 62. Open Mon.-Fri. 9am-6:30pm, Sat. 9am-2pm.

Laundry: Wasch Center, Brückenstr. 19-21, down the street from Karl Marx's house. Wash DM7 according to your abilities, dry DM2 per 20min. according to your needs. Soap included. Open Mon.-Sat. 7am-11pm.

ACCOMMODATIONS AND CAMPING

Jugendgästehaus (HI), An der Jugendherberge 4 (tel. 292 92, fax 240 80). Bus #2 or 8 (direction "Trierweilerweg" or "Pfalzel/Quint"): Moselbrücke and walk 10min. downstream on the path along the top of the river embankment. Or a 30min. walk from the station; take Theodor-Heuss-Allee to the Porta Nigra, right on Paulinstr., the 1st left onto the narrow, poorly-marked Maarstr., and follow it until it ends. All the comforts of home—and they sell beer. Reception open 3-11:30pm. Lockout 9:30am-1pm. Loose midnight curfew. DM24-31.50, over 26 DM28-35.50. Wash DM5. Credit cards accepted. Wheelchair access.

Jugendhotel Kolpinhaus/Hotel Kolpinhaus, Dietrichstr. 42 (tel. 751 31, fax 746 96). Well-located 1 block off the *Hauptmarkt.* The *Jugendhotel* has dorm rooms; the hotel offers doubles and singles. Clean 'n friendly. Reception open 8am-11pm. Key available for late returns. Dorm bed DM22. Singles DM30. Doubles DM60. Breakfast included. Call ahead.

Hotel Handelshof, Lorenz-Kellner-Str. 1 (tel. 739 33). Huge rooms. From Porta Nigra follow Simeonstr., then Fleischstr., then Brückenstr., and just before Karl-Marx-Str. turn left. Singles DM40. Doubles DM80.

Camping: Schloß Monaise, Monaiser Str. (tel. 862 10). On the grounds of an 18th-century castle. DM5 per person, DM6 per car.

FOOD AND DRINK

Kolpinhaus Restaurant, in the Kolpinhaus Hotel. Lunch specials DM5.50-7.50. Open 11:30am-2pm and 5:30-9pm.

Warsberger Hof, Dietrichstr. 42, serves up good meals including vegetarian fare for under DM12. Open Mon.-Sat. 11am-2:30pm and 5-11pm, Sun. 11am-3pm.

Astarix, Karl-Marx-Str. 11, is a relaxed student hangout that serves meals for ridiculously low prices *(tortellini* DM6.90). Open Mon.-Sat. 11am-1am, Sun. 6pm-1am.

La Strada, Fleischstr. 77. Just off the Marktplatz. Excellent food, including pastas for under DM10 and hearty lunch specials for under DM15. Open 10am-11pm.

Zum Domstein, across from the cathedral's main entrance. An excellent place to partake of the joys of wine-tasting *(Weinprobe,* DM6.50-10). Open daily 9am-1am.

Bier Akademie, half a block down from the train station on Christophstr. Over 100 beers, including a Danish one that'll knock your socks off.

SIGHTS AND ENTERTAINMENT

The natural point of departure for any tour of the city is the 2nd-century **Porta Nigra** (Black Gate). Named in honor of the centuries of grime that have turned its sandstone face varying shades of gray, the gate once served as the strongest line of defense against attacks on the city. (Open daily April-Sept. 9am-5:30pm, Oct.-Nov.

and Jan.-March 9am-4:30pm. Admission DM2, students DM1.) Inside the neighboring courtyard is the **Simeonstift,** a former monastery that dates back to the 11th century. On the second floor is the **Städtisches Museum,** a moderately interesting collection of mostly local historical artifacts and artwork (open Tues.-Fri. 9am-5pm, Sat.-Sun. 9am-3pm; admission DM2, students DM1).

Stroll down Simeonstr. to the **Hauptmarkt;** this busy street represents just the northern leg of Trier's remarkably large pedestrian shopping district, lined with a wide variety of attractive old buildings from various architectural epochs. The most interesting of the lot is the colorful Gothic **Dreikönigshaus** (House of the Three Magi). A medieval merchant's home, the dwelling's structure says a great deal about the ambivalent relationship that the original owner must have had with the rest of the town. The front door is located on the second story above street level, accessible only by a ladder that could be pulled up into the house when it was under siege by an angry *lumpenproletariat.* A left turn onto Sternstr. from the produce stands of the *Hauptmarkt* brings you to the 11th-century **Dom,** whose interior design is as impressive as any in Germany. Enclosed in a shrine at the eastern end of the cathedral is what is traditionally claimed to be the **Tunica Christi** (Holy Robe of Christ). Tradition has it that this relic was brought from Jerusalem to Trier around AD 300 by St. Helena, mother of Emperor Constantine. You may have to wait an awfully long time to see the actual robe—it was last shown to the public in 1959. (Cathedral open daily 6am-6pm; Nov.-March 6am-noon and 2-5:30pm. Free.) Also in the *Dom* is the **Schatzkammer** (treasury), which houses a variety of religious artifacts (open Mon.-Sat. 10am-noon and 2-5pm, Sun. 2-5pm; open Mon.-Sat. 10am-noon and 2-4pm, Sun. 2-4pm; admission DM1).

Adjacent to the *Dom* is the gloomy Gothic **Liebfrauenkirche.** From here, Liebfrauenstr. leads to the **Konstantin Basilika,** originally Emperor Constantine's throne room. Lavishly decorated in its 4th-century prime, this massive single-roomed edifice is now about as exciting to look at as an airplane hangar (open Mon.-Sat. 9am-1pm and 2-6pm, Sun. 11am-1pm and 2-6pm; free). Next door is the **Kurfürstiches Palais,** a former residence of the archbishop-electors of Trier that today houses municipal government offices. It overlooks the well-kept **Palastgarten** (palace garden). Along the eastern edge of the garden is the **Landesmuseum,** Ostallee 44, an impressive collection of Roman stonework, sculpture, and mosaics as well as a few other random relics, including a 2700-year-old Egyptian casket complete with its own mummy (museum open Mon. 10am-4pm, Tues.-Fri. 9:30am-4pm, Sat. 9:30am-1pm, Sun. 9am-1pm; free). Nearby at the southeast end of the park are the **Kaiserthermen,** the ruins of the Roman baths where Constantine once washed. From here, it's a five-minute walk uphill along Olewigerstr. to the remains of the 2nd-century **Amphitheater.** Had the Rolling Stones toured in AD 169, this 20,000-seat venue—one of the largest in the Roman Empire—definitely would have been on the itinerary. As it was, the arena was the scene of a variety of bloody, staged battles between beasts of the human and non-human varieties. Jackson Browne fans and other incorrigible Marxists will want to make a pilgrimage to the **Karl-Marx-Haus,** Brückenstr. 10, the birthplace of the great philosopher; unfortunately the museum contains only a dry account of Chuck's life and work. Just remember: recent events in Eastern Europe do *not* contradict the Marxian theory of history, which holds that capitalism's penetration into every corner of the globe is inevitable, and that only *after* this stage of history is reached will the internal contradictions of the machinery of commodification be exposed so that the proletarian revolution can occur (open Tues.-Sat. 10am-6pm, Mon. 1-6pm; admission DM3, students DM2).

Several annual festivals merit a visit to Trier in themselves. **Altstadtfest,** during the fourth weekend in June, has live music and plenty of wine and beer in the streets of the old city. The second weekend in July is home to the **Moselfest,** with fireworks on the water on Saturday night. The first weekend in August sees the arrival of **Weinfest,** with fireworks on Friday.

■■■ MOSEL VALLEY (Moseltal)

An arresting landscape, a comparable number of ancient castles, and a lot fewer tourists make the Mosel Valley as intriguing as the Rhine to the east. The headwaters of the Mosel are located in the Vosges Mountains of France; from there, the river follows a northeasterly course that meanders acrosss over 200km of German territory from Trier on the Luxembourg border to Koblenz, where it spills into the Rhine. The valley's slopes aren't quite as steep as the Rhine's narrow gorge, and the countless vineyards that crowd the gentle hillsides have been producing quality vintages since the Romans first cultivated them around the time of Christ.

The best way to see the valley's splendid scenery is by boat, bus, or bicycle; the train line between Koblenz and Trier strays frequently from the course of the river, passing through a lot of remarkably dull countryside. Although passenger **boats** no longer make the complete Koblenz-Trier run, several companies run daily trips along shorter stretches during the summer; local tourist offices provide details. Some train stations will rent you a sturdy one-speed **bike** for DM12 per day, DM6 per day if you have a train ticket or railpass. You can drop off the bike at another train station at no extra charge and have your baggage sent ahead.

COCHEM

The town of Cochem appears to exist solely to produce wine and coddle tourists. The majestic turrets of the **Reichsburg** castle (tel. 02671) dominate the setting from a lofty perch high on a vineyard-carpeted hill above the town. Originally built in the 11th century, the castle—like much of the Palatinate—was destroyed in 1689 by French troops under Louis XIV. In 1868, it was rebuilt by a wealthy Berlin merchant in a neo-Gothic style. The interior can be seen today as part of a guided tour. (Open mid-March to Oct. daily 9am-5pm. Frequent tours last 40min.; written English translations available. Admission DM4, students DM3.50.) Even if you don't want to shell out for the tour, the view from the castle grounds alone is worth the 15-minute uphill climb along Schloßstr. from the *Marktplatz*. Every Sunday evening at 10:30pm (April-Oct.), the castle is illuminated and the tale of Sleeping Beauty (*Dornröschen*) is retold to the tune of Tchaikovsky's ballet. The performance is best heard from the opposite side of the river.

Most of Cochem's 6,000 inhabitants are apparently dedicated to capitalizing on the tourist trade—hence the high concentration of hotels and souvenir stands. The flower-lined **Promenade** along the river offers some respite from the endless train of beer *Steins* and postcards, and the **Sesselbahn** (chairlift) on Endertstr. will take you up to **Pinnerkreuz** for a tremendous view of the area (lift runs April-Oct. daily 9am-6pm; DM5, round-trip DM7.50). Down the street from the train station, at the foot of the *Moselbrücke* (Mosel Bridge), **Endertplatz** is the site of open-air markets.

Cohem is perched on a bend in the river one-third of the way from Koblenz to Trier and well connected to both by rail. The **tourist office** (tel. (02671) 39 71 or 39 72) is on Endertplatz right next to the bridge; from the train station, go to the river and turn right. The office books rooms for no fee. (Open Mon.-Fri. 9am-1pm and 2-5pm, Sat. 10am-3pm; Nov.-May Mon.-Fri. 9am-1pm and 2-5pm.) Cochem's friendly but unadorned **Jugendherberge (HI),** Klottener-Str. 9 (tel. (02671) 86 33 or 85 68)), is 30 minutes from the station on the opposite shore. Cross the Mosel Bridge and turn left on Bergstr., which turns into Klottener-Str. (Reception open 8-9am and 6-6:30pm. Late arrivals should ring bell. Curfew 10pm. DM17, over 26 DM21.) The most convenient camping to the train station is **Camping Schausten-Reif,** Endertstr. 124 (tel. (02671) 75 28). From the station, take a right to the Mosel Bridge; instead of crossing the bridge, take the road in the opposite direction into the hills. (Reception open 8:30am-midnight. DM7.50 per person. Open Easter-Oct.) On the other side of the river, camp at **Campingplatz am Freizeitzentrum** (tel. (02671) 44 09), on Stadionstr. just below the youth hostel. (Reception open 8am-10pm. DM4.50 per person, DM3.50-7.50 per site. Open April-Oct.) **Weinhaus Gräfin,** Endertstr. 27 (tel.

(02671) 44 53), is reasonable and well-located. (Open Fri.-Wed. Singles DM28, with shower DM45. Doubles DM70, with showers and bathroom DM40.)

The **Mosel-Wein-Woche** begins a week and a half after Pentecostal Monday and features some of the Mosel's finest vintages (0.1L DM1-2). During the last weekend in August, the **Weinfest** takes place, culminating in a dramatic fireworks display on Saturday night. During the wine harvest (Sept. and Oct.), visitors can often find work (from a few days to a few weeks) if they can do the back-breaking labor of a wine harvester. For information contact the tourist office, or **Weingut Winzerhof** (tel. (02671) 72 97) directly to register—in German—at least four weeks in advance.

BEILSTEIN

Ten km upstream from Cochem lies Beilstein, a tiny hamlet whose half-timbered houses and crooked cobblestone streets are more attractive and less touristed than those of their larger neighbor. A private bus line (railpasses not valid) makes several trips a day between Cochem (bus stops at the train station and on Endertplatz) and Beilstein (15min., DM3.60). The passenger boats of **Personenschiffahrt Kolb** (tel. (02673) 15 15) take you there (4 per day, 1hr., round-trip DM15, railpasses not valid). Wine cellars abound in Beilstein; take your pick and settle down with one of the tasty local whites. The broken-down edifices of the ruins of **Burg Metternich,** a casualty of the French troops offer a sweeping view of the valley for kilometers around. (Open April-Oct. daily 8:30am-7pm. Admission DM2, students DM1.) Also worth a look is the Baroque **Karmelitenkirche** and its carved wooden altar.

BURG ELTZ

Deep in the hilly vineyards 35km west of Koblenz stands Burg Eltz, a medieval castle practically undisturbed for eight centuries because of its remote location. From the nearest train station at Moselkern, the castle is a difficult 40-minute walk. No regular buses are available, but **Moselland-Busreisen Knieper,** Endertstr. 30 (tel. (02671) 408 12), in Cochem, runs buses to the castle when enough people express interest (1hr., round-trip DM13, not including castle admission). This castle, in the Eltz family's hands for 30 generations, displays every architectural style from the 11th to the 17th centuries. The original arabesques and religious frescoes still cover the walls of rooms filled with 16th-century furniture; the state room is decorated with a vast Gobelin tapestry. (Open April-Oct. Mon.-Sat. 9am-5:30pm, Sun. 10am-5:30pm. Admission DM6.50, students DM4.50. 45min. tours depart every 15min.)

TRABEN-TRARBACH

The double town of Traben-Trarbach occupies both banks of a bend in the Mosel about halfway between Koblenz and Trier. The town is accessible by train via Bullay on the Koblenz-Trier line, as well as by passenger boats from both directions. Castle Grevenburg, on the south shore above Trarbach, was once of some strategic importance; today, its two surviving walls don't provide nearly as much protection and are billed in their post-mortem incarnation as **Ruine Grevenburg.** The castle ruins are the high point—literally and figuratively—of the city's sights. Among the distinctive, stately half-timbered houses that dot the streets of Trarbach are a few examples of *Jugendstil* architecture, most notably the twin-towered **Brückentor** at the south end of the bridge between the two towns. A map pinpointing the high spots, as well as a free room-finding service, is available at the **tourist office,** Bahnstr. 22 (tel. (06541) 90 11), three blocks from the train station. (Open Mon.-Fri. 8am-noon and 2-5pm, Sat. 10am-noon; Nov.-June closed Sat.) The **Jugendherberge (HI),** am Hirtenpfädchen (tel. (06541) 92 78 or 37 59), is a 15-minute walk from the station; take Bismarckstr. from behind the station to the end, turn left on Laugasse, right on Am Laubloch, and left on Am Hirtenpfad. (Reception open 8am-midnight. Curfew midnight. DM21.50-27, over 26 DM25.50-31. Big breakfast included. Dinner DM8. Wash DM5.) **Gasthaus Germania,** Kirchstr. 101 (tel. 93 98), a few blocks above the station, has top-notch rooms; go up the hill from the train station and turn right onto

MOSEL VALLEY (MOSELTAL)

Kirschstr. (Open Tues.-Sun. Singles DM27.50. Doubles DM55.) **Camp** at Rißbacher-Str. 165 (tel. (06541) 31 11), along the river 2km downstream on the Traben side of the river. From the train station follow Bahnhofstr., which becomes Rißbacherstr. (Reception open 8am-noon and 3-8pm. DM5 per person, DM10 per site.) Traben-Trarbach's annual **Weinfest** pours forth on the second weekend in July.

BERNKASTEL-KUES

Upstream from Traben-Trarbach is another double town, Bernkastel-Kues, whose gorgeous natural environment and picturesque streets make it the gem of the valley. By some freak of nature—or maybe provincial engineering—the road connecting Traben-Trarbach and Bernkastel-Kues stretches some 24km, yet a footpath separating the two towns traipses through several hillside vineyards to the tune of 6km. The path is too steep to navigate carrying a heavy backpack, but otherwise it's an easy and gorgeous hike. Rail service no longer connects Bernkastel-Kues to the outside world; instead, a private **bus** runs from this wonderland to Trier (DM11.40, round-trip DM17.20) and Traben-Trarbach (DM6.90), leaving approximately every two hours. Passenger boats also make the trip (May-Oct. daily; round-trip from Trier DM41, from Traben-Trarbach DM18). The **tourist office,** Am Gestade 5 (tel. (06531) 40 23), in Bernkastel, is across the street from the main bus stop and boat docks and will help find rooms. (Open Mon.-Fri. 8:30am-12:30pm and 1-5pm, Sat. 9:30am-noon and 2-5pm.) The Bernkastel **Marktplatz,** located one block from the bridge, is a 400-year-old half-timbered *tour de force.* Around the corner is the **Spitzhäuschen,** a narrow steep-roofed edifice that leans to one side and looks like it came straight out of a children's cartoon. From here, it's a scenic but grueling 20-minute climb along a vineyard-lined path to the ruins of **Burg Landshut** overlooking the town and valley. A summer home for the archbishops of Trier until it was gutted by fire in 1693, the ruins have since been rudely usurped by an outdoor café. While you may want to pass on the food, the view from the castle walls in incomparable.

Across the river, the town of Kues is relatively unremarkable except for a few stately 19th-century mansions along the river and the **Cusanusstift** next to the bridge. Also known as the **St.-Nikolaus-Hospital,** this home for the aged and destitute was founded in the 15th century by a local humanitarian and contains an elaborately decorated chapel. The number of boarders is kept at a constant 33 in honor of the life expectancy of messianic Nazarene carpenters. Next door at Cusanusstr. 1 is the **Moselweinmuseum,** which pays loving tribute to the tools of the wine-making trade (open daily 10am-5pm; admission DM2, students DM1). Bernkastel's **Jugendherberge,** Jugendherbergestr. 1 (tel. (06531) 23 95), is a scenic but traumatically high up on a hill; on foot, head to the castle and then follow the sign farther uphill. A bus starting at the *Busbahnhof* runs up to the hostel. (Reception open 4-9:45pm. Curfew 10pm. DM17, over 26 DM21. Breakfast included.) Camp at **Campingplatz Kueser Werth,** Am Hafen 2 (tel. (06531) 82 00), on the Kues side of the river; from the bridge, turn left and follow the road along the river (1.5km. Reception open 8am-noon and 3-6pm, DM6 per person, DM5 per tent.) Thousands pour into town for Bernkastel-Kues's **Weinfest,** held the first weekend in September.

BADEN-WÜRTTEMBERG

Two of the most prominent German stereotypes—the brooding romantic inaugurated by the Brothers Grimm and the more modern economic variety exemplified by Mercedes Benz—come to a head in Baden-Württemberg. Pretzels, cuckoo clocks, and cars were all invented here, and the region is as diverse as its products. Existing as three distinct states—Baden, Württemberg-Hohenzollern, and Württemberg-Baden—at the founding of the Federal Republic, the lands now comprising Baden-Württemberg were conglomerated in 1951 in a shotgun wedding engineered by the Allies to forge a conservative counterweight to socialist-leaning North Rhine-Westphalia. Although the merger was legitimated by a referendum, Badeners and Swabians (never Württembergers) stubbornly cling to their distinct identities. Rural custom and tradition are still widely evident in the scenic, foreboding hinterlands of the Black Forest and the Swabian Jura, while the modern capital city of Stuttgart exemplifies the latter-day ascendency of the German industrial machine. The province also hosts the millionaires' resort of Baden-Baden, the vacation getaways of Lake Constance, and the ancient university towns of Freiburg, Tübingen, and Heidelberg.

■■■ HEIDELBERG

Many German cities claim to be rich in tradition, but few have retained that tradition with as much blatant style as Heidelberg. From the crumbling walls of the once-majestic *Schloß* to the historic gabled buildings and cobblestone streets of the *Altstadt,* Heidelberg cries out to be seen. And seen it is, around 32,000 times a day, by the estimated three million tourists who pass through town in any given year. The home of Germany's oldest university (founded in 1386) and a short hike down the road from one of the largest U.S. Army posts in Europe, Heidelberg accommodates all kinds. Alas, this inclusiveness has its price; crowded even in the quietest of seasons, the city is best avoided altogether in late July and August, when the students disappear and a vast human carpet of tourists rolls over the city.

ORIENTATION AND PRACTICAL INFORMATION

Heidelberg is built on both sides of the Neckar River, about 20km east of its convergence with the Rhine. To get to the *Altstadt* from the train station, take almost any bus or streetcar going into the city (from Bismarckplatz, bus #33 (direction "Köpfel"): Bergbahn, or bus #11: Universitätsplatz). The main drag is the heavily touristed **Hauptstraße**, which runs straight down the middle of the *Altstadt,* beginning at **Bismarckplatz**, running through the *Marktplatz* and the Dornmarkt and ending at the **Karlstor**.

> **Tourist Office:** Directly in front of the station (tel. 277 35). Rooms reserved for a DM4 fee plus a 5% down payment. Maps DM1. You may want to call the lodgings yourself, as the tourist office may steer guests toward more expensive places. Open Mon.-Sat. 9am-7pm, Sun. 10am-6pm; Nov.-Dec. Mon.-Sat. 9am-7pm, Sun. 10am-3pm; Jan.-Feb. Mon.-Sat. 9am-7pm.
> **Budget Travel: HS Reisebüros,** am Bismarckplatz (tel. 271 51), next to Woolworth's. Student deals and specials; any student ID will do. Open Mon.-Fri. 9am-12:30pm and 2-6pm, Sat. 9am-noon.
> **American Express:** Friedrich-Ebert Anlage 16 (tel. 290 01). Mail held, but not packages. All banking services. Open Mon.-Fri. 9:30am-5:30pm, Sat. 9am-noon. Banking services closed noon-2pm.
> **Post Office:** Hauptpostamt, Belfortstr., 69115 Heidelberg, diagonally to the right across from the front of the station. Held mail can be picked up at counter 17. Open Mon.-Fri. 7am-6pm, Sat. 7am-noon. Limited services Mon.-Fri. 6-9pm.
> **Telephones:** At the post office, and at the main train station. **City Code:** 06221.

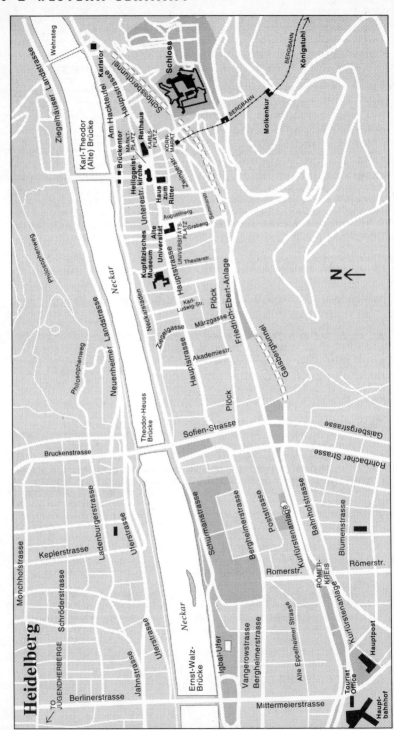

Trains: Frequent trains run from Stuttgart (45min.) and Frankfurt (1hr.); Mannheim is less than 10min. away. Other trains run to towns in the Neckar Valley.

Public Transportation: To get in, out, and around Heidelberg, buy a 24hr. pass good for two people on all streetcars and buses (DM7), available at the HSB Kiosk, halfway across the street that runs by the side entrance to the train station or from any bus or streetcar. Single-ride tickets are a serious DM2.70.

Ferries: Rhein-Neckar-Fahrgastschiffahrt, in front of the Kongresshaus, runs cruises up and down the Neckar. One popular destination is **Neckarsteinach.** (May-Sept. 7 per day, 9:30am-5:30pm, 1¼hr. each way, round-trip DM15.50.) **Rent boats** on the north shore of the Neckar by the Theodor-Heuss Brücke DM7-12 per ½hr., DM12-16 per hr.

Taxi: tel. 30 20 30.

Bike Rental: At the *Expreßgut* counter at the back of the train station. DM12, with railpass DM8. Open April-Sept. Mon.-Fri. 7am-7pm, Sat. 7-11:30am.

Hitchhiking: *Let's Go* does not recommend hitchhiking as a safe method of travel. People have been known to walk to the western end of Bergheimerstr. for all directions. The **Mitfahrzentrale,** Kurfürstenanlage 57 (tel. 246 46 or 194 44), 200m in front of the station, matches drivers and riders in a more orderly fashion. Open Mon.-Fri. 9am-6:30pm, Sat. 10am-2pm, Sun. 11am-2pm.

Bookstore: Bücher Braun, Sofienstr. 3. Selection of English books on second floor. Open Mon.-Fri. 9am-6:30pm, Sat. 9am-2pm.

Women's Resources: Information for women (tel. 213 17); **Women's café** (Frauencafé), Blumenstr. 43 (tel 213 17); **Women's bookstore,** Theaterstr. 16.

Laundromat: Wasch Salon SB, Post Str. 49, next to Kurfürst Hotel. Wash DM7, dry DM1 per 20min. Open Mon.-Sat. 7am-11pm.

Emergencies: tel. 110 for all emergencies, including medical. **Police:** Rohrbacher-str. 11 (tel. 52 00).

ACCOMMODATIONS AND CAMPING

Finding accommodations—even expensive ones—can be a nightmare in Heidelberg. In the summer, save yourself a major headache by arriving early in the day. If Heidelberg fills up, the tourist office's listings in nearby Kirchheim (bus #40, 20min.) may be worth investigating. Heidelberg's tourist office does not always have correct information about whether or not a place is full; check again by phone.

Jugendherberge (HI), Tiergartenstr. 5 (tel. 41 20 66). Bus #33 (from Bismarck-platz or train station, direction "Zoo-Sportzentrum"): Jugendherberge (1st stop after Zoo). After 8pm streetcar #1: Chirurgisches Klinik, then bus #33 as per above. Fairly far from the action. Members only. Reception open 7-9am, 1-3:30pm and 4:30-11pm. Curfew 11:30pm. Lockout 9am-1pm. DM18.20, over 26 DM22.20. Sheets DM5.50. Partial wheelchair access. Reserve ahead if possible.

Jeske Hotel, Mittelbadgasse 2 (tel. 237 33). Bus #33 (from the train station, direction "Köpfel") or #11 (direction "Karlstor"): Bergbahn, then backtrack, but not on the same street. Instead, veer a little to the right, and onto Mittelbadgasse. Absolutely perfect location. The youth hostel has met its match. Helpful management and amazingly low price draw students and others to this quiet, respectable over-nighter in the heart of Heidelberg. 2- to5-bed rooms DM22 per person. To sleep on the floor in one of these rooms with sleeping bag and cushion (included), DM11. Showers DM2. No breakfast, but there's a bakery around the corner. Open Feb. to mid-Nov.; other times call ahead; the owners may be on vacation.

Hotel-Pension Schmitt, Blumenstr. 54 (tel. 272 96). A 10min. walk from the train station and the *Altstadt*. From the station walk down Kurfrsten-Anlage, take a right on Rönerstr. and then a left onto Blumenstr. From Bismarckplatz, walk away from the river on Sofrenstr., turn right onto Kurfürsten Anlage then left onto Römerstr. Large rooms. Singles DM60. Doubles DM110, with shower DM120. Triples DM150. Breakfast included.

Hotel-Pension Elite, Bunsenstr. 15 (tel. 257 33). From Bismarckplatz, follow Rohrbacher Str. away from river, turn right onto Bunsenstr.; it's on the left. Truly sweet rooms. Singles DM75. Doubles DM95, DM15 per extra person. Shower and breakfast included. Reservations by mail and phone.

Pensione Brandstätter, Friedrich-Ebert Anlage 60 (tel. 239 44). Bus #33: Peterskirche. Be more than sure to call way in advance. Doubles DM79. Larger rooms available.

Camping: Haide (tel. (06223) 21 11), between Ziegelhausen and Kleingemünd. Bus #35: Orthopedisches Klinik, and cross the river. DM7 per person, DM6 per tent, DM2 per car. Cabins DM14-16 depending on number of people. If you don't like this side of the river, you can camp on the other at **Camping Heidelberg-Schlierbach** (tel. (06221) 80 25 06) near the Orthopedic Clinic. Bus #35 (direction "Neckargmünd"): Im Grund. DM7 per person, DM6 per tent, DM3 per car.

FOOD AND NIGHTLIFE

Eating out is rarely cheap in Heidelberg. Most of the restaurants in the pedestrian zone are exorbitantly priced. However, just outside the zone are historic student pubs and student restaurants that offer better values. Or try filling a picnic basket at **Handelshof,** 60 Kurfürsten-Anlage, a grocery store 200m in front of the train station on the right (open Mon.-Wed. and Fri. 8am-6:30pm, Thurs. 8am-8:30pm, Sat. 8am-2pm). The true nightlife of Heidelberg basically dies when those innumerable cafés strewn all up and down **Hauptstraße** close around midnight. You can, if you search, find places open later in the little alleyways that scurry off this main drag.

Restaurants

Mensa, in the Marstall, on Marstallstr. perpendicular to the river. State-subsidized cafeteria turns into a café in the afternoon. Cheap food, beer, cheesecake. Best to have a student ID.

Higher Taste, Kornmarkt 9. Owners subscribe to the "Give it an English Name, No Matter How Inane" school of restaurant naming. The food doesn't suffer, though. Vegetarian dishes DM5-8. Open daily 10:45am-6:30pm.

Goldener Hecht, Steingasse 2, Am Brückenker, by the Alte Brücke. A 270-year-old Wagnerian pub. Filling meals DM20, appetizers DM7. Credit cards accepted.

Wirsthaus Zum Spreisel, Neckarstaaden 66, in Hotel Holländischer Hof, next to Goldener Hecht. Individual meals are not cheap (DM15-40) but the portions are so huge and the food so good that it may be a good hunch to split a dish. Open Sun.-Thus. 5pm-midnight, Fri.-Sat. 2pm-midnight.

Bars

Roter Ochsen, Haupstr. 217. A student hangout, family-owned for over a century. Bismarck and Mark Twain dissipated themselves here, and so can you for DM4.50-25. It was conversations in this bar and in other settings that inspired Twain's caustic, more-funny-than-we-can-convey essay, "The Awful German Language." Open Mon.-Sat. 5pm-midnight.

Zum Sepp'l, Hauptstr. 213. Next door to Roter Ochsen with a similarly loud crowd. Meals DM6-20, beer DM4.20. Open daily 11am-midnight.

Max Bar, Marktplatz 5. You'll hear no English here. Big, happy, mostly young German crowd. Sit down with a tall *Hefeweizen* (0.5L DM5) and listen to the warble of voices. Bring cigs if you don't want to feel left out. Open daily 5pm-1:30am.

SIGHTS

19th-century American author Mark Twain's descriptions of Heidelberg are the high point of his travelogue *A Tramp Abroad*; Twain recorded, with rare respect, his impression of the beauty of this university town. The fact that his description is still on target is a testament to both his skill as a writer and Heidelberg's rare, enduring stateliness. The **Heidelberger Schloß** is the jewel in the crown of an already striking city. Its construction began early in the 14th century and stretched out over 400 years; consequently, the styles of its various components vary from Gothic to High Renaissance. Thrice destroyed, first by war (1622 and 1693) and later by nature (lightning struck the tower arsenal in 1764), the castle's regal state of disrepair is best viewed from the *Philosophenweg* high above the northern bank of the Neckar. The castle's broad terraces offer a breathtaking view of the town and valley below, and its spacious gardens are prime. Once a month during the summer, fireworks illuminate the sky around the castle for an occasion known as the *Schloßbelenchtung*. The *Schloß* is easily accessible by foot or by **Bergbahn** (cable car), which runs from the Bergbahn/Rathaus bus stop (bus #11 or 33) to the castle (round-trip DM4.50) and farther up to Königstuhl (every 10min. 9am-6:20pm; DM7; departures from the Kornmarkt parking lot next to the bus stop). The obligatory tour includes a visit to the **Faß,** one of the world's largest wine barrels. Local lore tells of a court jester and guardian of the *Faß* who drank nearly 18 bottles a day and died after "accidentally" drinking a glass of water. (Castle open daily 9am-5pm; Nov.-March daily 9am-4pm. Tours in English and German 9am-4pm. Admission DM5, students, children DM2.50, including a visit to the *Faß.* Just a visit to the *Faß* is DM2 for adults, DM1 for students, children, seniors *Faß* open daily 9am-5pm; Nov.-March daily 10am-4pm.) The **Apothekenmuseum,** also in the castle, features a 17th-century pharmacy and alchemist's laboratory (open daily 10am-5pm; Nov.-March Sat.-Sun. 11am-5pm; admission DM3, students DM1.50).

In town, several sights are clustered near the **Marktplatz,** a cobbled square that holds an open air market (Wed. and Sat.) with food and fruit stands. In the center of the square stands **Hercules' Fountain,** where accused witches and heretics were burned in the 15th century. The two oldest structures in Heidelberg border the *Marktplatz.* The 15th-century **Heiliggeistkirche,** built in the 14th century, is the largest Gothic church in the Palatinate and contains the tomb of Ruprecht I as well as an ancient library. Across from the church's southern face, the ornate façade of the swanky **Hotel zum Ritter** dates back to the 16th century, when it was built by a wealthy Huguenot refugee. Across from the church, the stately **Rathaus** presides over the far end of the square.

From the *Marktplatz,* take Haupstr. west for more Heidelbergian views; five blocks down, the **Universitätsplatz,** centered about a stone-lion fountain, is the former headquarters of the **Alte Universität.** In the aristocratic tradition, students at the university were exempt from prosecution by civil authorities; instead, the various crimes of their misspent youth were tried and punished by the university faculty. Between 1778 and 1914, naughty students were jailed in the **Studentkarzer** (enter via Augustinergasse behind the old university building). Covered with graffiti, the wall tells of a group of honest students who were unjustly imprisoned for returning a loose cobblestone to its rightful owner—through a window. (Open Tues.-Sat. 10am-noon and 2-5pm; Nov.-March Sat. 10am-1pm. Admission DM1.50, students and children DM1.) At Haupstr. 97, the **Kurpfälzisches Museum** is crammed with artifacts such as the jawbone of an unfortunate *homo Heidelbergensis,* or "Heidelberg man" (one of the oldest humans yet unearthed), works of art by Van der Weyden and Dürer, and a spectacular Gothic altarpiece by 15th-century sculptor Tilman Riemenschneider. (Open Tues.-Sun. 10am-5pm, Wed. 10am-9pm. Admission DM4. Students DM2. Children free; Sun. free for all.) Between Hauptstr. and the river is the new **Friedrich-Ebert Gedenkstätte,** Pfaffengasse 18, the birthplace of Germany's first president, Friedrich Ebert. The exhibit details the rise of Ebert from saddle-maker to Social-Democratic agitator to ill-fated-Weimar-Republic President (open Tues.-Wed. and Fri.-Sun. 10am-6pm, Thurs. 10am-8pm; free).

No trip to Heidelberg would be complete without a visit to the northern bank of the Neckar, opposite the *Altstadt.* Walk across the elegant **Karl-Theodor-Brücke;** on the south side of the bridge stands a statue of the Prince-Elector himself, which he commissioned as a symbol of his modesty. From the far end of the bridge clamber up the **Schlangenweg,** a tortuously steep stone stairway, to the **Philosophenweg.** The climb is worthwhile: the Philosophenweg provides an excellent view of Heidelberg by day and by night. Georg Hegel, Max Weber, and Karl Jaspers—among other intellectual luminaries—indulged in afternoon dialectical promenades along this path.

Atop the **Heiligenberg,** the mountain traversed by the Philosophenweg, lie ruins of the 9th-century **St. Michael Basilika,** the 13th-century **St. Stephen Kloster,** and an **amphitheater** built under Hitler in 1934 on the site of an ancient Celtic gathering place. Ascending this mountain is most easily begun near the **Tiefburg,** a moated castle in neighboring Handschuhsheim, reached by taking streetcar 1 or 3.

Heidelberg's **Faschings Parade** struts through the city on Shrove Tuesday, the day before Ash Wednesday. The two-week **Spring Festival** begins at the end of May. A wine festival is held in mid-September, and the **Christmas market** runs from late November to December 22.

■■■ NECKAR VALLEY (Neckartal)

A scenic range of narrow, thickly wooded ridges springs up around the Neckar River as it meanders along its path from Heilbronn to Heidelberg. This is the Neckar Valley *(Neckartal)*, much of which has been incorporated into the German Castle Road *(Burgenstraße)* that travels all the way to Nuremburg in the heart of Bavaria. Not surprisingly, the hills surrounding the river are peppered with castles built during the Middle Ages to protect merchant vessels from pirates. Still largely unspoiled by tourism, the valley makes an excellent daytrip from Heidelberg, and its charms can be absorbed by land or water. Two different train lines connect Heidelberg and Heilbronn regularly, stopping frequently in the many smaller towns along both sides of the valley. The **Rhein-Neckar Fahrgastschiffahrt** runs boat tours from June through early September between Heidelberg (departing from in front of the *Stadthalle)* and Neckarsteinach (daily, round-trip DM15.50) and between Heidelberg and Hirschhorn (Sun. DM21.50 round-trip; Tues. and Thurs. via Eberbach, round-trip DM26.50). For information and departure times, call (06221) 201 81.

NECKARSTEINACH

At the north end of the valley, 14km upstream from Heidelberg is Neckarsteinach, whose four medieval **castles** lie within 3km of one another along the north bank of the river. All built by the same ruling clan during the 12th and 13th centuries, the two westernmost castles today stand in ruins, while the two to the east are privately occupied. Tourists may visit all but the first castle on the path. The castles can be reached on foot—a journey of anywhere between 30 minutes and a few hours, depending on how many of the four you want to see—via the **Schloßweg** (castle path). From the train station, turn right on Bahnhofstr. until you reach Hauptstr., then turn left and follow the bend in the road to the Pizzeria Castello; the *Schloßweg* begins at the brick path leading upward to the right (open March-Oct. Mon.-Sat. 9am-8pm). Neckarsteinach's **tourist office** *(Verkehrsamt)*, Hauptstr. 7 (tel. (06229) 920 00), inside the *Rathaus,* is one block down from the Bahnhofstr. in the same direction as the *Schloßweg.* The tourist office has a list of hotels, *pensionen,* and private homes offering inexpensive rooms (open Mon.-Wed. and Fri. 8am-noon, Thurs. 8am-noon and 4:30-5:30pm). A **fireworks display** illuminates the castles on the last Saturday night in July.

HIRSCHHORN AND BURG GUTENBURG

Just south of Neckarsteinach is Hirschhorn am Neckar, ruled for centuries by the Knights of Hirschhorn from their hilltop castle until an enterprising young capitalist bought them out and turned the whole place into a pricey hotel/restaurant complex. Nevertheless, the surrounding countryside is good for hiking, and the former **castle of the knights of Hirschhorn** is still worth a look in spite of its defeat at the hands of market forces. To reach it (15min. hike), follow the grey brick of Schloßstr. upward from the Bürgerhaus intersection. The castle's terraces offer a fine view of the city and its environs; an even better one is available from the top of the castle tower for a mere 20 *pfennig*. Stone stairs wind from the castle down into the *Alts-*

tadt; along the way, they pass the 15th-century **Karmeliter Klosterkirche,** a Gothic church whose venerable interior will inspire awe in even the most devout atheists. A variety of interesting craft shops in the *Altstadt* below make for good shopping and browsing.

Detailed maps of the local trails are available at the **tourist office,** Alleeweg 2 (tel. (06272) 17 42; open Mon.-Fri. 8am-noon and 2-5pm; April-Oct. Sat. 9am-noon). To reach it from the train station, turn left on Neckarsteinacherstr. and follow it to the intersection in front of Bürgerhaus hotel. The tourist office is across the street to the right, inside the **Haus des Gastes,** which also houses an art and natural history museum. (Office open Mon.-Fri. 8am-noon and 2-5pm, Sat. 8am-noon; Sept. to mid-April Mon.-Fri. 8am-noon and 2-5pm. They also book rooms for no fee. Haus des Gastes museum open Tues. and Thurs.-Sat. 2-4pm, Sun. 10am-noon and 2-4pm; free.) **Rent bikes** at Readel, Hainbronnerstr. 6 (tel. (06272) 20 18 or 20 17; DM10 per day). For overnight accommodations, check the hotels and *Pensionen* along Hauptstr. **Zur Burg Hirschhorn,** Hauptstr. 10 (tel. (06272) 26 60), is right across from the Bürgerhaus and offers bed and breakfast. (Reception open until 9pm. Singles DM32. Doubles DM64.) Camping is possible between April and October at **Odenwald Camping** (tel. (06272) 809 or 25 80), 1km outside of town in the direction of the castle; follow the signs from the tourist office (DM6 per person).

Thirty km south of Hirschhorn along the German Castle Road *(Burgenstraße)* is **Burg Guttenberg,** one of the few castles on the Neckar in constant use since the Middle Ages. Miraculously untouched by the various and sundry sackings, sieges, bombings, and general plunder that laid waste to most of its peers along the Castle Road, Guttenberg today is home to both a museum detailing its long history and a unique aviary of birds of prey that features exhibitions of **eagles** and **vultures** in free flight. (Museum open March-Oct. daily 10am-5pm; admission DM6 for aviary and bird show, DM9 for castle and aviary. Bird performances daily 11am and 3pm.) To reach Castle Guttenberg by rail, get off at Gundelsheim. The castle is on the opposite side of the river approximately 2km from the bridge; follow the winding bus path (10-15min.) up the hill.

BAD WIMPFEN

Just downriver from Heilbronn along an alternative train route between Heidelberg and Heilbronn is the little village of Bad Wimpfen, one of the best-kept secrets in Southwest Germany. Set against the ruins of a Roman imperial castle on a ridge high above the Neckar, Bad Wimpfen is a living fairy tale where cobbled streets and rough-worked half-timbered houses are the rule rather than the exception.

From the station, the *Altstadt* is a 10-minute walk to the right, laid out along the southern side of the old castle walls. Several easily accessible points on the ancient battlements offer incredible views of the valley and surrounding countryside. Along the castle ruins between the *Marktplatz* and the train station are the **Blauer Turm** and the **Steinhaus.** The former, a watchtower that dates back to medieval times, offers a commanding view of the town and its environs to those willing to climb its 169 steps. Next door, the sandstone Steinhaus is home to a museum of artifacts left behind by the Romans. (Both open Tues.-Sun. 10am-noon and 2-4:30pm; Nov.-April Mon.-Fri. 10am-noon. Admission DM2, students DM1.) The miniature **Puppenmuseum** (puppet museum) is across from the evangelical church (open Wed., Sat., and Sun.).

The **tourist office,** Hauptstr. 45 (tel. (07063) 531 51), can be reached from the Marktplatz. Take Salzgane down the hill, then spin a sharp left onto Hauptstr. and it is be on the right about 200m down the street. They do not book rooms (open Mon.-Fri. 9am-noon and 2-5pm, Sat.-Sun. 10am-noon and 2-4pm). Two doors down from the Steinhaus is Bad Wimpfen's less-than-bright **Jugendherberge (HI),** Im Burgviertel 21 (tel. (07063) 70 69), housed in a pair of half-timbered houses directly in front of the castle ruins. Call ahead—like the rest of Bad Wimpfen, the youth hostel is very popular with German tourists in the know, and space is always scarce.

(Reception open at 5:30pm or by arrangement. Curfew 10pm or by arrangement. DM17.70, over 26 DM22.70. Lunch or dinner DM8. Family rooms available. Breakfast included.) **Hotel Garni Neckarblick,** Erich-Salier-Str. 48 (tel. (07063) 70 02, fax 85 48), offers handsome accommodations at affordable rates. To reach it from the *Marktplatz,* follow Mathildenbadstr. out of the pedestrian zone to the street, hang a right, and proceed for 10 minutes along Erich-Salier-Str. as it curves around the hillside (past the park). The hotel is on the right. (Singles DM40, with shower and TV DM61. Doubles DM73, with shower and TV DM102. Triples with TV DM108. Call ahead or fax reservations.)

■■■ HEILBRONN

Halfway between Heidelberg and Stuttgart, where the narrow valley of the Neckar broadens into gently sloping vineyards, and castles stop appearing around every bend in the river, lies the little city of Heilbronn. To be honest, this is a pretty unexciting place unless you're around for one of the town's many festivals; it's well worth a visit during the **Heilbronner Herbst** wine festival. Heilbronn is officially known as the *Weinstadt* (wine city), a fact that the city's residents dutifully remind themselves of each fall with the Herbst fest. For nine days each year in mid-September (Sept. 8-16 in 1994), the *Marktplatz* becomes a *Weindorf* (wine village) where as many as 200 vintages are quaffed by the glass (DM1) or by the liter (DM9) to the wheezing accompaniment of accordions. The **Neckarfest** or the **Stadtfest** (in June of alternate years), and the **Pferdemarkt** (February), are other reasons to visit, but otherwise you won't want to do much more than spend the night here. Most of Heilbronn's historic sites were permanently destroyed during World War II; the few that do remain lie within a block or two of one another in the area surrounding the Marktplatz.

The **tourist office** (tel. (07131) 56 22 70) is located in the corner of the square to the right of the *Rathaus* (open Mon.-Fri. 9am-5:30pm, Sat. 9am-12:30pm). From the left side of the train station, follow Bahnhofstr. (which turns into Kaiserstr. once you cross the river) straight ahead 500m across the bridge to the Marktplatz. A **bus ticket** in Heilbronn costs DM2, but you can buy a day pass (*Tageskarte*) for a mere DM3. Heilbronn's **Jugendherberge,** Schirrmannstr. 9 (tel. (07131) 729 61), lies east of town. Take bus #1 (direction "Trappensee") to Trappensee, continue uphill 200m and take a left where you see the sign. (Lockout 9-11am. Severe 9:45pm curfew, but you can leave a 50DM deposit and land yourself a key. Members only. DM17.70, over 26 DM22.70. Sheets DM5.50. Laundry DM8 per load. Breakfast included.) For inexpensive Italian food, check out **La Spaghetteria,** 90 Weinsbergerstr. Good-sized bowls of spaghetti go for DM6 (open daily 11am-2pm and 6pm-midnight).

Round-trip **river cruises** down the Neckar to Bad Wimpfen and Gundelsheim depart twice per day from just below the bridge near the *Marktplatz.* For information, call (07131) 854 30. Trains depart for Stuttgart and Heidelberg every hour (May-Oct. DM13-25).

■■■ SCHWÄBISCH HALL

Schwäbisch Hall's steep *Altstadt* threatens to slide off the side of the Galgenberg and into the Kocher River below. A former capital of the region's salt trade, the town takes its name from the archaic word for salt, *Hall.* Back when the salt business was booming, Schwäbisch Hall was a pretty lively place, but once the industry lost its flavor (so to speak), the city fell promptly off the fast track. Virtually ignored during the various and sundry wars that ensued over the next few centuries, Schwäbisch Hall today boasts a remarkably well-preserved *Altstadt* that may be one of the prettiest in Germany.

Practical Information Schwäbisch Hall's **tourist office** (*Tourist-Informa-tion*), Am Markt 9 (tel. (0791) 75 12 46), next to St. Michael's, has free maps and finds rooms for no fee (open Mon.-Fri. 9am-5pm, Sat. 9am-noon; Nov.-March Mon.-Fri. 9am-5pm). The **post office** is behind the *Rathaus* at Hafenmarkt 2. (Open Mon.-Fri. 8:30am-noon and 2:30-5:30pm, Sat 8:30am-noon.) The town's **telephone code** is 0791. The **Mitfahrzentrale** is at Bahnhofstr. 13 (tel. 848 40; open Mon.-Fri. 8am-5pm, Sat. 10am-1pm). To rent a **bike**, which may not be useful in this very steep city, try **Zweirad-Zügel**, Johanniterstr. 5 (tel. 890 66; DM10 per day and up). Schwäbisch Hall has two **train** stations. The larger and more important is in **Schwäbisch Hall-Hessental**, which lies on the main rail line to Stuttgart. Frequent buses (DM2.50) connect Hessental to Schwäbisch Hall proper. Schwäbisch Hall lies directly on the train route between Stuttgart and Nuremburg.

Accommodations and Food Schwäbisch Hall's **Jugendherberge (HI)**, Lan-genfelderstr. 5 (tel. 410 50), is past the Marktplatz on the Galgenberg (Galgenberg means "Gallows Mountain"). Follow Crailsheimer-Str. up and take a left onto Lan-genfelderstr. Clean rooms and cleaner bathrooms. (Reception at desk 5-7pm, after that in kitchen until curfew at 10pm. DM18, over 26 DM22.50. Sheets DM5.50. Breakfast included.) **Gästehaus "Sölch,"** Hauffstr. 14 (tel. 118 07), has neat rooms, a cheap restaurant downstairs (entrées DM6-12) and a fully-stocked bakery; quite an attractive place to stay. From the *Bahnhof,* take a right and walk away until you come to an intersection. Take the railed walkway up over the hill to a tiled plateau and then take a left up stairs up the hill. At the top of the hill turn right, take an immediate left onto the street, then turn right onto Hauffstr. (Singles DM35, with shower DM59. Doubles DM65, with shower DM95.) **Gasthof Dreikönig,** Neuestr. 25 (tel. 74 73), offers large, simply furnished rooms with eerie yet appealing creaky floors. (Singles DM39. Doubles DM78, with shower DM88.) There is a **Camping-platz** (tel. 29 84) at Steinbacher See. (DM7 per person, under 18 DM5; DM9 per tent. Open April to mid-Oct.) **Metzgerei Hespelt,** on the corner of Spitalbach and Rosmaringasse, churns out cheap stand-up meals (DM8; open Mon.-Fri. 8:30am-4pm, Sat. 8am-12:30pm).

Sights To reach the marvelously preserved *Altstadt* from the train station, cross Bahnhofstr. and go down the stone steps and footpath toward the river. Turn left on Mauerstr. and cross the wooden footbridges that connect the islands in the Kocher. Follow the winding cobblestone streets to the **Marktplatz,** using the church tower for direction. During summer evenings, the *Marktplatz* is used as an amphitheater for the staging of the renowned **Freilichtspiele** (see below). The restrained Baroque *Rathaus,* restored to its original form after being destroyed in 1944, faces the Romanesque **Kirche St. Michael,** which perches precariously atop a wide, steep set of **stone steps.** The high altar is a Dutch-influenced series of painted panels. Behind the altar one of the paving stones has been removed to reveal a medieval ossuary (a depository for bones). The view from the **tower** reveals a sea of red-tiled roofs slop-ing down into the Kocher Valley. (Open Tues.-Sun. 9am-noon and 2-5pm, Mon. 2-5pm; mid-Nov. to April Tues.-Sun. 11am-noon and 2-3pm. Church admission free. Tower admission DM1.)

A Gothic spirelet tops the early 16th-century square **fountain** standing to one side of the market square. A number of 15th- and 16th-century *Fachwerk* edifices reside on narrow Obere Herrngasse, which leads off the *Marktplatz,* and along Untere Herrngasse, connected by stone steps. The old **Keckenburg** harbors the eight-story Romanesque **Keckenturm** and the **Hällisch-Fränkisches Museum,** on Keckenhof, one street lower. The museum takes home many transient exhibits, as well as some permanent displays like its noteworthy collection of medieval sculpture. (Open Tues. and Thurs.-Sun. 10am-5pm, Wed. 10am-8pm. Tours in German Sun. 11am and Wed. 6:30pm. Free.) The best spot from which to appreciate Schwäbisch Hall as a whole is the **Henkersbrücke** (Hangman's Bridge—do you sense a trend here?), down Neuestr. from the *Marktplatz.* A few blocks farther into the lower city is the **Henkersturm** (Hangman's Tower), disappointingly ungrisly in appearance.

Entertainment On summer evenings from mid-June to mid-August the **Freilichtspiele,** a series of old and modern plays that run the gamut from Shakespeare to Brecht, are performed on the steps of Kirche St. Michael. For schedules and tickets (DM20-42, student discounts available), contact Freilichtspiele Schwäbisch Hall, Am Markt 8 (tel. 75 13 11). On Pentecost (Whit Sunday, the 7th Sun. after Easter, May 22-23 in 1994) and the following Monday Schwäbisch Hall celebrates the **Brunnenfest** (fountain festival), in which locals get decked out in 16th-century salt-boilers' costumes and dance a traditional jig.

■■■ SWABIAN JURA
(Schwäbische Alb)

The limestone plateaus, sharp ridges, and pine-forested valleys stretching from Tübingen in the north to Lake Constance in the south are collectively known as the Swabian Jura, a region often understood as an ugly cousin to the adjacent Black Forest. But the outline is colored by the brush of the exotic, and by a bit of the uncanny. Its rough-hewn landscape is scenic yet stubborn, with a harsh climate that often vents its wrath on travelers. The powerful medieval dynasties that held the area in their sway found the Swabian peaks perfect sites for fortification, as they command panoramic views of the surrounding valleys. Families like the Hohenstaufens spangled the region with castles and abbeys. The **Swabian Jura Road** *(Schwäbische Albstraße)* bisects the plateau, intersecting the Romantic Road at Nördlingen. A web of trails serves hikers well; maps are available at regional tourist offices in most major towns. Towns exude a tranquil aura that is ideal for rest and rejuvenation; nightlife, as in any rural area, doesn't have much of a place in the Jura. Train service to many points—in contrast to the norm for most of Germany—is roundabout and often incomplete. More frequent bus routes pick up the slack.

SCHWÄBISCH GMÜND

Baroque **Schwäbisch Gmünd,** located on the northern cusp of the range, provides the best base for excursions into the region. The town itself has been a center for metalworking—particularly silversmithing—since the 18th century. Beautifully wrought jewelry and ornaments can be found in many of the shops in the town center. The blossoming of this industry in the 18th century resulted in a building boom that left the town with a market square surrounded by Baroque plaster façades and *Fachwerk* buildings. One reason for all of the Americans: there is a military base in the town's Mutlangen suburb. It was here that protests erupted in the early 80s over the stationing of U.S. Pershing missiles in Germany, protests which drew the likes of writer and conscience of Germany Günter Grass to Schwäbisch Gmünd. However, most GI's have left since the fall of eastern Germany, leaving the calm, aesthetically stunning, and almost ancient town behind them.

The 14th-century **Heiligkreuzmünster** (Holy Cross Cathedral), on Münsterplatz, is an architectural freak in that it has no towers—the roof was too weak to support one. The Gothic interior is filled with statues, most dating from the 15th and 16th centuries. Most visitors to the **Silberwaren- und Bijonteriemuseum,** right across from the tourist office (see below), grow quiet as they watch the museum's craftworkers tool silver in the traditional style. Exhibits cover the history of the silver trade, silver age, and silver arts. (Open Wed.-Sat. 2-5pm, Sun. 10am-noon and 2-5pm. Admission DM5, students DM2.) The 16th-century **Kornhaus,** an old grain storage building right off the square and one block behind the *Rathaus,* now houses the **tourist office** (tel. (07171) 60 34 15; open Mon.-Fri. 9am-5:30pm, Sat. 9am-noon). The **post office** is across from the train station (open Mon.-Fri. 8:30am-noon, 2:30-6pm, Sat. 8:30am-noon).

Schwäbisch Gmünd's **Jugendherberge (HI),** Taubentalstr. 46-41 (tel. (07171) 22 60), is located on the edge of a forested region crisscrossed by footpaths, only 10 minutes from the train station. Turn left and pass underneath the railroad tracks. Follow the road and then veer right onto Taubentalstr. and keep on truckin' for quite a while. Way at the end of the street before you reach the recreational park parking lot, turn right up the hill toward that big yellow building in the sky with the letters DJH on it. The air is fresh, and the jogging is great if you don't mind hills. (Reception open 5-8pm. Curfew 10pm. DM17.70, over 26 DM22.70. Sheets DM5.50. Breakfast included.) **Gasthof Weißer Ochsen,** Parlerstr. 47 (tel. (07171) 28 12), has discreet singles (DM27) and one double (DM46). Another accommodation option is the hostel in Hohenstaufen (see below).

THE KAISERBERGE

Just south of Schwäbisch Gmünd lie three conical peaks, **Hohenstaufen, Hohenrechberg,** and **Stuifen,** which make up the **Kaiserberge.** This curtain of mountains marks the beginning of the Swabian Jura. Hohenstaufen was named after the castle that once graced its summit, built by the Hohenstaufens, one of Germany's great medieval dynastic families. The castle is gone, but the view of the other two Kaiserberge peaks and of the Swabian Jura in the distance is spectacular. To reach Hohenstaufen, take the bus from Schwäbisch Gmünd to either Straßdorf (bus #12) or the village of Hohenstaufen (bus #13, Sun. and holidays only). The trail to the top takes about 30 minutes. Or, take the bus to the Hohenstaufen Jugendherberge ("Juhe") stop and put yourself right in the middle of the hill action around **Jugendherberge Hohenstaufen,** Schottengasse 45 (tel. (07165) 438, fax 14 18). Be sure to call ahead. (Curfew. DM17.70. Over 26 DM22.70. Sheets DM5.50.)

Hohenrechberg, to the east, has a mysterious **castle ruin** and a Baroque **Wallfahrtskirche** (pilgrimage church). The old castle wall now functions as the foundation for a footpath. To reach Hohenrechberg, take the bus from Schwäbisch Gmünd to the village of **Rechberg.** It's about a one-hour climb from there. **Stuifen,** also close to Rechberg, can also be hiked, though there are no flashy ruins and the view is nowhere as compelling as it is from the other peaks. The **tourist office** in Schwäbisch Gmünd has a number of hiking maps with routes that take from four to six hours to complete. All buses to the Kaiserberge from Schwäbisch Gmünd run from the train station.

HAIGERLOCH

Haigerloch exemplifies both the rural charm and the lack of rail access that mark much of the Swabian Jura. Buses connect Haigerloch to the rest of the world via Horb to the northwest (DM4.60) and Hechingen to the east several times per day. Having evolved around an S-shaped bend in the Eyach River, Haigerloch's layout may prove somewhat confusing. The town is divided into an *Unterstadt* (lower city) on the valley floor and an *Oberstadt* (upper city) along the crescent-shaped southern ridge. The result can be either picturesque or confusing, depending on your position and the quality of your map.

To reach the **Schloß,** set on the northern ridge above the *Unterstadt,* follow the wide stairs heading upwards from the central Marktplatz. Since its conversion into a hotel and restaurant, there hasn't been much of interest to see in the *Schloß* itself. However, halfway to the top is the **Schloßkirche,** a Gothic cathedral whose interior walls and ceiling are adorned with Biblical and historical scenes rendered in the sort of Technicolor splendor that's faintly evocative of a ride at Disneyworld. At the top of the ascent, the terrace of the *Schloß* offers a good view of the area; an even better one can be had by following the path marked **Kapf,** a three-minute walk from the main courtyard. The remainder of the castle is rather disappointingly occupied by a few galleries and shops. Back in the valley below, an old beer cellar underneath the *Schloßkirche* houses the **Atomkeller Museum.** During the final stages of World War II, German physicists, Heisenberg and von Weizsäcker among them, struggled unsuccessfully to generate a self-sustaining nuclear chain reaction. Today, the reactor can be seen much as it was when American troops marched into Haigerloch in April 1945. (Open May-Sept. daily 10am-noon and 2-5pm; March-April and Oct.-Nov. Sat.-Sun. 10am-noon and 2-5pm. Admission DM1, students DM0.50.)

Maps and other information are readily available at the **tourist office,** Oberstadtstr. 11 (tel. (07474) 697 27), inside the *Rathaus* (open Mon.-Wed. 8am-noon, Thurs. 8am-noon and 4-6pm, Fri. 8am-noon). Buses from the outside deposit passengers at several different points in Haigerloch, the most common of which are the *Marktplatz* in the *Unterstadt* and the *Schulzentrum* on the outskirts of the *Oberstadt*. To reach the tourist office from the *Marktplatz*, cross the bridge, walk two blocks to Oberstadtstr., and turn right. From the *Schulzentrum,* follow Oberstadtstr.'s curving descent for 10 to 15 minutes. Watch out for an "S" on bus schedules, which indicates buses that don't run on school holidays. Overnight visitors should try staying at **Krone,** atop the hill at Oberstadtstr. 47 (tel. (07474) 411), between the *Römerturm* and St. Anna. (Singles with shower DM38. Doubles DM68. Breakfast included.)

On a solitary hill 3km south of nearby **Hechingen** stands **Burg Hohenzollern,** the ancestral home of the Hohenzollern family that ruled a unifed Germany from 1871 to 1918 in the persons of Kaisers Wilhelm I and II. The current edifice—most of it built during the first half of the 19th century—is a tremendous conglomeration of spiraling towers and imposing battlements that puts Snow White's castle to shame. The castle's treasury contains a variety of pricey monarchical hand-me-downs, including the former crown of Prussia. (Open daily 9am-5:30pm; Nov.-March 9am-4:30pm. Admission DM6, students DM3.) Unfortunately, no public transportation connects Hechingen to the castle. For the genuinely dedicated, the castle office (tel. (07471) 24 28) has recommendations about other means of transit, including information about private buses. One line runs from Parkplatz to Burg; follow the signs from the stop to a second bus, which drives up the hill.

■■■ STUTTGART

What Stuttgart lacks is a wealth of those familiar architectural attractions most other large German cities offer. This does not detract from Stuttgart's appeal. Rows of excellent museums, a colorful theater scene, and an uncommonly vibrant multinational culture fill Stuttgart's promenades with vitality. As a state capital, Stuttgart enshrouds itself in both industry and bureaucracy, while at the same time containing the throngs on busy streets and in peaceful parks. Porsche, Mercedes and a whole host of high-tech coffee makers all live out their corporate lives here.

ORIENTATION AND PRACTICAL INFORMATION

At the heart of Stuttgart lies an enormous pedestrian zone where shops and restaurants stretch as far as the eye can see, and then some. Königstr. and Lautenschlagerstr. are the main pedestrian thoroughfares; from the train station, both are accessible through the underground Arnulf-Klett-Passage. To the left lies the tranquil swath of green called the *Schloßgarten,* to the right the thriving business sector. Stuttgart sells itself as a compact city, and in comparison to many American sprawlers it is, but sooner or later you will probably have to ride a train or U-Bahn.

Tourist Office: I-Punkt, Königstr. 1 (tel. 222 82 40), directly in front of the escalator down into the Klett-Passage. Professional staff books rooms for no fee, sells excellent maps (DM1), and distributes bus and train schedules. Their *Monatsspiegel* (German only, DM2.80) lists museum hours, cultural events, and musical performances and includes a guide to restaurants and nightlife. Open Mon.-Sat. 9am-8pm, Sun. 11am-5pm; Nov.-Dec. Mon.-Sat. 8:309am-8pm, Sun. 1-5pm; Jan.-April Mon.-Sat. 9am-8pm. **Tips 'n' Trips,** Hohe Str. 9 (tel. 226 80 01), has a number of informative pamphlets for all facets of the Stuttgart experience (in English as well

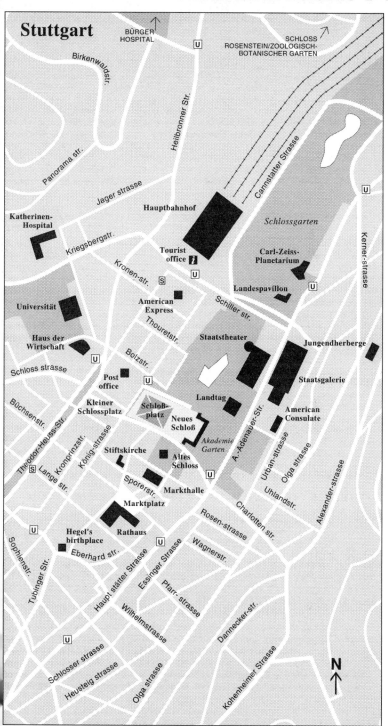

Stuttgart

STUTTGART

BÜRGER HOSPITAL

SCHLOSS ROSENSTEIN/ZOOLOGISCH-BOTANISCHER GARTEN

Birkenwaldstr.

Panorama str.

Heilbronner Str.

Jager strasse

Cannstatter Strasse

Katherinen-Hospital

Kriegsbergstr.

Hauptbahnhof

Schlossgarten

Kerner-strasse

Kronen-str.

Tourist office

Carl-Zeiss-Planetarium

Universität

American Express

Schiller str.

Landespavillon

Haus der Wirtschaft

Thouretstr.

Staatstheater

Jungendherberge

Schloss strasse

Bolzstr.

Büchsenstr.

Post office

Staatsgalerie

Theodor-Heuss-Str.

Kleiner Schlossplatz

Schloß-platz

Neues Schloß

Landtag

American Consulate

Lange str.

König-strasse

Stiftskirche

Altes Schloss

Akademie Garten

A.-Adenauer-Str.

Urban-strasse

Olga strasse

Alexander-strasse

Sophienstr.

Kronprinzstr.

Sporerstr.

Markthalle

Charlotten str.

Uhlandstr.

Marktplatz

Hegel's birthplace

Rathaus

Eberhard str.

Rosen-strasse

Wagnerstr.

Tubinger Str.

Haupt-stätter Strasse

Essinger Strasse

Pfarr-strasse

Wilhelmstrasse

Dannecker-str.

Schlosser strasse

Heusteig strasse

Olga strasse

Kohenheimer Strasse

N

as German). Helpful staff also has much info on travel and youth-oriented matters. Open Tues.-Fri. 10am-5pm.

Consulates: U.S., Urbanstr. 7 (tel. 215 40 or 214 52 39). **U.K.,** Breite-Str. 2 (tel. 16 26 90). **Canada,** Charlottenplatz 17 (tel. 226 19 91). New Zealand citizens and Aussies are directed to Munich or Frankfurt.

American Express: Lautenschlagerstr. 3 (tel. 187 50), 1 block south of the station. Holds mail, cashes traveler's checks. Open Mon.-Fri. 9am-5:30pm, Sat. 9am-noon.

Post Office: Lautenschlagerstr. 17, 70173 Stuttgart (tel. 20 67 or 20 61). Open Mon.-Fri. 8am-6pm, Sat. 8:30am-12:30pm, Sun. 11am-noon. **Postlagernde Briefe** (window 32) open Mon.-Fri. 8am-7pm, Sat. 8am-5pm, Sun 11am-noon.

Telephones: At the post offices. **City Code:** 0711.

Flights: To every major city in Germany and other countries (tel. 948 33 88 or 948 27 90). Buses shuttle passengers to the airport from the main train station 5am-11:30pm every 15-30min. DM6, children DM2.

Trains: tel. 194 19 for 24hr. schedule information. Transportation hub of south-western Germany, Stuttgart has direct rail links to most major German cities. Trains roll to Munich 30 times per day.

Public Transportation: Information office, Arnulf-Klett-Passage 1 (tel. 250 53 03), next to the escalator up to Königstr. Bus, streetcar, U-Bahn, and S-Bahn maps and schedules, along with needed map-and-schedule deciphering. Open Mon.-Sat. 8am-9pm, Sun. 9am-6pm. A **single-ride ticket** is DM3 for the inner city, DM4 for outlying parts of town. 4-ride *Mehrfahrkarten,* DM10. *Tageskarte*—valid for all trains and buses for 24hr.—DM14. Railpasses are valid only on the S-Bahn. **Nächtbus** (night bus) lines run through the night; stops are marked with a purple and yellow sign. The tourist office has a free night bus schedule.

Ferries: Neckar-Personen-Schiffahrt (tel. 54 10 73). Boats cruise from **Bad Cannstatt** (across the river) to little towns along the Neckar (1-2 per day, round-trip DM8.40-DM44). Tours of the harbor Sun.-Fri. 9am and 11am (2hr., DM13).

Car Rental: Auto-Rent, Molchweg 109 (tel. 86 11 75), rents from DM55 per day.

Luggage Storage: Lockers in the train station, DM2; large lockers, DM4.

Lost and Found: Fundbüro der Stadtvewaltung, Eberhardstr. 61a (tel. 216 20 16). **Fundbüro der Deutschen Bundesbahn,** Wolframstr. 19 (tel. 20 92 or 24 68).

Mitfahrzentrale: Stuttgart has 2 **Eurostop** offices, Stuttgart West, Lerchenstr. 65 (tel. 194 48), and Falbenheunenstr. 5 (tel. 636 80 36).

English Bookstore: Buchhaus Wittwer, Königstr. 30 (tel. 250 70), right off the *Schloßplatz,* has the largest selection. Open Mon.-Wed. and Fri. 9am-6:30pm, Thurs. 9am-8:30pm, Sat. 9am-2pm. **English library: America Haus,** Friedrichstr. 23a (tel. 229 83 17). U-Bahn 9 or 14: Keplerstr. Open Tues. and Thurs. 1-7pm, Wed. 1-5:30pm.

Laundromat: This is an expensive city to do laundry. If you must, try **Waschsalon Siegfried Rausch,** Techstr. 8 (tel. 26 11 91). Streetcar #4: Ostendplatz, walk up Haußmannstr., and take the first right. Wash DM10.50, dry DM2.50 per 10min.

Gay Information Line: Rosa Telefon (tel. 48 43 03), Fri. 7-9pm.

Rape Crisis Hotline: tel. 29 64 32.

24-Hour Pharmacy: For schedules of service, either buy **Amtsblatt** for DM1 from the tourist office (it comes out each Thurs.), or have a cheaper look at the copy posted at the *Rathaus.*

Hospital: Bürgerhospital, 1 Hohenheimerstr. Tunzhoferstr. 14-16 (tel 25 99 0).

Emergency Lines: Police: 1 Hahnemannstr. (tel. 899 01). **Emergency:** tel. 110.

ACCOMMODATIONS AND CAMPING

Most of Stuttgart's budget beds are located on the two ridges surrounding the downtown area and are easily accessible by streetcar. Accommodations around the pedestrian zone and train station cater to customers used to paying top mark for creature comforts. Contact **Tips 'n' Trips** for much info on cheap overnighting in Stuttgart.

Jugendherberge Stuttgart (HI), Haußmannstr. 27, 70188 Stuttgart (tel. 24 15 83, fax 60 83 51). Entrance on Kernerstr. U-Bahn 15, 16 (direction "Heumaden"):

Eugensplatz and walk right down Kernerstr. Or, walk left from the station on Schillerstr. and up and up and up the hill (follow stairs and signs). It's also possible to walk through the *Schloßgarten* along Schillerstr. where you'll find a sidewalk, in case you want to avoid the worrisome experience of walking on the edge of the road. Maddeningly full rooms may take their toll on the demeanor of the hardworking staff. One redeeming factor is the huge balcony, which invites *al fresco* breakfasting. Reception open 7-9am and noon-11pm. Strict lockout 9am-noon. Curfew 11:30pm. DM18.50, over 26 DM23.50. Sheets DM5.50. Sleepsack DM3.50. Breakfast included. If you intend to stay here, make a reservation by mail or by fax.

Jugendgästehaus Stuttgart, Richard-Wagner-Str. 2 (tel. 24 11 32). U-Bahn 15 or 16 (direction "Heumaden"): Bubenbad. Continue in direction of U-Bahn on right side of street, veer right immediately; the place is on the right. The dorm-hostel hybrid run by the International Association for Social Work has comfortable, spacious rooms in a quiet residential neighborhood. Reception open Mon.-Fri. 9am-8pm, Sat.-Sun. 11am-8pm. No curfew. Singles DM35, with bath DM45. Doubles DM60, with bath DM70. Triples DM90, with bath DM100. Breakfast, showers, and lockers included. Key deposit DM20.

Jugendherberge Ludwigsburg (HI), Gemsenbergstr. 21 (tel. (07141) 515 64). S-Bahn 4 or 5 (direction "Marbach" or "Biegetheim"): Ludwigsburg, or DB train from Stuttgart to the Ludwigsburg *Bahnhof*, then bus (direction "Schlößesfeld"): Schlößesfeld (30min.), continue down the hill, and follow signs. Clean, quiet rooms—more spacious than Stuttgart's hostel, and often has free beds when Stuttgart is full. Reception open 5pm until shortly before curfew at 10pm. DM17.70, over 26 DM22.70. Sheets DM 5.50. Breakfast included.

Pension Märklin, Friedrichstr. 39 (tel. 29 13 15), 2 blocks right from the train station. Convenient and cheap. What more can we say? Singles DM40. Doubles DM80. You get what you pay for: no breakfast thrown in.

Camping:

Campingplatz Stuttgart, Mercedesstr. 40 (tel. 55 66 96), Cannstatter Wesen, on the river in Bad Cannstatt. Streetcar #1, 2 (direction "Obere Ziegelei" or "Fellbach"). DM6 per person, DM5 per tent, DM3 per car. Showers DM2.

International Stuttgart Camp, Wienerstr. (tel. 817 74 76). U-Bahn 6 or 16 (direction "Gerlingen"): Sportpark Feuerbach. The camp is 2 blocks south of the stop. Shack up here under a big tent. Reception open through the night 5pm-9am. DM8 gets you an *Iso-Matte,* wool blankets, and shelter from the rain. Showers available. Breakfast DM3.50-4.50. Wash DM3, no dryers. 3-day max. stay. Open late June or early July to August or early September. Call **Tips 'n' Trips** (see Tourist Office listing) for exact dates.

FOOD

Thanks to a sizable contingent of foreign *Gastarbeiter* (guest workers), Stuttgart's restaurant scene is spiced with Greek, Turkish, African, and Asian eateries. But the cuisine of the *Schwaben* region is itself a step up from typical German food. *Spätzle* (thick fried noodles) and *Maultaschen* (pasta pockets filled with meat and spinach) were born here. Ask at **Tips 'n' Trips** (see Tourist Office listing) for a pamphlet of inexpensive eateries and pubs (in German or English). Stuttgart also has a **Wochenmarkt** on Marktplatz and Schillerplatz (Thurs. and Sat. 8am-3pm). For groceries, try the basement of **Kanfhof,** two blocks in front of the train station (open Mon.-Wed. and Fri. 9am-6:30pm, Thurs. 9am-8:30pm., Sat. 8:30-2pm).

University Mensa, Holzgartenstr. 9-11. From the *Bahnhof,* take Kriegsbergstr. to Holzgartenstr., turn left, and go down right side of street over the underpass; it is immediately on the right. Quantity compensates for quality (meals DM3-4). You must get a *Mensa* credit card at the entrance and leave a DM20 deposit. Open daily 11:15am-2pm; Aug.-Sept. 11:15am-1:30pm. Student ID required.

Iden, Eberhardstr. 1 (tel. 23 59 89). Cheap, good vegetarian fare served cafeteria-style. Entrees DM7-10. Open Mon.-Wed. and Fri. 11am-8pm, Thurs. 11am-9pm, Sat. 10am-4pm.

Litfass, Eberhardstr. 37 (tel. 24 30 31). From Eberhardstr. 37 descend the steps next to the "Rathaus" sign. Masses of Stuttgarters cram into Litfass for delicious and relatively inexpensive Turkish and Swabian food. Keeps on serving into the wee hours. Live bands Fri. and Sat. after midnight (sorry, hostelers). Try the green pepper filled with beef and yogurt sauce (DM12). Open daily 11:30am-5am.

Bernd's Ladle, Charlottenstr. 5 (tel. 24 02 02). One of the few places outside the train station for early morning coffee, with non-German open hours. But yes, German food. Breakfast favorites (DM3-10) served all day. Open 6am-9pm.

Weinhaus Stetter, Rosenstr. 32 (tel. 24 01 63). A great find. Offers intriguing Swabian specialties like *Ochsenmaulsalat* (DM7), *Maultaschen* (DM7.40), and *Saure Kutteln* (DM6.90) Incredible wine selection (DM3-7). Open Mon.-Fri. 3-11pm, Sat.-Sun. 10am-2pm.

SIGHTS

The **Schloßgarten,** Stuttgart's main municipal park, runs from the train station southward to the *Neues Schloß* and northeast to the Neckar. On warm summer days, the park is very popular with sunbathers in their birthday suits. The north end of the *Schloßgarten* contains the expansive **Rosensteinpark,** which also holds the **Wilhelma,** Stuttgart's famous zoo and botanical garden (open daily 8am-6pm; April and Sept. 8am-5:30pm; March and Oct. 8am-5pm; Nov.-Feb. 8am-4pm; admission DM10, students DM5). At the other end of the *Schloßgarten* is the **Schloßplatz,** upon which reposes the elegant, Baroque **Neues Schloß,** now infested with bureaucrats. This and the 16th-century **Altes Schloß** across the street on Schillerplatz comprise the whole of Stuttgart's architecturally notable sights. There is one world-spirit spot: **Hegel's birthplace**—just a few doors down from a busy porn shop—is at Eberhardstr. 53, a few blocks down Konrad-Adenauer-Str. The house provides a thorough, if somewhat inscrutable, exegesis of his life through letters, manuscripts, and notes (open Tues and Fri. 11am-5pm, Thurs. 11am-8pm, Sat. 11am-4pm).

MUSEUMS

Stuttgart's dearth of venerable buildings is more than compensated for by numerous excellent museums, most of them free.

Across from the *Schloßgarten,* the **Staatsgalerie Stuttgart,** Konrad-Adenauer-Str., is, simply put, superb. The museum is comprised of the *Staatsgalerie,* holding paintings from the Middle Ages to the 19th century, and the **new wing,** with an excellent group of moderns including Picasso, Kandinsky, Beckmann, and Dalí. A masterpiece of postmodernism, the new wing was designed by English architect James Stirling. (Open Wed. and Fri.-Sun. 10am-5pm, Tues. and Thurs. 10am-8pm. Free.) The glass collection is the highlight in a quite decent assembly of regional art and artifacts at the **Württembergisches Landesmuseum,** in the *Altes Schloß.* (Open Tues. and Thurs.-Sun. 10am-5pm, Wed. 10am-7pm. Free.)

The **Gottlieb Daimler Museum** (bus #56: Stadion, *or* S-Bahn 1: Neckarstadion) is the actual workshop where Herr Daimler, automobile innovator extraordinaire, built the first generation of Mercedes-Benz, and covers the history of the automobile from its invention to the strange and unusual experimental models now on the drawing board. Gottlieb's daughter was named Mercedes. (Open Tues.-Sun. 9am-5pm. Free.) Not to be outdone, Dr. Porsche's **Porsche-Museum** (S-Bahn 6, direction "Wielderstadt": Neuwirkshaus), tells much the same story, only with different cars. (Open Mon.-Fri. 9am-noon and 1:30-5pm. Free.) Unless you are a serious car freak, going to *both* of these museums will probably prove to be a mistake; choose your make and stick with it.

The **Schwäbisches Brauereimuseum Stuttgart** features state-of-the-art technology of a different flavor. The examination of the history of beer culminates in a look at current brewing processes. Take S-Bahn 1, 2, or 3 (direction "Vaihingen") to the last stop. (Sorry, no free samples—otherwise we'd put it on the back cover. Open Tues.-Sun. 10:30am-5:30pm. Last tour at 4pm. Free.) For more high-value-added exhibits, visit the **Haus der Wirtschaft,** Willi-Bleicher-Str. 19, which showcases the region's contributions to technology and product innovation. The exhibits on automobile and communications technology require an engineering degree to understand, but anyone can appreciate the *Bauhaus* synthesis of form and function manifested in the design exhibit, which features such dear mundanities as the Bic lighter, the Mag-lite flashlight, and Fiskars scissors. (U-Bahn 4: Berlinerplatz. Open Tues.-Sun. 11am-6pm. Free.)

ENTERTAINMENT

The **Staatstheater,** just across the plaza from the *Neues Schloß*, is Stuttgart's most famous theater (box office open Mon.-Fri. 9am-1pm and 2-5pm; DM10-90). There are at least 25 other local theaters, and tickets for them are usually much cheaper (DM10-25, students DM5-15). The tourist office provides schedules and sells tickets, which can also be purchased at the **Kartenhäusle,** Kleiner Schloßplatz (tel. 29 55 83; open Mon.-Fri. 9am-6pm, Sat. 9am-1pm, tel. lines open 9am-noon and 2-5pm).

Keep up with Stuttgart's nightlife if you can. To find out what's hot, get the **Tips 'n' Trips** (see Tourist Office listing) flier *Discos* or *Kneipen*, which list exhaustively, in both German and English, what's to do. When you've had your fill, take in either of Stuttgart's two **public baths** (U-Bahn 14, direction "Mühlhausen": Mineralbäder). The spectacular facilities of **Mineralbad Leuse** (tel. 28 32 27 or 28 32 24) have to be seen to be believed. (DM9.50 per 2hr., students DM6; DM12 per 3hr., students DM8; DM16 per day, students DM11.50; sauna DM6; massage DM29, **underwater massage** DM42.50. Open Mon.-Fri. 7am-8pm, Sat.-Sun. and holidays 7am-7pm.)

OZ, Büchsenstr. 10 (tel. 29 55 85), entrance on Kronprinzstr. The walls sweat and the music blasts at this very popular dance club. Nothing at all like Kansas. Open Fri. 8am-5am, Sat. 8pm-8am, Sun. 6am-midnight.

Perkins Park, Stresemannstr. 39. The place to see, be seen, etc. Do what you can. Open Fri.-Sat. 9pm-5am, Wed.-Thurs. and Sun. 9pm-4am.

Das unbekannte Tier, Bolzstr. 10, caters to society's square pegs. *Alternativ*, as they say. Hip-hop, acid jazz and degenerated reggae. Open daily 10pm-5am.

Kings Club, Calverstr. 21 (tel. 22 45 58). Gay men's disco. Lots of Erasure fans. Open daily 10pm-5am.

Lauras Club, Lautenschlagerstr. 20 (tel. 29 01 60). A women's disco. Open daily 10pm-5am.

■ Near Stuttgart: Esslingen am Neckar

Bounded by steep, terraced vineyards on one side and the Neckar River on the other, Esslingen nurtures a durable *Altstadt* surrounded by sizable remnants of the original town fortifications. Medieval Esslingen thrived as a way station on the main commercial route between Flanders and Venice. These days it lies within Stuttgart's hegemonic arena of industrial sprawl; still, modern Esslingen retains an air of decided grace.

To reach the *Altstadt* from the train station, walk down Berlinerstr. over the bridge and to the right. The pink Renaissance façade of the **Altes Rathaus** looks out over one corner of the square. The **Glockenspiel** sitting atop it has a repertoire of more than 200 songs, including "Yankee Doodle." The asymmetrical towers of the **Stadtkirche St. Dionys,** connected by a small footbridge, guard the other corner of the *Marktplatz*. The church holds a gorgeous 15th-century rood screen and *pietà*. Up on the hill rises the Gothic stone spire of the **Liebfrauenkirche,** which contains striking 14th-century stained glass. Farther up the ridge, among the vineyards, stands the **Burg,** or what's left of the city wall. From the **Dicker Turm,** the squat, round, half-timbered tower at one end, soak up the view of the town with a backdrop of the Swabian Jura. Footpaths crisscross the *Weinberge,* and maps identifying the grape-type for each section of the vineyard are available at the tourist office.

Esslingen is on the **train** line between Stuttgart and Ulm, and can also be reached by Stuttgart's **S-Bahn** (every 15-20min., 20min., DM4, railpasses valid).The **tourist**

office, Marktplatz 16 (tel. (0711) 351 24 41), provides free maps and books rooms for no fee (open Mon.-Fri. 8am-6pm, Sat. 9am-noon). Esslingen's clean but aging **Jugendherberge (HI),** Neuffenstr. 65 (tel. 38 18 48), is in the Zollberg section of town, about a 30-minute walk behind the train station. Take bus #3 (2-3 times per hr.) to Zollbergstr., then cross the street and follow the signs (10min.); overflow from Stuttgart's hostel is usually sent here. (Reception open 4-9:30pm. Curfew 10pm. DM17.20, over 26 DM22.20. Sheets DM5.50. Breakfast included.) In central Esslingen, try **Gasthof Falken,** Bahnhofstr. 4 (tel. 35 72 88), which has good clean rooms two blocks from the station (singles DM30, doubles DM50, no breakfast). A **market** fills the square with fruit and vegetable stalls (Wed. and Sat. 7-11am).

Esslingen overflows with *Weinstuben* serving the local *vino.* **Weinstuben Einhorn,** Heugasse 17 (tel 35 35 90), past the *Rathaus* from the square, serves warm meals (DM9.50-12.80) and cold wine from a medieval cellar daily after 6pm. Just down the street at Heugasse 27, **Goldenes Fäßle** cooks Swabian style. (Meals DM13.50-14.80. Open daily 11:30am-2pm and 5pm-midnight.) Back up the street and to the right on Landolinsgasse, **Goldener Pflug** (tel. 35 20 45) serves pizza (DM8-13) and Greek dishes (DM10-16.50) at more reasonable prices (open daily 5pm-1am).

■■■ TÜBINGEN

Left-wing graffiti smeared across 15th-century public buildings leaves no doubt that Tübingen is one of Germany's venerable academic towns. Because nearly one-half of the city's residents are affiliated with the 500-year-old university, Tübingen has retained the graceful aloofness of its intellectual origins; this is where literary giant Herman Hesse did his book-dealing internship. But university life has added unpredictability from the Middle Ages to the student uprisings of the late 60s, when the students of Tübingen's university boycotted classes to protest everything from the educational system and the Nazi past of many politicians to American involvement in the Vietnam War. The students leave in August and September, but at other times the buzz of young people and the relative lack of tourists enhance Tübingen's appeal. The city stands on the Neckar River, just before it disappears into the Black Forest.

Practical Information Tübingen's **tourist office** (*Verkehrsverein*) (tel. 350 11) sits on the south side of the Eberhardsbrücke. From the front of the train station, turn right and walk to Karlstr., then turn left and walk to the river. The office will book rooms in hotels (DM4.50 fee) or private homes (DM25-40; DM3 fee). (Open Mon.-Fri. 9am-6:30pm, Sat. 9am-5pm, Sun. 2-5pm; Oct.-April Mon.-Fri. 9am-6:30pm, Sat. 9am-5pm.) **Tours** of the city leave from the *Rathaus* entrance (April-Oct. Wed. 10am, Sat.-Sun. 2:30pm; DM4, students DM2). The **Mitfahrzentrale,** Münzgasse 6 (tel. 267 89 or 50 81), can hook you up with a ride to Munich for about DM9, plus DM15-20 for gas. (Open Mon.-Fri. 9am-6:30pm, Sat. 9am-2pm, Sun. 10am-1pm. Call 1-2 days in advance.) The **post office** and **telephones** are located 100m east of the train station on the opposite side of the street (open Mon.-Fri. 8am-6pm, Sat. 8am-noon). The **city code** is 07071. Rent a boat from **Bootsvermietung Tübingen** (tel. 315 29), on the river under the tourist office. (Open mid-April to Sept. daily 11am-8pm. Rowboats for 1-3 people, DM9.90 per hr., DM1 per each additional person.) The **Steinlach Waschsalon** at Albrechtstr. 21 (tel. 720 67), two blocks south of the main station, is part of a self-sufficiency project run by disabled citizens. (Wash DM7-8.50, dry DM4. Open Mon.-Fri. 8am-6:15pm, Sat. 8am-1pm.)

Accommodations The large, worn **Jugendherberge (HI),** Gartenstr. 22-2 (tel. 230 02, fax 250 61), overlooks the Neckar just downstream from the bridge at the tourist office. It's a 12-minute walk or take bus #11 (from the station, DM2.50) to Jugendherberge. (Reception open 7:30-9am, noon-1pm, 5-8pm, and 10-10:15pm.

Curfew midnight. Members only. DM17.70, over 26 DM21. Breakfast included. Wheelchair access.) On the hill leading to the *Schloß*, the lovely **Hotel am Schloß,** Burgsteig 18 (tel. 210 77, fax 520 90), has newly renovated singles. The sign above the bench outside is exaggerated Schwäbisch for "here sit those who always sit here" (*dohoggeddiadiaimmerdohogged*). (Singles DM50, with shower DM65, with bath DM95. Doubles DM95, with bath DM135. Breakfast included.) Most of the other accommodations in the city are not priced to please; however, the rooms rented out by private families and listed at the tourist office are usually economical. Camping is possible at **Rappernberghalde** (tel. 431 45), on the river. Go upstream from the old town or left from the station, cross the river on the Alleenbrücke, and turn left again. Follow the blue camping signs. (20-25min. by foot. DM7 per person, DM5-6 per tent. Open April to mid-Oct. daily 8am-12:30pm and 2:30-10pm.)

Food and Nightlife Tübingen's students keep a number of superb yet inexpensive restaurants busy. The student-run **Marquardtei,** Herrenbergstr. 34 (tel. 433 86; bus #8 or 9: Rappstr.), serves whole-wheat pizza and a vast selection of outstanding vegetarian and meat dishes to a mostly Red and Green clientele. (Entrees DM6-15. Open Sun.-Fri. 11:30am-1am, Sat. 6pm-1am.) For the severely budget conscious, the **Mensa,** at Wilhelmstr. and Keplerstr., offers generic fare at low prices. (Open late Aug.-late July Mon.-Fri. 11:30am-1:30pm and 6-8:15pm. Tübingen University ID theoretically required.)

Nightlife is not hard to find in Tübingen; nearly every block claims one or two student pubs. The **Zentrum-Zoo** disco, Schliefmühleweg 86 (tel. 405 39), a 10-minute walk from the old city, brings down the house nightly. It's popular with college students, but occasionally gets overrun by a still younger crowd. (Open Tues.-Sat. 8pm-2am, Sun. 8pm-midnight. Beer DM3.50-4. Cover varies, usually DM5.) On the other side of town, **Cinderella,** Düsseldorfer-Str. 4, serves up Europop and other snacks until 3am. Take bus #3 to Düsseldorfer-Str., in the heart of the industrial zone. Be prepared; it's a long walk back to the old city (open Wed. and Fri.-Sat. 10pm-4am, Mon.-Tues. and Thurs. 10pm-1am). Inside the *Altstadt,* **Alter Simpel,** Haaggasse 24, proffers the standard assortment of beer, beverages, and beer (DM3-4, wine DM5-7) from 6pm to 2am.

Sights The focal point of the old city, the 15th-century **Stiftskirche,** is surrounded by winding alleys and gabled houses. In the chancel at the east end of the church lie the tombs of 14 members of the former House of Württemberg underneath life-size stone sculptures of the deceased, the men decked out in their finest suits of armor. From an entryway to the left of the chancel, the rickety stairs of the church tower can be climbed for a commanding view in all directions. (Church open daily 9am-5pm. Chancel and tower open April-July and Oct. Fri.-Sun. 10:30am-5pm; Aug.-Sept. daily 10:30am-5pm. Chancel admission DM1, students DM0.50; tower DM1, students DM0.50.) Just down the road from the Stiftkirche on Kronenstr. is the **Evangelischer Stift,** a seminary unremarkable except for the fact that at one time Hegel and Schelling studied there. In the center of the *Altstadt,* the ornate, incredibly painted façade of the **Rathaus** faces the old market square.

On top of the hill that rudely separates the university from most of the city stands the **Schloß Hohentübingen,** a castle with a rough stone balcony overlooking the old town. (Open April-Oct. Obligatory tour Sat. 5pm, Sun. 11am and 3pm. Admission DM3.) From the *Rathaus,* follow the signs marked "*Schloß*" leading up to the right in order to reach the castle. Along the river, the tree-lined path of the **Platanenallee**—which runs the length of a man-made island on the Neckar—makes for a pleasant walk with a view of the *Altstadt.* On the northern riverbank is the **Hölderlinturm,** a tower where the great 18th-century poet Friedrich Hölderlin lived out the final 36 years of his life in a state of clinical insanity. The tower now contains a museum dedicated to his life. (Open Tues.-Fri. 10am-noon and 3-5pm, Sat.-Sun. 2-5pm. Tours Sat.-Sun. 5pm. Admission DM2, students DM1.) Tübingen also has a small, interesting-to-enthusiasts **Auto Museum "Boxenstop,"** Brunnenstr. 18. (Open Wed. and Fri.-Sun. 10am-noon and 2-5pm; Nov.-March Sun. 10am-noon and 2-5pm. Admission DM3.50.)

■■■ KARLSRUHE

By European standards, Karlsruhe was born yesterday—it was established in 1715 by a local nobleman, Margrave Karl Wilhelm, who built a castle retreat there (hence "Karlsruhe," meaning "Karl's Rest"). Karl then designed a planned city around his castle's perimeter, the original layout of which remains to this day; from the castle, a series of streets radiate outward in the shape of a giant fan. Modern Karlsruhe is notable as a center of culture—exemplified by its many excellent museums—and as the home of Germany's two highest courts, the Federal Supreme Court and the Federal Constitutional Court.

Practical Information The **tourist office,** Bahnhofplatz 6 (tel. 355 30 or 355 311), located across the street from the train station, finds rooms for no fee and offers a good map for DM2 (open Mon.-Fri. 8am-7pm, Sat. 8am-1pm). The main **post office** sprawls at Europaplatz. *Postlagernde Briefe* (Poste Restante) reception has a room of its own with booths 21-24 (or, if those are closed, room E105). The **telephone city code** is 0721. (The **S-Bahn** costs DM2.50 for 1hr. going in one direction and DM6 for a 24hr. ticket for 2 adults and 2 children.)

Accommodations Karlsruhe's **Jugendherberge (HI),** Moltkestr. 2b (tel. 282 48), is conveniently located near the *Schloß* and university. Take S-Bahn 3 or 4 (from the station): Europaplatz, then follow Karlstr. and Seminarstr. to Moltkestr. (Reception open briefly at 5, 7, and 9:30pm. Curfew 11:30pm. Members only. DM17.20, over 26 DM22.20. Breakfast included.) **Kolpinghaus,** Karlstr. 115 (tel. 314 34), is near the station; from the *Bahnhof,* turn left onto Ebertstr. and right onto Karlstr. This place has 142 beds, so many that it rents a floor to students. Plain rooms but surprisingly spacious doubles. (Singles DM40. Doubles DM80. Mandatory breakfast DM8.50.) **Camp** at **Türmbergblick,** Tiengerer Str. 40 (tel. 440 60), in the nearby village of Durlach. S-Bahn 3: Durlacher Tor, then change to S-Bahn 1 or 2: Durlach. (Reception open daily 8am-1pm and 3-9pm. DM6.50 per person, DM4 per tent.) Accommodations are cheaper in outlying villages; ask the tourist office for a list.

Food and Nightlife The **Mensa** (university cafeteria) sells cheap snacks. From Europaplatz go up Karlstr. and continue up Seminarstr. Turn left into the bleak blue grey school complex (open Mon.-Thurs. 8:30am-3pm, Fri. 8:30am-2pm). For reasonably priced, traditional German fare, try **Goldenes Kreuz,** Karlstr. 21a (tel. 220 54; open Thurs.-Tues. 11am-midnight). Around the corner on Ludwigplatz is the trendier **Krokodil,** Waldstr. 63, a restaurant and café that offers salad buffets for DM7 (specials DM12-18; open daily 8am-1am). The **main market** caters to the people camping in Durlach (open Mon.-Sat. 7:30am-12:30pm). Several cafés on Ludwigsplatz remain open until 1am, and the tourist office has a list of all local pubs, discos, and live music venues. **Harmonie,** Kaiserstr. 57 (tel. 37 42 09), is a good student pub that serves cheap eats and occasionally features live music (open daily 10am-1am). Brush up on your beer-drinking at **Bierakademie,** Douglasstr. 10, a *Kneipe magna cum laude* (open Mon.-Fri. 11am-1am, Sat. 7pm-1am, Sun. 7pm-midnight).

Sights In the center of the Marktplatz stands a red sandstone pyramid housing the **tomb of Karl Wilhelm.** From here, it's a three-minute walk to his former getaway, the giant yellow **Schloß,** aloof from the surrounding municipal buildings (and backed by a landscape). Today, it houses the **Landesmuseum** (State Museum). This collection of antiques is dominated by the third floor's *Türkenbeute* (Turkish Booty), a dazzling display of Turkish artifacts brought back by a local count from his campaigns in the late 17th century. (Open Tues.-Wed. and Fri.-Sun. 10am-5:30pm, Thurs. 10am-7:30pm. Free.) Around the corner are the **Kunsthalle,** Hans-Thomas-Str. 2, and **Kunsthalle Orangerie,** Hans-Thomas-Str. 6, a pair of top-notch art museums (tel. 133 33 55). The Kunsthalle boasts a variety of European masterpieces from the 15th to the 19th century, while the Orangerie contains a smaller collection of modern art (both open Tues.-Fri. 10am-5pm, Sat.-Sun. 10am-6pm; free). The *Markt-platz,* designed by architect and city planner Friedrich Weinbrenner, is bordered on the west by the broad pink **Rathaus** and on the east by the imposing columns of the **Stadtkirche.** (From the station, the town center is a 25-minute walk away from the train tracks on Ettlinger Str. and Karl-Friedrich-Str.; or, S-Bahn 3 or 4: Marktplatz or Europaplatz.)

Located in the upper floors of a former mansion, the **Prinz Max Palais** museum, Karlstr. 10 (tel. 133 36 70), has loaned exhibitions and a local history display that includes what purports to be the world's first bicycle, though the resemblance to your 10-speed is minimal. To reach the museum from the Orangerie, take Stephanienstr. to Karlstr. (Open Tues.-Sun. 10am-1pm and 2-6pm, Wed. 2-8pm. Free.) The quirkiest of Karlsruhe's museums is undoubtedly the particularistic **Oberrheinisches Dichtermuseum** (Upper Rhine Poets' Museum), Röntgenstr. 6, dedicated to lyrical legends such as von Scheffel, Hebel, and Flake. Don't worry—we haven't read them either (open Mon.-Fri. 9am-noon and 2-5pm; free). More universally appealing is Karlsruhe's **zoo,** in the Stadtgarten across the street from the train station. The elephant feeding is at 4:30pm. (Open daily 8am-7:30pm; last entry 6:30pm. Admission DM4.50, students DM3.50.)

The unremarkable **Bundesverfassungsgericht** (Federal Constitutional Court) is next to the *Schloß.* Look carefully at this institution, because it embodies Germany's legal safeguard against the return of totalitarian rule, but don't look too closely, or you may find yourself under interrogation by machine-gun-toting guards. Take a moment to savor the irony. Near Friedrichsplatz is the **Bundesgerichtshof** (Federal Supreme Court), whose security apparatus makes its counterpart five blocks to the north look open by comparison. Germany's most sensational postwar criminal trials have been held here, including those of the infamous Baader-Meinhof terrorist gang.

■■■ BADEN-BADEN

If you're fabulously wealthy, Baden-Baden can be a lot of fun. Even if you're not, it can still be a great place to visit—provided that you get at least an inkling of pleasure out of watching rich people on vacation. During its 19th-century heyday, Baden-Baden's guest list read like a who's who of European aristocracy. Although its status has since fallen somewhat, this spa town on the northern fringes of the Black Forest remains more or less a playground for the well-to-do; minor royalty, *Wirtschaftswunderkinder,* and the like convene here year-round to bathe in the mineral spas and drop fat sums of money in the elegant casino. The humble tourist can nevertheless enjoy the curative beauty of the pampered, relaxed town.

Practical Information The appropriately opulent **tourist office** is at Augusta-platz 8 (tel. 27 52 00, for room reservations tel. 299 99), with its large reading room and multiple TV rooms, inside the massive Haus des Kurgastes (open Mon.-Sat. 9am-10pm, Sun. 10am-10pm). The **post office** on Leopoldplatz has phones (daily 8am-7pm) and **exchanges** money, as does the casino. The **telephone city code** is 07221. Baden-Baden's **train station** is inconveniently located several km northwest of the town center. To avoid the blistering 90-minute walk, take bus #1 (direction "Lichtental/Oberbeuern," DM2.50; 24hr. pass DM6.50). A large public **swimming pool** (open 10am-8pm; admission DM3, after 5pm DM1.50) sits next door to the hostel.

Accommodations and Food The cheapest bed in town is at the modern **Jugendherberge (HI),** Hardbergstr. 34 (tel. 522 23, fax 600 12), halfway between the station and the town center (bus #1: Grosse-Dollen-Str.; follow the signs uphill). The hostel has family apartments and is wheelchair accessible. (Reception open 5-6pm and briefly at 8 and 10pm. Curfew 11:30pm. Members only. DM18.20, over 26 DM23.20.) Rooms in the center of the town are ritzy and overpriced, with the exception of the **Hotel Löhr**, Adlerstr. 2 (tel. 313 70 or 262 04); reception is 1½ blocks away at **Café Löhr**, Lichtentaler Str. 19, across the street from the Augustaplatz bus stop. (One single at DM35, other singles DM50, with shower DM55. Doubles DM85, with shower DM90.) **Hotel Deutscher Kaiser (Lichtental)**, Hauptstr. 35 (tel. 721 52, fax 721 54), about 1.5km south of the town center, has reasonable prices and large rooms. (Singles from DM42. Doubles from DM65.)

You're probably not wealthy enough to eat out in Baden-Baden. But **Pfankuch** at Augustaplatz has groceries, and fast food joints serve cheap arteriosclerosis all over town. Similarly, nightlife in Baden-Baden is intended primarily for the rich, with several cabarets filling the bill. If you're in search of young, rich, marriageable Europeans, look no further than **Club Taverne**, located in the basement of the Kurhaus, under the casino (admission a steep DM10; open 9pm-3am).

Sights and Spas Baden-Baden's history as a resort goes back nearly two millennia, to the time when the Romans built the first **thermal baths** here. Everybody knows that Germans are obsessed with ineffectual natural cures of all sorts. The **Friedrichsbad**, Römerplatz 1 (tel. 27 59 20), a palatial 19th-century bathing palace where you can enjoy a two-hour-long "Roman" "Irish Bath" in 14 different luxuriating stages. It's guaranteed to cure any malady, almost. Not a stitch of clothing is permitted. (Open Mon.-Sat. 9am-10pm. Last entry 7:30pm. Baths are coed Tues. and Fri. 4-10pm and all day Wed. and Sat. DM28, with soap and brush massage DM38. Credit cards accepted, of course.) More modest and budget-minded cure-seekers should try next door at the also astoundingly beautiful **Caracalla-Therme**, Römerplatz 11 (tel. 27 59 40), which offers placid soaking in the same water (and in bathing suits) at half the price (DM18, DM14.40 with youth hostel coupon; open daily 8am-10pm).

When they're not busy getting all pruney at the baths, Baden-Baden's affluent guests head to the **Casino**, whose opulent decor—modeled after the palace at Versailles—can be viewed via daily guided tours (open daily 10am-noon; Oct.-March 9:30am-noon; last tour leaves at 11:30am; DM3). Bus #1 stops just outside the door. Attendance during gaming hours (Sun.-Thurs. 2pm-2am, Fri.-Sat. 2pm-3am) costs DM5 with a laundry list of restrictions: you must be 21 (or the spouse of someone who is), present ID proving you're not a Baden-Baden resident, and wear appropriate dress (coat and tie for men). Technically, students are not allowed in. Minimum bets are DM5; the maximum bet is DM20,000. (Yeah, we were disappointed, too.) If you live in Baden-Baden and want to bet, you need a note from the mayor. Next to the casino is the massive Neoclassical **Trinkhalle** (Pump Room), which contains a gallery of paintings that immortalize area folk tales and a gold-plated fountain (open daily 10am-5:30pm; tours and a drink DM4, students DM2). A few blocks in the opposite direction of the casino down the leafy paths of the Lichtentaler Allee is the **Kunsthalle**, which houses visiting exhibits of modern art (open Tues. and Thurs.-Sun. 10am-6pm, Wed. 10am-8pm; admission DM5, students DM2).

For a sumptuous view of the Black Forest, mount the 668m **Merkur** peak east of town. Take bus #5 to Merkurwald, then take the steep railway to the top (combined round-trip DM6). On the hill above the baths and the pedestrian zone—accessible by a steep set of stairs—is the **Neues Schloß**, which houses a museum of the town's history (tours Mon.-Fri. 3pm; open Tues.-Sun. 10am-12:30pm and 2-5pm; admission DM2, students DM1). From the neighboring garden, you can get an excellent view of the entire town; an even better one, extending all the way into France, can be had from the 12th-century ruins of the **Altes Schloß** (tel. 269 48) in the upper hills a few km from the rear of the *Neues Schloß*. Bus #15 makes two loops per day at 2 and 5:30pm between Augustaplatz and Altes Schloß (open Tues.-Sun. 10am-10pm).

■■■ FREIBURG IM BREISGAU

In May 1940, a squadron of *Luftwaffe* pilots accidentally bombed Freiburg when they mistook it for a French border town. Historically and culturally, at least, this is an easy mistake to make; ruled by the Habsburg empire for much of its 800-year existence and frequently usurped by the French up until the 19th century, Freiburg is more cosmopolitan and less distinctively German than perhaps any city in the country. Potted palm trees line the city's streets, as do a large contingent of street musicians, artists, and university students. Freiburg is the undisputed metropolis of the Black Forest, which is not to say that this old university town is distant from the life of the forest, or that, with all of its urbanity, it lords its status over those dark woods. It is in fact surprising how quickly Freiburg's suburbs lose themselves in the Black Forest.

ORIENTATION AND PRACTICAL INFORMATION

Freiburg lies on the track between Karlsruhe (2hr.) and Basel, Switzerland (1hr.), and is connected to both by frequent trains. Local trains and buses leave for scattered Black Forest towns. Freiburg is also a natural point of departure for excursions into the Massif. Most of the city's sights and restaurants are within easy walking distance of one another in the *Altstadt,* a 15-minute walk straight ahead from the main train station.

Tourist Office: Rotteckring 14 (tel. 368 90 90 or 368 90 97), 2 blocks down Eisenbahnstr. from the station. Finds rooms (no fee), sells tickets to area events, has a free map, but prefers to sell the comprehensive *Freiburg Official Guide* (German or English, DM5). Also has Black Forest information. Open Mon.-Sat. 9am-8pm, Sun. 10am-noon; Nov.-April Mon.-Fri. 9am-6pm, Sat. 9am-3pm, Sun. 10am-noon.

Budget Travel: Schwarzwald Reisebüro, Rotteckring 14 (tel. 31 90 10), in the tourist office building, arranges planes, trains, and spas. Open Mon.-Fri. 9am-6pm, Sat. 9:30am-12:30pm.

Currency Exchange: At the main train station. Open Mon.-Sat. 7am-8pm, Sun. 9am-1pm. Slightly better rates are available at the post office.

Post Office: Eisenbahnstr. 58-62, 79098 Freiburg, 1 block straight ahead from the train station. Open Mon.-Fri. 8am-6pm, Sat. 8am-noon, Sun. 9-10am. **Late open** window for limited services Mon.-Fri. 6-9pm, Sat. noon-9pm, Sun. 10am-8pm.

Telephones: At the post office. Open Mon.-Sat. 8am-9pm, Sun. 9am-8pm. **City Code:** 0761.

Taxis: Frauentaxi (tel. 240 40), only women drivers and riders.

Public Transportation: Single fares on Freiburg's many bus and streetcar lines DM2.50; invest in one of several day passes available at the tourist office or from any driver. 24hr. ticket valid for 2 adults and 2 children DM6.50, and 48hr. ticket DM9, 72hr. ticket DM12.

Mitfahrzentrale: Belfortstr. 55 (tel. 194 44), sets riders up with drivers for a fee. South of the station, just off Schnewlingstr. Open Mon.-Fri. 9am-7pm, Sat. 9am-1pm, Sun. 10am-1pm.

Hitchhiking: Hitchers report that public transportation can get one to the necessary starting spots. *Let's Go* does not recommend hitchhiking as a safe means of transportation. North: S-Bahn 2 or 5 (direction "Zähringen"): last stop, then those who hitch walk back some 50m. West: S-Bahn 1: Padua-Allee, then bus #31 or 32: Hauptstr. East: S-Bahn 1 (direction "Littenweiler"): Lassbergstr., then bus #18 (direction "Ebnet"): Strandbad.

English Bookstore: Walthari, Bertholdstr. 28. A fairly large but pricey collection of English-language paperbacks. Carries guides to the Black Forest region as well as a full *Let's Go* selection. Open Mon.-Fri. 9am-6:30pm, Sat. 9am-1pm.

Bike Rental: (tel. 21 43 37), at the *Reisegepäck* counter at the train station. DM12 per day, DM8 with rail ticket.

Laundromat: Café Fleck, Predigerstr. 3 (tel. 268 29). Laundro-café—get a drink or sandwich at the adjacent bar. Wash DM6, dry DM1 per 10min. Laundromat open daily 7am-1am. Café open Mon.-Fri. 7am-6:30pm, Sat. 8am-2pm.

Emergencies: Police and **ambulance:** tel. 110. **Fire:** tel. 112.

ACCOMMODATIONS AND CAMPING

Most of Freiburg's hotels and *pensionen* are expensive, and nearly all are located outside of the city center. The tourist office books cheaper rooms (DM22-40 for singles, DM40-80 for doubles) in private homes, but a stay of at least three nights is usually required. Fortunately, Freiburg's youth hostel is one of the largest in Germany.

Jugendherberge (HI), Kartäuserstr. 151 (tel. 676 56). S-Bahn 1 (direction "Littenweiler"): Römerhof, then walk down Fritz-Geiges-Str., cross the stream, and follow the footpath to the right. Modern institutional accommodations in an arboreal setting. Unfortunately, the huge summer vacation groups often displace the mere individual. Reception open 7am-11:30pm. Curfew 11:30pm. Members only. DM17, over 26 DM22.50.

Hotel Schemmer, Eschholzstr. 63 (tel. 27 24 24). From the train station, take the overpass that crosses over the tracks, then go past the church and turn left. Friendly management and a central location. Fine rooms, some with balconies. Singles DM45. Doubles DM75, with shower DM80. Breakfast included.

Hotel Hirschen, Hirschstr. 2 (tel. 293 53). S-Bahn 2 or 4 (direction "Günterstal"): Klosterplatz, then walk back 1 block; the hotel is in the upper floors of the Dionysos restaurant. Reception open Mon.-Sat. noon-3pm and 5:30pm-midnight, Sun. noon-midnight. Singles DM34. Doubles DM59, with shower DM64.75.

Gasthaus Hirschen, Breisgauer Str. 47 (tel. 821 18). On the other side of town from the hotel of the same name. S-Bahn 1: Padua-Allee, then walk down Breisgauerstr. for 5min. Beautiful old house in a quiet farm neighborhood. Comfortable rooms have been managed by the same family since 1740. Reception open Fri.-Wed. Singles DM40. Doubles DM70, with shower DM90. Triples DM110.

Pension Gisela, Am Vogelbach 27 (tel. 811 52). Bus #10 (direction "Padua-Allee"): Hofackerstr., then double back 2 blocks and turn left. The tacky *Schwarzwald*-theme wall on the outside wall (almost Realism except for a touch of amateurism) conceals large, comfy rooms. Reception next door at the Schnogeloch restaurant. Singles DM40. Doubles DM76.

Hotel Alleehaus, Marienstr. 7 (tel. 348 92). From the town center, follow Kaiser-Joseph-Str. past the Martinstor, turn left on Adelhauser Str., and walk 2 blocks. Near some of central Freiburg's most beautiful little streets, and with breakfast buffet to compensate for the room prices. Singles DM55, with shower DM65. Doubles DM80, with shower DM100.

Haus Lydia Kalchtaler, Peterhof 11 (tel. 671 19). S-Bahn 1 (direction "Littenweiler"): Lassbergstr. Then bus #17: Kleintalstr., and follow Peterhof up to the large wooden farmhouse. Located in the boondock suburb of Kappel, but Lydia's lovely old home and generous hospitality make it well worth the extra effort to get there. DM18 per person, showers included. No breakfast, but use of kitchen is included. Laundry facilities.

FOOD

In the early 15th century, the humanist Dietrich von Nieheim noted admiringly that "the supply of victuals is good and readily available" in Freiburg. With more than 20,000 university students to feed, Freiburg's budget eateries carry on the tradition. During the daytime, the **Freiburger Markthalle** next to the Martinstor is home to a variety of food stands serving ethnic specialties for under DM10 (Mon.-Fri. 9am-6:30pm, Sat. 9am-2pm). At the open-air **market** on Münsterplatz, you can find everything from fresh radishes to handmade crafts (open Mon.-Sat. 7am-1pm; Oct.-May 7:30am-1pm).

Mensa: 2 university *Mensen*—**Rampartstr.** in the *Altstadt* (lunch) and **Albertstr.** on the main campus north of the city center (lunch and dinner). Both serve hot meals for under DM4, but only to those who can successfully impersonate a German college student—or better yet, get a real one to buy them a meal ticket.

Meals DM3.50, strip of 5 tickets DM13.50. Rampartstr. open Mon.-Fri. 11:30am-2pm, Sat. 11:30am-1:30pm. Albertstr. open Mon.-Fri. 11:30am-2pm and 6-7:30pm.

Toast Reich, Münsterpl. 14 (tel. 279 33), in the shadow of the cathedral. Europe's first—and probably last—toast fest, featuring a variety of eclectic open-faced combinations, and noodle dishes for under DM10. Tennis fans should try "Boris-Becker-Toast" (DM8.50) or "Toast Steffi" (DM12.50). Open daily 9am-11pm.

Salat Stube, Löwenstr. 1 (tel. 351 55), near the Martinstor. A health food heaven-on-earth. Load up on salad, DM1.89 per 100g. Soup DM4.70 per ½L. Open Mon.-Fri. 11am-8pm, Sat. 11am-4pm, first Sat. of the month 11am-6pm.

Milano, Schusterstr. 7. Surprisingly inexpensive pasta dinners (DM9-15) and friendly service. Open daily 11am-midnight.

Papalapub, Moltkestr. 30. Near the Stadttheater. A student pub through and through, Papalapub serves extremely cheap pasta and pizzas (DM6-11) under the pensive gaze of Jake and Elwood. Open Mon.-Sat. noon-1am and Sun 6pm-1am.

SIGHTS

The pride of Freiburg is the **Münster,** a tremendous stone cathedral whose 116m spire dominates the skyline. With various sections constructed at intervals between the 13th and 16th centuries, the chapel's interior is a wealth of architectural and artistic achievement. Many of the stained-glass windows represent different medieval guilds that financed the cathedral's construction, and the group of sculptures on the interior west porch, depicts all manner of Biblical characters. You can climb the tower to marvel at its delicate, lattice-like stonework and see the view that made philosopher Wilhelm von Humboldt swoon: "One cannot conceive of a more beautiful view than the blue heavens peeking through the thousand openings of the cupola." Gazing up from near the south entrance, you can see one of the gargoyles mooning the city. (Cathedral open daily 9am-7pm. Tower open Mon.-Sat. 9:30am-5pm, Sun. 1-5pm; Nov.-April Tues.-Sat. 9:30am-5pm, Sun. 1-5pm. Admission DM1.50. Cathedral tours depart regularly from the south entrance.)

What buildings the errant *Luftwaffe* bombers didn't hit, the Allies finished off one night in 1944, when most of the old city was obliterated. Since then, the citizens of Freiburg have painstakingly recreated the city's architecture and public spaces. On the south side of Münsterplatz is the pink-tinted **Kaufhaus,** a merchants' hall dating from the 16th century. Two medieval gates—the **Schwabentor** and the **Martin-stor**—still stand within a few blocks of one another in the southeast corner of the *Altstadt.* The latter is indelibly profaned by a McDonald's sign. From the *Schwaben-tor,* you can take the pedestrian overpass across the heavily trafficked Schloßbergring and climb the glorified hill known as the **Schloßberg** for an excellent view of the city. Tucked away in the blocks between the *Münster* and the tourist office are the **Rathaus,** an amalgam of older buildings from whose tower a carillon plays daily at noon, and the oddly named **Haus zum Walfisch** (House of the Whale), where Erasmus of Rotterdam lived in exile from Basel for two years following the Reformation. This gold-trimmed wonder is actually a careful recreation of the original, which was destroyed during World War II.

Freiburg's museums cater to a variety of interests. Even better, most of them are free. The **Augustiner Museum** (tel. 216 33 00), housed in a former monastery on Augustinerplatz two blocks south of the *Münster,* has a large collection of mostly medieval artifacts. Many original works of stained glass and statuary from the *Münster* are here along with other religious art, and there is a section devoted to folk art from the Black Forest. (Open Tues.-Fri. 9:30am-5pm, Sat.-Sun. 10:30am-5pm. Admission DM4, students DM2.) Further south is the **Museum für Neuekunst** (Museum of Modern Art), Marienstr. 10a (tel. 216 36 71), which displays the works of 20th-century German artists (open Tues.-Fri. 9:30am-5pm, Sat.-Sun. 10:30am-5pm; free). Around the corner from the tourist office is the **Zunfthaus der Narren** (Carnival Fools' Guildhall), Turmstr. 14 (tel. 226 11), whose second floor showcases a colorful assortment of Carnival costumes (open Sat. 10am-3pm and by arrangement).

Freiburg's unique look stems from the system of narrow streams—known as **Bächle**—that run through the city. In medieval times, these swift-flowing gutters were used to water cattle and protect against fires—and to serve as open-air sewers. Today, they appear to exist only to soak the shoes of unwary tourists.

ENTERTAINMENT AND NIGHTLIFE

Freiburg proclaims itself to be a city of wine and music, and, true to its word, is awash with *Weinstuben* and clubs. The annual three-week **Zeltmusikfestival** (Tent Music Festival), held in June and July, brings big-name classical, rock, and jazz performers to three circus tents pitched at the city's edge. Tickets sell fast (DM15-40). (S-Bahn 5: Bisserstr. and catch the free shuttle bus to the site.) **Freiburger Weintage** (Wine Days) is a 10-day festival held on Münsterplatz in late June and early July where you can stagger around sampling some 300 different vintages (DM3-6 per glass). In addition, the **Narrenfest** (Fools' Festival) is held in mid-February, and the **Christkindlmarkt** runs from late November until just days before Christmas.

Freiburg's nightlife keeps pace with the city's 27,000-plus students. Jazz fans should check out the **Jazzhaus,** Schnewlingstr. 1 (tel. 349 73).

Far Out, Universitätstr. 3, next to the old university. Hole-in-the-wall disco, packed nightly. Open Tues.-Sun. 11pm-3am. Cover DM5 after midnight; no cover before.

Greiffenegg-Schlößle, Schloßbergring 3 (tel. 327 28). Beer and wine on a hillside terrace above the city. Open April-Oct. Tues.-Sun. 10am-midnight.

Cafe Atlantik, Schwabentorring 7. Spacious pub that plays a wide variety of American FM rock from the mid-70s (open daily 5pm-1am).

zum Schlappen, Löwenstr. 2. Serious beer drinkers head here. For DM15 you can prove your mettle by polishing off the 2L **Stiefel,** known to English-speakers as "the Boot." Open daily noon-1am.

■■■ BLACK FOREST (Schwarzwald)

The Black Forest (*Schwarzwald*) looms large in the German cultural consciousness. Fairy tales, storybooks, and Romantic lyrical poetry all owe their inspiration to the tangled expanse of evergreens where Hänsel and Gretel were left to their own devices. Stretching west of the Rhine from Karlsruhe to Basel, the region owes its name to the eerie darkness that prevails under the thick canopy of vegetation; a generation's worth of acid rain has rapidly thinned this natural cover by at least half, and today parts of the forest show the unmistakable signs of environmental decay. Tradition and custom still play a leading role here—not surprisingly, since the area remained remarkably isolated from the rest of Germany and the larger world until early in this century. Venerable farm houses sporting trademark straw roofs appear around every other turn in the road, as do venerable farmers sporting trademark rural garb. The cuckoo clock originated here, and the tourist shops, which penetrated the various towns in the area soon after indoor plumbing, all proffer local renditions of the classic timepiece. Hiking is a favorite pastime; trails are frequent and well-marked throughout the forest and are used in winter for cross-country skiing. There are downhill slopes at Feldberg and near Schwarzwälderhochstr.

The main entry points to the Black Forest are Freiburg, at its center, Baden-Baden to the northwest, Stuttgart to the east, and Basel, Switzerland to the southwest. Public transportation is sparse in this mountain region: rail lines run along the perimeter from Baden-Baden to Freiburg and east from Freiburg to Donaueschingen and Stuttgart, but many of the innermost regions are accessible only by the infrequent bus service. Travelers making daytrips should check their return connections in advance to avoid getting stranded overnight. Also, many bus lines are privately owned, rendering railpasses invalid. The most scenic route through the Black Forest is the stretch from northern Waldkirch to southeastern Hinterzarten, where the vistas extend to the Alps in the south and the Rhine Valley in the west.

HIGH BLACK FOREST (Hochschwarzwald)

High, rounded mountaintops and a thick carpet of trees maintain the centuries-old isolation of the remote villages of the **High Black Forest** (*Hochschwarzwald*), also known as the High Black Forest. Hospitable and traditional residents will confound you with their dialect and impress you with their generosity. The best source of general information about the area is probably the **Freiburg tourist office,** Potteckring 14 (tel. (0761) 216). The tourist offices of all the local towns will provide maps and information.

The best **skiing** in the Black Forest is on the **Feldberg**—at 1493m the Schwarzwald's highest mountain—although by Alpine standards it's little more than a big hill. The ski lift runs in summer and winter (round-trip DM5). At 1234m above sea level, Feldberg's **Jugendherberge Hebelhof (HI),** Passhöhe 14 (tel. (07676) 221, fax 12 32), may be the highest in Germany. Take the Titisee-Schluchsee train to Feldberg-Bärental, then the bus to Hebelhof stop. (Reception open 8am-10pm. Curfew 10:45pm. Members only. DM17.20, over 26 DM22.20. Reserve in advance in winter.) For tourist information about Feldberg and the other 16 ski lifts in the area, call the **tourist office** at (07655) 80 19; for a **ski report,** call (07676) 12 14.

Titisee and Schluchsee

Thirty kilometers east of Freiburg lies the resort town of **Titisee,** situated along the lake of the same name. Twice-hourly trains connect Freiburg to Titisee; along the way, the train ride through the **Höllental** (Hell's Valley) is one of the most scenic rail voyages in Germany. Titisee itself is an attractive lake set against a backdrop of dark pine-forested ridges. This beauty is somewhat marred, however, by a massive influx of consumer tourism; the pedestrian zone along the lakeside **Seestraße** is crammed with stands peddling kitsch. Somewhat miraculously, the lake and its surroundings still manage to assert their charms, and few other areas combine such natural beauty with so many modern conveniences. The **tourist office** is in the *Kurhaus,* Strandbadstr. 4 (tel. (07651) 81 01); to reach the building, turn right in front of the train station, walk to the first intersection, and turn right at the entrances to the pedestrian zone. Look for the flags dotting the *Kurhaus* lawn. During especially busy times the office books rooms for a DM4 fee; otherwise, the service is free. Also available are detailed maps (DM7.80-DM9.80) of the 130km of hiking trails surrounding the lake (open Mon.-Fri. 8am-noon and 1:30-5:30pm, Sat.-Sun. 10am-noon). Rent paddleboats from several vendors along Seestr. (DM11-15 per hour). Guided boat tours of the lake depart from the same area (25 min., DM5).

Titisee's **Jugendherberge Veltishof (HI),** Bruderhalde 27 (tel. (07652) 238, fax 756), is comfortable but inconveniently located at the far end of the lake. (From the train station, Sudbaden bus, direction "Todtnau" (every 2hr., DM2): Feuerwehrheim.) By foot, it's a 30-minute walk along the main road from the *Kurhaus.* At DM8, the hostel serves the cheapest meal in the area. (Reception open 5-6pm and 7:30-8pm. Curfew 10pm. DM17.50; over 26, DM22.50.) Several campgrounds lie along the same road: **Campingplatz Weiherhof** (tel. (07652) 14 68) is on the water near the hostel and has laundry facilities. (April-Oct. DM6.50 per person, DM8.50 per tent.) Bastion of tourism that it is, Titisee has its fair share of expensive accommodations. One exception is **Gasthaus Rehwinkel,** Neustädter-Str. 7 (tel. (07651) 83 41), which offers comfortable rooms (some with terraces) less than a 10-minute walk from the train station. Walk one block to the right from the station, follow the underpass, and take Neustädler-Str. to the left. The hotel is on the right past the fire station. (Singles from DM45. Doubles from DM66.) Fill up on pasta and pizzas (DM10) at **Toscana Pizzeria** in the orange building on the corner of Parkstr. and Seestr. (open Tues.-Sun. 11:30am-2:30pm and 5:30pm-midnight). Enjoy beers

(DM4.50) and traditional German fare (DM9-15) on the overvisited terrace of **Berg-see am Titisee,** overlooking the lake on Seestr. (open daily 8am-midnight).

South of Titisee is the larger, less touristed **Schluchsee.** Eight round-trip **trains** make the 30-minute jaunt daily from Titisee to the towns of Schluchsee and See-brugg, both on the lake. The Schluchsee **tourist office** (*Verkehrsamt;* tel. (07656) 77 32) is a few blocks up the hill from the station in the *Rathaus* on the corner of Fischbacherstr. and Lindenstr. The office provides maps and finds accommodations (open Mon.-Fri. 8am-6pm, Sat. 10am-noon and 4-6pm, Sun. 10am-noon). The **Jugendherberge Schluchsee-Wolfsgrund (HI)** (tel. (07656) 329, fax 92 37) is ide-ally situated on the shore; from the station, with your back to the water, turn left and follow the tracks across the bridge to Wolfsgrund 28. All of the rooms here are named after flowers. (Reception open all day. Curfew 11pm. DM17.70, over 26 DM22.70. Dinner DM8. Laundry DM6). **Boat rental** near the hostel is considerably cheaper than in neighboring Titisee (DM9 per hr.). There are 10 **bikes for rent** at the train station (DM12 per day, DM8 per day with train ticket; open daily 8:15am-5:15pm). Three km down the lake at the end of the train line, **Seebrugg** consists of nothing but a train station, a beach, and the **Jugendherberge Schluchsee-Seebrugg (HI)** (tel. (07656) 494). Then again, what more could you want? (Reception at noon, 5, 6:30, and 9:45pm. Curfew 10pm. Members only. DM16.70, over 26 DM21.70.)

St. Peter and St. Märgen

North of Titisee and about 20km due east of Freiburg, the twin villages of St. Peter and St. Märgen lie well within the High Black Forest. Buses run regularly between St. Peter and St. Märgen, and eight times per day buses depart from Freiburg's Omni-bushof adjacent to the train station to reach these scenic locales (line #7216; DM5.50 to St. Peter, DM6.50 to St. Märgen). **St. Peter's,** designed by architecht Peter Thumb, sits high where the air is curative, and where a halo of green farmland breaks through the dark crust of pine forests. Its Klosterkirche may not be much on the outside, but the inside is rocking with Baroque angels. (Abbey and its library tours in summer Tues. 2:30pm and Sun. Bus: St. Peter Post.) The bus puts you right in front of the **tourist office** (*Kurverwaltung;* tel. (07660) 274), which has a list of affordable overnight accommodations as well as maps detailing the many mountain paths in the region. (Open Mon.-Thurs. 8am-noon and 2-5pm, June-Oct. also Sat. 11am-1pm.) Many of these paths depart from the tourist office and the abbey; they are well marked with colored triangles, circles and diamonds. Following the blue diamond signs from the abbey takes one over an 8km footpath to **St. Märgen,** much of it directly through the forest. Known as a *Wanderparadies* (hiking paradise), St. Märgen is a popular base from which to hike into the wilderness. St. Märgen's **tour-ist office** (*Kurverwaltung;* tel. (07669) 10 66) is located in the *Rathaus,* 100m from the St. Märgen "Post" bus stop. (Open Mon.-Thurs. 8am-noon and 2-5pm, Fri. 8am-noon and 2-4pm, Sat. 10am-noon; mid-Dec. to June and Oct. closed Sat.; Nov. 1-Dec. 15 Mon.-Fri. 8am-noon.)

CENTRAL BLACK FOREST

Donaueschingen

At the tender yet prodigious age of 10, while traveling from his native Vienna to Paris, Wolfgang Amadeus Mozart stopped in Donaueschingen and, according to leg-end, played three concerts in the castle. Since that time a variety of other famous personalities have passed through Donaueschingen; most, like Mozart, were on their way somewhere else. Located on the Baar Plateau between the Black Forest and the Swabian Jura, Donaueschingen is an ideal starting point for forays into the Black Forest or to the **Wutach Schlucht** (Wutach Gorge) 15km to the south.

The town's renown comes from its status as the "source" of the 2840km Danube River, the second-longest in Europe and the only major European river to flow west to east. While Donaueschingen's claim has little basis in geographical fact (the head-waters of the Brigach and Breg Rivers which converge here are each more likely sources), the town built a monument to the Danube. The **Donauquelle** (Source of the Danube) is an oversized, rock-bottomed puddle encased in 19th-century stone-work in the garden of the **Fürstenberg Schloß,** conveniently located next to a sou-venir stand. The *Schloß,* with its marbled floors and tapestried walls, is moderately interesting. (Garden always open. Tours Easter-Sept. Wed.-Mon. 9am-noon and 2-5pm. Admission DM5, students DM4.) In the block behind the *Schloß* is the **Fürstenburg Sammlungen,** Karlsplatz 7, a museum displaying the former collec-tions of the princes of Fürstenburg. The art collection is especially strong in its late Gothic holdings: Hans Holbein the Elder, Cranach the Elder, and Mathias Grünewald are represented. (Open Dec.-Oct. Tues.-Sun. 9am-noon and 1:30-5pm. Admission DM5, students DM4.)

The museum, *Schloß,* and adjacent puddle are all a 10-minute walk from the train station; take a right in front of the station, walk one block, turn left at Josefstr., cross the bridge and walk a few hundred meters more. On the way, you'll pass the **Johan-niskirche** just above and behind the *Donauquelle;* the church's tame exterior con-ceals an amazing gold and marble altar. Donaueschingen is also home to the **Fürstliche Fürstenberger Brauerei,** between Haldenstr. and Poststr. (tel. 863 58). Single tourists can accompany larger groups on tours through the brewery, which culminate in **free samples** and sandwiches. (Open Aug. to mid-June Mon.-Fri. Call for daily tour schedule. Free.)

To reach the **tourist office,** Karlstr. 58 (tel. (0771) 38 34), veer right up the hill past the *Schloß* and turn left at Karlstr. (open Mon.-Fri. 8am-noon and 2-5pm, Sat. 9am-noon; Sept.-May Mon.-Fri. 8am-noon and 2-5pm). Information about Donaue-schingen's annual **Internationales Dressur-, Spring-, und Fahrturnier** (Sept.), four days of horses, and the **Musiktage** (Oct.), a modern music festival, is available at the tourist office. Two minutes from the train station, Donaueschingen's brand new, privately owned **Southern Cross Hostel,** Josefstr. 8/13 (tel. (0771) 33 27), comes complete with full kitchen facilities and an adjacent budget travel agency. Run by people who spent a great deal of time Down Under (and speak perfect English), this hostel is one of the only places in Southern Germany where you can get a Foster's Lager on tap. Ask for John if you want any part of your body pierced. (No curfew. DM15. Sheets and breakfast included.) Other budget accommodations are scarce. 8km southeast of town **Reidsee Camping** (tel. (0771) 55 11) colonizes lakefront property (DM6 per person, DM12 per tent). Alternatively, the tourist office has a list of private homes with rooms for rent. Although most of the restaurants in the area are expensive, you can fill up on food at **Krone,** a huge supermarket on Mühlenstr., the continuation of Karlstr.

Running alongside the river, one end of the Danube bicycle trail connects the city to Vienna, hundreds of kilometers away. Take Josefstr. from the station, turn right onto Parkstr., cross one of three bridges to the left, then follow the path to where the official trail begins.

Triberg

At the center of the High Black Forest is Triberg, accessible by a half-hour train ride from Donaueschingen to the southeast. Bounded on all sides by steep hills, Triberg is a hiker's paradise, boasting more than 200km of trails in its immediate vicinity. When the clouds roll in from the east and the mist begins to cover the trees, the city's hillside beauty multiplies tenfold. Triberg is in the middle of the region's cuckoo clock manufacturing territory, as evidenced by the dozen or so clock stores that line the **Hauptstraße.**

From the train station, the city center is a 15-minute uphill walk; turn right in front of the station, head down the stairs at the overpass, and follow the road past the large post office building, where the road becomes Hauptstr. At the top of Hauptstr. is Triberg's prime attraction, the largest **waterfall** in Germany. It's a gorgeous sight, but the crafty local authorities have roped off the area and added a turnstile at the entrance, charging visitors to see the water plunge 162m in seven separate drops (open daily 9am-7pm; admission DM2, students DM1). One-and-a-half blocks to the left of the waterfall's entrace is the **tourist office,** Luisenstr. 10 (tel. (07722) 812 30), in the *Kurhaus.* It books rooms and sells city maps (in English, DM1) and hiking maps (DM5.50). (Open Mon.-Fri. 8am-noon and 2-5pm; May-Oct. also Sat. 10am-noon.)

One block from the waterfall in the opposite direction is the **Schwarzwald Museum,** Wallfahrtstr. 4, which details the art, culture, and daily life of Black Forest denizens past and present (open daily 9am-6pm; admission DM4, students DM2). A few blocks up the street, Clemens-Maria-Hofbauer-Str. forks off of Wallfahrtstr., leading uphill to the **Wallfahrtskirche St. Maria in der Tanne.** This church has been a popular destination for pilgrims since its construction in 1704, owing to the miraculous properties that legend ascribes to the image of the Virgin embedded in the altar.

The **youth hostel (HI)** in Triberg is a 20 minute trudge uphill from the waterfall to the hostel, Rohrbacherstr. 37 (tel. (07722) 41 10), will be richly rewarded with a scenic vista. (Reception open 5-7pm and 9:45pm. Curfew 10pm. Members only. DM17.20; over 26, DM22.20.) Other accommodations are a bit more accessible; **Zum Bären,** Hauptstr. 10 (tel. (07722) 44 93), offers singles from DM31, doubles from DM62. **Krone,** Schulstr. 37 (tel. (07722) 45 24), one block off Hauptstr. to the left, has singles for DM32 (with shower, DM40) and doubles with showers for DM76. (Reception open 9am-3pm and 5pm-midnight.) Get Italian victuals for rock-bottom prices (DM8-13) at **Sonne,** Hauptstr. 27. Up the street at Hauptstr. 51, **Tick Tack Stube** serves traditional German fare (open Thurs.-Tues.; entrees DM9-25).

Furtwangen

Buses depart hourly from Triberg's train station this small town 15km to the south (line #7270; DM4.80). Here, in the heart of cuckoo clock territory, is perhaps the definitive statement on timepieces—the **Deutsches Uhrenmuseum** (German Clock Museum), Gerwigstr. 11 (tel. 65 61 17). Take the bus to Friedrichstr., and walk to the traffic light. The museum is home to over 1000 different watches and clocks from around the world. When the hour strikes, it's pure cuckooing pandemonium. (Open daily 9am-5pm, Nov.-March Mon.-Sat. 10am-4pm. Admission DM4, students DM2.) Further information on Furtwangen and its surroundings is available from Furtwangen's **tourist office** (*Verkehrsamt*), Marktplatz 4 (tel. (07723) 93 91 11), in the *Rathaus.* (Open Mon.-Fri. 8am-noon and 1:30-5pm, Sat. 10am-noon; Oct.-April Mon.-Fri. 8:30am-noon and 2-4pm.)

NORTHERN BLACK FOREST
(Nördlicher Schwarzwald)

Freudenstadt

The dark, meandering valleys of the Northern Black Forest, spanned by an extensive network of trails, make for wonderful hiking. The area is easily accessible from the north; direct trains make the two-hour trip from Karlsruhe to Freudenstadt every hour, and the final 45-minute stretch of the journey offers tremendous scenery. For information on the entire region, the tourist offices (*Kurverwaltung*) in nearby Baden-Baden (tel. (07221) 27 52 00) and Freudenstadt (tel. (07441) 86 40) are helpful. The area's two transportation hubs—Freudenstadt and Pforzheim—aren't too interesting in themselves, and should probably be used only as a place to spend the night.

Near the center of the northern Black Forest, semi-industrial **Freudenstadt** is a pretty boring place, but it does have a swimming pool. If long hours on the train or the trails have left you feeling less than clean, head for the **Panorama Bad** on Ludwig-Jahn-Str. 60, just up the hill from the youth hostel (tel. (07441) 576 20). This swimming pool, hot tub, and sauna complex is considerably cheaper (but a lot less fun) if you avoid the sauna. (Open Mon.-Fri. 9am-10pm; Sat.-Sun. 9am-8pm. Admission with sauna DM17, students DM13. Without sauna DM9, students DM7. Add DM1 to all prices on Sun.) Freudenstadt has two railway stations, the **Hauptbahnhof** and the **Stadtbahnhof.** The *Stadtbahnhof* is considerably closer to the town center and to the youth hostel. From the *Stadtbahnhof,* Freudenstadt's **tourist office** (*Kurverwaltung*), Promenade Platz 1 (tel. (07441) 86 40), can be reached by following Forststr. away from the station, crossing the largest *Marktplatz* in Germany, and following Loßburgerstr. past the Volksbank; the office is in the modern-looking Kurhaus complex. They book rooms for travelers for no fee. (Open Mon.-Fri. 9am-noon and 2-5pm, Sat. 9:30am-12:30pm. Extended hours in summer.) From the *Stadtbahnhof,* hang a left, follow the train tracks to a set of steps, pass under the bridge, and turn right at Gottlieb-Daimler-Str. (about 10min. all told) to reach the **Jugendherberge (HI),** Eugen-Nägele-Str. 69 (tel. (07441) 77 20, fax 857 88). (Reception open 5-7pm and 9-9:45pm. Curfew 10pm. Members only. DM17.70, over 26 DM22.70. Laundry DM5.) **Hotel-Garni zur Stadt,** Loßburgstr. 19 (tel. (07441) 27 19), one block away from the tourist office, has well-kept rooms and a kindly manager. (Singles DM43, with shower DM48. Doubles DM80, with shower DM90.) **Gasthof See,** Forststr. 17 (tel. (07441) 26 88), has handsome rooms and accepts credit cards. (Singles with shower DM58. Doubles DM80, with a shower DM96.) **Camp** at **Langenwald** (tel. (07441) 28 62), 3km west of town on the B28 highway; follow the path along Schwarzwaldhochstr. for about 3km. (Reception 8am-noon and 3-9:30pm. DM8 per person, DM6 per tent. Open May-Sept.)

The Black Forest Highway

The **Schwarzwaldhochstraße** (Black Forest Highway), which contains parts of the two *Bundesstraßen* B28 and B500, stretches 65km from Freudenstadt in the south to Baden-Baden in the north and contains some of Germany's most gorgeous scenery. Even more arresting is the accompanying footpath, the **Westweg,** which runs along the spine of the mountains overlooking the Rhine Valley and the Vosges Mountains in France. Along the Westweg, 17km northwest of Freudenstadt and 2km from the crossroads at Alexanderschanze, stands one of Germany's most comfortable youth hostels, the **Jugendherberge Zuflucht (HI)** (tel. (07804) 611, fax 13 23), a large, converted hotel built in imitation of a Black Forest farmhouse. Lodgers bask in spotless, carpeted six-bed dorm rooms. The hostel rents ski equipment and bikes. Twice daily, bus T77 from Freudenstadt to Baden-Baden stops just outside the hostel doors; other buses run more regularly from both Freudenstadt and Baden-Baden. (No lockout. Curfew 10pm or by prior arrangement. Members only. DM18.20, over 26 DM23.20. Sheets DM5.50.) From the nearby settlement of **Ruhestein,** the Westweg leads over Seiblesecke and the **Mummelsee** to **Unterstmatt,** traversing the **Hornisgrinde** (1164m), the highest peak in the area. Unbeknownst to the busloads of tourists that have been known to frequent it, the Mummelsee is tiny and boring. Down the hill after a rigorous hike rests the **Wildsee,** a more attractive lake inaccessible to automobiles.

■■■ ROTTWEIL

Known in Roman times by the name *Avae Flaviae* (Flavius's Altar), Rottweil bears the distinction of being the oldest city in Baden-Württemburg. A free and independent city in the Holy Roman Empire, Rottweil is now known less as the site of the invention of flameless gunpowder (one Herr Duttenhofer ushered in this new era of weaponry) than as the home turf of the fearsome canines.

Along the way from the train station to the city center stand a number of the picturesque old homes that make Rottweil a visual treat; the contrasting colors, meticulously crafted oriel windows, and occasional historic murals on their façades have turned nearly every building into a work of art. A walk uphill on Hauptstr. yields a more impressive array of structures. At the top of the street is the 13th-century **Schwarzes Tor**. Halfway up Hauptstr. across from the **Altes Rathaus** is the **Stadtmuseum,** Hauptstr. 20, whose prizes include a 15th-century treaty made between Rottweil and nine Swiss cantons—still valid to this day—and a collection of wooden masks from the town's renowned *Fastnet* celebration—a wild affair on Ash Wednesday (open Mon.-Thurs. 9am-noon and 2-5pm, Fri. 9am-noon, Sun. 10am-noon; free).

Higher up, the ancient **Hochturm,** once a lookout tower, stands impenetrable (unless you picked up the key from the Teufel family, Hochturmgasse 9, open 10am-noon and 2-6pm; free with ID deposit). Behind the *Altes Rathaus,* the Gothic **Heilig-Kreuz-Münster** (Cathedral of the Holy Cross) impresses with its altar and ornamentation. One block down from the *Münster,* vibrant ceiling paintings give the **Evangelische Predigerkirche** a bright Baroque look. Next to the Predigerkirche is the newly constructed **Dominikanermuseum.** Its collection includes a large variety of religiously inspired stone and wood sculptures and a 2nd-century Roman mosaic made of approximately 570,000 tiles (open Tues.-Sun. 10am-1pm and 2-5pm; admission DM3).

Lying on the Stuttgart-Zürich rail line, Rottweil is easily accessible by train, though the location of the train station itself is out-of-the-way; the city center is a 15-minute uphill walk. Turn right in front of the station, head upward until you reach the 12th-century bridge, and take another right, crossing the bridge. A walk down Hochbrücktorstr. brings you to Hauptstr., the center of the *Innenstadt.* Halfway up Hauptstr. through a side door of the *Rathaus* is the **tourist office** (tel. (0741) 49 42 80), which offers maps and a guide to the city in English and books rooms for DM3 (open Mon.-Fri. 9:30am-12:30pm and 2-6pm, Sat. 9:30am-12:30pm). A few doors down from the Predigerkirche is the **Jugendherberge (HI),** Lorenzgasse 8 (tel. (0741) 76 64), near the Obere Hauptstr. bus stop. Many of the hostel's rooms overlook the Neckar. (Reception open 5-10:30pm. Curfew 10:30pm. Members only. DM17.20, over 25 DM22.20. Reservations recommended.) **Goldenes Rad,** Hauptstr. 38 (tel. 74 12), is often booked solid several weeks in advance. (Singles DM30. Doubles DM55.) **Gasthof Löwen,** Hauptstr. 66 (tel. 76 40), is another option (singles DM40, with shower DM45; doubles DM70-80). For excellent regional cooking at low prices, head to **zum goldenen Becher,** a family-run restaurant at Hochbrücktorstr. 17 (meals DM10-25; open Tues.-Sun.). To uncover Rottweil's elusive nightlife, turn to the *Freizeit Spiegel,* a monthly publication available at the tourist office.

■■■ LAKE CONSTANCE (Bodensee)

The third-largest lake in Europe, the Bodensee forms a graceful three-cornered border at the conjunction of Austria, Switzerland, and Germany. Ancient castles, manicured islands, and endless opportunities to tan to a melanomic crisp draw residents of all three countries to the vast lake all summer long. Konstanz is the principle city on the lake, but ferries and roads lead from its gates to a ring of striking water-front towns.

Ships depart about once per hour from behind the Konstanz train station to all the ports on the Bodensee. Consider the cruise ship that stops at Meersburg, Mainau, Unteruhldigen, and Überlingen (June-late Sept. daily, round-trip DM19.20, with railpass half-price). For more information and schedules, contact the **Weiße Bodenseeflotte** counter (tel. (07531) 28 13 89), in the harbor behind the train station.

CONSTANCE (Konstanz)

Spanning the Rhine's exit from the Bodensee, the elegant university city of Konstanz is just about the largest German city never struck by a bomb; the city extends into neighboring Switzerland, and the Allies were always leery of accidentally striking neutral territory. That, and the fact that Konstanz belonged to Austria until 1805, give it the feel of an open, international city. The narrow streets wind around beautiful painted Baroque and Renaissance façades in the central part of town, while along the river promenades, gabled and turreted 19th-century houses create an aura of undeniable gentility. Meanwhile, local students and visitors crowd the old resort beaches on the edge of town.

Practical Information The **tourist office** *(Tourist-Information)* in the arcade to the right of the train station (tel. (07531) 28 43 76) provides an excellent walking map and lots of information about the area. (Open Mon.-Fri. 9am-8pm, Sat. 10am-1pm and 4-7pm, Sun. 10am-1pm; Oct. and April Mon.-Fri. 9am-6pm, Sat. 10am-1pm and 4-7pm, Sun. 10am-1pm; Nov.-March Mon.-Fri. 9am-noon and 2-6pm.) Konstanz's **Mitfahrzentrale,** Münzgasse 22, can help you find a ride (open Mon.-Fri. 10am-1pm and 2pm-6pm, Sat. 10am-2pm, tel. (07531) 214 44), or check the **rideboard** at the university. **Buses** in Konstanz cost DM2. You can buy a six-ride ticket (DM9) for the Meersburg-Konstanz ferry, or a four-ride ticket (DM6) from any machine. The tourist office offers a two-day pass (DM28) including transportation on buses, the ferry, the *Weiße Flotte* ship-line to Meersburg and Mainau and back, a tour of the city, and admission to Mainau (see below).

Accommodations Konstanz has two youth hostels: far and away the top choice is the clean, comfortable **Jugendherberge Kreuzlingen (HI)** (tel. (072) 75 26 63; remember the Swiss access code, 0041), which rests in an old manor on the water south of the border in Kreuzlingen, **Switzerland**—actually the closer hostel to downtown Konstanz. The best way there is on foot; you won't get there any faster by bus (but you can try: take bus #8 to the Kreuzlingen train station and follow Bahnhofstr. left until you see signs for the hostel). From the Konstanz station cross the tracks over the rusted bridge to the back of the station. This relatively deserted road runs to the border checkpoint "Klein Venedig." Get directions from the guard or keep walking, bearing left on Seestr. until you reach the wooded paths along the shoreline. Follow them to the hostel. (Reception open 8-10am and 5-11pm. DM19. Breakfast and sheets included. If you call, remember you're dialing Switzerland! Access code is 0041.) The hostel in Konstanz proper, **Jugendherberge "Otto-Moericke-Turm" (HI)**, Allmannshohe 18 (tel. (07531) 322 60), is not as close as Kreuzlingen. Take bus #4 from the "Markstätte" stop (just around the corner from the post office in front of the station) to "Jugendherberge." (Reception open 5-5:30pm, 7-7:10pm and 9:45-9:55pm. Curfew 10pm. DM16, over 26 DM18.50. Breakfast included. Sheets DM5.50. Call ahead.) If you can't get a bed in a hostel, spending the night in Konstanz can be expensive. Budget singles run DM40-60, doubles DM60-85, and those on the lower end of the scale fill up fast. The tourist office finds rooms for a DM5 fee, and after 6pm, a queue forms at the counter. **Campingplatz Konstanz-Staad,** Fohrenbühlweg 50 (tel. (07531) 313 88 or 313 92), offers a cheaper alternative; take bus #4 to Staad. The campground is along the water. Call ahead; like the hotels, it fills up fast.

Food The **University Mensa** dishes out Konstanz's cheapest food. Lunches, including dessert and a view of the lake, cost DM3-4 (DM1 discount with students ID). Take bus #9 from the station. (Open Mon.-Fri. 8am-6pm, in Aug. open Mon.-Fri. 11am-2pm.) Stroll through the area around Rheingasse, the oldest part of Konstanz, and now the center of its vibrant alternative scene—complete with health-food stores, left-wing graffiti, and student cafés. **Sedir,** Hofhaldestr. 11, serves big bowls of vegetarian noodles for DM9 (open Mon.-Fri. 11am-2pm and 6pm-midnight, Sat.-Sun. 6pm-2am). For Greek food, try **Syrtaki,** St.-Stephans-Platz 5 (entrees 10-20DM).

Sights The **Münster,** built over the course of 600 years, has a soaring Gothic spire and 17th-century vaulting. From the tower, the panorama of the town and the lake is riveting. (Open mid-April to mid-Oct. Mon.-Fri. 9am-5pm, Sat. 10am-5pm, Sun. 1-

5pm. Free. Admission to tower DM2, students DM1.) The elaborate frescoes on the **Rathaus** depict the history of Konstanz, and the delightful inner courtyard merits at least a glance. Wander down **Seestraße,** near the yacht harbor on the lake, or **Rheinsteig** along the Rhine, two picturesque waterside promenades. The tree-filled **Stadtgarten,** next to Konstanz's main harbor, provides an opportunity to catch your breath while taking in the unbroken view down the length of the Bodensee.

Konstanz boasts a number of **public beaches;** all are free and open from May to September. **Strandbad Horn** (bus #5), the largest and often the most crowded, sports a section for nude sunbathing. **Strandbad Konstanz-Litzelstetten** and **Strandbad Konstanz-Wallhausen** can both be reached via bus #4. The twenty-something set frolics on the beach at the university (bus #4: Egg, and walk past the *Sporthalle* and playing fields). In inclement weather, head next door to **Freizeitbad Jakob,** Wilhelm-von-Scholz-Weg 2 (tel. (07531) 611 63), an ultra-modern indoor-outdoor pool complex with thermal baths and *faux*-summer sun lamps. Walk thirty minutes along the waterfront from the train station, or take bus #5 (open daily 9am-9pm; admission DM8, students DM5). **Boats** run every hour from behind the train station to the **Freizetbad** and the **Freibad Horn** (June-Aug. daily 10:50am-5:50pm, May and Sept. Sun. only, each way DM2.50, children half-price). Paddleboats, rowboats, and motorboats can all be rented at **Am Gondelhafen** (tel. (07531) 218 81). All can be rented for about DM14 per hour, with the exception of motorboats (DM60 per hour).

MAINAU

Off the northeast corner of Konstanz is the island Mainau, connected to the mainland by a footbridge. The lush and exquisitely manicured garden that covers the island is the result of the horticultural prowess of generations of Baden princes and the Swedish royal family. An arboretum, greenhouses, and huge animals made out of flowers surround a lovely Baroque palace, built by the Knights of the Teutonic Order who lived here from the 13th to the 18th centuries.

To reach Mainau, take bus #4 from the Konstanz train station to "Staad," or follow the water from the train station for a good hour. (Island open 7am-7pm. Admission DM13, students DM6, seniors DM10, children DM3; Oct.-March DM5, children free.) In spring and summer the tourist office offers a special ticket covering admission and bus transportation to and from the island (DM13, children DM4).

FRIEDRICHSHAFEN

A former construction base for zeppelins, Friedrichshafen was almost entirely leveled by Allied bombing in 1944. The current town was rebuilt with relaxingly wide promenades and tree-lined boulevards. The expansive **Graf-Zeppelin-Haus,** right on the water, commemorates the contraption that made the town such a popular target. The museum inside details the development of the flying machines and the life of their inventor. (Open Tues. and Thurs.-Sun. 10am-5pm, Wed. 10am-7pm; Nov.-April Tues. and Thurs.-Sun. 10am-noon and 2-5pm, Wed. 10am-noon and 2-7pm. Admission DM2; Wed. free.) Down the street from Graf-Zeppelin-Haus is the **Schulmuseum Friedrichshaven,** which documents school life in Germany over the last five centuries. See report cards of Bertolt Brecht and Karl Marx, whose teacher once commented "In history and geography, Karl is a bit lost." (Open daily 10am-5pm; mid-Nov. to mid-March Tues.-Sun. 2-5pm.) Also catch the **Bodensee-Museum,** the town art museum in the *Rathaus* (hours and prices same as Zeppelin Museum). Hit the beach at the **Strandbad Friedrichshafen,** Königshafen 11 (open mid-May to mid-Sept. daily 9am-8pm; admission DM2).

The **tourist office** is on Friedrichstr. (tel. (07541) 217 29), on the shore directly in front of the train station. They provide free maps, rent **bicycles** (DM7 per day), and help find rooms (DM28-40 per person). Friedrichshafen's **Jugendherberge "Graf Zeppelin" (HI),** Lindauer Str. 3 (tel. (07541) 724 04), is clean, modern, and 50m from water's edge. Call ahead; this place fills up just like the rest, especially in summer. Take the bus towards Lindau from the train station. (Reception open 5-10pm. DM17.70, over 26 DM22.70. Breakfast included. Sheets DM5.50.) Friedrichshafen is connected by frequent **buses** and less frequent **trains** to Lindau, Meersburg, and Ravensburg. The town also has unusually good tourist orientation signs, so you can find almost everything noteworthy from the *Bahnhof.*

MEERSBURG

Meersburg clings to the hillside directly across the lake from Konstanz. This glorious medieval town is graced by the **Altes Schloß,** Germany's oldest inhabited castle. Begun in the 7th century, the huge, mostly medieval edifice now houses a pile of armor. (Open daily 9am-6pm; Nov.-Feb. 10am-5pm. Admission DM7, students DM6, children DM3, groups receive DM1 discount.) Next door stands the pink baroque **Neues Schloß,** which contains an arresting staircase (!) by 18th-century architect Balthasar Neumann. (Open April-Oct. daily 10am-1pm and 2-6pm. Admission DM3, students and children DM1.50.) Beyond the new castle, along the **Uferpromenade,** you can catch a mind-occluding view of the Bodensee against a backdrop of the Alps. Climb the steep **Steigstraße** from the harbor past the crowded half-timbered houses. The **tourist office** *(Kur- und Verkehrverwaltung)* at the top of the climb, Kirschstr. 4 (tel. (07532) 823 82 or 833 83), provides token maps and books rooms (DM30-50) for DM2.50. (Open Mon.-Fri. 8am-noon and 1-5:30pm, Sat.-Sun. 10am-2pm and 4-6pm; Nov.-April Mon.-Fri. 8am-noon and 1-5:30pm.) Meersburg is half an hour from Konstanz by **boat** (DM2) and an hour from Lindau by **bus** and **rail** (change at Friedrichshafen).

LINDAU

Connected to the lake shore by a narrow causeway, the romantic medieval city of **Lindau im Bodensee** peers across the Bodensee from a small island close to the shore. Though most of the Bodensee borders Baden-Württemberg, Lindau is technically part of Bavaria. The central part of town, particularly **Maximilianstraße,** features captivating half-timbered houses. The footpaths along the harbor beg to be strolled. The **Städtische Kunstsammelung** (town art museum) is located in **Cavazzen-Haus,** an ornate Baroque *Patrizierhaus.* (Open April-Nov. Tues.-Sat. 9am-noon and 2-5pm, Sun. 10am-noon. Admission DM2.)

The **tourist office** (tel. (08382) 260 00), across from the station, finds rooms for a DM3 fee (open Mon.-Fri. 9am-6pm, Sat. 9am-1pm, holidays 3-6pm). **Ferries** link Lindau with Konstanz, stopping at Meersburg, Mainau, and Friedrichshafen (5-7 per day, 3hr., round-trip DM19.20, half-price with railpasses).

The **Jugendherberge** in town will be closed until early 1995 for renovations, so try the **Gästehaus Lädine,** in der Grub (tel. (08382) 53 26), on the island, an avatar of comfort. (Singles DM39-44, with shower DM44-49. Doubles DM69-79, with shower DM80-90. DM3 extra per person for 1-night stays. Showers included.) You can eat off the floor of the fine rooms at **Gästehaus Holdereggen,** Näherweg 4 (tel. (08382) 65 74). Follow the railroad tracks across the causeway to the mainland. Turn right onto Holdereggengasse, and then left on to Jungernburg. Näherweg is on the left. (Singles DM32. Doubles and more: DM30 per bed.) Camp at the **Campingplatz Lindau-Zech,** Frauenhoferstr. 20 (tel. (08382) 722 36), on the mainland 3km south of the island, within spitting range of the Austrian border. (DM7 per person, DM3.50 per tent. Showers included. Cars DM3.50. Open May-Sept.) Take bus #3 or 6 from the station. One of the cheapest places to eat in this expensive Bodensee town is the **Pizzeria "Alte Schüle,"** right off in der Grub at the Alter Schüleplatz. Large bowls of pasta are DM7-12.

■■■ RAVENSBURG

Largely spared the ravages of World War II, Ravensburg is a white-stucco and red-tile gem of a town, nicknamed the "town of towers." The tallest of these towers, rising from the bluff above the town below, is the so-called **Mehlsack** (flour sack), built by the citizens of Ravensburg in order to keep tabs on the constable of the **Veitsburg,** the castle that once stood farther up the bluff. Ravensburg itself had been a free city since the Middle Ages, but the higher castle remained in the hands of the former lords of the town, and the truce between them had grown uneasy (it's now long gone; a restaurant stands in its place). The Mehlsack can be reached via the steps leading up the hill from Marktstr. close by the fountain (open March-Oct. on third Sun. of month 10am-noon). During the last schoolweek, Ravensburg's schoolchildren and their teachers get to medievally act out their enmity with the lords on the hill in the humorous **Rudenfest** (Jul. 1-Jul. 5, 1994).

The **Evangelische Stadtkirche** (Protestant town church), on Seestr. just below the Veitsburg, is a strikingly simple late Gothic church containing comely 15th-century stained glass. One block farther is the long **Marienplatz,** the central market square, lined with historic buildings including the late Gothic **Rathaus** and the charming, colorful Renaissance **Lederhaus,** the former quarters of the leather workers' guild. At the other end of the Marienplatz is the **Liebfrauenkirche** (Church of Our Lady), a small, graceful Gothic church from the late 14th century that was completely renovated in the 1960s. It houses a copy of the noteworthy 15th-century *Virgin of Ravensburg,* the original of which has been moved to Berlin.

Ravensburg is easily reached by **train** from Ulm (1hr., DM20), and is an ideal base for trips to Lake Constance (DM8-19). The **tourist office** *(Verkehrsamt),* Kirchstr. 16 (tel. (0751) 823 24), is in a building called Weingartner Hof. From the train station, walk straight down Bahnhofstr. which becomes Eisenbahnstr., take a left on Marienplatz then a right down Herrenstr. to the side of the church; the office is on your right. The staff does the usual, finds rooms for free (open Mon. 8am-12:30pm, Tues.-Fri. 2-5:30pm, Sat. 9am-noon). The town's **public library,** Marienplatz 12 (tel. (0751) 822 60), in the historic *Kornhaus,* has reading rooms, **lockers** (DM1; although you're not supposed to leave the library with the key), and public restrooms (open Tues.-Fri. 10am-7pm, Sat. 10am-1pm). The main **post office** is at Eisenbahnstr. 44, 88212 Ravensburg (open Mon.-Fri. 8am-noon and 2-6pm). Ravensburg's **Mitfahrzentrale,** Charlottenstr. 3 (tel. (0751) 232 38), hooks up riders and drivers. The friendly neighborhood **Jugendherberge (HI),** Veitsburgstr. 1 (tel. (0751) 253 63), commands a breathtaking view of the valley with spotless rooms and a cheerful staff. The quickest way (although getting there is never very quick from the *Bahnhof)* up is to take the stairway, to the Mehlsack and follow it on up to the Veitsburg area. (Reception open 5-9pm. Curfew 10pm. DM17.70, over 26 DM22.70. Breakfast included. Sheets DM5.50. Open April-Oct. Call ahead.)

■■■ ULM

Perhaps best known as the birthplace of Albert Einstein, Ulm was also home to another, less rigorously scientific dreamer, the ill-fated "Tailor of Ulm." Albrecht Ludwig Berblinger, tailor by day, inventor by night, drowned in 1811 while trying to fly across the Danube with his "kite-wings" in one of the earliest serious attempts at human flight. The tailor's destination, Neu Ulm, was originally part of Ulm until Napoleon designated the Danube as the border between Bavaria and Württemberg, splitting the 800-year-old city. Despite the cartographical nitpicking, Ulm remains Bavarian to its core.

Practical Information The **tourist office** (tel. (0731) 641 61) can be found by walking toward the *Münster* spire; it's the squat, rectangular building next to the cathedral. Plenty of free and not-free maps and brochures, and they book rooms for DM5. The **main post office** is just to the left of the station, 89073 Ulm. The **telephone code** is **0731.** Rent **bikes** from the *Bahnhof* (DM12 per day, with rail pass DM8 per day) or from **Reich Fahrradverlieh,** Frauenstr. 43 (tel. 211 79; DM15 per day). Your choice. Check on the window of the tourist office for the **late-night pharmacy** telephone number(open Mon.-Fri. 9am-6pm, Sat. 9am-12:30pm).

Accommodations and Food Ulm's Jugendherberge "Geschwister Scholl" **(HI)**, Grimmelfinger Weg 45 (tel. 38 44 55), is near the edge of town behind the train station. Bus #9 (from the train station) or bus #4 (across from the *Rathaus*) to Schulzentrum, continue in the same direction and through the underpass (just up the road). Walk all the way around the athletic complex, past the tennis courts and to the road, where you should see the sign. The hostel is named in memory of a brother and sister, students at the University of Munich, executed in 1943 for conspiring against Hitler. (Reception open 4:30-7pm and 7:15-8pm, 9:30-9:45pm. Lockout 9-10am. DM18, over 26 DM23. Sheets DM5.50. Breakfast included.) **Münster-Hotel**, Münsterplatz 14 (tel. 641 62), is located, where else, near the Münster. (Singles DM45. Doubles DM80.) Across the river in Neu Ulm, **Gasthof Rose**, Kasernstr. 42a (tel. 778 03), has lovely rooms in a quiet district. (Singles DM40. Doubles DM80. Breakfast included). Ulm's restaurants reflect the culinary influences of both Swabia and Bavaria. **Gaststätte Franziskauer**, Neuestr. 56 (tel. 680 13), serves platters from both regions along with hefty steins of local brew (entrées DM12-25; open daily 9am-midnight). **Allgäuer Hof**, Fischerstr. 12 (tel. 674 08), in the fisher's quarter, serves 41 types of pancakes (DM8-15; open daily 11am-2pm and 5pm-midnight, Sat. until 1am). Across from the *Rathaus*, the **#1 Ulmer Weizenbierhaus**, Kronengasse 12 (tel. 624 96), pours more than 20 varieties of *Weizenbier* (open daily 4pm-3am). Ulm has a **farmer's market** on Münsterplatz (Wed. and Sat. morning).

Sights At 161m, the steeple topping the **Ulm Münster** is the highest in the world. Next to the front portal of the cathedral is *The Man of Sorrows*, a famous representation of Christ by 15th-century sculptor Hans Multscher. Inside the Gothic walls, extravagantly carved choir stalls (by Jörg Syrlin the Elder) bemuse onlookers with a small community of busts arranged in pairs along the corridors. The lowliest tier, at eye level, depicts Greek and Roman philosophers and various sibyls, supposedly modeled after Syrlin's friends and relatives. Climb the 768 dizzying corkscrew steps of the spire and you'll remember it—on a clear day you can see the Alps. (Open daily 9am-7:45pm; fall-spring daily 9am-4:45pm. Church interior free. Daily organ concerts 11am-noon. Free. Spire admission DM2, children DM1.) Toward the river along Neuestr. the fabulously painted **Rathaus**, built in 1370, is decorated with brilliantly colored murals from 1540. The old **Fishermen's Quarter** *(Fischerviertel)*, down Kronengasse from the *Rathaus*, has the classics: half-timbered houses, narrow cobblestone streets, and footbridges spanning a network of canals. The **Shiefes Haus** (Crooked House) is the most interesting of the lot. Continuing the trend of askew construction, the 14th-century **Metzgerturm** (Butcher's Tower) has some psychedelic shingles, and the **Schiefer Turm** (Crooked Tower) leans out precariously next to the Danube. The remnants of the city wall run along the river here, and the bank has been turned into an alluring park.

On the other side of the *Rathaus* is the **Ulmer Museum**, with a historical exegesis of the region from prehistory to the present. (Open Tues.-Sun. 10am-5pm, Thurs. until 8pm. Free. Special exhibits DM7, students, children and seniors DM5.) The **Deutsches Brotmuseum** (German Bread Museum), Salzstadelstr. 10, documents 6000 years of breadmaking and waxes philosophical about "the *Leitmotiv* of Man and Bread" (open Tues.-Sun. 10am-5pm; admission DM4.50, students DM3). A monument marking **Albert Einstein's birthplace** stands in front of the station. He only lived here a year, and the house has long since given way to a glass-and-chrome savings and loan establishment. Every year on the penultimate Monday of July (July 18 in 1994), the mayor of Ulm takes the stand at the **Schwörhaus** (Oath House), to carry on a centuries-old tradition by swearing allegiance to the town's 1397 constitution. The whole affair is accompanied by excessive drinking.

Central Southern Germany: Black Forest and Romantic Road

Mannheim

Ludwigshafen

Neckar

Heidelberg

Speyer

Neckar-Steinach

Burg Guttenburg

Bad Wimpfen

Heilbronn

Goldenes Adler

Karlsruhe

FRANCE

Pforzheim

Baden-Baden

Stuttgart

Esslingen

Strasbourg

500

Freudenstadt

Tübingen

Neckar

Rhine

Gutach

Triberg

Rottweil

Breisach

Furtwangen

Danube

Federse

St. Peter

Donau-eschingen

Freiburg

St. Märgen

Titisee

Feldberg

Schluchsee

Bodensee (Lake Constance)

Meersburg

Konstanz

Friedrichs-hafen

0   25 miles

N

0   25 kilometers

SWITZERLAND

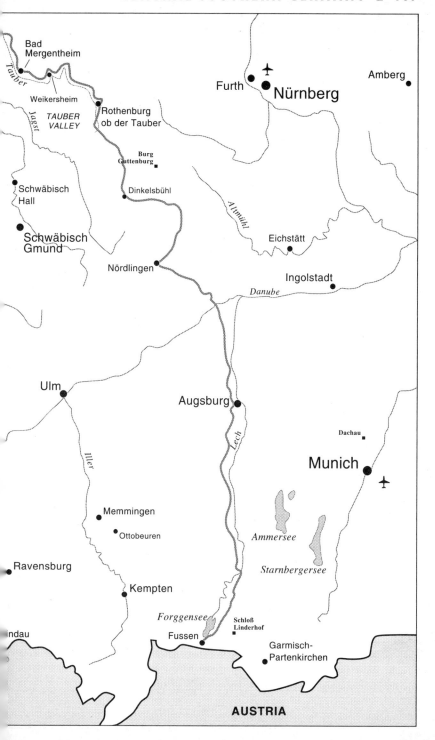

BAVARIA (BAYERN)

From the villages of the Bavarian Forest and the Baroque cities along the Danube to the turreted castles perched in the Alps, Bavaria is the Germany of fairy tale, Teutonic myth, and Wagnerian opera. In fact, the region is often the only part of Germany that visitors see, a tradition that traces its roots to the invading Roman Legions of the first century who never made it past the Danube. When most foreigners conjure up images of Germany, they are thinking of Bavaria-land of beer halls, oom-pah bands, and Lederhosen. The fact that they do is partly a relic of the geography of German division, which shifted the balance of West Germany southward and hindered Berlin from acting as a counterweight to straight-edge Munich. The independent local residents have always been Bavarians first and Germans second; it took wars with France and Austria to pull the Kingdom of Bavaria into Bismarck's orbit, and local authorities still insist upon using the *Land*'s proper name: the Free State of Bavaria. Germany's central government has still not overcome Bavarian particularism. Bavaria was the only state to refuse to ratify the Federal Republic's Basic Law in a plebiscite, and the ruling Christian Democratic Union still abides by a long-standing agreement not to compete in Bavarian elections (instead, a related Bavarian party, the Christian Social Union, represents the Right in the region). Though mostly rural, Catholic, and staunchly conservative (save Munich), this largest of Germany's federal states is also home to commerce and industry, including such renowned companies as Bayerische Motor-Werke (BMW).

> Reminder: HI-affiliated hostels in Bavaria do not admit guests over age 26.

■■■ MUNICH (München)

By most accounts, Munich is Germany's Second City. The capital and cultural center of Bavaria, Munich is a sprawling, liberal cosmopolis in the midst of solidly conservative southern Germany. Western Germany's postwar economic glory suffuses this place. World-class museums, handsome parks and architecture, a rambunctious theater and art scene, and an urbane populace collude to create a city of astonishing vitality. An ebullient, arrogant mixture of sophistication and earthy Bavarian *Gemütlichkeit* keeps the city awake all hours. *Münchners* party particularly zealously during *Fasching,* Germany's equivalent of Mardi Gras or Carnival, and during the legendary *Oktoberfest.* Before reunification, Munich was the shadow capital of Germany; now that the Wall has fallen, its popularity has been eclipsed by the cutting-edge energy of Berlin. Though it has plenty to offer in terms of beer and architecture, Munich may have to take a back seat from here on out.

HISTORY

Those stately monuments and public buildings that survived World War II testify to the imperial aspirations of the House of Wittelsbach, the dynasty that ruled Bavaria from the 12th to the late 19th century as dukes, prince-electors, and later kings. Though *Münchners* are loath to admit it, the city was actually founded by a northerner, Heinrich der Löwe (Henry the Lion), who built a bridge across the Isar in 1158 to consolidate his hold on the Austrian salt trade. By the end of the century, the town was fortified behind a city wall and rapidly growing in power. Even after the Wittelsbachs moved their court to Munich in the late 13th century, several other cities, including Landshut and Straubing, continued to rival Munich for supremacy in Bavaria. But the dynasty's ruthless acquisition of territory and privileges trickled down into growing wealth and grandeur for Munich. The Reformation was mercilessly suppressed in the lands under Wittelsbach domain, and when the Protestant King Gustav Adolphus of Sweden occupied Munich in the Thirty Years War, the city only managed to save itself by paying ransom in blood. Several heads of prominent hostages rolled. Periodic war, revolt and intrigue failed to shake Wittelsbach rule through the 18th century, when by Friedrich the Great kept Munich from falling under Austrian control. Napoleon's romp over the European continent included a brief occupation of Munich, which sided with the French against the Holy Roman Empire. When Napoleon dissolved the anachronistic empire, Bavaria was rewarded with the status of Kingdom, with Munich as its capital.

The Kingdom period is still remembered as the Bavarian Golden Age, when enlightened (though still absolutist) rulers rationalized state administration, promoted commerce and patronized the arts. The most famous king, Ludwig II, spent little time in Munich, preferring to find solace in his extravagant castles. In 1871, after Bismarck's successful wars solidified Prussian dominance, Ludwig presided over the absorption of Bavaria into the greater German Reich (a process somewhat lubricated by Prussia's generous subsidization of Ludwig's building schemes). With all of Germany now under Prussian dominance, Bavaria was a kingdom in name only. Munich, however, remained a cultural power that rivaled hated Berlin (a city that *Münchners* regarded as a glorified garrison town). Franz Wedekind, Paul Klee, Wassily Kandinsky, and Franz Marc (among others) stimulated the vibrant artistic and intellectual scene that flourished in Munich at the turn of the century.

The Golden Age came to an abrupt end with Germany's ignominious defeat in World War I. In the chaos following the war, Munich briefly became the capital of an independent Bavarian Soviet Republic, until the revolutionaries were brutally suppressed by right-wing *Freikorps*. Weimar Munich was something of an incubator for reactionary and anti-Semitic movements. Adolf Hitler found the city such a fertile recruiting ground for the new National Socialist German Workers Party (Nazis) that he later called Munich "the capital of our movement." In 1923, Hitler attempted to overthrow the municipal government and lead a march on Berlin to topple the Weimar Republic. His "Beer Hall *Putsch*" was quickly quashed and its leaders arrested, but Germany had not seen the end of the Austrian corporal. Munich carries a number of other unsavory associations with the Third Reich: Neville Chamberlain's attempted appeasement of Hitler over the Sudetenland is (erroneously) remembered as the "Munich Agreement," and one of the Nazis' first concentration camps was constructed just outside the city at Dachau.

Despite Munich's fortuitous location deep inside German air defenses, Allied bombing did a particularly thorough job of destroying the city, and the post-war building boom was so intense that many salvageable old buildings were demolished anyway. The only substantial portion of Munich that looks the same as before the War is the area around the Marienplatz. When Munich hosted the 1972 Olympics, it was hoped that the Games would rehabilitate the city's tattered image once and for all. A tragic attack by a Palestinian terrorist group called *Black September*, which led to the death of 11 Israeli athletes in a police shoot-out, tarnished those hopes.

ORIENTATION AND PRACTICAL INFORMATION

South-central Bavaria is Munich's ground; only a short distance away lie Augsburg, Füssen, and Garmisch-Partenkirchen. Nüremberg is to the north, and trains to Vienna run through Passau. The **Isar River** flows basically north-south through Munich; it traces a line along the edge of the enormous **Englischer Garten** to the east, and the central district of the city.

Touring by foot is easy in Munich's compact center. **Schützenstraße,** straight ahead from the main train station, leads towards **Neuhauser Straße,** the main pedestrian shopping street. Neuhauser Str. connects **Karlsplatz am Stachus** and the famed **Marienplatz.** Im Tal leads further to Isartorplatz on the Thomas-Wimmer-Ring stretch of the large and busy sectional highway that roughly encircles central Munich. From here it's only three blocks down Zweibrückenstr. to the Isar River, which the monumental **Deutsches Museum** guards from the long, thin **Museuminsel.** North of Marienplatz, the pedestrian zone ranges to **Odeonsplatz,** next to the *Residenz* palace. **Ludwigstraße,** Munich's strip of iniquity and chic nightlife, leads to the University, from which Leopoldstr. continues north through **Schwabing,** the

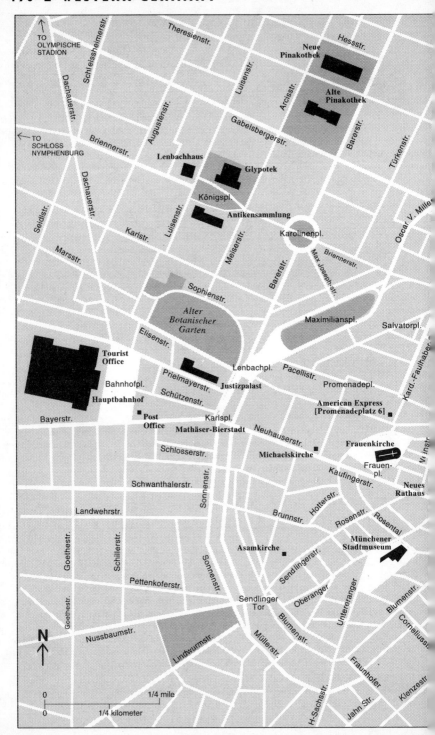

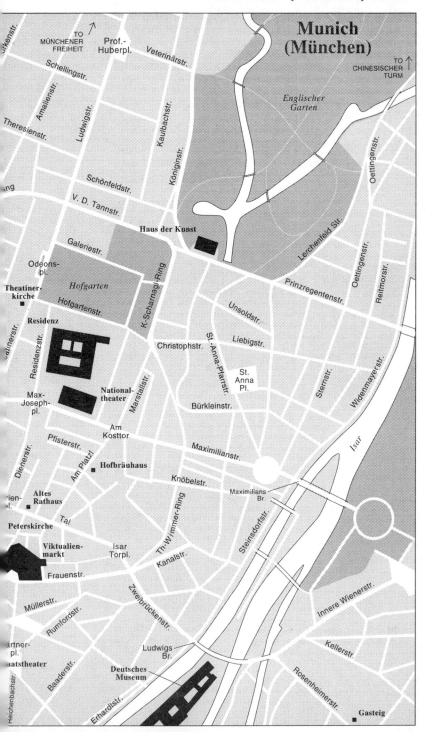

Munich (München)

TO MÜNCHENER FREIHEIT

Prof.-Huberpl.

Veterinärstr.

TO CHINESISCHER TURM

Englischer Garten

Schellingstr.

Amalienstr.

Ludwigstr.

Theresienstr.

Kaulbachstr.

Königinstr.

Schönfeldstr.

V. D. Tannstr.

Oettingenstr.

Galeriestr.

Haus der Kunst

Odeons-pl.

Hofgarten

Theatiner-kirche

Hofgartenstr.

K.-Scharnagl-Ring

Lerchenfeld Str.

Oettingenstr.

Reitmorstr.

Prinzregentenstr.

Residenz

Residenzstr.

Unsoldstr.

Liebigstr.

Christophstr.

St.-Anna-Pfarstr.

St. Anna Pl.

Sternstr.

Widenmayerstr.

Max-Joseph-pl.

National-theater

Marstallstr.

Bürkleinstr.

Isar

Am Kosttor

Maximilianstr.

Pfisterstr.

Dienerstr.

Am Platzl

Hofbräuhaus

Knöbelstr.

Maximilians Br.

Altes Rathaus

Th.-Wimmer-Ring

Steinsdorfstr.

Tal

Peterskirche

Viktualien-markt

Isar Torpl.

Kanalstr.

Frauenstr.

Innere Wienerstr.

Müllerstr.

Rumfordstr.

Zweibrückenstr.

ärtner-pl.

...aatstheater

Ludwigs Br.

Kellerstr.

Baaderstr.

Deutsches Museum

Rosenheimerstr.

Reichenbachstr.

Erhardtstr.

Gasteig

student district. To the east of Schwabing sprawls the *Englischer Garten*; to the west is the **Olympiazentrum**, a hyper-modern settlement built for the 1972 games, surrounded by the verdant Olympiapark. Further southwest lies posh **Nymphenburg**, built around **Nymphenburg Palace.** Southwest of Marienplatz, **Sendlingerstraße** leads past shops and the Baroque **Asamkirche** to the Sendlingertor. Lindwurmstr. proceeds onward to Goetheplatz, from which Mozartstr. leads to **Theresienwiese,** site of the annual *Oktoberfest.*

There are several publications to help you find your way around Munich. The most comprehensive one (in English) is *Munich Found* (DM3.50), which itself can be found at the **Internationale Presse** booth in the center of the train station, at the Anglia English Bookshop (see Bookstores, below), and elsewhere. The tourist office distributes the encyclopedic *Monatsprogramm* (DM2) in German with basically the same info as *Munich Found*, though without current articles.

Tourist Offices:
Main office: Fremdenverkehrsamt (tel. 239 12 56 or 239 12 57), opposite track 11 in the main train station. A near must, but expect to wait 15min. or more in the summer. EurAide (listed below) is usually faster and just as helpful. The *Fremdenverkehrsamt* staff books rooms (DM5 per room plus DM3 deposit) and sells accommodations lists (DM0.50). Pick up the excellent free map, or buy one with a street-name index for DM3. *Munich for Young People* (DM1) is cute but a little out of date. Call for recorded information on museums and galleries (tel. 23 91 61) or on sights and castles (tel. 23 91 71); for English recordings call (tel. 23 91 62) and (tel. 23 91 72) respectively.
Branch offices: At the new ultra-modern **Flughafen Munich** airport (tel. 97 59 28 15) in the *Zentralgebäude*. Provides general information, but no room bookings. Open Mon.-Sat. 8:30am-10pm, Sun. 1-9pm. **Ruffinihaus,** on Pettenbeckstr. at Rindermarkt, has the same free maps and many of the same brochures and also finds rooms for DM5. Open Mon.-Fri. 9:30am-6pm.
EurAide in English: In the station at track 11 next to the train police (tel. 59 38 89). Provides train information, makes room reservations (DM6), and will generally facilitate your passage through the tourist bureaucracy. Their *Inside Track* (free) is available in their office and at the *Reisezentrum*. *Thomas Cook Timetables* sold (DM37), and Eurailpasses validated. They also offer outings to the Royal Castles (Königsschlößer). Open daily 7:30-11:30am and 1-6pm.
Regional office: Fremdenverkehrsverband München-Oberbayern, Sonnenstr. 10 (tel. 59 73 47). Has brochures, maps, and information for the upper Bavaria region.
Tours:
Radius Touristik: opposite track 35 in the train station (tel. 59 61 13). Offers the most adventurous tours of Munich during the tourist season (the summer months plus a little extra around the edges). 2hr. **walking** tour of the old city daily 10:30am; DM12. Also, a **bike** tour (16km) which takes advantage of Munich's web of cycling paths Sat. 10am.; DM25, DM18 with own bike. The "Munich in a Day" tour covers most major sights.
Panorama Tours: Arnulfstr. 8 (tel. 120 42 48), offers bilingual **bus** tours of varying lengths which leave from across the street from the train station's main entrance. 1hr. tour daily 10, 11:30am and 2:30pm; Oct.-May daily 11:30am; DM15, children DM8. 2½hr. tour daily 10am and 2:30pm, with a special visit to either the Alte Pinakothek (Tues.-Sun. 10am), the Olympic Park (Mon. 10am), or the Nymphenburg palace (Tues.-Sun. 2:30pm); DM27, children DM14.
Deutsche Gewerkschaftsbund (German Trade Union Federation): gives free historical tours of the city on the first Sat. of every month. German only. Tours depart from Schwanthalerstr. 64 at 10am.
Jugendlage Kapuzinerhölzl (see Accommodations, below): Earthy walking tours depart from the Tent every Wed. 9am. Free.
Budget Travel: Studiosus Reisen an der Uni, Amalienstr. 73 (tel. 50 06 05 40, ext. 544), near the university. Open Mon.-Fri. 9am-6pm. FIYTO cards and ISICs sold Mon.-Fri. 10am-2pm. **Travel Overland,** Leopoldstr. 13 (tel. 34 67 21 or 27

27 60) behind the pink library in the university cafeteria. Open Mon.-Fri. 10am-2pm. **abr Reisebüro,** at the train station (tel. 55 34 46). Open Mon.-Fri. 9am-6pm and Sat. 9am-noon.

Consulates: U.S., Königinstr. 5 (tel. 288 80). **Canada,** Tal 29 (tel. 22 26 61). **U.K.,** Bürkleinstr. 10 (tel. 21 10 90). **Ireland,** Mauerkircherstr. 1a (tel. 98 57 23 25).

Currency Exchange: Use the **post office** across from the station to exchange large denomination traveler's checks (DM3 fee per check). **Deutsche Verkehrs-Bank (DVB),** at the main station, also changes currency and checks, and advances cash on MC and Visa. Pick up the free publication *Inside Track* at the EurAide office and receive a 50% commission reduction for U.S. traveler's checks totalling above $50 at the DVB. Open daily 6am-11:30pm.

American Express: Promenadeplatz 6 (tel. 219 90). From the station, walk straight through Karlsplatz to Neuhauserstr., then turn left on Ettstr.; follow it 2 blocks and across the little park. Holds mail and cashes AmEx "Traveler's Cheques" for no kiquebaque. Personal check-cashing service of up to US$1000 for cardholders. Open Mon.-Fri. 9am-5:30pm, Sat. 9am-noon.

Post Office: Post/Telegrafamt, Bahnhofplatz 1, 80335 München (tel. 53 88 27 32), directly opposite the main train station. **Poste Restante** counter near the back wall open daily 7am-11pm. All other services open 24hrs.

Telephones: International phone booths are located on various tracks and elsewhere in the train station. Make credit card and collect calls from the post office on the 2nd level of the station or across the street. **City code:** 089.

Flights: Munich's spiffy airport, **Flughafen München,** is accessible from the train station by S-Bahn 8 (every 20min. daily 3:13am-11:13pm). DM12, or 8 stripes on a 12-stripe ticket *(Streifenkarte);* railpasses valid.

Trains: The transportation hub of southern Germany, Munich has connections to all major cities in Germany and throughout Europe several times per day. To: Frankfurt (40 per day, 3½hr.), Berlin (25 per day, 9½hr.), Cologne (37 per day, 6½hr.), Hamburg (20 per day, 7hr.), Prague (10 per day, 7hr.), Zürich (5 per day, 4½hr.), Vienna (19 per day, 5½hr.), Paris (8 per day, 10hr.), Amsterdam (18 per day, 9hr.). Call for **schedules** (tel. 194 19); **fare information** (tel. 55 41 41); **reservations** (in German only, tel. 128 59 94). **EurAide** (see Tourist Offices, above), in the station, provides free train information in unaccented English. Otherwise, the best source of information is a **destination leaflet,** available from a stand in the station's information office. These list all the possible connections between Munich and scores of other cities. Station open daily 5am-12:30am.

Public Transportation:

Basic Information and Fares: Munich's public transport system runs from about 5am-12:30am on weekdays, 5am-1:30am on weekends. Eurailpasses and German rail passes are valid on any S-Bahn (commuter rail), but neither is valid on the U-Bahn (subway), *Straßenbahn* (streetcars), or buses. Single rides within the *Innenraum* (inner city) cost DM3. Cancel your ticket in the boxes marked with an "E" *before you go to the platform.* If you plan to jump the fare, bring along an extra DM60 to hand over to the frequent, unforgiving inspectors. If you can't pay up on the spot, you go to jail.

Special Passes and Maps: The *Tageskarte Innenraum* (inner-city day pass), valid on all public transport for up to 2 people until 4am (DM10), is usually the most convenient and economical way to get around. Don't bother with the day-pass for the entire Munich area *(Gesamttarifgebiet).* 12-ride *Streifenkarte* (DM14) can be more economical and more flexible than the day ticket (ride length determines the number of stripes you must cancel). For *Streifenkarten,* you must cancel 2 sections for every zone you travel in (i.e., for traveling within the city center *(Innenraum)* you need cancel only 2 sections per trip). **Transit maps** can be picked up in the tourist office or EurAide, and at MVV counters near the subway entrance in the train station.

Taxi: Taxi-Zentrale (tel. 216 10 or 194 10) forwards your call to the nearest cab stand. Women can request a female driver. Large **stands** in front of the train station, and every 5-10 blocks throughout central Munich. Rides DM2.20 per km.

Car Rental: Autovermietung München, Auguststr. 13 (tel. 18 40 30), rents compacts for DM79 per day, with the first 200km included. **Flach's Leihwagen,**

Landsberger Str. 289 (tel. 56 60 56), rents cars from DM84 per day, with no mileage charge. Open Mon.-Fri. 8am-8pm.

Bike Rental: Bikes can be rented from the Deutsche Bahn at 15 S-Bahn locations and returned to train stations throughout Upper Bavaria. They cost DM12 per day, DM8 for rail-ticket holders. Cheapest and most convenient to the town center is **Radius Touristik** (tel. 59 61 13), near platform 35 at the station, owned by a friendly English couple. Owners loan raincoats to bikers in inclement weather. Bikes DM5 per hr., DM20 per day. DM50 deposit. Students and Eurailpass holders receive a 10% discount. Open daily 9am-6:30pm. They also run a bike rental at the southern entrance to the *Englischer Garten* (same prices and phone). **Jugendlage Kapuzinerhölzl** (see hostels listings) also rents bikes. DM8 per day; distribution open 7-9am, returns 5pm.

Lost and Found: Städtisches Fundbüro, Ruppertstr. 19 (tel. 23 31). Open Mon.-Fri. 8:30am-noon, Tues. also 2-5:30pm. For items lost on trains, **Fundstelle der DB,** Bahnhofplatz 2 (tel. 128 66 64), across from track 26. Open daily 6:30am-11:30pm.

Hitchhiking: Let's Go does not recommend hitchhiking as a safe mode of transportation. Those who choose to hitchhike often can scan the bulletin boards in the *Mensa,* Leopoldstr. 13. Otherwise, they try the *Autobahn* on-ramps; *those who stand behind the blue sign with the white auto may be heavily fined.* Hitchers who've gotta get to *Autobahn* E11 (direction "Salzburg-Vienna-Italy") start with U-Bahn 1 or 2: Karl-Preis-Platz. For E11 in the opposite direction ("Stuttgart/France"), they take U-Bahn 1: Rotkreuzplatz, then streetcar #12: Amalienburgstr.; or S-Bahn 2: Obermenzing. Either way, some are said to take bus #73 or 75: Blutenburg. Thumbers who want to get to the *Autobahn* E6 interchange for all points north take U-Bahn 6: Studetenstadt and walk 500m to the Frankfurter Ring. For the *Autobahn* to Lake Constance and Switzerland, these intrepid souls take U-Bahn 4 or 5: Heimeranplatz, then bus #33: Siegenburgerstr. For Garmisch-Partenkirchen, hitchers head for the *Autobahn* E6 south; U-Bahn 3 or 6: Westpark, and from bus #33: Luise-Kesselbach-Platz.

Mitfahrzentrale: Lämmerstr. 4 (tel. 59 45 61), near the train station. Open daily 8am-8pm. **Känguruh,** Amalienstr. 87 (tel. 194 44), in the Amalienpassage. Open Mon.-Fri. 8:30am-7pm, Sat. 9am-3pm, Sun. 10am-3pm. Both match drivers and passengers for a small fee. **Frauenmitfahrzentrale,** Klenzstr. 57b (tel. 201 46 90). U-Bahn 1: Frauenhoferstr., then walk up Frauenhoferstr. away from the river and turn right. For women only. Open Mon.-Fri. 8am-8pm.

Bookstores: Anglia English Bookshop, Schellingstr. 3 (tel. 28 36 42), has a gloriously chaotic atmosphere. Open Mon.-Fri. 9am-8:30pm, Sat. 9:30am-2pm. **Wordsworth,** a bit farther down at Schellingstr. 21a (tel. 280 91 41), offers more obscure English novels as well as a full range of literature from the greats. **Internationale Presse,** in the train station, sells a large variety of English-language materials. **Lillemor's Frauenbuchladen,** Arcisstr. 57 (tel. 272 12 05), is a women's bookstore (open Mon.-Fri. 10am-6pm, Sat. 10am-2pm).

Libraries: Bayrische Staatsbibliothek, Ludwigstr. 16 (tel. 28 63 80). Reading rooms open Mon.-Fri. 9am-7:30pm, Sat. 9am-4:30pm.

Cultural Centers:

Amerika Haus, Karolinenplatz 3 (tel. 59 53 67, fax 55 35 78). Cultural resources, advice for Americans wishing to teach. Full library. Open Mon.-Fri. 1-7:30pm.

British Council, Rosenheimer Str. 116b (tel. 40 18 32).

Deutsch-Kanadische-Gesellschaft, Gräfelfinger Str. 20 (tel. 71 51 46).

Munich Scottish Association, Schleißheimer Str. 394 (tel. 354 36 46).

Deutsch-Japanische Gesellschaft in Bayern, Marienplatz 1 (tel. 22 18 63).

Women's Centers: Frauenzentrum Treibhaus mit Café, Güllstr. 3 (tel. 77 40 41). *Kaffee und Küchen* in addition to the information. **Frauenbibliothek und Frauenzentrum,** Nymphenburgerstr. 182 (tel. 16 04 51), is more of a resource for pamphlets and books. Open Mon.-Fri. 8am-7pm.

Ticket Agencies: Tickets for concerts in the **Olympiapark** and soccer games are available on the 3rd floor of the **Kaufhof** department store (tel. 260 32 49) on Marienplatz. Open Mon.-Fri. 11am-6pm, Sat. 11am-2pm. **Studiosus Reisen** (tel. 28 07 68) sells student tickets for theater and concerts. Open 9:30am-12:30pm.

Laundromat: Wasch-Center, Klenzestr. 18. S-Bahn (from the main station): Isartor (2 stops). Walk 1 block down Rumfordstr. and turn left. Wash DM6, dry DM0.50 per 15min. Soap included. Open daily 6am-10:30pm. **Münz Wäschsalon,** Amalienstr. 61, near the university. Wash DM6, dry DM1. Soap DM1. Open Mon.-Fri. 8am-6:30pm, Sat. 8am-1pm. **Wäscherei,** Landshuter Allee 77. U-Bahn 1: Rotkreuzplatz, follow Leonrodstr. to Landshuter Allee and turn left. The laundromat is located about a block away, on the corner of Volkartstr. Open 24hrs. Wash DM6, dry DM0.50 per 15min. *Bring your own change for all laundromats.*
Pharmacy: Bahnhof Apotheke (tel. 59 41 19), on the corner outside the station. Open Mon.-Fri. 8am-6:30pm, Sat. 8am-2pm. 24hr. service rotates among the city's pharmacies—call 59 44 75 for recorded information (German only). The tourist office and EurAide also have free monthly schedules.
Medical Assistance: University clinic, across the river on Ismaningerstr. VD and AIDS tests free and anonymous at the **Gesundheitshaus,** Dachauerstr. 90 (tel. 520 71). Open Mon.-Thurs. 8-11am and 1-2pm, Fri. 8-11am. U.S. and British consulates carry a list of English-speaking doctors.
Rape Crisis: tel. 76 37 37.
Emergencies: Police: tel. 110. **Ambulance:** tel. 192 22. **Emergency medical service:** tel. 55 86 61.

ACCOMMODATIONS AND CAMPING

Accommodations in Munich generally fall into one of three categories: seedy, expensive, or booked solid. During *Oktoberfest,* there is only one category. During the summer, the best strategy is to start calling around before noon, or to book a few weeks in advance, especially for longer stays. Remember, **Bavarian HI hostels do not accept guests over age 26.** At several of Munich's hostels you can check in all day—start your search well before 5pm. Sleeping in the *Englischer Garten* is unsafe and illegal; the police sometimes patrol. If you have a railpass, Augsburg's hostel (30-45min. by train) is a viable option, but be mindful of the 11pm curfew. Many wandering backpackers who arrive too late to find lodging cluster in the train station; this practice is extremely unsafe for body and property. If you have no other alternative but to fall in with one of these groups, don't fall asleep unless someone you know and trust is awake and watching you—cherubic-looking backpackers may turn out to be thieves or worse. A safer though by no means risk-free alternative for railpass-holders is hopping a late train. The 12:41am train to Stuttgart works best because it runs direct. Arrive in Stuttgart at 4:39am and catch the 4:54am train back to Munich. Arrive in Munich at 7:27am, and start looking for a real room as soon as you arrive. *Double check* an up-to-date train schedule before trying this stunt.

Hostels and Camping

Jugendlage Kapuzinerhölzl ("The Tent"), Frank-Schrank-Str. (tel. 141 43 00). U-Bahn 1: Rotkreuzplatz, then streetcar #12 (direction "Amalienburgstr."): Botanischer Garten. *Don't ride without a ticket*—inspections are especially rigorous on this route. Sleep with 400 other people in a big tent. Gets you a foam pad, blankets, a dry spot on the floor, bathrooms, a shower (not necessarily warm), hot tea, and enthusiastic management. Spontaneous merrymaking around the bonfire in the evening. Unfortunately, the Tent's future is in doubt; call ahead. 3-day max. stay (flexible). Reception open 5pm-9am. No lockers—use the ones at the station. Under 24 only (flexible). DM7. No reservations. Open late June to early Sept. If you have thoughts of staying without paying, forget them. They'll find you.
Jugendherberge Burg Schwaneck (HI), Burgweg 4-6 (tel. 793 06 43), in a castle far from the city. S-Bahn 7 (direction "Wolfratshausen"): Pullach (last train at 10:40pm), and follow the signs that begin on Margaretenstr. (15min.). Unmajestic but entirely adequate. Swarms of schoolchildren. 6- to 8-bed dorms. Reception open 5-11pm. Curfew 11:30pm. Under 27 only. DM14.50. Buy a shower token (DM2) early, as there are a limited number. Sheets DM4.50 Breakfast included.
Jugendgästehaus München (HI), Miesingstr. 4 (tel. 723 65 50). U-Bahn 1 or 2: Sendlinger Tor, then U-Bahn 3: Thalkirchen (Tierpark), walk south on Pognerstr.

and turn left on Frauenbergstr. Cross Plinganserstr., then walk 2 blocks and turn right onto Miesingerstr. Crowded and distant, but the rooms are spacious and immaculate. Reception open 7am-1am; rooms available after 3pm. Curfew 1am. Under 27 only. 8- to 15-bed dorms DM23. Singles DM31. Doubles DM54. Triples DM75. Quads DM100. Sheets and breakfast included.

Jugendherberge (HI), Wendl-Dietrichstr. 20. (tel. 13 11 56). U-Bahn 1: Rotkreuzplatz; enter on Winthirplatz. Central location attracts noisy crowds. Management has just installed new safes in the reception area. *Use them*, and keep all keys on your person at *all* times. Check-in starts at 10am, but lines form before 9am. Reception open 10am-1am. Lockout 9am-noon. Curfew 1am. Under 27 only. DM19.80-21. Breakfast and sheets included.

Haus International Youth Hotel, Elisabethstr. 87, 80797 München (tel. 12 00 60, fax 12 00 62 51). U-Bahn 2 (direction "Dülferstr."): Hohenzollernplatz, then streetcar #12 or bus #33: Barbarastr. Bare concrete interior design, reminiscent of dorm life except that everything is delightfully clean. Disco, swimming pool, cafeteria. Singles DM51, with shower DM79. Doubles DM96, with shower DM132. Triples DM129. Quads DM156. Quints DM190. Reservations by mail or fax.

CVJM (YMCA) Jugendgästehaus, Landwehrstr. 13, 80336 München (tel. 552 14 10), 2 blocks south of the station. Convenient, with clean, no-frills rooms and a pristine moral environment. Slightly seedy neighborhood. Reception open 8am-12:30am. Curfew 12:30am. Singles DM45. Doubles DM78. Triples DM108. Over 27 add 15% surcharge. Breakfast included. Reservations by telephone and/or mail.

Kolpinghaus St. Theresa, Hanebergstr. 8 (tel. 12 60 50). U-Bahn 1: Rotkreuzplatz, then walk down Leonrodstr., and turn left at Platz der Freiheit onto Landshuterstr. Walk 4 blocks and turn left. Simple, tidy rooms and communal showers. Reception open 8am-3pm. Singles DM43. Doubles DM75. Triples DM92.

Jugendhotel Marienberge, Goethestr. 9 (tel. 55 58 91), less than a block south of the train station. Rough neighborhood but secure building. The rooms in this Catholic hostel are comfortable and spotless. Kitchen and laundry facilities (wash DM2, dry DM2). *Open only to women between ages 18 and 25*. Reception open 8am-noon and 4pm-midnight. Curfew midnight. Singles DM31. Doubles DM54. Triples DM81. Giant 6-bed dorms DM25 per person. Showers included.

Camping: Campingplatz Thalkirchen, Zentralländstr. 49 (tel. 723 17 07), in the Isar River Valley Conservation Area. U-Bahn 1 or 2: Sendlinger Tor, then U-Bahn 3: Thalkirchen. Large and crowded. Curfew 11pm. DM6 per person, DM3-4.50 per tent, DM5 per car. Showers DM1. Laundry facilities and a cheap restaurant (meals DM2-6). Open mid-March to Oct.

Hotels and Pensionen

When the city is full, finding singles under DM50-60 or doubles for less than DM80-100 can be nearly impossible. Some places refuse service to English-speaking backpackers, the owners having cleaned up one too many puddles of collegiate beer. The tourist office charges DM5 to find lodgings. When they say they have nothing available under DM60, believe them. EurAide at the station also finds rooms for a DM6 fee. If seedy is okay, poke around the neighborhood around the train station (during the daytime, please) where many small, less-than-spotless *Pensionen* can be found. Always ask to see the room before committing yourself to such a place.

Hotel-Pension am Markt, Heiliggeiststr. 6 (tel. 22 50 14), between Viktualienmarkt and Im Tal, next to Heiliggeist Kirche, in the town center. Aging photographs recall the celebrities who have graced the hotel's sparsely furnished, thoroughly clean rooms. Singles DM62, with shower DM89. Doubles DM110, with shower DM124-150. Reserve rooms 3-4 weeks in advance by phone only.

Pension am Kaiserplatz, Kaiserplatz 12 (tel. 34 91 90). U-Bahn 1 or 2 (from the main station): Odeonsplatz, then U-Bahn 3 or 6: Münchner Freiheit, take the escalator to Herzogstr., follow it until you take a left onto Viktoriastr., walk to Kaiserplatz (10min.). Sweet; carefully decorated, elegant, high-ceilinged rooms in a small *Pension*. Reception open daily 7am-8pm. Singles DM45-49. Doubles DM69-

So, you're getting away from it all.

Just make sure you can get back.

AT&T Access Numbers
Dial the number of the country you're in to reach AT&T.

*ANDORRA	19◇-0011	GERMANY**	0130-0010	*NETHERLANDS	06◇-022-9111
*AUSTRIA	022-903-011	*GREECE	00-800-1311	*NORWAY	050-12011
*BELGIUM	078-11-0010	*HUNGARY	00◇-800-01111	POLAND¹◆²	0◇010-480-0111
BULGARIA	00-1800-0010	*ICELAND	999-001	PORTUGAL¹	05017-1-288
CROATIA¹◆	99-38-0011	IRELAND	1-800-550-000	ROMANIA	01-800-4288
*CYPRUS	080-90010	ISRAEL	177-100-2727	*RUSSIA¹ (MOSCOW)	155-5042
CZECH REPUBLIC	00-420-00101	*ITALY	172-1011	SLOVAKIA	00-420-00101
*DENMARK	8001-0010	KENYA¹	0800-10	SPAIN	900-99-00-11
*EGYPT¹ (CAIRO)	510-0200	*LIECHTENSTEIN	155-00-11	*SWEDEN	020-795-611
*FINLAND	9800-100-10	LITHUANIA◆	8◇196	*SWITZERLAND	155-00-11
FRANCE	19◇-0011	LUXEMBOURG	0-800-0111	*TURKEY	9◇9-8001-2277
*GAMBIA	00111	*MALTA	0800-890-110	UK	0800-89-0011

Countries in bold face permit country-to-country calling in addition to calls to the U.S. *Public phones require deposit of coin or phone card. **Western portion. Includes Berlin and Leipzig. ◇Await second dial tone. ¹May not be available from every phone. ◆ Not available from public phones. ²Dial ''02'' first, outside Cairo. ³Dial 010-480-0111 from major Warsaw hotels. © 1993 AT&T.

Here's a travel tip that will make it easy to call back to the States. Dial the access number for the country you're visiting and connect right to **AT&T USADirect®** Service. It's the quick way to get English-speaking operators and can minimize hotel surcharges.

If all the countries you're visiting aren't listed above, call **1 800 241-5555** before you leave for a free wallet card with all AT&T access numbers. International calling made easy—it's all part of **The *i* Plan.**℠

THE *i* PLAN™

AT&T

Let's Go wishes you safe and happy travels

These people are only a third of the 150 students who bring you the *Let's Go* guides. Most of us were still out on the road when this photo was taken, roaming the world in search of the best travel bargains.

Of course, *Let's Go* wouldn't be the same without the help of our readers. We count on you for advice we need to make *Let's Go* better every year. That's why we read each and every piece of mail we get from readers around the globe — and that's why we look forward to your response. Drop us a line, send us a postcard, tell us your stories. We're at 1 Story Street, Cambridge, Massachusetts 02138, USA. Enjoy your trip!

79. Triples DM98-105. Quads DM120. Quints DM140. 6-person room DM160. Showers and breakfast included. Phone reservations only.

Pension Geiger, Steinheilstr. 1 (tel. 52 15 56), across the street from the Technische Universität. Walk up Luisenstr. from the train station 5 blocks and it's on the left. Homey, with big fluffy pillows. Singles DM45-59. Doubles DM74-90.

Pension Theresia, Luisenstr. 51 (tel. 52 12 50), 40 paces up Luisenstr. from Pension Geiger. Rooms plain but clean. Singles DM47, with shower DM54. Doubles DM80, with shower DM92. Showers DM3. DM3 surcharge on single night stays.

Pension Agnes, Agnesstr. 58 (tel. 129 30 61, fax 129 17 64), near Haus International Youth Hotel. U-Bahn 2 (direction "Dülferstr."): Josefsplatz, and follow Adelheidstr. 2 blocks north (away from church tower) and left on Agnesstr. Cramped singles, huge doubles with lace curtains. Reception open 8am-noon and 5-9pm. Singles DM49-57. Doubles DM83-88. No breakfast. Reservations by phone or fax.

Pension Frank, Schellingstr. 24, 80799 München (tel. 28 14 51). U-Bahn 3 or 6 (from Odeonsplatz or Marienplatz): Universität. A curious combination of scruffy backpackers and dolled-up models. Singles DM55. Doubles DM75-85. Share a room wherever a bed is available, DM40 per person. Showers and breakfast included. Book in advance during the summer. Reservations by phone or mail.

Hotel Haberstock, Schillerstr. 4, 80336 München (tel. 55 78 55, fax 550 23 81), right below the train station. Snazzy rooms with soft, expansive pillows. Reception open 24hrs. Singles DM60-66, with shower DM79, with bath DM98. Doubles DM104, with shower DM125, with bath DM165. Written reservations only.

Hotel Helvetia, Schillerstr. 6 (tel. 55 47 45), next door to Hotel Haberstock. Bare walls, smiling hostess. Singles DM65. Doubles DM95. Triples DM120. Quads DM160. Quints DM200. Showers and breakfast included. Phone reservations only. In summer call ahead for singles and doubles.

FOOD

Munich's gastronomic center is the vibrant **Viktualienmarkt,** two minutes south of Marienplatz, with a rainbow of bread, fruit, meat, pastry, cheese, wine, vegetable, sausage, and sandwich shops (open Mon.-Fri. 6am-6:30pm, Sat. 6am-noon). Most **beer gardens** (see Beer Drinking, below) sell tasty, inexpensive snacks along with the brew. Grab a *Brezel* (a giant soft pretzel) and spread it with *Leberwurst* or cheese for a cheap and authentic German lunch. One of the cheapest meals in town is also a Munich specialty: two *Weißwürste* (white veal sausages) served in a pot of hot water with sweet mustard and a soft pretzel on the side. Don't eat the skin off the sausage. Traditionally, *Weißwürste* is supposed to be consumed before noon, but you can find it any time of the day. Another German lunch is a slice of *Leberkäs,* a pinkish, meatloaf-like compound of ground beef and bacon which, despite its name, contains neither liver nor cheese. Buy a 100g portion from one of the stands at the Viktuelienmarkt or from butcher shops. **H.L. Markt,** Im Tal 13, on the corner of Hochbrückenstr., is a discount supermarket (open Mon.-Fri. 8:15am-6:30pm, Sat. 8am-2pm). **Vinzenzmurr,** on Karl-Theodor-Str. at Bonnerplatz; at Karlsplatz on the corner of Sonnenstr. and Adolf-Kolping-Str.; and at Schellingstr. 21 near the university, is a budget-deli chain with a salad bar (DM1.49 per 100g), *Brötchen* (4 for DM1), meat, and cheese (open Mon.-Fri. 8am-6:30pm, Sat. 7:30am-12:30pm).

> **University Mensas** are located at **Arcisstr. 17,** near the Pinakothek Museums; **Leopoldstr. 13; Dachauer-Str. 98b,** and **Helene-Mayer-Ring,** in the former Olympic village. Large portions of institutional food, DM2.70-4, would be a bargain at twice the price. Buy your token from the booths *before* getting your meal. Open Mon.-Fri. 11am-1:45pm. At Leopoldstr. 15, there's also a student café with sandwiches (DM2-3). Open Mon.-Fri. 9am-5pm. *Mensas* and cafeterias open Nov.-July; student ID sometimes required.
>
> **Münchner Suppenküche,** at the Viktualienmarkt; also at Schellingstr. 24 near the university. A Munich institution; the soups are authentic and eat like a meal. Soups DM49. *Krustis* DM3.50-4.80. Open Mon.-Fri. 8am-6:30pm, Sat. 10am-5pm.

Türkenhof, Türkenstr. 78, west of the university. A favorite hangout for the university crowd. Packed evenings. Varying daily menu. Fried rice with chicken and vegetables DM13.80. Creative entrees DM6.50-16.80. Open daily 11am-1am.

Gaststätte Engelsburg, Türkenstr. at Schellingstr. A mix of students and Bavarian locals. Many Bavarian specialties including *Weißwürste, Nürnberger Rostbratwürstl,* and *Spätzle.* Daily special 3-course lunches DM9.90-15.90. Salads DM11-14. Take-out window with its own menu, including pizza. Don't miss their *Apfelstrudel* with whipped cream (DM3.80). Open daily 9:30am-1am.

Metternich, Lindwurmstr. 21. What a café. Major med student hangout (brush up on human physiology next door at the medical bookstore). Simple menu, entrees DM5-14. Open daily 7am-10pm.

Beim Sendlmayr, Westenriederstr. 6, just off the Viktualienmarkt. Very Bavarian, with terrific local specialties DM8.50-21.50. Open daily 11am-11pm.

Jahreszeiten, Sebastianplatz 9, the Zen of vegetarian dining. Sublime, but the prices aren't. Entrees DM18-25. Open Mon.-Fri. 5-11pm, Sat.-Sun. 11:30am-11pm.

Café Frischhut, Prälat-Zistlstr. 8, just off the Viktualienmarkt. *The* breakfast place for early risers and late-night convalescents alike. *Schmalznudel* (fried pastry, a Munich specialty) with coffee, DM5.10. Open Mon.-Fri. 5am-2pm, Sat. 5am-1pm.

Mango, Rosental 3-4, between Marienplatz and the Viktualienmarkt. Self-serve vegetarian (DM6-12). Open Mon.-Fri. 11am-7pm, Thurs. 11am-9pm, Sat. 11am-4pm.

Café Oase, Amelienstr. 89. Quirky mixture of intellectual and whimsical. Sandwiches DM6.80-7.80. Salads DM5.10. Entrees DM9-15. Open Mon.-Fri. 8:30am-1am, Sat.-Sun. 9:30am-1am.

bux-am viktualienmarkt, Frauenstr. 9 (tel. 22 94 82). Fine self-serve vegetarian food. Happy, healthy. Open Mon.-Fri. 10am-6pm, Sat. 10am-2pm.

Frauentreffenpunkt Neuperlach, Oskar-Maria-Graf-Ring 20/22 (tel. 670 64 63). A women's café; feminist rendezvous. Open Tues. and Thurs.-Fri. 10am-1pm, Wed. 10am-1pm and 3-6pm.

SIGHTS

The Catholic Church was long the preeminent institution in Munich; the name of the city itself is a bastardization of *Mönch* (monk), referring to the small Benedictine order around which the village appeared in the 9th century. Over the centuries, the relationship proved to be architecturally fruitful, and the city is now graced with a variety of impressive sacred edifices, most within blocks of the **Marienplatz.** The square, an interchange for the major S- and U-Bahn lines as well as the social nexus of the city, takes its name from the **Mariensäule,** an ornate 17th-century column dedicated to the Virgin Mary. The 15th-century **Frauenkirche,** whose onion-domed towers have long been one of Munich's most notable landmarks, dominates the skyline (interior closed for renovations until mid-1994). At the neo-Gothic **Neues Rathaus,** the **Glockenspiel** steals the show with an elaborate mechanized display of jousting knights and dancing coopers. At 9pm, a mechanical watchman marches out and the Guardian Angel escorts the *Münchner Kindl* (the symbol of Munich) to bed (performances daily 11am, noon, 5, and 9pm; Nov.-April 11am and 9pm only).

Munich's ritual past is represented by the 11th-century **Peterskirche,** at Rindermarkt and Petersplatz, whose interior was *barockiziert* (Baroquified) in the 18th century. The church tower, christened *Alter Peter* (Old Peter) by locals, affords a splendid view of the city from atop 294 steps (admission DM2). Ludwig II of Bavaria rests in peace in a crypt of the 16th-century Jesuit **Michaelskirche,** on Neuhauserstr. Its construction, designed to emphasize the city's Catholic loyalty during the Reformation, almost bankrupted the state treasury. Father Rupert Mayer, one of the most heroic of the few German clergy to speak out against Hitler, preached in this church (admission to crypt DM0.50). A Bavarian Rococo masterpiece, the **Asamkirche** is named after the brothers who designed and built it; Cosmas Damian Asam painted the frescoes while Egid Quirin Asam carved the sculptures.

The dozens of richly decorated rooms built from the 14th to the 19th centuries in the magnificent **Residenz,** Max-Joseph-Platz 3 (U-Bahn 3, 4, 5 or 6: Odeonsplatz), form the earthly remains of the Wittelsbach dynasty. The grounds now house several museums (see Museums, below). The **Schatzkammer** (Treasury) contains jeweled baubles, crowns, swords, china, ivorywork, and other trinkets. (Open Tues.-Sun. 10am-4:30pm. Admission DM4, students and groups DM2, children under 15 with adult free.) The **Residenzmuseum** comprises the former Wittelsbach apartments and State Rooms, a collection of European porcelain, and a 17th-century court chapel. The walls of the **Ahnengalerie** (Gallery of Ancestors), hung with a hundred and twenty "family portraits," show an utter loss of perspective. Charlemagne would have been more surprised than any to find his own face here, held accountable before the world for the genesis of the Wittelsbach family (hours and admission same as *Schatzkammer*).

Schloß Nymphenburg, the royal summer residence, is worth the trip northwest of town (U-Bahn 1: Rotkreuzplatz, then streetcar #12, direction "Amalienburgstr."). A Baroque wonder set in a winsome park, the palace hides a number of treasures, including a two-story granite marble hall seasoned with stucco, frescoes, and a Chinese lacquer cabinet. Check out King Ludwig's "Gallery of Beauties"—whenever a woman caught his fancy, he would have her portrait painted (particularly scandalous considering many of the women were mere commoners; particularly touching given the fact that Ludwig grappled with his affection for men all his life). The palace also contains both a wonderful collection of antique porcelain (as well as a modern porcelain manufacturing studio's selling room) and the strange **Marstallmuseum** (Carriage Museum, see below). (Main palace open Tues.-Sun. 9am-12:30pm and 1:30-5pm; Oct.-March 10am-12:30pm and 1:30-4pm. The pagodas and palaces have similar hours. Admission to main palace DM2.50, students DM1.50; to entire complex DM6. Wander the grounds for free.) Just next door is the immense **Botanischer Garten,** whose greenhouses shelter rare and wonderful plants from all over the world. Check out the water lily room and the unassuming moss room, with an exquisitely **romantic alcove** in the back. (Open daily 9am-7pm. Greenhouses open 9am-11:45am and 1-6:30pm. Admission DM3, students DM1.50.)

Abutting the city center is the vast **Englischer Garten,** one of Europe's oldest landscaped public parks. On sunny days, all Munich turns out to bike, play badminton, go horseback riding, or sunbathe. Nude sunbathing areas are designated "FKK" *(Freikörperkultur)* on signs and park maps. The newest thing to do is to hop on a surf board and ride the Eisbach, which flows through the park. The force of the water springing out of the ground causes a mighty wave, and swarms of wetsuited daredevils ply the waters just under the bridge between the Haus der Kunst and the Bayerisches Nationalmuseum (see Museums, below).

MUSEUMS

Munich is a supreme museum city, and many of the city's offerings would require days to peruse exhaustively. Several museums are contained on the grounds of the *Residenz* and *Schloß Nymphenburg* (see Sights). Many of these museums are closed on Mondays.

Museumsinsel-Isartor

Deutsches Museum (tel. 217 91 or 217 94 33 for recording in German), on the *Museumsinsel* (Museum Island) in the Isar River. Streetcar #18: Isartor. One of the world's most extensive museums of science and technology, filling the entire island with displays on just about anything ever invented. Particularly well-conceived are the 1st-floor exhibits on aerospace, the 2nd-floor exegesis of the development of photography, and the 5th-floor displays on astronomy. Lose yourself in the labyrinthine mine shafts beneath the museum, gawking at the immense subterranean machinery. The planetarium (DM2) and the daily electrical show will warm the cockles of any young physicist's heart. Open daily 9am-5pm. Admission DM8, students DM3.

Konigsplatz

Alte Pinakothek, Bärenstr. 27 (tel. 238 05 215 or -216). U-Bahn 2 or streetcar #18: Königsplatz. Built to house the collections of the Wittelsbach family, the museum covers the 13th through the 17th centuries, counting among its extensive collection works by Giotto, Titian, da Vinci, Dürer, Rembrandt, and Rubens. The stunningly detailed *Battle of Alexander at Issus* by Albrecht Altdorfer is displayed here. Open Wed. and Fri.-Sun. 9:15am-4:30pm, Tues. and Thurs. 9:15am-4:30pm and 7-9pm. Admission DM5, students DM3.50. Joint admission with the Neue Pinakothek DM10, students DM5. Sun. free.

Neue Pinakothek, next to the Alte Pinakothek (tel. 238 051 95). The newer, sleeker museum covers the 18th and 19th centuries, including a fine collection of French Impressionists and works by Van Gogh, Gauguin, and Gustav Klimt. Hours and admission same as Alte Pinakotek.

Lenbachhaus, Luisenstr. 33 (tel. 52 10 41, recorded information in German tel. 52 82 50). U-Bahn 2: Königsplatz. Houses an extensive collection of Munich cityscapes, along with the works of Kandinsky, Klee, and the *Blaue Reiter* school (Münter, Marc, Macke, and others), which disdained the perfumed Impressionism of late 19th-century painting and forged the modernist aesthetic of abstraction. Open Tues.-Sun. 10am-6pm. Admission DM5, students DM2.50, Sun. free.

Glypothek, Königsplatz 3 (tel. 28 61 00), around the corner from the Lenbachhaus. U-Bahn 2: Königsplatz. Holds half of Germany's best collection of ancient art, especially Greek, Etruscan, and Roman sculptures. Open Tues.-Wed. and Fri.-Sun. 10am-4:30pm, Thurs. noon-8:30pm. Admission DM5, students DM3. Joint admission with Antikensammlung DM8, students DM4. Sun. free.

Antikensammlung, Königsplatz 1 (tel. 59 83 59), across Königsplatz from Glypothek and around the corner from the Lenbachhaus. U-Bahn 2: Königsplatz. Holds a first-rate exhibit of vases and the other half of Germany's best collection of ancient art. Open Tues. and Thurs.-Sun. 10am-4:30pm, Wed. noon-8:30pm. Tours Thurs.-Tues. 2pm, Wed. 2pm and 6pm. Admission DM5, students DM3. Joint admission with Glypothek DM8, students DM4. Sun. free.

Elsewhere in Munich

Staatsgallerie Moderner Kunst, Prinz-Regenten-Str. 1 (tel. 29 27 10), in the Haus der Kunst, right below the Englischer Garten. Showcases the work of Beckmann, Kandinsky, Picasso, and Dalí, among others. Ironically, the building was originally constructed by the Nazis as the Museum of German Art, which housed the famous exhibit of *entartete Kunst* (degenerate art), including works of Cubists, Expressionists, and Dadaists. Many of the same artists denigrated as Jews and Bolsheviks then are glorified in the museum today. Renovations closed the museum in summer 1993; should be ready for visitors in 1994, but call or inquire at the tourist office. Open Tues.-Wed. and Fri.-Sun. 9:15am-4:30pm, Thurs. 9:15am-4:30pm and 7-9pm. Admission DM3.50, students DM1.80, Sun. free.

Zentrum für außergewöhnliche Museen (Center for Unusual Museums), Westenriederstr. 26 (tel. 290 41 21). S-Bahn 1-8: Isartor. The museum hogties under one roof such treasures as the Corkscrew Museum and the Museum of Easter Rabbits. Open daily 10am-6pm. Admission DM8, students, seniors, and children DM5.

Museum for Erotic Art, Odeonsplatz 8 (tel. 228 35 44), in same building as the Filmcasino. U-Bahn 3, 4, or 6: Odeonsplatz. For those lonely days when you're 5000km away from your lover back home, this museum covers all four bases around the world and through the centuries. Featuring a French illustrated book of sex gags entitled *The Circus,* hot and heavy chess pieces, American postcards featuring the "dream women of the 20s," and a whole set of Japanese illustrations. Open Tues.-Sun. 11am-7pm. Admission DM8, students DM6.

BMW Museum, Petuelring 130 (tel. 28 95 33 07). U-Bahn 3: Olympiazentrum. The ultimate driving museum. Features a fetching display of Bavaria's second-favorite export. Open daily 9am-5pm. Admission DM4.50, students DM3.

Münchener Stadtmuseum, St.-Jakobs-Platz 1 (tel. 23 32 23 70). U-or S-Bahn: Marienplatz. Houses the **Deutsches Brauereimuseum** (Beer Museum), showcase for Bavaria's favorite export. (Brewery museum closed for renovation until mid-1994.) Also at the museum, **classic films** roll every evening at 8pm (DM7). Foreign films are shown with subtitles; call for program (tel. 233 55 86). Open Tues. and Thurs.-Sun. 10am-5pm, Wed. 10am-8:30pm. Musuem admission DM5, students, seniors, and children DM2.50. Stop at the **Stadtmuseum Café** for dark clothes, lots of smoke, and stone-faced intellectuals.

Siemens Museum, Prannerstr. 10 (tel. 234 26 60). From Odeonsplatz, streetcar #19 or bus #53: Marienplatz. Takes an intensive look at electronics. Displays include the shamelessly self-promoting multi-media extravaganza *Siemens Throughout the World.* Open Mon.-Fri. 9am-4pm, Sat.-Sun. 10am-2pm. First Tues. of every month open 9am-9pm. Free.

ENTERTAINMENT

Munich's cultural offerings rank with the world's best. Eleven large theaters and countless smaller stages throughout the city run the gamut of styles and tastes from dramatic classics at the **Residenztheater** and the **Volkstheater,** to comic opera at the **Staatstheater am Gärtnerplatz,** to experimental at the **Theater im Marstall,** in Nymphenburg. Munich's **Opera Festival** runs throughout July, as does a concert series in the Nymphenburg and Schleissheim palaces.

The *Monatsprogramm* lists schedules for all of Munich's stages; newspapers and posters in the subway stops list **movie** showings. English-language films that are listed with the title in English are screened in English with German subtitles. **Cinema Programmkino,** Nymphenburgerstr. 31 (tel. 55 52 55; U-Bahn 1: Stiglmaierplatz), and **Ricky's Hollywood,** Schwartalerstr. 2-6 (tel. 55 56 70), screen foreign-language films in the original tongue. Smack in the middle of the student district, **Türkenclolch,** Türkenstr. 74, has mini-film festivals of a particular director or theme all the time. Foreign films are shown in the original tongue with German subtitles (admission DM9). Munich's **film festival** generally runs for about a week at the end of June. For schedules and ticket information, contact **Internationale Filmwoche GmbH.,** Türkenstr. 99, 80799 Munich (tel. 381 90 40).

Gasteig, Rosenheimerstr. 5 (tel. 48 09 80). S-Bahn (all except 27, direction "Ostbahnhof"): Rosenheimerplatz. A cultural center with quite a history, it hosts musical performances ranging from classical to non-Western avant-garde on the former site of the *Bürgerbräukeller* where Adolf Hitler launched his abortive "Beer Hall *Putsch.*" Contains the **Munich Philharmonic's** performance space as well as that of numerous others, featuring a wide range of events such as concerts, public readings, recitals, and ballet. Box office (tel. 48 09 86 14) open Mon.-Fri. 10:30am-2pm and 3-6pm, Sat. 10:30am-2pm. Located in the Glashalle and is also open 1hr. before the beginning of a program.

Bayerische Staatsoper (Bavarian State Opera), Max-Joseph-Platz (tel. 22 13 16). U-Bahn 3, 6: Odeonsplatz or S-Bahn: Marienplatz; the Opera lies right between these two next to the *Residenz*; or streetcar #19: Max-Joseph-Platz. Standing-room (DM9) and reduced-rate student tickets to the numerous operas and ballets sold at Maximillianstr. 11 (tel. same as above), behind the Opera House, or 1hr. before the performance at the side entrance on Maximilianstr. Box office open Mon.-Fri. 10am-1pm and 3:30-5:30pm, Sat. 10am-12:30pm.

Staatstheater, Gärtnerplatz 3 (tel. 201 67 67). U-Bahn 1 or 2: Frauenhoferstr., then follow Reichenbächstr. to Gärtnerplatz; or streetcar #8 or 20: Gärtnerplatz. Stages comic opera and musicals. Tickets available max. 4 weeks before each performance at the Staatstheater box office, open Mon.-Fri. 10am-6pm, Sat. 10am-1pm; 1hr. before performance at the night counter (tel. 20 24 11); or at the Bavarian State Opera counter (see above). Standing room tickets start at DM6.

Residenztheater, Max-Joseph-Platz 1 (tel. 22 57 54). Same directions as Bavarian State Opera. Also stages dramatic works. Ticket counter open Mon.-Fri. 10am-6pm, Sat. 10am-1pm and 1hr. before performance. Tickets start at DM8.

Drehleier, Balanstr. 23 (tel. 48 43 37). A mixture of theater, cabaret, and performance art romps across this offbeat stage. Kitchen serves inexpensive salads and noodle dishes (DM6-15) until 10pm. Open Tues.-Sat. 7pm-1am. Cover DM15-20. Reservations required.

BEER AND BEER HALLS

To most visitors, Munich is synonymous with beer. Even before Duke Wilhelm IV decreed the **Beer Purity Law** *(Reinheitsgebot)* in 1516, Bavaria was already something of a Holy Land for connoisseurs of frothy malt beverages. Bavaria doesn't even have a close competitor for the title of largest producer and consumer of beer in Germany (which is itself the largest per capita producer and consumer of beer in the world). The six great Munich labels are *Augustiner, Hacker-Pschorr, Hofbräu, Löwenbräu, Paulaner-Thomasbräu,* and *Spaten-Franzinskaner.* With a little footwork you can try them all—each brand supplies its own beer halls. Beer is served by the *Maß* (about a liter, DM8-11). If you want a half-*Maß* (DM4-6) you must specify it. *Helles Bier* is your standard golden-colored beer; *dunkles* is sweeter and darker in color. *Weißbier* is the Bavarian name for what is elsewhere called *Weizenbier,* or wheat beer, and is traditionally served in tall glasses rather than mugs. To pour it, tilt the glass to avoid foaming up, and pour all but a few tablespoons into the glass; then swirl what remains in the bottle to mix up the dregs, pour in the rest, and watch the glass cloud up. *Helles Weißbier* is a smooth light beer; *dunkles Weißbier,* a rich, brown beer, is the dark variety. *Hefeweizenbier* is a mix of half-light and half-dark *Weizenbier. Bockbier,* not served everywhere, has a high alcohol content (5.5%). A *Radler* is a mixture of *Helles* beer and *Limonade* (a light-colored soft drink), a favorite among German lightweights—don't knock it 'til you've tried it. *Russen* is another version of *Radler* made with *Weizenbier* instead of *Helles.*

The biggest keg party in the world, Munich's **Oktoberfest,** runs from the second to last Saturday in September to the first Sunday in October (Sept. 17-Oct. 2 in 1994). The festival got started in 1810 when Prince Ludwig married Princess Therese von Sachsen-Hildburghausen. (The fairgrounds where the partying takes place are known as Theresienwiese, or Therese's Meadow; U-Bahn 4 or 5: Theresienwiese.) The revelry accompanying the wedding was so much fun that *Münchners* decided to do it again next year, and every year after that. The festivities kick off with speeches, a parade of horse-drawn beer wagons, and the mayor tapping the first ceremonial barrel. The Hofbräu tent is the rowdiest and the most touristy, but can be dangerous; fights break out more often here than in other tents.

Hofbräuhaus, Am Platzl 9 (tel. 22 16 76), 2 blocks from Marienplatz. Established on the Platzl in 1644, Munich's world-famous beer hall was originally reserved for royalty and its invited guests (the name means "court brewery house"). The Hofbräuhaus has been tapping barrels for the general public since 1859, and is now hopelessly touristy. Nazi party meetings were held here, and it was in the *Festsaal* that Hitler was proclaimed the first chair of the Nazi party. Regulars (those who come at least 5 times a week) get their own personal mugs. *Maß* DM9. Oom-pah band after 7pm. Open daily 10am-midnight.

Hofbräukeller, Innere Wiener Str. 19 (tel. 448 73 76). Pours the same brew as the Hofbräuhaus, only this time with Germans. It also has a beer garden. *Maß* DM8.50. Open daily 9am-midnight.

Augustiner, Neuhauserstr. 16 (tel. 55 19 92 57) and Arnulfstr. 52 (tel. 59 43 93). The Neuhauserstr. location has a superior atmosphere as well as a beer garden in back and sidewalk tables on the pedestrian zone. The sweet brew is touted by many natives as the finest in the city. On *Bierhalle* days *Maß* DM9.20, on restaurant days DM10. Open daily 10am-midnight.

Hacker-Keller, Theresienhöhe 4 (tel. 50 70 04). More relaxed than the Hofbräuhaus. Come here to chat with friendly locals. *Maß* DM10.80. Open daily 5pm-1am. Live music and dancing after 7pm.

Pschorr Keller, Theresienhöhe 7 (tel. 50 10 88). Along with the Hacker-Keller down the street, an outpost of the Hacker-Pschorr brewery. Come here for your breakfast beer. *Maß* DM10.80. Open daily 8am-midnight.

Löwenbräukeller, Nymphenburgerstr. 2 (tel. 52 60 21). Festive and loud. Come here to taste the real *Löwenbräu. Maß* DM9.50. Open daily 9:30am-1am.

Franziskaner-Keller, Perusastr. 5 (tel. 231 81 20). Jubilant *Münchners* and harried servers. *Maß* DM10.80. Open daily 8am-midnight.

Forschungsbrauerei, Unterhachingerstr. 76 (tel. 670 11 69). Serves up some very strange brew—the name means "research brewery." Pleasant atmosphere, and pours varieties of beer you can't find anywhere else. *Maß* DM8-8.80. Open Tues.-Sat. 11am-11pm, Sun. 10am-10pm.

Chinesischer Turm (tel. 39 50 28), in the *Englischer Garten.* U-Bahn 3 or 6: Giselastr., follow Giselastr. into the park and then take any one of the paths to the right and look for the pagoda, or bus #54 (from *Südbahnhof*): Chinesischer Turm. A large beer garden next to the pagoda. Munich shows up in all its splendour. *Maß* DM9.40. Open daily in balmy weather 10am-11pm.

Hirschgarten, Hirschgartenallee 1 (tel. 17 25 91). The largest beer garden in Munich is boisterous and verdant. *Maß* DM8.50. Open daily 10:30am-11pm.

NIGHTLIFE

Munich's nightlife is marked by the odd co-existence of Bavarian *Gemütlichkeit* and trendy cliquishness. What's odd about it is the ease with which the two mix. The streets erupt with raucous beer halls, loud discos, and exclusive cafés every night of the week; many places are as likely to be packed on a weeknight as on a Saturday.

The locals tend to approach their nightlife as an epic voyage. The odyssey begins at one of Munich's beer gardens or beer halls (see above), which generally close before midnight and are most crowded earlier in the evening. The discos and dance clubs, soporific before midnight, suddenly come to life and continue to throb relentlessly until 4am. The **Schwabing** district, especially on the majestic Leopoldstr. and Ludwigstr., is littered with bars, cafés, cabarets, discos, and galleries. This is the trendy part of town notorious for its "door standers"—neurotic bouncers with orders to protect the clientele from unwanted association with chic-less individuals. Single men will have a harder time than single women. The best strategy is to look bored and, while avoiding eye contact with the bouncer, try to walk in. Early in the evening (before 9-11pm), bouncers aren't as picky. The area in Schwabing around **Münchener Freiheit** is the most touristy, but you'll also find the most serious partying and loudest discos here. More low-key is the southwestern section of Schwabing, directly behind the university on Amalienstr. and Türkenstr.; this area is drowned in student cafés, cheap restaurants, and mellow bars. When they close, hard-core types head for the late-night/early-morning cafés to sip a last beer or first cup of coffee. Culture and nightlife resource guides are available to help you sort out the Munich scene. Pick up the *Young People's Guide to Munich,* or buy a copy of the *Münchner Stadtmagazin* (biweekly), the *Münchner Stadtzeitung* (weekly), or *Prinz* (monthly) at any newsstand to find out what's up. For smaller rock clubs, scope bulletin boards and posters around the university. Big-name pop artists often perform at the **Olympia Halle,** while the open-air **Olympia Stadion** on the northern edge of town hosts mega-concerts. Check listings for dates and ticket information.

Dance Clubs

Nachtwerk, Landesberger Str. 185 (tel. 570 43 74). Any S-Bahn except 27: Donnersberger Brücke. Huge warehouse with lots of floor where younger people dance. Occasionally live music on weekends. Open Mon.-Thurs. 8pm-2am, Fri.-Sun. 8pm-4am.

Babalu, Luitpoldstr. 19 (tel. 39 94 57). U-Bahn 3 or 6: Giselastr. Technoblast of a time. Occasional live music, raving off and on. Note that it's well into Sun. before the Sat.-nighters go home. Open Sun.-Fri. 10pm-4am, Sat. 10pm-11am.

Far Out, Am Kastor 2 (tel. 22 66 61) U- or S-Bahn: Marienplatz. Reputedly this was once a Hare Krishna hangout. Now a mixed crowd moves to mainstream dance tunes. Open daily 8pm-3am.

P-1, Prinz-Regenten-Str. 1 (tel. 29 42 52). Bus #53. Located in the House der Kunst off of the *Englischer Garten,* the place is predictably *trés chic* and well guarded by nervous bouncers. Very very Munich; no square heads allowed. Open daily 10:30pm-4am

Cadillac, Theklastr. 1 (tel. 26 69 74). Streetcar # 18: Müllerstr. Supposedly popular among Munich's Rastas. Rock n' Roll is the sound, calm and cool the attitude. Open daily 7pm-4am.

Oly, Helene-Mayer-Ring (tel. 351 77 33), in the Olympic village. U-Bahn 2 (direction "Olympiazentrum"): last station, then walk past the bus depot to the tall high-rise buildings to your left. A recently-renovated slick student disco. Cheap beer (DM3.90) and a bohemian crowd. Student ID required. Open daily 9pm-3am. Cover Sun.-Thurs. DM3, Fri.-Sat. DM5.

Mrs. Henderson, Rumfordstr. 2 (tel. 260 43 23). Lively dance hall/cabaret hybrid—somewhere between kitsch and nostalgia.

Jazz Bars

Allotria Jazz Saloon, Türkenstr. 33 (tel. 28 58 58). Excellent jazz wails through to the wee morning hours. Beer DM5.50. Open Tues.-Sun. 10:30pm-whenever. Cover varies, sometimes free.

Schwabinger Podium, Wagnerstr. 1 (tel. 39 94 82). Live jazz and Dixie draws a somewhat younger crowd than at Allotria. Beer DM5.40. Opens at 8pm, music starts at 9pm. Cover DM5-8.

Nachtcafé, Maximiliansplatz 5 (tel. 59 59 00). Live jazz and blues until the wee hours. Things don't get really rolling until 2am. Breakfast served after 3am. No cover, just a bouncer. Beer DM4-6, coffee DM3. Open daily 7pm-5am.

Gay and Lesbian Munich

Although Bavaria is reckoned to be the region in Germany least tolerant of homosexuality, Munich sustains a respectably vibrant gay nightlife. The blocks between the Viktualienmarkt and Gärtnerplatz are the center of the gay and lesbian scene. Bars, cafés, and clubs of all atmospheres abound. A guide to gay life, *München von Hinten* (Munich from Behind), can be found at **Max und Milian bookstore,** Gabelsbergerstr. 65 (tel. 52 74 52). For lesbian information, call **Lesbentelefon** at 725 42 72 (open Fri. 6-10pm). **Sapphovision,** a lesbian film center at the **Frauenzentrum Treibhaus mit Café** (see Women's Centers, in Practical Information, above), shows films every second Friday of the month. (Call Lesbentelefon for information; see Practical Information listing for Frauenzentrum information.)

New York, Sonnenstr. 25 (tel. 59 10 56). U-Bahn 1-3 or 6: Sendlinger Tor. Fashionable gay men dance this disco into the ground. Open daily 11pm-4am.

Together, Hans-Sachs-Str. 17 (tel. 26 34 69). U-Bahn 1-3 or 6: Sendlinger Tor, then streetcar #18 or 20: Müllerstr. Glitzy, campy disco. Features occasional transvestite shows. Open Fri. 9pm-3am, Sun. and Tues.-Thurs. 9pm-1am.

Villani's Café-Bistro, Kreuzstr. 3b (tel. 260 79 72), in the passage *(Asamhof)* between Sendlinger Str. and Kreuzstr. Raucous revelers of all genders and sexual orientations every night, though Sunday is unofficially "gay night." Beers DM4. Open Mon.-Sat. 10am-1am, Sun. and holidays 11am-1am.

■ Near Munich: Dachau

"Once they burn books, they'll end up burning people," wrote the 19th-century German poet Heinrich Heine. This eerie statement is posted at the **Konzentrationslager-Gedenkstätte,** the concentration camp at Dachau, next to a photograph of one of Hitler's book burnings. Though most of the buildings at the camp were destroyed in 1962, but the walls, gates, and crematorium remain. Dachau was the first concentration camp in Germany, built in an average residential neighborhood.

Dachau has, to a jarring extent, become a major sight on the routes of packaged tours. It is important for visitors to realize that while the KZ Gedenkstätte is treated as a tourist attraction by many, it is primarily a memorial; Jews and Germans alike come here for personal reasons; often to grieve over the horrors of the former Nazi concentration camp. Take a moment to read the sign-in log at the end of the exhibit; you'll find that visitors from all over the world come here to remember lost relatives or to pay their respects to those who perished, but interwoven into the multitude of names and addresses from different countries are statements of resilience and hope. Respectful behavior by those having only an historical interest is in order.

The museum, located in the former administrative buildings, examines pre-1930 anti-Semitism and reconstructs the rise of Nazism, the establishment of the concentration camp system, and the lives of prisoners through photographs, documents, and artifacts. The expensive (DM37) guide, available in English, translates the propaganda posters, SS files, documents, and letters, though many exhibits are accompanied by short captions in English, primarily for identification purposes. Also on display are the texts of the letters from prisoners to their families and internal SS memos. A small, annotated map is available for DM1.50. A short film (22min.) is screened in English at 11:30am and 3:30pm. The two reconstructed barracks and the crematoria can also be viewed. The wrought-iron gate at the *Jourhaus,* formerly the only entrance to the camp, reads *"Arbeit Macht Frei"* (Work Makes One Free). It was the first sight for prisoners as they entered the camp. There is also a Jewish memorial, a Protestant commemorative chapel, and the Catholic *Todesangst Christ-Kapelle* (Christ in Agony Church) on the grounds. Behind the back wall is a Carmelite convent. For more discussion about issues surrounding concentration camps, see Germany History: The Living Archives. Take S-Bahn 2 (from Munich, direction "Petershausen") to Dachau, and board bus #722 (DM2) in front of the station to KZ Gedenkstätte, a 20min. ride (grounds open Tues.-Sun. 9am-5pm).

In the mid-19th century, painters like Carl Spitzweg and Max Lieberman traveled to Dachau. A 16th-century castle tops the *Altstadt.* The **tourist office,** Konrad-Adenauer-Str. 3 (tel. (08131) 845 66) sells maps for DM1. EurAide offers a guided tour in English at 9:30am, starting from the train station (June-Aug. 21 on Tues. and Thurs., Aug. 22-Sept. on Wed.; tour costs DM25, DM17 for railpass-holders)

■ The Lake Region and Andechs

Münchners frequently get away to the nearby glacial lakes, particularly the **Starnbergersee** and the **Ammersee.** Take S-Bahn 6 out to the beautiful lakeside promenade of **Starnberg,** an old resort town. The castle to which Ludwig II was confined after he was deposed is just around the tip of the lake in **Berg.** His body was found shortly thereafter, mysteriously drowned in the Starnbergersee—a cross in the water now marks the spot. Take S-Bahn 5 to **Herrsching** on the Ammersee. Herrsching is the start of one of the many *Wanderwege* (hiking paths) established by the transit system in connection with the S-Bahn. Ask at the tourist offices at Herrsching (tel. (08152) 374 44) or Starnberg (tel. (08151) 132 74) for more information.

The monastery at **Andechs** combines Bavaria's two most acclaimed attributes—Catholicism and beer gardens—on a gorgeous mountaintop. To get to Andechs, take S-Bahn 5 to Herrsching; switch to the private bus line **Omnibus-Verkehr Rauner** (Mon.-Sat. outbound 7-10 per day 7am-6:30pm, inbound 9-12 per day, last return Mon.-Tues. and Thurs.-Fri. at 5:50pm, Sat. at 5:30pm, Wed. at 6:45pm; Sun. 11 per day 7:56am-6:33pm, returning 9:55am-6:45pm), or take the 3km hiking trail up the mountain. Follow signs marked *"Fußweg nach Andechs"* and stick to the trail; a sign reminds hikers of 11 people who met their deaths short-cutting down the precipitous slope. The monks here brew up a **light beer** and an rocking *Bock-bier* which, piously, is not served on Sundays. The secular brewing industry is currently up in arms over what they charge is an unfair competitive advantage: as a religious institution, the monastic brewers are exempt from the beer tax. A *Maß* costs only DM6.20 (open daily Mon.-Sat. 10am-7pm). More than 250 centuries-old giant votive candles—commemorating departed brothers—are stored in the adjacent **Klosterkirche Heiliger Berg** (Abbey Church of the Holy Mountain),. The mortal remains of composer Carl Orff rest in the building. Orff was best known for *Carmina Burana,* a profane oratorio which featured, ironically, a drunken abbot.

■■■ BAVARIAN ALPS (Bayerische Alpen)

South of Munich, the land buckles into a series of dramatic peaks and valleys that stretches through Austria and into Italy. It was through this magical terrain that Ludwig II of Bavaria, the assertively batty "Fairytale King," chose to build his theatrical palaces. Mountain villages, glacial lakes, icy waterfalls, and world-class ski resorts dot the forested slopes. This is also the place where people authentically, even nonchalantly, wear *Lederhosen*. Rail lines are sparse; buses fill the gaps. For regional information, contact the *Fremdenverkehrsverband Oberbayern,* Sonnenstr. 10 (tel. (089) 59 73 47) in Munich (open Mon.-Fri. 9am-4:30pm, Sat. 9am-noon).

GARMISCH-PARTENKIRCHEN

Once, Garmisch and Partenkirchen were unassuming Bavarian villages whose location at the foot of the **Zugspitze,** Germany's highest mountain, kept them in tranquil isolation. As the mid-19th-century back-to-nature contingent discovered the mountains, the two towns became a popular resort area (they united in 1935 in preparation for the following year's winter Olympics). Hiking trails of every grade radiate from town. One of the most popular trails leads up to the dramatic, 100m-deep **Partnachklamm** gorge (admission DM2). Walk up to the gorge from behind the Olympic ski stadium (35min.). Garmisch-Partenkirchen is now a thriving resort whose lifeblood is the Zugspitze's ski slopes.

There are two ways up the peak; the first is a cog railway from the Zugspitzbahnhof (50m behind the Garmisch main station) via Grainau to Hotel Schneefernerhaus, then a cable car, the Gipfelseilbahn, to the top (entire trip 80min., 65min. to the ski area; round-trip DM60). Another cable car, the Eibseeseilbahn, runs from Eibsee to the summit (10min.). Tickets are interchangeable and include the cog railway between the two base stations. To get a view of, rather than from, the Zugspitze, the Osterfelderbahn goes up the neighboring **Alpspitze** (9min., round-trip DM35). The cog railway leads to the cable-cars.

Pick up free maps of hiking trails at the **tourist office** *(Verkehrsamt der Kurverwaltung),* Richard-Strauss-Platz (tel. (08821) 18 06). From the station, walk to the left and turn left onto Von-Brug-Str. (Open Mon.-Sat. 8am-6pm, Sun. and holidays 10am-noon.) When the office is closed, check out the automat in front of the building or call (08821) 194 12 for recorded information on vacancies. Procure **mountain bikes** at **Sportfreizeit Werdenfels,** Münchnerstr. 11, (tel. (08824) 81 62; DM25 per day). For a **snow report** (German only), call (08821) 79 79 79. Of the six ski schools, the cheapest **equipment rental** is at **Sepp Hohenleitner's,** at the Zugespitzbahnhof (tel. (08821) 506 10), a 20-minute walk to the slopes. (DM23 per day, DM90 for 5 days.) **Ski passes** in the Zugspitzgebiet cost DM51 per day, DM44 with Eurail.

Garmisch-Partenkirchen hosts dozens of private rooms for under DM20 per night and scores more rooms in *Gasthäuser* and *Pensionen* (DM20-30). Unfortunately, few will rent for fewer than three nights. Also, prices rise about DM5 during the winter. At the **Jugendherberge (HI),** Jochstr. 10 (tel. (08821) 29 80), 4km from town in Burgrain (bus #6 or 7, direction "Farchant": Burgrain), you can awake to the tolling of church bells. (Reception open 7-10am and 5-10pm. Curfew 11:30pm. Under 27 only. Dorms DM15.50. Breakfast included. Sheets DM5. Open late Dec.-Oct.) **Camping Zugspitze** (tel. (08821) 31 80) is on highway B24 at the base of the Zugspitze; take the blue-and-white bus (from the station, direction "Eibsee/Grainau") to Schmölzabzweigung. (DM6.50 per person, DM9.50 per site. In summer, DM5.70 and DM8.50, respectively. Call ahead.) At **Vinzenzmurr,** a chain-store delicatessen off Bahnhofstr. at Rathausstr., assemble a sandwich platter from the selection of *Wurst* and cheese, or fill up on cafeteria-style meals. (Open Mon.-Fri. 8am-6:15pm, Sat. 7:30am-12:30pm.)

BERCHTESGADEN

At the easternmost point of the Bavarian Alps, near Salzburg and the Austrian border, Berchtesgaden profits from a somewhat sinister and unjustifiably overtouristed attraction—Hitler's *Kehlsteinhaus,* a mountaintop retreat christened "Eagle's Nest" by occupying American troops. A disconcertingly large crowd of tourists—many of them American soldiers—besieges the Bavarian town to examine this small slice of World War II history. Historically and geographically, Berchtesgaden belongs more properly to Austria and the Archbishophric of Salzburg than to Germany, but Bavaria snatched the area away in 1809 to take possession of its salt deposits.

Practical Information The Berchtesgaden **tourist office** *(Kurdirektion;* tel. (08652) 50 11), is opposite the train station on Königsseerstr. in the off-white building with blue shutters. Ask for their *Berchtesgadener Land: General Information* pamphlet, which lists sights, concerts, and other activities. (Open June-Oct. Mon.-Fri. 8am-6pm, Sat. 8am-5pm, Sun. 9am-3pm; Nov.-May Mon.-Fri. 8am-5pm, Sat. 9am-noon.) Most materials are available in English. The **post office,** Bahnhofplatz 4, is adjacent to the train station. (Open Mon.-Fri. 9am-noon and 2-6pm, Sat. 9am-noon.) In the southeasternmost corner of Germany, Berchtesgaden is three hours from Munich by train, with a transfer in Freilassing. (Day excursion Tues.-Thurs. and Sat.-Sun. DM50. Round-trip DM82, under 26 DM70.) Most establishments will accept payment in Austrian *Schillings;* you can also change oney at the Salzburg train station post office before departing. The fare for a bus ride is DM2.20.

Accommodations and Food The **Jugendherberge (HI),** Gebirgsjägerstr. 52, (tel. (08652) 21 90), is 20 minutes down the road to the right as you emerge from the train station; take the first right and follow the steep, gravel path to the left, or take bus #9539. (Direction "Strub Kaserne" (DM2.20): Jugendherberge. Reception open 5-7pm. Flexible curfew 10pm. DM15.50. Breakfast included. Sheets DM4.50. Open Dec. 27-Oct.) **Haus Alpina,** Ramsauerstr. 6 (tel. (08652) 25 17), five minutes to the right on the same street as the station, lures guests with clean rooms and down comforters. Most rooms with bath and balcony. (DM27.50, DM25 per each additional night. Breakfast included.) Berchtesgaden is filled with restaurants for tourists—wealthy tourists. Pick up a *Wurst* sandwich from a vendor, or groceries at the **Edeka Markt,** Dr.-Imhof-Str. near Griesstätterstr. (Open Mon.-Fri. 8am-6pm, Sat. 8am-noon.) The casual, relaxed **Martinklause,** 20 1/3 Ludwig-Ganghofer-str., offers inexpensive soups (DM3-5.50), *Wurst* sandwiches (DM7.80), and beer. Old rock music and pinball, too (open daily 10am-2pm, 5pm-midnight).

Sights The **Kehlsteinhaus** was built at the behest of Hitler's secretary Martin Bormann as a place to entertain the *Führer.* In fact, Hitler only visited the mountaintop retreat a few times, but that doesn't deter a parade of tourists. There's no museum at the site, just an Alpine panorama from the 1834m summit. Buses depart irregularly between 7:20am and 3:35pm from the Berchtesgaden train station (ask for the current bus schedule at the tourist office; round-trip DM5.50) to "Obersalzberg-Hintereck." There you must switch to a special bus (7:40am-4pm, every 25-30min.; round-trip DM18) that winds up the stomach-wrenching one-lane road to the mountaintop. The road itself is something of an engineering marvel, hewn into solid rock by an army of 3,000 (un)fortunate men excused from military conscription for health reasons. Where the bus ride ends, ride an elevator up the last 400 vertical feet; orwalk for 20 minutes and take the elevator back down (DM3). On the way back down, you can inspect what little remains of another Nazi retreat which was bombed by the Allies on April 25, 1945; the **Berghof** in Obersalzberg, was used by Hitler to entertain foreign dignitaries. It was here on February 12, 1938, that the Nazi dictator browbeat Austrian Chancellor Kurt von Schuschnigg into giving the Nazis control of the Austrian police, which paved the way for the *Anschluß* by the Third Reich. Seven months later, British Prime Minister Neville Chamberlain visited to strike an agreement with Hitler, erroneously called the "Munich Agreement," that Chamberlain claimed would guarantee "peace in our time."

The **Schloß** itself was a monastic priory until the Bavarian rulers usurped the area and appropriated the property. It now houses a fairly interesting collection of art and weaponry. (Open Sun-Fri. 10am-1pm and 2-5pm; Oct.-Easter Mon.-Fri. 10am-1pm and 2-5pm. Admission DM5, students DM3.) Next door to the *Schloß* is the **Kirche St. Peter,** which boasts an unusually interesting vaulted ceiling. To reach the castle and the rest of the *Altstadt,* cross over the traintracks on the footbridge behind the station and continue to Bahnhofweg until you hit Maximillianstr.; continue straight ahead. At the **salt mines** *(Salzbergwerke)* near town, you can dress up in an old salt miner's outfit, slide down snaking passages in the dark, and go on a raft ride on a salt lake. From the station, take bus #9547 to Salzbergwerk. (Open daily 8:30am-5pm; mid-Oct. to April Mon.-Sat. 12:30-3:30pm. Admission DM14, children DM7. 90-minute tours. Call (086521) 600 20 for information.) Wedged deep into extraordinary Alpine cliffs, the **Königssee** is a lake so calm that its blue-green surface mirrors the landscape. Ships glide across the lake iregularly (to St. Bartholomä, DM15.50; to Obersee DM19); the best view is at the **Malerwinkel** (Painter's Outlook), around the left of the lake. Take bus #9541, direction "Königssee" from the main train station to the end of the line (3 per hour, DM2.80, Eurail valid).

OBERAMMERGAU AND ETTAL ABBEY

Since 1634, the tiny Alpine town of Oberammergau has been the site of the world-famous **Passion Plays.** After the town was spared from a plague which swept through Europe, the inhabitants promised to perform the crucifixion and resurrection of Christ every 10 years. The cast is composed of about 1000 locals who begin rehearsing long in advance, often growing long beards and hair months ahead. The plays last all day, with a short break for lunch. The next Passion Plays will be presented from May to mid-September, 2000, and just about the most exciting thing to do in Oberammergau in the meantime is to watch the grass grow and visit nearby Ettal Abbey (below). Reserve tickets and accommodations for the plays a good two years in advance. Information and tickets can be obtained from the **tourist office,** Eugen-Papst-Str. 9a (tel. (08822) 10 21 or 47 71), which also finds rooms (DM1 fee, rooms DM20-30 per person, DM30-40 with bath) and provides maps (open Mon.-Fri. 8:30am-8:30pm, Sat. 8:30am-noon and 4-8:30pm, Sun. 4-8:30pm). For Oberammergau's **Jugendherberge (HI),** Malensteinweg 10 (tel. (08822) 41 14), follow the right bank of the Ammer upstream (7min. from train station). The mood is a bit loud and unpredictable. (Reception open 5-9:30pm. Curfew 10pm. Under 27 only. DM15.50. Sheets DM4.50. Open Dec. 27 to mid-March and April to mid-Nov.)

In 1330, Ludwig I of Bavaria founded the enormous, domed **Abbey Church** in the tiny village of **Ettal,** about four km south of Oberammergau. Since then, the abbey has conducted a brisk business of spirits and beer. Buy a sampler six-pack for DM15.80 or cross the street and down a *Kloster Ettal Dunkles* (DM3.80). Beautifully stuccoed and gilded, the rectangular sanctuary assumed its present shape after 18th-century renovations. Buses to Ettal from Oberammergau (DM4) leave from the train station about once per hour (30min., round-trip DM4.20, Eurail valid).

FÜSSEN

Füssen was built on the crossway of an old imperial Roman road, where the Lech River leaves the mountains on its way to the Danube. At the southern end of the Romantic Road at the base of the Alpine foothills, Füssen has since the 19th century mainly been known as a resort for ordinary Germans as well as for Mad King Ludwig. The town's proximity to Ludwig's famed *Königsschlösser* (royal castles; see below) is part of what daws folds of visitors here each year. Under Heinrich VII, the town found itself an unwilling player in a game of European intrigue and politics. In order to help finance his Italian campaign, Heinrich put up the town against 400 silver marks from the prince-bishop of Augsburg. Heinrich died without having repaid the debt, so in the year 1313 the town came into the prince-bishop's hands, where it remained until the great German Secularization in 1802.

Evidence of the prince-bishops' medieval reign is everywhere. The artifacts the bishops left behind include the inner walls of the courtyard of the **Hohes Schloß** (High Castle) are decorated with arresting *trompe l'oeil* windows and towers. Inside is the **Gemäldegalerie** and its collection of regional late-Gothic and Renaissance art, housed in what were once the offices and bedrooms of late-medieval bishops and knights. (Open Tues.-Sun. 11am-4pm; Nov.-March Tues.-Sun. 2-4pm. Admission DM3, students and seniors DM2.) In the Romanesque basilica **St. Mangkirche** (Church of St. Magnus) and its abbey, just below the castle, an ancient fresco, discovered during renovations in 1950, lights up the church's 10th-century subterranean crypt (guided tour each Tues. 4:30pm). Inside the **Chapel of St. Anne,** a series of skeleton-bedecked panels illustrate the *Totentanz* (death dance), a plague-era public frenzy. (Open same hours as *Hohes Schloß*; free.)

The **tourist office** *(Kurverwaltung;* tel. (08362) 70 77) is on the Augsburger-Tor-Platz. Turn left out of the *Bahnhof* and continue down the length of Bahnhofstr., the follow Luitpold-Str. to the big yellow building. The staff gives advice on hiking and finds rooms for no fee. The office organizes 5-6 guided hikes of the surrounding area (DM4 per person; ask about departure times), as well as other expeditions to the Königschlößer. (open Mon.-Fri. 8am-noon and 2-6:15pm, Sat. 10am-noon and 2-6:15pm, Sun. 9am-12:30pm; Oct.- May Mon.-Fri. 8am-noon and 2-6pm, Sat. 10am-noon.) **Rent bikes** at the *Bahnhof* (tel. 63 13) or **Radsport Zacherl,** Rupprechtstr. 8-1/2. Budget singles in *Gasthäuser* run DM30-35; in *Pensionen,* DM40 and up. Despite a bit of wear, Füssen's **Jugendherberge (HI),** Mariahilferstr. 5 (tel. 77 54, fax 27 70), is clean and well-kept. Turn right from the station and follow the railroad tracks. It's often packed, so double-check *before* you arrive to make sure you have a bed to sleep in; if you've made a reservation, they're obligated to find a place for you to sleep. (Reception open 5-7pm. Lockout 9-11am. Curfew 10pm, in summer 11pm. Under 27 only. DM17.80. Breakfast included. Sheets DM5. Wash DM2.50, dry DM2.50, soap DM2. Open mid-Dec. to Oct.; reservations recommended. They prefer reservations by fax, but also take them by phone.) On Reichenstr. (which leads away from the tourist office toward the Schloß) is **Kaiser's supermarket,** where you can fill a picnic basket for a nice bike ride into the surrounding countryside.

Wieskirche (Church of the Meadow)

A daytrip from Füssen or Oberammergau to the Ammergau Alps ought to include the **Wieskirche** (Church of the Meadows), a splendid Rococo pilgrimage church surrounded by forests and farmland. Vendors of religious paraphernalia and sinful funnel-cakes have set up shop near the church, infringing on the tranquility of its location in the middle of nowhere. The church has two unusual aspects. A light pastel color scheme, uncommon in religious architecture, dominates the richly stuccoed and painted interior. The church's windows admit as much light as possible, even into the choir. Thus the entire church exudes an astonishing lightness, particularly in the morning and evening when the sun shines directly through the arching windows. The fresco on the central dome depicts a skillfully rendered *Gate to Paradise*. To fully appreciate the way in which the painter's use of perspective and the concave shape of the ceiling collude to trick the eye, first stand directly underneath the dome, then observe it again from the gallery next to the choir. Better yet, stand directly underneath, look up, and twirl around three times. Buses to the Wieskirche leave the Füssen train station Monday through Saturday at 11:15am, 1:05 and 4:15pm, and on Sunday at 1:05 and 4:15pm. A bus returns at 3:50pm (bus #106). From Oberammergau, buses leave Monday through Saturday at 8:40am (change at Echlesbacher Brücke) and 12:57pm, and return at 3:40pm and 5:10pm (change at Echelsbacher Brücke for the 6:10pm bus). Railpasses are valid on all buses. The trip lasts one hour from Füssen and two to three hours from Oberammergau.

THE ROYAL CASTLES (KÖNIGSSCHLÖSSER)

■■■ THE ROYAL CASTLES
(Königsschlösser)

In 1864, when Ludwig II inherited the Kingdom of Bavaria, he was young and shockingly handsome. The commonly accepted word is that Ludwig was a bit bonkers. Unlike many dreamers, he had the cash to make his visions solid, and spent his own private fortune building fantastic castles to the Alpine skies. In 1886, a band of upstart nobles and bureaucrats formed an Arrest Commission that deposed Ludwig in a *coup d'état* and imprisoned him in Schloß Neuschwanstein on the Starnbergersee lake. Three days later, the King and a loyal adviser were found drowned in the lake under mysterious circumstances, possibly in an escape attempt. According to Bavarians, Ludwig gets a bad rap. The king was a bit eccentric, they concede, but only because he was bored and indifferent to politics, not because he was mentally ill. They claim that his enemies fabricated the story of his madness as an excuse to seize power.

HOHENSCHWANGAU AND NEUSCHWANSTEIN

These *Königsschlösser* are about 5km across the Lech River, in the village of Hohenschwangau. It was in **Schloß Hohenschwangau,** the neo-Gothic castle rebuilt by his father Maximilian II, that Ludwig II grew up and no doubt acquired his taste for the romantic German mythologies of the Middle Ages. Despite the excessive decorative use of swans and a number of terrifyingly tasteless *objets d'art* that were state gifts to the family, the furnishings—particularly the Biedermeier—are truly lovely. Truly.

Ludwig's desperate building spree across Upper Bavaria peaked with the construction of **Schloß Neuschwanstein,** the neo-feudal inspiration for Disneyworld's "Fantasyland" castle. The first sketches of the anachronistic castle were reportedly drawn by a set designer, not an architect, which explains a lot. The young Ludwig II lived a mere 170 days within the castle's extravagant rooms, which include a byzantine throne-room, a small artificial grotto, and an immense *Sängersaal* (Singer's Hall) lined with murals depicting the *Parzifal* legend. The king's bed is topped by a carved wooden depiction of a familiar-looking, yet somehow unrecognizable city skyline; the models represent most of the famous towers of the world. The lines for the brisk, heavily accented **tours** (no fee additional to admission price) tend to be endless, but they are the only way to get inside. The best time to arrive is first thing in the morning, but even then, expect to wait an hour or more. (Admission prices and open hours same for both castles. Open daily 9am-5:30pm; Nov.-March daily 10am-4pm. Admission DM8, students, seniors, and persons with disabilities DM5.) Consider spending the rest of the day hiking around the spectacular environs. For the daddy of all views, hike up to the Marienbrücke spanning the **Pöllat Gorge** behind the castle. Those with stout hearts and legs continue uphill from there for about two and a half hours for a knockout overlook of the castle and the nearby lake. Sane people ride up the **Tegelbergbahn** cable car for a glimpse at the same panorama. (One-way DM13, round-trip DM21; students DM12.50 and DM20 respectively. Open daily 8:30am-5pm, in winter 9am-4:30pm.)

From Füssen, take the bus marked, appropriately enough, "Königsschlösser," which departs from the train station more or less hourly (DM2.10, Eurail valid). The quickest way to Hohenschwangau is path #18 which runs behind Hotel Müller on Alpseestr. (about 10min.; many steps). To Neuschwanstein take path #32, which begins at Car Park D (a.k.a. *Parkplatz Königsschlösser,* right across the street from the bus stop), for the shortest, but steepest, route to the top (20min.). Alternately, clip-clop your way to the top on a horse-drawn carriage (uphill DM7, downhill DM3.50, daily 9am-5pm) from Car Park D or Hotel Müller. Consider trekking down path #33 (open only in summer) from Neuschwanstein (35-40min.). Virtually untouristed, this route winds its way down through the dramatic **Pöllat Gorge.** For maps or more information on trails, check out the information booth where the bus to the castles (direction "Hohenschwangau village") stops. **Buses** depart from the

Garmisch-Partenkirchen train station and stop directly in Hohenschwangau village (3 per day at 8am (bus #1084), 12:10pm (bus #106 via Echelsbacher Brücke), and 4:50pm (bus #1084, 2hr., DM14.70, round-trip DM23.40, free with Eurail); return at 1:13pm (bus #97, with a change of buses at the Wieskirche and a layover of 1½hr.), or 5:24pm (direct). From Munich, take a **train** to Buchloe or Kaufbeuren and transfer to the regional train to Füssen (trip lasts about 2hr.; DM30).

THE CASTLES: HYPERTRAVEL

Seeing all three of the **royal castles** (*Königsschlösser*) during a daytrip from Munich requires some fancy footwork, and it can only be done Monday through Friday. Take the 8am train from Munich to Murnau, then transfer on the 9:06am train to Oberammergau (1¾hr. total; DM21.40). Catch bus #9622 to Linderhof at 10am (30min.; Mon.-Fri., non-holiday departure-only; DM3.80). Catch the 12:30pm bus back to Oberammergau Post/Bahnhof (arrives 12:55pm), then take bus #1084 at 12:57pm to Hohenschwangau. Yes, this does mean you only have two minutes to change buses. If you miss the bus to Hohenschwangau, you're done. You've failed. Pray for an on-time bus. Hohenschwangau is the site of the Neuschwanstein and Hohenschwangau castles, transferring at the Echelsbacher Brücke at 1:41pm (90min.; DM10.20). Leave on the 6:42pm bus to Füssen (10min., DM1.80), then catch the train back to Munich at 7:30pm (via Buchloe; 2hr.; DM31). Realize that this schedule allows you at the most three hours to see Neuschwanstein and Hohenschwangau. In summer the line to Neuschwanstein alone may take half that time, and *even German* trains and buses are late on occasion. Railpasses are valid only on train rides, not buses; double-check your schedule with a timetable before departing. A simpler option, particularly if you don't have a railpass, is to sign on with **EurAide, Inc.** for a charter bus ride to Neuschwanstein and Linderhof. (Tours June 5-Aug. 10 Wed. and Sat. 7:45am; round trip bus and tour DM70, with railpass DM54. Reserve a day ahead at the EurAide office in Munich (see Munich Practical Information, above). Or, take them one at a time; specific directions are after the description of each castle.

SCHLOß LINDERHOF

Halfway between Garmisch-Partenkirchen and Oberammergau lies Ludwig II's small hunting palace, Schloß Linderhof, surrounded by an elegant, manicured park. Through busts and portraits, Ludwig paid copious homage to the French Bourbon kings, as he did at his Herrenchiemsee palace. The royal bedchamber contains an unbelievable amount of gold leaf and a huge crystal chandelier. Don't miss the tribute to Louis XIV, the "Sun King," in the vestibule. On the ceiling is written *"Nec pluribus impar,"* which roughly translates as "I am the greatest; I am the best." Also note the two malachite tables given by Russian Csarina Marie Alexandrovna, whose goal it was to match Ludwig (a bachelor to his death) with one of her daughters. Ludwig decided just to keep the tables.

More impressive than the palace itself, however, is the magnificent **park.** The sheer force of water cascading down steps behind the palace powers the fountain in front. About once every hour, water shoots higher than the top of the palace. Paths weave through the beautifully landscaped grounds. To the right of the palace and up the slope is an enormous artificial **grotto,** complete with a "subterranean" lake and a floating shell-boat, as in Wagner's *Tannenhäuser.* Farther along the same path, brilliant red and blue stained-glass windows richly illuminate the **Maurischer Kiosk** (Moorish Pavilion), an elaborate, mosque-shaped building, which, incidentally, was the only building on the palace grounds not built expressly for Ludwig. Ludwig saw it at the 1867 World Exposition in Paris and liked it so much he brought it back with him. Within these walls, Ludwig would smoke his water pipe and have his servants, dressed in costume, read him tales from *1001 Arabian Nights.* Following the path down the hill and to the left is the newly reconstructed **Hunding-Hütte** (20min.), another of Ludwig's flights of fancy, modeled after a scene from Wagner's

Die Walküre. (Palace and grounds open daily 9am-5:30pm, Oct.-March 10am-12:15pm and 12:45-4pm. Admission to all 4 buildings in summer DM7, students and seniors DM4; in winter DM5 and DM2.50 respectively.)

Buses run between Oberammergau and the park (7 per day 10am-7:02pm, last bus leaves Linderhof at 5:35pm; round-trip DM7.20). Get to Oberammergau by bus from Garmisch-Partenkirchen (round-trip DM10.40), Schongau (round-trip DM12.60), or Füssen (round-trip DM18). Eurail is valid on all routes. Trains run from Munichto Oberammergau, switching at Murnau (1¾hr.; 11 per day; DM21).

■■■ ALLGÄU ALPS

MEMMINGEN

A former imperial town and the gateway to the Allgäu region, Memmingen is generally as staid as only true Swabians can be. But very four years in late July and early August, Memmingen's citizens take to the streets in a ten-day celebration of the summer of 1630, when Commander-General Albrecht von Wallenstein brought his camp to Memmingen and with it a respite from the ravages of the Thirty Years War. (The next "Wallenstein-Sommer" will take place in 1996; for more information, write Wallenstein-Sommer '96, Verkehrsamt im Parishaus, Ulmerstraße 9, 87700 Memmingen.) In between those frenzies, few visitors disturb Memmingen, its Marktplatz and pedestrian zone, crisscrossed by tiny creeks, and overflowing with painted and molded façades.

The Rococo **Rathaus,** topped by three onion domes, looks over the market square. On the other end of the pedestrian zone at Gerberplatz stands the half-timbered **Siebendächerhaus** (Seven-Gabled House), a 17th-century former tannery. To the extent that *Fachwerk* is ever magnificent, this building is. Two blocks south of the Marktplatz, the **St.-Martinskirche,** the symbol of Memmingen, rises in Gothic grandeur. Of particular interest are the carved 15th-century choir stalls. (Open May-Sept. daily 2:30-5pm except Sat. 10am-noon; Oct. Sun.-Fri. 2-4pm Sat. 10am-noon. If closed, call (08331) 22 53 for information.) Farther south, on Frauenkirchplatz, stands the eponymous **Frauenkirche** (Church of Our Lady), a 14th- and 15th-century church with an exquisite fresco cycle and dramatic vaulting over the apse.

Memmingen's **tourist office,** Ulmer Str. 9 (tel. (08331) 85 01 72), is one block north of the *Rathaus* (open Mon.-Fri. 8am-noon and 2-5pm, Sat. 9:30am-12:30pm). The **Jugendherberge (HI),** Kempter Str. 42 (tel. (08331) 49 40 87), is easily reached from the train station. Follow Bahnhofstr. left from the station until you reach the park. Turn right into the park and walk the length of it, cross the street and the building is there in the building with the tower, somewhat recessed from the street. (Reception open 5-10pm. Curfew 10pm. Lockout 9am-5pm. Under 27 only. DM15. Breakfast included. Sheets DM3.) The conveniently located **Gasthaus Weißes Lamm,** Hallhof 9 (tel. (08331) 21 02), four blocks down Maximilianstr. from the train station, has cozy singles (DM34, with bath DM38) and doubles (DM60, with bath DM68). There are two swell **campsites** in the area. **Camping am See International,** Am Weiherhaus 7 (tel. (08331) 718 00) in Buxheim, is quite close. Take the bus (direction "Buxheim") to Oben am Weiher (DM5.50 per person, DM4 per tent, DM9 per car). The **Familien-Ferien-Campingplatz Iller,** Illerstr. 57 (tel. (07565) 54 19), is farther out. (DM6.50 per person, DM8 per car. Open April to mid-Oct.) Memmingen is connected by **train** to Augsburg (1hr., DM20) and Ulm (45min., DM13).

OTTOBEUREN

A little town with a big church, Ottobeuren rests lazily in the rolling alpine foothills of the Allgäu. The **Benedictine Abbey Church,** on a grassy rise in the middle of town, is about as inconspicuous as an American tourist. The largest Baroque church in Germany, its towers are 82 meters high, the nave 90meters long, and the transept 60 meters wide. The façade is dramatic...from afar. As you approach, however, the marvelous stonework flattens out into what turns out to be a moderately skillful painting job. The interior, however, is dazzling. Intricately molded relief-work, gilded scrolling, colored marble, and a line of frescoed domes lead visitors to a high altar which takes Baroque fantasy to its pinnacle. The side-altars contain countless relics—skulls, bones, bone shards—neatly labeled and displayed. The four altars under the central dome each contain the complete skeleton of a saint associated with the abbey, every one neatly dressed in ecclesiastical garments (including embroidered slippers) and artfully arranged atop velvet pillows. Behind the church is the palatial **prelature,** including a lavish library. (Open March-Nov. daily 10am-noon and 2-5pm. Admission DM3.)

The **tourist office** *(Kurverwaltung)* (tel. (08332) 68 17), on Marktplatz, right across from the abbey, provides free maps, finds rooms (DM20-30) for no fee, and sells tickets for the abbey concerts (open Mon.-Thurs. 8am-noon and 2-5pm, Fri. - Sat. 8am-noon and 2-4pm.) To reach Ottobeuren's tidy **Jugendherberge (HI),** Faichtmayrstr. 24 (tel. (08331) 368), walk down Silachweg along the church, turn right onto Luitpoldstr., and left onto Faichtmayrstr. The hostel is four blocks down to the right. (Reception open 5-7pm. Under 27 only. DM13. Breakfast included. Sheets DM5. Open March-Oct.) Buses (DM3.40; railpasses not valid) run about once per hour between Ottobeuren and Memmingen, 15km to the northwest. Ask at the tourist office for a map of hiking and cycling trails to nearby sights and resorts.

KEMPTEN

First a Celtic settlement, then the site of a Roman military post, Kempten centers around an unusually well-preserved *Altstadt* encircled by forested hills. Across the street from the *Altstadt* is the large 17th-century **St. Lorenz Basilika,** built shortly after the Thirty Years War. The elegant Baroque **Fürstäbtliche Residenz** (Prince Abbot's Residence) is a sizable former Benedictine cloister with colorfully painted window frames. The building has served the town as everything from barracks to law courts. Behind the *Residenz* stretches the terraced **Hofgarten,** webbed by paths leading to the 18th-century **Orangerie.** (Guided tours Tues.-Sun. 10 and 11am, 2 and 3pm; Oct.-Apr. Sat. 2pm). To reach the town center from the distant train station, take bus #5, 7, 8, 10, 11, or 13 to Residenz stop (DM2). Klostersteige leads from the *Residenz* to the cobbled pedestrian zone. Fisherstr. and Rathausstr. are lined with Baroque and Rococo *patrizier* façades.

Across from the basilica on Residenzplatz, in the elegant patrician **Zumsteinhaus,** are the **Römische Sammlung Cambodunum** (Roman Museum of Kempten) and the **Naturkunde Museum** (Museum of Natural History of the Allgäu), which has rocks and animals and things. (Both open Tues.-Sun. 10am-4pm; admission DM4, students and seniors DM2, on Sundays and holidays admission is free.) Along Burgstr. is a large forested park containing the **Burghalde,** the oldest part of the city, which includes a late Roman **Castell** and a Gothic castle tower, as well as an amphitheater. More Roman ruins are across the Iller River along Kaufbeurerstr. at the **Cambodunum Archeological Park;** the park boasts some Gallo-Roman temple remains, a basilica, and thermal baths. Guides give tours of all partially restored structures, and the nearby museum contains exhibits. (Open Tues.-Sun. 10am-5pm, Nov.-April Tues.-Sun. 10am-4:30pm. Admission DM4, children DM2. Free 1½hr. tours in German only Mar.-Dec. Sun. at 11am from the kiosk.)

Kempten's **tourist office** *(Verkehrsamt),* Im Rathaus (tel. (0831) 252 52 37), provides city and hiking maps, accommodation listings, and 1½- to 2-hr. city tours for free. (Open May-Oct. Mon.-Fri. 8am-noon and 1:30-5pm, Sat. 10am-1pm. Tours in German every Sat. 11am.) The **Mitfahrzentrale,** Bodmanstr. 1 (tel. (0831) 230 72) matches riders and drivers. Built on a bend in the Iller River, Kempten can be reached by train from Lindau and Ulm, and from Munich. The noisy **Jugendherberge (HI),** Saarlandstr. 1 (tel. (0831) 736 63), is usually packed with school groups, but opens out onto a sweeping view of the Alps beyond the Allgäu. Take bus #4 from the train station to Lenzfriederstr./Altersheim. Or, take Bahnhofstr. to Schumacherring, turn right and follow this large street (30min.) until you see signs for the Jugenderherberge on the right. Note that this route crosses a somewhat doubtful district, and travelers may not feel safe walking it, especially at night. (Reception open 5-10pm. Curfew 10pm. Under 27 only. DM15.50. Breakfast included. Sheets DM5. Open mid-Dec. to Oct.) To reach **Camping Oeschlesee** (tel. 08376) 621), take bus from the *Altbahnhof* at Sulzberg (about 20min., DM4.20) and walk to the lake (DM5 per person, DM4-7 per tent). For cheap eats in the *Altstadt,* try **Kochlöffel** at 22 Fischerstr. Along the river past the St. Mary bridge on Brennergasse, **Pilsbar Platz'l** serves standard lunchtime fare for under DM10.

IMMENSTADT AND BÜHL AM ALPSEE

The small town of **Immenstadt** and the even smaller hamlet of **Bühl am Alpsee** huddle deep in the Allgäu near Kempten, a world distanced from the resorts to the south. Streams flowing down from the Alps feed two lakes, the **Große Alpsee** and the **Kleiner Alpsee** (Greater and Lesser Alpine Lakes) whose cool, clear waters are unspeakably refreshing after a hike into the surrounding hilly countryside.

The **tourist office,** Marienplatz 3 (tel. (08323) 804 81), has loads of hiking maps and suggested routes, many of which will land you at a mountain **Gaststätte** at about lunchtime. (Open Mon.-Fri. 8:30am-noon and 2-5:30pm, Sat. 10am-noon.) The Kleiner Alpsee, a 15-minute walk down Badeweg towards Bühl, has a large public beach. The Großer Alpsee is dotted with swimming spots, but certain stretches are off-limits to swimmers. Boat and surfboard rental on the Großer Alpsee is possible but rather expensive. Immenstadt is close to three huge skiing areas: **Gschwender Horn, Alpsee Skizirkus,** and **Mitlag Ski-Center.** The season runs roughly from December to March. Day passes run about DM25 in each area; weekpasses DM140. Contact the tourist office in either Bühl or Immenstadt for more information on buses and special offers. The **tourist office** in Bühl (tel. (08323) 804 83) has many of the same maps and brochures as its counterpart in Immenstadt (open Mon.-Fri. 8:30am-noon and 2-5pm, Sat. 10am-noon). Both tourist offices find accommodations. (In Immenstadt DM25-45 per person; in Bühl DM18-30 per person. Breakfast included.) Camp directly on the Großer Alpsee at **Bucher's Camping,** Seestr. 25 (tel. (08323) 77 26) in Bühl. (DM5 per person, DM3.80 per tent, DM3 per car. Open Mar. 25-Nov. 5.) Immenstadt can be reached by **train** from Kempten along the Munich-Zürich route, or from Ulm along the Stuttgart-Oberstdorf route.

■■■ THE CHIEMSEE

Artists, architects, and musicians have chosen the **Chiemsee** (Lake Chiem), with its picturesque islands and dramatic crescent of mountains, as a setting for their work for almost 2000 years. The region first lured the 9th-century builders of the cloisters on **Fraueninsel,** and later King Ludwig II of Bavaria, who built **Herrenchiemsee,** his third and last "fairy-tale castle" (his unfinished attempt to surpass Versailles) on the Herreninsel. The poet Maximilian Haushofer lived and died on the shores of Chiemsee in **Prien** (see below), and an 11-year-old Mozart composed a mass in Seeon while on holiday. Most modern visitors to Bavaria's largest lake (approximately 32 square miles) are artists of leisure, as the area has become overrun with resorts and prices have risen. Don't expect to find very many foreigners; Chiemsee is where Munich goes on vacation. Prien, the largest lake town, offers easy access to ski areas in the **Kampenwand,** the curtain of mountains that surrounds Chiemsee.

HERRENINSEL AND FRAUENINSEL

The main attractions of the Chiemsee are its three islands. The smallest is uninhabited, but the other two teem with streams of visitors. Ferries ply the waters of the Chiemsee from the port in Prien to the Herreninsel (Men's Island), the Fraueninsel (Women's Island) and towns on the other side of the lake. Both islands are co-ed, although this wasn't always the case; way back when, there was a monastery on Herreninsel in addition to the still-extant nunnery on Fraueninsel. (Round-trip to Herreninsel DM8, to Fraueninsel DM9.50.) To get to the dock, hang a right coming out of the Prien train station's main entrance and follow Seestr. (the major thorough-fare on your right) for about 25 minutes. The train station **information booth,** though visible, has very limited open hours (July-mid Sept. 12:45-5pm). Or, a special **green steam train** takes visitors from the train station (take underpass from plat-form 1 at station to other side, or look for the huge Chiemseebahn sign) to the dock every 20 minutes. (DM3, round-trip DM4.50. Total package, including train shuttle and ship passage, DM17.) Be sure to read the schedules carefully to avoid gettting stranded. As the ferry moves away from the shore, the ridge of perpetually snow-capped mountains bordering the lake to the south comes into full view.

Schloß Herrenchiemsee

"Never can as unsuitable a location have been chosen for something as tasteless as this unfortunate copy of the palace at Versailles," Bavarian poet Ludwig Thoma once wrote. Once on Herreninsel, either walk along the paved footpath to the pal-ace (20min.) or take one of the horse-drawn carriages that run every 15 minutes (DM3.50, children DM2.50). The architecture of **Königsschloß Herrenchiemsee** (Herrenchiemsee Royal Palace) is as fabulously overwrought as only King Ludwig II could manage. The entire U-shaped palace (70 rooms total, less than one-fifth of which were ever completed), artwork included, is a shameless attempt to be larger, better, and more expensive than the main wing of Versailles, the abode of France's Louis XIV. Ludwig II was so obsessed with the "Sun King" that he commissioned paintings, copied directly from the French originals, to grace the walls of his palace. Surprisingly, there isn't a single image of Ludwig in the place, though a tiny bust of him stands far in the back of the palace grounds. There's even a Versailles-style **Hall of Mirrors,** only Ludwig's is longer than Louis's. Throughout the summer, concerts are given in this room. The enitre palace was meant to be a superlative—it was very important to Ludwig that he spend more money than Louis on chandeliers, gold leaf, marble, and everything else available to the rich and famous. In the process, Ludwig bankrupted Bavaria's treasury and then promptly drowned, having spent only 9 days in the palace. (Entrance to the palace DM6, which requires a guided tour; seniors, students, and disabled DM3.50; under 15 free with adult. German tours every 10min.; English tours 10:30, 11:30am, 2, and 3pm.)

Fraueninsel

Fraueninsel offers subtler pleasures. From the boat dock, a marked path weaves toward the island's cloister, dating back to at least 866. St. Irmengard, the great-granddaughter of Charlemagne and the earliest known abbess at the cloister, has a **memorial chapel** in her honor behind the main altar in the cloister church. Her sar-cophagus was exhumed in the 17th century, and since 1928 her remains have been on view behind glass within the altar. They're not very interesting, but that's what 1000 years will do to you. The old **Torhalle** (gate) is the oldest surviving part of the original cloister. Various artifacts, including the impressive 8th-century Merovingian **Cross of Bischofhofen,** are on display in the room above the gate. (Open Mon.-Sat. 11am-6pm. Admission DM3, students and seniors DM1.50.)

PRIEN AM CHIEMSEE

Truth be told, the best thing about Prien is the Chiemsee. Located on the northwest-ern corner of the Chiemsee, Prien has a convenient and direct rail link to Munich (a 52-minute ride through lush but occasionally Bavarian farmland). Go here to orient yourself for trips to the real sights elsewhere on the lake. There is also a bus to Salzburg, Austria (45min.), which runs weekdays almost on the hour. The train sta-tion is a few blocks from the city center and a 20-minute walk north of the lake. If the **information booth** at the train station is closed, head out the main exit and ten paces to your right is a city map (open July-Sept. Mon.-Fri. 12:45-5pm). To reach the

Altstadt, walk northeast to Seestr. (exiting the train station, you face north). Past the four-way intersection, Seestr. becomes Alte Rathausstr. The large **tourist office** (Alte Rathaus 11, tel. (080) 690 50, fax 69 05 40), five minutes up Alte Rathausstr. on the left side of the street, is full of free maps and brochures. Call to hear which **pharmacy** is open on a particular night (tel. (080) 10 37).

The cheapest bed in town is at the raucous, overflowing-with-pre-teens **Jugendherberge (HI),** Carl-Braun-Str. 15 (tel. (080) 29 72), a 10-minute walk from the lake. (6 bunk rooms. Reception open 5-7pm. Lockout 9am-1pm. Curfew 10pm. Members DM16.50. Showers, lockers, and breakfast (8-9am) included. Open Jan.-Oct.) The tourist office finds a rooms in private houses (starting at DM25) for no fee. There is a **campsite** just outside of town at Bernauer Str. 110 (tel. (080) 41 36). Walk up Bahnhofstr. from the train station and turn left, then walk 800m. Most of the restaurants in Prien cater to the vacationing bourgeoisie. The cheapest eats can be found at **La Spaghetteria Tricolore,** Seestr. 7, one block down from the train station along the way to the lake. They make a decent pizza (DM7), and better tortellini (open Tues.-Sun. noon-2pm and 6pm-midnight). Hoard groceries from **Norma's,** on Hallwanger Str. coming from the station take Seestr., and then the first left after the railroad tracks (open Mon.-Fri. 8am-noon and 2-6pm, Sat. 8am-noon).

■■■ BURGHAUSEN

Separated from Austria only by the Salzach River, the town of **Burghausen** is dominated by the proverbial castle on a hill—in this case, the longest medieval fortress in Germany. Built in the 13th century, the **Schloß** was considered impregnable, and indeed, it was only breached once. In 1742 the Hapsburg Empire, eager to extend its borders into Bavaria, approached the border town of Burghausen. Cowed by the Austrian show of arms, and lacking outside reinforcements, Burghausen opened its gates without a fight. However, some short days later on October 16, 1742, in Burghausen's moment of glory, the brash 26-year-old *Hofkaminkehrermeister* (King of Chimney Sweeps) Karl Franz Cura recruited 40 grenadiers for the seemingly impossible task of breaking through the castle walls. In a commando-type assault on the occupied castle, Cura freed the castle and the city in one fell swoop. Until the Habsburgs decide to mount another assault, Burghausen will remain one of the undiscovered gems of Bavaria, amply rewarding all who make the visit with some of the most attractive scenery in the region.

These days, the **castle** ramparts can be walked with little fear of violent reprisals, and the upper halls contain the town's **historical museum.** For the price of a punishing climb up the steep footpath which starts near the church across from the **Rathaus,** the castle also offers a ravishing view of the *Altstadt* roofscape of red tiles and colorful gables. (Open Mon.-Fri. 9am-5pm, Sat. 9am-1pm. Admission DM4, students, seniors, and with disabilities DM2.) Directly below the castle, in all its technicolor splendor, lies the town plaza and main thoroughfare, **Stadtplatz.** Simply put, the view from the castle sets toe-hairs tingling; it rambles outward in all directions.

Stepping off the train, you'll find yourself seemingly in the middle of nowhere. Don't panic. Walking directly to your left coming off the train (100m) through the parking lot brings you to the street **Marktlerstraße.** Following that to the right (taking the left fork 400m from the train station to remain on Marktlerstr.) is good for a 30-minute hike to the *Altstadt;* or, you can opt to take the bus on Marktlerstr. just around the corner of the train station (every 30min., DM 1.50).

Back on *terra firma,* the **tourist office** (*Fremdenverkehrsamt;* tel. (08677) 24 35) is located in the light-green *Rathaus* at the far end of the Stadtplatz. On the ground floor are free maps, brochures, and information on tours of both Burghausen and the surrounding area. To your left exiting the *Rathaus* is an archway which opens onto a narrow cobblestone street called In den Grüben; the **post office** (no currency exchange) is located at #162 (tel. 45 80). There is one international **phone booth** in the post office (open Mon.-Fri. 10am-noon and 2:30-5pm). The **telephone city code** is 08677. **Police** are at Tittmonigerstr. 6 (tel. 20 46). Burghausen is most easily reached from Munich by **train,** though buses run from Mühldorf, the center for train and bus transportation in eastern Bavaria.

The **Jugendherberge Burghausen (HI)** (tel. 41 87), hands-down the cheapest place in town, is in the castle (see directions above). At the top, turn right and walk 100m. The dorms are roomy and clean and the view astounding. (Reception open 5-7pm. Lockout 10am-1pm. Curfew 10pm. DM11, with breakfast DM15, with morning and evening meals (*Halbpension*) DM21.50, with full board DM25.50. Sheets DM5. Reservations recommended during summer.) The tourist office can help you find quieter accommodations for no fee; *Pensionen* in Burghausen start at DM25.

Many of the restaurants and cafés which dot the Stadtplatz are downright pricey. Sip a beer at the **Hotel Post** on the Stadtplatz for DM3.80 and ask the manager about Franz Cura's scuffle with the Austrians in that very same inn. Buy supplies at the **Edeka Markt,** In den Gruben (open Mon.-Fri. 8:30am-6:30pm, Sat. 9am-noon).

■ ■ ■ PASSAU

Situated on the two peninsulas formed by the confluence of the Danube, Inn, and Ilz rivers, elegant Passau fulfills every dream of what an Old World continental city should be. The strategic potential of the bluff overlooking the Austrian-German border first caught the eye of Roman generals in AD 80. By 739, Passau was the seat of a diocese, and centuries of peaceful church and cathedral building had begun. In the 12th century, Wolfger, the bishop of Passau, supervised the written recording of the epic *Nibelungenlied* for the first time, thereby establishing Passau in the minds of all once and future tourism boards as the *Nibelungenstadt;* today, the great hall of Passau's *Rathaus* contains extravagant frescoes depicting scenes from the famous epic. The castle, palaces, and monasteries all bear witness to Passau's past as an influential center of administrative, commercial, and religious power in central Europe. Its beautiful Baroque cathedral, the *Stephansdom,* was the mother church that founded the *Stephansdom* in Vienna.

ORIENTATION AND PRACTICAL INFORMATION

Passau is accessible by direct rail lines from both Munich and Vienna. Buses duplicate most rail routes and are often less expensive, but can nearly double the travel time of an already lengthy journey, especially from Vienna. Passau proper is located almost entirely on the peninsula formed by the Danube and the Inn. The adjacent peninsula between the Danube and the Ilz is home to the castle. These two areas contain most places of interest to the traveler. The local dialect, which resembles Austrian German, can be quite difficult for foreigners to understand. To get to the *Altstadt* from the train station, turn right and follow the brown *Jugendherberge* signs; they will take you right past the *Rathaus;* or try catching a **City-Bus.** Before heading out, though, pick up a map of the city at the tourist office 50m to the left of the train station. Passau lies close to the border between Germany and Austria, but is only one hour away by train from Regensburg and two from Nuremberg.

Tourist Office: Fremdenverkehrsverein, Rathausplatz 3, 94032 Passau (tel. 334 21). Facing away from the *Rathaus,* look to your left and down the street. Mind-occluding assortment of free maps, brochures, schedules, and tour information. Room-finding service DM2.50. Distributes *Aktuell,* a free monthly guide to everything going down in Passau. Open Mon.-Fri. 8:30am-6pm; Sat.-Sun. and holidays 10am-2pm. Also a branch at the train station called **Infostelle Passau/Oberösterreich** (tel. 75 14 63). Open Apr.-Oct., Mon.-Fri. 9am-5pm, Sat., Sun., and holidays 9am-1pm. An **automat** in front of the tourist office gives maps and a brochure for DM1.

Budget Travel: ITO Reise, Bahnhofstr. 28 (tel. 540 48), across the street from the train station in the *Donau Passage,* a mall-type establishment.

Currency Exchange: In the train station (tel. 512 68), across from the ticket counters. Open Mon.-Fri. 8:30am-1pm and 1:45-4:30pm. Also at the **post office** next door.

Post Office: Next door to the train station on Bahnhofstr., 94032 Passau (tel. 50 50). Also offers **banking** services: changes money, cashes traveler's checks. Open Mon.-Fri. 8:30am-12:30pm and 2-5:30pm, Sat. 8am-noon.

Telephones: In the post office, in front of the *Rathaus,* and next to the youth hostel. All are international phone booths. **City Code:** 0851.

Trains: Station located west of downtown on Bahnhofstr. (tel. 550 01). Trains run to both Munich (DM46) and Vienna (DM64; 8 per day, fewer on weekends). Trains also run to nearby Regensburg (1hr.) and Nuremberg (2hr.).

Buses: To various towns on the outskirts of Passau and a number of stops within the city (DM4-7). For schedules call 56 02 72. **City-Bus** runs from the train station to the *Rathaus* every 15min. Mon.-Fri. 6:30am-6:30pm, DM0.50.

Ferries: Danube steamers cruise to Linz, Austria (5½hr., round-trip DM47), where connections can be made for Vienna (full round-trip DM221.40). One must stay overnight in Linz and the next morning move on to Vienna. The "Three Rivers Round Trip" tour of the city runs March to early Nov. whenever enough people show up (45min. tour DM7, children DM3.50). All ships depart from the docks along the Fritz-Schäffer-Promenade in front of the *Rathaus.*

Bike Rental: In the **Deutsche Bahn's** half of the train station, bikes DM12 per day, DM8 with a valid ticket of same date. At the **Österreichische Bundesbahn** half, bikes are AS45 per day, AS120 for a mountain bike; with a valid ÖBB ticket of same date, AS45 and AS51.50 respectively.

Laundromat: Wasch-salon, Neubergerstr. 34a. Big new German washers and dryers. Open Mon.-Fri. 7:30am-8pm, Sat. 7:30am-6pm. Wash DM5, dry DM2. Detergent DM1, fabric softener DM0.30.

Hospital: Klinikum Passau, Bischof-Pilgrim-Str. 1 (tel. 53 000). 24hr. **pharmacy** service rotates among the city's pharmacies; check the listings in the notices section of the daily newspaper, either the *Tagespresse* or the *Passauer Neue Presse.*

Emergencies: tel. 110. **Police:** Nibelungenstr. 17 (tel. 50 30).

ACCOMMODATIONS, CAMPING, AND FOOD

Passau's numerous *Pensionen* and cheaper hotels fill up during the summer, thanks to travelers from both East and West. The only youth hostel in town is often full of German schoolchildren, especially during June and July, so enter at your own risk.

Jugendherberge (HI), Veste Oberhaus 125, 94034 Passau (tel. 413 51, fax 437 09), in the castle on the mountain across the Danube. Cross the bridge by the docks and brace yourself for a steep hike to the top, or take the infrequent shuttle from Rathausplatz to the front door (after Easter-mid-Oct. every 30min. 11:30am-5pm). Aging but tidy rooms. Open 6:30am-11:30pm. Reception 9am-2pm and 4-11:30pm; open to phone calls all day. Curfew 11:30pm. DM16.50. Sheets DM5.50. Breakfast included. Reservations recommended.

Rotel Inn, 94012 Passau (tel. 951 60, fax 951 61 00). Right on the bank of the Danube in front of the train station, this far-out modern hotel was built in 1993 in the shape of a sleeping man. Small rooms, big comfortable beds, amazingly cheap. Reception open 24hrs. Singles DM25. Doubles DM50.

Gasthof Zum Hirschen, Im Ort 6 (tel. 362 38), 94032 Passau. Follow the Fritz-Schäffer-Promenade as far as possible toward the tip of the Passau peninsula, then turn right. Threadbare, clean rooms with comfortable beds. Central location on a cobblestone street. Check-out 11am. Singles DM30. Doubles DM55, with shower DM65. Breakfast included. Reservations by phone or mail recommended.

Gasthof Pension Zur Brücke, Hals Landrichterstr. 13 (tel. 434 75). 1hr. north of town, but a nice hike. Best for bike tourists. Follow directions for camping (below) but don't bear right at the "Kann/Camping" sign. Instead take the left fork and follow until you come to a small square; turn right, walk across the bridge and head right and up the hill and it will be immediately on your right. Singles DM22. Doubles DM36. Booking in advance by phone is a must.

Camping: Zeltplatz der Faltbootabteilung, Halserstr. 34 (tel. 414 57). Downhill from the youth hostel. Follow Angerstr. right from Luitpoldbrüke, walk left through the tunnel onto F.-Wagner-Str., veer left up the hill and take the right fork at the "Kahn/Camping" sign. Reception open 8-10am, 3-10pm. DM8.50, under 17 DM6.50, including shower. No camping vehicles. Open May-Oct.

FOOD

Passau is brimming with street vendors, sidewalk cafés, and bistros. For a sugar infusion, stroll down the Ludwigsplatz and sample the baked goods *(Krapfen* DM1, cakes DM3-8) and *gelato* (DM1.40 per scoop).

Mensa, Innstr. 29. Complete cafeteria meals (DM4-5). Most student IDs will do. Open Mon.-Thurs. 11:15am-1:45pm and 5-6:30pm, Fri. 11:15am-1:45pm and 5-6pm. Over term break (July-Aug.) open Mon.-Fri. 11:15am-1:30pm and 5-6pm.
Café Duft, Theresienstr. 22. Modern café, mostly young adult clientele, breakfasts DM7.80-16.50. Soups DM4.50. Salads DM10. Entrees DM8-12.50. Open Mon.-Fri. 9am-1am, Sat.-Sun. and holidays 10am-1am. Kitchen open 6-11pm.
Ristorante Zi Terisa, Theresienstr. 26. A long room with well-dressed waiters and cheery, colorful menu. Pasta DM13 and under. Pizza not so cheap at DM7-DM20. Open daily 11am-midnight.

SIGHTS

Passau's beautiful Baroque architecture reaches its apex in the sublime **Stephansdom** (St. Stephen's Cathedral). Hundreds of cherubs are sprawled across the ceiling, and the world's **largest church organ,** gilded and filigreed, looms above the choir. (Cathedral open Mon.-Sat. 8-11am and 12:30-6pm. Free. Organ concerts May-Oct. Mon.-Fri. noon, DM3, students and seniors DM1, Thurs. 8pm, DM6, students and seniors DM3; no concerts on holidays.) Behind the cathedral is the **Residenzplatz,** lined with formerly patrician dwellings as well as the **Residenz,** erstwhile home of Passau's bishops. The **Domschatz** (cathedral treasury) housed within the *Residenz* has an extravagant collection of gold and tapestries purchased by the bishops with the wealth they tithed from their flocks. (Open May-Oct., Christmas to early Jan., and the week after Easter Mon.-Sat. 10am-4pm. Admission DM2, children DM1.) Also on the Residenzplatz is the **Spielzeugmuseum** (Toy Museum), offering a little something for the kid in all of us (open daily 9am-6pm; admission DM3).

Nearby stands the Baroque church of **St. Michael;** the Jesuits built it and covered much of it with gold (open Tues.-Sun. 9am-5pm; Nov.-Jan. and March 10am-4pm; admission DM3, students DM1.50). The 14th-century Gothic **Rathaus** is decorated with less opulent colors, but is still stunning. (Great Hall of *Rathaus* open Easter-Oct. Mon.-Fri. 10am-noon and 1:30-4pm, Sat.-Sun. 10am-4pm. Admission DM1.) The renowned **Passauer Glasmuseum,** next to the *Rathaus,* houses more than 20,000 examples of glasswork, documenting the last 150 years of glass-making. (Open daily 10am-5pm. DM3, students DM2, children under 10 accompanied by parents free.) Across the river and up the footpath is the **Veste Oberhaus,** the former palace of the bishopric. Once both a place of refuge for the bishop when the local residents got too surly and a prison for various enemies of the cloth, the stronghold now contains the magnificent **Cultural History Museum,** 54 rooms of art and artifacts spanning the last 2000 years. (Open March-Jan. Tues.-Sun. 9am-5pm. DM3, students DM1.50; free on Sun.)

■■■ STRAUBING

Near the Danube on the fringe of the Bavarian Forest, Straubing hasn't undergone a major development for 400 years. If you get the feeling that everyone (with the exception of you) knows everyone else, you're right. If you're in or around Straubing during mid-August, don't miss the massive ten-day **Gäubodenvolksfest,** the second-largest public festival in Bavaria, with carnival rides and beer gardens everywhere(Aug. 12-22 in 1994; check with the tourist office, below, for specifics). The **watchtower** in the middle of the market square, erected in the 14th century, is the symbol of the city. The oldest (1104 AD) and most famous Church in town is the **Wallfahrtskirche St. Maria** (pilgrimage church). The other churches around the market square were originally built in the Gothic style and adapted to the Baroque style centuries later. Walk from the square down the Frauenhoferstr. and bear right to reach the **Herzogsschloß** (ducal palace), parts of which date to 1356. The interior of the palace is closed to the public.

The *Altstadt* lies northwest of the train station, only minutes away on foot. To get there, follow the street in front of the train station to your left. To pick up a free map of the city, head to the small **tourist office** (*Verkehrsamt*) (tel. (09421) 163 07), Theresienplatz 20, in the square across from the tower. Brochures on Straubing, neighboring towns and cultural events are available; they will also track down a room for you for no fee. (Open Mon. 9am-5pm, Tues.-Fri. 9am-6pm, Sat. 10am-2pm, Sun. 10am-noon.) The **post office** is right across from the train station. Cash traveler's checks, exchange foreign currency, or call pa; you never call him; he'd love to hear from you (open Mon.-Thurs. 9am-6pm, Fri. 9am-1pm and 2-6pm, Sat. 9am-1pm, Sun. and holidays 10-11am). The **telephone city code** is 09421.

The **Jugendherberge (HI),** Friedhofstr. 12 (tel. 804 36), is close to the train station. Turn right from the front entrance to the station and follow the curve of the main road. Turn right onto Schildhauerstr. and cross over Außere-Passauer-Str.; the hostel is on your right, at the end of the path through the trees. The building is old and the rooms are cramped, but cleanliness is king. (Reception open 7-10pm. Lockout 9am-1pm. Curfew 10pm. Under 27 only. DM13. Breakfast included. Sheets DM5.) **Gabelsberger Hof,** a *Pension* to the left of the train station down Gabelsbergerstr. (tel. 333 63) has tidy, spacious rooms. (Singles DM30, with bath DM33. Doubles DM55, with bath DM65.) The nine-bed **Falter,** Chamerstr. 34, has rock-bottom prices and is worth a shot (singles DM25, doubles DM50). A bit of a walk south of the train station is the **Weißes Rößl** (tel. 325 81), Landshuterstr. 65 (singles DM30; doubles DM60). There's a **Campingplatz** (tel. 129 12) north of the *Altstadt,* across the Donau River and to the left at Dammweg 17 (open May-Oct. 15). The small and modest **Straubinger Suppenhaferl,** Bahnhofstr., has extremely filling soups; try the *Leberspätlesuppe* (DM4.20; open Mon.-Fri. 8am-10pm, Sat. 8am-3pm).

Straubing and its surroundings produce some royally distinctive **wine**. Bernauergasse, a small street two blocks from the market square, has *Heurigen,* small **wine shops** that sell the local vintage, generally wine that has been produced within the last year. The easiest to find is **Zum Heurigen** at the Rohrmayer Tanzcafé on Theresienplatz 29 (tel. 107 18), comfortable though slightly murky.

■■■ REGENSBURG

Located at the northernmost point on the Danube's long passage to the Black Sea, much of Regensburg's *Altstadt* spills onto the numerous islands created by that river as it converges with the Regen. An enchanting city of patrician houses and Imperial administrative houses, Regensburg is near two extraordinary sights: **Walhalla,** King Ludwig I of Bavaria's tribute to German heroes, and the **Donaudurchbruch,** where the Danube has carved a deep gorge between high church- and cloister-filled grassy banks. What began as a fortress built by Marcus Aurelius in 179 became the first capital of Bavaria, later the seat of the Perpetual Imperial Diet, the parliament of the Holy Roman Empire and of the first German parliament. The rooms once used for the Imperial congresses are now rented out for conventions, concerts, and parties, but the rest of the *Altstadt* seems untouched by time.

ORIENTATION AND PRACTICAL INFORMATION

Regensburg is easily reached by train or bus from either Nuremberg or Passau. The historic old city lies north of the train station, between the station and the Danube, bounded on either side by Kumpfmühlerstr. and Maximilianstr. Maximilianstr. leads straight from the train station into the heart of Regensburg.

Tourist Office: Altes Rathaus (tel. 507 44 10, 11, 12). Walk down Maximilianstr. from the station to Grasgasse. Take a left and follow it even after it turns into Obermünsterstr. Take a right onto Obere Bachgasse and follow it 5 blocks to Rathausplatz. The tourist office is to your left across the square. They will provide you with a free map, find you a room (DM1.50), and sell you tickets to local places and happenings. Open Mon.-Fri. 8:30am-6pm, Sat. 9am-4pm, and Sun. 9:30am-2:30pm; Nov.-March Mon.-Sat. 9am-noon and 2-6pm, Sun. 10am-noon. Pick up info on the Bavarian forest at the **Fremdenverkehrsverband Ostbayern,** Landshuterstr. 13 (tel. 571 86). Open Mon.-Fri. 9am-noon and 2-6pm, Sat. 10am-noon.

Post Office: Next door to the train station. The best exchange rates in Regensburg. Open Mon.-Fri. 8am-6pm, Sat. 9am-noon, Sun. 11am-noon.

Telephones: In front of the train station and the post office. **City Code:** 0941.

Trains: Station at Bahnhofsplatz (tel. 194 19). To: Munich (via Landshut, 2-3hr., DM31), Nuremberg (1½hr., DM24), Passau (1hr., DM29). Ticket office open Mon.-Fri. 7:30am-7:15pm, Sat. 7:30am-6:30pm, Sun. and holidays 7:30am-7pm.

Public Transportation: Very good public bus system. Schedules available at Ernst-Reuter-Platz 2 (tel.797 66 75). Single ride DM2. No night buses.

Ferries: Boats leave from the banks of the Danube between the Eiserne and Steinerne bridges for **Passau** (1 per day, 7:30am; 8hr., DM32) and **Straubing** (1 per day, 9am; 3½hr., DM20, round-trip DM26). There is also a boat to **Walhalla** every few hours from Apr.-Oct. (45min., DM8.50, children DM4.50; round-trip DM12, children DM6).

Bike Rental: At the tourist office. DM10 per day.

Lockers: Next to the train tracks; DM2, larger lockers DM4.

Lost and Found: At the *Altes Rathaus* (tel. 507 21 05).

Library: Zentralbibliothek, Thon-Ditmar-Palais, Haidplatz 8 (tel. 507 24 16 and 507 22 41). Open Mon.-Fri. 10am-6:30pm, Sat. 10am-12:30pm.

Crisis Hotline: In case of rape and other traumas, contact **Caritas** (tel. 50 210).

Pharmacy: 24-hr. service rotated among the city's pharmacies. To find out which pharmacy is on duty, visit a pharmacy during the day and look at a schedule.

Hospital: Evangelische Krankenhaus, Obere Bachgasse (tel. 504 00); is the most centrally located.

Emergency Medical Assistance: tel. 192 22.

Emergency: tel. 110. **Police:** Minoritenweg (tel. 192 22).

ACCOMMODATIONS AND CAMPING

Most of Regensburg's cheap lodgings are centrally located, but they fill up in the summer. Reservations, preferably at least a week in advance, are always a good idea. If the hotels and *Pensionen* are full, the tourist office might find you a room in a private home. Otherwise, try the hotels in the outlying parts of town, all of which are linked to the center by reliable bus service.

Jugendherberge (HI), Wöhrdstr. 60 (tel. 574 02), on an island in the Danube. Bus # 5 (from Maximilianstr. in front of the station): Weißenburgstr., begin crossing the Eiserne Bridge, and turn left down the steps at the eagle statue. Renovated into pleasant, roomy modernity. Reception open most of the time 7am-11:30pm. Lockout 9am-1pm. Curfew 11:30pm. DM16.50. Sheets DM5. Dinner DM5.50. Breakfast included. Reservations encouraged. Partial wheelchair access.

Spitalgarten, St. Katharinenplatz 1, 93059 Regensburg (tel. 847 74), inside the walls of the old hospital. Cross the Danube at the Steinerne Bridge, go inside the gate to St. Katherine's, go through another gate, past the left side of the church, and on the left you'll see the entrance to the *Biergarten*. Inside, direct all inquiries about the *Pension* to the people behind the counter. Reception until midnight. Singles DM30. Doubles DM60. Breakfast included. Only 18 clean, simple rooms, and they're usually full, so call well ahead. Reservations by phone or mail.

Stadlerbräu, Stadtamhof 15 (tel. 857 24), over the Steinerne Brücke; follow the street for about 5min. It's on the right. Clean and orderly rooms. Reception 7:30am-midnight. Singles DM58, doubles with shower DM110. Breakfast included. Only 14 beds so call ahead.

Camping: Campingplatz, Weinweg 40 (tel. 268 39). Take the Hochweg or bus #6 out of town and turn right onto Hans-Sachs-Str., which will turn into Weinweg. Keep walking (about 2.5km) and the campsite will be on your right. DM5 per person, children DM3, DM3.50 per tent, DM6.50 per tent and car. Free showers. Open March-Oct.

FOOD

To stock up on fruit, vegetables, and other basics, wake up early and head to the daily **market** on Donaumarkt (open 5-8am, Nov.-March 6-9am).

University Mensa, on the University campus. The cheapest meal in Regensburg. Take Universitätstr. south from behind the train station about 2km; or take bus #11 or 4 (DM2). The university is on your left. Any student ID will do. Open Mon.-Fri. 11:30am-1:30pm. Lunch DM3.60, drinks DM0.50-1. Open Oct.-July.

Würstküche, Goldene-Bärenstr., next to the bridge. The oldest operating fast-food joint in Europe—the 12th-century workers who built the bridge took their lunch breaks here. Very busy place; be patient. Four small *Wurstl* from the smoky kitchen with sauerkraut and bread, DM5.20. Open daily 8:30am-7pm.

Münchener Hofbräuhaus, Rathausplatz (tel. 512 80), serves hefty traditional meals (DM8-15.50) and the same brew as the Munich original. Open mid-May to mid-Sept. Mon.-Sat. 9am-1am.

Antagon Kneipe, Rote-Hahnen-Gasse 2. Home away from home for Regensburg's students and alternative set. The only communists this side of China or Berkeley dine on the tasty vegetarian dishes (DM8-12). Complimentary copies of radical newspapers on every table. Open Mon.-Sat. 1pm-midnight.

Kneitinger Keller, Galgenbergstr. 18. Regensburg's largest beer garden (1200 seats). People get rip-roaring drunk here. Food, too. Open daily 9am-midnight.

SIGHTS

A tour of Regensburg will take you on a time-trip from the monuments built during the last centuries of the Roman Empire to the Gothic, Baroque, and Rococo of another, later Empire. The **Porta Praetoria,** a Roman gateway, and parts of its accompanying wall sketch a hazy outline of the city's original fortifications. They have been built into a house located on Unter-den-Schwibbögen-Gasse. One block away from the river on Niedermünstergasse is the Domplatz, which holds the soaring high-Gothic **St. Peter's Cathedral** and, inside the church, the **Diocese Museum.** Begun in 1276, the cathedral—marked by delicately carved twin sandstone towers—was finished in its current form by 1486, but periodic renovations took place until 1859. The now-dark gray stone exterior is currently being cleaned, and car traffic is no longer allowed in the vicinity. Inside the cathedral is the **Domschatz** (cathedral treasury), a priceless collection of gold and jewels purchased by the Regensburg bishops back in the good old days of indulgences and economic exploitation by the clergy. (Cathedral open 6:30am-6pm; Nov.-March 6:30am-4pm. Tours Mon.-Fri. 10, 11am, and 2pm, Sun. noon and 2pm; Nov.-April Mon.-Fri. 11am, Sun. noon. *Domschatz* open Tues.-Sat. 10am-5pm, Sun. 11:30am-5pm; Dec.-March Tues.-Sat. 10am-4pm, Sun. 11:30am-4pm.)

A few blocks away from the cathedral, the Gothic **Altes Rathaus** served as the capital of the Holy Roman Empire until 1803. The sycophantic and impotent Imperial Parliament, the first of many similar bodies in German history, lives on in the **Reichstag Museum,** housed in the *Altes Rathaus.* The differing heights of the chairs reflect the political hierarchy of the legislators. (Tours every ½hr. Mon.-Sat. 9:30am-4pm, English tour 3:15pm; Nov.-March Mon.-Sat. 9:30a, 10:30am, 2, 3, and 4pm, Sun. 10am, 11am, and noon. Admission DM3, students DM1.50.)

The **Fürstliches Thurn und Taxissches Schloß,** originally a Benedictine cloister, was the residence of the Duke of Thurn und Taxis after 1812. Little remains of the Gothic cloister; it's almost completely covered by later Baroque additions. The Thurn und Taxis family built a franchise granted by Kaiser Maximillian in 1490 into a feudal postal empire which tightened its grip over much of Central Europe, until the Prussian Post—backed by Bismarck's armies—displaced it in 1867. The Duke is now dead, but his very young and *trés chic* widow has been the darling of German tabloids for several years. They met in a disco. The **Alte Kapelle,** on Alter Kornmarkt, has an exceptionally frothy and gilded Rococo interior. The fabulous marble high altar and the rich frescoes on the walls and ceilings make it worth your time (open daily 7am-5pm; Dec.-March 7am-4pm). The duke's beer-making namesake, the **Fürstliches Brauerei Thurn und Taxis,** Galgenbergstr. 14 (tel. 134), next door to the Kneitinger Keller, guides visitors through a demonstration of the brewer's art and hands out free samples at the end (reservations requested several weeks in advance; free).

The iconoclastic astronomer and physicist Johannes Kepler died in 1630 at the site of the **Kepler Memorial House,** Keplerstr. 5. Period furniture, portraits, and facsimiles of Kepler's work are on display. (Tours Tues.-Sat. 10am, 11am, 2pm, and 3pm, Sun. 10 and 11am. Admission DM2.50, students DM1.) Up the street at #2 is a colorful house, **Kepler's Wohnhaus,** where he hung his hat and spent time with his family.

Down the river from Regensburg is **Walhalla,** an imitation Greek temple posed dramatically on the steep northern bank of the Danube. Ludwig I of Bavaria built the monument to honor Germans past and present whom he admired. Modeled after the Parthenon in Athens and named after the final resting place of Norse heroes, Walhalla looks down imposingly on the river as the boat from Regensburg approaches the dock (see Practical Information, above, for ferry information). The climb up the steep steps to the monument itself is tough going, but the view of the river and the opposite bank is a golden Photo Opportunity. Inside the monument are a series of busts of German leaders and military heroes, most of whom you've thankfully never heard of.

■■■ BAVARIAN FOREST
(Bayerischer Wald)

Central Europe's largest range of wooded mountains, the Bavarian Forest is considered a national treasure. The 6000 square km of wooded peaks (60 of them over 1000m high) and countless rivers and creeks between the Danube and the Austrian and Czech borders compose the vast hook that lures hikers, campers, and cross-country skiers the year through. The **Bavarian Forest National Park,** the first national park on German soil, is strictly protected from any activities that might alter the forest ecosystem. Clearly marked trails criss-cross 8000 hectares (20,000 acres) of forest. You can hoof it alone or sign up for guided hiking tours, botanical tours, natural history tours, and tours of virgin woodlands. For information and schedules, contact either the **Nationalparkverwaltung Bayerischer Wald,** Freyunstr. 94481 Grafenau (tel. (08552) 427 43); the **Dr. Hans Eisenmann Haus,** Böhmstr. 94556 Neuschönau (tel. (08558) 13 00); or the **Landratsamt,** Wolfkerstr. 94078 Freyung (tel. (08551) 571 22). For news of the rest of the forest, contact the Fremdenverkehrsverband Ostbayern, Landshuterstr. 13 (tel. (0941) 571 86), off Maximillianstr., a 10-minute walk from the train station in Regensburg (open Mon.-Sat. 9am-noon and 2-6pm, Sun. 10am-noon).

The Bavarian Forest offers much more than just verdant paradise. Palaces, churches, and castle ruins are tucked away in tiny villages throughout the region. **Burgruine Hals,** an extensive castle ruin high on a woody cliff north of Passau dating from the 12th century and 18th-century **Wiesenfelden** are surrounded by a lush palace garden—for information contact **Herr Hubert Weinzierl** at (09966) 777, or the **tourist office,** 94344 Wiesenfelden (tel. (09966) 262). **Frauenzell's** 15th-century Benedictine church has been lavishly *barokiziert* (Baroquified), while parts of the **Annunciation Church** in **Chammünster** date from the 12th century.

This region is also famous for its crafts, particularly **glass-blowing,** which has been associated with the Bavarian Forest for 700 years. The glass produced here, most specially the green *Waldglas* (forest glass), is prized throughout the world. To visit a *Glashütte,* contact the **Bergglashütte Weinfurter,** Ferienpark Geyersberg (tel. (08551) 60 66), in Freyung or the **Freiherr von Poschinger Kristallglasfabrik,** Moosauhütte (tel. (09926) 703), in Frauenau, or **Joska Waldglashütte** in Bodenmais (tel. (09924) 19 90).

The towns of **Cham, Deggendorf,** and **Regen** can all be reached by **train** (Cham from Regensburg or Nuremberg via Schwanndorf; Deggendorf and Regen from Regensburg, Munich, or Passau via Platting). **Buses** run from Regensburg and Straubing to Cham and from Passau and Straubing to Deggendorf and Regen. There are 17 **HI youth hostels** in the Bavarian Forest; Regensburg's tourist office has an omniscient brochure. **Jugendherberge Waldhäuser (HI),** Herbergsweg 2 (tel. (08553) 300, fax 45 81), is in the heart of the forest, a 17km bus ride from the train station at Grafenau. Take the bus from Spiegelau or Neuschönau. (Under 27 only. DM17.50. Sheets DM5.) **Jugendherberge Mauth (HI),** Jugendherbergestr. 11 (tel. (08557) 289), is accessible from Passau. (Under 27 only. DM16.50. Breakfast included. Sheets DM5.) Most towns within the Bavarian Forest offer several *Pensionen* and *Gasthöfe* which cost DM18-30 per person, breakfast included; prices are slightly higher in summer and around Christmas. The **Nationalparkverwaltung Bayerischer Wald** offers a whole brochure on **camping** in the Bavarian Forest. Drop by their offices in Regensburg or write for it. For further info, contact the **Verkehrsamt Cham,** Propsteistr. 46 (tel. (09971) 49 33); **Kultur und Verkehrsamt Deggendorf,** Deggendorf (tel. (0991) 38 01 69); or the **Haus des Gastes** in Regen (tel. (09921) 29 29).

■■■ EICHSTÄTT

Sheltered in the valley of the Altmühl river and surrounded by the **Naturpark Altmühltal** (the largest nature preserve in Germany), the small university and episcopal town of Eichstätt is blessed with moments of inspired, lavish architecture. Most conspicuous is the **Willibaldsburg,** which watches over the town from its perch atop a ridge across the river. The 14th-century castle now houses the **Jura-Museum** (Jurassic Museum), filled with fossils from that geological period found in the Altmühltal valley (once covered by the vast Jurassic Sea) and dinosaur movies. The **Historisches Museum,** also in the Willibaldsburg, picks up the story at the debut of *Homo sapiens* and continues it through the Roman presence in the area (both musuems open Tues.-Sun. 9am-noon and 1-5pm; Oct.-March Tues.-Sun. 10am-noon and 1-4pm). To reach the castle, walk up Bergstr. behind the tracks.

Across the river, Eichstätt proper is built around the extravagant **Residenzplatz,** surrounded by the Rococo episcopal palaces. The west wing has a particularly magnificent portal, and the interior is just as richly decorated. Tours of the **Residenz** begin here. (Easter-Oct. Mon.-Thurs. 10, 11am, 2, 3pm; Fri. 10 and 11am; Sat.-Sun. every ½hour 10-11:30am and 2-3:30pm.) In a corner of the Residenzplatz, in the middle of a fountain, stands the **Mariensäule** (Madonna Column). Behind the *Residenz* is the 14th-century **Hohe Dom** (High Cathedral), part Romanesque, part Gothic, and part Baroque. The east apse features richly colored stained glass, and the north aisle shelters the intricate 15th-century stone **Pappenheim Altar.** On the other side of the high altar is the entrance to the **Moritorium** (Mortuary), resting place of Eichstätt's bishops, in which the carved Gothic **Schöne Säule** (Beautiful Column) rises to meet the 15th-century groin vaulting. The windows contain stained glass by Hans Holbein the Elder. Also in the cathedral complex is the **Diözesan-Museum,** an examination of the history of the diocese since its founding in 741 by St. Willibald. (Open April-Oct. Tues.-Sat. 9:30am-1pm and 2-5pm, Sun. 11am-5pm. Admission DM0.50.) Two blocks farther, on Leonrodplatz, is the Baroque **Schutzengelkirche** (Church of the Guardian Angel), built during the Thirty Years War, containing richly carved wooden altars and a striking golden sunburst above the high altar. The **Kapuzinerkirche** (Capuchin Church), at the end of Gottesacker-gasse, holds a 12th-century replica of Jerusalem's Holy Sepulchre. Across the pedestrian zone stands the **Abtei St. Walburg** (Abbey of St. Walburg), a Benedictine convent whose exquisite Baroque church boasts a lavishly stuccoed ceiling.

The Eichstätt **train station** is a 25-minute ride from Ingolstadt. Perhaps in anticipation of a growth spurt which has not yet come to pass, Eichstätt's train station is 5km from the edge of town. A train shuttles back and forth between Eichstätt *Bahnhof* and Eichstätt town (6am-10pm, every ½-1hr., 15-25min.). The **tourist office,** Kardinal-Preysing-Platz 14 (tel. (08421) 79 77), has excellent free maps and helps find rooms for free. Walk through Residenzplatz—the office is to the left past the *Schutzengelkirche.* Eichstätt's **Jugendherberge (HI),** Reichenauerstr. (tel. (08421) 44 27), is clean, modern, and spacious. Walk behind the train station and turn left up the hill onto Herbergshöhe. (Reception open 5-8pm. Curfew 10pm. Under 27 only. DM17.50. Breakfast included. Sheets DM5. Open late Jan. to mid-Dec.) Cheapest after the hostel is one of the many beds available in private homes (DM18-25); the tourist office has a list.

■■■ **INGOLSTADT**

Site of the first Bavarian university from 1472 to 1800, the old Danube city of Ingolstadt is now best known as the home of the Audi. The name of this luxury car company was originally *Horch,* German for "eavesdrop." After World War II it was changed to *Audi,* Latin for "listen," to help exports on an international market which was thought to be resistant to harsh German-sounding products. It would take much more than a name-change to shake the traditional German look of this old town. A stroll through the compact *Altstadt* reveals lovely Renaissance façades and half-timbered streetscapes.

Practical Information Ingolstadt's **tourist office,** in Alten Rathaus, Rathaus-platz 2 (tel. (0841) 30 54 15), hands out free maps and brochures and provides a free **24-hour room finding service** (tel. 30 54 17; desk open Mon.-Fri. 8am-noon and 1-6pm, Sat. 8am-noon). To reach the tourist office and the rest of the old city from the distant train station, take bus #10 (DM2.30) to Rathausplatz. The telephone **city code** is 0841. **Public bus** routes center around the **Omnibusbahnhof,** located in the middle of the city (single fare DM2.30; day tickets DM7). **Trains** roll between Ingolstadt and Munich (2-3 per hr., 45min.).

Accommodations and Food Ingolstadt's superb **Jugendherberge (HI),** Friedhofstr. 4½ (tel. 341 77), is located in a renovated section of the old town fortifications. From the tourist office, turn right and right again onto Moritzstr.; the third left should place you on Theresienstr. Follow it all the way to Kreuztor. Walk through the Kreuztor and cross Auf-der-Schanz. Or, bus #10 to Omnibusbahnhof, and change to bus #50, 53, or 60 to Jugendherberge/Kreuztor. Then follow Herderstr. one block to Unterer Graben, where you turn right and follow Oberer Graben in a left-curving stretch all the way to the Kreuztor. (Reception open 3-9pm. Curfew 10pm. Under 27 only. DM16.50. Sheets DM5. Open Feb. to mid-Dec., but closed every 2nd and 4th weekend from Nov. 11-Dec. 15 and Feb. 1-March 15.) Campers head out to **Campingplatz Auwaldsee** (tel. 68 911). *Car a must* (off the E45/Autobahn A9). (DM4 per person, DM6 per tent, DM4 per car. Open April-Sept.) Ingolstadt's few *Pensionen* and *Gasthöfe* tend to cost dearly. **Pension Lipp,** Feldkirchenerstr. (tel. 587 36), down Schloßländestr. along the Donau and left up Frühlingstr., is pleasant, if out-of-the-way. (Singles DM35, with bath DM38.

Doubles DM70, with shower DM80.) **Gaststätte Herzog Wilhelm,** Theresienstr. 29 (tel. 351 93), in the pedestrian zone, serves an enormous salad with ham and egg slices (DM10.50) and the traditional favorite, *Leberkäs,* with potato salad (open Mon.-Sat. 8am-1am, Sun. 2pm-1am).

Sights The old city wall is magnificently represented by the turreted **Kreuztor,** topped by dainty caps and moderate stone ornamentation. Around the city are scattered other remnants of the city's medieval fortifications. Two blocks east of the Kreuztor stands the late Gothic **Liebfrauenmünster,** full of fabulously ornate altars and dramatic, even inspiring, vaulting. A few blocks south on Anatomiestr. is the **Alte Anatomie,** an 18th-century building which now houses the **Deutsches Medizinhistorisches Museum** (German Museum of Medical History), a fascinating and somewhat grisly look at medical "instruments" of the last few hundred years. 18th-century coral-handled scalpels and 19th-century portable surgery kits, not to mention the "skeleton room," attract visitors with stolid imaginations. (Open Tues.-Sun. 10am-noon and 2-5pm. Admission DM3, students and seniors DM1.50, Sun. free.) North of the *Münster,* at the corner of Jesuiten and Neubaustr., is the "Rococo jewel," the **Maria-de-Viktoria-Kirche** (Church of Our Lady of Victories). This formerly spartan chapel for students of the nearby Catholic school was Rococoed with a vengeance in 1732, and an awe-inspiring frescoco now adorns the ceiling. (Open Tues.-Sun. 9am-noon and 1-6pm. Ring for the caretaker. Admission DM1.) Across town on Paradeplatz is the 15th-century **Neues Schloß,** Paradeplatz 4, a red-tiled affair which now houses the **Bayerisches Armee-Museum** (Bavarian Military Museum), collected under King Ludwig "If-I-weren't-crazy-I'd-be-dangerous" II. The display of old firearms and suits of armor is notable among military museums for its size rather than its particular interest. (Open Tues.-Sun. 8:45am-4:30pm. Admission DM3.50, students DM1, seniors DM2, children DM0.50.) Right off of Donaustr., near the Konrad-Adenauer-Brücke, is the brand new **Museum für Konkrete Kunst** (Museum for Concrete Art), Tränktorstr. 6-8. Stare at bold geometric designs in primary colors until your eyes get screwy. (Open Tues.-Wed. and Fri.-Sun. 10am-1pm and 2-6pm, Thurs. 10am-1pm and 2-8pm. Admission DM3, students DM1.50.)

Those fascinated by Audi's automobiles can call **Audi** for information on tours (tel. 89 12 41).

■■■ AUGSBURG

Founded by Caesar Augustus in 15 BC, Augsburg had become the financial center of the Holy Roman Empire and a major commercial city in Central Europe by the end of the 15th century. Augsburg's commercial prestige was due mainly to the Fuggers, an Augsburger family who virtually monopolized the banking industry, particularly Jakob Fugger the Rich, personal financier to the Habsburgs. Augsburg was also the birthplace of Bertolt Brecht; in 1945—after years in exile—he addressed the angry, haunting poem "Epistle to the Augsburgers" to the residents of the town. Today Augsburg is a relaxing and interesting break from the tourist trail: a city small enough to discourage crowds, but large enough to cater to many different interests.

Practical Information The resourceful **tourist office,** Bahnhofstr. 7 (tel. (0821) 50 20 70), about 300m from the train station down Bahnhofstr., finds rooms for DM3 (open Mon.-Fri. 9am-6pm). There's also a tiny one-person information window directly in front of the train station (open Mon.-Fri. 10am-8pm, Sat.-Sun. 9am-8pm), and an office at the *Rathaus* (tel. (0821) 502 07 24; open Mon.-Fri. 9am-6pm, Sat. 10am-6pm, Sun. 10am-1pm). The **telephone city code** is 0821. The **Mitfahrzentrale,** Barthof 3 (tel. (0821) 15 70 19), arranges ride-shares for a small fee (open Mon.-Sat. noon-9pm). Augsburg has excellent train connections to Munich (1-2 per hr.), and the **Europabus** for the Romantic Road stops at the Augsburg train station— get schedules from the tourist office.

Accommodations To reach Augsburg's **Jugendherberge (HI)**, Beim Pfaffen-keller 3 (tel. 339 03), take streetcar #2 from the *Bahnhof* (direction "Kriegshaber") to Stadtwerke, and continue on foot in the same direction up Hoher Weg, and go right onto Inneres Pfaffengäßchen; follow the left side of this small alley along the wall until you the reach the marked hostel driveway. Try to walk it by day, as this alley is not well-lit. Alternately, walk straight up Bahnhofstr. from the station to Konigsplatz, bear left on Annastr., then right on Karlstr., straight on to Hoher Weg, turn left and follow the above directions from there. Clean, cramped, and centrally located. (Reception open 7:30am-11pm, though you may have to seek out the pro-prietors. Curfew 11pm. Under 27 only. DM15.50. Sheets DM5. Excellent breakfast included. Call ahead. Open Jan. 1-Dec. 12.) Apart from the hostel, Augsburg has a dearth of inexpensive centrally located rooms. Try **Gasthof Lenzhalde**, Theolottstr. 2 (tel. (0821) 52 07 45); from the *Bahnhof,* bear right onto Halderstr., take a sharp right onto Hermannstr., cross the Gögginger bridge and take the first right onto Rosenaustr., and follow it for several blocks directly to the hotel (singles and dou-bles DM37 per person). Or have the tourist office find a room in the suburbs (singles DM32-42; doubles DM70-80). To camp at **Campingplatz Augusta** (tel. (0821) 70 75 75), take the bus (direction "Neuburg") to Autobahnsee (DM6 per person, DM5 per tent).

Food and Entertainment Don't miss the **Stadtmarkt** (farmer's market) between Fuggerstr. and Annastr. (right past the St. Anna Kirche on Fuggerstr.; open Mon.-Fri. 7am-6pm, Sat. 7am-1pm). For hot and meaty items, check the **Fleis-chmarkt** in the middle of the *Stadtmarkt*. There's one of those pricey and historic restaurants right in the *Rathaus* (open daily 11:30am-1am), and most corner joints sell the local beer, *Riegele Augsburg*. From late June to early July, Augsburg's *Alts-tadt* from Königsplatz down Maximilianstr. is filled with food and craft stalls for the **Historisches Bürgerfest.** The vendors don traditional peasant garb and serve Fran-conian favorites.

Sights Old Jakob Fugger founded the **Fuggerei** quarter in 1519 as the first welfare housing project in the world. The narrow cobblestone streets and little gabled houses are still a haven for the elderly destitute, who earn their keep by praying for the departed souls of the Fuggers. To reach the Fuggerei from the *Rathaus,* walk behind the Perlachturm tower on Perlachberg, which becomes Barfüßerstr. and finally Jakobstr. The Fuggerei opens out on the right at the "Fuggereistube." The gates to the Fuggerei close at dusk. The **Fuggerei Museum** documents this classic piece of urban planning, as well as the financial adventures of its patrons. (Open Mar.-Dec. daily 9am-6pm. Admission DM1, students, seniors, and groups DM0.50.) Augsburg's medieval period unfolds at the brightly frescoed **Guildhaus,** down Burgermeister-Fischer-Str., now part of the marketplace area, lying down Bahnhof-str. from the train station, along the edge of the park and past the street cars. From the Guildhaus, a left down Maximilianstr. leads to the huge Renaissance *Rathaus* (open daily 10am-6pm; free). The brightly painted ceiling of the **Goldener Saal** depicts tradesmen and women, impressing upon visitors the importance of com-merce in Augsburg's history. Down Hoher Weg and to the left is the **Hoher Dom** (cathedral), the seat of the region's bishop. Originally built in the 9th century, the cathedral was renovated in the Gothic style in the 14th century. Heavily damaged in the war, many items were lost or destroyed. The current chancel and high altar are very attractive examples of the Bauhaus-inspired architecture, so prevalent in Ger-man churches since the war. (Open daily 6am-5pm except Sundays and holidays.) If you go to the left of the Perlachturm, down Perlachberg and then left onto Auf dem Raim, you'll arrive at the **Bertolt Brecht Haus,** the birthplace of one of the most influential 20th-century playwrights and poets. In 1925, with Augsburg and Bavaria well behind him, Brecht wrote "I, Bertolt Brecht, came out of the black forests/ My mother moved me into the cities as I lay/ Inside her body. And the coldness of the forests/ will be inside me till my dying day." The house chronicles his life through photographs, letters, and his poetry. (Open Tues.-Sun. 10am-5pm; Nov.-Apr. Tues.-Sun. 10am-4pm. Admission DM2.50, students and children DM1.50.) The area of town where the Brechthaus stands is the old trader's quarter, and numerous small channeled creeks rush between the houses and under the streets.

■■■ ROMANTIC ROAD
(Romantische Straße)

Between Würzburg and Füssen, in the Lechtal at the foothills of the Alps, lies a beautiful countryside of walled cities, castles, and elaborate churches. Sensing opportunity, the German tourist industry christened these ancient, bucolic backwaters the Romantic Road in 1950 and set about exploiting them. Be warned—this is the most heavily touristed area in Germany, and although the region is beautiful, it will be a group experience. Deutsche Bahn's **Europabus** runs buses daily from Frankfurt to Munich (11hr.) and from Würzburg to Füssen (11hr.) from mid-March to late October (only 1 per day March-May). The trip can be done in segments, or stop anywhere along the line and catch the bus the next day (must be specified in your reservations). DB and Eurail passes are valid on these routes. The DB's regular *Linienbuses* go to all the towns on the Europabus route and then some (3-10 per day); and are far less crowded. Schedules are posted in every train station or, in towns with no station, at the local tourist office.To bike the Romantic Road, plan carefully. Any tourist office in the area can provide detailed maps and lists of camping sites, hostels, and *Pensionen*; most campgrounds are 10-20km apart. Some travelers reportedly hitch the route successfully. For general information, contact the Romantische Straße Arbeitsgemeinschaft, Marktplatz, 91550 Dinkelsbühl (tel. (09851) 902 71). Almost all of their brochures are available in English.

ROTHENBURG OB DER TAUBER

If you can visit only one town on the Romantic Road, you will probably focus on Rothenburg ob der Tauber—and bring lots of film. Expect a camera-clicking family of four from Cedarville, Illinois on every corner (no offense to Cedarville intended), for this is the most-touristed town in the country—perhaps in the western world. Bumperstickers reading *Ich bin doch kein Tourist; Ich wohne hier!* (I am not a tourist; I live here!) grace many fenders. The hype is almost justifiable; Rothenburg is your only chance to see a nearly intact medieval walled city without a single modern building within. The town became a first-class tourist mecca by making a virtue out of a necessity. After the Thirty Years War, major commercial routes shifted away from the town and Rothenburg was left to stagnate, lacking money to expand or finance new building projects. At the end of the 19th century, strict preservation laws were set in place to maintain a typical 16th-century town for the enjoyment of a shocking number of tourists. Rothenburg narrowly escaped destruction in World War II only because of the intervention of John J. McCloy (later the Allied High Commissioner to Occupied Germany), who loved the town and prevailed upon American commanders not to destroy it. The 14th-century fortified walls and towers are thus almost perfectly preserved and can be walked in their entirety. Smile and look at the camera.

Practical Information Rothenburg's **tourist office,** Marktplatz 1 (tel. (09861) 404 92), next to the *Rathaus,* supplies handy maps in English and books rooms (usually for free, DM2 during peak times; open Mon.-Fri. 9am-noon and 2-6pm, Sat. 9am-noon and 2-4pm). **Tours** in German depart from the steps of the *Rathaus* (April-Oct. daily 11am and 2pm; DM5). The English-language tours meet at the Hotel Riemenschneider (daily 1:30pm; DM6), and there's a special "tour with the night watchman" in German leaving from the market square (nightly 9pm).

Accommodations Housed in medieval buildings, Rothenburg's two youth hostels stand a stone's throw from one another. The **Jugendherberge Rossmühle (HI),** Mühlacker 1 at Rossmühleweg (tel. (09861) 45 10), is in a former horse-powered mill, and the worn stone exterior shelters immaculate, carpeted rooms. From the station, turn left and then take a right onto Ausbacher-Str. Go through the opening in the wall and turn left at Marktplatz onto Obere Schmiedgasse. Go straight until you see the **Jugendherberge** sign to the right. (Reception open 7-9am, 5-7pm, and 8-10pm. Curfew 11:30pm. DM 17.50. Under 27 only. Sheets DM5.50. Showers, breakfast, with simpler and cheaper quarters. (Same reception and curfew. DM13. Under 27 only. Sheets DM5. Breakfast and showers included.) Rothenburg has an unbelievable number of *Pensionen* for a town its size, but most of them are very expensive. There are a few exceptions, however. **Pension Raidel,** Wengasse 3 (tel. (09861) 31 15), has bright rooms and fluff featherbeds. Fluff like this town. (Singles DM33-37. Doubles DM57-61. Breakfast included. Call ahead.) **Pension Hofman,** Stollengasse 29 (tel. (09861) 33 71), has rooms next to the town wall. (Singles with shower DM38-45. Doubles DM58, with shower DM65-75. Breakfast included. Call ahead.) A number of private rooms (DM18-30) not registered with the tourist office are also available—marked by signs in house windows reading *"Zimmer frei."* Though most are fine, make sure that you look at any such room before committing.

Food Reasonable meals—a rarity in this town—can be found at **Zum Schmolzen,** the restaurant at Pension Hofman. Try the *Schweinbraten,* two scrumptious pork medallions with dumplings on the side (DM11). They also have the cheapest beer (0.5L DM2.70). **Pizzeria Roma,** Galgengasse 19, serves hefty pasta dishes (DM8-15) and pizzas long after the rest of town is in bed (open daily 11:30am-midnight).

Sights Of course, the main attraction in Rothenburg is the town itself, taken as an aesthetic whole. On Marktplatz stands the Renaissance **Rathaus** (open daily 8am-5pm; free). Scope the town from the tower. On this site in 1631, the invading Catholic general Johann Tilly offered to spare the town if any local resident could chug a *Stein* containing almost a gallon of wine. *Bürgermeister* Georg Nusch successfully met the challenge—then passed out for several days. His *Meistertrunk* (master drink) is celebrated every year at Pentecost (50 days after Easter) with a parade and reenactment of the event. The **Reichsstadtmuseum,** housed in a former 13th-century Dominican convent, displays a number of rooms whose contents are preserved from the Middle Ages (open daily 10am-5pm; Nov.-March 1-4pm; free).

The town's **Medieval Crime Museum,** Burggasse 3, exhibits "eye for an eye" jurisprudence with displays on special punishments reserved for bad musicians, dishonest bakers, and frivolous gossips. (Open daily 9:30am-6pm; Dec. and March 10am-4pm; Jan.-Feb. 2-4pm. Admission DM4.50, students DM3.) Lots of old toys displayed in neat little rows and glass cases are most of what the **Doll and Toy Museum,** Hofbronnengasse 13, has to offer. Nevertheless, the numerous dolls, dollhouses, and rocking horses are fun to look at. They can't help where they are (open daily 9:30am-6pm; Jan.-Feb. daily 11am-5pm). Rothenburg has a number of churches worth a glance, as long as you are in town. Next to the *Rathaus,* **St. Jakobskirche,** begun in 1311, features Tilman Riemenschneider's enigmatic *Altarpiece of the Holy Blood,* in which Judas is depicted from behind, facing Jesus and his disciples during the Last Supper. Down Klingengasse is **St. Wolfgangskirche,** a fortified church built—for reasons unknown—by 15th-century shepherds. From the ramparts, the **city wall** is accessible by way of a platform constructed in 1587. To extract yourself from the maddening crowd, visit the **Burggarten,** at the end of Herrngasse. The site of the former castle affords a tranquil view of the valley below the town.

DINKELSBÜHL

Though not as pre-packaged as Rothenburg, Dinkelsbühl (40km to the south) maintains a full complement of half-timbered houses. The Gothic **St. Georgskirche** boasts a Romanesque tower and striking fan vaulting. A few blocks away on Martin-Luther-Str. is the **Deutsches Haus,** with a richly painted and ornamented façade dating from the 15th century. On **Nördlingerstraße,** none of the old houses are perfectly rectangular; medieval superstition correctly held that houses with 90° angles were homes of demons. **Kinderzeche** (children's weeping), a nine-day celebration of the town's rescue during the Thirty Years War, takes place in late July. The tears of the town's children reportedly persuaded Swedish King Gustav Adolph to spare it. A recreation of the historical event accompanies parades, fireworks, and dances.

The **tourist office** (tel. (09851) 902 40), on the Marktplatz, finds rooms for free and distributes free maps and schedules to the *Kinderzeche* festival (open Mon.-Fri. 9am-noon and 2-6pm, Sat. 10am-noon and 2-5pm, Sun. 10am-1pm; Nov.-March Mon.-Fri. 9am-1pm and 2-6pm, Sat. 10am-1pm). The **post office,** the **police station** (tel. (09851) 888), and the **train station** (tel. (09851) 22 27) are across the river from the *Altstadt,* one block down highway B25 (also known as the Romantic Road). **Buses** leave from the train station and from Am Stauferwall to Rothenburg (3-5 per day, DM21, railpasses valid) and Würzburg. Schedules can be picked up and deciphered at the tourist office. As in any Romantic Road town, be wary of **Europabus** tour groups (especially if you have arrived with one).

The **Jugendherberge (HI),** Koppengasse 10 (tel. (09851) 509), is an old half-timbered house three blocks from the town center. (Reception open daily 5-10pm. DM16. Under 27 only. Sheets DM5.50. Breakfast included. Open March-Oct.) **Pension Gerda,** Nestleinberg 24 (tel. (09581) 18 60), has clean rooms a 15-minute walk from the Marktplatz (DM30 per person; breakfast included). Over the river north of the city on Dürrwanger-Str. is the **DCC Campingpark Romantische Straße** (tel. (09851) 78 17; DM5.50 per person, tents DM7.50, DM13 per tent and car.).

NÖRDLINGEN IM RIES

The walled city of Nördlingen im Ries, 35km south of Dinkelsbühl, is located near the center of a circular meteor crater, the **Ries.** At nearly 12km in diameter, the crater is the largest of its kind in the world. The former Carolingian royal city was built on and from these rock deposits, geologically similar to rocks found on the moon. The **Rieskrater Museum,** Hintere Gerbergasse 3 (tel. (09081) 841 43), a state-of-the-art geological museum housed in a large 15th-century barn, offers tours of the crater by appointment. (Open Tues.-Sun. 10am-noon and 1:30-4:30pm. Admission DM5, students DM2.50. Tours DM40.) The crater can also be seen from **Der Daniel,** the flamboyant tower of the 15th-century **St. Georgskirche,** which contains a beautiful Gothic statue of Mary Magdelene. (Tower accessible Mon.-Fri. 9am-noon and 2-5pm, Sat.-Sun. 9am-5pm; winter Mon.-Fri. 9am-noon and 2-5pm, Sat.-Sun. 9am-11:30am and noon-5pm. Tower admission DM2, children and groups DM1.) The 14th-century city wall is nearly 3km long and can be walked in its entirety. It's the only completely preserved city wall in Germany. Napoleon stopped at the **Berger Tor** on his way to Austerlitz, and so can you.

Change trains at Donauwörth (45min.) for connections between Nördlingen and Augsburg or Munich, and at Aalen for trains to Stuttgart. The town is connected by **bus** (Europabus! Europabus! Europabus!) with the rest of the Romantic Road. The **tourist office** *(Kultur- und Verkehrsamt),* Marktplatz 2 (tel. (09081) 43 80 or 841 16), next door to the *Rathaus,* provides a list of overnight options (from DM25) with a city map attached, and books rooms for free (open Mon.-Thurs. 9am-6pm, Fri. 9am-4:30pm, Sat. and holidays 9:30am-12:30pm). **Rent bikes** at Jet-Tankstelle, auf der Kaiserwiese (tel. (09081) 80 10 92), near the hostel. Nördlingen's small and largely un-enthralling **Jugendherberge (HI),** Kaiserwiese 1 (tel. (09081) 841 09), is, if nothing else, conveniently located a few paces outside the city wall. From the *Marktplatz* walk up Baldinger-Str. through the gate (Baldinger Tor) until you come to an underpass on the right. Follow the underpass down and under the street, then up along the sidewalk about 50m straight (first veering a little to the left) and it's on your left. (Reception open 4:30-7pm. Currency exchange open 12:15-12:30pm. Showers open 7-8am and 6-7:30pm. Curfew 10pm. DM15. Sheets DM5. Breakfast included. Open March-Oct.) There is a produce **market** in the pedestrian zone (Wed. and Sat. morning).

■ ■ ■ WÜRZBURG

Würzburg dominates the Franconian countryside with its massive stone façades. The largest and most imposing is the 13th-century Marienburg Fortress, testament to the immense secular power of Würzburg's *Fürstbischöfe* (prince-bishops). On the other side of the river, the bishops' Residenz is one of the largest Baroque palaces in Germany. Declared a bishopric in 742, Würzburg grew steadily as a reiigious center; it now houses seventeen churches in addition to the main Cathedral. Wartime bombing swept away the town's rail terminals, but its older giants remained, and have not, by the looks of them, changed much since the town's first centuries.

ORIENTATION AND PRACTICAL INFORMATION

Würzburg is a frazzled traveler's dream come true, with three separate tourist information offices, one situated conveniently in front of the train station. The wonderfully compact *Altstadt* unfolds right out of the train station. To get to the city's center, the **Markt,** follow Kaiserstr. to the walkway under Juliuspromenade, take a right, then hang a left onto Schönbornstr., the main pedestrian and streetcar route; the *Markt* should be a few blocks down and to your right. The Main River separates the green, steep hills on which the Fortress is stands, and the city.

Tourist Office: Main Office, in front of the train station (tel. 374 36). Provides a packet with a map of the city and a hotel list (DM0.50). They also help find rooms for DM3. Open Mon.-Sat. 8am-8pm. Another tourist office is in the pink **Falkenhaus,** at the Marktplatz (tel. 373 98). Open Mon.-Fri. 9am-6pm, Sat. 9am-2pm. Yet a third is located in the **Palais am Congress Centrum** (tel. 373 35), right near the Friedensbrücke where Röntgenring intersects the Main. Open Mon.-Thurs. 8:30am-4pm, Fri. 8:30am-noon. **24hr. accommodations hotline:** tel. 194 14.

Post Office: Bahnhofplatz 2, 97070 Würzburg. Exchange money, cash traveler's checks, and call home. Open Mon.-Fri. 6am-9pm, Sat. 6am-8pm, Sun. 9am-8pm.

Telephones: At the post office. **City code:** 0931.

Trains: Würzburg lies on a major rail line between Frankfurt and Nuremburg. Trains also leave frequently for Hamburg.

Buses: Europabuses head down the Romantic Road to Veitshöchheim Castle daily at 9am and 10:15am, departing from beside the station. The 10:15 bus fills quickly. Reservations must be made 3 days in advance with the **Deutsche Touring Büro,** Am Römerhof 17 (tel. (069) 790 32 56), in Frankfurt.

Public Transportation: (tel. 363 52). **Streetcars** are the fastest and most convenient way around, but large sections of the city are not covered. The **bus** network is comprehensive, but most routes do not run nights and weekends. Ask for **night bus** schedules at the WSB kiosk in front of the train station. Single fare DM1.80, 4-fare ticket DM5, 24hr. ticket DM6, weekend day ticket DM3.50.

Ferries: Schiffstouristik Kurth & Schiebe (tel. 46 29 82, dock kiosk tel. 585 73), or **Veitshöchheimer Personenschiffahrt Heinrich Herbert** (tel. 915 53, dock kiosk tel. 556 33). Both lines depart from the **Alter Kranen** wharf near the Congress Centrum to Veitshöchheim 40min.; DM8, round-trip DM11.

Bike Rental: At the train station (DM12 per day, DM8 per day with valid train ticket). **Max und Moritz,** Pleicherkirchplatz 11 (tel. 576 00), also rents; DM15 per day. Open Mon.-Sat. 8am-12:30pm, Sun. 10am-noon.

Mitfahrzentrale: in kiosk in front of train station (tel. 194 48). Arranges ride shares. Open Mon.-Fri. 9am-6pm, Sat. 9am-2pm, Sun. 11am-1pm.

24-Hour Pharmacy: Look for listings of rotating late-openers in the weekly *Main Post* or *Fränkisches Volksblatt*.
Emergencies: Medical Aid: tel. 192 22. **Police:** tel. 110. **Fire:** tel. 112.

ACCOMMODATIONS AND CAMPING

The one drawback to this otherwise excellent city is the lack of budget accommodations—rooms for under DM40 are a rarity. Würzburg's least expensive beds are around the train station, on (or just off) Kaiserstr. and Bahnhofstr.

Jugendgästehaus (HI), Burkarderstr. 44 (tel. 425 90), near St. Burkard's Basilica, across the river from downtown. Streetcar #3 or 5 (direction "Heidingsfeld"): Löwenbrücke, then backtrack, down the stairs marked by the "Jugendherberge/ Käppele" sign, turn right, walk all the way down through the underpass and it's immediately on your left. Note: If you're walking at night, take precautions, and be especially aware of loiterers. Between the river and the fortress, modern, huge. Reception open 2-10pm. Lockout 9am-2pm. Curfew 1am. Under 27 only. Top floor beds DM20, others DM24. Breakfast and sheets included.

Pension Siegel, Reisgrubengasse 7, 97070 Würzburg (tel. 529 41), a block down Kaiserstr. from the train station, on your left. The best bet. Reception open 2-10:30pm. Splendid singles DM42. Doubles DM79. Reservations recommended.

Hotel Groene, Scheffelstr. 2 (tel. 744 49). Streetcar #1 or 4 (direction "Randersacker"): Ehehaltenhaus, then take a left onto Sonnenstr., and a right onto Scheffelstr. A bit cheaper, but a lot farther away. Rooms are comfortable and clean. Singles DM35-37. Doubles DM59-64. Phone reservations accepted.

Camping: Camping Kalte Quelle, Winterhäuserstr. 160 (tel. 655 98). Streetcar #3 (direction "Heidingsfeld"): last stop, then hike 2km. Reception open 2-9:30pm. DM6 per person, DM7 per caravan. **Camping Kanu Club,** Mergentheimerstr. 13b (tel. 725 36). Streetcar #3 (direction "Heidingsfeld"): Judenbühlweg. Reception open noon-8pm. DM5.50 per person.

FOOD AND NIGHTLIFE

For run-of-the-mill *Imbiß* fare, the lowest prices are near the train station. To sample some of the region's distinctive wines, try **Haus des Frankenweins Fränkischer Weinverband,** Krankenkai 1 (tel. 120 93).Würzburg's answer to *Oktoberfest,* the **Kiliani Festival,** is held in July, while the huge annual **Wine Festival** takes place in fall (Sept. 16-26, 1994). Braver souls should snoop around the back alleys of the city's south side, the heart of the university subculture. Strange people, strange food, and ridiculously low prices abound in these smoke-laden dens and grottos.

University Mensa, in the *Studentenhaus* on Friedrich-Ebert-Ring, at Münzstr.; through the doors to your left. Assembly line eating. Würzburg University ID technically required, but try your luck. Meals run about DM2.90. Open mid-Oct. to mid-July Mon.-Fri. 11am-2pm, Sat. 11:30am-2pm; evening meals Mon.-Thurs. 5:30-7:30pm.

Kult, Landwehrstr. 10 (tel. 531 43), is the largest and most mainstream bar-cafe-*kneipe* of the local underground alternatives. Who knows, your meal might include Indian rice with salad and yogurt dip (DM8.20) or Mexican peanuts with corn kernels in hot chili oil with bread (DM7). Open Mon.-Fri. 9am-1am (if too hot outside open 9am-2pm and 6pm-1am), Sat. 6pm-1am, Sun. 11am-1pm.

Holzapfel Brauerei, Klinikstr. 2. Bring your own food and they'll serve you up some local wine and bear at great prices. Open Mon.-Fri. 10am-8pm, Sat. 2-8pm.

SIGHTS

Marienburg Fortress, the striking symbol of the city, keeps its vigil high on a hillside over the Main. The footpath to the fortress starts a short distance from the **Alte Mainbrücke.** The **Fürstenbau Museum** contains an extensive collection of German paintings, furniture, and *objets d'art.* (Open Tues.-Sun. 9am-12:30pm and 1-5pm; Oct.-March Tues.-Sun. 10am-12:30pm and 1-4pm. Admission DM3, students DM2, under 15 accompanied by adult free.) The fortress also houses the **Mainfränkisches Museum,** with a large collection of statues by Würzburg's native son, Tilman Riemenschneider, known as the **Master of Würzburg.** A genius of Gothic styling, Riemenschneider sided with the peasants in their 16th-century revolts against Luther and the powers that were. When the insurrection was suppressed, the sculptor's fingers were broken as punishment, and he was never able to work again. (Open Tues.-Sun. 10am-5pm; Nov.-March Tues.-Sun. 10am-4pm. Admission DM3, students DM1.) Masochists can make the climb to the fortress in under an hour; ortake bus #9 from the "Spitäle" bus stop at the western end of the bridge on up (every ½hr.; May to mid-Oct. 9:43am-5:43pm; DM1.80). On the next hill stands the **Käppele,** a graceful 18th-century church built by the Würzburg architect Balthasar Neumann.

In 1168, twelve years after he married Beatrix of Burgundy in Würzburg, Friedrich Barbarossa raised the local bishop to the rank of "Prince." The **Residenz** Palace, Neumann's masterpiece, was the base camp for Würzburg's prince-bishops during the Enlightenment. It stands over the sweeping Residenzplatz (15min. walk down Kaiserstr. and Theaterstr. from the station). Note the ceiling fresco by Johannes Zick in the first-floor garden room. Its brilliant colors are original—it has never been restored. It was precisely this extravagant use of color that got Zick fired. The Italian painter Giovanni Tiepolo was hired to finish the job in hopes that his paintings would be a little more sedate. His ceiling fresco in the grand staircase is the largest in the world, and certainly among the most ostentatious. In the *Kaisersaal,* Tiepolo and the sculptor A. Bossi combine their crafts flawlessly with fiendishly disorienting results. The question is, where does the painting end and the sculpture begin? (Open Tues.-Sun. 9am-5pm; Oct.-March Tues.-Sun. 10am-4pm. Last admission ½hr. before closing. Admission DM4.50, students and seniors DM3.) The **Residenzhofkirche** is astounding: the gilded moldings, pink marble, and frescoes make this little church the apex of Baroque fantasy (open Tues.-Sun. 9am-noon and 1-5pm; Oct.-March Tues.-Sun. 10am-noon and 1-4pm; free).

Behind the Residenz complex is the **Hofgarten,** a studiously laid-out park with a large rose garden (open dawn-dusk; free). In front of the Residenz, down Hofstr., stands the 900-year-old **Dom** of St. Killian, rebuilt in the mid-1960s after obliteration in 1945. St. Killian, an Irish missionary bishop who became the city's patron saint, was killed with two other missionaries in the ducal court in the year 689. The cathedral is supposed to hold his remains. Tilman Riemenschneider (see above) is responsible for the many fetching Gothic figures that grace this large, light Romanesque cathedral. (Open Mon.-Fri. 10am-5pm, Sun. 1-6pm; Nov.-Easter Mon.-Fri. 10am-noon and 2-5pm, Sun. 12:30-1:30pm and 2:30-6pm. Tours April-Oct. Mon.-Sat. at noon, Sun. at 12:30pm. Admission DM2, children DM1.) The **Stift Haug,** at the end of Bahnhofstr., is a great find with its moving altarpiece, Tintoretto's *Crucifixion.* Two different operators run cruises (tel. 556 33 or 585 73; round-trip DM11) to the **Veitshöchheim Castle** (tel. 915 82). The palace grounds have become a public park (open April-Sept. Tues.-Sun. 9am-noon and 1-5pm; admission DM2.50, students DM1.50).

■■■ NUREMBERG (Nürnberg)

Although the city's official tourist pamphlet cites *Bratwurst,* Albrecht Dürer, and the local soccer team as its most memorable attractions, in the eyes of many Nuremberg is a city inextricably bound to a darker side of its past: Adolf Hitler and the Third Reich. The very mention of Nuremberg—which provided the setting for massive annual Nazi party rallies between 1927 and 1935, and lent its name to the 1935 racial purity laws that paved the way for the Holocaust—still conjures up totalitarian imagery of the sort immortalized in Leni Riefenstahl's film *Triumph des Willens* (Triumph of the Will). Because of Nuremberg's tight affiliations with the power of Nazi Germany, the Allies chose this city as the site of the war-crime trials.

Originally, it was Nuremberg's long association with the imperial traditions of the Holy Roman Empire that attracted Hitler to the city. It was declared a "free city" by Kaiser Ludwig the Bavarian in 1332, after which the local government answered to no authority lower than the Emperor. The imperial *Reichstag* was held here until 1543, the imperial jewels were kept locked in a tower over the Spital, and each of the more than thirty Holy Roman Emperors paid an obligatory visit to Nuremberg's *Kaiserschloß* (imperial castle) at some point during his reign.

Its checkered past aside, contemporary Nuremberg is a model of postwar Teutonic prosperity. The second-largest city in Bavaria (after Munich), Nuremberg's various industries employ over 265,000 people, and the city is equipped with both a bustling regional airport and a dizzyingly large and efficient public transportation system. Its wide variety of attractions—you know, they really do have a pretty good soccer team here—beckon to visitors of every stripe.

ORIENTATION AND PRACTICAL INFORMATION

Nuremberg's thriving central district is neatly encircled by the old city wall. From the train station, cross the street onto Königstr. and you'll find yourself in the middle of the main shopping district. Both Lorenzerplatz and the Hauptmarktplatz lie directly ahead. Most of this part of the *Altstadt* is a pedestrian zone. The far end of the old city is marked by the *Burg*. Nuremberg is 2½-hour north of Munich by train.

Tourist Offices: Verkehrsverein, (tel. 23 36 32), in the central hall of the **Hauptbahnhof.** (Mailing address: Congress und Tourismus Zentrale, Frauenburggraben 3, 90443 Nürnberg.) City map (DM0.30), free brochures, schedules of events, and guides for young people. They also find rooms (DM3 fee). Open Mon.-Sat. 9am-7pm. **Branch office** across the river, Hauptmarktplatz (tel. 23 36 35); same services. Open Mon.-Sat. 9am-1pm, 2-6pm; March-Sept. Sun. 10am-1pm and 2-4pm.

Budget Travel: ABR Reisebüro, (tel. 201 00), across from the tourist office in the train station. Deciphers train schedules. Open Mon.-Fri. 9am-6pm, Sat. 9am-noon.

American Express: Adlerstr. 2 (tel. 23 23 97), off Königstr. near Lorenzerplatz. Great rates and no service charges for changing cash and AmEx traveler's checks. Members may cash personal checks and receive held mail. Open Mon.-Fri. 9am-5:30pm, cashier closed noon-2pm, Sat. 9am-12:30pm.

Currency Exchange: The **AmEx** office is the cheapest opportunity for those with or without the Card; the post office is another good bet (see below). DM traveler's checks can be cashed for no fee at one of the many **Sparkasse** banks. Beware *Wechsel* stands due to their often high rates and/or absurd fees.

Post Office: Bahnhofplatz 1, 90402 Nürnberg. Cash traveler's checks and exchange money. **Poste Restante** and international **telephones.** Open Mon.-Fri. 8am-6pm, Sat. 8am-noon. Late teller open until 11pm.

Telephones: City Code: 0911.

Airport: Located north of the city on Flughafenstr. (tel. 350 62 00). **City-Airport-Express** runs shuttles from the train station to the airport (20min., DM5). Follow signs at the train station to traffic island in front of the station.

Trains: Hauptbahnhof (tel. 194 19). To: Munich (DM24); Frankfurt (DM57).

Public Transportation: A variety of possibilities: subway, streetcar, bus, regional train (R-Bahn) and S-Bahn. Single ride tickets DM2.30-DM13.80 (depending on distance). Day or weekend card DM6.50. 5-stripe card (stamp at least 2 sections each time; more for longer rides) DM7.60; 10-stripe card DM11.20. Pick up a map and schedule at the tourist office.

Hitchhiking: *Let's Go* does not recommend hitchhiking as a safe means of transportation. Hitchers headed to Munich and Austria take U-Bahn 1 or 11: Bauernfeindstr., then bus #59: Am Zollhaus and the *Autobahn* interchange. Those going to Würzburg and Frankfurt take U-Bahn 1: Stadtgrenze and walk to the A-3 interchange. A safer idea is to arrange a ride through the **Mitfahrzentrale.** Allersbergerstr. 31a (tel. 194 44). Take the Allersberger *Unterführung* (under the tracks) and walk 10min. Open Mon.-Fri. 9am-6pm, Sat. 8:30am-1pm, Sun. 11am-2pm.

Pharmacy: Check the city notices in the *Nürnberger Zeitung* for 24-hr. pharmacy.

Rape Crisis: tel. 28 44 00.
Hospital: Städtische Klinikum, Flurstr. 17 (tel. 39 80). **Medical Assistance:** tel. 53 32 11 or 53 37 71.
Emergency: tel. 110. **Police:** Jakobspl. 5, Nuremberg Mitte 1. Open 24hrs.

ACCOMMODATIONS AND CAMPING

There are a number of inexpensive *Pensionen* in Nuremberg's *Altstadt,* but they tend to fill up fast in summer, so call ahead. The tourist office will help you find a room for a DM1.50 fee; price guides to area hotels and *Gasthöfe* are also available.

Jugendgästehaus (HI), Burg 2 (tel. 22 10 24). Exit the train station, continue north all the way through the *Altstadt* to Burgstr.; hostel is on top of the hill. Built into the Stadtburg section of the imperial castle, the hostel affords the best view in town. The 300-bed building was destroyed in 1945 and rebuilt in 1952. Once a grain storage house, but now the interior is incorporated into the old Romanesque arches and wooden beams. With starched sheets and fans, this place is for you. Reception open 7am-1am. Curfew 1am. Checkout 9am. Theoretical quiet time 10pm-7am; vociferous theory at other times. Under 27 only. DM22. Sheets and breakfast included. Reservations strongly recommended.
Jugend-Hotel Nuremberg, Rathsbergstr. 300 (tel. 521 60 92, fax 521 69 54). Streetcar #3: Ziegelstein, or bus #41: Felsenkeller. 25min. north of town. Dorm-rooms DM21-24 per person, with bath DM22-26. Breakfast included. Call ahead.
Pension Vater Jahn, Jahnstr. 13 (tel. 44 45 07). From the train station, walk left down Eilgutstr., then turn left under the Tafelfeld Tunnel. When you emerge you'll see *Vater Jahn* written on the side of the tall *Pension* building. Comfort-able, tidy rooms. Singles DM40. Doubles DM70, with shower DM80, with shower and toilet DM90. Breakfast included.
Pension Melanchthon, Melanchthonplatz 1 (tel. 41 26 26 66), behind the train sta-tion, 5 blocks west of Vater Jahn. Quiet pleasant rooms. Singles DM40. Doubles DM70, with bath DM80. Breakfast included. Call at least 1 day in advance.
Pension Fischer, Brunnengasse 11 (tel. 22 61 89), 2 blocks from Königstr. Quiet and clean. Singles DM42. Doubles DM72, with shower DM82. Showers DM2. Breakfast included. Reservations absolutely necessary.
Pension Alt-Nürnberg, Breite Gasse 40 (tel. 22 41 29), 1½ blocks from Pension Fischer. In the pedestrian zone. Slightly cramped, but some rooms have great views. Singles DM35-40. Doubles DM60-70. Reservations a few days in advance strongly recommended.
Pension Brendel, Blumenstr. 1 (tel. 22 56 18). Small rooms are bright and tidy. Sin-gles DM37. Doubles DM87. Breakfast included. Reservations recommended.
Camping: Campingplatz am Stadion, Hans-Kalb-Str. 56 (tel. 81 11 22), behind the soccer stadium. U-Bahn south: Messenzentrum. DM7 per person, DM6 per tent, DM5.50 per car. Call ahead. Open May-Sept. Another option is **Camping-platz Am Kreuzweiher** (tel. 56 79 75), in a neighboring town west of Nurem-berg. Take the bus (from the train station): Kalereuth Röckenhof. DM5 per person, DM4 per tent, DM4 per car.

FOOD

Nuremberg is famous for its specialty foods—particularly *Rostbratwurst,* boiled *Sauerwurst,* and *Lebkuchen,* traditionally eaten at Christmas. Another regional offering, particularly in the cafe-bistro-pub scene, is *überbacktes Camembert.*

University Mensa, Andrej-Sacharov-Platz 1. New, modern, efficient, spanking white. Cheapest bearable meal in town. Lunch DM4-5, salad DM1.50. Other loca-tions: Regensburgerstr. 160, Kesslerplatz 12, and at the University Erlangen-Nürn-berg im Haus. All open mid-Sept. to mid-July daily 11:30am-2pm.
Bratwurst Häusle, Rathausplatz 1, next to St. Sebald's Church. The most famous and crowded *Bratwurst* restaurant in Nuremberg for a reason. As they say, "when in Rome…." 6 *Rostbratwürste* DM8-15, served with sauerkraut or spiced potato salad. Open Mon.-Sat. 9:30am-10pm.

Gänskrong I, Innerer Laufer Platz 2-4, in the northeast corner of the *Altstadt* off Theresienstr. To call it a pizzeria and restaurant is an understatement. Serves 165 different dishes. A whopping 44 go for under DM10, not including the pizza selection. Great spaghetti *carbonara.* Open daily 11am-2:30pm, 5pm-midnight.

Amaranth, Färberstr. 11, on the 5th floor of the Fachmarktcenter Maximum. They offer cafeteria-style vegetarian dishes in a whacked-out teal-and-mauve Bauhaus space. Great salad bar. Open Mon.-Fri. 11am-8pm.

Ceres, Vordere Sterngasse 1. This elegantly pastel restaurant is Nuremberg's oldest vegetarian joint, and the food is delicious. Entrees DM10-18. Open Tues.-Fri. 11am-10pm.

SIGHTS

Allied bombing didn't leave much of old Nuremberg for posterity. After a single air raid on January 2, 1945, 90% of the *Altstadt* was wiped out. The churches, castle, and buildings were all reconstructed from the original stone between 1945 and 1966. Most of the churches show empty pedestals where the exterior statues were lost in the bombing. From the train station, the closest part of the *Altstadt* is a walled-in area filled with cottages and shops. This is the **Handwerkhof,** a tourist trap masquerading as a historical attraction. The real sights lie farther up Königstr.

Around the Altstadt and Castle

Nuremberg has three churches which are definitely worth exploring. The **Lorenz-kirche,** on St. Lorenzplatz, was originally Catholic; like all of Nuremberg's churches, it later converted to Protestantism. During WWII, all of the transportable artwork was removed to the cellar, and the church itself was completely destroyed except for the towers. The beautiful Gothic church has been completely restored and once again displays its priceless works of art. Of particular interest is the 20m-high **taber-nacle,** with delicate stone tendrils curling up into the roof vaulting. The large wooden carving hanging in front of the altar is the 1517 *Engelsgruß* (angel-greeting), Veit Stoß's masterpiece (open Mon.-Sat. 9am-5pm, Sun. 2-4pm).

Across the river on Hauptmarktplatz is the **Frauenkirche** (Church of Our Lady), a Catholic church since 1916, though prior to that it had been Protestant since Luther's time (open Mon.-Sat. 9am-5pm, Sun. and holidays 12:30-6pm). The clock in the center of the façade is the site of the *Männleinlaufen* every day at noon: seven little figures, the **Kurfürsten** (nobles), walk three times around the seated figure of Kaiser Karl IV, the emperor who had the *Frauenkirche* built in 1350. Also on the Hauptmarktplatz is the **Schöner Brunnen** (Beautiful Well), which resembles nothing so much as the steeple of a Gothic church. Check out the 40 imaginatively carved figures. On the side of the fountain facing into the market, a golden ring has been incorporated into the wrought-iron railing. The trick is that there is no seam or joint in either ring or rail. One of the stories has it that a young metal-worker had fallen in love with the king's daughter, and fashioned the ring-rail in tribute, whereupon her father was so impressed that he allowed them to marry. The real **wish ring,** made of wrought iron, is hidden somewhere in the bannister. Nuremberg superstition says that if you turn it three times, your wish will come true. It can't hurt to try.

Walk uphill from the *Schöner Brunnen* and the **Rathaus** will be to your right. Built between 1616 and 1622 in early Baroque style (with a little Renaissance classicism thrown in), Nuremberg's *Rathaus* once held the largest council chamber in central Europe, destroyed by fire in 1945. Beneath the building are the **Lochgegäng-nissen** (dungeons), containing an exhibit of medieval torture instruments. (Obligatory 25min. tour every 30min. Open April 1 to Oct. 18 Mon.-Fri. 10am-4pm, Sat.-Sun. 10am-1pm. Admission DM3, students DM1.50.) Across from the *Rathaus* is the **Sebalduskirche,** also a Protestant church. Once a year the Catholic congregation is allowed to fetch St. Sebaldus's relics (that is, his corpse) for his feast-day, whereupon they parade through the streets with him. In front of the altar is the gilded cast-bronze tomb of St. Sebaldus (open daily 9am-6pm, Nov.-Feb. 10am-4pm). Up Burgstr. from the church is the fabulous **Fembo-Haus,** a lavishly ornamented patrician house which now contains the **Stadtmuseum.** (Open March-Oct. and during *Christkindlmarkt* (Nov. 30-Dec. 24) Tues. and Thurs.-Sun. 10am-5pm, Wed. 10am-9pm; Nov.-Feb. except *Christkindlmarkt* Tues. and Thurs.-Fri. 1-5pm, Wed. 1-9pm, Sat.-Sun. 10am-5pm. Admission DM3, students DM1.50, children DM1.)

Up the hill is the castle, which has three parts: the **Kaiserburg** (Emperor's castle), the **Burggrafenburg** (the castle count's castle), and the **Stadtburg** (the city castle). Kaiser Konrad III originally erected the Kaiserburg and the next Emperor, Friedrich I ("Barbarossa"), added to it in the 13th century. The spartan chambers of the *Kaiserburg* have the distinction of having housed all of the Holy Roman Emperors after Konrad III. It was law that every German Kaiser spend at least his first day in office here. However, as the castle had no heating, the Kaisers usually spent their nights in the warm patrician homes of the *Altstadt.* Inside lurk the Romanesque Emperor's **Chapel** and the imperial living quarters. (40min. tour (in German) covers all parts of the Kaiserburg. Admission DM3, children DM2. Open daily 9am-noon and 12:45-5pm; Oct.-March 9:30am-noon and 12:45-4pm.)

Ruins of the Third Reich

The ruins of **Dutzendteich Park,** site of the *Parteitage* (Nazi Party Convention) rallies in the 1930s, remind visitors of a darker time in German history. (R-Bahn #5, direction "Neumarkt": Dutzendteich Bahnhof; or streetcar #9, direction "Luitpoldhain": last stop, and continue walking to your left until you reach the artificial lake, which is Dutzendteich. Many areas are fenced off, using electrified barbed wire, so be careful.) **Zeppelin Field** is across the lake to your left, near the massive marble platform from which Hitler addressed throngs. The faint remains of a swastika, stained into the marble, can still be seen on the central promontory, despite numerous attempts to efface the symbol. The poles spaced intermittently along the desolate field once held enormous banners. The overwhelming emotional power of these events—which injected elements of Wagnerian theater and Catholic ritual into Fascist grandiosity—can be seen in the exhibit *"Faszination und Gewalt"* located atop the Zeppelin **Tribune.** (Open July-Oct. Tues.-Sun. 10am-6pm. Free.) The rest of the park still envelops the Nazi-era **New Congress Hall** and the broad, untrafficked **Great Road.** The building style represents the apogee of Fascist architecture: massive and harsh, mixing modernist straight lines with Neoclassical grandiosity. The litter strewn about and the overgrowth along the paths and buildings defines the mood today. On the other side of town, Fürtherstr., 22 (U-Bahn 1: Bärenschanze, and continue on Fürtherstr., walking away from the old town) Nazi leaders faced Allied military judges during war-crime trials in room 600 of the **Justizgebäude.** Soon after the trials, in October of 1946, twelve men were hanged for their crimes against humanity. The building still serves as a courthouse.

Museums

The **Albrecht Dürer Haus,** right off of Albrecht-Dürer-Platz, is the last residence of Nuremberg's favorite son. The *Fachwerk* house contains period furniture along with Dürer etchings and copies of his paintings, as well as an exhibit of Dürer-derived works by modern artists displayed alongside the originals. (Open Tues. and Thurs.-Sun. 10am-5pm, Wed. 10am-7pm. Admission DM3, students DM1.)

Back down Bergstr. at #19 is the **Altstadthof,** which features an historical brewery. No free samples, but tempting liter bottles of the house brew cost only DM5.50, including a DM2 deposit. (Tours hourly Mon.-Fri. 2-7pm, Sat.-Sun. 11am-7pm; during *Christkindlmarkt* (Nov. 30-Dec. 24) daily 11am-7pm. Admission DM4.50, children DM2.50.) Across the river is the **Germanisches Nationalmuseum,** Kornmarkt, a huge collection chronicling the last millennium of German art. (Open Tues.-Sun. 10am-5pm, Thurs. until 9pm. Admission DM5, students DM2; Sun. free.)

NIGHTLIFE

The nightspots of Nuremberg run the gamut from ultra-traditional to hyper-modern. The Altstadt is packed with bars and clubs. Or grab an outdoor patch of cobblestone at **Albrecht-Dürer-Platz,** a favorite summer hangout of the teeny-bopper crowd. On weekend nights they're like swarms of well-scrubbed locusts.

> **Kaiserburg,** Obere Krämergasse 20 (tel. 22 12 16), is a bar which works hard at being *gemütlich*—there's lots of heavy wood furniture and the beer is tapped out of wooden barrels (DM3.50). It occasionally features live jazz or blues. Open Sun.-Tues. 7:30pm-1am, Wed.-Sat. 6pm-3am. The Keller is open daily 8pm-whenever.
>
> **Flohmarkt,** Obere Wörth Str. 19 (tel. 22 53 17), a chaotically cluttered, junky bar near the river where everything—the furniture, the knick-knacks, the dishes—is for sale (the name means "flea market" in German). Beer DM3.80. Live blues or folk after 8pm; it's free, but add DM1 to your first three beers.
>
> **Komm,** Königstr. 93, is the unofficial center for the city's post-teen nightlife. It has everything under one roof—a movie theater, a disco, a bar, a café, cheap beer, music video. Multi-colored hair, leather-jacketed types hang out at the front door. Different areas open different times; cover varies (generally DM4-5). Things start happening at 5:30pm and stop Mon.-Thurs. at midnight, Fri.-Sat. at 1am.
>
> **Comeback,** Engelhardsgasse 2 (tel. 22 24 88), is one of the best gay bar-discos around, with lots of videos. Almost all-male crowd. Open Mon.-Sun. 8pm-4am.
>
> **Ruhestörung,** Tetzelgasse 21 (tel. 22 19 21), Nuremberg's big student hangout, is 5min. from St. Lorenz Church. Open Mon.-Fri. 7:30am-1am, Sat.-Sun. 9:30am-1am.

■■■ BAYREUTH

Once you've turned off of Meistersingerstr. onto Nibelungenstr., walked past Walküregasse, and headed into the Parsifal Pharmacy, there can be little doubt that you're in Bayreuth, the adopted home of Richard Wagner and the site of the annual *Festspiele* of his music. When the composer first moved here in 1872, he saw in this small provincial town the perfect setting for his music. He also saw the perfect wealthy patroness, the Margravine Wilhelmine, to support him. Meanwhile, King Ludwig II conveniently paid off all Wagner's debts and kept him out of jail. As with most "sacred" cities, the urge to build on a grandiose scale has left Bayreuth a treasure trove of gorgeous buildings. An affection for grandiosity or a desire to mock the Wagner groupies makes Bayreuth a worthwhile visit even for those less than enthralled with the man and his music.

Practical Information For general orientation, the *Altstadt* lies south of the train station, to the left as you exit. The **tourist office,** Luitpoldplatz 9 (tel. (0921) 885 88), to the left and about four blocks from the train station, provides a free map of the city, a list of hotels, information about the surrounding area, a monthly calendar of events, and walking tours of the city. **Branch office** at Jean-Paul Platz 1 (same telephone number; DM3 accommodation-finding fee). They, too, sell tickets to Bayreuth's lively year-round theater, opera, and musical performances. (Open Mon.-Fri. 9am-6pm, Sat. 9am-noon. Tours May-Oct. Tues.-Sat. 10am. DM7, students DM4) The **post office,** Bürgerreutherstr. 1, 98444 Bayreuth (tel. 78 00), is across from the train station and to the right (open Mon.-Thurs. 8am-noon and 1-3:30pm, Fri. 8am-noon and 1pm-2:25pm, late teller 6-8pm, Sun. 11am-noon). The **telephone city code** is 0921. The town is an easy day trip; frequent **trains** connect it to Nuremberg.

Accommodations If you visit during the *Festspiele* and you didn't book your room last year, don't even try to stay in Bayreuth. During any time other than the *Festspiele,* prices are reasonable and there are lots of beds in town. Bayreuth's brand–new-but-eerily-sedate-and-spacious **Jugendherberge (HI),** Universitätstr. 28 (tel. 252 62), is way out in the boonies next to the vast university. Take bus #4 (DM1.60) from the Marktplatz and get out at the "Mensa" stop. Walk past the buildings straight ahead; the *Mensa* should be to your right up the steps; past its entrance, go down the stairs, pass the first left and then take the left fork in the stone road leading under the bridge. Then make a right; after a few twists and turns you will be able to see a wild yellow building with clashing green windows. Follow the path around to the front, and you're there. The path is neither well-lit nor populated at night; you might want to avoid the semi-industrial area after dark. (Open March to mid-Dec. Reception open 9-11:30am and 6-10pm, though notoriously understaffed. Curfew 10pm. Under 27 only. DM11, with breakfast DM16.50. Sheets DM5, wash DM3.) The **Gasthof Vogel**, Friedrichstr. 13 (tel. 682 68), is in the old city and offers pleasant rooms. (Singles DM30. Doubles DM60. Call ahead). Or try **Gasthof Hirsch**, St. Georgen 26 (tel. 267 14), a little farther out but clean, crisp, and excellent. Walk left from the station to Tunnelstr., follow it until it becomes Brandenburgerstr., and left onto St. Georgen. (Singles DM35-40, Doubles DM70-80.)

Food Fill up at the **University Mensa** for DM3; any student ID should do. (Open Mon.-Thurs. 11am-1:45pm, Fri. 11am-1:30pm; August-Sept. open Mon.-Thurs. 11:15am-1:30pm, Fri. 11:15am-1:15pm. See *Jugendherberge*, in Accommodations, for directions.) The **Gaststätte Zum Oberen Tor,** Richard-Wagner-Str. 14, serves appropriate and delicious Teutonic fare (meals DM13-25; open Tues.-Wed. and Fri.-Sat. 10am-8pm, Thurs. 10am-10pm, Sun. 10am-3pm). The **Schützenhaus,** Am Schießhaus 2, features authentic Franconian delights and a sprawling beer garden where you can get pleasantly buzzed (open Tues.-Sat. 9:30am-midnight; kitchen open Tues.-Sun. 9:30am-2pm and 5-10pm). **Braunbierhaus,** Kanzleistr. 15, beyond Bayreuth's Stadtkirche, is a delight, and at almost 900 years, the oldest house in the city. *Holzfällersteak* (woodchopper's steak) with *Bratkartoffeln* (hash browns), DM17.80 (open daily 11:30am-2pm and 5:30-10:30pm; Sun. 11:30am-2:30pm). There is a morning **market** in the Rotmainhall near Hindenburgstr. (Wed. and Sat.).

The Wagner Fest For Wagnerians, traveling to Bayreuth is nothing short of a pilgrimage. Every summer (late July through late Aug.), thousands of visitors pour in for the **Bayreuth Festspiele,** a vast and bombastic—in a word, Wagnerian—celebration of the composer's works in the **Festspielhaus,** the theater Wagner built for his "music of the future." Tickets (DM35-255, obstructed view DM17-25) for the festival go on sale a year in advance and sell out almost immediately. For the 1995 festival, you must order tickets in writing by November 15, 1994. Write to Bayreuth Festspiele, 95402 Bayreuth, preferably *well* before the deadline. Your request will be processed when it is received and notification will take place some time after November 15. Reserve a room in town as soon as you get tickets.

Sights Visitors without tickets to the *Festspiele* can console themselves with a tour of the *Festspielhaus;* go right at the train station and up at the end of Siegfried-Wagner-Allee. (Open Tues.-Sun. 10-11:30am and 1:30-3pm, Oct.-March Tues.-Sun. 10-11:30am. Closed during rehearsals and performances. Admission DM2, students DM1.50.) As you might imagine, these tourists are serious Wagnerophiles. Those who fail to appreciate Wagner's "Total Works of Art" (as he so modestly styled them) should recall Mark Twain's fiendishly accurate assessment of Wagner's music: "It's better than it sounds."

The composer's house, **Villa Wahnfried,** Richard-Wagner-Str. 48 (tel. 757 28 16), houses an inexhaustible collection of scores, opera costumes, stage sets, and personal effects. Check out the two death masks on display—one is Wagner's and the other is that of his friend and patsy, Ludwig II. Sound bites of Wagner's compositions are performed in the drawing room daily at 10am, noon, and 2pm. (Open daily 9am-5pm. Admission DM4, students DM1.50; Sept.-June DM3, students DM1.50.) Behind the house lie the graves of Wagner, his wife Cosima, and their dog. Even farther behind is the **Hofgarten,** a park in the English style. Turn right as you enter, and your first right leads to the **Freemason's Museum** (tel. 698 24; ring the bell). If you've wondered what's inside those windowless temples or what those strange symbols mean—and particularly if you've ever read *Foucault's Pendulum*—this is the place for you, complete with floor plans. (Open Tues.-Fri. 10am-noon and 2-

4pm, Sat. 10am-noon. Admission DM2.) Lead yourself down the garden path to the 18th-century Baroque **Neues Schloß,** former residence of Friedrich the Great's sister, the Margravine Wilhelmine. Considered one of Europe's most brilliant and cultured women, she married the Margrave of Bayreuth and ended up stuck in what must have seemed a provincial cowtown, frustrated with her dull husband and craving the cultural accoutrements of a cosmopolitan city. At this point, Wagner entered the picture. The interior of her palace is lavishly Rococo and richly furnished. (Open Tues.-Sun. 10-11:30am and 1:30-4:30pm; Oct.-March Tues.-Sun. 10-11:30am and 1:30-3pm. Admission DM2, students free.) The mind-shatteringly ornate **Margravian Opera House** is the tangible result of such frustration combined with more money than is good for a person. (Open Tues.-Sun. 9-11:30am and 1:30-4:30pm; Oct.-March Tues.-Sun. 10-11:30am and 1:30-3pm. Admission DM2, students free.)

■■■ COBURG

Coburg only joined Bavaria in 1920, having previously been part of Saxony. In so doing, the city avoided inclusion in the GDR. The division of Germany shifted the town's geographical location from the heartland to the margins, and with the shift went much of Coburg's political importance. Coburg is at the center again; its residents put together an unofficial Welcome Wagon for East Germans in the brief, heady period in which reunification seemed like a problem-free idea.

Head down Mohrenstr. from the train station to reach the Renaissance-influenced **Altstadt,** with its frescoed **Rathaus.** Down Herrengasse is the part Renaissance, part neo-Gothic **Schloß Ehrenburg** (Castle of Honor). When the *Herzog* (Duke) built the palace, he did so without borrowing money and without oppressing his peasantry too badly; thus, when the Kaiser toured the site, he remarked that it stood as a monument to the *Herzog's* honor, and the name stuck. The palace came into the hands of the Saxe-Coburg-Gothas, and Prince Albert (Queen Victoria's husband) spent his childhood within its walls. Victoria's private quarters during her frequent visits can be toured. (Tours Tues.-Sun. 10, 11am, 1:30, 2:30, 3:30, and 4:30pm; Nov.-March Tues.-Sun. 10, 11am, 1:30, 2:30, and 3:30pm. Admission DM3, students DM2.)

Paved footpaths wind through the **Hofgarten,** a shaded, grassy expanse which stretches from Schloß Ehrenburg to the **Veste** (fortress). Allow 30-45 minutes to hoof it up the deceptively steep hill to the fortress. Otherwise, take bus #8 (from in front of the Rathaus, DM1.60) to the Veste stop and walk up about 50m. The 16th-century fortress, encircled by a double set of fortified walls, was inhabited until 1918, when Karl Eduard abdicated the dukedom. The main buildings are the **Fürstenbau** (prince's palace) and the **Coburg Art Museum.** The half-timbered *Fürstenbau* contains a chapel commemorating Martin Luther's 1530 stay in Coburg, as well as the beautifully furnished ducal living quarters. (Open April-Oct. Tues.-Sun. 9:30-noon and 2-4pm. Required tours every ½hr. Nov.-March Tues.-Sun. tours 2, 2:45, and 3:30pm. Admission DM3.50, students DM2.50, children DM1.50.)

Coburg's **tourist office,** Herrngasse 4 (tel. (09561) 741 80), off the Marktplatz, offers free city maps and will find you a room. (Open Mon.-Fri. 9am-noon and 1:30-7pm, Sat. 9am-noon; Nov.-March Mon.-Fri. 9am-noon and 1:30-5pm.) The **post office** is at Hindenburgstr. 6 (tel. 910) and has lots of **telephones** and good **exchange** rates (open Mon.-Fri. 8:30am-6pm, Sat. 8:30am-1pm). The **telephone city code** is 09561. Coburg is connected to Bamberg by frequent **trains** (DM13) and to Nuremberg (4-7 per day; DM28).

Jugendherberge Schloß Ketschendorf (HI), Parkstr. 2 (tel. 153 30, fax 286 53), is in a beautiful converted palace. The rooms are large, modern, spotless, and wow— Ketschendorf proudly displays plaques proclaiming itself the "Best Bavarian Youth Hostel." (Reception open 5-7pm and 9-9:30pm. Phone lines closed after 5pm. Curfew 6pm or by prior arrangement. Lockout 10am-noon. Showers available 7-9am and 3-10pm. Under 27 only. DM17.50. Sheets DM5. Breakfast included.) The **Gasthof Goldenes Kreuz,** Herrngasse 1 (tel. 904 73), is on the Marktplatz. Its cramped but tidy singles (DM42) and doubles (DM80) are centrally located. Try the bargain prices at **Zum Hohenfels,** Geleitstr. 12 (tel. 385 79). Follow Lossaustr. left from the train station under the underpass, then right, then left onto Geleitstr. (singles DM30, doubles DM60). **Frankenbräu**, Mauer 4 (tel. 952 31) has reasonable prices and a great location (singles DM35-45, doubles DM65-75). Two specialty foods in Coburg are *Thüringer Klößer* (dumplings) and *Coburger Bratwurst*. Billowing clouds of smoke and the smell of grilled *Coburger Bratwürste* (sausages) hang thick in the air over the market square. The **Münchner Hofbräu,** Kleine Johannisgasse 8, serves just what you think it would—beer (DM4-6).

■ Near Coburg: Vierzehnheiligen

About 20 minutes south of Coburg is the resplendent Rococo masterpiece, **Vierzehnheiligen Church** (14 Saints' Church), which stands on a broad grassy rise above the Main River. The hill was the site of the visions of a local shepherd in 1445-46, the last one involving the *"Fourteen Saints of Intercession."* The spot became an important center of pilgrimage, and in the 18th century the present church was erected. The façade is a sumptuous example of ornate detailing, with unusually high towers for a church of this period and a golden-yellow glow to the stone. The interior of the church is dominated by the huge altar (*Nothelfer-Altar*) to the Saints of Intercession, which contains statues of all 14, each one in action interceding for a particular cause. Pray to St. Catherine if you want to get married, or to St. Christopher for budget travel tips. To reach Vierzehnheiligen from Coburg, take the **train** to Lichtenfels (30min., DM5). The church is about 6km outside of town. A **bus** runs from the Lichtenfels station to the church (Tues.-Thurs. 8:15am and 2pm, returns 10:40am and 5:40pm). A **taxi** costs about DM12-15 from the stand outside Lichtenfels train station. The **walk** takes about 1½ to two hours; the return, at least, is downhill.

■■■ BAMBERG

Packed with sights and yet largely overlooked by most travelers, this little city on the Regnitz boasts a history that spans a thousand years. Emperor Heinrich II liked Bamberg so much that he made it the center of his empire and crowned it with a cathedral of daunting proportions. The cathedral is but one example of the city's incredible bounty—take the time to behold the city's imperial palace, frescoes, and Romanesque-Gothic-Baroque-Rococo architecture. Bamberg's remarkable architectural treasures owe a great deal to the city's sheer luck; unlike most of its German counterparts, Bamberg survived two virulent wars relatively unscathed. During the Thirty Years War, Bamberg withstood two sieges by the Swedish King Gustav Adolphus; three centuries later, the city emerged from WWII with comparably minor bruises. Incidentally, the residents of Bamberg consume more beer per capita than any other city in Germany. We're not really sure why.

ORIENTATION AND PRACTICAL INFORMATION

The heart of Bamberg lies on an island between the Regnitz and the Rhine-Main-Danube Canal (the Regnitz is cleverly named for its location at the confluence of the *Reg*en and the Peg*nitz*). Across the canal is the train station, and across the Regnitz is the *Dom*. From the train station, the *Altstadt* lies directly ahead. Follow Luitpoldstr. over the Luitpoldbrücke, the bridge spanning the **Rhein-Main-Donau Kanal.** Immediately take your first right onto Heinrichsdamm and your second left (not counting small alleys), and you will find yourself on the main strech of the *Altstadt* (it starts out as Hauptwachstr., but the name is wont to change deeper into the city).

Tourist Office: Fremdenverkehrsamt, Geyerworthstr. 3 (mailing address: Postfach 120163, 96033 Bamburg; tel. 87 11 61), on the island in the Regnitz. To get there, follow the above directions to the *Altstadt* explicitly. Walk down Hauptwachstr. over the bridge and through the *Alte Rathaus,* the building with the frescoes. Take 2 lefts and cross a wooden footbridge, and you're on Geyersworthstr.; the tourist office is just a few hops, away. Dispenses city maps (DM0.30), hiking and cycling maps, and schedules. Open Mon.-Fri. 9am-7pm, Sat. 9am-5pm.

Walking tours of the city meet at the tourist office, Mon.-Sat. 2pm. DM6, students DM3. Tour of the cathedral and the *Neue Residenz* meets at the *Neue Residenz*, DM3, students free.

Post Office: Hauptpostamt, Ludwigstr. 25, 96052 Bamberg (tel. 83 62 81), across from the train station. International telephones, telegrams, currency exchange; also cashes traveler's checks (DM3). Open Mon.-Fri. 8am-6pm, Sat. 8am-2pm, Sun. 11am-1pm and 6-7pm.

Telephone: City Code: 0951.

Trains: Main station on Ludwigstr. (tel. 194 19). Lockers DM2-4. Frequent trains to Würzburg (DM24), Nuremberg (DM15), and all the way to Munich (DM61).

Bike Rental: At the main station; DM12 per day, with valid ticket DM8.

Public Transportation: Excellent transportation net centers around the **ZOB (Zentral Omnibus Bahnhof)** on Promenadestr. in the central part of town. For schedules, ask at the tourist office. Bus fare DM1.30, 5-ride ticket DM5.

Ferries: Boat tours of Bamberg leave from the **Klein-Venedig Hafen** on Am Kranen. 4 per day; 80min.; DM7, children DM5.

Laundromat: SB Waschsabon, in the Atrium mall near the train station, 2nd floor (tel. 20 29 40). Wash DM6, 10min. dry DM1. Open Mon.-Sat. 8am-10pm.

Pharmacy: Look in the paper's notices section for the pharmacy on 24-hr. duty.

Rape Crisis: tel. 5 82 80.

Emergency: tel. 110. **Police:** Schildstr. 81 (tel. 18 50).**Hospital: Klinikum Bamberg,** Burgerstr. 80 (tel. 50 30).

ACCOMMODATIONS AND CAMPING

Since—for no discernible reason—it is forbidden here to rent rooms in private homes, Bamberg's accommodations tend to be very expensive. Fortunately, there are two hostels a little way out of town, both on direct bus routes from the Zentral Omnibus Bahnhof (ZOB).

Jugendherberge Stadion (HI), Pödeldorferstr. 178 (tel. 123 77). Bus #2 (from ZOB): Stadion. This hostel's been on the scene for a while, but it's loads of fun. In a quiet residential neighborhood. Reception open 5-7pm. Lockout 9am-4pm. Curfew 10pm. Under 26 only. DM15. Sheets DM4.50. Breakfast included. Open April-Sept. Call ahead.

Jugendherberge Wolfsschlucht (HI), Oberer Leintritt 70 (tel. 560 02). Bus #18 (from ZOB): Am Regnitzufer. Older and farther out, but tidy and larger than Stadion. Reception open 3-5pm and 6-10pm. Curfew 10pm. Under 26 only. DM15.50. Sheets DM5. Breakfast included. Open Feb. to mid-Dec.

Maiselbräustübl, Obere Konigsstr. 38, 96052 Bamberg (tel. 255 03). Large rooms overlooking a serene courtyard. Reception 11am-midnight. Singles DM35. Doubles DM65, with shower DM75. Breakfast included; delectable dinners start at DM11. Reservations by phone or mail.

Hospiz, Promenade 3, 96047 Bamberg (tel. 20 00 11, fax 20 04 68). Large doubles, some with balconies, great breakfast. Reception noon-9:30pm. Singles DM45, with shower DM60. Doubles DM80, with shower DM88. Triples with shower DM100. Always call ahead. Checkout 11am. Reservations by phone, fax, or mail.

Camping: Campingplatz Insel (tel. 563 20), bus #18 (direction "Klinikum"): Bug. Prime riverside locale. DM5 per person, DM4 per tent, DM8 per car.

FOOD

University Mensa, Ausstr. 37, off central Grüner Markt. Serves the cheapest edible meals in town at DM3.50. Any student ID will do. Open Nov.-July 11:30am-2pm.

Polarbär, Judenstr. 7 (tel. 536 01). Vegetarian dishes for under DM12 and a beer garden (0.5L DM3.60). Hip student scene. Open daily noon-11pm. Kitchen open noon-3pm.

Hofbräuschänke, Karolinestr. 7 (tel. 533 21), will satisfy any vegetarian with DM9.20-17.50 meals. Open Sun.-Fri. 10am-1am, Sat. 10am- 2am.

SIGHTS

The **Altes Rathaus** guards the middle of the Regnitz River like an anchored ship. Stand on one of the two bridges to get a look at this building, half *Fachwerk* (half-timber) and half Baroque fresco, with a Rococo tower in between. You'll notice a number of visual oddities in the frescoes—painted cherubs have three-dimensional limbs and bodies that jut from the wall where sculpted stone has been attached. From the bridges, fisherhouses can be seen crowded up against the water.

Across the river and up the hill are the **Dom** (cathedral) and the **Neue Residenz,** the former episcopal palace. Construction on the cathedral began in 1004, and the transition from Romanesque to Gothic can be traced in the architecture of the building. The most famous object within the *Dom* is the equestrian statue called the **Bamberger Reiter** (the Bamberg Knight), which dates from the 13th century and depicts the chivalric ideal of the medieval warrior-king. Many stories have grown up around the statue over the years, including one that the statue was a prophecy of Hitler's rise to power. People just like to tell stories. The tomb of Heinrich II and Queen Kunigunde of the Holy Roman Empire lies near the east apse. Heinrich sponsored the construction of the cathedral and was later canonized. At the west apse is the grave of the only pope buried in Germany—Clement II, who died in 1047. Heinrich and Kunigunde's crowns are also on display, each in a glass box on its own altar. (Open daily 9am-6pm except during services. Closed June 29-30. ½hr. organ concerts Sat. noon. Free. Call 50 23 30 for info on group tours.)

Across the square the **Neue Residenz** poses Baroquely; from its rose garden, the town is a sea of roofs. The air smells like roses from 40 paces, and the palace is lavishly decorated and furnished. (Open daily 9am-noon and 1:30-5pm; Oct.-March daily 9am-noon and 1:30-4pm. Admission DM3, students DM2.) In town, the streets between the *Rathaus* and the *Dom* are lined with 18th-century Baroque houses, many of them not yet renovated. **Böttinger Palace,** on Judenstr., has a 1713 façade inspired by a Venetian palace, and a similarly exotic courtyard. Farther down the street is the lovely **Concordiahaus,** now the local Institute for Geochemical Research. Across the river at Schillerplatz 26 is the **E.T.A. Hoffmann House.** Hoffmann, author of the nightmarish "Sandman," wrote his uncanny stories here for five years. He and his wife rented two little rooms, one directly over the other, and often chatted with each other through a small opening in the floor. (Open May-Oct. Tues.-Fri. 4-6pm, Sat.-Sun. and holidays 10am-noon. Admission DM1, students DM 0.50.)

■■■ ASCHAFFENBURG

Aschaffenburg was once second home to the Electors of Mainz, and their Renaissance palace still overlooks the river, amid labyrinthine cobblestone streets. Nowadays, "A-Burg" is home to about 8000 U.S. soldiers, and if you ever get the feeling walking through town that you're surrounded by Americans, it's probably because you are. Past Aschaffenburg's tightly packed *Altstadt* are the famous **Schönbusch Gardens** and the newly reopened **Schloß Schönbusch,** a country house built in 1780 for the archbishop of Mainz. The view from the **Chamber of Mirrors** takes in the surrounding city against a backdrop of the Spessart forests (open April-Sept. Tues.-Sun. 9:30am-12:30pm and 2-4:30pm; admission DM3, students DM2). The park itself was built by Elector Friedrich Karl Joseph in 1775 as an experiment in the then-new English style of landscape architecture, which involved natural-looking tree placement. The park is littered with ponds, islands, and fake ruins and temples known as "follies." (Bus #3 from the station: Schönbusch. Open daily 9am-dusk.)

Schloß-Johannisburg, the former domain of the Mainz bishops, now contains an extensive art museum and a particularly nice set of bells, thus being home to the yearly **Carillion-Fest** (first weekend in Aug.) when renowned ringing artists (i.e., people who ring bells as an art) come from all over the world, and hear the tintinnabulation that so musically swells. (Castle open Tues.-Sun. 9am-noon and 1-5pm; Oct.-March Tues.-Sun. 10am-noon and 1-4pm. Museum open Tues.-Sun. 9-11:30am and 1-4:30pm; Oct.-March Tues.-Sun. 10-11:30am and 1-3:30pm.) Across from the palace lies the tourist office (see below) and a new performance center.

To get to the **tourist office,** Schloßplatz 1 (tel (06021) 304 26), cross Ludwigstr. in front of the station, walk through Duccastr., cross the street and take a left down Friedrichstr. and the next right down Erthalstr. The office, in the library, has free maps and a free room-finding service (open Mon.-Fri. 9am-noon and 1:15-4:30pm, Sat. 9am-noon). The **post office** (tel. (06021) 36 90), next to the train station, changes money and traveler's checks(open Mon.-Fri. 8am-noon and 1:30-5:30pm, Sat. 9am-noon). Built on a high bank at a bend in the Main, Aschaffenburg is reached by **train** from Frankfurt or Würzburg. Aschaffenburg's **Jugendherberge (HI),** Beckerstr. 47 (tel. (06021) 927 63), is reached by bus #5 or 15 (from the station) to Schroberstr., then left up Kneippstr. and take a right onto Beckerstr.; it's on the left. (Reception open 5-8pm. Curfew 10pm. DM15. Under 27 only. Breakfast included. Sheets DM4.50.) Aschaffenburg has a few budget hotels and *Pensionen,* and the tourist office finds rooms in private home. In town, **Gasthof zum Heißen Stein,** Am Heißen-Stein (tel. (06021) 269 61), has comfortable rooms (singles DM37; doubles DM74). Rooms at **Café Central,** Steingasse 5 (tel. (06021) 233 92), are just plain lovely. (Singles DM40. Doubles DM78. Call ahead.) Swing by the **Dahlberg Weinstube** on Pfaffengasse. They offer delicious Franconian entrees (DM7.50-21), beer and wine (DM3.50-6; open daily 2:30pm-midnight).

HESSE (HESSEN)

Prior to the 20th century, Hesse was most commonly known for the mercenary soldiers that its various potentates farmed out to such needy despots as King George III, who then sent them to America to put down an unruly gang of colonial hicks in 1776. Absorbed by Bismarck's Prussia in 1866, Hesse ceased to exist as a political entity until the Allies resurrected it in 1945. Somewhere along the line, the Hessians apparently made a collective decision to exchange their guns for briefcases; today, Hesse is the busiest commercial center in the country, led by the banking metropolis of Frankfurt. Overshadowed by Frankfurt, the rest of Hesse attracts remarkably little attention from tourists—a shame, considering that Hesse is also home to the medieval university town of Marburg, the Baroque city of Fulda, and the villages of the Taunus and Lahn Valley.

■■■ FRANKFURT AM MAIN

A city of skyscrapers and investment bankers, Frankfurt belongs more properly to the Germany of tomorrow than the Germany of yesterday. Although the city only recently acquired the derisive nickname "Bankfurt," its reputation as a financial and commercial center reaches back for centuries. The Rothschild family's mammoth banking empire began as a fledgling lending house here. Intellectuals Max Horkheimer, Theodor Adorno, and Walter Benjamin chose Frankfurt as home to the *Institut für Sozialforschung*, better known as the Frankfurt School, whose members started out trying to explain the failure of Germany's socialist revolution and ended up revolutionizing modern social theory. Frankfurt has the reputation among Germans and non-Germans alike of being the most Americanized city in Europe—residents joke that Frankfurt is an American city on German soil populated by Turks— and this title remains something of a mixed blessing given Frankfurt's reputation as the crime capital of Germany. Rest assured, however, that it's still *Kindergarten* compared to New York City, and recent efforts to increase police activity in the city have made it safer than in recent years. Although very little of historic Frankfurt survived the carpet bombings of World War II, there's a fairly wide range of offerings —a compact section of the *Altstadt* is still intact, the zoo is among the best in the world, and the city's liberal expenditures on culture and the arts are reflected in an extraordinary variety of museums. If that isn't enough to make you come to Frankfurt, the immense likelihood of your flying into Rhein-Main Airport probably is.

ORIENTATION AND PRACTICAL INFORMATION

A sprawling conglomeration of steel, concrete, and glass, Germany's fifth-largest city bridges the Main River 35km east of its confluence with the Rhine, in the heart of central Germany. Frankfurt's airport and main train station *(Hauptbahnhof)* are among the busiest in Europe. The train station lies at the end of Frankfurt's moderately sleazy red-light district. From the station, the town center is a 20-minute walk down Kaiserstr. or Münchener Str. The commercial heart of the city—which itself becomes somewhat seedy after dark—is centered around **Hauptwache** (S-Bahn 1-6, 14; 2 stops from the main station), while the historical center revolves around **Römerberg** (U-Bahn 4, direction "Seckbacher Landstr.": Römer).

Tourist Office: In the main train station across from track 23 (tel. (069) 21 23 88 49 or 21 23 88 51). A whole library of maps and brochures. Rooms booked for a DM5 fee, plus a DM8 deposit, applied to your hotel bill when you check in, just to help you show up. Open Mon.-Sat. 8am-9pm.

Consulate: U.S. Siesmayerstr. 21 (tel. 74 53 50 emergency 753 53700). **U.K.** Bockenheimer Landstr. 42 (tel. 170 00 20). **Australia** Gutleutstr. 85 (tel. 273 90 90).

Currency Exchange: In Airport Halle B (open daily 7:30am-9pm) or in the main train station (open daily 6:30am-10pm).

American Express: Kaiserstr. 8 (tel. 210 50). Holds mail 4 weeks. Open Mon.-Fri. 9:30am-5:30pm, Sat. 9am-noon.

Post Office: Main branch, Zeil 110, 60313 Frankfurt. U- or S-Bahn: Hauptwache. **Poste Restante** can be picked up at counter 6 or 7. Open Mon.-Fri. 8am-6pm, Sat. 8am-noon. Post office on the upper level of the main station, open 24hrs.

Telephones: In the main train station and the airport. Open 24hrs. **City code:** 069.

Flights: Flughafen Rhein-Main is a major hub for destinations in Europe, across the Atlantic, and around the world. Call 69 01 for information. From the airport, S-Bahn 14 and 15 travel every 10min. to the main train station. Buy tickets (DM4) from a blue automat; Eurail and Tramper-Monats valid.

Public Transportation: For unlimited access to S-Bahn, U-Bahn, and buses, 24hr. (DM6) and 72hr. (DM15) passes are available from machines in almost every station in the city. Eurail and the Tramper-Monats passes valid on all S-Bahn trains.

Hitchhiking: *Let's Go* does not recommend hitchhiking as a safe mode of transportation. Those headed to Munich take bus #36 or 960 from Konstablerwache south to the *Autobahn* interchange. Those bound for Cologne or Düsseldorf take S-Bahn 1 or 14 to the Wiesbaden *Hauptbahnhof*, then a local train to Auringen-Medenbach; from there they turn right, walk 800m, proceed under the *Autobahn,* and take the access road to the *Autobahn* rest stop. Hitching on the highway itself is strictly forbidden. Hitchers headed in all other directions take streetcar #13 or 61: Stadion, and continue along Mörfelder-Landstr.

Mitfahrzentrale: Baselerstr. 7 (tel. 23 64 45, 23 61 27, or 23 10 28) is 200m from the side exit (track 1) of the main train station. For a fee, connects riders with drivers. Call ahead. Open Mon.-Fri. 8am-6:30pm, Sat. 8am-2pm.

English Bookstores: Süssman's Internationale Buchhandlung, Zeil 127 (tel. 29 89 04 10). Open Mon.-Wed. and Fri. 9am-6:30pm, Thurs. 9am-8:30pm, Sat. 9am-2pm. **British Book Shop,** Börsenstr. 17 (tel. 28 04 92). Open Mon.-Fri. 9am-6:30pm, Sat. 9am-2pm. **Women's bookstore:** Kiesstr. 27 (tel. 70 52 95).

Cultural Institute: Amerika Haus, Staufenstr. 1 (tel. 72 27 94). Open Tues. and Thurs.-Fri. 12:30-5:30pm, Wed. 12:30-7:30pm.

Laundromat: SB Waschen, Wallstr. 8, in Sachsenhausen near the youth hostel. Wash DM7, dry DM1 per 15min. Soap included. Open daily 6am-10pm.

Pharmacy: In the main station near the entrance. Open Mon.-Fri. 6:30am-9pm, Sat.-Sun. 8am-9pm. Newspapers and pharmacies list the pharmacy on 24hr. duty.

Rape/Battered Women's Hotline: tel. 70 94 94.

Emergencies: Police: tel. 110. **Fire** and **ambulance:** tel. 112.

ACCOMMODATIONS

Hotel prices in Frankfurt can be as high as the skyscrapers. The cheapest options are near the main train station in the worst part of town, or in the outlying suburbs. If all else fails, there are four other hostels less than 45 minutes away. The hostels in Bad Homburg (S-Bahn 5, direction "Friedrichsdorf"), Darmstadt (S-Bahn 12), Mainz (S-Bahn 14, direction "Wiesbaden"), and Wiesbaden (S-Bahn 14 or 1) are all in reach.

Jugendherberge (HI), Deutschherrnufer 12, 60594 Frankfurt am Main (tel. 61 90 58). Bus #46 (from main station; DM2.10, DM2.80 during morning and evening rush hours): Frankensteinerplatz. The hostel is 50m west in the large yellow building. After 7:30pm, streetcar #16: Lokalbahnhof, then walk north on Dreieichstr. and take a left on Deutschherrnufer. Clean and conveniently located near the Sachsenhausen pubs and the museum district. 3-day max. stay. Reception open 11am-10pm. Lockout 9am-1pm. Curfew midnight. DM19.50, over 20 DM23.50. Double DM35.50 per person, additional nights DM 33.50, but doubles are *rarely* available. Sheets DM10. Key deposit for smaller rooms DM10. Written reservations accepted.

Pension Backer, Mendelssohnstr. 92 (tel. 74 79 92). U-Bahn: Westend, take the Mendelssohnstr. exit, walk two blocks down Bockenheimer-Landstr. and turn left onto Mendelssohnstr. Clean rooms; pleasant locale near the university and the Palmengarten. Singles DM30-40. Doubles DM60. Showers available 7am-10pm, DM3 per 8min. Breakfast included.

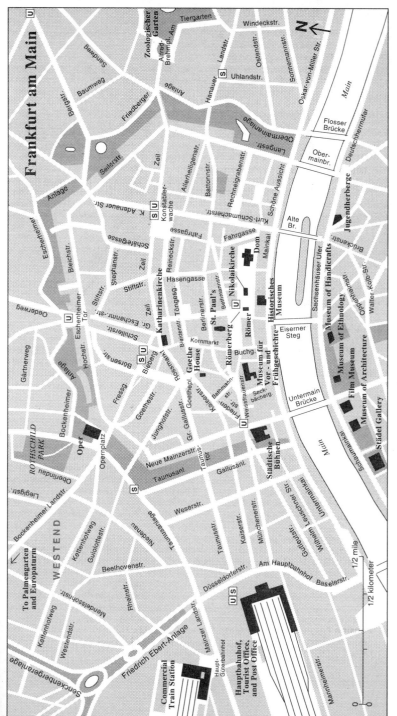

FRANKFURT AM MAIN

Frankfurt am Main

Pension Bruns, Mendelssohnstr. 42 (tel. 74 88 96). Bus #33: Bettinaplatz; or, facing the train station, turn right down Düsseldorfer Str., which will become Friedrich-Ebert-Anlage, turn right on Mendelssohnstr., and it's on the right. Tastefully decorated, comfortable rooms. Singles DM54. Doubles DM76. Showers and breakfast included. Also has rooms for groups.

Hotel Goldener Stern, Karlsruher Str. 8 (tel. 23 33 09). One block behind the station to the right. Neighborhood is somewhat foreboding at night. Decent rooms, worth a try in a pinch. Reception open until 11pm. Singles DM39-50. Doubles DM60-75. Showers DM4. Breakfast included.

Pension Fennisfuchser, Mainzerlandstr. 95 (tel. 25 38 55). From the north entrance to the station, head left (facing away from the tracks) and walk 2 blocks. Acceptable rooms furnished predominantly with unexciting green decor. Singles DM60. Doubles DM92. Triples DM130. Quads DM145. Breakfast included.

FOOD

Like hotel rates, food prices vary inversely with the distance to the city center. Many of the taverns and pubs in the Alt Sachsenhausen district also serve food, and you can always find cheap cuisine around Leipziger Str. in the Bockenheimer district (U-Bahn 6 or 7). Frankfurter sausages (hot dogs; the locals know them as *Wieners*) are not a Frankfurt specialty and should probably be avoided; *Äpfelwein* (apple wine, a.ka. *Äppelwei* or *Ebbelwei*) is a specialty. Also popular are *gegrillte Rippchen* (grilled ribs) and *Handkäse mit Musik*, a kind of curd cheese with raw onions.

University Mensa, Bockenheimer Landstr. 120. U-Bahn 6 or 7: Bockenheimer Warte. Just outside the subway stop. This excellent student cafeteria offers 2 standard dishes for DM3 and DM3.50, and has a grill which prepares *Würste* for DM3 and steaks for DM7. Salads DM2.50 and DM4.50. Technically, you must have a Hessian university student ID, but try your luck. Open Mon.-Fri. 11am-2pm.

Ulli's Backstube, Jordanstr. 1, near the university. Small outdoor café serves sandwiches, salads and quiche as well as breakfasts, all for under DM8. Open Mon.-Fri. 6am-7:30pm.

Green Hill, Gutzkowstr. 43, on the corner of Laubestr. in Sachsenhausen. Upmarket vegetarian food at slightly high prices. Entrees DM11-22. Open Tues.-Sun. 6pm-1am. Kitchen open until 11:30pm. Credit cards accepted.

Atschel, Wallstr. 7 (tel. 61 92 01), in Sachsenhausen. A quiet local establishment serving good food at reasonable prices. *Handkäse mit Musik* (DM4), *Frankfurter Rippchen* (DM12.80). Open daily 5:30pm-1am.

SIGHTS

"Everywhere one looks," wrote the 18th-century author Johann Kaspar Riesbeck, "one sees the signs of a high standard of living. The furnishings of the houses, the yards, the carriages, the clothes, the jewelry of the women—in short, everything exceeds the bourgeois and borders on the most unimaginable splendor." The logical starting point for a tour of this city of consumption is the **Römerberg,** the name given to the cluster of surviving historical buildings in the city center. The eastern end of the Römerberg is dominated by the **Dom,** a huge red sandstone Gothic cathedral that was the site of coronation ceremonies for German emperors between 1562 and 1792. (Under renovation until mid-1994. Open daily 9am-1pm and 2:30-6pm. Tours 3pm.) The view from the *Dom's* tower is well worth the punishing climb to the top (tower admission DM2, students and children DM1). The **Dom Museum** inside the main entrance contains some of the venerated robes of the imperial electors and not much else of interest (open Tues.-Fri. 10am-5pm, Sat.-Sun. 11am-5pm; admission DM2). Directly in front of the *Dom* is the **Historischer Garten,** a mixed bag of ruins from Roman to medieval times, all discovered by chance when workers digging up a sewer line happened upon them.

The **Römer,** a distinctively gabled red sandstone structure at the west end of *Römerberg,* has been Frankfurt's city hall since 1405. The upper floors contain the **Kaisersaal,** a former imperial banquet hall whose walls are adorned with portraits of the 52 German emperors from Charlemagne to Franz II (open Tues.-Sun. 11am-3pm; obligatory tour on the hour DM3). Next to the Römer on Paulsplatz stands the **Paulskirche** (St. Paul's Church). In the wake of a wave of revolution that swept through Europe in 1848-49, Germany's first democratic National Assembly convened in the church to draw up a constitution for a German republic. Recognizing that Germany could not be unified without the assent of powerful Prussia, the liberal assembly attempted to flatter Prussia's Friedrich Wilhelm IV into accepting the crown of a constitutional monarchy. The king replied that he ruled by the grace of God, not by the approval of a parliament, and the whole episode ended with the democracy movement being bloodily repressed in the streets of Frankfurt.

Of the half-dozen or so German cities that claim to be the home of Goethe, Frankfurt has the best case. The great author and poet was born here in 1749, he found his first love here (a girl named Gretchen, said to be the inspiration for Marguerite in *Faust),* and he wrote some of his best-known works here, including *The Sorrows of Young Werther.* A few blocks northwest of the Römer stands his birthplace and family home, the **Goethe Haus,** Großer Hirschgraben 23-25 (tel. 28 28 24), now a carefully preserved museum. The sumptuous interior is evidence that you don't necessarily have to suffer to produce great art. (Open Mon.-Sat. 9am-6pm, Sun. 10am-1pm. Tours Mon.-Sat. 10:30am and 2pm, Sun. 2pm. Admission DM3, students DM2.) The *Museumsufer* is home to a row of high-powered collections (see Museums, below) and Frankfurt's weekly flea market, held on Saturdays.

Over 650 species from the banal to the exotic are represented at the **Zoo,** on the eastern side of town (U-Bahn 6 or 7). The feeding of the apes (daily at 4:30pm) and of the big cats (daily at 5pm) excite a certain visceral pleasure. (Zoo open daily 8am-7pm; Oct. to mid-March daily 8am-5pm. Admission DM9.50, students and under 18 DM4.50.) On the northwest side of town, the vast **Palmengarten's** greenhouses (U-Bahn 6 or 7: Bockenheimer Warte) are home to tropical and subtropical flora (open daily 9am-6pm; Nov.-Feb. daily 9am-4pm; admission DM5, students DM2). A few blocks away is the **Naturmuseum,** Senckenberganlage 25 (tel. 754 20), with some amazing prehistoric skeletons (open Mon.-Fri. 9am-5pm, Sat.-Sun. 9am-6pm).

MUSEUMS

Walk down the **Museumsufer,** a row of museums along the *Schaumainkai* on the southern bank of the Main. Other collections, including Frankfurt's cache of modern art, are in what's left of the *Altstadt.*

Museumsufer, on Schaumainkai, an easy 10min. walk across the Eiserner Steg foot bridge from the Römerberg. All 7 museums are open Tues. and Thurs.-Sun. 10am-5pm, Wed. 10am-8pm. Tours are offered each Sun. at 11am and Wed. at 6:30pm.

Museum für Kunsthandwerk, Schaumainkai 71 (tel. 21 23 40 37). Full of furniture, china, and other forms of utilitarian art from the 18-20th centuries. In the museum's courtyard stands the tiny **Museum für Volkerkunde** (Museum of Ethnology), which explores several African and South American cultures. Both are free.

Deutsches Filmmuseum, Schaumainkai 41 (tel. 21 23 88 30), 1 block down on the corner of Schweizerstr., chronicles the development of the filmmaking industry—old movies play continuously on the 3rd floor. Free.

Bündespostmuseum, Schaumainkai 53 (tel. 606 01). A multimedia presentation detailing the history of the German mail system. The truth about the House of von Thurn und Taxis, whose hold on the post crumbled when the Prussians marched into Frankfurt in 1866. Free.

Architektur Museum, Schaumainkai 83 (tel. 21 23 88 44), next door to the Filmmuseum, with special exhibits and a survey of architecture from the Sumerians to today. Admission DM4, students DM2.

Städel, Schaumainkai 63 (tel. 605 09 80), a block downstream, possesses an excellent collection of old masters is one of Europe's leading art museums. This one is not to be missed. Admission DM6, students DM3. Sun. free.

Liebighaus, Schaumainkai 71 (tel. 21 23 86 17), 2 blocks down from the Städel, is home to all the sculptures the covetous museum collectors in Frankfurt could get their hands on. Free.

Museum für Moderne Kunst (Museum of Modern Art), Domstr. 10, north of the *Dom*. In a triangular building that's as bizarre as some of the art it houses. Open Tues., Thurs., Fri., and Sun. 10am-5pm; Wed. 10am-8pm; Sat. noon-7pm. Last entry ½hr. before closing. Admission DM6, students, seniors, and children DM3, Sat. free.

Schirn Kunsthalle, beyond the *Dom* to the west, its entrance tucked in a narrow alley. A postmodern art gallery hosting visiting exhibits. Open Mon. 2-6pm, Tues.-Fri. 10am-10pm, holidays 10am-7pm. Admission varies; student discounts available.

Historisches Museum, Saalgasse 19, back toward the river from the Römer. Presents a first-rate series of exhibitions on the history of the city and the larger German nation. Open Tues. and Thurs.-Sun. 10am-5pm, Wed. 10am-8pm. Admission DM3, students DM1.

ENTERTAINMENT AND NIGHTLIFE

Frankfurt wields a nightlife commensurate with its size. There are two major theaters, the **Alte Oper** and the **Städtisches Theater,** as well as several smaller ones. Performances are detailed in two publications, *Frankfurter Woche* (DM3.50) and *Journal Frankfurt* (DM3.20), both available at newsstands as well as at the tourist office. Students can often purchase leftover tickets at reduced prices one hour before the beginning of a performance. Frankfurt has a renowned **jazz** scene that centers around Kleine Bockenheimer Str., also known as **Jazzgasse** (Jazz Alley).

If you're looking for a drinking night out, the **Alt Sachsenhausen** district, between Brückenstr. and Dreieichstr., is home to a huge number of rowdy pubs and taverns specializing in *Äpfelwein* (apple wine), the local drink of choice. Frankfurt also has a number of thriving discos in the city, many if not all of which are marked by neurotic bouncers, high cover charges and drink prices that may make going out on the town more pain than pleasure. Gay nightlife is mainly centered around the area between Zeil and Bleichstr. **Zum Schwejk,** Schäfergasse 20, is a relaxed gay men's bar (open Mon. 4pm-1am, Tues.-Thurs. 11am-1am, Fri.-Sat. 11am-2am, Sun. 3pm-1am). **Pferdestall,** Ulmenstr. 20, is a café-bar for women only, with a mixed lesbian and straight crowd; **La Gata,** Seehofstr. 3 (tel. 61 45 81), is a women's disco.

Omen, Junghofstr. 14 (tel. 28 22 33). One of the hippest discos in town. Unfortunately, it's also one of the hardest to get into. House music. Open Fri.-Sat. 10pm-6am. Admission DM12.

Cooky's, Am Salzhaus 4 (tel. 28 76 62), off Goetheplatz. Disco with live music every Mon. night. Attracts the alternative crowd. Is there no alternative? Open Sun.-Thurs. 10pm-4am, Fri.-Sat. 10pm-6am. Cover DM6, more with live band.

Wagner, Schweizerstr. 71, near Schweizerplatz. Extremely friendly *Äpfelwein* brewery with a *Biergarten*. Also serves a broad selection of local specialties (DM5.50-30). *Äpfelwein* DM2 for 0.3L. Open daily 11am-midnight.

Zum Gemalten Haus, Schweizerstr. 67. This *Äpfelwein* joint has less to eat but is equally *gemütlich*. Watch out for the complicated door system. *Äpfelwein* DM2 for 0.3L. Open Wed.-Sun. 11am-midnight.

Irish Pub, Kleine Rittergasse 11-13 (tel. 61 59 86), in Sachsenhausen. Live music every night at 9pm and Guinness on tap (DM6) in this English-speaker's home away from home. Open Mon.-Thurs. 2pm-1am, Fri. 2pm-2am, Sat.-Sun. noon-2am.

Der Jazzkeller, Kleine Bockenheimer Str. 18a (tel. 28 85 37). Near Hauptwache. Frankfurt's most renowned jazz club; often has world-class jazz. Call for schedule and cover prices. Open Tues.-Sun. 9pm-3am.

Jazz Life Podium, Kleine Rittergasse 22 (tel. 62 63 46), in Sachsenhausen. Poor person's jazz club with lesser known acts;they still know how to swing. No cover.

■ Near Frankfurt: Wiesbaden

The capital of Hesse, Wiesbaden historically has a lot in common with Baden-Baden. Both are spa towns with ritzy casinos that served as highbrow amusement parks for the aristocracy of Europe during the heady years of the 19th century. When the royalty fell from grace, so did Wiesbaden, and today the city is but a shadow of its former self. It's now largely a residential town without much of interest to travelers and remarkable mostly for its huge U.S. military base, from which the Berlin airlift was launched. You can still test the curative waters of the thermal baths and, provided that you're formally attired, gamble away your life savings at the casino.

The original **Kurhaus,** now used for business conventions, is situated off of Wilhelmstr. and bordered on two sides by the expansive and serene **Kurpark,** where locals sprawl under century-old willow trees during the summer. (Bus #1 or 8, from the station: Kurhaus/Theater.) The **casino** (Spielbank) is inside the Kurhaus; compulsive gambler Fyodor Dostoevsky squandered the last 30 dollars that stood between him and poverty while visiting Wiesbaden, and so can you (coat and tie rental DM10). To the right of the Kurhaus is the stately **Staatstheater.** Around the corner and up the street just off Taunusstr. is the **Kochbrunnen,** a fountain dispensing the town's renowned thermal water. If the smell doesn't deter you, you're welcome to drink the water—its curative powers are, after all, legendary.

The **Neroberg,** a low hill at the north end of town that offers good views of the city below. Bus #1 ends at the "Nerotal" stop; from there, a **hydraulic funicular** (DM2) or a short walk will take you to the top. There's a **public swimming pool** up there, and 100m beyond it stands the **Russische-Griechische Kapelle,** probably the most impressive monument in the city. This painstakingly decorated Greek Orthodox chapel was built in 1855 as a mausoleum for Princess Elizabeth of Nassau, the niece of a Russian tsar who was married off to a local duke and died in childbirth at age 19. Her tear-jerking tomb dominates the chapel's inspiring interior (open daily 10am-5pm; admission DM1). Back in town, the **Museum Wiesbaden** houses a run-of-the-mill collection of art and natural history (open Tues. 10am-8pm, Wed.-Sun. 10am-4pm; admission DM5, students DM3).

At the corner of Rheinstr. and Wilhelmstr. you'll find Wiesbaden's **tourist office** (*Verhkehrsburo*), Rheinstr. 15 (tel. 172 97 80; open Mon.-Fri. 9am-6:30pm). There's a **branch office** in the train station (tel. 172 97 81; open Mon.-Fri. 8:30am-1pm and 1:30-8pm, Sat.-Sun. 9am-7pm). **American Express** does its thing at Webergasse 8 (tel. 391 44; open Mon.-Fri. 8:45am-5:30pm and Sat. 9am-noon; financial services closed 1-2pm). The **telephone city code** is 0611. The **Mitfahrzentrale** (tel. 37 33 52 or 194 40), in a camper on Bahnhofstr. halfway between the pedestrian zone and the train station, connects riders with drivers going the same way (open Mon.-Fri. 7:30am-6pm, Sat. 8am-1pm). The **Jugendherberge (HI),** Blucherstr. 66 (tel. 486 57), has laid-back management and a downstairs bar. From the station, take bus #14 to Gneisenaustr. or Elsasser Platz. (Reception open 1-11:30pm. Curfew 11:30pm. DM18.50, over 26 DM22.) Cheap hotels in the city center simply don't exist, but the tourist office will help find reasonable accommodations in one of the nearby suburbs. The **pedestrian zone** west of the Kurhaus is brimming with pubs and restaurants. **Schanke zur Hauptwache,** Faulbrunnenstr. 8, near the Platz der Deutschen Einheit, has satisfied middle-aged German appetites for 60 years.

■■■ BAD HOMBURG AND THE TAUNUS

Bad Homburg vor der Höhe, a medium-sized spa town at the base of the diminutive Taunus Mountains, is short on sights but long on atmosphere. Bad Homburg is clean, comfortable, almost deathly quiet, and best known for its **Schloß.** This castle was the summer residence, between 1871 and 1918, of Kaiser Wilhelm II, the last German Emperor. Prince Friedrich II of Homburg built the *Schloß* in the mid-17th century as a residence for himself and his successors. To reach the castle from the train station, follow Marienbaderplatz to Schöne Aussicht and take a left. (Obligatory tours every hr. Tues.-Sun. 10am-5pm; Nov.-Feb. Tues.-Sun. 10am-4pm; English translations available. Admission DM4, students DM2.) Across from the front of the castle is the **Evangelische Klosterkirche,** built by Wilhelm and decorated with mosaics (open April-Oct. Fri. 3-5pm, Sat. 10am-5pm, Sun. after service-5pm). Inside the large **Kurpark** in the center of town are a Roman temple, a Siamese pagoda, and the 150-year-old **Spielbank** (tel. (06172) 17 01 70), a casino that bills itself as the "Mother of Monte Carlo." François Blanc, who founded Monte Carlo in 1863, opened this casino in 1841, after all casinos were banned in France. (Open daily 3pm-2:30am. Admission DM5. Must be 21 or older. Coat and tie required; no jeans or sneakers.)

Bad Homburg's **tourist office,** inside the **Kurhaus,** Louisenstr. 58 (tel. (06172) 12 13 10 or 12 13 11), provides accommodation information for no fee (open Mon.-Fri. 8:30am-6pm, Sat. 9am-1pm). There is a **laundromat** *(Waschsalon)* on the corner of Wallstr. and Elisabethenstr. (wash DM12, dry DM6 for mandatory full service; open Mon.-Tues. and Fri. 8am-12:30pm and 2-6:30pm, Wed. 8am-noon and 3-6:30pm, Thurs. 8am-noon and 3-8:30pm, Sat. 8am-3pm). The **Jugendherberge (HI),** Meiereiberg 1 (tel. (06172) 239 50), is near the *Schloß* and about 15 minutes from the station. Facing the castle, turn left and follow Löwengasse to the bottom of the hill. (Curfew 11:30pm. DM18, over 26 DM23.50. Breakfast included.) The only hotel in the city center with rooms for less than DM50 per person is **Hotel Johannisberg,** Thomasstr. 5 (tel. (06172) 213 15). (Singles DM38, with shower DM50. Doubles DM70, with shower DM95.) A market takes place Tuesdays and Fridays in front of the Kurhaus from 8am to 1:30pm.

Thirty minutes north of Frankfurt (S-Bahn 5), Bad Homburg makes a good base for excursions into the nearby **Taunus** mountains, which run from the Rheingau vineyards on the banks of the Rhine to the Lahn Valley 40km to the northeast. While they're really little more than foothills, the Taunus mountains were sufficiently charming to make tough-guy Otto von Bismarck lachrymose. "I never thought I would ever again feel homesick for Frankfurt am Main," wrote the Iron Chancellor, "but when the last Taunus peak that can be seen from our windows faded from view, I became downright wistful." The highest mountain in the region is **Grosser Feldberg,** an 880m peak with a tower at its summit that affords a panoramic view of the surrounding area. Two buses (#59 and 42) run daily from Bad Homburg to the mountain. There's a **Jugendherberge (HI),** Limestr. 14 (tel. (06082) 24 40), in the nearby village of Oberreinfenberg. (Reception open 5:30-11:30pm. Curfew 11:30pm. DM17.50, over 26 DM20.50.) The largest town in the Taunus is **Königstein im Taunus** (accessible by train from Frankfurt or Wiesbaden), famous for the crumbling ramparts of its **Festungsruine** (fortress ruins).

■■■ DARMSTADT

In 1830, when Grand Duke Lewis was caught by the passion for urban renewal; a new visitor incredulously remarked that Darmstadt "is difficult to recognize, it has become so beautiful and grand, everywhere new buildings, new streets and new squares." This center of art and literature was reduced to rubble in 1944, but the drab, postwar architecture only partially obscures a variety of worthwhile sights.

At the turn of the century, the Grand Duke Ernst Ludwig founded the **Mathildenhöhe,** an artists' colony on a hill in Darmstadt, about 800m east of the city center. The Duke had fallen in love with *Jugendstil* (art nouveau) forms during his travels, and paid for the lavish complex to advertise the style, and show how the Jugendstil could transform the urban landscape. Now, the houses that once housed the colony's artists are inhabited by a variety of institutes and organizations, as well as a smattering of artists. The **Hochzeitsturm,** a 48m tower built in 1908, boasts an excellent view from the top (open daily 10am-6pm; elevator DM1.50).

To reach Mathildenhöhe, walk east along Erich-Ollenhauer-Promenade, or take Bus D from either the *Hauptbahnhof* or Luisenplatz to the "Grosser Woog" stop and head north on Beckenstr. (open Wed.-Sun. 10am-5pm; admission DM5, students DM2). At the east end of the district stands the **Russische Kapelle,** imported stone by stone from Russia at the behest of Czar Nicholas II upon his marriage to Darmstadt's Princess Alexandra. Eastern Orthodox services are still celebrated under the church's two gilded domes (open daily in summer 9:30am-6:30pm; admission DM1, DM0.80 for students). Also on the Mathildenhöhe are two art museums: the **Austellungsgebäude,** which houses rotating exhibits; and the **Museum der Kunstkolonie,** with its collection of *Jugendstil* works. **Rosenhöhe** park contains the tombs of the ducal family and a rose garden four minutes east of Mathildenhöhe.

Two squares anchor the rest of downtown Darmstadt. In the center of **Luisenplatz** stands a 39m high monument to Grand Duke Ludwig I; **Ernst-Ludwig Platz** lies one block to the east. The Duke actually lived here in, of course, a **Schloß.** Rebuilt after World War II, the Schloß houses a museum detailing the history of the ruling class of Hesse. Luisenplatz and Ernst-Ludwig Platz border the east end of Rheinstr. and can be reached by taking Bus D (DM2) from the main train station. (Museum open Mon.-Thurs. 10am-1pm and 2-5pm, Sat.-Sun. 10am-1pm. Admission DM2.50.) Two of Darmstadt's main attractions are momentarily closed. The **Porzellansammlung** (Porcelain Collection) is fixing a collapsed ceiling until 1996, and the **Wella Museum** (of hairdressing) is spraying together some collapsed dos.

The **tourist office** is in front of the main train station (tel. (06151) 13 27 82). They provide good city maps and hotel guides, and find rooms (open Mon.-Fri. 9am-5pm, Sat. 9am-noon). The **post office,** 64293 Darmstadt, across the street from the tourist office, **exchanges currency** and sells traveler's checks (open Mon.-Fri. 7am-8pm, Sat. 7am-6pm, Sun. 9am-12:30pm). The **telephone city code** is 06151. **S-Bahn** and **bus** tickets start at DM1.60 (24-hr. ticket DM6; 7-day ticket DM13, students DM10). Darmstadt is accessible from Frankfurt by frequent trains (25min.) or S-Bahn 12.

The **Jugendherberge (HI),** Landgraf-Georg-Str. 119 (tel. (06151) 452 93), is conveniently located next to the swimming pool and artificial lake at Grosser Woog. (Bus D: Grosser Woog. Reception open until 10pm. Curfew 1am. Members only. DM17.50, over 26 DM29.) **Zentral Hotel,** Schuchardstr. 6 (tel. 264 11), is behind the *Neues Rathaus* at Luisenplatz. Clean, with nicely renovated rooms. (Singles DM55, with shower DM90. Doubles DM90, with shower DM120-140. Breakfast included.) The University cafeteria, **Studentenwerk Stadtmensa,** Alexanderstr. 4 , is the most economical food option. (Open Mon.-Thurs. 9am-5pm, Fri. 9am-3:40pm. Kitchen open 11:45am-2pm.) Also check the square in front of the *Schloß* for the open-air **produce market** (Wed. and Sat. morning).

■■■ THE LAHN VALLEY

Although its subdued natural beauty pales in comparison to the towering majesty of the Rhine Gorge, the Lahn Valley has a deep wooded landscape and a few undertouristed villages. Rail service runs frequently between Koblenz and Wetzlar at the eastern extremity of the valley; trains also run between Frankfurt and Limburg.

LIMBURG

Limburg an der Lahn is remembered primarily as the manufacturer of a smelly cheese, but the town downplays that gastronomic distinction. The **St. Georg-Dom,** a strangely orange-and-white painted edifice, easily ranks as one of the most attractive cathedrals in Germany. Up on a rocky embankment above the Lahn River, this architectural commingling of Romanesque and Gothic styles contains a series of galleries and carefully restored frescoes. The **Diözesanmuseum,** Domstr. 12, has a small but occasionally dazzling collection of medieval religious artifacts that includes the **Staurothek,** a Byzantine reliquary cross that a local knight spirited away from Constantinople during the Crusades (open mid-March to mid-Nov. Tues.-Sat. 10am-1pm and 2-5pm, Sun. 11am-5pm; admission DM2, students DM1).

Limburg's **Altstadt,** a mass of medieval, half-timbered houses, has weathered the centuries extraordinarily well. Limburg's **tourist office** *(Verkehrsamt),* Hospitalstr. 2 (tel. (06431) 61 66), helps track down rooms (open Mon.-Fri. 9am-12:30pm and 2-6pm; Nov.-March Mon.-Thurs. 8am-12:30pm and 2-5pm, Fri. 8am-1pm). The **Jugendherberge (HI),** auf dem Guckucksberg (tel. (06431) 414 93), offers spartan lodgings after a marathon walk (30min.); from behind the train station, take the pedestrian underpass to Im Schlenkert, turn left and walk to Frankfurter Str., turn right and follow the road to Am Hammerberg; or bus #3 (from the tourist office) to Am Hammerberg. (Reception open 5-11:30pm. Curfew 11:30pm. DM18.50, over 26 DM23.50.) There's a **Campingplatz** (tel. (06431) 226 10) on the far side of the Lahn. Take the Alte Lahnbrücke across the river and turn right, or bus #4 (from train station) to Alte Lahnbrücke (open May to mid-Oct; DM6 per person, DM5 per tent).

RUNKEL AND WEILBURG

Traveling up the valley (10km), you cross the Lahn at the impossibly picturesque 15th-century village of **Runkel,** which is dominated by the towering stone **Schloß Schadeck.** Continuing 15km later, you arrive at **Weilburg,** a lovely little Baroque town that grew up around the huge complex of the **Schloß,** a former residence of the Counts of Nassau (open 10am-noon and 1-4pm; Nov.-Feb. 10am-noon and 1-3pm). Inside the *Rathaus* is the **tourist office,** Mauerstr. 8 (tel. (06471) 314 24). The **Jugendherberge (HI),** Am Steinbühl (tel. (06471) 71 16), sits on the edge of the woods 2km outside of town. Take the Odersbach bus (from the station) to Kranken-haus Odersbach, then walk 10 minutes up the path. (Reception open 7:30am-1:30pm and 5-7pm. Curfew 10pm. DM16.50, over 26 DM19.)

WETZLAR

From Weilburg, it's another 20km to Wetzlar, the former seat of an imperial legal court of the Holy Roman Empire and a place of pilgrimage for Goethe aficionados. In 1772, the man who would one day be known as Germany's Shakespeare came to Wetzlar as a legal clerk and had his heart stomped on by a young woman named Charlotte Buff, who was engaged to a local diplomat and friend of Goethe's named Kestner. Goethe's tale of woe and that of a young man in the area who, also a victim of an unhappy love, killed himself, were assimilated in the enormously popular *Sorrows of Young Werther,* and the real Lotte Buff soon dissolved into literary legend. One (now classic) revisionist view of old Lotte is Thomas Mann's novel, *Lotte in Weimar.* A large number of first editions of *Werther* are enshrined today in the **Lottehaus,** a museum located inside the house where Lotte lived with her parents (open Tues.-Sat. 10am-1pm and 2-5pm, Sun. 10am-1pm). Wetzlar's **tourist office** *(Verkehrsamt)* is at Domplatz 8 (tel. (06441) 40 53 38; open Mon.-Fri. 8am-noon and 2-4:30pm, Sat. 9:30-11:30am). To reach the **Jugendgästehaus (HI),** Richard-Schirmann-Str. 3 (tel. (06441) 710 68), walk from the station (35min.), or save yourself the trouble by taking bus #12 or 13 (direction "Krankenhaus") to Sturzkopf. (Reception open 8am-4pm and 6-10pm. Curfew midnight. DM21, over 26 DM25.50. Breakfast included. Full board available. Definitely call ahead.)

■■■ MARBURG

The brothers Grimm spun their tales in these rolling hills; from a distance Marburg an der Lahn seems more of their world than ours. The world's first Protestant university was endowed here in 1527 and is still the heart of the town. Its alumni list reads like a syllabus for an intellectual history course: Martin Heidegger, Boris Pasternak, T.S. Eliot, Richard Bunsen (of burner fame), and José Ortega y Gasset are but a few. The 15,000 students who follow their example pore over books, conversation, and each other on the banks of the Lahn River. On the first Sunday in July, costumed citizens parade onto the Markt for the rowdy **Frühschoppen festival**. Drinking officially begins at 11am when the brass rooster on top of the 1851 **Rathaus** flaps its wings. Unofficially the Alt Marburger Pils is tapped around 10am, and ribald old Marburger *Trinklieder* (drinking ballads) are sung throughout. It was on this square in 1248 that St. Elisabeth's daughter Sophie lifted her four-year-old son up to the market crowd and declared him heir to the newly founded Landgrave of Hesse.

ORIENTATION AND PRACTICAL INFORMATION

Built around a bend in the river, Marburg is served by frequent **trains** from Frankfurt (1hr.) and Kassel (1hr.); check travel agents and, occasionally, the Bundesbahn information office for greatly discounted weekend fares to these hubs.

Tourist Office (tel. 20 12 49 or 20 12 62), to the right of the station, finds rooms (from DM35) free of charge. List of rooms also posted outside the office; call (06421) 194 14 for 24-hr. hotel information. Open Mon.-Fri. 8am-12:30pm and 2-5pm, Sat. 9:30am-noon; Nov.-March Mon.-Fri. 8am-12:30pm and 2-5pm.
Post Office: To reach the postmodern *Hauptpostamt* (main **post office**), turn right on Neue Kasseler Str. from the train station and continue for 5min.
Telephone city code: 06421.
Laundromat: Either branch of computerized, ecoconscious **Wasch Center laundromat,** one at the corner of Gutenberg and Jägerstr., the other at Bahnhofstr. 22, will do, but the former location is far more inviting; sip a beer in the adjacent **Bistro Waschbrett** during the rinse cycle. Bahnhofstr. branch open Mon.-Sat. 8am-10pm. Gutenbergstr. branch open Mon.-Sat. 8am-10pm, Sun. 5-10pm. Wash DM6, dry DM1 for 15min. Bistro open Mon.-Fri. 9am-1am, Sat. 9am-midnight, Sun. 5pm-midnight.

ACCOMMODATIONS

Jugendherberge (HI), Jahnstr. 1 (tel. (06421) 234 61). Bus #1-6, 16, or S: Rudolfplatz, cross the river, turn immediately right onto Trojedamm, and follow the riverside road until you turn left onto Jahnstr. (10min.); to find Rudolphsplatz on foot, head up Bahnhofstr., left on Elisabethstr., which becomes Pilgrimstein, and walk for 10min. The *Jugendherberge* catches the nighttime music of the *Altstadt* from across the Lahn. Reception officially open 3:30-11:30pm but house keys can be checked out by leaving an ID or a DM50 deposit. No lockout. DM 20.50, over 26 DM24. Breakfast buffet included. Call ahead.
Tusculum-Gästehaus, Gutenbergerstr. 25 (tel. (06421) 227 78). This well-kept hotel was renovated to embody the spirit and look of Spanish painter Joan Miro. To arrive, turn right where Am Grün becomes Frankfurter-Str. and walk to the end of Jägerstr. Each room explores (exploits?) a different color. Singles DM50-60, with shower DM80-90. Doubles with shower DM100-125. Breakfast included.
Camping Lahnaue (tel. (06421) 213 31) is on the Lahn River; take bus #1 toward Sommerbad to "Mensa" and walk 10min. DM5 per person, DM4 per tent.

FOOD

Marburg's food life is tied up with academic life; students give the many cafés in the *Altstadt* their flavor. See Nightlife, below, for cafés with less respect for food than for drinks. The **Markt** is crowded with vendors every Saturday, 8am-1pm. *Wurst* stands, along with junk and gems, can be found past the Wettergasse pedestrian zone at the Steinweg **flea market,** held on the first Saturday of every month. A **Plus** Supermarket can be found on Bahnhofstr.

Café Barfuß, Barfüßerstr. 33, fills up at night, with Jever on tap (DM3), Guinness in bottles, and "American coffee" (i.e. free refills) at breakfast. Quirky antiques dangle from the ceiling. Meals from DM12. Open daily 10am-1am.

Café Vetter, Reitgasse 4, is a big traditional café, very proud of its terrace over-looking Pilgrimstein. *Kaffe und Kuchen* (coffee and cake), Germany's 4pm sugar break, DM6.20. Open Mon. and Wed.-Sat. 8:30am-6:30pm, Sun. 9:30am-6:30pm.

Brasserie, Reitgasse 8 (from Rudolphsplatz go down Untergasse and take the first right). This classy establishment serves filling pasta and baguette meals for under DM10. Vegetarian options and outdoor seating; eight beers on tap. Hot meals 10am-midnight. Open until 1am.

University Mensa cafeteria is in the *Studentenwerk* building; from Rudolphsplatz, cross the Lahn and turn left on Lingelgasse, then follow the students converging to the token booth. The food line moves with ruthless efficiency and speed; think fast. Meals cost DM2.40-6.80 for students, DM4.40-8.80 for guests; snacks down-stairs in the "Buffeteria" are less expensive. Open during the semester, October 16-July 14 Mon.-Thurs. 11:30am-2:15pm and 6-8:15pm, Fri. 11:30am-2pm and 6-8:15pm, Sat. 11:30am-1:30pm; when school is out, Mon.-Fri. noon-2pm and 6-7:45pm, Sat. noon-1:30pm. Buffeteria open during school Mon.-Fri. 8:15am-8pm, when school is out, Mon.-Fri. 8:15am-7:30pm.

SIGHTS

Jakob Grimm ordered visitors to Marburg to "move your legs and walk the stairs up and down;" the hillside **Oberstadt** (similar to the *Altstadt* in other towns) is a maze of narrow staircases and alleys. **Enge Gasse,** an old sewer, is now as suitably scenic and half-timbered as the rest. Climb more than 250 steps or take bus #16 from Rudolfsplatz (every 45min.) to the exalted **Landgrafenschloß,** former haunt of the infamous Teutonic knights. Count Philip brought rival Protestants Martin Luther and Ulricht Zwingli to his court in 1529 in an attempt to convince them to kiss and make up, but failed to bring about a reconciliation. Towering over Marburg, the castle is illuminated until 11pm. The castle houses the university's **Museum für Kulturge-schichte** (Cultural Museum), with exhibits of Hessian history and religious art (open Tues.-Sun. 10am-6pm; admission DM3, students DM2). Occasional performances are given in the open-air theater of the **Schloßpark,** the gardens stretching to the west of the fortress; check for schedules at the tourist office.

Walk past a strikingly ugly boar's head and down the 140 steps of Ludwig-Bickell-Treppe to the 13th-century **Marienkirche** with its amber stained glass and elaborate organ (open daily 9am-6pm; 1-hour organ concert Sat. at 6:30pm). Save some eccle-siastical awe for the oldest Gothic church in Germany (c. 1285), the **Elisabeth-kirche,** named for the town's patron, a widowed child-bride—engaged at 4, married at 14—who took refuge in Marburg, founded a hospital, and snagged sainthood four years after she died. The **reliquary** for her bones is so overdone, it's glorious (in the *Kunstschätze*). (Church open Mon.-Sat. 9am-6pm, Sun. 11:15am-6pm. Tours Mon.-Fri. at 3pm, Sun 11am and 3pm; DM1. Reliquary admission DM2, students DM1.) To get there, cross the bridge opposite the train station and take a left at Elisabethstr. The church kicks off the free guided tour of the town (April-Oct. Sat. at 3pm).

The main university building in use today was built in 1871, but the original **Alte Universität** on Rudolfsplatz was built over the rubble of a monastery, conveniently vacated when Reformation-minded Marburgers ejected the resident monks. The houses decked with technicolor flags are university fraternities, now home to aristo-cratic pretensions and some fine collections of old fencing equipment. Riled by a nascent sense of nationalism, these Prussian frat boys fought regular pseudo-duels to defend their pieces of sidewalk well into the 19th century. The idea of the duels was to get sliced in the face, leaving a scar that was considered a badge of aristocratic "honor." Student members still strut around town in dubious, overdone suits and colorful ribbons to match their house colors (and their arrogance). Modern *verbin-dungen* (lifetime networking fraternities) are formed around sports, religion, and the politically conservative *burschenshaften* (student associations).

NIGHTLIFE AND ENTERTAINMENT

Live music, concert, theater, and movie options abound and can be found listed in the weekly *Marburger Express*, but be sure to ask at the tourist office about a bi-monthly program of live music and theater in the Schloßpark. The nightly choice for most students, however, is sitting for hours in a *kneipe* (café) drinking, smoking, and chatting.

Pegasus, Schloßtreppe 2. At the intersection of Markt and Ritterstr., and in bad weather people cram indoors. A big tree shelters the popular outdoor Biergarten. No food, but lots of drinks. Open Mon.-Fri. 2pm-1am, Sat.-Sun. noon-1am.

Bolschoi Café, Ketzerbach-Str., is a bit of a trip, in more ways than one; from Rudolphsplatz walk up Pilgrimstein and turn left onto Ketzerbach-Str. It's up a block on the left side of the street. Then prepare for the *real* left...this capsule of communist kitsch warms the cold war with red candles, red walls, a red foil ceiling, and 19 types of domestic and imported vodka (DM2.30 - DM4.80). Lenin's bust is stenciled on the wall. *Rollmops*, raw pickled herring, high in fat and salt, may help your tolerance. Open Sun.-Tues. 10pm-1am, Wed.-Sat. 10pm-2am.

Slot, Steinweg 9. At Rudolphsplatz, find Untergasse and wrap around Universitäts Kirche to take a right onto Reitgasse, which first becomes Wetterg., then Neustadt, then Steinweg. On your right the small crowded disco gets a crowd jumping to a different beat every night. Open Sun.-Thurs. 8pm-2am, Fri.-Sat. 8pm-3am; cover DM3.

■■■ FULDA

In the grim old days, Fulda had the dubious distinction of being the most likely point of a Warsaw Pact invasion (the "Fulda Gap"). Today Fulda is simply a graceful Baroque city and former university town that offers an unusual number of large parks and public gardens for a place of its size. Its compact Baroque quarter was built by some of Germany's most famous 18th-century architects at the behest of the local Prince-Abbots, who had a monopoly on both secular and spiritual authority for nearly 700 years. The extravagant **Schloß** was built between 1700 and 1737 as the residence for the Prince-Abbots. Inside, the white **Kaisersaal** displays the portraits of 16 Habsburg emperors. To reach the palace from the main train station, head down Bahnhofstr. and turn right onto Friedrichstr. just after the Karstadt. (Open Sat.-Thurs. 10am-6pm, Fri. 2-6pm. Admission DM3, students DM1.50.) Behind the palace is a lush **park** edged with terraces and home to the 18th-century **Orangerie;** its stately rooms demonstrate the restrained side of Baroque.

Across the Pauluspromenade stands the magnificent 18th-century **Dom** (cathedral), built to house the tomb of St. Boniface, an 8th-century English monk who came to Germany to spread the gospel and founded the abbey in Fulda. A low-relief funeral monument supposedly depicts St. Boniface surrounded by angels raising his coffin lid on Judgement Day, though it actually looks like the cherubs are trying to stuff him back in. (Open Mon.-Fri. 10am-6pm, Sat. 10am-3pm, Sun. 3-6pm; Nov.-March Mon.-Fri. 10am-5pm, Sat. 10am-3pm, Sun. 3-5pm. Free.) The **Dommuseum,** accessible through the crypt, contains the dagger with which St. Boniface was martyred and the poor man's head. (Open Mon.-Fri. 10am-5pm, Sat. 10am-2pm, Sun. 12:30-5:30pm; Nov.-March Mon.-Fri. 10am-12:30pm and 1:30-4pm, Sat. 10am-2pm, Sun. 12:30-4pm. Admission DM3, students DM1.50. Closed Jan.)

The **Feuerwehr-Museum (Fire Department Museum),** St. Laurentius-Str., across the Fulda River from downtown, displays extinguishers and vehicles that date from the 14th century. Locals take it too seriously. (Open Tues.-Wed. and Fri.-Sun. 10am-5pm, Thurs. 2-9pm. Admission DM3, students and seniors DM2.)

For free maps of Fulda and the nearby hiking area of the **Rhön,** contact the **tourist office** (tel. (0661) 10 23 45, fax 10 27 75), entrance D2 of the *Schloß.* (open Mon.-Fri. 8:30am-noon and 2-4:30pm, Sat. 9:30am-noon.) Rent **bikes** (tel. (0661) 183 77) at the train station (DM8-10 per day). Due to its erstwhile military importance, Fulda has unusually good rail connections for a city its size. However, many departing trains are ICE, superfast but expensive. **Trains** to Hamburg (hourly), Nuremburg (hourly), and Frankfurt (2-3 per hour). To reach Fulda's **Jugendherberge (HI)**, Schirmannstr. 31 (tel. (0661) 733 89, fax 748 11), take bus #18 (direction "Niederrode" from the central bus station across from the *Schloß* to the "Stadion" stop (DM1.30), then walk five minutes to the other side of the stadium. The rooms are clean and simple. (DM19; over 26 DM23. Breakfast included.) Behind the *Dom*, the **Gasthof "Zum Kronhof,"** Am Kronhof 2 (tel. (0661) 741 47), proffers pleasant quarters in an antique house. (Singles DM33. Doubles DM65. Breakfast included.)

■■■ KASSEL

Kassel has been wrapped up in industry ever since 1706, when an exiled French tinkerer played parlor tricks for the Landgrave's court with one of the earliest steam engines; even the Grimm brothers shut themselves up to work when they were here. But at the edge of town, the lavish Wilhelmshöhe park-and-castles complex is a monument to 18th-century fancy (and a real crowd-pleaser). It is fitting that, since 1955, a city rebuilt almost from the ground after World War II has hosted the world's premier exhibit of (post-) modern art. Held every five years, Kassel's documenta regularly transforms the art world, challenges the 20th-century imagination, and leaves the city a still-emerging, and very visible, artistic legacy.

PRACTICAL INFORMATION AND ORIENTATION

Kassel is a wildly spread-out city, a notorious post-war-housing-shortage-building-boom nightmare. Somehow the boom never stopped. Transportation powers-that-be chose Kassel as an InterCity Express connection and rebuilt the outlying **Bahnhof Wilhelmshöhe-Kassel** to streamlined postmodern specs. Wilhelmshöhe is the point of entry to Kassel's ancient castles and immense parklands on the west side; the older **Hauptbahnhof** is the gateway to the tightly packed and entirely modernized *Altstadt*. Frequent trains and the RKH and #11 buses shuttle between stations; you can catch most other bus and streetcar lines at either "Rathaus" or "Am Stern." IC, ICE, and most IR trains only stop at Wilhelmshöhe. **Treppenstraße**, on the east side of town, was Germany's first pedestrian zone, but the **Markt** at Herculestr. and Goethestr. attracts hipper crowds. Kassel is in northern Hesse on the banks of the Fulda River, accessible by trains from Hanover (1hr.) and Frankfurt (1-1/2 to 2hr.).

Tourist Office: In the Wilhelmshöhe *Bahnhof* (tel. 340 54), and as modern as the rest of the station. Doles out slick catalogs and maps and offers a DM5 room-finding service. An automat outside vends maps and hotel lists in the off-hours (DM1). Open Mon.-Fri. 9am-6pm, Sat. 9am-1pm. The **Arbeitsgemeinschaft "Deutsche Märchenstraße"** (German Fairy-Tale Road), Obere Königstr. 8 (tel. 787 21 30), covers the Brothers-Grimm picturesque towns in the surrounding region.

Post Office: Hauptpostamt, Untere Königsstr., 34117 Kassel, near Hollandischer Platz and the University. Open Mon.-Fri. 8am-6pm, Sat. 8am-noon.

Telephones: City Code: 0561.

Public Transportation: KVG-Info, Königsplatz 36b, houses the information offices of the local public transportation conglomerate. Pick up a free map to make sense of the extensive streetcar and bus system. Open Mon.-Fri. 8am-6pm, Sat. 8am-1pm. Day and weekend tickets for streetcar and buses DM6.50, family card DM8.50; single fares DM1.90-2.60 depending on distance, under 11 DM1.40.

Mitfahrzentrale: 3 ride-share offices:: **Mitfahrzentrale des Westens,** Friedrich-Ebert-Str. 107 at Querallee (tel. 77 33 05), open Mon.-Fri. 9am-1pm and 2-6pm, Sat. 10am-2pm, Sun. 11am-1pm. **Sun-Drive,** Frankfurterstr. 197 (tel. 24 03 12), open daily 9am-7pm. **Mitfahrladen** at **Ikarus-Reisebüro,** Wilhelmshöher Allee 106 (tel. 10 33 71) open Mon.-Fri. 10am-2pm and 2:30-6pm, Sat. 10am-1pm.

Car Rental: Avis, 77 Leipziger Str. (tel. 57 10 06), on the other side of the Fulda.

Bike Rental: At **Edelman-Fahrräder,** Goethestr. 37-39 (tel. 177 69). City bikes DM29 per day, mountain bikes DM39 per day.
Ferries: Ferries run from the Rondell-Altmarkt dock; 2 firms are especially prominent. **Personenschiffahrt Söllner** (tel. 77 46 70) offers Fulda Valley tours in 3hr. flat (mid-June to Aug. daily 2pm; May to mid-June and Sept. Sat.-Sun. and Wed. 2pm. Round-trip DM16, under 14 DM8). Sail up to the junction of the Fulda and Werra rivers. Departures May to mid-Sept. Sun. and Wed. 9:30am; round-trip DM30, one-way DM20; children half-price.
English Bookstore: Buchladung Vaternahm, Königsstr. opposite the *Rathaus.* Open Mon.-Fri. 9am-6:30pm, Sat. 9am-2pm. **Buchladung Lometsch,** Kölnischestr. 5. Open Mon. 10am-6pm, Tues.-Fri. 9am-6pm, Sat. 9am-1pm.
Laundromat: Bio-Wasch Center, at Friedrich-Ebert-Str. 83 near the hostel, is ecologically friendly and computerized. Open Mon.-Sat. 5am-midnight. Wash DM6, dry DM1 per 15min.
Rape Crisis Hotline: tel. (0561) 77 22 44.
Fire/Ambulance: tel. 112, **Police:** tel. 110.

ACCOMMODATIONS

Hotels in Kassel are actively seeking conventions and the ICE-riding business crowd. One option for humbler guests is the **Mitzwohnzentrale,** Elfbuchenstr. 5 (tel. 77 99 97), an office which matches apartment needers with apartment holders, for stays ranging from several days to several months. (Open Mon.-Thurs. 9am-2pm and 3-6pm, Fri. 9am-2pm, Sat. 9am-1pm.)

Jugendherberge, Schenkendorfstr. 18 (tel. 77 64 55), on Tannenwälder Park. S-Bahn 1, 3, or 6 (from Kassel-Wilhelmshöhe): Kirchweg, change around the corner for bus #27: Jugendherberge. From the *Hauptbahnhof* it's faster to walk than hop streetcars: go straight through the *Südausgang* (South Exit), turn right on Kölnische Str., and on to Schenkendorf (25-30min.); or bus #10, 42, or the RKH line: Achenbachstr., turn around and walk down Kölnische Str. one block to Schenkendorfstr. This pristine, friendly hostel beats many hotels. Reception open 7am-midnight. No Lockout. Curfew 1am; no curfew when a night guard is on duty. DM21, over 26 DM24.50. Satisfying breakfast buffet (included) pleases carnivores and herbivores alike. Coffee and soft drink bar open until midnight.
Hotel-Restaurant Palmenbad, Kurhausstr. 27 (tel. 326 91). Streetcar #3 or 4: Brabanter Str., turn around, and walk down Kurhausstr.; or, walk from Bahnhof Wilhelmshöhe up Wilhelmshöher Allee (towards Herkules), turn left on Baunsbergstr., and right on Kurhausstr. Clean, fairly pleasant, near the Wilhelmshöhe monuments. Singles DM40. Doubles DM80-98. Breakfast included.
Hotel-Restaurant Lenz, Frankfurter Str. 176, (tel. 433 73), is too far to walk from either main station, but the Bahnhof Niederzwehren station and bus stop right around the corner is serviced by DB trains or bus #24 (from Wilhelmshöhe) and streetcar #7 or buses #5 and 5250 (from the *Hauptbahnhof).* Rooms are small but clean, with huge bathrooms. Reception open Mon.-Sat. 7am-1am. Singles DM40, with shower DM80. Doubles DM80, with shower and toilet DM130.
Hotel zum Katzensprung, Kurt-Walters-Str. 27 (tel. 87 49 27). Streetcar #1 or 5: Hollandische Platz, and head right. Cozy rooms, near the university, and over a lively restaurant. No private baths. Singles DM55. Doubles DM100.Call ahead.
Camping: Kurhessen-Kassel, Giepenallee 7 (tel. 224 33), has a stunning spot right on the Fulda and unbelievably close to the Island of Flowers, in the Karlsaue park. Reception open March-Oct. daily 7am-noon and 3-10pm. DM5 per person, under 15 DM3, DM5 per car, DM4 per tent.

FOOD

Like everything else in Kassel, food gems are scattered wildly. Friedrich-Ebert-Str. and the upper part of Wilhelmshöher Allee have supermarkets and bargain cafés sprinkled among department stores and fashion boutiques. To go easy on your wallet, shop in the **Markethalle,** off of Steinweg on Wildemangasse (open Mon.-Fri. 7am-6pm, Sat. 7am-2pm). The **City Center,** to the left of Kassel-Wilhelmshöhe station, is a haven for basic foodstuffs, with two bakeries, an **Okay** supermarket (open Mon.-Fri. 9am-6:30m, Sat. 8:30am-2pm), and **Fraiche,** a pleasant restaurant with tables in the sun, a breakfast bar, and vegetarian buffet (open Mon.-Wed. and Fri. 8:30am-6:30pm, Thurs. 8:30am-8:30pm, Sat. 8:30am-2pm).

Student Mensa, Arnold-Bode-Str. on university grounds north of the *Altstadt;* look for the sign—it's the only way to tell this brick building from the 50-odd others. Students DM2.60-3.80, others tack on DM2. Lunch Mon.-Fri. noon-2pm. The **Moritz-Terasse** shop outside serves snack treats. **Studentwerks-Pavillon,** Diagonale 13 inside the university bounds; this campus restaurant has a more flexible ID policy than the *Mensa.* Wholesome meals in a sunny rotunda, DM4.40 for students, DM5.40 for guests. Open Mon.-Fri. 8am-10pm, hot food 5-9pm.

Avocado, Schönfelderstr. 3 (tel. 253 01), explores the creative limits of vegetarian food. Try the delectable dips and dressings. Full meals DM12 and up. Open Tues.-Sat. noon-2pm and 7pm-midnight; Tues. night is women only.

Restaurant and Imbiß Holomed Vollwertkost, Kurfürstenstr. 10, right by the *Hauptbahnhof.* The place to grab some organic greens between trains. Meals hover at DM8.50, and the extensive salad bar costs only DM1.89 per 100g. Open Mon.-Fri. 11am-6pm, Sat. 11am-2pm.

Schalander Bräu, on the corner of Mauerstr. and Gießbergstr., brews its own beer behind the bar; you can drink it there for DM3.60-11, depending on size (0.3-1L), or take it home in 2L flasks or 10 and 30L kegs (DM10-135). Open Mon.-Fri. 11am-1am, Sat. 5pm-2am, Sun. 5pm-1am.

SIGHTS

Kassel's sights fall into three areas: those around Wilhelmshöhe; those elsewhere in Kassel; and the collections of cultural institutions associated with the documenta.

Wilhelmshöhe

Wilhelmshöhe is a hillside park with one giant Greek hero, two castles, three museums, and five waterfalls, punctuated with rock gardens, mountain streams, and innumerable hiking trails. The whole park experience—a cross between the halls of Montezuma and a Baroque theme park—takes up half a day in itself; approach it with humor or cynicism if that is your wont (love of castles is also acceptable), but do approach. Bring a picnic, bring your lover and a bottle of wine. Streetcars #1 and 4 stop at the foot of the park near **Schloß Wilhelmshöhe,** the mammoth main attraction and former home of the rulers of Kassel. Napoleon III was imprisoned here once after being captured in the Battle of Sedan. The **Schloß Museum,** located in the right wing, records the extravagant royal lifestyle. (Open Tues.-Sun. 10am-5pm; Nov.-Feb. Tues.-Sun. 10am-4pm. Tours of private suites DM2, students DM1, and leave when there are "enough" people.) Before you trek up the hill, take in some artistry at the **Gallery of Old Masters** (tel. 360 11), in the center of the *Schloß.* Ramble through the room of studies, or view the finished works of Dürer, Rubens, Jordaens, Rembrandt, and, Tintoretto. (Open Tues.-Sat. 10am-5pm; studies on the 3rd floor visible Thurs. and Sat. 10am-noon and 2-5pm. Free.)

All paths lead up to the **Herkules,** a massive octagonal amphitheater topped by a figure of the Greek hero himself, clearly visible from almost anywhere in the park. Built between 1701 and 1717, it has become Kassel's emblem; climb the scores of steps to the feet of the statue, past the spectacular steps of the water **Cascades.** The less robust can take streetcar #3 to Druseltal, and then bus #43 to the rear of the monument. (Admission to the interior of the amphitheater DM2, students DM1.) If you arrive at the top of Hercules a bit after 2pm on a Sunday or Wednesday, you'll see the **fountain displays** that start at 2:30pm; they're timed so that a walk down the clearly designated path will land you at the next waterfall as the show begins—if the crowds didn't throng together. Battle the masses or stake out a vantage point early.

The more subtle **Schloß Löwenburg** is an amazing piece of architectural fantasy. It was built in the 18th century with stones deliberately missing in order to achieve

LET'S GO® Travel

1994 CATALOG

We give you the world
at a discount!

•Discount Flights •Eurails •Travel Gear

LET'S PACK IT UP

Let's Go Supreme

Innovative hideaway suspension with parallel stay internal frame turns backpack into carry-on suitcase. Includes lumbar support pad, torso and waist adjustment, leather trim, and detachable daypack. Waterproof Cordura nylon, lifetime guarantee, 4400 cu. in. Navy, Green or Black.

A · · · · · · · · · · · · · **$175**

Let's Go Backpack/Suitcase

Hideaway suspension with internal frame turns backpack into carry-on suitcase. Detachable daypack makes it 3 bags in 1. Waterproof Cordura nylon, lifetime guarantee, 3750 cu. in. Navy, Green or Black.

B · · · · · · · · · · · · · · · **$130**

Let's Go Backcountry

Full size, slim profile expedition pack designed for the serious trekker. New Airflex suspension. X-frame pack with advanced composite tube suspension. Velcro height adjustment, side compression straps. Detachable hood converts into a fanny pack. Waterproof Cordura nylon, lifetime guarantee. Main compartment 6530 cu. in. extends to 7130 cu. in.

C · · · · · · · · · **$210**

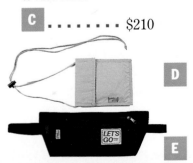

Undercover NeckPouch

Ripstop nylon with soft Cambrelle back. 3 pockets. 6 x 7". Lifetime guarantee. Black or Tan.

D · · · · · · · · · · · · · · **$9.95**

Undercover WaistPouch

Ripstop nylon with soft Cambrelle back. 2 pockets. 12 x 5" with adjustable waistband. Lifetime guarantee. Black or Tan.

E · · · · · · · · · · · · · · **$9.95**

LET'S GO BY TRAIN

Eurail Passes

Convenient way to travel Europe. Save up to 70% over cost of individual tickets.

EURAILPASS

FIRST CLASS

15 days	$498
21 days	$648
1 month	$798
2 months	$1098
3 months	$1398

EURAIL FLEXIPASS

FIRST CLASS

Any 5 days in 2 months	$348
Any 10 days in 2 months	$560
Any 15 days in 2 months	$740

EURAIL SAVERPASS**

FIRST CLASS

15 days	$430
21 days	$550
1 month	$678

**Price per person for 2 or more people travelling together. 3 people required between April 1 - September 3.

EURAIL YOUTHPASS*

SECOND CLASS

15 days	$398
1 month	$578
2 months	$768

*Valid only if passenger is under 26 on first date of travel.

EURAIL YOUTH FLEXIPASS*

SECOND CLASS

Any 5 days in 2 months	$255
Any 10 days in 2 months	$398
Any 15 days in 2 months	$540

*Valid only if passenger is under 26 on first date of travel.

LET'S GO BY PLANE

Discounted Flights

Over 150 destinations including:

LONDON

MADRID

PARIS

ATHENS

ROME

Domestic fares too!
For prices & reservations

EURAIL COUNTRY PASSES

POLAND HUNGARY
AUSTRIA FRANCE
SCANDINAVIA
FINLAND
LUXEMBOURG
GREECE SPAIN
CZECHOSLOVAKIA
GERMANY PORTUGAL
NETHERLANDS
BRITAIN SPAIN

Call for prices, rail n' drive or rail n' fly options. Flexotel passes too!

WE GIVE YOU THE WORLD...
AT A DISCOUNT!

LET'S GO TRAVEL
**53a Church St.
Cambridge, MA 02138**
(617) 495-9649 or 1-800-5-LETS-GO
FAX (617) 496-8015

LET'S GO HOSTELING
1994-95 Youth Hostel Card
Required by most international hostels.
Must be a U.S. resident.

F1 Adult (ages 18-55) $25

F2 Youth (under 18) $10

Sleepsack
Required at all hostels. Washable durable
poly/cotton. 18" pillow pocket. Folds into
pouch size.

G $13.95

1993-94 Youth Hostel Guide (IYHG)
Essential information about 4000 hostels in
Europe and the Mediterranean.

H $10.95

LET'S GET STARTED
Please print or type. Incomplete applications will be returned

Last Name   First Name   Date of Birth

Street   *We do not ship to P.O. Boxes. U.S. addresses only.*

City   State   Zip Code

Phone   Date Trip Begins

Item Code	Description, Size & Color	Quantity	Unit Price	Total Price

Shipping & Handling		
Shipping & Handling	Total Merchandise Price	
If order totals: . . . . . . Add	Shipping & Handling (See box at left)	
Up to $30.00. . . . . . $4.00	For Rush Handling Add $10 for continental U.S., $12 for AK & HI	
30.01-100.00. . . . . . $6.00	MA Residents (Add 5% sales tax on gear & books)	
Over 100.00 . . . . . . $7.00	**Total**	

Mastercard/Visa Order

Cardholder name_____

Card number_____

Expiration date_____

Allow 2-3 weeks for delivery. Ru'
orders delivered within one wee'
our receipt.

Enclose check or money order
payable to:
Harvard Student Agencies, Inc.
53a Church St. Cambridge, MA

Prices subject to change without notice

the effect of a crumbling medieval castle; it works, oddly enough. Inside a **Museum of Chivalry** (tel. 342 86) reflects the local knight-life. (Open Tues.-Sun. 10am-5pm; Nov.-Feb. 10am-4pm. Required tours on the hour, except noon. Admission DM2, children DM1.) For a more private walk through the playground of Hessian nobility, avoid fountain days or walk the park's longer trails which lead to the edge of the nearby Waldeck Forest. Ask at the tourist office for more information.

Elsewhere in Kassel

The English Garden of **Karlsaue Park** sprawls along the Fulda. At its north end, the bright yellow **Orangerie** manor house (built 1701) is home to the **Museum of Technological History,** crammed full of mechanical and optical marvels (open Tues.-Sun. 10am-5pm; free). Lavishly illustrated, the **Brüder Grimm Museum** is in Palais Bellevue, Schöne Aussicht, near the Orangerie. Exhibits include the brothers' handwritten copy of *Kinder- und Haus-Märchen.* (Open daily 10am-5pm. Free.) But nothing quite matches the **Deutsches Tapeten Museum** (German Wallpaper Museum) in the same building (tel. (0561) 77 57 12). No joke, no sarcasm, this place is *great;* it's an unabashed celebration of everything that's ever covered a wall. Surprises include 16th-century embossed leather and gold Spanish hangings, a rare depiction of the battle of Austerlitz, a six-color wallpaper printer, and a letter from Goethe to Schiller mentioning an order of wallpaper. Classic figures from Virginia Woolf to Rosa Luxemburg, photographed beside "their" wallpaper, populate the museum along with world wallpaper masters. Not surprisingly, this is the only museum of its kind in the world (open Tues.-Fri. 10am-5pm, Sat.-Sun. 10am-1pm; free).

documenta Museums

Every five years, Kassel gets to walk in the sun, dominating the art world for a summer with the **documenta,** an international art assembly of the most modern moderns. The next one isn't until 1997, but a good part remains at the **documenta-Archiv,** in the nearby **Gerhard-Hauptmann Schule** (open Mon.-Fri. 10am-2pm). Also during off years, the **Museum Fredericanum,** on Friedrichsplatz, hosts visiting modern exhibits (open Tues.-Sun. 10am-5pm; admission DM5, students DM3). Other remnants of past documenta years include the immense **Spitzhacke** (ice pick) on the banks of the Fulda and the **Rahmenbau** (frame construction) next to the Staatstheater. The **Neue Galerie,** Schöne Aussicht 1 (tel. 152 66), when not exhibiting documenta work, houses other modern European art and a tiny collection of 19th-century canvases (open Tues.-Sun. 10am-5pm; free). The **Neue documenta-Halle,** adjacent to the Staatstheater, was completed for use during the last documenta in 1992; plans for future use are as yet uncertain.

NIGHTLIFE

Kassel's most accessible nightlife is concentrated on one main drag downtown. **Irish Pup,** the German chain that circulates live bands, and **Prigogine,** a colorful disco, share a corner at Bürgermeister-Brünner-Str. and Friedrich-Ebert-Str. Around the bend, Friedrich-Ebert-Str. becomes Fünffenstr. and at the intersection with Wilhelmshöher Allee, the **New York** offers darker rhythms and a cool café. The **Hypodrom,** under the intersecting streets, does the disco and concert scene (open Mon.-Sat.). All discos change their music selection on a daily basis. If your particular scene isn't represented, you can bop into **Hyposports,** upstairs from the Hypodrom, and play pool (DM10 per hour) or snooker (DM14 per hour; open Sun.-Thurs. noon-3am, Fri.-Sat. noon-4am). If you're into drinking instead of sweating and talking instead of screaming, the **Créperie** at 116 Friedrich-Ebert-Str. is a chatty warm bar, complete with palm trees.

LOWER SAXONY (NIEDERSACHSEN)

Embracing the North Sea coast and the deep Harz Mountains, Lower Saxony has glorious landscapes undisturbed by many foreign visitors. Since the Middle Ages, the region has been the seat of striking individualism and innovation. Christianity first gained a German foothold here, following in the wake of Charlemagne's march around the fringe of the deep-purple Lüneburger Heide. Lower Saxony continues on a path of independence pioneered by the Hanseatic traders, who made the region's fortune. A pocket of Lower Saxony's area belongs to Bremen and Bremerhaven, two seafaring cities united in a unique case of state federalism to form one of Germany's smallest *Länder*.

■■■ HANOVER (Hannover)

Levelled during World War II, Hanover would have made General George Marshall and his team of post-war planners proud; it is now the picture of a tidy modern commercial center. Novelist Walter Abish had a way of describing cities like Hanover: "Innovative? Hardly. Imaginative? Not really.... Still, something must be said in favor of the wide expanse of glass on the buildings...reflecting not only the sky, but also acting as a mirror for the older historical sights, those clusters of carefully reconstructed buildings..." Hanover does have some strikingly beautiful architecture and just about the finest Baroque garden in Europe, but the city is renowned as a modern conference center, and often looks it. The purest German is supposedly spoken in Hanover—this in a city which recalls, more than any other, the traditional connections between Germany and Britain. The city has its urban problems, especially around the train station where a sizeable young population gathers to loiter. For all this, Hanover, with its wealth of museums, almost matchless opera hall, and tradition of outdoor festivals, continues to serve as the cultural capital of Lower Saxony.

ORIENTATION AND PRACTICAL INFORMATION

Hanover's *Hauptbahnhof* lies in the center of the city. **Bahnhofstraße** extends from the front of the station, intersecting with the landmark **Kröpcke café**. Beneath Bahnhofstr. lies the surreal **Pasarelle,** a sprawling underground shopping mall. A pedestrian zone connects most of the middle city, including the major shopping districts along **Georgstraße** and the *Altstadt*.

Tourist Office: Fremdenverkehrsamt, Ernst-August-Platz 8 (tel. 30 14 22, fax 30 14 14), outside the train station and to the left. The splendid staff finds rooms for a DM5 fee, provides maps and information on cultural events, sells tickets to concerts and exhibits, and has a full travel agency. Open Mon.-Fri. 8:30am-6pm, Sat. 8:30am-2pm.

Student Travel Office: RDS, Limmerstr. (tel. 44 60 37), or at Asternstr. 34 (tel. 70 24 54). Basic bargains for the budget traveler, including flights and train packages.

Consulate: U.K., Georgsplatz 1 (tel. 388 3808). From the train station, walk up Bahnhofstr. to Kröpcke and left onto Georgstr. At the intersection of Georgstr. and Georgswall, Georgsplatz will be in front of you and to either side of the main road.

Currency Exchange: The bank in the train station offers the most convenience, the longest hours, and small commissions. Open Mon.-Fri. 7:30am-8pm, Sat. 7:30am-5pm, Sun. 10am-3pm.

American Express: Georgstr. 54, 30159 Hanover (tel. 36 34 28), across from the Opera House. Travel agency and full card member services. Mail held for 4 weeks. Open Mon.-Fri. 9am-5:30pm, Sat. 10am-1pm.

Post Office: Just to the right of the train station. Open Mon.-Fri. 8am-6pm, Sat. 8am-1pm, Sun. 11am-noon.

Telephones: In the post office, with longer hours. Open Mon.-Fri. 6am-10pm, Sat.-Sun. 7am-10pm. **City Code:** 0511.

Airport: The Hanover airport is about 15-20min. from the city center. By car, take highway B522 from the *Innenstadt. Schnellbuslinie* (express bus line) #60 runs from the *Hauptbahnhof* to the airport (every 20min. on weekdays, every 30min. on weekends; DM5). Flights depart to Berlin, Dresden, Frankfurt, Leipzig, Munich, Nuremberg, and Stuttgart, as well as to other European centers. Call for flight information (tel. 977 1223).

Public Transportation: You can set your watch by the green **buses** and **streetcars** that speed through Hanover, above its **U-** and **S-Bahn** lines. Single ride DM3, but consider a pass, valid on any of these lines (24-hr. card DM7, week card DM13; groups of 6 cards can be purchased at reduced rates). Tickets can be purchased on board except at U-Bahn stations, where you *must* buy your ticket before boarding. Many of the lines run all night on Fri. and Sat. The **ÜSTRA** office in the Pasarelle (the underground mall running through the city) has information on tickets. Office open Mon.-Fri. 8am-6pm, Sat. 9am-1pm.

Mitfahrzentrale: Citynetz, Weißekreuzerstr. 18 (tel. 194 44). Open Mon.-Fri. 9am-6pm, Sat. 9am-2pm, Sun. 10am-3pm.

Bike Rental: Erich Möller Fahrrad, Lavesstr. 71 (tel. 32 23 78). DM10 per day, DM18 per 2 days, DM24 per 3 days, DM35 per week. DM50 deposit required. Open Mon.-Fri. 9am-6pm, Sat. 9am-2pm.

Bookstores: Georgsbuchhandlung, Georgstr. 52, has plenty of English-language books. Open Mon.-Wed. and Fri. 9am-6:30pm, Thurs. 9am-8:30pm, Sat. 9am-2pm.

Pharmacy: Europa Apotheke, Georgstr. 16, near the train station. English spoken. Open Mon.-Wed. and Fri. 8am-6:30pm, Thurs. 8am-8:30pm, Sat. 8am-2pm. Information about *Notdienst* during closed hours at the doorway.

Emergencies: Police: tel. 110. **Medical Information:** tel. 115 02.

Rape Crisis Line: tel. 33 21 12

ACCOMMODATIONS AND CAMPING

Hanover's accommodations are either feast or famine. The three youth hostels offer decent respite for budget travelers, but beyond that you're screwed; the average room here costs well over DM100. The hostels in Braunschweig or Celle are always options; if the tourist office can't find you anything inexpensive here, train fare may be less than your hotel bill.

Naturfreundhaus Stadtheim, Hermann-Bahlsen-Allee 8 (tel. 69 14 93). U-Bahn 3 or 7 (direction "Lahe" or "Fasanenkrug"): Spannhagengarten; cross the street away from the tracks and follow Hermann-Bahlsen-Allee to the left for about 700m. Tucked along the edge of Hanover's monstrous Eilenriede Park, the hostel is a sort of sylvan EconoLodge. Reception open 8am-10pm. No curfew. Doubles DM25 per person, non-members DM30. Breakfast included. Reservations recommended.

Jugendherberge Hannover (HI), Ferdinand-Wilhelm-Fricke-Weg 1 (tel. 131 76 74, fax 185 55). U-Bahn 3 or 7 (direction "Mühlenberg"): Fischerhof/Fachhochschule, cross the tracks and walk past the school along the bike path until you cross the bridge; the hostel will be on the right. Or, bus #24 (direction "Stadionbrücke") to the front door. Within walking distance of the Maschsee, the Schützenfestplatz, and the *Altstadt.* The roses out front don't quite compensate for the institutional rooms. You're unlikely to have a peaceful slumber due to crowded quarters, but a friendly staff usually manages to keep the noise level bearable. Small lockers will not hold extra-large backpacks. Curfew 11:30pm. Sheets DM5.50. DM18.30, over 26 DM22.30. **Camping** places DM12 per person. Mini-breakfast included. Reservations recommended.

Hotel Flora, Heirichstr. 36 (tel. 34 23 34, fax 34 58 99). From the train station, turn left on to Joachimstr. Turn left at Thielenplatz and continue straight, crossing Berliner Allee, then go left at Emmichplatz. Heinrichstr. is the second street on the left and the hotel is on your left (15min.). Alternatively, U-Bahn 2 (direction "Kleefeld/Nackenberg"): Emmichplatz, turn right on Hohenzollernstr., and take your second left. Clean and very convenient to the city center. Singles DM50-75. Doubles DM80-110. Breakfast included.

Hospiz am Bahnhof, Joachimstr. 2, 30159 Hanover (tel. 32 42 97). The best value for the price in Hanover; less than a 5min. walk from the train station. Run by a church group, so it's closed on major religious holidays, but a steal the rest of the year. Singles with phone and sink DM50, with shower and toilet up to DM87. Doubles DM96-110. Reservations emphatically suggested.

FOOD

Starting at **Kröpcke**—the world-renowned café in the center of Hanover's pedestrian zone where you can find everything from take-out sandwiches (DM4) to sit-down meals (from DM12)—and spiraling outwards, restaurants go from not expensive to really expensive. If you can't find something within three blocks of Kröpcke, try one of the *Kneipen* in the *Altstadt*. The **CO-OP,** a market on the end of the Pasarelle, sells inexpensive groceries.

Bavarium, Windmühlstr. 3 (tel. 32 36 00), on a small side street in front and to the left of the Opera House. This indoor-outdoor *Biergarten* and restaurant rocks with locals enjoying big portions and bigger beers. Try the *Wienerschnitzel* (DM15.20) or the rack of ribs (DM14.80). Open daily 11am-11pm.

da ciaudio, Andreasstr. 2a. Satisfying Italian food by candlelight. The *Pizza 2000* (DM12) has everything but the kitchen sink sliced and diced onto it. The *Spaghetti Mare* (DM13) features Hanover's daily catches. Open Mon.-Sat. 10am-midnight, Sun. 11am-midnight.

Restaurant Marché, Galerie Luise, Luisenstr. 5. This all-day self-service café features lots of fresh produce and hearty meals. Open daily 11am-10pm. Entrees from DM7.

Café Klatsch, Lummerstr. 58 (tel. 45 52 31). Alternative, ecologically friendly café that serves fresh sandwiches and salads. Board games available in addition to socialist and feminist periodicals. A good place to find out about women's and gay/lesbian activities in Hanover. Open Mon.-Fri. 9am-6:30pm, Sat. 10am-6:30pm, Sun. 11am-6:30pm.

Altstadt Café, Kramerstr. 4 (tel. 32 03 77). Wonderful, just plain wonderful little café. Sprawls out onto the street. Serves pizzas and pasta (DM9-16) as well as Italian ice cream. Open daily from 11am.

SIGHTS

In 1714, the son of Electoral Princess Sophie ascended to the throne of England as George I; the joint rule of Hanover and Britain continued until 1837 when the Hanoverians refused to accept Victoria as queen. The city owes much to Sophie, who furnished it with the **Herrenhausen Gardens** (U-Bahn 4 or 5, direction "Stöcken": Herrenhausengarten). This is one attraction that is more an experience than a sight; if you're going to get lost anywhere in Hanover, do it here. The Baroque landscaping is wildly, ambitiously decorative, without being gaudy in the least. The theater in the centerpiece **Herrenhausen Palace,** built in the 18th century, hosts frequent concerts, ballets, and plays which often spill over into the gardens during the warmer months (snap up advance tickets at the tourist office, or buy tickets at the door on the evening of the performance). The daily "illuminations," when geyser-like fountains shoot from the ground to glow in the warm backlighting, are a must-see; among these is Europe's highest garden fountain, the **Große Fontäne** (Great Fountain), originally 32m high but gradually built up to 80m. Adjacent to the Great Garden, the smaller **Georgengarten** and **Berggarten** are equally bewitching. (Open daily 8am-8pm; in winter 8am-4:30pm. Fountains run May-Sept. Mon.-Fri. 11am-noon and 3-5pm, Sat.-Sun. 11am-1pm and 3-6pm. Illuminations May-Sept. Wed. and Fri.-Sat. at dusk.)

The 14th-century **Marktkirche,** Haus-Lilie-Platz, presides over the almost totally reconstructed **Altstadt** (from the station, follow Bahnhofstr. to the Markt; church open daily 10am-4pm). City government outgrew the **Altes Rathaus** (Old Town

Hall, just off the Markt) in 1913, but its trellised facade and mosaic work are kept bright. On seeing the **Leibnizhaus,** a ridiculously Baroque mansion and home to the thinker and man-of-letters Gottfried Leibniz until his death in 1716, one gets the impression that philosophy paid pretty well back then. Nearby, the ivy-covered shell of the wrecked **Aegidienkirche,** on Aegidenplatz, stands as a monument to the destruction of Hanover in 1943.

Against the remains of Hanover's medieval fortifications, the **Friedrichswall** (down Marktstr. from the *Altstadt*), stands the more modern, and quite spectacular **Neues Rathaus.** Hanoverians painstakingly recreated this palatial turn-of-the-century complex after World War II, with unqualified success. The slanting elevator definitely merits a go—you can see the entire city from the top. (Elevator open April-Oct. daily 10am-12:30pm and 1:30-4:30pm. Admission DM3, students DM2.) From on high, scout out Hanover's many parks, including the woods around the **Maschsee.** This artificial 2-km lake just south of the Rathaus is covered with sailboats and rowboats during the summer, and ice skaters in winter. Hanover's links with Britain are espoused in the **Waterloo Monument** (from the Neues Rathaus, cross the Leine River bridge), a high column which commemorates those from Lower Saxony who fought with the British against Napoleon.

In order to help you find your way to Hanover's various attractions, the city has constructed the **Red Thread,** a walking tour indicated by a red line drawn on the pavement which connects all the major sites. The accompanying *Red Thread Guide* (DM3) explains the sights and is available at the tourist office.

MUSEUMS

Hanover prides itself on its cultural tradition, exemplified by the city's 10 museums; six are listed here.

Landesmuseum, Am Maschseeplatz 5 (tel. 88 30 51). Between the lake and the *Rathaus.* Has just about everything including an aquarium/terrarium and a natural history branch. If that's not enough, there are history and art exhibitions focusing on art up to the 20th century. Open Tues.-Wed. and Fri.-Sun. 10am-5pm, Thurs. 10am-7pm. Free.

Sprengel Museum, (tel. 168 38 75), next door from the Landesmuseum, continues the artistic collection with a hefty section of modern and abstract works. Open Tues. 10am-10pm, Wed.-Sun. 10am-6pm. Free.

Kestner-Museum, Trammplatz 3 (tel. 168 21 20). Cross through the park behind the *Rathaus* and you'll find yourself at the museum. Numismatic fetishists will go wild over the ancient coin collection; here you can also find some extremely creative antique and modern vases. The centerpiece is the ancient Greco-Roman and Egyptian art, a touch out of place in this ultra-modern building. Open Tues. and Thurs.-Fri. 10am-4pm, Wed. 10am-8pm, Sat.-Sun. 10am-6pm. Admission DM 2, Sun. Free.

Historisches Museum am Hohen Ufer, Pferdestr. 6 (tel. 168 30 92), is housed in a 1960s replica of a 10th-century fortress. Inside, the cultural history of Hanover and Lower Saxony, along with the explanation of the intertwined Hanoverian and British royal lineage, is presented in agonizing detail. Open Tues. 10am-8pm, Wed.-Fri. 10am-4pm, Sat.-Sun. 10am-6pm. Free.

Wilhelm-Busch Museum, in the Georgengarten (tel. 71 40 76), U-Bahn 4 or 5 (direction "Stöcken"): Schneiderberg, proves that caricatures and political cartoons evoke chuckles, and occasionally rage, in any language. Also see the definitive history of Max and Moritz, two nasty cartoon children who play practical jokes on everyone but who are eventually ground into meal and eaten by geese. Open Tues.-Sun. 10am-5pm; Nov.-Feb. Tues.-Sun. 10am-4pm. Admission DM2, students DM1.

Staatstheatermuseum, on Prinzenstr. in the **Schauspielhaus** has a standing exhibit on the history of theater in Lower Saxony from the 17th century to the present. Open Tues. 10am-10pm, Wed.-Fri. 10am-6pm, Sat.-Sun. 10am-2pm.

GÖTTINGEN

ENTERTAINMENT AND NIGHTLIFE

If you're within a 100km radius of Hannover in late June or early July, make a detour to Hanover's **Schützenfest (marksmanship festival),** the largest such fête in Germany. Every summer since 1539, Hanoverians have congregated—firearms in hand—to test their markspersonship and then retreat to the beer gardens and get *Schützen*-faced. The 10-day festival comes complete with a parade, fireworks, chintzy stuffed animals, and creaky amusement-park rides. The festival's main attraction is the *Lüttje Lage,* a feisty little drink. Without spilling, you must drink from two shot glasses at the same time, held side by side in one hand; one glass contains *Weißbier,* the other *Schnapps.*

The **Kneipen,** quiet during the day, warm up quickly at night with Hanover's young and beautiful. The **Altstadt** area is especially fun. Around Am Marstall however, Hanover's sex district attracts its distinctive, unnerving clientele. **Waterloo Biergarten,** Waterlooplatz 1, is a large, fully-outdoor beer garden. Stands around the perimeter sell gyros, pretzels, and currywurst (open daily from 11am). **Kalauer Bierpub Bistro,** Ballhofstr. 12, overlooks the cobblestone Ballhofplatz. In summer you can sit outside with trendy student-type locals (open daily from 10am). **Schwüle Sau,** Schaufeldstr. 29 (tel. 70 00 525) is a gay bar and nightclub in the University district (open evenings from 9pm).

The **Flohmarkt (flea market)** on the Leibnizufer comes to town every Saturday from 7am to 4pm. People gather on the banks of the mud-brown river to sell household odds-and-ends. While at this weekly carnival, pick up a *Schinkenbrötchen* (ham on a hard roll) and beer from the **Bonanza Western Grill** that appears with the market; be warned: the Wild Teutonic West is a bizarre place.

Hanover is not quite as philistine as it may appear. Over twenty theaters find their homes here, supplying Hanoverians with everything from ballet and opera to Broadway musicals and dramas. The **Opera House,** Opernplatz 1, the **Ballhof,** Ballhofstr. 5, the **Schauspielhaus,** and the **Theater am Aegi,** Aegienterplatz, are the four largest. Tickets (starting at about DM15) for most of the theaters may be purchased at the tourist office. (Advance tickets for the Opera house and the Schauspielhaus may be purchased at the Opera House Mon.-Fri. 10am-1:30pm and 3-5:30pm, Sat. 10am-1pm, Sun. 11am-1pm or by calling 368 17 11 one hour after the box office opens.)

■■■ GÖTTINGEN

Göttingen is home to Europe's first free university. The institution has turned out 31 Nobel Prize winners, Otto von Bismarck, and the quantum theory of physics. Even the Brothers Grimm had chairs here. In the years after its founding by England's King George II in 1737, the university was reputed to be one of the most liberal and free-thinking in the German lands. By the end of World War I, however, it had degenerated into a hotbed of reactionary nationalism (with the notable exception of the physics faculty); when one professor resigned to protest Nazi anti-Semitism, 33 of his colleagues rose up to denounce him. A few years later, the shift reversed and Göttingen was considered a *"rote uni"* (red university). Now it has settled into moderate liberalism along with the Clinton administration. The crowded squares are inviting for students, while architectural draws are few and far between; Göttingen has its pleasures, but most are outside of the museums.

PRACTICAL INFORMATION

Tourist Office: in the *Rathaus* (tel. 540 00; fax 400 29 98). Makes room reservations for a DM3 service charge. Open Mon.-Fri. 9am-6pm, Sat.-Sun. 10am-4pm, Nov.-March Mon.-Fri. 9am-1pm and 2-6pm, Sat. 10am-1pm. There's also a smaller office across from the train station (tel. 56 000). Open Mon.-Fri. 10am-1pm and 2-6pm, Sat. 10am-1pm.

Post Office: To the left of the station, 37073 Göttingen. Open Mon.-Fri. 6am-10pm, Sat. 6am-5pm, Sun. 9am-noon.

Telephones: City Code: 0551.

Mitfahrzentrale: Mitfahrbüro Cheltenham House, Friedrichstr. 1 (tel. 485988.), hooks up riders and drivers, and includes a budget travel office. English spoken. Open Mon.-Fri. 10am-6pm, Sat.-Sun. 10am-2pm.

Car Rental: Sixt-Budget, Rodeweg 18c (tel. 910 76).

Bike Rental: Hotel-Restaurant "Zur Rose," Kurze Geismarstr. 11 (tel. 570 50) rents for DM10 per day and DM50 per week. The **youth hostel,** Habichtsweg 2 (tel. 576 22), also rents bikes for DM8 per day for the first 2 days, DM5 per day thereafter. DM30 deposit.

Bookstore: Deuerlich, with the main store at Weenderstr. 33, but smaller specialized branches at Weender Landstr. 6, Theaterstr. 25, and Gotmarstr. 3 (main tel. 49 50 00). A rich selection of English, French, and even Russian paperbacks. Open Mon.-Wed., Fri. 9am-6pm, Thurs. 9am-7:00pm, Sat. 9am-2pm.

Library: Staats- und Universitäts-Bibilothek, corner of Papendiek and Prinzenstr. (tel. 39 52 31). Reading room open Mon.-Fri. 9am-8pm, Sat. 9:30am-2pm.

Laundromat: Wasch Center, Ritterplan, opposite the Städtisches Museum. Wash DM5, dry DM1 per 15min. Soap included. Open Mon.-Sat. 7am-10pm.

ACCOMMODATIONS

The abundance of students and visitors at Göttingen means that the long-term housing market is tight, and hotels tend to be expensive. There are, however, ways to get around this: the hostel is excellent, and those wishing to stay anywhere from a few days to a few months can check the **Mitwohnzentrale,** Jüdenstr. 10 (tel. 19445) which matches potential roomers (open Mon.-Thurs. 10am-noon and 3-6:30pm).

Jugendherberge (HI), Habichtsweg 2 (tel. 576 22). From the station, walk left up Berlinerstr. to Nikolausberger Weg, and follow the signs (40min.); or, walk *right* on Berlinerstr., then left at Groner-Tor-Str. and follow it to the pedestrian zone, and take bus #6 from the Kornmarkt stop all the way to the hostel. The hostel is pleasant and thoroughly modern. Reception open 1-10pm. Lockout 9-11:30am. Curfew 11:30pm. DM17.50, over 26 DM21.50. Breakfast included; vegetarian meals available. Laundry DM4.50 per load, but there's just a clothesline, no dryer. Bike rental available (see above listings). Wheelchair access.

Hotel-Gastätte Berliner Hof, Weender Landstr. 43 (tel. 313 40 and 31 411). Bus #2, 3, 7, 10, 17, 18, or 24: Kreuzberg Ring, or walk left on Berlinerstr. from the station and turn left on Weender Landstr. Neatly fitted by the university, and backed by a pleasant *Biergarten*. Singles DM40, with shower and TV DM50. Doubles DM70, with shower and TV DM95.

Hotel "Zum Schwan," Weender Landstr. 23 (tel. 448 63). Another nice place in a great location, with a few more rooms than Berliner Hof. Reception open Mon.-Fri. 7am-10pm, Sat.-Sun. 7am-2pm. Singles DM42, with shower DM49. Doubles DM65, with shower DM79.

Hotel zur Rose, Kurze Geismarstr (tel. 570 50). Three charms in one—hotel, restaurant, and bike rental—in the heart of the *Altstadt*. The owner, who claims to know 7 languages including fluent English, serves up 13 kinds of beer. Reception closed on Sun. Restaurant open Mon.-Fri. 10am-1pm and 5pm-1am, Sat. 10am-2:30pm. Singles with shower DM50. Doubles with shower DM100. Call ahead.

FOOD

Göttingen is blessed with two great German culinary institutions, the **Mensa** (university cafeteria) and the **Markt.** An impressive array of farm-fresh peddlers haggle on the square between Lange and Kurze Geismarst (Tues., Thurs., and Sat. 7am-1pm; the **supermarkets** around town, mostly **Helco** and **Plus,** are fair substitutes. Goethe-Allee, near the station, has a string of late-night Greek, Italian, and Turkish restaurants in every price range.

Zentral Mensa, follow Weenderlandstr., turn right at the University complex, and follow the starving students. The cavernous *Mensa,* swarming with people and plastered with listings of local events, is on the left. Cafeteria meals DM2-4 for stu-

GÖTTINGEN

dents (any student ID will do), DM4-7 for other visitors. Shorter lines at the less wholesome snack bar. Automats also sell non-student meal vouchers downstairs. Lunch served Mon.-Fri. 11:30am-2pm.

Alte Mensa, on Wilhelmsplatz back in the *Altstadt,* is cozier than Zentral (above), but with the same prices and ID policy. Open mid-April to mid-July and mid-Oct. to mid-Feb. Mon.-Fri. 11:30am-2pm; adjacent *Taberna* café open 11:30am-2:15pm and 5:30-8:30pm.

Naturell Vollwert-Milchcafé, Lange Geismarstr. 40. Come at lunch or for an herbal-tea tray from the vegetarian kitchen. Thick *Bio-Kartoffelpuffen* (organic potato puffs) with applesauce, DM6.50. Fresh-squeezed juices, *naturell* milk-shakes; located appropriately among the beautiful body boutiques of the *Altstadt.* Open Mon.-Fri. 10:30am-6pm, Sat. 10:30am-2:30pm.

Cron & Lanz, Weenderstr. 25, on the main pedestrian drag, is one of Germany's sweetest pastry shops. Deciding which elaborate confection to order will be the hardest part. If you're feeling extravagant, try their specialty: *Baumkuchentorte* ("tree-cake," DM2.50), or marzipan monkeys, elephants, and pigs (DM6-7.50). Open Mon.-Sat. 9am-6:30pm, Sun. 1-6:30pm.

Pfannkuchen Haus, Speckstr. 10 (tel. 41870). German pancakes are grilled without yeast, so they're incredibly heavy and filling. This spacious restaurant serves sweets, meats, and health-conscious toppings (DM4-14).

Waffelstube, On the corner of Papendieck and Johannisstr. If pancakes are too substantial for you, try a waffle snack. A basic waffle, fresh off the iron, costs DM1.20. Open Mon.-Fri. 1-6pm, Sat. 10am-1pm.

SIGHTS

The courtyard of the **Altes Rathaus** serves as meeting place for the whole town—punker, professor, and panhandler alike. Radical students and evangelists preach to the converted, with tracts for passers-by. The diminutive **Gänseliesel** (goose-girl) fountain in front of the *Rathaus* is Göttingen's symbol; graduating doctors kiss the bronze beauty after receiving their diplomas. The repressed city council imposed a "kissing ban" in 1926, prompting one incensed student to sue. He lost, but town officials now turn a blind eye to the extracurricular fountain activity. The murals inside the *Rathaus* depict 19th-century work-a-day life in Göttingen. Free tours of the city depart from the *Gänseliesel* (April-Oct. Wed. and Sat. at 3pm). Göttingen's renowned **University** is outside the city wall, scattered throughout the area bounded by Nikolausbergerweg and Weender Landstr.

The **Bismarckhaus** is a tiny stone cottage, also outside the city wall, where 17-year-old law student Otto von Bismarck took up residence after authorities expelled him from the inner city for boozing it up (open Tues. 10am-1pm, Thurs. and Sat. 3-5pm). A **Bismarckturm** in Kleperberg (tel. 742 13; along the Stadtforest) commemorates the larger-scale trouble-making of his later career. From the top of the old stone tower, there's a Göttingen-wide view. Take bus A to "Bismarckstraße/Reitsall." (Open Wed.-Sat. 10am-5:30pm except in bad weather; Oct.-March Wed.-Sat. 10am-dusk.) The **Stadtisches Museum,** at Ritterplan 7/8, spices up features on local culture with visiting shows of modern art (open Tues.-Fri. 10am-5pm, Sat.-Sun. 10am-1pm; free).

Göttingen also hosts a few notable medieval churches. At the corner of Prinzenstr. and Weenderstr., right by the stone lambada sculpture called "Der Tanz," is **St. Jacobi's** 72m tower. The gargoyle-ridden monument's best feature is probably its main door, with six colorful concentric arches. (Open May-Oct. Mon.-Sat. 10am-1pm. Free organ concerts Fri. at 6pm.) Down Weenderstr. and behind the *Altes Rathaus* stands the fortress-like **St. Johanniskirche** (open May-Oct. Mon.-Sat. 10:30-11:30am). The interior is fairly typical; the more interesting tower is open Saturday from 2 to 4pm. On Untere Maschstr., is a twisting, spiraling pyramid erected as a **memorial** to the Göttingen synagogue, razed in 1938. Numerous venerable houses mark the town's zenith as a member of the Hanseatic League from 1351 to 1572.

The university runs seven separate museums: the **Völkerkundliche Sammlung** (primitive art collection), Theaterplatz 15, the **Zoologisches Museum,** Berliner Str. 28, the **Kunstsammlung** (art collection), the **Musikinstrumentensammlung,** the **Archäologisches Museum,** the **Museum der Göttinger Chemie (Chemistry Museum),** and the **Museum für Geologie und Paläontologie.** A brochure at the tourist office has information on each; note the limited hours.

ENTERTAINMENT AND NIGHTLIFE

Peukert, Jüdenstr. 13a (tel. 433 11), sells **concert tickets** (some for out-of-town events) and a variety of student magazines (open Mon.-Fri. 9am-6pm, Sat. 9am-1pm). For drama, check with the **Deutsches Theater box office** (tel. 49 69 11; open Mon.-Thurs. 10am-1pm and 5-6:30pm, Fri. 10am-1pm and 2-6:30pm, and Sat. 10am-noon). **Gummi-Zelle,** Nikolaistr. 20, promotes safety first; buy your condom greeting cards, wind-up toys, and costume kits here (open Mon.-Wed. and Fri. 10:30am-6:30pm, Thurs. 10:30am-8:30pm, Sat. 10:30am-2pm). **KAZ** is an indoor/outdoor pub right next to the mostly experimental **Junges Theater,** Hospitalstr. 6 (theater tel. 49 69 11; box office open Mon.-Sat. 10am-1pm). The pub has snacks and small meals, up to DM10 (open daily 11am-early morning). **Blue Note,** adjacent to the **Alte Mensa,** draws students as the **Mensa** closes. Every day there's a new musical theme, with occasional live bands (open daily 7:30pm-2am).

■■■ GOSLAR

In 922 AD, Holy Roman Emperor Heinrich stumbled upon Goslar, hidden in the northern fringe of the Harz Mountains. Heinrich III, his successor, asked that his heart be kept here, though the rest of his body was buried at Speyer. This dusty city still considers itself the *Kaiserstadt,* unofficial capital of the region. Luckily, some traces of the town's former glory remain.

Practical Information The **tourist office,** Markt 7 (tel. (05321) 28 47, fax 230 05), across from the *Rathaus,* finds rooms (from DM30) for a DM3 fee. From the station, walk to the end of Rosentorstr. (open Mon.-Fri. 9am-6pm, Sat. 9am-2pm; Nov.-April Mon.-Fri. 9am-5pm, Sat. 9am-1pm). The **post office** is at Klubgartenstr. 10, 38640 Goslar (open Mon.-Fri. 8:30am-12:30pm and 3-6pm, Sat. 9am-noon). The **telephone city code** is 05321. **Harzbike Goslar-Baßgeige,** Bornhardtstr. 3-5 (tel. 820 11), rents **bicycles** (DM25-35 per day; open Mon.-Fri. 9:30am-6pm; Sat. 9am-2pm). **Trains** from Hanover (16 per day) and Göttingen (14 per day) stop at Goslar. Near the now-defunct border, Goslar is a good base for a bus or hiking tour of the lush Harz Mountains.

Accommodations and Food The half-timbered **Jugendherberge (HI),** Rammelsbergerstr. 25, 38644 Goslar (tel. 222 40), wins a prize for the most confusing address of the year. From the bus C stop at "Theresienhof," walk up Rammelberger-str., passing house numbers 27-49 on your left. After #49, make a sharp left at the *"Jugendherberge"* sign and walk all the way back up the hill to #25. (Reception open 8:30-11am, 4-7pm, and 9:30-10pm. Curfew 10pm. Members only. DM17.80, over 26 DM21.80. Breakfast included. Vegetarian meals available.) **Gästehaus Möller,** Schieferweg 6 (tel. 230 98), has comfortable rooms and windowsill flower boxes. Take Klubgartenstr. and Am Heiligen Grabe west from the train station, cross Von Garssen Str., and right on Schieferweg. It's sweet. (Singles DM35-40. Doubles DM70-90.) **Gästehaus Schmitz,** Korustr. 1 (tel. 234 45), attracts many with its warm atmosphere and central location. From the *Markt* take a left on Korustr. (Reception open 9am-7pm. Singles DM50. Doubles DM60. Breakfast included. Reservations highly recommended.)

Campingplatz Sennhütte, Clausthalerstr. 28 (tel. 224 98), 3km from town along the B241, has a restaurant and sauna (DM4 per person, DM3.50 per tent, showers

DM1). A mountain **Markt** brightens the town with fresh baked goods and produce (open Tues. and Fri. 7am-1pm). Try the homemade pasta at **Rigoletto,** Marktstr. 38-39, on the other side of the Marktkirche from the *Marktplatz*. Savory pizzas run DM9.50-12 (open Mon.-Tues. and Thurs.-Sun. noon-3pm and 6pm-midnight).

Sights Guarded by oversized stone lions, the **Kaiserpfalz,** Kaiserbleek 6, is a massive Romanesque palace that served as the ruling seat for 11th- and 12th-century emperors. Heinrich IV was actually born within its walls. The interior of the **great hall** is plastered with decorous 19th-century murals. Wander through massive oaken doors and twisting medieval passages to the palace's **Ulrichskapelle,** where Heinrich III's heart lies tucked away inside a massive sarcophagus (open daily 10am-5pm; Nov.-March 10am-4pm; admission DM3.50, students DM2). Below the palace is the **Domvorhalle** (Cathedral Foyer), Kaiserbleek 10, the sad remains of a 12th-century imperial cathedral destroyed 170 years ago. In summer of 1993, the tiny hall was closed for renovations; still visible, however, is the plaque on the outer wall with the engraved equivalent of a scrawled "Heinrich Heine wuz here."

The central **Marktplatz** is a rush of ornate woodwork and trellices, especially on the Hotel Kaiserworth and on the gables of the treasury building. Each day, the small mechanical figures of court nobles, and the miners whose work made the region prosperous dance to the chime of the **Glocken- und Figurenspiel** at 9am, noon, 3, and 6pm. Directly opposite is the **Rathaus,** with its wonderfully preserved **Huldigungssaal** (Hall of Homage). This 15th-century city council chamber swims with depictions of town elders and pre-Renaissance biblical scenes; the **Bergkanne,** an unbelievably ornate silver and gold-encrusted tankard, and the similarly bejeweled **Goslarer Evangeliar,** a 1230 illuminated manuscript, are stashed in a secret safe inside. A perfectly elaborate copy of the book is on display in the Hall. The Hall's **imperial eagle,** on the other hand, is real, dating back to 1220; it's the one atop the *Markt* fountain that's a copy. (Hall tours are given every 30min. from 10am-5pm; Oct.-May every 30min. from 10am-4pm. Admission DM3, students DM1.50.)

The reconstructed 12th-century **Marktkirche** dominates the Goslar skyline from right behind the *Rathaus*. Inside, you can see the stained-glass saga of St. Cosmas and St. Damian, 3rd-century twin doctors. In a classic case of medieval religious overkill, the saints were put to death by drowning, burning at the stake, stoning, crucifixion, *and* transfixion by arrows (church open Tues.-Thurs. and Sat. 10:30am-3:30pm, Fri. 10:30am-2pm, Sun. noon-3:30pm).

The **Mönchehaus,** Mönchestr. 3, is an outstanding modern art museum inside a small house with a sculpture garden in back (open Tues.-Sat. 10am-1pm and 3-5pm, Sun. 10am-1pm; admission DM3.50, students and children DM2). Don't miss the fantastic **Musical Instrument Museum,** Hoherweg 5. The owner has spent more than 40 years collecting musical items, as well as an impressive assortment of dolls and African tribal art, and has amassed the largest private instrument collection in Germany (open daily from 11am-5pm; admission DM3.50, children DM1.50). Gambol through the **Zinnfiguren Museum,** Münzerstr. 11, with its collection of more than 10,000 hand-painted tin figures arranged in fun dioramas (open daily 10am-5pm; admission DM3.50, students DM2).

■■■ WESTERN HARZ MOUNTAINS

Germany's 40-year division allowed the Harz Mountains to flourish; since the region straddled the Iron Curtain, East and West declared much of it off-limits, effectively protecting the region's natural gifts from development. Border guards have since given way to the occasional masked raccoon, and with political divisions gone, the mountains can be seen for what they are—a dreamy-looking but rugged heartland. The range stretches from the northwestern **Oberharz** area to the wind-sheltered, mineral-rich valleys in the south and Wernigerode in the east. The more historic villages cluster in the Eastern Harz; the attraction on the western side of the mountains is mainly outdoors. With the first snows, sublime hiking terrain becomes a splendid winter playland for skiing, skating, and tobogganing. For information on area towns on the other side of the former border, see the Eastern Harz, Sachsen-Anhalt, below.

If at all possible, try to be deep into the Harz in the last week of April to join in the immense region-wide celebration of **Walpurgisnacht**. The April 30th hedonistic festivities—immortalized by Goethe—center around legendary **witches** who sweep through the sky on broomsticks and land on Brocken, the Harz's highest peak. They dance with the devil until midnight, at which point the May King arrives and cleans house. Apparently, this is also a major Norse festival; the head-god Odin married Freya on the last night of April. The Christian clergy sought to usurp the ritual merrymaking by calling the party "Walpurgisnacht" after St. Walpurga, born May 1, but the pagan pleasures have endured. The Harz explodes on Walpurgisnacht with festivals, demonic skits, wilderness spook treks, and witch paraphernalia.

There is a **regional tourist office** in Goslar, the Harzer Verkehrsverband, Markstr. 45 (tel. (05321) 34 040), inside the **Industrie und Handels Kammer** building (open Mon.-Thurs. 8am-4pm, Fri. 8am-1pm). Their indispensable *Gruner Faden fur den Harz-Gast* pamphlet (DM3) lists attractions, as well as everything from ski schools, rentals, and lifts to tours on horseback. *Jugend und Freizeitheime im Harz und im Harzvorland* is a complete compilation of youth hostels and student centers in the area. The *Museumsfuhrer: Harz und Umgebung* booklet will tell you about every museum in every village. Also pick up the *Auto- und Wanderkarte der ganzen Harz*, the map to hike, bike, or drive through the region (DM9.80).

When in the Harz, always be prepared for bad weather, especially sudden and violent rainstorms. Call (053212) 200 24 for daily Harz **weather reports,** tourist information, and, in winter, ski condition reports.

From train stations at Braunlage and **Bad Harzburg,** buses zip to towns and hamlets deep in the Harz. In addition to the towns listed below, consider expeditions to **Hahnenklee,** a ski-area village known for its unusual Norwegian Church (built without nails), **Lauterberg,** with tours of the abandoned Grube Samson mining works, and **St. Andreasberg** and Bad Sachsa for more hiking and skiing. The easiest way to get to head east is with the bus line between Bad Harzburg and Wernigerode.

BAD HARZBURG

The train from Hanover to the mountains ends at the Bad Harzburg *Bahnhof*, about 10 minutes past Goslar. The ruins of the original imperial town of Harzburg are in the hills above, but there really isn't much left. Bad Harzburg is a perfectly good place to stock up and recoup before hitting the Harz interior, but does not boast much else, other than private spas which draw Germans for mud baths. The other attraction is the **Marchenwald** (Fairy-Tale Forest), Nordhauser Str., a little play-park of mechanical houses relating 25 of the Grimm Brothers' finest (open daily 9am-6pm; admission DM3, children DM2).

The **tourist office** (tel. (05322) 2927) to the left of the station will find rooms for a DM5 fee (rooms from DM35; open Mon.-Fri. 9am-1pm and 3-6pm, Sat. 10am-1pm). The **post office** and **phones** are in the tree- and restaurant-lined **pedestrian zone,** where Bummel Allee meets Herzog-Wilhelm-Str. (open Mon.-Fri. 8am-12:30pm and 3-5:30pm, Sat. 8am-noon). **All-Time Rent,** Herzog-Julius-Str. 40 (tel. (05322) 44 86) rents **mountain bikes** for DM25 per half-day, and DM35 per day; helmet included (open Mon.-Fri. 9am-1pm and 3-6pm, Sat. 9am-1pm). Take in a breath of fresh air and some spectacular treetop scenery with the **Bergbahn,** located at the end of the pedestrian zone. Hauling skiers in the winter and snap-shooting tourists in the summer, the Bergbahn runs up to the Burgberg (say that 5 times fast), 482m above sea level. (DM4, round-trip DM5; students DM1.50, round-trip DM2. Open mid-Dec. to mid-Nov.) For **ski** rentals and courses, see Torfhaus, below.

A retreat owned by the "Naturfreunde" society, **Braunschweiger Haus,** Waldstr. 5 (tel. (05322) 45 82), doubles as Bad Harzburg's **Jugendherberge (HI).** From the station, take bus #73 and ask the driver for the Larchenweg stop (the bus drives in 2 rings around the town and may not hit Larchenweg until the second go-around), then take Im Bleichental to Waldstr., then go up the stone steps at the "Naturfreunde" sign. On foot, head right from the station to Silberbornstr. and follow its curves uphill to Im Bleichental (about 35min.), and follow the above directions from there. The mountainside complex is disproportionately inhabited by school groups in June. (Reception open 9am-1pm and 3-8pm. DM23, ages 12-18 DM20, children under 12 DM16. Sheets and breakfast included.) The bus to Goslar only stops at **Campingplatz Gottingerode** (tel. (05322) 812 15) if you ask the driver ahead of time. At the stop, head left. All the modern amenities: pool, sauna, hot showers, solarium, restaurant. (DM7 per tent, DM6.50 per person. Call ahead.)

There is a **supermarket** to the right of the train station; people heading to Torfhaus and trails beyond should pick up food and camping supplies here and in the pedestrian zone, as none can be found in Torfhaus. A mountain-produce **Markt** appears in the park at Herzog-Julius-Str. and Schmiedstr., purveying breads, cheeses, teas, four varieties of *Bad Sachsa* honey, and other local goods (open Thurs. 7am-1pm). Vegetable-indifferent Germans watch the vendors from the **Bad Harzburg Biergarten** (tel. (05322) 62 30) over a *Reichelbrau* (DM2.50) and a pair of *Wiener Wurstchen* (sausages, DM4).

TORFHAUS AND ALTENAU

Torfhaus, a humble crossroads 3km from the former inter-German border, has little to offer worldly sophisticates except an airy mountain hostel, near-perfect hiking trails, and the Harz's highest mountain (the 1142m **Brocken**). The Bad Harzburg-Braunlage bus pauses here every 90 minutes (weekdays 7:45am-9pm, DM3.90). A left turn at the "Altenau-8km" sign will take you to the **Goetheweg;** the 16km path to Brocken's peak jumps the stream that used to divide Germany and occasionally follows the old patrol road along the Iron Curtain. About two hours from Torfhaus along the trail, you can stop by and gawk at the at the local haunted house, an abandoned **Soviet Radar Station.** The high fence around the garrison was erected after the border was opened—not so much to keep tourists out as to keep soldiers in. The **Brockenbahn,** a narrow-gauge train, runs from the peak of the mountain to the Eastern Harz; scramble up and steam down the other side (for information see Nordhausen, in Thuringia, below). **Skizentrum Torfhaus,** Birkenweg 11 (tel. (05320) 2275) offers weekend courses in Alpine and cross-country skiing (DM160 per 20hr., children DM140). The affiliated **Skischulburo Stuhlpfarrer** (tel. (05320) 201), rents equipment next door (cross-country skis DM15 per day). Turn right at the "Altenau-8km" sign for the exceptional **Jugendherberge (HI),** Torfhaus 3 (tel. (05320) 242). The rooms here are designated by bird species rather than number. Proprietors will guide non-ornithologists to their rooms. (Reception open 12:15-1pm, and 6:15-7pm. Curfew 10pm. DM18.20, over 26 DM22.20. Breakfast included.)

The road from Torfhaus to **Altenau** is 8km of classic downhill, twisting, hairpin, mountainside, car-commercial terrain. Altenau itself is only slightly larger than Torfhaus, but it has an all-important bus connection to Goslar, in addition to the skiing and hiking; buses also make the Altenau-Torfhaus trip once a day. (At last notice, buses left Altenau at 8:45am and left Torfhaus at 3:15pm and 5pm; call (05328) 262 or 80 20 for updated times and more details.) The Altenau **tourist office** is at Schultal 5 (tel. (05328) 802 22), and will find you a room in the area at no cost (open Mon.-Fri. 8am-5pm, Sat. 10am-noon). The **post office** is on the opposite side of the Busbahnhof, at Breitestr. 1, 38707 Altenau. **Jugendherberge Altenau (HI),** Auf der Rose 11 (tel. (05328) 361), is actually more crowded in winter than in summer; it's right next to the skiing. Bus #2432 from Goslar and bus #2451 from Osterode both stop at "Jugendherberge," the starting point of a seemingly endless **hiking trail** up and into the forest. (Reception open 11am-10pm. Curfew 10:30pm. DM17.30, over 26 DM121.30. Breakfast included.) To reach **Campingplatz Okertalsperre,** Kornhardtweg 1 (tel. (05328) 702), take Huttenstr. (B498) north from town until you see the Oker-Stau-See. (Reception open 7:30am-1pm and 3-8pm. DM4.50 per tent, DM6.60 per person, DM5.10 per child.)

BRAUNLAGE

The larger town of Braunlage, 12km south of Torhaus, also makes an ideal launch-pad for hikes and winter sports near the Bronze Age **Kultstatten** (burial mounds and religious rock formations) on the Wurmberg mountain. The **Wurmbergseil-bahn,** a cable car (tel. (05520) 725), ascends the mountain from just off of Harzburger Str. (DM8, round-trip DM12; students DM6, round-trip DM8.50; under 15 DM4, round-trip DM5.50. It's also possible to stop at the mid-station. Cars run daily 9am-5:30pm.) The **tourist office** (Kurverwaltung), Elbingeroderstr. 17 (tel. (05520) 10 54), attends to accommodations (open Mon.-Fri. 7:30am-12:30pm and 2-5pm, Sat. 9:30am-noon). After hours, the big board outside the office lists prices, addresses and availability of *Pensionen* and hotels in Braunlage. The **Jugendher-berge (HI),** von Langenstr. 63 (tel. (05520) 22 38), is an uphill climb from anywhere in town, but the resulting view is to die for. Take the bus to the Marienhof stop and walk up Am Marienhof to the dirt path, or walk up Von-Langen-Str. past the dirt soc-cer fields and turn left on the first paved path. (Reception open 9am-1pm and 5-7pm. DM17.30, over 26 DM 21.30. Breakfast included.) **Hotel Berliner Hof,** Elbin-geroderstr. 12 (tel. (05520) 427), is much closer to the center of town. Comfortable rooms, rock-bottom prices. (Reception open Mon.-Tues. and Thurs.-Sun. 7am-10:30pm. Singles with various amenities DM30-42. Doubles DM60-84. Breakfast included.) **Camp** at **Ferien vom Ich** (tel. (05520) 413), in the forest near Braunlage. From the Braunlage center, walk towards Lauterberg; on Lauterbergerstr. turn left and follow the signs. (40min. Reception open 8am-noon and 3-6pm. DM6 per per-son, DM4 per tent, DM2.50 per auto.) The **Braunlage Eisstadion** (ice rink) rents **ice skates.** (Open Tues. and Thurs.-Fri. 10am-noon, 2-4pm, and 5-7pm; Wed. and Sat. 10am-noon, 2-4pm, and 8-10pm; Sun. 9:30am-noon, 1:30-3:30pm, and 4-6pm. Spe-cial times for **disco-skate** and senior-skate, though regrettably not overlapping. Admission DM5, students DM4.50. Skates DM4.)

■■■ HAMELIN (Hameln)

Hamelin is a town still living—somewhat cynically—off of the legend of the Pied Piper. Why any town would celebrate the fact that they cheated someone and then had their kids stolen is open to question. The **Rattenfänger** (rat-catcher), as he's known in Germany, supposedly marched off with 130 children in 1284 after the town skimped on exterminator fees. Less mainstream historians hold that the citi-zens themselves drove the children out because of overcrowding, while another theory is that the children were pressed into forced labor in the East. But the more fanciful version made it into the Grimms' *Deutsche Sagen,* and the town's fortune was made. Strolling along the souvenir-choked streets today, you can almost hear the town mayor consoling the grieving parents: You haven't lost a child, you've gained a tourist industry.

If you're averse to small rodents or small flute players in colorful capes, Hamelin is probably not the best vacation spot; the Pied Piper motif adorns everything. Ironi-cally, one of the few buildings unadorned by Piper paraphernalia is the modern **Rathaus.** In the courtyard in front of the town hall, though, several elfin children hang suspended in mid-air, following a piper statue to the fountain at the end of the **Rattenfänger-Brunnen.** The **Bürgergarten,** right down the street, is a small but soothing relief from tourist-trap-central, but be careful as you exit *not* to notice the **Rattenfänger-Relief.** This fresco celebrates a supposed metaphysical link between the exodus of the children and the 1945 return of soldiers; it actually just looks like a large conglomeration of strange people. (Fountains in the garden run mid-May to mid-Sept. daily 11am-noon and 3-4pm and 7:30-8pm.) The grim tale itself is reen-acted each Sunday at noon (May-Sept. weather permitting) in a **Freilichtspiel** (open-air show) at the **Hochzeithaus** (wedding house). Small children dressed as rats chase a man in a multicolored suit. The Hochzeithaus itself, built in 1610 as the town apothecary, is much more attractive than the performance. Other Weser-Renaissance survivors, products of Hamelin's brief fling with the Hanseatic League, give the old town some life. The **Rattenfängerhaus** (built in 1602) is decked out with dozens of startled-looking figureheads recalling the sudden demographic aging of the town. Between the Hochzeithaus and Rattenfängerhaus, **Museum Hameln,** Osterstr. 8/9 (tel. 202 215 216), specializes in fairy tales and dabbles in local history. (Open Tues.-Fri. and Sun. 10am-4:30pm, Sat. 10am-12:30pm; Nov.-April Tues.-Fri. 10am-4:30pm, Sat.-Sun. 10am-12:30pm.) The relatively overlooked **Münster** is a beautiful church in the east corner of the *Altstadt;* best of all, no stone rats scamper around the altar. At 8:35am the **Glockenspiel** on the Hochzeithaus plays the *Rattenfängerlied* (Pied Piper Song); at 11:05am you're serenaded with the *Weserlied*; and at 1:05, 3:35, and 5:35pm, rats run in circles around a peculiar wooden flautist.

The **tourist office,** on the Bürgergarten at Deisterallee (tel. (05151) 20 26 17 or 20 26 18) tracks down rooms for a DM2 fee. From the station, cross Bahnhofplatz, go up Bahnhofstr., and turn left onto Diesterallee. Maps of paths, roads, and bike trails to even smaller towns around Hamelin are available here (open Mon.-Fri. 9am-1pm and 2-6pm, Sat. 9:30am-12:30pm and 3-5pm, Sun. 9:30am-12:30pm; Oct.-April Mon.-Fri. 9am-1pm and 2-5pm). A smaller booth in the **Hochzeithaus** has **summertime information** (open mid-April to mid-Oct. Mon.-Fri. 11am-2pm and 2:30-5pm, Sat.-Sun. 10am-2pm). The **telephone city code** is **05151.** Keep your feet off the ground with a **bike** from the **Troche Fahrräder repair shop,** Kreuzstr. 7 (tel. 136 70; hours and bike supply somewhat irregular). **English books,** including multiple renditions of the Pied Piper legend, are available at **Buchhandlung Matthias,** on Bäckerstr. (open Mon.-Fri. 9am-6pm, Sat. 9am-1pm). Hamelin bridges the Weser River, 45min. from Hanover by frequent **trains** (4am-midnight). **Ferry** down the Weser along the Fairy-Tale road, from Hamelin to Hannoversch Münden, with **Oberweser-Dampfschiffahrt,** Inselstr. 3 in Hamelin (tel. 220 16, fax 230 40) for prices and times.

The spacious but Piper-decorated **Jugendherberge (HI),** Fischbeckerstr. 33 (tel. 34 25) sits on a dreamy bend in the *Weser;* it fills up quickly, so call ahead. From the station, take bus #2: Wehler Weg, and turn right onto Fischbeckerstr. By foot (35min.), cross Bahnhof Platz to Bahnhofstr., turn left on Deisterallee, right around 164-er Ring (along the Hamel rivulet) to Erichstr., which bends into Fischbeckerstr. (Reception open 5-10pm. Curfew 10pm. Check-out 8:30am. DM17.80, over 26 DM21.80. Breakfast included.) Southeast of the city center, on the Tönebön lake, lies **campground Jugendzeltplatz,** Tönebönweg 8 (tel. 262 23). From the *Bahnhof* or the *Altstadt,* take bus #34 (direction "Hagenohsen"). The hotels in the *Altstadt* are decent, but not cheap; Neue Marktstr. has a number of adequate (but expensive) hotels. The bright and modern **Hotel Garni Brauns,** Sandstr. 3a (tel. 650 55, fax 453 99), feels like a sunny art museum. Go down Deisterstr. from the main station and turn right onto Sandstr. (Singles DM65, with shower DM75. Doubles DM100, with shower and bath DM110. English spoken.)

An outstanding selection of baked potatoes awaits at the **Alte Post,** Hummenstr. 23 (tel. (05151) 434 44), just off of Neue Marktstr. The tubers range from DM4.50-6.50; full meals cost DM7.50-11.50 (open daily 11am-2am). Hamelners come out for fruit, vegetables, and other treats from the open-air **Markt,** Wednesday mornings from 8am to 1pm on the Bürgergarten. And of course, Hamelin boasts an impressive array of edible rodents. To catch these rats, you have to pay something to the tune of DM0.35 for tiny marzipan critters, and up to DM6 for jumbo pastry rats. Little crusty bread-rats cost DM3 at **Schäfer's,** Osterstr. 12 (open Mon.-Fri. 8am-6pm, Sat. 8am-1pm). **Steding,** the butcher next door, has stuffed them with *Wurst.*

■■■ HANNOVERSCH MÜNDEN

Wedged between severe, forested inclines at the junctions of the Werra and Fulda Rivers, Hannoversch Münden is just about the prettiest of Germany's six zillion half-timbered towns—Alexander von Humboldt called it one of the seven "most perfect cities" in the world. The impeccable *Altstadt* remains relatively free of tourists, which is not to say that the town hasn't tried to draw extensively on its position at the foot of the *Deutsche Märchenstraße* (German fairy-tale route). To gather the flavor of the town, it's more appropriate to breathe the atmosphere of geniality than to drag yourself from sight to sight. Nevertheless, Hannoversch Münden presents an extremely attractive façade.

Orientation and Practical Information Get hiking maps *(Wanderkarten)* and the extremely valuable *Weg & Fähre* newsletter, a complete guide with all the information you need for the town and its environs, at the **tourist office** (tel. (05541) 753 13) in the *Rathaus*. The staff will book you a room (DM30) for a DM5 fee (open Mon.-Fri. 8:30am-5pm, Sat. 8:30am-12:30pm; Oct.-April Mon.-Thurs. 8:30am-12:30pm and 1-4pm, Fri. 8:30am-12:30pm). Aid is also on hand from the *Auskunftschalter* (information counter) in the same building, after the office closes (tel. 750). When one closes, the other opens (mid-May to mid-Sept. daily until 9pm; Oct.-April daily until 8pm). There's also a smaller tourist office in the **Rotunda,** a massive round fortification where Langestr. becomes Kasselerstr. (open April 16 - Sept. 13 daily 10:30am-12:30pm and 3-5pm). **Bicycles** are rented at **Fahrrad Wieland,** Ägidiiplatz 14 (tel. (05541) 48 72; DM10 per day; open Mon.-Fri. 9am-1pm, Sat. 9am-noon); the hostel (see below) also rents bikes for DM6 per day.

Ferries set sail for Kassel (May-Aug. Wed. and Sun. 3pm, DM20, children DM10) from the dock between the Löwenbrücke and the Pionierbrücke. (Call Personenschiffahrt Söllner at (0561) 77 46 70 for more information.) The paths along the Weser River leading to the *Tillyschanze* continue on toward the **Reinhardswald forest** area. Formidable **hiking maps** are available at the youth hostel and the tourist office for DM9.80. Hannoversch Münden is easily accessible by train from Göttingen (35min.) or Kassel (20min.).

Accommodations and Food The lace-curtained **Jugendherberge (HI),** Prof.-Oelkers-Str. 8 (tel. (05541) 88 53), is located just outside the town limits on the banks of the Weser. From the station, walk down Beethovenstr., turn left at Wallstr., cross the Pionierbrücke, turn right along Veckerhägerstr. (B3), then left onto the B80 (45min.); or take bus #35 (direction "Holzhausen/Kassel") to the Jugendherberge stop—buses run more or less hourly until about 7:30pm. (Reception open 5-10pm. Curfew 10:30pm. DM16.50, over 26 DM20. Breakfast included.) Close by the Mühlenbrücke, **Gasthaus "Im Anker,"** (tel. 4923) Bremer Schlagd 18, 34346 Hann. Münden, has moderately priced rooms with a fantastic view of the Werra. Call for info on vacancies, then come in person or write for reservations (DM30-35 per person. Breakfast included.) **Gasthaus zur Hafenbahn,** Blume 54 (tel. (05541) 40 94), up Langestr. from the *Rathaus* and across the Werrabrücke, offers well-kept rooms from DM27 per person. Reception open Wed.-Mon. 9am-6pm.

You can pitch your tent in view of the city walls at **Campingplatz Tanzwerder** (tel. (05541) 122 57), 10 minutes from the train station, on an island in the River Fulda off Pionierbrücke. There is a small **restaurant** on the premises, and **canoe rentals** and hot showers are on tap. (Reception open daily 7am-1pm and 3-10pm. DM6 per person, DM3 per tent. Open April-Sept.)

Sights Weave through the angled sidestreets to admire the 14th-century **Fachwerkhäuser** (half-timbered houses); some of the oldest and most impressive are tucked away on **Ziegelstraße**. The 16th-century **Hinter der Stadtmauer 23,** a Jewish School since 1796, was gutted in 1938; there is a plaque outside in memoriam.

Later owners restored it and uncovered a ritual bath (*Mikwe*) in the basement. The ornate **Rathaus** is a leading example of the Weser-Renaissance style that arose in this area around 1550. To reach the *Rathaus* from the train station, walk straight down Bahnhofstr., take a right at Burgstr., and continue on until you reach Markstr.; take a left here and the *Rathaus* is on your left. Past centuries-old markings of Weser flood heights on the *Rathaus* corner walls, the **Rathaushalle** is lined with coloring-book scenes out of the city's past. The striking **St. Blasiuskirche,** opposite the *Rathaus,* is decked out in periwinkle and emerald, with ornate Solomonic columns around the altar (open Mon.-Sat. 10am-noon and 3-6pm, Sun. 2-6pm).

Hannoversch Münden's three islands, **Doktorwerder, Unterer Tanzwerder,** and **Oberer Tanzwerder** are all easily accessibly by small, historic bridges at the outskirts of the *Altstadt.* At the tip of Unterer Tanzwerder, the **Weser Stone** marks the spot "where the Fulda and Werra kiss each other" and the Weser River is born (from the *Markt,* cross the Muhlenstr. bridge). England's hired guns, the famous Hessian mercenaries—19,300 of them—took off from the islet's former pier to face off against the upstart American colonists. With different dreams, some 57,000 German emigrants set sail from Doktorwerder between 1844 and 1857, up the Weser and straight on to America. The best view of the valley is from across the Fulda, atop the **Tillyschanze,** an 1882 tower built to commemorate May 30, 1626; on this day during the Thirty Years War, General Tilly stormed through Hannoversch Münden, slaughtering over 2000 citizens. The climb to the tower base is exhausting; to make sure you stay on the small, demanding, and unmarked path, follow the occasional concrete-slab steps and wire fences. At the base, you've got farther to go; platforms are at steps 26, 55, 76, and 98 for those too exhausted to go all 130 to the top. (Normally open May-Sept. daily 10am-sunset, contingent on the weather; if the tower's flag is flying, all is well. Admission DM1, children DM0.50.)

■■■ HILDESHEIM

Hildesheim has never attracted as many tourists as it deserves. Although it has boomed into a *Großstadt* (major metropolis) since World War II, Hildesheim seems to have more residents than energy, and the city's greatest treasures are still those of the past. Sort of. The entire *Altstadt* was leveled in World War II, and reconstruction was completely finished only four years ago, but the new-old structures do radiate beauty and majesty. Follow the white roses stenciled onto the street to the **St. Michaeliskirche,** tucked away in the northwest corner of the city center. This massive Romanesque church was completely rebuilt after the war; for its sake and that of the *Dom* (cathedral), UNESCO lists Hildesheim as one of the "historic legacies of mankind." (Open Mon.-Sat. 8am-6pm, Sun. 11:30-6pm; Oct.-March Mon.-Sat. 9am-4pm, Sun. 11:30am-4pm. Multicolor lighting weekend evenings.)

The *Dom,* built around a tiny chapel erected by Ludwig der Fromme in 815, dominates the old town center. According to legend, the emperor was on a hunting trip in the area when he lost the cross he wore around his neck. His servant, who had been sent out on a search, found the cross hanging on a rosebush blooming in the snow. What is said to be the same bush, the **1000-jährige Rosenstock,** now climbs a pillar in the open courtyard at the *Dom's* center. Jakob Grimm (one of the Brothers, who recorded the *Rosenstock* legend) kept one of its blossoms pressed in his library. The branches were burnt during World War II; the cathedral staff claims that the roots were preserved among the stones and blossomed again as soon as the *Dom* was restored. The life-from-death motif is repeated in the keystone phoenix carving of the **Annenkapelle,** Ludwig's old chapel, also in the courtyard. (*Dom* open May-Sept. Mon.-Fri. 9:30am-5pm, Sat.-Sun. 9:30am-noon and 2-5pm; Oct.-April Mon.-Fri. 10am-4:30pm.) Around the corner of the Dom, the **Diözesan Museum** showcases relics (i.e. saints' body parts) and over 100,000 books including prewar holdings dating back to 815, as well as tomes by the famed mathematician René

Descartes. (Museum open Tues.-Sat. 10am-5pm, Sun. noon-5pm. Admission DM4, students DM1.50.)

Near Neustädter Markt in the city's southeast section, at the intersection of Lappenberg and the appropriately named **Gelber Stern** (yellow star), is the beautiful marble **memorial** to Hildesheim's **synagogue.** The synagogue was built in 1819 and razed on *Reichskristallnacht* in 1938, the night of country-wide Nazi raids; now, only parts of the temple's foundation remain. The crooked, warped façade of the 1606 **Wernerhaus** (down from *Gelber Stern* to Brühl) conveys age but also artistry, untouched by bombs or modernizing renovations. If ostentation suits you more, the fairly majestic *fachwerk* (half-timbered design) of the **Knochenhaueramtshaus,** in the middle of the *Marktplatz*—a plaza of reconstructed half-timbered buildings and archways—should suffice. The upper floors of the *Knochenhaueramtshaus* also hold the city history portion of the **Römer-und Pelizaeus-Museum** (tel. (05121) 936 90). The museum features one of the continent's most colorful collections of Egyptian art, as well as frequent and extensive special exhibits; the other sections are located at Am Steine 1, around the corner from the *Dom.* (Open Tues. and Thurs.-Sun. 9am-4:30pm, Wed. 9am-9pm. Admission DM4, students DM2. Hours and admission vary for special exhibits.)

About two blocks from the *Rathaus,* the **tourist office,** Am Ratsbauhof 1c (tel. (05121) 159 95), reserves rooms for a DM3 fee. From the station, take bus #1: Schuhstraße, or walk from Bahnhofplatz to Bernwardstr. and bear left onto Osterstr. Walk "the wrong way" on this one-way street until the end, and look for information signs. An automat outside of the office dispenses hotel and city information for DM1 (open Mon.-Fri. 9am-6pm, Sat. 9am-1pm). The **post office** and **telephones** are just left of the train station (open Mon.-Wed. and Fri. 7-11:30am and 2-7pm, Thurs. 7-11:30am and 2-8:30pm, Sat. 7-10am and noon-2:30pm, Sun. 10am-noon). Hildesheim is 35km southeast of Hanover, with good *Autobahn* connections and almost hourly trains.

To reach Hildesheim's pastoral **Jugendherberge (HI),** take bus #1: Am Dammtor and change for the #4: Triffstr. Bring your trail mix for your trek uphill. The pale mauve hostel will be visible after a minute. Walking from the *Bahnhof* is an option for marathoners only. (Open 8am-2pm, 5pm, 7pm, and 9:30pm. Curfew 10pm. Partial wheelchair access. DM17.80, over 26 DM21.80. Sheets DM5.50. Breakfast included.) As far out as the hostel is, not much else in the affordable range is any closer; it's best to let the tourist office match price and distance in this case. The Hildesheim **pedestrian zone** stretches from the train station to Heilig Kreuz church. Much of that expanse in lined with *Imbiß* (snack) and fruit stands.

■■■ BRAUNSCHWEIG

Before Heinrich der Löwe (Henry the Lion) settled in Braunschweig in 1166, the merchants of this sleepy trading post on the River Oker slumbered in Dark-Age obscurity. After Heinrich unpacked his bags and erected his famous catty statue, he catalyzed the explosive rise of Braunschweig (sometimes called "Brunswick" in English) into a thriving center of medieval religion and commerce. Close on the hanging of Heinrich's hat, eight churches and cathedrals sprouted up, soon to be followed by the guildhouses, which mark the free city's economic importance to the Holy Roman Empire. An alumnus of the Hanseatic League, Braunschweig's robust economy and self-conscious bids for tourism make it one of Lower Saxony's most vital cities.

ORIENTATION AND PRACTICAL INFORMATION

Braunschweig lies close between the Lüneburger Heide and the Harz Mountains. It is the crossing point for high-speed trains connecting Frankfurt and Hanover to Berlin, and for other regional lines. Within the city, the *Hauptbahnhof* lies southeast of the inner city, an island ringed by the east and west branches of the Oker River. A concentric ring of streetcar tracks and four-lane traffic contains most of the city's attractions and its three pedestrian zones; most of the transit lines funnel through either the "Rathaus" or the "J.F.-Kennedy Platz/K. Schumacher-Str." stops.

Tourist Offices: There are 2 tourist offices in town, one immediately in front of the **train station** and the other a block from the **Rathaus**, Pavillon Bohlweg (tel. 792 37). Both provide maps of the city, and from a kiosk in the middle of the street, book rooms for a DM3 fee. Open Mon.-Fri. 8am-6pm, Sat. 9am-noon.

Currency Exchange: The post office offers decent rates and cashes travelers checks for a charge of DM3 per check.

Post Office: The main post office is the enormous building to the right of the train station. Open Mon.-Fri. 8am-6pm, Sat. 8am-1pm.

Telephones: Outside post office. **City Code:** 0531.

Public Transportation: A thorough system of **streetcars** and **buses** laces Braunschweig and its environs. 90-min. tickets, valid for any number of line changes within the hour and a half, are sold as single cards (DM2.60), double cards (DM4.20), or in packs of 10 (DM18); 24-hour (DM6), 48-hour (DM10), week- and month-passes are also available. Pick up a network map *(Liniennetzplan)* at the tourist office.

Car Rental: Hertz (tel. 710 55) near the station; turn left from Lathe Bahnhof and you'll see the office, Berliner Platz 1D. Open Mon.-Fri. 7am-6pm, Sat. 8am-1pm.

Mitfahrzentrale: Citynetz, Bohlweg 43-44 (tel. 194 44). Open Mon.-Fri. 10am-6pm, Sat. 10am-2pm, Sun. noon-4pm.

Bike Rental: Glockman, Ölschlägen 29-30 (tel. 469 23) rents bikes for DM10 per day. No deposit required.

Student Agency: ASTA (tel. 391 45 55), to the right of the cafeteria on Katharinenstr. This university-sponsored office finds summer housing and has information on women's and gay/lesbian activities. Open Mon.-Fri. 10am-2pm.

Bookstores: Pressezentrum Salzman, in the Brugpassage Galerie mall, has paperback trash novels as well as English and American magazines and newspapers. Open Mon.-Fri. 8:30am-6:30pm, Sat. 9am-2pm.

Library: Öffentliche Bücherei (tel. 470 29 14), at Hintern Brüdern 23, right off Langestr. Main building open Mon.-Fri. 11am-7pm, but the **foreign language library** is open Tues. noon-6pm and Fri. 11am-4pm.

Laundromat: Göttingstr. 1, near the university. Wash DM6. Open Mon.-Sat. 6am-11pm.

Emergencies: Police: tel. 110. **Ambulance:** tel. 440 33.

ACCOMMODATIONS

The charm of Braunschweig's inner city has not rubbed off on its budget accommodations. Little that is inexpensive can be found within walking distance; most require a 10- to 15-minute bus or streetcar ride. Pick up a free copy of *Hotels und Gaststätten* at the tourist office. It includes a listing of all accommodations and some cafes, with prices, phone numbers, and helpful city maps.

Jugendgästehaus (HI), Salzdahlumerstr. 170 (tel. 622 68 or 622 69, fax 636 54). Bus #11 (from the main station, direction "Welfenplatz") or #19 (weekdays only, direction "Glogaustr."): Krankenhaus-Salzdahlumer. On foot, walk left from the station on Berliner Platz to H.-Büssing-Ring, and turn left on Salzdahlumer Str.; the hostel is under the overpass and then 20min. down the road. Despite the look of a former industrial-park, the antiseptic buildings house bright and spacious rooms. Kitchen facilities and pool available (DM2). Members only. Reception open 7-10am and 4-10pm. No curfew. A variety of accommodation options are available from DM23-46, depending on number of roommates and proximity of showers, over 26 DM26-46. Sheets and breakfast included. Key deposit DM30.

Hotel-Pension Wienecke, Kuhstr. 14 (tel. 464 76, fax 464 64). From the station, walk up Kurt-Schumacher-Str. to J.F.-Kennedy Platz, bear left onto Auguststr. and then Kuhstr. (5min.). Quiet, comfortable rooms with big windows and TVs. Singles DM55-80. Doubles DM100-120. Reservations strongly recommended.

Simoné, Cellerstr. 111 (tel. 57 78 98). Bus #11 (from the *Hauptbahnhof*, direction "Paracelsusstr.") or #18 from the *Rathaus* (direction "Wendeschleife"): Maschstr., and continue up Cellarstr. If you must walk it, head up Kurt-Schumacher-Str. to J.F.-Kennedy Platz, bear left onto Konrad-Adenauer-Str. until Europa Platz, and then turn right on Gieseler Str., which becomes Güldenstr.; at Radeklint, turn left onto Celler Str. On the opposite side of town from the station, but close to the city center. Singles DM39-65. Doubles DM75-95

Elch, Wolfenbüttler Str. 67 (tel. 730 79). A 5-min. stroll from the train station, left on Berliner Platz to Heinrich-Büssing-Ring, and then right on Wolfelbüttler Str. The rooms feature plush carpets, plush chairs, and even plush lampshades. Definitely call ahead. Singles DM55-80. Doubles DM85-120.

FOOD

A plethora of *Kneipen* (bars) and *Imbiß* kiosks in the *Stadtmitte* offer salads, soups, and small sandwiches at reasonable prices. To quench your thirst, try the local favorite, a **Krefelder,** a sumptuous concoction of dark beer and Coke that tastes like root beer with a kick. There's a produce market in the *Altstadt* every Wednesday and Saturday from 8am to 1:30pm.

Student-Mensa, Katharinenstr. If it looks like a large, institutional cafeteria, you're in the right place. Hardly gourmet, but 5 selections are offered (DM1.50-4.20). Hang inside the doorway and observe before you saunter up to the *Kasse* to purchase a ticket voucher for your meal; only students get discounted rates, and you're supposed to be University-affiliated to dine at all. Open for lunch Mon.-Fri. 11:15am-2:25pm, Sat. 11:15am-1:55pm; for dinner Mon.-Thurs. 4:30-8pm.

Atlantik's Früchtchen, in the Burgpassage Galerie mall. With the frequent sales , the prices are unbelievably low. An impressive assortment of fresh fruits and veggies, with a sprinkler-mist system simulating sparkling morning dew.

Café L'Emigré, Hinter Liebfrauen, near St. Ägidienkirche. A *papier-mâché* centaur is the centerpiece of this Turkish bistro, which features a fully stocked vegetarian menu and an almost shocking number of kebabs. Meals from DM9-15. Open Mon.-Thurs. and Sun. 3pm-2am, Fri.-Sat. 3pm-3am.

Braunschweiger Hof, Kohlmarkt 10 (tel. 40 03 22). Winsome restaurant with a tiny courtyard surrounded by half-timbered houses. German specialties such as *spargel* and *wurst* from DM8. Open Mon.-Sat. noon-midnight.

SIGHTS

All of Braunschweig was once crowded on a small island formed by offshoots of the Oker River; the streams now form a moat-like line around the *Altstadt*. Braunschweig's medieval sights encircle the cobbled **Burgplatz,** over which the city's (and Heinrich's) emblem, a **bronze lion,** stands guard. It was first cast in 1166 as a symbol of Heinrich's regional dominance. The lion is challenged by the **St. Blasius Cathedral,** which towers over the inner city. Walk in and be awestruck. The 12th-century *Dom* contains twisting Gothic columns, spectacular stained-glass windows, an original 12th-century wooden crucifix, a dragon-supported candelabra, and, to top it all off, choir columns of Albert the Fat (no kidding). The **crypt** beneath holds the sarcophagi of Heinrich der Löwe, his consort, and his fan club (open daily 10am-1pm and 3-5pm; admission DM1, students DM0.50). The original Braunschweiger lion has retreated to the confines of the **Dankwarderode Castle,** also on the Burgplatz. Originally Heinrich's 12th-century den, it now keeps a modest trove of saints' relics to stand by the lion (open Tues.-Sun. 10am-5pm; free). To reach the historic center, take streetcar #1 from the train station, or walk (15 min.) along Kurt-Schumacher-Str., and bear right at J.F.-Kennedy Platz through Ägidienmarkt onto Bohlweg.

The **Braunschweig Landesmuseum,** across from the castle, also has a copy of the bronze lion; more copies can be found in the Rathaus in the *Altstadt*, in squares of neighboring villages, and, *ad infinitum,* in the tourist office. If the sight of the cat grows tiresome, give time to other exhibits: a 200,000,000,000 Rentenmark bill, coined in the inflationary 1920s, and the reconstructed Trabant and Volkswagen parked upstairs (open Tues.-Wed. and Fri.-Sat. 10am-5pm, Thurs. 10am-8pm; free). The Landesmuseum also has a branch at Hinter Ägidien devoted to **Jewish culture.** A reconstruction of the main room of the old synagogue hauntingly complements memorials to victims of the Holocaust. The furniture is all authentic, taken from the deteriorating temple in the 1920s (open Tues.-Wed. and Fri.-Sun. 10am-5pm, Thurs. 10am-8pm; free). The **Herzog Anton Ulrich Museum,** on Museumstr. in the eastern part of town, was the first European museum to open its doors to the general public. Its painting galleries are papered with Dutch masterpieces, including works by van Dyck, Vermeer, and Rembrandt (open Tues. and Thurs.-Fri. 10am-1pm and 2-4pm, Wed. 10am-1pm and 2-6pm, Sat.-Sun. 10am-4:45pm). Down the street, the world's first motorcycle is poised at the entry to the **Städtisches Museum,** on Am Löwenwall (tel. (0531) 470 24 50); holdings include historical originals of just about everything in your living room (open Tues.-Wed. and Fri.-Sun. 10am-5pm, Thurs. 10am-8pm; free).

The **Staatstheater,** built in 1861 to replace the Court Theater on Haymarkt where Lessing's *Emilia Galotti* and Goethe's *Faust* were premiered, has an extensive and inexpensive repertoire. Tickets start at DM7 and students get in for half-price. Write or call (tel. (0531) 484 28 00) for tickets at least one month prior to the show, or beg for leftover seats one hour before the performance (box office open Tues.-Fri. 9-10am and 4-5pm, Sat. 9-10am).

■■■ LÜNEBURG HEATH

Between Hamburg and Hanover stretches the flat, heather- and birch-covered Lüneburg Heath *(Lüneburger Heide).* Journeying, by bicycle or on horseback, from one mist-shrouded town to the next during the still morning hours is a tranquil escape from the worries of backpacking. The Heath evokes a child's crayon drawing of what the countryside should be like; green gives way to purple in August and September, when the bushes flower. The most important towns in the region are Lüneburg and Celle. In Lüneburg, the **Fremdenverkehrsverband Lüneburger Heide,** Lüner Weg 22 (tel. (04131) 520 63), finds rooms in hamlets barely on the map, with overnight stays at barnyard B&Bs and horse farms. Their barnhouse-hotel list even tells you what animals each has. Bike and riding maps and calendars of Heath events are also available (office open Mon.-Thurs. 8am-5pm, Fri. 8am-1pm).

LÜNEBURG

The city of Lüneburg made a 13th-century fortune with its natural stores of "white gold"—otherwise known as salt—and hasn't forgotten it. The *Bürgers'* monopoly held Northern Europe in an iron grip until plague and war broke in the 1620s; the salt has lately been channeled into healing baths. Poet Heinrich Heine grew up in Lüneburg but really didn't like it—he wrote the *Lorelei* here with thoughts of distant places. All that's left of the saline wealth and power is the town's structural beauty. The cut-out façades of the Gothic brick *Altstadt* are geometrically playful, and the quiet elegance of the half-timbered houses lends the city a graceful air.

Practical Information The **tourist office,** Am Markt (tel. 30 95 93 or 322 00, fax 30 95 98), in the *Rathaus,* will search for a room for a DM5 fee, but it often comes up empty in the summer; call ahead. From the train station, head downhill, away from the post office, and take a left onto Lünertorstr., which becomes Lüner Str.; turn left on Bardowicker Str. at the end, and you'll find yourself at the Markt-platz. (Open May-Sept. Mon.-Fri. 9am-6pm, Sat.-Sun. 9am-1pm.) There's a separate **regional tourist office** serving the entire Heath area (see Lüneburg Heath listings). The main **post office** is on the corner of Soltauer and Saltztorstr., 21335 Lüneburg. (Open Mon.-Fri. 8am-6pm, Sat. 8am-noon); the **telephone code** is 04131. **Hertz,** Lunerstr. 11 (tel. 581 30), rents cars near the train station. Open Mon.-Fri. 7:30am-1:30pm and 3-6pm. For a **Bike Rental,** try **Laden 25,** Am Weder 25 (tel. 379 60;

DM12 per day, DM60 per week; DM50 deposit required; open Mon.-Fri. 9am-noon and 1-6pm, Sat. 9am-1pm). Lüneburg lies at the northeast corner of the *Lüneburger Heide* region, and serves as the main transportation axis for the Heath. With 60,000 citizens, the city is only 30 minutes by frequent commuter trains from Hamburg and just over an hour from Hanover, on route to Hamburg.

Accommodations and Camping Although hotels fill up with alarming speed as the Heath blooms in July, August, and September, they're still available for a price. At other times, cheap and charming go hand in hand. The only camping in town is at **Campingplatz Rote Schleuse** (tel. 79 15 00), 3.5km south of Lüneburg on the Ilmenau River. Take the rail bus toward Deutschevern. (DM5 per person, DM3 per tent. Warm showers DM0.5. Sauna DM7.50.) **Jugendherberge Lüneburg (HI),** Soltauer Str. 133 (tel. 418 64), is adequate and offers above average breakfast. To get there during the week and Sat. morning, bus #1 runs from Am Sande to the hostel. Off hours, brace yourself for a long haul: from the train station, take Altenbrückertorstr. to Am Sande, turn left on Rotestr., and right on Lindenstr.; then hike 35 minutes down Solltauer Str. (Reception open 5-7pm. Curfew 10pm. DM17.80, over 26 DM21.80. Sleepsack DM2, complete linen DM5. Breakfast included. Call ahead. Partial wheelchair access.) **Hotel Lübecker Hof,** Lünertorstr. 12 (tel. 514 20), is right near the *Hauptbahnhof* and features bright, recently renovated rooms. (Reception open daily 6am-9pm. Singles DM50, with shower and toilet DM54-75. Doubles DM82, with shower and toilet DM92-118. Breakfast included.) **Hotel "Stadt Hamburg,"** Am Sande 25 (tel. 444 38), is smack in the center of the "other" market square. Well-kept rooms with portraits of famous Lüneburgers over the stairway (singles from DM35; doubles from DM65).

Food Beer seems to have lately replaced salt as the staple of choice in Lüneburg, as several area breweries will attest; during meals at **Kronen-Brauerei,** Heiligengeiststr., pound freshly-brewed beer in an early 15th-century beer hall (open daily 11am-midnight). Sample one of the local brands in the pedestrian zone around the **Brauerei-Museum,** or at the pubs of the **Stintmarkt** along the waters of the Ilmenau. **Legumes,** Rothenhamstr. (tel. 32 20), is very nouveau-vegetarian. Soothing new-age music is piped in as you select a meal from the weekly "suggestions" menu (every meal DM10.20) or from the impressive standard list (DM9-15; open Tues.-Sun. noon-3pm and 6-11pm). **Lüneburger Nudel Kontor,** Auf dem Kauf 1, (tel. 314 69), is a great Italian deli with fresh pasta, wine, cheeses, and olives. Prepared dishes run DM6-9 (open Mon.-Fri. 7am-6pm, Sat. 7am-1pm). Lüneburg possesses its fair share of street-side *Eiscafés,* often with pizza or gyros in the back. An open-air **market** springs up at Am Markt (Wed. and Sat. 7am-1pm).

Sights Tradition has it that salt was discovered in Lüneburg when a wild boar fell into a pit and, when he clawed his way out, shook salt loose from his bristles. At the **Deutsches Salz Museum (German Salt Museum),** Sülfmeisterstr. 1, you can see, touch, taste, smell, mine, melt, experience, and generally be at one with salt. From the Rathaus, take Neue Sülze to Salzstr.; at Lambertiplatz, take the path behind the supermarket. The quite well done and piquant museum features exhibits on salt production, ancient salt ships, salt use, and its medieval salt mill. (Open Mon.-Fri. 9am-5pm, Sat.-Sun. 10am-5pm; Oct.-April daily 10am-5pm. Tours Mon.-Fri. 11am, 12:30, 3, and 3:30pm, Sat.-Sun. 11:30am and 3pm. Admission DM4, children DM2.50. Add DM1.50, children DM1 for tours.)

The **Kloster Lüne** (cloister), on Domänehof just over the Lünetor bridge (tel. 523 18), proudly displays its 15th-century face and even older innards. (Open April-Oct. Mon.-Sat. 9-11:30am and 2:30-5pm, Sun. 11:30am-12:30pm and 2-5pm. Admission DM4.) The Gothic **Michaeliskirche** on Johann-Sebastian-Bach-Platz in the *Altstadt* is an impressive brick church built in 1418 on a foundation of salt; since then, the massive pillars have warped. (Open Mon.-Sat. 10am-noon and 2-5pm.) The **Nico-**

laikirche is the youngest of the churches—it was built in the 1430s (open daily 8am-6pm; Oct.-April daily 9am-5pm). Towering over the gables of the main streets is the spire of the **Johanniskirche**, Am Sande (tel. 445 42). The late Gothic altar and Baroque organ rest within the late 13th-century walls (open Mon. 1-4pm, Tues.-Thurs. 10am-5pm, Fri. 10am-5:30pm, Sat. 10am-6pm, Sun. 9:30am-5pm). Two other offbeat museums keep up the pace set by the shrine to salt (see above). The **Brauereimuseum (Brewery Museum)**, Heilgengeistr. 39-41 (tel. 410 21), was a working brewery for 500 years until the copper vats became museum pieces in 1985. This shows you exactly how hops, malt barley, and some extras become the magic potion that keeps Germany going (open daily 10am-noon and 3-5pm; free). The **Ost-preußiches Landemuseum**, Ritterstr. 10 (tel. 418 55), celebrates the sometimes dubious history and culture of East Prussia (open Tues.-Sun. 10am-5pm; admission DM2, children DM1). From the top of the **Kalkberg** hill, view Lüneberg's red roofs and small crooked buildings. The Kalkberg was once the site of a Benedictine monastery, destroyed in 1371. Gypsum, extracted from the rock for several centuries, works with the natural salt to produce the distinct, often weirdly colorful, vegetation on this and other hills around Lüneburg. Today it is a nature preserve; details on specific trails are available from the tourist office.

CELLE

Celle's most striking characteristic is its narrow cobble streets lined almost entirely with half-timbered houses. Even department stores and fast-food restaurants lurk behind traditional façades. Although some observant visitors might notice a little fake *Fachwerk* thrown in with the rest, the attraction of the area is genuine. In the heyday of *Fachwerk,* men had to pay a tax for each pair of crossed diagonal beams on their houses—they were coveted status symbols. Celle's homes have survived the wear of centuries and urban renewal better than most any in this part of Germany, making the town both a respite and a good base for expeditions through the wild landscape of the Southern Lüneburg heath, and to the remains of the Bergen-Belsen concentration camp.

Practical Information The discordantly non-half-timbered **tourist office**, Markt 6 (tel. (05141) 12 12; fax 124 59), across from the *Rathaus,* reserves rooms for DM2. From the station, head up Bahnhofstr. around Westceller-Tor-Str., then left on Poststr. to the Markt. Pick up a copy of *Jahresveranstaltung,* a list of concerts and musical productions, or *Celler Land Gastgeberverzeichnis,* a fantastic compilation of information for all the towns of Celle's administrative district. (Open Mon.-Fri. 9am-6pm, Sat. 9am-1pm and 2-5pm, Sun. 10am-noon; mid-Oct. to April Mon.-Fri. 9am-5pm, Sat. 10am-noon.) The telephone **city code** is 05141. The **post office** is on Schloßplatz, next to the park. You can motor through the greater Celle region in a **car** rented from **AutoHansa**, Braunschweiger-Heerstr. (tel. 290 44). Or rent a **bicycle** for DM10 per day from **2-Rad-Meier GmbH**, Neustadt 42a (tel. 413 69), just behind the station. This loudly self-proclaimed "Romantic Half-Timbered City" is 40km northeast of Hanover, 20 minutes by frequent trains.

Accommodations and Food Celle's stark but spic-and-span **Jugendher-berge (HI)**, Weghausstr. 2 (tel. 532 08) is in a large wood building; go from the station on Biermanstr. as far as you can, then turn left on Bremer Weg (30min.), or take bus #3 to "Dorfstr." (Reception open 5-7pm. Curfew 10pm. DM18.50, over 26 DM22.50. Breakfast included. Sheets DM5.50. Partial wheelchair access.) **Hotel Blühende Schiffahrt**, Fritzenwiese 39 (tel. 227 61) is considerably closer to the *Altstadt* and right on the Aller River. It effuses an old-world ambience. (Singles DM50-70. Doubles DM80-120. Breakfast included.) **Campingplatz Silbersee** (tel. 312 23), the nearest tent-pitching spot, is 7km northeast of the town proper; take the bus (direction "Vorwerk") from the station. Cafés line the cobbled streets of the *Alts-*

tadt; many have outdoor terraces. **Ararat**, Maunstr. 29 (tel. 254 13) serves amazing Turkish dishes from DM15.

Sights Some of the best *Fachwerk* houses are tucked away on **sidestreets**, such as Im Kreise, though Poststr. and Mauernstr. are also scenic. Don't miss the oldest house in the *Altstadt*, at Am Heiligen Kreuz 26. The **Stadtkirche** is just outside of the massive pedestrian zone comprising most of the *Altstadt*. The climb up the church tower yields an impressive view of plenty of red- and brown-shingled roofs. (Admission DM1, children DM0.50. Church open Tues.-Sat. 9am-12:30pm and 3-6pm; tower open April-Oct. Tues.-Sat. 3-4pm.) In the *Altstadt*, the exterior of the **Rathaus** is richly decorated in the *Weserrenaissance* style. Directly across the road, moving mechanical people chime the hours on a **Glockenspiel**.

The **Herzogschloß** (Duke's Castle), just west of the **Altstadt**, has foundations dating back to 1292. One of the most renowned residents of the castle was Caroline-Mathilde who was given asylum here in 1772 after her politically expedient marriage to the King of Denmark collapsed and her affair with the King's minister was exposed. (Tours daily every hr. 10am-4pm, except 1pm. Admission DM2, children DM1. Caroline-Mathilde's personal rooms open Mon.-Sat. 10am-4:30pm, Sun. 10:30am-12:30pm. Call 123 73 for more information.) A monument to the queen cries stone tears in the **Französischer Garten,** south of the *Altstadt*; when the rhododendron bloom in the summer, it's breathtaking. The gardens also contain the active hives of the **Niedersächsisches Landesinstitut für Bienenforschung** (Bee Institute; tel. 60 54; open Mon.-Fri. 9am-noon and 2-4pm; free).

BERGEN-BELSEN

Twenty km north of Celle, near the town of Bergen, lies the former site of the **Bergen-Belsen concentration camp.** Fear of a typhus epidemic led British military authorities to burn down the camp buildings in May 1945; memories of what they had seen there inspired a monument in November of that year. The German government agreed to care for and expand it in 1952. A somber stone obelisk commemorates the 30,000 Jewish victims and mass graves flank the massive stone dedicated to 50,000 Soviet prisoners of war who perished here. All in all, Bergen-Belsen claimed more than 100,000 lives. The document room presents the camp's history in detail; the photographs taken by the liberating British troops are powerful and moving reminders of the atrocities that occurred here. Most inmates were political insurgents, West European Jews, and women. One of the many victims was young Anne Frank, immortalized by her famous diary in which she wrote that "in spite of everything I still believe that people are really good at heart."

The site of the camp is difficult to reach. While the Bergen-Belsen Memorial (tel. (05051) 60 01) is open daily 9am-6pm, you must take two buses: #2 to Belsen and #9 to the camp. Schedules change regularly; call (05141) 88 11 30 for exact schedules. By car take the B3 toward Hamburg to Hinweisschild (about 20km from Celle), turn left, and continue straight to Bergen-Belsen, following the *Gedenkstätte* (memorial) signs. See Germany's History section for more discussion on this topic.

■■■ BREMEN

Happy is the man who has reached the harbor and left the sea and storm behind and now sits warm and peaceful in the good Ratskeller of Bremen.

—Heinrich Heine, "Im Hafen"

Bremen has lived by sailing all its life, and will likely end that way. Of course, there's no reason to believe that Bremen's star will fall any time soon. A longtime member of the Hanseatic League with spots of gritty *Weserrennaisance* beauty, the port has preserved its medieval heritage while capitalizing on such modern assets as the

BREMEN

Beck's Beer brewery and the enormous ships that pass through its harbor. Politically, the city constitutes a *Land* of its own, the smallest in Germany, contained entirely within the *Land* of Lower Saxony. Bremen's independence was famously expressed in 1980, when it was the sight of large scale, violent battles between the police and anti-war demonstrators. This harbor city is more dynamic than rough, both hardworking and cosmopolitan.

ORIENTATION AND PRACTICAL INFORMATION

Bremen lies along the Weser River south of its mouth at the North Sea, a little more than an hour by frequent trains from both Hamburg and Hanover. Much of central Bremen is walkable, but be wary should your forays bring you to the few blocks surrounding Ostertorsteinweg and Am Dobben: the farther you are from the *Altstadt,* the more likely you are to enter a high-crime and high-drug-use area.

Tourist Office: The souvenir-jammed central office (tel. 30 80 00, fax 308 00 30) across from the *Hauptbahnhof* has guides to museum exhibits and theater schedules, and sells tickets for concerts and the like. Open Mon.-Wed. and Fri. 9:30am-6:30pm, Thurs. 9:30am-8:30pm, Sat. 9:30am-2pm.

Consulate: U.K., Herrlichkeit 6 (tel. 590 90). From the *Hauptbahnhof,* go down Bahnhofstr. and bear right at the end onto Herdentorsteinweg; follow this as it becomes Sögenstr. and turn left onto Obenstr. At the *Dom,* turn right onto Bagebrückstr., go up and over the Weser River, onto the island, across the Wilhelm-Keisen-Brücke, and turn right on Herrlichkeit.

Currency Exchange: DVB, in the train station cashes travelers checks and exchanges currency. Open Mon.-Fri. 8am-6pm, Sat. 9am-noon and 12:30-4pm.

American Express: Am Wall 138, 28195 Bremen (tel. 141 71), at the lower end of the old city. Travel agency and full cardmember services. Open Mon.-Fri. 9am-5:30pm, Sat. 9am-noon.

Post Office: Main office at Domsheide 15, 28195 Bremen, near the *Markt.* Open Mon.-Wed. and Fri. 8am-6pm, Thurs. 8am-8:30pm, Sat. 8am-1pm, Sun. 9-10am. There is also an office on Bahnhofplatz 5 to the left of the train station.

Telephones: In the main post office and the branch office near the station. **City Code:** 0421.

Flights: Bremen's airport (tel. 559 50) is only 3.5km from the city center; take S-Bahn 5 or drive south on Oldenburger Str. and follow the signs. Frequent flights to major German cities, the East Frisian Islands, and out of the country.

Public Transportation: An integrated system of streetcars and buses covers city and suburbs. Information and many connections in front of the train station. The best deal by far is the **Bremer Kärtchen**, unlimited rides for one calendar day *(not* 24 hours from time of purchase). DM6 per card; fold the card in half (so day scene meets night scene) and insert arrow side up into the orange canceling machines the first time you board a bus or train. Single rides DM2.70, 4 tickets DM8, 10 tickets DM20.

Ferries: Shuttle to the suburbs and towns up the Weser, ending at Bremerhaven. Departures late May and mid-Aug. to mid- Sept. Wed.-Thurs. 8:30am; June to mid-Aug. Wed.-Thurs., Sat. 8:30am. One-way to Bremerhaven DM19, round-trip DM30. More info at the tourist office. Also combined bus/ship trips to Helgoland. Departures April-Sept. at 8:20am; check with the tourist office or a travel agent for departure dates. One-day return DM60, under 18 DM40, under 12 DM30.

Car Rental: Avis, Kirchbachstr. 200 (tel. 21 10 77).

Bike Rentals: Leave a DM50 security deposit and pedal away from the **Fahrrad Station** (tel. 30 21 14), a bright red stand with a bright yellow bike on top, to your left as you exit the station. DM13 per day, children DM8; DM52 per week, children DM40. Bicyclists' city map DM9.80. Open Mon. and Wed.-Fri. 9:30am-1pm, 2:30-5pm, Sat. 9:30am-noon, Sun. 9:30am-noon and 5-5:30pm.

Mitfahrzentrale, Citynetz, Hornerstr. 63 (tel. (0421) 194 44). Open Mon.-Fri. 10am-6pm, Sat. 10am-3pm.

Bookstores: Storm, Langestr. 10 (tel. 32 15 23). Has a selection of English books, dictionaries, and travel writing. Open Mon.-Fri. 9am-6:30pm, Sat. 9am-2pm. Also,

Frauenbuchladen Hagazussa, Friesenstr. 12 (tel. 741 40) stocks over 3000 titles of particular interest to women. Open Mon. 10am-2pm, Tues.-Fri. 10am-6pm, Sat. 10am-2pm.

Laundromat: Wasch Center, Vor dem Steintor, S-Bahn 2, 3, and 10: Brunnenstr. DM7 for wash, soap, and spin dry, and another DM1 to dry in a standard machine. Open daily 7am-10pm.

Pharmacy: Päs Apotheke, Bahnhofplatz 5-7 (tel. 32 10 15). Pick up a map of the city's pharmacies, with their rotating schedule of late and emergency openings. Open Mon.-Wed. and Fri. 9am-6:30, Thurs. 9am-8pm, Sat. 9am-2pm.

Gay Information Line: (tel. 70 41 70), has information about gay events and services.

Women's Center: Frauenstadthaus, Am Hulsberg 11 (tel. 498 95 00) has information for women. See Bookstores for a women's bookstore.

ACCOMMODATIONS AND CAMPING

The key words for Bremen are "call ahead." Small and inexpensive hotels are out there, but they fill up without warning. Otherwise, rooms in Bremen are ruinously expensive. **Camping** is distant, but it is an option.

Jugendgästehaus Bremen (HI), Kalkstr. 6 (tel. 17 13 69, fax 17 11 02). Bus #26 or streetcar #6: Am Brille, then walk along Bürgermeister-Smidt-Str. to the river, turn right and walk 2 blocks. To walk from the train station, take Bahnhofstr. to Herdentorsteinweg, go right at Am Wall, turn left on Bürgermeister-Smidt-Str., then right along the water to the 160-bed hostel. Sleek riverside real estate near the city center. The glowing Beck's Brewery sign, directly across the Weser, is your night light. Reception open 24hrs. No curfew. DM24, over 26 DM28. Breakfast and sheets included.

Jugendherberge Bremen-Blumenthal (HI), Bürgermeister-Dehnkamp-Str. 22 (tel. 60 10 05), in Blumenthal. Bus #10 from the *Hauptbahnhof* (direction "Großelingen") to the end of the line, then change for the #70 or 71 (direction "Farge/neuenkirchen" or "Blumenthal"): Kreinsloger (45- to 50-min. trip). Bürgermeister-Dehnkamp-Str. is down the stone steps through the trees. An oasis on a businesslike wharf, the hostel's small park overlooks the river. Call ahead to make sure it isn't filled with schoolchildren. Reception open 5-7pm. Curfew 10pm. DM18.50, over 26 DM22.50. Breakfast included.

Hotel Enzensperger, Brautstr. 9 (tel. 50 32 24). From the *Markt,* cross the Wilhelm-Keisen Bridge over the Weser, turn right on Osterstr., and right again on Brautstr. Blue-flowered quilts cover tidy beds, and some rooms have small streetside terraces. Singles DM42, with shower DM47. Doubles DM68, with shower DM78. Breakfast included.

Hotel Weltevreden, Am Dobben 62 (tel. 78 015, fax 70 40 91), just off Ostertorsteinweg. A more than adequate resting place with immediate access to late-night Bremen. Reception open until 10pm. Singles DM58. Doubles DM95, with shower DM100. Breakfast included. Call a few days in advance.

Hotel-Pension Haus Hohenlohe, Hohenlohestr. 5 (tel. 34 23 95). Under the bridge between the station and the post office branch, down Hermann-Bösestr., and right on Hohenlohe. If German charm exists anywhere, it's here. Highceilinged rooms with a jumble of old-fashioned furniture. Singles DM45-65. Doubles DM70-75. Triples DM105. Breakfast not included. Definitely call ahead.

Camping at Am Stadtwaldsee 1 (tel. 21 20 02) Bus #22 or 23 to the last stop (15min.), then walk along Kuhgangweg to Anwieseck and turn left. DM6.50 per person, DM4-8 per tent. Washers and dryers DM3 each. Open Easter-Oct.

FOOD

In the *Rathaus* itself visit Bremen's renowned **Ratskeller,** one of the oldest wine bars in Germany (1408). It keeps 600 German wines on hand; most are reasonably priced (DM3-10 per 0.2L glass), but the meals run about DM20. Competition comes from an open-air **Markt** on Tuesdays and Saturdays from 7:30am to 3pm. The restaurants that pack the **Schnoorviertel** are charming-all-too-charming, and exceedingly pricey; shop around. Bronze pigs herd pedestrians into shops and take-out cafés on **Sögerstraße**, yielding everything from chocolate truffles to *Fisch-Brötchen*. Student pubs await farther east, on and around **Ostertorsteinweg**; see Nightlife listings, below. Bremen is the coffee capital of Germany; over half of the nation's java passes through and is roasted in Bremen.

Feinbäckerei Janssen, Landherrnamt 7 (tel. 32 56 17). Put Janssen's *Bremerkaffeebrot* (slivers of toast with butter and cinnamon sugar, DM2.50 per 100g) on your temporary tea table, or the thick *Bremerklemen* (raisin bread) in your picnic basket. The best deal in the Schnoor since 1890. Open Mon.-Fri. 7am-6:30pm, Sat. 7am-2pm.

Café Torno, Am Dobben 71 (tel. 70 06 11). Try a rich *panini* sandwich (DM5-9, your choice of filling) after a few beers around the corner. The crowds fill the back, and the gyro window is always busy. Pasta dinners DM9-12. Open Mon.-Fri. noon-2am, Sat. noon-4am, Sun. noon-1am.

Engel, Ostertorsteinweg 31/33 (tel. 766 15). More graceful than most; *Jugendstil* gateway onto the Ostertor district. Coffee, cakes, and conversation inside, beer on the terrace outside; both spots come with a view. See what happens. Artful meals for DM10-15. Open daily 7am-4am.

Harlekin Bookshop/Café, Lahnstr. 65b (tel. 50 19 11). Bus #5: Theater am Leibnizplatz, walk over the bridge and continue down Friedrich-Ebertstr. Bremen's best breakfast selection (served all day) is spread out alongside a fine alternative bookstore. The generous *Käse-Brötchen* (DM4) and the *Turkische Frûbstück* (*Fladenbrot*, feta, olives, and cucumbers, DM7) make invigorating lunches. *Milchkaffee mit biscotti*, DM2.70. Café open daily 10am-6:30pm. Bookstore open Mon.-Fri. 10am-6:30pm, Sat. 10am-2pm.

SIGHTS

The best way to see Bremen is simply to wander around the city, drifting from one historic street to another. The **Altstadt** revolves around the **Rathaus,** its 15th-century base decorated by an amazingly ornate Renaissance façade. It survived WWII only because the English pilot who bombed the area deliberately missed this target. (Tours, the only access to the interior of the building, Mon.-Fri. at 10am, 11, and noon; Sat.-Sun. at 11am and noon. Admission DM4, children DM2.) Just left of the town hall is sculpture by Gerhard Marcks, *Die Musikanten,* which illustrates the Brothers Grimm's tale of a donkey, a dog, a cat, and a rooster who guilefully deceived a gang of robbers on their way to Bremen.

Also a war survivor, the achingly beautiful **St. Petri Dom,** Sandstr. 10-12 (next to the *Rathaus*, tel. 36 50 40), has a mosaic interior of orange, gold, and gray stone arches. The foundation dates to 798, when Charlemagne, North Germany's number-one missionary, had the first stone placed there. If gilded chandeliers and artwork are too overwhelming, descend into the subterranean crypts at the front and rear of the church. (Cathedral open Mon.-Fri. 10am-5pm, Sat. 10am-noon, Sun. 2-5pm. Tower open, all 265 steps, May-Oct. same times as cathedral. Tower admission DM1.) In a corner of the cathedral is the **Dom Museum** (tel. 365 04 75), housed in part of the original foundation with frescoes dating back 500 years. (Open Mon.-Fri. 10am-5pm, Sat. 10am-noon, Sun. 2-5pm; Nov.-April Mon.-Fri. 1-5pm, Sat. 10am-noon, Sun. 2-5pm. Admission DM2, children DM1.) Your ticket from the museum is good for half-price on the ticket for the **Bleikeller,** in the basement of the **Dom.** In 1695 the mummified corpses of workers who had fallen from the roof of the cathedral were discovered here; they have been on exhibit—alongside desiccated church luminaries—for three centuries. (Open May-Oct. Mon.-Fri. 10am-5pm, Sat. 10am-noon, Sun. 2-5pm. Combined ticket for museum and *Bleikeller* DM2.)

Just past the *Domshof*, turn left on Domsheide for the medieval **Schnoorviertel**, a district of red-roofed gingerbread houses and shops. Between the Marktplatz and the Weser River lies the narrow red brick and cobblestone **Böttcherstraße**, a winding labyrinth of boutiques and craft shops. The **Glockenspiel** right next to **Roselius**

Haus chimes at noon, 3pm, or 6pm, when part of the building opens up to tell the story of early aviators. Some very modern offices are now housed in very beautiful Renaissance buildings; one which stands out is the **Gerichtsgebäude** (municipal court), Domsheide 16. As you work the streets, stop by the **Bremer Nachrichten** building on Langenstr., where the daily paper can be read page by window-display page. For more of a cultural education, see museum listings, below.

MUSEUMS

Kunsthalle, Am Wall 207 (tel. 32 90 80), between the Marktplatz and the Ostertorsteinweg. A collection of artworks ranging from the Renaissance to the present; the ensemble of bright, guilty German Expressionist pieces is especially strong. Open Tues. 10am-9pm, Wed.-Sun. 10am-5pm. Admission DM6, students DM3.

Neues Museum Weserburg Bremen, Teerhof 20 (tel. 59 83 90), on the small island that splits the Weser River. Modern artistic attempts from the Angst-ridden 60s to the Angst-ridden 90s. Open Tues.-Fri. 10am-6pm, Sat.-Sun. 11am-6pm. Admission DM6, students DM3.

Übersee Museum, next to the train station at Bahnhofsplatz 13 (tel. 397 83 57). The gilded Baroque façade makes for a strange welcome to its multicultural exhibits. Highlights include a mock South Sea island village. Open Tues.-Sun. 10am-6pm. Admission DM2, students DM1.

Rundfunkmuseum, Findorffstr. 85 (tel. 35 74 06). A large-scale center which chronicles the development of telecommunications, with the sorts of exhibits which light up and whirl when touched. Open Mon.-Tues. and Thurs.-Fri. 9:30am-1pm and 2-5pm, Sun. 10am-12:30pm. Admission DM2, children DM1.

ENTERTAINMENT

Bremen rounds it all out with a strong cultural scene, encompassing opera in the **Theater am Goetherplatz,** Am Goetheplatz 1-3 (tel. 365 33 33), new drama in the **Schauspielhaus,** Ostertorsteinweg 57a (tel. 365 33 33) and the **Bremer Shakespeare Company,** Theater am Leipnizplatz (tel. 50 03 33). The **Theater im Schoor,** Wüste Stätte 11 (tel. 32 60 54) offers cabarets and revues. Discount tickets are usually held for students. Contact the tourist office or the theaters for schedules and prices. During the last two weeks of October, Bremen celebrates its trading heritage with the colorful **Freimarkt** fair, an annual event since 1095. The **Weserflohmarkt** (flea market), an organized cacophony of vendors, sets up shop every Saturday on Schlactel and Weserpromenade (on the banks of the river) 8am-2pm. The Bremen **casino** is at the heart of Böttcherstr. (tel. 32 90 00; open daily 3pm-3am; 18 or older).

NIGHTLIFE

Bremen rocks. Concerts are often held in the **Weserstadion** behind the train station. The tourist office will have current information about concerts and where to find tickets. Many clubs also host live music nights which feature American bands making their European debut. Check out *Mix,* a free entertainment magazine available at the information office for details. **Modernes Complex,** Neustadtswall 28 (tel 50 55 53) has, at different times, cinema, theater, concerts, and dancing (times and cover charges vary). If you want to sample Bremen's pub culture, wander along the **Ostertorsteinweg** at night. This is the major haunt for Bremen students and trendies.

Litfass, Ostertorsteinweg 22 (tel. 70 32 92). An all-day, all-night bastion of alternative chic. Its extensive outdoor terrace and open facade make it the place to be and be seen—if that's what you're into. Open Sun.-Thurs. 10am-2pm, Fri.-Sat. 10am-4pm.

Aladin, Hannoverschestr. 11. A bar which often hosts live music. Open Wed. 8pm-2am, Fri.-Sat. 8pm-7am.

Café Honolulu, Theodor-Körnerstr. 1. Gay bar/club usually crowded with students. Open Tues.-Wed., and Fri. from 8pm, Sun. from 3pm.

TheaLit, Im Krummen Arm 1(tel. 70 16 32). Evening club and center for women and lesbian events. It also contains a bar. Open Sun.-Fri. 4pm-midnight.

■ Near Bremen: Bremerhaven and Cuxhaven

Both Bremerhaven and Cuxhaven are departure points for **Helgoland** (see below). Bremerhaven was founded in 1827 to serve as Bremen's harbor on the North Sea. Friedrich Engels called the city a "young place" in 1841, "quite nice, quite convenient, quite Bremian."The **Deutsches Schiffahrts Museum** (National Maritime Gallery), pays tribute to boats boats boats with models and sea relics inside the main building, and **Museumschiffe** (Museum ships) moored outside. (Ships and main building open Tues.-Sun. 10am-6pm; main building only Oct.-April Tues.-Sun. 10am-6pm. Combined admission DM4, children DM2.) Docked nearby, but with separate admission, is the **U-Boot Wilhelm Bauer,** the only submarine of its (rather infamous) late WWII class neither sunk nor scrapped (open April-Oct. daily 10am-6pm; admission DM2.50, under 18 DM1.50). Bremerhaven is a half-hour away from Bremen by train; a **ferry** also leaves Bremen each morning at 8:30am. The **tourist office** (tel. (0471) 420 95), fax 482 07 55) receives guests at Van-Ronzelenstr. 2.

Cuxhaven has the North Sea at its back and not much else. At the **Alte Liebe** pier (named for the sunken ship, the *Olivia*, on whose bulk and bones it was built) board the *MS Flipper* for **Neuwerk Island,** a pocket of land only separated from mainland Germany in high tide. (Round-trip DM26, under 17 DM20. One-way DM20, under 17 DM15. Call (tel. 322 11) for schedule and other information.) Low tide exposes the sinking ground of the **Watt,** Northern Germany's unique sandmarsh landscape. Be careful not to cross alone the somewhat eerie plain alone; the best route is by one of the **Wattenpost horse-drawn carriages.** (Departures vary with the tides. 2hr., leaving about 8 hrs. on the island before return; tel. (04721) 290 43 for more information. Round-trip DM43, ages 10-17 DM38.) Of the eleven district **tourist offices,** the closest to the train station is on Lichtenbergplatz; take buses #1-4, 21 (direction "Duhnen") to Lichtenbergplatz. Cuxhaven's **Jugendherberge (HI)** is a block and a half from the deep blue sea (tel. (04721) 485 52, fax 457 94). From the station take bus #1, 2, or 4 (direction "Döse-Duhnen") to Seelust, and backtrack to the *Jugendherberge* sign. The rooms are sparse but adequate. Save your room receipt to get onto the beach for free. (No securable lockers. Curfew 11:30pm. DM16.50, over 26 DM20. Breakfast included. Partial wheelchair access.) Near the hostel, **Campingplatz Seelust,** Cuxhavenerstr. 65/67 (tel. (04721) 40 25 04; DM9.20-11.50 per site, DM6.90 per person) is little more than a place to park yourself between trips to the surf, but for that it will do.

■■■ HELGOLAND

Helgoland is a rocky red island off the coast of Germany, accessible by ferries from **Bremerhaven** and **Cuxhaven** (see above), both easy commutes from Bremen. For Northern Germans, the red cliffs rising steeply from the sea give Helgoland poetic cachet, similar to that of its pale cousin Dover. The island itself has at various times been controlled by pirates, Frisians, the Hanseatic League, Danes, and Britons; the Germans traded Zanzibar to England for Helgoland in 1890. The MS *Helgoland* leaves Bremerhaven daily from April to September at 9:45am from the Seebäderkaje (Regular round-trip DM68, ages 12-18 DM38, ages 4-11 DM34. Day excursions DM55, ages 12-18 DM35.50, ages 4-11 DM27.50. Call (04464) 80 21 for more information.) From May to September, the *Wappen von Hamburg* sails from Cuxhaven's *Fährhafen* harbor; from October to April, the transit is on other, smaller vessels out of the *Alte Liebe* docks (departures daily at 10:30am). A daytrip includes four hours at sea and four hours on shore, arriving back in Cuxhaven by 6:30pm. (Call (0461) 864 17 for information and bookings. Regular round-trip DM72, ages 12-18 DM40, children DM34. Day excursions DM55, under 18 DM36. One-way DM41, ages 12-18 DM25, children DM21.) Helgoland's **Jugendherberge "Haus der Jugend" (HI)**, Postfach 580, is a 15-minute walk from the ferry dock. (Reception open 6-8pm. Curfew 10pm. DM16.50, over 26 DM19.50. Open April-Oct.)

■■■ OLDENBURG

The center of the Weser and Ems River region, polite little Oldenburg was a Danish foothold from 1667 to 1773, when it blossomed in independence. Not far from Bremen (frequent trains; 25min. trip), Oldenburg is on an offshoot of the Weser River; the moated old city opens the way to East Frisia, and serves as the take-off point for most excursions. The painting collection in the **Landesmuseum,** on Schloßplatz, is extensive. Goethe friend and fan Johann Tischbein, extremely well-represented on the first floor, tried to paint everything the author described (open Tues.-Fri. 9am-5pm, Sat.-Sun. 10am-5pm; free). The **Augusteum,** Elisabethstr. 1 (tel. (0441) 220 26 00), is an extension of the Landesmuseum with two floors of half-awake Surrealist dreamscapes and Kirchener's Expressionist street scenes (open Tues.-Fri. 9am-5pm, Sat.-Sun. 10am-5pm; free). On the **Markt,** the 13th-century **Lambertikirche** has a worn Gothic façade, but the interior is a Neoclassical version of the Pantheon (open Tues.-Fri. 11am-12:30pm and 2:30-5pm, Sat. 11am-12:30pm; free).

The **tourist office,** Wallstr. 14 (tel. (0441) 157 44), finds rooms from DM35 for free and plies visitors with numerous North Sea brochures (open Mon.-Fri. 9am-6pm, Sat. 9am-noon). Visit the **Fremdenverkehrsverband Nordsee-Niedersachsen-Bremen,** Bahnhofstr. 19-20 (tel. 92 17 10), for invaluable information on the East Frisian islands, as well as regional information for the area between Holland and Hamburg (open Mon.-Thurs. 8am-5pm, Fri. 8am-4pm). Rent **bikes** at **Die Speiche,** Donnerschweerstr. 45 (tel. 84 123). The city's modernist **Jugendherberge (HI)** is at Alexanderstr. 65 (tel. (0441) 871 35); bus #7, 9 or 12 to Lappan, then bus #2 or 3 to von Finckhstr. To walk from the station (1.5km), go down Moslestr. and turn right on Am Stadtmuseum; the hostel is straight ahead down an *Imbiß*-restaurant lined street. The hostel fills up, so call ahead. (Reception open 5-10pm. Curfew 10pm, sometimes 11pm. DM18, over 26 DM22. Breakfast included.) The **Hotel Hegeler,** Donnerschweerstr. 27 (tel. 875 61), has clean rooms and a bowling alley. From the station, cross the pedestrian bridge over the tracks (near the post office) and follow the road to Donnerschweerstr. Turn left and walk 100m. (Singles DM40-45, with shower DM60. Doubles DM70-80, with shower DM110. Call a few days ahead.)

■■■ EAST FRISIAN ISLANDS

Seven sandy islands bracelet the East Frisian (*Ostfriesische*) North Sea coast. Control of the East Frisian dunes has been passed among Russia, Prussia, Holland, and various Scandinavian countries for the past few centuries, but their value is more aesthetic than strategic. Though floods of Germans come here to be healed by the purifying air, be wary about gaining a false sense of seasonal stability—the climate here has been known to change dramatically in one day. A sweater and umbrella might be practical additions to warm-weather gear. If it is cold and wet outside, try some hot **East Frisian tea,** or catch a local telling a fish story in the totally incomprehensible (even to most Germans) *Plattdeutsch* dialect. Nature speaks more clearly—the *Seehunde* (seals), endangered by coastal development and oil exploration, victims of the filthy discharge of the Elbe River, are sometimes found washed up on the shore. When the tide is out, the Watts beaches appear, connecting the mainland to Baltrum, Norderney, Spiekeroog and Langeoog. *Never* venture out onto the Watts without a guide because the tide's quick return can be *extremely* dangerous. Do, however, take the 8 to 10km walk with a certified guide to witness the vast and splendid desolation of the ocean's floor.

There are **HI youth hostels** on six of the islands—Borkum, Juist, Norderney (two hostels), Langeoog, Spiekeroog, and Wangerooge—plus several more on the mainland coast. All are frequently swamped in summer, so remember to call ahead. Finding a place to eat should never be a problem, as most of the hostels require you to purchase *Vollpension* (full board; 3 meals per day). A resort tax slimes its way onto all accommodation bills. **Getting there** is the most vexing problem of East Frisian tourism: a variety of small independent companies run **ferries** to individual islands from separate mainland ports. There is no inter-island transport. Unadulterated air is ensured by **car bans** on all islands except Borkum and Norderney (where cars are highly restricted), but bikes or just sandals will transport you to the North Sea surf.

EMDEN TO BORKUM

Borkum is the largest and western-most of the islands, a perfect choice for idle per-ambulations. The island offers a spectrum of seaside pleasures, from the 1576 **light-house** on Richthofenstr. to the **nude beach.** For the latter, take the bus to stop 33: FKK-Strand. In case you're on the island in the winter, Borkum host the "**Klaa-sohm" folk festival** on December 5.

The **ferry** ride leaves from the Borkum dock in Emden, the first port on the train from Oldenburg. (2¼hr. Departures March 15-Oct. 17 daily at 8, 11am, 2, and 5pm; Oct. 18-March 14 Mon.-Thurs. and Sat. 8am and 3:30pm, Fri. and Sun. 8am and 5pm. Day excursion DM24, round-trip DM44; Fri. 5pm-Sun. round-trip DM35, ages 4-11 DM 17.50.) Double-hulled **katamarans,** which skim the water, also run to the island. (1hr. Departures irregular. DM15 surcharge on regular prices.) A second ferry runs from Borkum to **Eemshaven** in the Netherlands. (Day-excursion DM19, children DM9.50; round-trip DM35, children DM17.50.) For more information on the Emden-Borkum run, call (04921) 89 07 22, and for Borkum-Eemshaven informa-tion, call their office in the Netherlands (tel. 0031 (5961) 60 84). Make reservations for private **rooms** (DM30 and up) and pick up a bus map at the **Kurverwaltung,** Goethestr. 1 (tel. (04922) 30 31; for rooms (04922) 841). Predictably, Borkum's **Jugendherberge (HI),** Jann-Berghaus-Str. 63 (tel. (04922) 579, fax 7124) fills up with others seeking a prime location (5min. walk from the dock; call ahead; open March-Nov). **Insel-Camping** is at Hindenburgstr. 114 (tel. (04922) 10 88), about 15 min-utes from the island's train station by foot, or take the bus to stop #17. (DM16 per person, tent included. Open mid-March to Oct.)

If you end up stuck in Emden, don't despair; there's plenty to do while waiting for the next ferry. Call (04921) 86 23 90 to get on a tour of the mammoth **Volkswagen plant** (open Mon.-Fri. 9:30am-1:30pm). **Jugendherberge Emden (HI),** An der Kes-selschleuse 5 (tel. (04921) 237 97), is in a graceful old house; walk from the city cen-ter to the park (10min.); the hostel is near the outdoor pool. (DM17.50, over 26 DM21.50. Breakfast included.)

NORDDEICH TO NORDERNEY

The most accessible of the islands, **Norderney** is the oldest German North Sea spa and a former Hanoverian royal retreat. Bismarck and Heinrich Heine both vaca-tioned here. To follow in their illustrious footsteps, catch the boat from the main-land city of **Norddeich,** about half an hour by train from Emden to the "Norddeich-Mole" stop. Test a smoked-eel (DM4) or fresh crab sandwich (DM3) at the **seafood stand** outside the station while waiting for the next **ferry.** (Several departures daily, Mon.-Thurs. 6:45am-6pm, Fri.-Sun. 7am-8pm; just about hourly during the summer. Day excursion DM20, round-trip DM21; railpasses not valid.) Information and tick-ets are at the end of a long line at the **Aktiengesellschaft Reederei** on the wharf (tel. (04931) 18 02 24; Norderney office tel. (04932) 895 20); daily schedules are also posted (open Mon.-Thurs. 7am-6pm, Fri.-Sun. 7am-7:30pm).

Norderney has the standard East Frisian attraction of a **nude beach** at the east end of the island. Follow the FKK (Frei-Körper-Kultur) signs. The **tourist office,** Bülow-allee 5 (tel. (04932) 502), sniffs out rooms in *Pensionen* (DM30) or private homes (longer stays only, DM25) for a DM7.50 fee (open May-Sept. Mon.-Fri. 9am-12:30pm and 2-6pm, Sat. 10am-12:30pm and 2-4pm). Norderney's two **Jugendherbergen (HI)** are both extremely crowded. The hostel at **Südstraße 1** (tel. (04932) 24 51) is for members only. Follow Zum Fähranleger to Deichstr., then onto Südstr. (approx-imately 15min. walk). (Reception open 8:30-9am, 5-5:30pm, and 9:45-10pm. First night: DM20, over 26 DM23. Breakfast included. Subsequent nights: DM24, over 26

DM26. Full board included. Open March-Oct.) The other hostel is at **Am Dün-ensender 3** (tel. (04932) 25 74, fax 832 66), one hour from the ferry; rent a bike in town or suffer. (DM30, over 26 DM37.90. Full board included. **Camping** available in summer is for HI members only: DM10.25 per person with breakfast, DM24.15 with full board. For stays of more than 1 night, you must purchase full board for DM13 per day at the Jugendzeltplatz. Open March-Oct.) **Camping Booken,** Waldweg 2 (tel. (04932) 448), is expensive, but the next best thing to the hostels. Call ahead. (Reception open 10am-noon and 5-7pm. DM10 per person, DM8-10 per tent. DM40 per mobile home. Showers DM1.50. Open May-Sept.)

Norderney is especially thronged in late July, so staying overnight on shore at **Norddeich** is an inviting option for day-trippers. In the field past the tourist office (see below), the giant wind-energy towers are surprisingly impressive. The only mal-contents are the seal colonies which once owned the shore; two minutes farther up the way at the **Seehunde Station,** some specimens still have a petting-zoo home (admission DM2, children DM1). The Norddeich **tourist office,** Dörperweg (tel. (04931) 172 02) accepts donations to the Save-the-Seals fund and finds rooms in *Pensionen* (DM25-30). From the train station, head down the seaside Promenade and turn right on Dörperweg (open Mon.-Thurs. 8:30am-12:30pm and 2-4:30pm, Fri. 8:30am-4pm, Sat. 10am-4pm). The environmentally conscious **Jugendherberge (HI),** Strandstr. 1 (tel. (04931) 80 64, fax 818 28), is just over the dike from the beach. Head down to Badestr. from the ferry dock and turn right onto Strandstr. (Reception open 8:30am-2pm and 4:30-10pm. DM18, over 26 DM22. Breakfast included. Closed 1st weekend of each month Nov.-March.) The hostel's backyard tent sleeps eight (DM8 per person); they'll also let you set up on your own (DM7 per person). **Nordsee-Camp,** Deichstr. 21 (tel. (04931) 80 73), is 500m farther down Badestr., which turns into Deichstr. Impressive views, but dike-side camping gets chilly at night. (DM5 per day, DM7.75 per person, plus DM3 tourist tax.)

JUIST

Juist is 17km long, 500m wide, and famous for its birds. First settled in 1398, it's a bit tough to settle there now. Ferries leave at odd times, depending on tides and season; call (04931) 85 20 for details. (June-Oct. roughly 2 per day. Day excursion DM24, round-trip DM36.) The **tourist office** *(Kurverwaltung),* Friesenstr. 18, has maps and a room-finding service (tel. (04935) 80 90; for rooms tel. 80 92 22, fax 80 92 23). You can ride to and from the **Jugendherberge,** Loogster Pad 20, (tel. (04935) 10 94, fax 82 94), on a horse. (Reception open daily noon-10pm, or whenever a boat arrives. DM24.10 with breakfast, DM28.40 with full board; over 26 DM28.10, DM32.40.)

BALTRUM

From west to east, the islands get harder to reach. The ships that serve them follow the tides; be careful not to get marooned overnight. Departure times are available at any train station in the area and at most hostels. To reach **Baltrum,** the smallest island with only 500 people, take the bus from the Norden train station (1 short stop from Norddeich) to **Neßmersiel** to meet the ferry. Train, bus, and boat are all timed for a convenient rendezvous. (June-Nov. 2-3 per day; last ferry to the island does not have a corresponding ferry back.) Check the day-by-day schedule for exact times; call (04939) 235 for help. The **tourist office** *(Kurverwaltung),* Rathaustr. 130 (tel. (04939) 800; for rooms (04939) 80 48), in the *Rathaus,* offers hotel information.

LANGEOOG AND SPIEKEROOG

Trains from Oldenburg reach the inland town of **Esens,** from which you can pro-ceed to the 18th-century pirate base **Langeoog.** Take the bus (DM3.50) from the Esens train station to **Bensersiel,** the departure point for island ferries. (7 per day. Early June to late Sept. Mon.-Thurs. and Sat. 8:15am-5:30pm, Fri. and Sun. 8:15am-7pm; Day excursion DM25.) Langeoog's **Jugendherberge "Domäne Melkhörn"**

(HI) (tel. (07942) 276) is smack-dab in the middle of the island (45min. from port. Members only. Under 18 DM29.35, ages 18-26 DM30.70, over 26 DM34.70. Full board included.) The hostel also runs a **campground.** (Members only. DM25.70. Full board included. Reservation required. Open April-Oct.) Get exact walking directions to the hostel at the **tourist office** at the pier (tel. (04972) 69 30), or **rent a bike** and take the cycling path. Another bus leaves Esens for **Neuharlingersiel,** the departure point for **Spiekeroog,** an island which takes pride in its historic shipwrecks and its natural silence—"No festivals celebrated here," brags the official brochure. Call for seasonal ferry schedules (tel. (04976) 17 33). Its **tourist office,** Noorderpad 25 (tel. (04976) 17 25), has information on rooms and dune paths (open Mon.-Fri. 8am-12:30pm and 2-4pm, Sat. 8am-12:30pm). Spiekeroog's **Jugendherberge,** Bid Utkiek 1 (tel. (04976) 329), is a short walk (10min.) from either the port or the beach. (DM33.50 per person. Full board included. Write or call well in advance.)

WANGEROOGE

The journey to Wangerooge is a labor worthy of Ulysses. A bus from Esens (or a more convenient one from Wilhelmshaven, accessible by train from Oldenburg) stops at Carolinsel. There choose either a second bus or a boat ride up a narrow inlet to the sea-town of **Harlesiel.** Boats leave Harlesiel two to five times daily from April to October, and once or twice daily the rest of the year; exact times vary widely with the season. Call for up-to-date **ferry information** (tel. (04464) 345). Wangerooge's own **tourist office,** Strandpromenade (tel. (04469) 890), can direct you to the haunting **Westturm,** a landmark which has been converted into the region's most striking **Jugendherberge (HI)** (tel. (04469) 439), about a 20-minute walk from the station. Look for the old stone tower. (Reception open daily 7-9am, 1-2pm, and 5-7pm. DM17.60, over 26 DM22.20. With full board DM29, over 26 DM31.70. Breakfast included. Open May-Sept.)

SCHLESWIG-HOLSTEIN

The best parts of Schleswig-Holstein lie around its twin coastlines, where the gritty Baltic ports of Lübeck and Kiel contrast sharply with the North Sea beaches. Were it not for these cities, and for the urban decadence of Hamburg, Germany's northernmost province could well be described as a region of harbors and pastures. Between its seafaring coasts lies a flat, green countryside dotted with small towns and traversed by scenic cycling routes. Schleswig-Holstein finally became a Prussian province in 1867 following Bismarck's defeat of Denmark and chose to remain in Germany at the end of World War I. However, the state still has close links with the Danes; many Danish libraries and schools as well as plenty of tourists are scattered within its borders. Most of the major ports are connected by ferries to Danish, Swedish, and Norwegian docks. Hamburg, the great metropolis at the region's southern border, is politically its own Land, but nevertheless dominates the regional landscape.

■■■ HAMBURG

As the largest port city in Germany, Hamburg exudes a kind of mad recklessness. Calling Hamburg's atmosphere "liberal" or "alternative" might not do the city justice; with a licentious sex industry comparable only to Amsterdam, and a fire-eyed ecological movement which recently convinced the *Land* government to plant 6000 new trees each year, Hamburg merits both exploration and experimentation. Welcoming and bidding farewell to goods and passengers from all over the world for centuries, Hamburg has grown into a sea-side industrial center of almost three million inhabitants. Industry, however, isn't the only thing you'll notice when you visit—more visible is the unique way in which Hamburg has grown old gracefully as Germany's "Gateway to the World," preserving its time-worn structures while allowing ample room for the new.

HISTORY

Having gained the right to navigate the Elbe in 1189, Hamburg held off pirates and trading rivals to become a leading power in the Hanseatic League by the 13th century. Its position straddling several rivers made it a hub for overland trade from Lübeck and the Baltic Sea. The growing profits of the lucrative shipping trade naturally led Hamburg to dabble in other financial concerns—the first German stock exchange convened here in 1558, while the Bank of Hamburg dates back to the early 17th century. In 1618 the city was granted the status of Free Imperial City, a tradition of autonomy that endures to this day. The commercial city's jealously guarded neutrality came in handy during the Thirty Years War, when the destruction that swept northern Germany remained wholly outside its city gates.

Riding the crest of Germany's breakneck industrialization and naval construction, by the time World War I broke out Hamburg had become one of Europe's wealthiest metropolises and the *Hamburg-Amerika Linie* ruled the waves as the largest shipping firm in the world. The city suffered an unusually severe pummeling in World War II as the first stop after the North Sea for the Royal Air Force. Thousands of lower-class dockworkers lived in crowded tenements right up against the port, the primary Allied target; a single air raid killed 50,000 civilians. The conflagration in the streets reached temperatures of 1800°F (1000°C), leaving nearly half the city's buildings as heaps of charred rubble. Fortunately, Germany's richest city could afford to reconstruct much of the copper-roofed brick architecture so characteristic of northern Germany.

Urban planning has continued to be an issue for the city; since the late sixties an active conservation movement has lobbied for the restoration of historic buildings. In the early 1980s, violent riots erupted when police attempted to evacuate buildings occupied by anarchists and left-wing intellectuals protesting against property speculators who had acquired the buildings. Eventually, advice was taken to heart; today, Hamburg actively restores and renovates its historic sites even when they are privately owned.

ORIENTATION

Hamburg's world-renowned North Sea port is actually 100km inland on the north bank of the **Elbe River**. The city is squeezed between the river and the two city lakes, **Aussenalster** and **Binnenalster**, formed by the confluence of the Alster and Bille Rivers with the Elbe. Most major sights lie between the **St. Pauli Landungs-brücken** ferry terminal in the west and the tourist office and *Hauptbahnhof* (main station) in the east. Much of the city around the docks is part of the *freihafen* (duty-free zone), so be prepared for customs stops when traveling out of the duty-free zone. Both the **Nord-** and **Sudbahnhof** S-Bahn stations exit onto the *Hauptbahnhof*.

The **Hanse Viertel** is a *Passage* thick with shops, art galleries, and auction houses; you won't buy anything, but the glamour makes window shopping a study in popular aesthetics. The area around **Sternschanze** has a grittier feel; a flea market often buzzes there on Saturdays. The **Altona** district, with its own major train station, was once an independent city ruled by Denmark. But as Hamburg got bigger, the Germans beat the Danes out. At the south end of town, an entirely different atmosphere reigns in the **Fischmarkt** along the Elbe at St. Pauli, which comes crazily alive on Sunday mornings as the North Sea catch is brought in. This is Europe's largest fish exchange. People run amok for a few gray dawn hours hawking fish, produce, and everything from socks to CDs—come and prowl the chaos for a bargain (5-9:30am; off-season 7-9:30am; U- or S-Bahn: Landungsbrücken).

PRACTICAL INFORMATION

Tourist Offices: Hamburg has 4 tourist offices dotted throughout the city which all supply free maps and other pamphlets for nominal prices. The **Hauptbahnhof office,** Kirchenallee exit (tel. 30 05 12 30), open daily 7am-11pm, and the **Fühls-büttel airport office,** Terminal 3 arrivals (tel 30 05 12 40), open daily 8am-11pm, will book rooms for a DM6 fee. Information also available at the **St. Pauli Land-ungsbrücken,** between piers 4 and 5 (tel. 30 05 12 00), open daily 9am-6pm, Nov.-Feb. daily 10am-5pm; and in the **Hansa-Viertel mall,** Poststr. entrance 20 (tel. 30 05 12); open Mon.-Fri. 10am-6:30pm, Sat. 10am-3pm, Sun. 11am-3pm.

Budget Travel: SSR Reiseladen, Rothenbaumchaussee 61 (tel. 410 20 81), near the university. BIJ and student discounts. Open Mon.-Fri. 9am-6pm, Sat. 9am-noon.

Consulates: U.S.: Alsterufer 27 (tel. 41 17 12 14), open Mon.-Fri. 8am-noon. **U.K.:** Harvestehuderweg 8a (tel. 44 60 71), open 9am-noon and 2-4pm.

Currency Exchange: The **bank** at the Kirchenallee exit of the train station has long hours but high prices (1% on traveler's checks with DM7.50 minimum). Open daily 7:30am-10pm. Better rates at downtown banks (open 9am-4pm).

American Express: Rathausmarkt (tel. 33 11 41, refund service tel. 01 30 31 00). Mail held. All banking services. Open Mon.-Fri. 9am-5:30pm, Sat. 9am-noon.

Post Office: Branch at the Kirchenallee exit of the *Hauptbahnhof*, 20099 Hamburg. **Poste Restante** at window #1. Open Mon.-Sat. 7am-9pm, Sun. 8am-8pm. The **Hauptpostamt (main office),** Hühnenposten 12, 20097 Hamburg, is about 150m right from the Kirchenallee exit of the station. Open Mon.-Fri. 8am-6pm, Sat. 8am-noon.

Telephones: At the *Hauptbahnhof* post office. **City code:** 040.

Flights: Information: tel. 50 75 25 57. Buses zoom off to **Fuhlsbüttel Airport** which serves most major European and German cities from outside the Kirche-nallee exit of the *Hauptbahnhof* (5:40am-9:20pm, every 20min., 30min. travel time, DM8). Or take the U-Bahn to Ohlsdorf, and catch the bus to the airport (every 10min., DM3.40).

Trains: The **Hauptbahnhof** handles most traffic with connections to Berlin (3½hr.), Bremen (1½hr.), Munich (6hr. ICE), Copenhagen 5hr.) and Basel (6½hr.

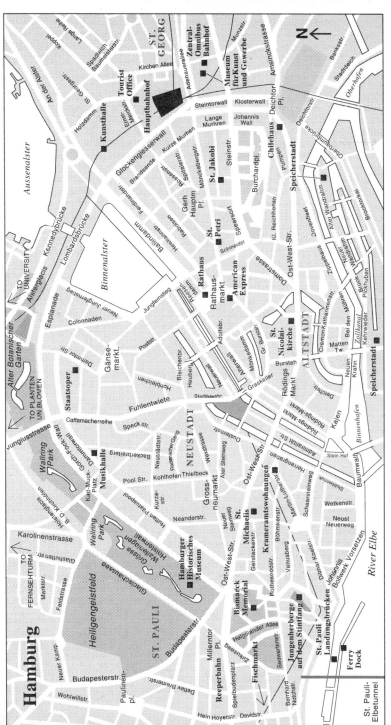

ICE). **Train information:** 194 19. **Dammtor** station is across the Kennedy/Lombards bridge, and **Altona** station is in the west of the city. Most trains to and from Kiel, Schleswig, Flensburg, and Westerland stop only at **Altona** station, which is also the end station for most intercity trains. Frequent trains and S-Bahn connect the three stations.

Buses: The long-distance bus station is near the *Hauptbahnhof* on Adenauerallee; buses go to Berlin (3½hr., DM50) and farther points.

Public Transportation: The efficient public transportation system (buses, U-Bahn, and S-Bahn) charges DM2.30-5.20 per trip, depending on distance. The U- and S-Bahn sleeps from midnight to 5am, when only a few **night buses** shuttle off from the Rathaus Markt.

Passes: Get **day tickets** DM6.90 for the U-Bahn and S-Bahn from orange automat machines or at the tourist office. A **family day ticket** (DM12.20) is good for up to 4 adults and 3 children under 12. A **3-day ticket** sells for DM20.The best deal is the **Hamburg Card** which gives 1st-class travel, including free night buses, and free admission to 11 museums and reduced admission to many other attractions and tours (**one-day card** DM9.80 for 1 adult and 3 children; DM20 for 4 adults and 3 children; **three-day card** DM19 or DM30). Cards may be purchased at tourist offices and One-day cards can be bought at *Automaten*. Railpasses are valid on the S-Bahn, but only for 2nd-class seating.

Ferries: Landungsbrücken, pier 9 (tel. 38 90 71), 2km west along the shore from St.-Pauli Landungsbrücken. **Scandinavian Seaways,** Rathausstr. 12 (tel. 389 03 71), runs overnight ferries to Harwich, England from mid-June to Aug. Tickets Sun.-Wed. from DM216, Thurs.-Sat. from DM240; reduced rate Sept.-June. Ages 4-15, 50% off; students under 26 and seniors 25% off. Less business-like **excursion** ferries sail for 50min. tours of the surrounding lakes and canals from the **Jungfernstieg** at Binnenalster (April-Oct. daily 10am-6pm. DM13, DM10 with Hamburg Card). Grand **tours of the port** are offered in English by **Hadag** steamer (tel. 56 45 23), running daily from pier #1. (March-Nov. at 11:15am; 1hr. ride; DM14, under 15 DM7.) Other cruises—minus the English—leave from Brücke 2-7 (DM8-18).

Boat Rental: You can rent sailboats and paddle-boats on the Aussenalster from **Alfred Seebeck** (tel. 24 76 52) or **H. Pieper** (tel. 24 75 78), both directly in front of the Hotel Atlantic, An der Alster, at the end of the Kennedy bridge. (S-Bahn to "Dammtor," then head west along Alsterglacis. Sailboats DM20 per hr., paddleboats DM15 per hr.)

Car Rental: Hertz, Kirchenallee 34-36 (tel. 28 01 20 103) is opposite the train station. Open Mon.-Fri. 7am-6pm, Sat. 8am-4pm, Sun. 10am-4pm.

Bike Rental: City Bike, Alte Feuerwache, Millentorplatz, Glacichaussee, near St. Pauli U-Bahn station. DM12 per day, DM60 per week. DM100 deposit and passport required. Open Mon.-Fri. 9am-noon and 4-7pm, Sat. 9am-noon.

Hitchhiking: *Let's Go* does not recommend hitchhiking as a safe mode of transportation. Those stubborn hitchers headed to Berlin, Copenhagen, or Lübeck take S-Bahn #1 to "Wandsbeker Chaussee," then walk along Hammerstr. up to the Hamburg Horn, a large, treacherous traffic rotary at the base of the *Autobahn*. Hitchers aiming for points south take S-Bahn 3 (direction "Harburg"): Veddel, and walk 5min. to the *Autobahn*. **Mitfahrzentrale,** Lobuschstr. 22 (tel. 39 17 21), at the Altona train station. Mon.-Wed. 8am-7pm, Thurs.-Fri. 8am-8pm, Sat. 9am-7pm, Sun. 10am-6pm. **City Netz Mitfahrzentrale,** Goterstr. 19 (tel. 194 44) is efficiently computerized. Open Mon.-Thurs. and Sat. 8am-7pm, Fri. 8am-9pm, Sun. 9am-9pm.

Bookstore: Internationaler Bücherladen, Eppendorferweg 1 (tel. 43 98 041), vends scads of English-language books at second-hand prices. Open Mon.-Fri. 10:30am-6pm, Sat. 10am-2pm.

Library: Staats- und Universitätsbibliothek, Von Melle Park 3 (tel. 41 23 22 33). Open Mon.-Fri. 9am-7pm, Sat. 10am-1pm. English-language section open Mon.-Wed. and Fri. 10am-noon and 2-4pm. Thurs. 10am-noon and 2-6pm.

Laundromat: Wasch-Center, Nobistor 34, near the Reeperbahn. Wash DM6, dry DM2 per 15min. Open 6am-10pm.

Rape Crisis Line: tel. 25 55 66, Mon.-Tues. 10am-1pm and 3-9pm, Wed. 10am-1pm and 3-4pm, Thurs. 10am-1pm and 3-5pm, Fri. 10am-1pm. **Opferhilfe Beratungstelle,** Paul-Nevermann-Platz 2-4 (tel. 38 19 93) offers advice to men and women who have been victims of sexually related crimes. Open Mon.-Thurs. 9am-5pm, Fri. 9am-2pm.

Lesbian and Gay Center: Magnus Hirschfeld Centrum, Borgweg 8 (tel. 279 00 60). U-Bahn 3 or bus #108 to Borgweg. Daily films and counseling sessions, as well as a good source for gay and lesbian community scene. Evening café open Mon.-Sat. 3pm-midnight, Sun. and holidays 4pm-midnight.

Pharmacy: Senator Apotheke, at the Kirchenallee exit to the train station (tel. 33 92 92) is open 8am-6:30pm, Sat. 9am-2pm. For emergency service, the addresses of late-night pharmacies are posted in the window.

Emergencies: Police: tel. 110. Headquarters at Kirchenallee 46, opposite the train station. **Ambulance:** tel. 112.

ACCOMMODATIONS AND CAMPING

Hamburg is not a cheap place to stay; single rooms start at about DM55, with doubles from DM75. Many of these, however, are tawdry establishments with few creature comforts. A stew of small, inexpensive *pensionen* line **Steindamm, Bremer Weg,** and **Bremer Reihe** north of the *Hauptbahnhof.* Check out your hotel before you accept a room—many of the establishments along this strip are of dubious repute. Let the tourist office's *Hotelführer* (DM0.50) help you steer clear. For longer stays, try the **Mitwohnzentrale,** Lobuschstr. 22 (tel. 39 13 73, open Mon.-Fri. 9am-6:30pm, Sat.-Sun. 10am-2:30pm).

Hostels and Camping

Jugendherberge auf dem Stintfang (HI), Alfred-Wegener-Weg 5 (tel. 31 34 88, fax 31 54 07). S-Bahn 1, 2, or 3, or U-Bahn 3 (from the main station): Landungsbrücke. Hike up the steps to the hill above. Large, busy hostel attracts travelers from all over the globe. View of the harbor, close to the Reeperbahn. Do take the hostel's security advice to heart. Kitchen facilities and lockers available. Reservations advisable. 3-day max. stay. Reception open 7-9am and 5:30pm-1am. Curfew 1am. DM18, over 26 DM22. Nonmembers DM5 extra. Breakfast included.

Jugendgästehaus Horner-Rennbahn (HI), Rennbahnstr. 100 (tel. 651 16 71, fax 65 56 516), U-Bahn 3: Horner-Rennbahn, then walk 10min. or take the bus (direction "Wandsbek;" DM2.80). Immaculately clean and very peaceful, a bit far from things. They serve a great buffet breakfast. Go for a 6-bed room; they're cheaper (DM23, over 26 DM27.50) and more than adequate. Lockers. Reception open 7:30-9am, 1-6pm, and 12:30pm-1am. Curfew 1am. DM25, over 26 DM29.50. Sheets and breakfast included. Open March-Dec.

Campingplatz Buchholz, Kielerstr. 374 (tel. 540 45 32). S-Bahn 3 (direction "Pinneberg") or S-Bahn 21 (direction "Elbgaustr."): Stellingren. Walk straight on Volksparkstr. and turn right on Kielstr. Reception open daily 7am-11pm; Oct.-May 8-10am and 4-8pm. DM5 per person, DM12.50-16.50 per tent. Showers DM2.50. Call ahead.

Hotels

Hotel Terminus Garni, Steindamm 5 (tel. 280 31 44), near the train station, around the corner from the Kunst- und Gewerbe Museum. Sprightly service and fetching rooms, but avoid the raisin-sized singles. Small, so call ahead. Singles DM65. Doubles DM100. Triples DM150. Showers DM1. Breakfast included.

Annerhof, Lange Reihe 23 (tel. 24 34 26). High corniced ceilings in spacious, comfortable rooms. Call ahead. Singles DM44. Doubles DM76. Breakfast DM8.

Pension Sarah Peterson, Lange Reihe 50 (tel. 24 98 26). Small, artsy pension in an old building with bohemian flair. Doubles DM89. Triples DM140.

Hotel-Pension Kieler Hof, Bremer Reihe 15 (tel. 24 30 24), on the corner. From the *Hauptbahnhof's* Kieler Allee exit, turn right, then left on Bremer Reihe. The shady bars farther down the street don't make ideal neighbors, but this is a visitor-friendly, welcoming spot. Tastefully done rooms. Singles DM65. Doubles DM90, with shower DM100.

Hotel Kochler Garni, Bremer Reihe 19 (tel. 24 95 11), 2min. from the *Hauptbah-nhof.* Clean, well-run, and very respectable. Comfortable and quite spacious rooms. Call ahead. Singles DM55-60. Doubles DM85-100. Triples DM110-130. Quads DM120-140. Breakfast DM10.

Pension Helga Schmidt, Holzdam 14 (tel. 280 21 19), off An der Alster, surprisingly near the *Hauptbahnhof.* Beautifully outfitted, large rooms in a classic building on a wind-swept street. Worth the money; you wouldn't mind your parents staying here. Call ahead for reservations. Singles with shower DM62-67. Doubles DM96-116.

FOOD

Walk along **St. Pauli's Quai**, **Landungsbrücke**, for small fish restaurants and fry stands. Right in the middle of the Rathausmarkt, the aptly named **Rathausmarkt** offers all things edible at honest prices. Numerous cheap dives sit along the **Kirchenallee**, serving everything from *Schnitzel* to gyros. Better deals are yours in the numerous inexpensive cafés and restaurants in the University area around **Renteelstraße, Grindelhof,** and **Grindallee.** In **Altona** a plethora of inexpensive cafés and restaurants can be found on **Schanzenstraße.** Sample the local specialty, *Labskaus,* a hash of mashed potatoes, herring, pickled beets and pickled cucumbers topped by a fried egg. It's better than it sounds.

Mensa, Schlüterstr. 7. Also a place to catch up with students and check bulletin boards for special events. Serves lunch Mon.-Fri. DM1.70-6. ID officially required.

Gröninger Braukeller, Ost-West-Str. 47 (tel. 33 13 81), south of the Rathausmarkt. A crowded watering hole featuring simple, local fare. Buffet served after 1pm. *Gröninger* beer is brewed on-site. Open Mon.-Fri. 11am-midnight, Sat. 5pm-midnight.

Fischerhaus, St. Pauli Fischmarkt 14 (tel. 31 40 53). Fresh fish and superb service explain this restaurant's appeal. Meals DM11-30. Open daily 11am-11pm.

Café Buckwahn, Grindallee 148 (tel. 410 61 41). Light food served all day with special *Mittagtisch* (lunch platter, DM9) in this very relaxed café. Open daily 10am-7pm.

Piceno, Hein-Hoyer-str. 8 (tel. 31 04 77). Simple Italian restaurant serves the classics (DM8-15). Their *maccaroni arabiata* comes in a spicy tomato sauce with peppers and basil. Open daily 5pm-midnight.

Gorki Park, Grindelallee 1 (tel. 45 70 17). The new face of socialism serves up a *proletarier* fest (DM8-15) amidst red velvet drapes, antique furniture, communist kitsch, and Russian folk music. Open daily 10am-after midnight.

Café Adagio, Marx-Brauer-Allee 114 (tel. 38 24 09). Trendy little café serves snacks and salads (DM3-10). Wildly huge cappucino DM4. Comfortable for gay, lesbian, and straight couples. Open Mon.-Fri. 9:30am-11pm, Sat. 5pm-1am, Sun. 11am-11pm.

Noodles & Mehr, Schanzenstr. 2-4 (tel. 439 28 40). Chic café serving, yes, reasonably priced food (DM7-15). Open Mon.-Thurs. 11am-1am, Fri.-Sat. 1pm-3am, Sun. 1pm-1am.

Golden Oase, Eppendorferbaum 34. A step beyond vegetarian: this vegan restaurant even avoids eggs and other borderline animal products. Steaming plates of "food" even taste good. Dishes DM10-18. Open Mon.-Sat. noon-10pm, Sun. 10am-6pm.

Libresso Antiquariat, Binderstr. 24 (tel. 45 16 63), U-Bahn: Hallerstr. Bookstore-café mixes up its dark espresso with a high grade of used printed matter, served up for students at the nearby university. Open Mon.-Fri. 10am-6pm.

Frauenbuchladung und Café, Bismarckstr. 98 (tel. 420 47 48). Pick up the *Hamburger Frauenzeitung* (DM5) if you can read German. Good food. Good books. Women only. Open Mon.-Fri. 10am-6:30pm, Sat. 10am-2pm). and

SIGHTS

At night the **Hamburg Hafen**, the largest port in Germany, is lit up by ships from all over the world. Over 100,000 dockers and sailors work the ports, and their presence fills the two most distinctive Hamburg scenes: the business of the sea and the unmatched parade of the city awake at night. When a ship leaves Hamburg's harbor, Hamburg's flag is lowered and the national anthem of the country in which the ship is registered is played. After sailing the East Indies, the 19th-century **Windjammer Rickmer Rickmers** was docked at pier 1 and restored as a museum ship. Come for the old navigation equipment, all brass and polished, alongside the newer technology. (Open daily 10am-6pm. Admission DM4, students DM3, children DM2.) Nearby, the **Old Elbe Tunnel** connects St. Pauli to Steinwerder. Constructed between 1907 and 1909, it was a feat of engineering for its time. Take an elevator down to the lower level and then walk the 426m of tunnel. Just east of the docks is the historic warehouse district known as the **Speicherstadt,** a late 19th-century civic project of elegant brick warehouses filled with cargo, spices, and swarms of stevedores. It still lives and breathes a storybook port scene, but the meter-thick walls now hold imported electronic equipment as well.

The richly ornamented **Rathaus,** a monstrous 19th-century palace, dominates the city center with its copper spire. From the train station, head down Mönckebergstr. Tours pass through the several gorgeous rooms still used for receptions and meetings; of course, they're canceled when city government is in session. (Hourly tours in English Mon.-Thurs. 10:15am-3:15pm, Fri.-Sun. 10:15am-1:15pm. Open Mon.-Thurs. 10am-3pm, Fri. 10am-1pm, Sat.-Sun. 10am-1pm. Admission DM1.) Built in 1932, the grim, imposing **column** to the left of the *Rathaus* is dedicated to the 40,000 Hamburg boys who died in World War I. To the north of the *Rathaus* are the two **Alster lakes** bordered by tree-lined walkways. The **Binnenalster** is a small quiet lake surrounded by elegant promenades and commercial façades, while the larger **Aussenalster** is dominated by windsurfers, sailboats, and leisure paddle-boats. Ferries, less business-like than the bigger Hamburg boats, sail from the Jungfernstieg on Binnenalster (see Ferries, in Practical Information, above).

After much of the old city was destroyed by fire in 1842, Hamburg's city government launched an ambitious reconstruction scheme which dictated much of the current urban landscape including its familiar six green copper spires. Just south of the *Rathaus* on Hopfenmarkt stand the somber ruins of the **St. Nikolaikirche.** One of the earliest examples of neo-Gothic architecture, it was flattened by Allied bombing raids in 1943. City officials have left the ruins unrestored as a reminder of the horrors of war. Just east of the *Rathaus* are two more churches with copper spires, the 12th-century **St. Petrikirche** (open Mon.-Fri. 10am-6pm, Sat. 9am-5pm, Sun. 9am-noon and 1-5pm) and **St. Jacobikirche,** with its 17th-century Schnitger organ (open Mon.-Fri. 10am-1pm, and 1:30-5pm). On the other side of the busy Ost-Weststr. stands a fourth copper tower, this one of the medieval **St. Katharinenkirche,** built over 75 years starting in 1350 (U-Bahn: Messberg; open 9am-6pm; Oct.-April 9am-4pm).

The imposing 18th-century **Große Michaeliskirche,** affectionately dubbed *"der Michael,"* is a tad further west. This tower, whose bulbous Baroque silhouette is the official emblem of Hamburg, is the only one of the city's six that can be ascended, and it even has an elevator. (Organ concerts April-Aug. Sat. 6pm; concert admission DM6, students DM3. Church free, elevator DM4, crypt admission DM2.50. Tower open Mon.-Sat. 9am-5:30pm, Sun. 11:30am-5:30pm; Nov.-April Thurs.-Tues. 10am-4pm.) Farther east along Ost-Weststr. is an architectural landmark of a different stripe, the **Chilehaus.** This striking *trompe l'oeil* office building is the work of Expressionist architect Fritz Höger, also responsible for the **Sprinkenhof** building across the street. The last block of **Peterstraße,** up Neanderstr. from the Michaeliskirche and then left, is a pedestrian zone for the ages, a quiet cobblestone street lined with 17th- and 18th-century High Baroque houses. A Hamburg philanthropist led a private initiative to restore the street after the war. The historic **Reep-**

HAMBURG: ENTERTAINMENT

erbahn district, originally a rope-manufacturing center, now has a different character; see Nightlife, below, for details and more on the St. Pauli district

Other elements of Hamburg history are less attractive. In 1923, communist labor-leader Ernst Thälmann led a march on the police headquarters, ending in a riot that left 61 protestors and 17 police officers dead and resulted in near one thousand arrests. Thälmann was later murdered by the Nazis at Buchenwald. His life, and some of Hamburg's rough-and-tumble history, are chronicled at the **Ernst-Thälmann Gedenkstätte**, on Ernst-Thälmann-Platz. (Open Mon.-Sat. 10am-5pm, Sat.-Sun. 10am-3pm. Free.)

The **KZ** (concentration camp) **Gedenkstätte Neuengamme**, Jean-Doldier-Weg (tel. 723 10 31) cannot be separated from the history of the port itself. The camp can be reached on S-Bahn 21: Bergdorff, then bus #227; about 50 minutes from the *Hauptbahnhof*. 55,000 of the 110,000 prisoners brought to the camp were killed or died under slave-labor conditions. Several of the camp buildings have been reconstructed, and the Dokumenthaus tells the story. The museum also sponsors occasional films and Sunday afternoon talks by Holocaust survivors; call for a schedule. (Open Tues.-Sun. 10am-5pm; April-Sept. Tues.-Fri. 10am-5pm, Sat.-Sun. 10am-6pm. Free.) The scale of KZ-Neuengamme can be overwhelming; the smaller **Gedenkstätte Janusz-Korczak-Schule**, Bullenhuser Damm 92 (tel. 78 32 95; S-Bahn: Rothenburgsort), is a museum study of Nazi medical experiments on prisoners. It also serves as a memorial to 20 Jewish children and 20 adolescents who were brought here from Auschwitz for "testing" and murdered by the SS hours before Allied troops arrived. Visitors can arrange to plant a rose for the children in the flower garden behind the school. (Open Mon.-Thurs. 9am-5pm, Fri. 9am-3pm, Sun. 10am-5pm. Free.)

Museums

If you plan on a longer stay, consider procuring a **week-long pass** to all of Hamburg's three dozen museums for just DM15.

Hamburger Kunsthalle, Glockengiesserwall 1, one block north of the *Hauptbahnhof*. Holds an extensive collection of paintings and drawings ranging from medieval to modern. The early medieval, Renaissance, and German Romantic collections are strongest, but every major artistic era is represented. The museum's **Café Liebermann** is set in the colorful Säulerhalle. Open Tues.-Wed. and Fri.-Sun. 10am-6pm, Thurs. 10am-9pm. Admission DM3, students DM0.70.

Museum für Kunst und Gewerbe, Steintorplatz 1, 1 block south of the *Hauptbahnhof*. A fantastic, rich collection of handicrafts, china, and furnishings ranging from ancient Egyptian and Roman to Asian and *Jugendstil*, sure to inspire you to new heights of interior decoration. You'll want to allow a few hours here. Open Tues.-Sun. 10am-6pm. Admission DM3, students and seniors DM0.70.

Museum of Hamburger History, Holstenwall 24, at the end of Peterstr., U-Bahn: St. Pauli. Recounts the city's past. Giant dioramas display the growth of the harbor, with anchors hanging precariously from the ceiling. The third floor is one big maze of model railroad tracks, mimicking Hamburg's own rail connections. Open Tues.-Sun. 10am-6pm. Admission DM2, students DM0.70. The museum is parent to the **Historic Emigration Office**, Bei den St. Pauli Landungsbrücken 3, 20359 Hamburg, a Germanically meticulous archive that has recorded the names, hometowns, and vital statistics of the 5 million Germans and East Europeans who emigrated through Hamburg between 1850 and 1914. Write or drop by if you're interested in tracking your roots. Open Tues.-Sat. 10am-2pm.

ENTERTAINMENT

The cultural capital of the North, Hamburg invests a lot of cash and effort in the arts. The **Staatsoper**, Dammtorstr. 28, houses one of the best opera companies in Germany, vying with Munich's for primacy. John Neumeier has directed the attached **ballet** company for the last decade, making it the acknowledged dance powerhouse of the nation. **Orchestras** abound for the music lovers who don't dig opera—the **Philharmonie,** the **Symphony,** and the **Nord-Deutscher-Rundfunk** are the big three. Lighter music, popular musicals, and transvestite cabarets play the **Operettenhaus Hamburg,** the **Neue Flora Theater,** and other smaller venues. Call the tourist office for information on dates, venues, and tickets.

The **Deutsches Schauspielhaus,** Kirchenallee 39, refuses to be overshadowed by the musicians of the city; the productions here are known all over Germany for their quality and for the controversy they inspire. Peter Zadek is one of the group of virtuoso directors who have become the main figures in German drama in the 1980s, producing both new plays and old with his own personal, and sometimes shocking, stamp. Most theaters sell **half-price tickets** to students at the **Abendkasse,** which generally opens one hour before performance times. In July and August, many theaters close down, but only to make way for the **Hamburger Sommer** festival of the arts. Check with the tourist office for performance schedules. The **Theaterkarten Last-Minute** kiosk in the Hansa-Viertel tourist office (see above) has tickets for regular and special events.

Hamburg has an extensive live music scene which spans all tastes. Traditional jazz is at its best at **Cotton Club** (see Nightlife, below), and on Sunday mornings at the Fish Auction Hall at the **Fischmarkt.** International rock groups play at **Große Freiheit,** Große Freiheit 36 (tel. 319 36 49) and at **Docks,** Spielbudenplatz 19 (tel. 319 43 78). The renowned **Fabrik,** Barnerstr. 36 (tel. 39 10 70) in Altona features everything from funk to punk. The best sources of information on what is happening are *Szene, Oxmox,* or *Prinz* (available at newsstands; hostels also keep copies).

As for special festivals, Hamburg's favorite event is the **Hafengeburtstag,** the celebration of the "Harbor Birthday." Hamburg owes its prosperity to the day in 1189 when Friedrich Barbarossa granted the town the right to open a port, and the city still sees fit to celebrate the anniversary for a weekend in early May with events on land and water. In 1994, the event will take place from May 6 to May 8. For three months each year (mid-March to mid-April, August, and November), the **Heiligengeistfeld,** just north of the Reeperbahn, is transformed into the **Dom,** a huge amusement park, with booths, kiosks, and rides.

NIGHTLIFE

The nexus of Hamburg's nightlife is at the heart of St. Pauli on the **Reeperbahn.** World renowned as the home of the St. Pauli girls, the area is packed with the best clubs and bars in Hamburg, as well as sleazy sex-clubs and peepshows. The **Große Freiheit,** a street lined with explicit revues and cabarets, might be one of the most concentrated sinks of sleaze in the world. **Herbertstraße,** just south of the Reeperbahn off Davidstr., is a legalized prostitution strip. Only men over 18 are permitted down the street; women who pass through the barricades are verbally abused and often have things thrown at them. The fact that women can't walk here points out one of the limitations of life in Hamburg. Many men on the street will address women as merchandise; if you're female and out late, take a cab. Men who walk down any of the sidestreets off the Reeperbahn will be approached by sex-industry workers seeking to transact business. These street-walkers are not subject to health inspections, as are the licensed prostitutes who pose behind windows. Despite this, men and women flock to the area at night to revel all night long. While aspects of the Reeperbahn may disgust and intimidate, the area is flooded with sultry energy. Police patrol extensively; the **Davidwache** police station, is on the corner of Davidstr. and Reeperbahn. The street comes alive after dark; packed S- and U-Bahn deliver hordes of pleasure-seekers at around midnight and the action goes until dawn.

Clubs and **bars** are scattered throughout the city. Clusters of popular student bars can be found along Grindelallee and Schanzenstr. Swarms of street-side cafés line the three squares **Gänsemarkt** (U-Bahn 2), **Rodningsmarkt** (U-Bahn 3), and **Großneumarkt** (S-Bahn 1 or 2: Stadthausbrücke). Much of the Hamburg gay scene is located in the **St. Georg** area of the city, near the *Hauptbahnhof.* A rather shady area itself, it lacks the bright lights and the throngs of tourists and couples which characterize the Reeperbahn. In general, clubs open late and close late, with some techno and trance clubs staying open until noon the following day. *Szene, Oxmox,* and *Prinz* all have listings of events and parties happening at the bars and clubs. Lesbians and gays alike are clued in on special events by the *Dorn Rosa* journal. A publication called *Gay Life* also has plenty of information.

Frank und Frei, Schanzenstr. 93 (tel. 43 48 03). Big bar where students go, and like it. Open Mon.-Sat. 11am-3am, Sun. 10am-3am.

La Paloma, corner of Gerhardt and Friedrichstr. At the heart of St. Pauli, but not a bit sordid; "art" is not just a euphemism here. A local painter opened this late-night bar-club-café to fill some walls with his friends' work. Despite the pretension, the mood is open-minded. Open 24hr.

Cotton Club, Alter Steinweg 10 (tel. 34 38 78). Offers a different traditional jazz band a chance every night at 8:30pm. Smoky and atmospheric; have a beer and truly feel the music. Open Mon.-Sat. 8pm-midnight. Cover varies with act, but usually DM5-10.

Mojo Club, Reeperbahn 1 (tel. 319 19 99) has been described as the best club in Germany by MTV. Go Mojo. The attached **Jazz Café** attracts the trendy and has sylish bar-tenders. Features jazz, dance-floor jazz, and acid-jazz (?) music. Club open Fri.-Sat. from 4pm; cover usually DM10. Café open Wed.-Sat. from 10pm; no cover.

Gröninger Braukeller, Ost-West-str. 47 (tel. 33 13 81) has been serving its own brew since 1750. Need we say more? Open Mon.-Fri. 11am-1am, Sat. 5pm-1am.

Front, Heidencampsweg 1 (tel. 23 25 23), plays house music to the hip. Substantial gay presence. Open Fri.-Sat. 11pm. Cover DM10.

Pleasure Dome, Ankelmanplatz 3, in the old Berliner Tor S-Bahn station, is a recently-opened club playing pop and dance music. Open Thurs.-Sat. 11pm. Cover DM10.

Logo, Grindelallee 5 (tel. 410 56 58). Dance hall near the university, with a correspondingly experimental sound and crowd. Features a host of alternative live music. Open nightly from 9:30pm, cover varies.

Café Schöne Aussichten, Gorch-Frock-Wall 2 (tel. 34 01 13). Everyone seems to meet here. Very popular and rolicking café-bar in **Planten un Blomen** park. Open Sun.-Thurs. 11am-2am, Fri.-Sat. 11am-4am.

Baluga, Lincolnstr. 6 (tel. 319 41 59), near the Reeperbahn. Trendy late-night bar. The action really only starts after midnight.

Frauenkneipe, Stresemanstr. 60, is a bar and meeting place for women only, where visitors who are disconcerted by the Reeperbahn and drunken-sailor scene realize that red-light workers do not, by any means, represent the whole of Hamburg.

■ Near Hamburg

Blankensee (S-Bahn Balnkensee), once a small fishing village, is still a picturesque hillside town that sweeps down to a strand at the banks of the Elbe. Narrow crooked steps lead from the top of the hill to the river through a collection of summer houses and thatched fisher-homes. From the top of Süllberg, there is a wonderful view of the mile-wide Elbe.

■■■ LÜBECK

Once the robust capital of the Hanseatic League, now Schleswig-Holstein's most exciting city (largely by default), **Lübeck** flourished in the Middle Ages as a link in the prosperous Baltic trade. The city's most famous brothers, Thomas and Heinrich Mann, drew the inspiration for their masterful dissections of the German bourgeoisie while living among the wealth and hypocrisy of Lübeck. Its merchants devoted their profits to red brick architecture and interior decoration, a pastime unrewarded until 1987 when UNESCO declared Lübeck's *Altstadt* a World Heritage Site. Another hometown hero, Herbert Frahm, was born an illegitimate child in 1914. He spent the Hitler years in exile in Norway and Sweden, where he changed his name to Willy Brandt before becoming mayor of Berlin and chancellor of the Federal Republic. Lübeck still thrives as a harbor and as a vital link between Germany and Scandinavia, witnessed by the abundance of Scandinavian restaurants and ATMs which dispense Swedish and Danish currencies.

ORIENTATION AND PRACTICAL INFORMATION

Lübeck lies on the Baltic Sea approximately 60km north east of Hamburg. It serves as a connection between eastern cities, such as Rostock and Schwerin, and Western Germany.

Tourist office: (tel. 86 46 75). In the train station. Open Mon.-Sat. 9am-7pm. Unless you want to book a room (DM3 fee), grab a free map and make for the larger **main office** at Am Markt 1 (tel. 122 81 06), across from the *Rathaus*. Open Mon.-Fri. 9:30am-6pm, Sat.-Sun. 10am-2pm.

Post Office: The main office, Am Markt, 23552 Lübeck, next to the main tourist office, is less crowded than the one to the left of the train station. Currency exchange available. Open Mon.-Fri. 8am-6pm, Sat. 8am-noon.

Telephones: City Code: 0451.

Trains: Lübeck serves as a main transfer point for travelers crossing the former border. Trains depart frequently for Schwerin (1½hr.), Rostock (2hr.), Hamburg (40min.), and Berlin (4hr.).

Public Transportation: Lübeck has an excellent bus network. A single ride is DM2.50. **Mehrfahrkarten,** books of 6 tickets, cost DM12. The **Tageskarte** is valid for 24-hr. travel in the city center (DM4). Best value is the **Lübeck-karte** which is valid for 24-hr. on all Lübeck buses, extending into Travemünde (DM7.50). Some lines run later on Fridays and Saturdays.

Ferries: Cruises around the **harbor** depart several times per day from the bridge in front of the *Holsentor* (DM5-10). **Poseidon Ferries** (tel. 40 00 50) steam to Helsinki and ever farther to Kotka every 4 or 5 days—inquire about departure times. Low season DM420, DM750 roundtrip. High season DM600, DM1020 round trip. Prices include cabin with shower and toilet. Better deals may be available from Travemünde or Kiel.

Taxi: tel. 811 22. **Frauen-Nacht-Taxi:** for women only (tel. 836 36), operates nightly 9pm-5am.

Car Rental: Hertz, Wallhalbinsel 1-5 near the train station (tel. 717 47, fax 751 97). Open Mon.-Fri. 7am-6:30pm, Sat. 7am-2pm, Sun. 9-10:30am and 8-9pm.

Mitfahrzentrale, Fischergrube 45 (tel. 710 74), matches riders and drivers. Open Mon.-Fri. 2-6pm, Sat.-Sun. noon-2pm.

Bike Rental: Leihcycle, Schwartuaer Allee 39 (tel. 426 60), close to the train station rents bikes for DM5 per day. Passport required.

Bookstore: Buchhandlung Weiland, Königstr. 67a (tel. 16 00 60) stocks English-language paperbacks in the basement. Open Mon.-Wed. and Fri. 9am-6pm, Thurs. 9am-8:30pm, Sat. 9am-2pm.

Laundromat: McWash, on the corner of An der Mauer and Hüxlerdam. McWash DM6, McDry DM1 per 15min. McOpen McDaily 6am-11pm.

Pharmacies: Apotheke am Lindenplatz, Lindenplatz. Near the train station. Open Mon.-Fri. 8am-6:30pm, Sat. 8am-1pm. Late-night pharmacies for emergencies are indicated in the windows of all *Apotheken*.

Rape Crisis Line: (tel. 70 46 40) open Mon. and Thurs.-Fri. 10am-noon and 5-9pm.

Emergencies: Fire/Ambulance: tel. 112. **Police:** tel. 110.

ACCOMMODATIONS AND CAMPING

Lübeck accommodations tend to be quite expensive and fill up quickly. Bargains, however, *do* exist, generally with sleep-and-run travelers in mind. **Camping** is somewhat distant from the city center. Try **Campingplatz Lübeck-Schönböcken,** Steinrader Damm 12 (tel. 89 30 90), which offers grassy sites north-west of the city. Showers, washing machines, cooking facilities, and kiosk available. From the ZOB Bus Terminal, take bus #7 or 8 (direction "Dornbreite") to Bauernweg, and walk along Steinrader Damm toward the city for about 300m.

Jugendherberge Lübeck (HI), Am Gertrudenkirchhof 4 (tel. 235 68, fax 345 40), northeast of the historic center, past the *Burgtor.* Bus #1 (direction "Roter Hahn) or bus #3 (direction "Brandenbaum"): Gustav-Radbruch-Platz. Walk approximately 100m along Travemünder-Allee and turn left. Situated in a calm neighborhood just outside the *Altstadt,* a cheerful staff make up for slightly cramped rooms. Reception open 8-9am and 1:30-11:30pm. Lockout 9-11:30am. Curfew 11:30pm. Members only. DM17.50, over 26 DM21.50. Breakfast included. Open Jan. 11-Dec. 9. Don't expect a room in summer without a written reservation.

Jugengästehaus Lübeck (HI), Mengstr. 33 (tel. 702 03 99). From the train station head for the *Holsentor,* cross the river and make a left on An der Untertrave, then make a right on Mengstr. Though more expensive, this hostel is ideally located, and singles, doubles, triples and quads are available in this wonderful historic-building-turned-hostel. Reception open 8am-midnight. Call ahead. DM24.50, over 26 DM29.50. Breakfast included.

Rucksack Hotel, Kanalstr. 70 (tel. 70 68 92) in the *Altstadt* by the canal. From the train station walk past the Holstentor, turn left on An der Untertrave and right on Beckergrube. The hotel is on the corner of Glockengießenstr. and Kanalstr. Peter and Kalli welcome you to their clean and friendly accommodation close to the bars and cafés of Glockengießenstr. Reception open daily 9am-10pm. Singles DM30, doubles DM120, quads DM120. Dormitory-style rooms also available; 6-bed room DM22, 8-bed room DM19.

Sleep-In (CVJM), Große Petersgrube 11 (tel. 789 82), near the Petrikirche. This shiny, earnest YMCA is right in the old area of town 10min. from the station: walk past the *Holsentor,* turn left on An der Obertrave, left again on Große Petersgrube, and look carefully to the right for the CVJM sign. Reception open Mon.-Fri. 9am-noon and 5pm-midnight, Sat.-Sun. 9-10am and 5pm-midnight. Sept.-June Mon.-Fri. 9am-noon and 5-10pm, Sat.-Sun. 9-10am and 5-10pm. 10-bed dorms for DM14 per person. Breakfast DM5.

Hotel Schönwald, Chasotstr. 25 (tel. 641 69) is amiable and pleasantly cheap in a quiet residential neighborhood. Take bus #3 (direction "Schlutup"): Königstr.; change to bus #4 (direction "Brandenbaum") or #14 (direction "Heiweg"): Gneisenaustr. Call first in summer; they may fetch you from the train station. Singles DM35. Doubles DM60, quads DM100. No breakfast.

FOOD

Lübeck's cuisine reflects the city's timeless seafaring tradition as well as the more recent onslaught of immigrants. During the summer, the **market** offers fresh fruit and vegetables, and on sunny days picnic tables on the Mengstr. are surrounded by booths offering gyros, vegetarian pitas, and *Bratwurst* for under DM10. A local specialty is *Lübecker Marzipan,* a gratifying candy concocted from sugar and almonds. **I.G. Niederegger,** Breitestr. 89, across from the *Rathaus,* is renowned all over Germany for its marzipan (open Mon.-Fri. 9am-6:30pm, Sat. 9am-6pm, Sun. 10am-6pm).

Ali Dayi, Am Kohlmarkt 2-7 (tel. 70 67 44), serves copious portions of Turkish specialties and vegetarian options. Entrees DM12-24. Open Sun.-Thurs. 10:30am-11:30pm, Fri.-Sat. 10:30am-12:30pm.

Schmidt's Gasthaus, Dr. Julius-Leber-Str. 60 (tel. 761 82), offers a broad international menu and an expansive selection of beer. Entrees DM8-16. Open Mon.-Thurs. 5pm-1am, Fri.-Sat. 5pm-2am, Sun. noon-1am.

Café Affenbrot, Glockengießerstr. 70 (tel. 721 93) is a fetching vegetarian café and bistro. Their *Salattasche,* a salad in *fladenbrot* (DM5) really quells hunger pangs. Open daily 9am-midnight.

"Bei Ulla," Mühlenstr. 19 (tel. 764 41), serves German fillers such as *Bratkartoffeln mit Spiegeleier* (fried potatoes with 2 fried eggs on top; DM8) and *schnitzel* (DM8-14). Open Sun.-Thurs. noon-midnight, Fri.-Sat. noon-2am.

Café Amadeus, Königstr. 26 (tel. 70 53 57), done up like an indoor tropical grotto, an interesting environment to enjoy a few brews. Open Sun.-Thurs. 8am-12:30am, Fri.-Sat. 8am-2am.

Café Heftia, on the corner of Fleischauer and St. Johannisstr. It's one big work of Expressionist-graffiti art. Sit at a fish-shaped table and gaze at the aliens on the wall. Crazy stuff. Open 10am-1am.

SIGHTS AND ENTERTAINMENT

On the eve of Palm Sunday, 1942, most of Lübeck was flattened by Allied bombers. Since then, Lübeck has been renovating and rebuilding its beautiful historic *Altstadt*. The core of the *Altstadt* is the **Rathaus,** a striking 13th-century structure of glazed black bricks that sets off the technicolor fruit and flower market in the square. (Tours Mon.-Fri. at 11am, noon, and 3pm. Admission DM3, students DM1.) Across the Marktplatz towers the North-German Gothic **Marienkirche;** inside, under the southern tower, the bent and broken pieces of the multi-ton church bells still rest where they fell during an air raid in 1942. The organ is the largest mechanical organ in the world. Only a partially restored section of its famous **Totentanzbild** (death-dance mural), dating from the days of the bubonic plague, remains (open 10am-6pm; off-season 10am-4pm; free).

Opposite the Marienkirche on Mengstr. is the **Buddenbrooks House,** from which Thomas Mann's ironic 1911 novel took its name. The house is now a museum dedicated to the life and works of Thomas and Heinrich Mann; the two brothers, both influential writers and swayers of Weimar culture, quarreled about politics in 1915 and were never completely reconciled. Mann's post-war works, notably *The Magic Mountain*, were built on his critique of Germany and deep ambivalence about its culture; he wrote: "Such musicality of the soul must be paid for dearly in other spheres—in the political, the sphere of the common life of human beings." Much of the exhibit is textual; reading knowledge of German is helpful although English guides are available. (Open Fri.-Wed. 10am-4pm, Thurs. 10am-7pm. Admission DM4, students DM2.)

The organ inside the **Jacobikirche,** farther north on Breitestr., is one of the oldest in Germany. (Open daily 10am-6pm. Half-hour organ recitals Sat. at 5pm. Admission DM3, students DM2.) Behind the Jacobikirche stands the **Heiligen-Geist-Hospital,** Königstr. 9. Built in 1280, the hospital served as an old-age home from 1518 to 1970. On display are some excellent North-German medieval murals (open Tues.-Sun. 10am-5pm, Oct.-April Tues.-Sun. 10am-4pm; free). The well-preserved houses of sea captains adorn **Engelsgrubestraße,** opposite Jacobikirche. Explore **Berrahn's Gang** at #73 and **Hellgrüner Gang** at Engelswisch 28, off Englesgrube; look for the footprints of cats and dogs who walked through the freshly laid mortar 800 years ago.

Between the inner city and the train station is **Holstentor,** one of the four gates built in the 15th century to guard the entrance to Lübeck. It appeared until recently on the back of the DM50 bill. Inside is the **Museum Holstentor** (tel. 122 41 29), with exhibits on ship construction, trade, and quaint local implements of torture. (Open Tues.-Sun. 10am-5pm; Oct.-March 10am-4pm. Admission DM3, students DM1.50, under 18 free.) The **Petrikirche,** on Schmiederstr., is approximately 750 years old. It has a lift to the top of the steeple, and a sweeping view of the *Altstadt*. (Church open Tues.-Sun. 11am-4pm. Lift open April-Oct. 9am-6pm. Admission DM2.50, students DM1.50.) The **Lübeck Marionette Theater** (tel. 700 60) and **Puppet Museum** (tel. 786 26), Kleine Petersgrube 4-6, just below the Petrikirche, has 13 rooms filled with puppets, dolls, and accompanying paraphernalia from Africa, Asia, and Europe. The theater puts on performances Tuesday through Sunday at 3:30pm for children, and Friday and Saturday at 7:30pm for adults (museum open daily 9:30am-10pm; admission DM3, students DM2).

At the southern end of the inner island lies the **Dom,** Domkirchhof (tel. 747 04), founded by Henry the Lion in 1173; the trademark **lion statue** out front is his insignia. (Open April-Sept. 10am-6pm, March and Oct. 10am-5pm, Nov. 10am-4pm, Dec.-March 10am-3pm. Free.) Lübeck is world-famous for its **organ concerts.** Most of the churches schedule concerts throughout the summer. Details are available in churches or at the tourist office.

■ Near Lubeck: Ratzeburg

The town of **Ratzeburg** is a sight in itself: a cluster of red-roofed houses built on an island in the middle of a lake connected to the mainland by three causeways. The old moated town is the training center for the German Olympic crew team and boats dot the lake in the summer. The town's 12th-century **Dom** was established by Henry the Lion soon after he colonized Schleswig-Holstein. (Open daily 10am-noon and 3-6pm; Oct.-Mar. Tues.-Sun. 10am-noon and 3-4pm. Free. Guided tours DM1.) The **Ernst-Barlach-Museum,** near the St.-Petri Kirche is devoted to the work of the Expressionist artist and writer who spent his childhood in Ratzeburg. Many of his sculptures and sketches are on view (open April-Nov. Tues.-Sun. 10am-noon and 3-6pm; admission DM2, children DM1). The works of another famous local, A. Paul Weber, are on display in the **A. Paul Weber Museum,** Danhof 5 (tel. 123 26); most famous amongst these is *Das Verhangis,* a satirical depiction of Hitler (open Tues.-Sun. 10am-1pm and 2-5pm; admission DM2, children DM1).

The **tourist office,** Schloßwiese 7 (tel. (04541) 53 27), is on the way from the train station to the island. Walk down Bahnhofsallee; the office is on the left-hand side by the lake. Ratzeburg's **Jugendherberge (HI),** Fischerstr. 20 (tel. (04541) 3707, fax 847 80), offers wonderful views of the lake. From the train station, take the bus to Am Markt, and turn right at Kaufhaus Mohr. (DM16, over 26 DM20. Curfew 10pm. Reception 5-7pm. Laundry facilities in basement, DM5.) The **Burg Theater café,** on Theaterplatz, is just around the corner from the hostel. Enjoy drinks, espresso, and light snacks in its elegantly decorated interior (open daily 2pm-midnight).

Ratzeburg lies on the former Luneberg-Lubeck salt line and is accessible by train from Lubeck (20min.) or Luneberg (40min.). The town is also accessible by ferry from Lubeck via Rothenhusen (6 per day, combined cost is DM18). Call **Lubecker Fahrgastschiffart** (tel. (0451) 39 37 34 or 738 84) for information.

■ Near Lübeck: Travemünde

Lübeck's daughter-on-the-Baltic, the small resort town of Travemünde, is notable primarily for its beach and its ferry connections to Scandinavia. Although over 800 years old, the town has few items to remind it of its past. The old **lighthouse** on Trelleborg Allee dates back to 1226. This former beacon is dwarfed by the nearby 35-story **Hotel Maritim.** Across the water the **Passat,** an old four-mast ship, is moored (open May 16-Sept. 20, 10am-5pm; free).

15km north of Lübeck, Travemünde is accessible by train and bus (Lübeck city line A; day pass valid); there are three stations. **Skandinavienkai** gives access to the Scandinavia-bound ferries, **Lübeck-Travemünde-Hafen** is close to the town center, and **Lübeck-Travemünde-Strand** leads directly to the beach. The **tourist office** is located in the Aqua-Top building, Hotel Maritim, Strandpromenade 1b (tel. (04502) 804 32); walk from the **Travemünde-Strand** station down Bertlingstr. and turn left on Strandpromenade. They will find rooms (for 5% of the first-night price) as well as provide information about the town. From the Skandinavienkai pier, the **Finnjet** ferry departs two to three times per week for **Helsinki** (23-27hr. trip, DM210-680, students DM195-620 depending on accommodation). The **TT-Line** sials to **Trelleborg, Sweden** (7-8hr., 2 per day, DM110, students DM82 on day of sailing; 50% reduction on standard price with Eurail pass). For more information on ferries and Scandinavia, contact **Nordische Touristik Information,** Skandinavienkai 1 (tel. (04502) 66 88; open Mon.-Fri. 9am-5:30pm).

Head for the hostel or a campsite; both have easy access to the beach. The **Jugendherberge (HI)**, Mecklenbergerlandstr. 69 (tel. (04502) 25 76) is lively by day but goes to bed early. From the Hafen train station, walk down Vogtelstr. and turn right on Rose, then left on Vorderreihe and take the Priwall ferry (DM6) to the other side. Finally, walk straight down Mecklenburgerlandstr.; the hostel is on the left. (Curfew 10pm. Reception open 2-10pm. DM19.50, over 26 DM21.50. Open April to mid-Oct.) Next door, you can pitch your tent at **Strandcamping-Priwall,** Dünenweg 3 (tel. (04502) 28 35). The campsite attracts city kids out for sun and sand as well as the eco-conscious, so the atmosphere is totally festive (DM6 per person, DM11 per tent; open April-Sept.). Along the Strandpromenade, food tends to be quite expensive. The harbor area yields better deals.

■ ■ ■ KIEL

Capital of Schleswig-Holstein, the busy Baltic port of Kiel is best known as the epicenter of German **U-Boot** (submarine) warfare in World War II, a distinction that invited ruinous Allied bombing attacks that destroyed 80% of the city. This unsavory aspect of Kiel's history is balanced out by the city's most heroic moment, when a mutiny of sailors in 1918, during armistice negotiations, touched off the revolution that sent the Kaiser packing and helped end World War I. Kiel's mainstay shipping industry still thrives on the traffic through the world's busiest inland waterway, the Kiel Canal, and the city's most dramatic face is seen around the harbor.

Practical Information and Ferries Kiel's **tourist office** (tel. (0431) 67 91 00) is across from the train station. Their room-finding service costs DM3.50. (Open Mon.-Sat. 9am-6:30pm, Sun. 9am-noon; Oct.-April Mon.-Fri. 9am-6:30pm.) The **post office** on Stresemannplatz is one block north of the train station on Sophienblatt. The **postal code** for this office is 24103. (Open Mon.-Fri. 8am-6pm, Sat. 8:30am-1pm.) The **Mitfahrzentrale**, Sophienblattstr. 54 (tel. (0431) 194 44), two blocks south of the train station, matches riders and drivers (open Mon.-Wed. and Fri. 9am-7pm, Thurs. 9am-8pm, Sat. 9am-3pm, Sun. 10am-3pm). If you plan on using **public transportation** often, invest in a **KielerKarte** (1 day DM10, 3 days DM15), which give unlimited use of Kiel's buses and the ferries which circulate through the harbor. Single day cards may be bought on board; three day cards must be purchased at any Kieler-Verkehrs-AG office or at the tourist office. Every two hours a **bus** leaves from the bus station for the Hamburg **airport** (1½hr., DM20); there is also a bus connection to the Hamburg train station, 100km to the south.

Ferries leave from the wharf on the west bank of the city: **Stena Line** (tel. (0431) 90 90) sails to **Gothenburg, Sweden,** daily at 7pm (14hr., DM98-194). **Baltic Line** (tel. (0431) 982 00 00) will take you to **St. Petersburg, Russia,** via Nynäshamn, Sweden, on weekly sailings (60hr., DM410-540). **Color Line** (tel. (0431) 97 40 90) to **Oslo** (daily, every other day in Jan., 18hr., DM1140-188, students 50% off selected sailings), and **Langeland-Kiel** (tel. (0431) 97 41 50) to **Bagenkop, Denmark** (DM7, in July DM8).

Accommodations and Food Reach Kiel's **Jugendherberge (HI),** Johannesstr. 1 (tel. (0431) 73 57 23) on bus #4 or 34. Get off at "Karlstr.," walk a block north, and go left on Johannesstr. The hostel's rooms may not be as shiny as the reception but the beds are clean and comfortable. (Reception open 2-10pm. Curfew 1am. Locker DM 17.50, over 26 21.50. Camping is distant at **Campingplatz Falckenstein,** Palisadenweg 171 (tel. (0431) 39 20 78) and difficult to reach by foot (about 10km north of the city center). From the train station, take bus #44 (direction "Strand"): Seekamp. Backtrack to Scheidekoppel and hike for about 20min. through wheat fields and meadows until Pallisadenweg. Turn left. The campsite is well-equipped and runs right down to the beach.The **Karstadt supermarket** at the corner of Eggerstedtr. and Kaistr. Wall has cheap eats (open Mon.-Wed. and Fri. 9am-

KIEL

6:30pm, Thurs. 9am-8:30pm, Sat. 9am-2pm, first Sat. of month until 4pm). **Ristorante San Marco,** Dänischestr. 12 (tel. (0431) 924 92) serves generous servings of pizza.

Sights and Entertainment The city lives on its fjord; the harbor cuts through the city and from any point you can see or hear the docks at work. One of the highlights of the city is a tour of the Kiel **locks,** the largest in the world. The locks regulate the *Nord-Ostsee Kanal,* making Kiel the only harbor to border both the North and Baltic Sea. Take bus #4, 14, or 44 north from the central bus station (*ZOB*) to the Kanal stop, and take the free ferry (every 15min.) to the other side, where the tour of the locks and the locks museum departs. (Tours 9, 11am, 1, 3pm. Admission DM1.) Closer to the center of town, hugging the west coast of the Kieler Forde, you'll find the **Kieler Schifffahrtsmuseum (Navigation Museum).** One of the three ships on display, the *Bussard,* was one of the last coal- and steam-driven ships in service when it was retired in 1979. (Open Tues.-Sun. 10am-6pm; mid-Oct. to mid-April Tues.-Sun. 10am-5pm. Free.) A bit north of the ship museum along Kiellinie is the **aquarium,** home to the greatest assembly of Baltic Sea creatures known to civilization—which isn't saying all that much—as well as good-looking sea lions. (Open daily 9am-7pm; Oct.-March 9am-5pm. Admission DM2.20, students DM1.)

To the left of the **St. Nicolaskirche** (open Mon.-Fri. 10am-1pm and 2-6pm, Sat. 10am-1pm; free) stands Barlach's haunting statue, the *Geistkämpfer* (ghost-fighter; see Güstrow, in Mecklenburg-Lower Pomerania, below, for more on the controversial artist). Every February, Kielers celebrate the *"Umschlag,"* when a flag, *"Der Bürgermeister sin Büx"* (which is *Plattdeutsch* for "the mayor's pants"), is hung outside of the Nikolaikirche. There are tours of the nearby **Rathaus,** on Waisenhofstr. between Rathausstr. and Treppenstr., including a trip up into the steeple during the summer. (Tours Wed. and Sun. 12:30pm; on Wed. from Pförtnerloge; April-Oct. Sun. only. Admission DM1.)

The last full week of June sees the annual **Kieler Festwoche,** an internationally renowned regatta that enlivens the harbor with prismatic sails. This event takes place in the **Olympia-Zentrum** to the north, where the sailing events were held for the 1936 and 1972 Olympic games; take bus #4 or 44. The entire city celebrates and concerts and many special events are coordinated with the regatta.

■ Near Kiel: Mölsee and Laboe

6km outside Kiel in **Molfsee** is the **Schleswig-Holsteinisches Freilichtmuseum,** an outdoor model of traditional life in Schleswig-Holstein. Windmills run, blacksmiths and potters work, and the bakery produces goods daily. Take bus #1: Schulensee, and walk another 1.8km. (Open June to mid-Sept. Mon.-Sat. 9am-5pm, Sun. 10am-6pm; mid-Sept. to mid-Nov. and April-May open Tues.-Sat. 9am-5pm, Sun. 10am-6pm; mid-Nov. to March open Tues.-Sat. 9am-5pm, Sun. 10am-dusk in fair weather. Admission DM7, students DM5, DM2 with the *Kieler Karte*.)

Swimming is possible in the **Kieler Forde,** but nicer **beaches** can be reached in about 90 minutes by ferry. The ferries leave directly across from the train station and continue to **Laboe.** You can take the ferry to any beach, but the trip to Laboe is worth the time. If you're in a rush, bus #4 will take you there from the ZOB terminal (45min.), but on a clear day, the view is better from the water. Laboe's primary attraction is the **Deutsche Marine-Ehrenmal** (Naval Memorial), an 85m tower in the shape of a ship's stern that commemorates sailors killed in the world wars. The lower level houses a **Navigation Museum,** including a wide collection of flags of sunken ships in the *Flaggenraum.* (Open daily 9am-6pm in summer, 9am-4pm in winter. Admission DM3.70, under 18 DM2.) Next door, a genuine vintage German submarine, **U-Boot 955,** documents the days when German "wolf packs" were the terror of the high seas(same hours as museum; admission DM1.70, under 18 DM1).

■■■ FLENSBURG

Flensburg, Germany's most northern city, lies only a few kilometers away from the Danish border. The town retains many of the vestiges of four centuries of Danish rule; cross-border traffic is heavy, especially from higher-taxed Denmark. Heading down from the train station along Bahnhofstr. brings you to the lively *Altstadt* and Flensburg's pedestrian zone along **Großestraße.** Along the way you pass the **Deutsches Haus,** a Bauhaus-style concert hall donated to Flensburg in recognition of the city's loyalty in the 1920 referendum (for an example of contrasting civic behavior in that period, see Kiel, above). In the **Südermarkt,** the beautiful 14th-century Nikolaikirche boasts the largest organ in Schleswig (open Tues.-Fri. 9am-5pm, Sat. 10am-1pm; free). Just north of the Nordermarkt stands the **Marienkirche,** with its superb stained-glass windows (open Tues. and Thurs.-Fri. 10am-1pm and 2-4pm, Wed. and Sat. 10am-1pm; free). From the top of the **Marientreppe,** off Norderstr., you can get a great view of the harbor and the masses of orange-roofed houses.

Many small alleys lead down to the harbor; here, you'll find the **Museumshafen,** a dock where several old ships have been laid mercifully to rest. At Schiffbrücke 39, an old customs house has become the **Schiffahrtsmuseum** (Navigation Museum), documenting Flensburg's nautical history and major role in Denmark's once-thriving Caribbean trade. The museum is especially proud of its rum exhibit; the city is renowned for the seafarer's drink (open Tues.-Sat. 10am-5pm, Sun. 10am-1pm; admission DM2, students DM1).

The **tourist office,** Amalie-Lamp-Speicher, Speicherlinie 40 (tel. (0461) 230 90, fax 173 52) lies off Großestr. (open Mon.-Fri. 9am-6pm, Sat. 10am-1pm). The main post office, Bahnhofstr. 40, near the train station, changes currency (open Mon.-Fri. 8am-6pm, Sat. 8am-1pm). Flensburg has a decent bus system which saves a lot of uphill walking. Most buses circulate through the ZOB (central bus station), which is close to the city center (one-way fare DM2.10, 24-hr. Tageskarte DM6). The telephone **city code** is 0461. You can **rent a bike** from the train station for DM8 per day. Call (0461) 235 28 to reserve a bike in advance. **Trains** link the city to Hamburg (2hr.) and Kiel (1½hr.) to the south while others head north to Copenhagen (5 hr.). **Buses** from the ZOB bus station also cross the border to Sønderberg (1¼hr.) and Aabenraa (50min.). From the west bank of the harbor, ferries country-hop between Flensburg and Glücksburg in Germany and Gravenstein and Kollund in Denmark with duty-free shopping on board (DM3).

Flensburg's **Jugendherberge (HI),** Fichtestr. 76 (tel. 377 42, fax 31 29 52), is in a nature reserve beside the local stadium. A buffet breakfast and a view of the fjord compensate for eight-bed rooms. From the train station take bus #1 (direction "Lachsbach") or #4 (direction "Klueshof") to the ZOB and change to #3 or 7 (direction "Twedter Plack"): Stadion. Restaurants around the *Altstadt* tend to be expensive; during the day bargains can be found at Imbiße and Steh-Cafés along Großestr. **La Paloma,** Großestr. 13 (tel 222 18) offers more-than-decent Italian and Greek food (DM6-12) on their street-side terrace. The **Nordermarkt** is filled with a slew of cafés and bars, many of which feature live music. **Hansen's Brauerei,** Broßestr. 83 (tel. 222 10) serves beer brewed in-house to tables inside an old streetcar parked opposite the bar. **Orpheus,** Marienstr. 1-5 (tel. 231 68) schedules cabarets and jazz.

Just 10km away from Flensburg, **Glücksburg** boasts beautiful beaches (DM4) and a fairytale **Schloß** surrounded on all sides by a lake. Glücksburg can be reached by bus from Flensburg (35min., DM3) or by ferry via Kollund, Denmark. (Mid-May to mid-Aug. 10 per day; 5 per day otherwise; 50min. Fare DM3. Passport necessary.) Skate around the waxed second floor in the provided carpet slippers while discovering just how inbred 19th-century royals were. On the third floor Gobelin tapestries depicting scenes from Ovid's *Metamorphoses* are on display over fabulous leather wallpaper. (Open May-Sept. 10am-5pm, Oct. 10am-4:30pm, April Tues.-Sun. 10am-noon and 2-4pm, March Sat. Sun. 11am-4pm, Nov.-Feb. Sat.-Sun. noon-3pm. Admission DM6, students DM4.)

■■■ HUSUM

The grey town by the sea.

—Theodor Storm

Husum, a town of just over 20,000 inhabitants, is the economic and cultural center of wind-swept North Friesia. The home-town of late 19th-century novelist Theodor Storm, its fishing boats and tourists venture into the **Wattenmeer** (swamp-sea) towards the **Halligen Islands,** a sparsely populated but attractive group of islands just offshore (see below).

Most of Husum's interesting features are within walking distance of the **Markt-platz** in the middle of town. From the train station, head up Herzog-Adolf-Str. and turn left on Norderstr., which becomes Großestr. On the north end of the square stands the 17th-century **Rathaus.** The **Theodor Storm Birthplace** is at Marktplatz 9. From that hallowed spot, a left on the Twiete or Hohle Gasse leads to the **Binnen-hafen,** or inner harbor, from which North Sea sailors have departed since god knows when. Nearby is the **Theodor Storm Haus,** Wassereihe 31, former residence of the writer and now a museum. (Open Sat.-Mon. 2-5pm, Tues.-Fri. 10am-noon and 2-5pm; Nov.-March Tues., Thurs., and Sat. 3-5pm. Admission DM2.)

The **Schloß vor Husum,** two blocks in the opposite direction from the markt-platz, was built by the Gottort dukes at the end of the 16th century but was later built up into a Baroque castle. It holds exhibits of Baroque interior over-decoration and hosts concerts in the summer evenings. (Open April-Oct. Tues.-Sun. 10am-noon and 2-5pm. Admission DM3, students DM1.50. Concert tickets DM10, students DM5.) The **Nissenhaus,** Herzog-Adolf-Str. 25, was donated by a wealthy German-American and houses the **North Friesian Museum.** Its collections will possess you—they include fascinating presentations on the art of dike-building in North Friesland and, for bird-watchers traveling through, an exhibit on migratory birds in the area (open daily 10am-5pm, Nov.-March Mon.-Fri. 10am-4pm; admission DM4, students DM2).

Husum has frequent rail connections to Hamburg (1¾hr.) and Kiel (1½hr.) The **tourist office** is in the *Rathaus,* and books rooms in private homes—the cheapest accommodation apart from the hostel—for a 10% down payment. For regional information, stop by the Nordseebäderverband, Parkstr. 7 (tel. (04841) 4089); they have ferry schedules, etc. **Bike rental** is at **Peter Schurr,** Schulstr. 4 (tel. (04841) 44 65. (Open Mon.-Fri. 8:30am-6pm, Sat. 8:30am-12:30pm. DM7 per day; DM35 per week. Passport required.) The walk to the **Jugendherberge Theodor Storm (HI)** is long and complicated. Instead, take the bus #51 (direction "Hattstedt via Scönbüll"): Westercampweg. Catch the bus at the ZOB (central station) just down the street from the train station. The spotless beds are new but often filled. Preference is given to those under 27. (Reception open 5-10pm. Lockout 9-11:30am. Curfew 10pm. Members only. DM17, over 26 DM21. Breakfast included. Closed Jan.15-Feb.15. Wheelchair access. Call ahead.) Sustain yourself with the *Matjesfilet,* a local specialty. **Seiers Gasthof,** Schiffbrücke 1 (tel. (04841) 29 63), on the harbor, serves traditional German dishes for less than DM12 (open daily 10am-2pm and 4:30-10pm). **Tire Café,** Schiffbrücke 17-19 (tel. (04841) 659 10), bakes tempting pastries (open Mon.-Sat. 7:30am-6:30pm, Sun. 10am-6:30pm).

■■■ SCHLESWIG

At the end of the Schlei inlet off of the Baltic Sea, Schleswig hides behind the boats and trees which line its harbor. Once a major Viking settlement, Schleswig was an important fishing and trade center in the Middle Ages. The city subsequently became the seat of Gottorfs, lesser German nobles who, despite their social status built a grandiose castle on the banks of the Schlei. When Bismarck annexed Schleswig-Holstein in 1867, he made Schleswig the capital, a post which it retained until 1945. Today, the city, with its Norse ruins, provides a beautiful base from which to explore the northern half of Schleswig-Holstein.

Schleswig's fishing heritage is obvious in the narrow street of the Holm district, which until March was an island. The large white Baroque **Schloß Gottorf,** on an island off the Schlei, now houses the **Landesmuseum,** with collections of artifacts dating back to the mad mad world of 12th-century Schleswig-Holstein. Also located in the complex are the **Nydamhalle** with archaeological finds dating back to the last Ice Age, and the **Kreuzstall,** a museum of modern art with an especially strong showing from the Expressionists. (Museums open Tues.-Sun. 9am-5pm; Nov.-March Tues.-Sun. 9:30am-4pm. Admission DM5, students DM2.) The copper steeple of the **St. Petri Dom** towers above Schleswig's *Altstadt.* Built between the 12th and 13th centuries, it houses a magnificent carved altar by Brüggeman. (Open Mon.-Thurs. and Sat. 9am-5pm, Fri. 9am-3pm, Sun. 1-5pm; Oct.-April Mon.-Thurs. and Sat. 10am-4pm, Fri. 10am-3pm, Sun. 1-4pm. Organ concerts DM4-6.)

Ferries travel from the Schleihallenbrücke near the Schloß to the **Wikinger Museum Haithabu;** picture tall rude blond men in hats with horns. The museum, built next door to an archeological excavation of the former **Viking settlement,** covers all aspects of Viking life. An ancient ship is under reconstruction in the **ship hall.** (Open daily 9am-6pm, Nov.-March Tues.-Fri. 9am-5pm, Sat.-Sun. 10am-6pm. Admission DM4, students DM2. ferries DM3, roundtrip DM5.)

The **tourist office** (tel. (04621) 81 42 26 or 81 42 27) is located at Plessenstr. 7, up the street from the harbor. (Open July-Aug. Mon.-Wed. 9am-12:30pm and 1:30-5pm, Thurs.-Sat. 9am-12:30pm and 1:30-8pm; Sept.-June Mon.-Fri. 9am-12:30pm and 1:30-5pm, Sat. 9am-noon.) Accommodation in Schleswig is not terribly expensive; information on hotels (DM40-60) is posted outside the tourist office. The **Jugendherberge (HI),** Steinkoppel 1 (tel. (04621) 238 93) lies close to the center of town. To get there, take any bus from the stop to the left of the station to the ZOB terminal, change to bus #2 (direction "Hühnhauser-Schwimhalle") to Schwimhalle. It has as a view of the Schlei and a binder of information about Schleswig. (Reception open 12:30-1pm, 4:30-5pm, 5:45-6pm, 7-7:30pm and 8-10pm. Curfew 10pm. DM16, over 26 DM19.50. Breakfast included.) For an experience in a former *Fischerhaus,* try **Pension Schleiblick,** Hafengang 4 (tel. (04621) 234 68). (Singles DM40-45. Doubles DM80-105 per person. Showers and breakfast included.) Cheap fish sandwiches are available at any *Fisch Imbiß* stand. Close to the pedestrian precinct and the hostel, **Patio,** Lollfuß 3 (tel. (04621) 299 99) serves solid food in an attractive **Hof** (open daily 11am-midnight; DM6-15). At the end of August, Schleswig celebrates its traditions with the colorful **Twiebakken-Regatta.** On Wednesdays and Saturdays there is a **market** in front of the *Rathaus* from 9am to 12:30pm.

■■■ NORTH FRIESIAN ISLANDS

SYLT

The sandy island of Sylt, connected to the mainland by a railtrack on an embankment stretches far into the North Sea to stake out Germany's northernmost point. For the most part desolate and bare, the island is a perennial favorite spot for seekers of that elusive German goal, a "return to nature." All too fashionable Germans paste labels cut in the Island's distinctive shape on the back of their cars, to show that they are in on the secret—along with hundreds of their closest friends. Accommodation is in demand—it is never too early to book a room here. Apart from the hostels, accommodations in private homes are most reasonable but for summer months should be reserved in advance. Because the island is almost entirely beach, quiet secluded spots can still be found near the extremities of the island. The best way to get around Sylt is by bicycle; the Westerland train station (see below) rents bikes from a booth opposite Platform 1 (DM6-8 per day).

Somewhere between the dunes lie holiday homes and the cosmetics and jewelry stores of **Westerland,** the island's largest town. Trains from Hamburg travel to Westerland via Niebüll (about 15 per day, 3¼hr.). Cars must be left in Niebüll or Klanxbüll or must take an *Autozug* (car-toting train) from Niebüll across the Hindenburgdamm. To use any of the beaches, or to spend a night there, you must pay a *Kurtaxe* (DM5.50, under 18 DM2.75). The **tourist office** (tel. (04651) 240 01, fax 240 60) to the left of the train station will reserve rooms for a DM5 fee. Prices start at DM25 for private rooms and small guest houses (open Mon.-Sat. 9am-6pm, Sun. 10am-6pm). Public transportation on the island is quite expensive (DM5 to reach either hostel). Buses leave from the **ZOB** terminal to the left of the Westerland station; pick up a bus schedule from the bus ticket office.

Westerland has no youth hostel; Sylt's two youth hostels are located in **List** and **Hörnum,** 16km to the north and south of Westerland respectively. List's **Jugendherberge Mövenberg** (tel. (04652) 397, fax 10 39) is close to the beach but very little else. To get there catch the bus (direction "List") from the Westerland ZOB to List-Schule. If you're lucky you can change for the infrequent List Strand bus to Mövenberg; otherwise, return to the intersection, turn right and walk for 2.5km. among sheep and dunes. (Reception open 4-8pm and 9-10pm. Closed Nov. to mid-March. Curfew 11:30pm. DM16.90, over 26 DM20.40. Written reservations strongly advised; definitely call ahead.) On the other end of the island **Jugendherberge Hörnum (HI),** Friesenplatz 2 (tel. (04653) 294, fax 13 92) is a little more accessible to the bus stop and life in general. From the ZOB take the bus (direction "Hornum") to Hörnum-Nord and continue along Rantumerstr., turning left at the Jugendherberge sign. (Closed Dec. 12-Jan13. Reception open 5-7 and 9-10pm. Curfew 11:30pm. DM16.90, over 26 DM20.40. Reservations strongly recommended.)

From List, a **ferry** sails on the hour from the "Fähre" stop to **Havneby** on the Danish island of **Rømø** (less frequently in winter; one-way fare DM4, round-trip DM6). Call **Rømø-Sylt Linie** at (04652) 475 in List for reservations and information. Several **duty-free shopping cruises** sail daily from the List harbor (DM3.50); call **Adler-Schiffe** in Westerland (tel. (04651) 257 58) for more information or visit them at Wilhelmstr. 22 (on the right, halfway to the beach).

HALLIGEN ISLANDS

To the south of Sylt lie the **Halligen Islands,** a sparsely-populated group of islands surrounded by the **Wattenmeer.** The low-lying islands are constantly threatened by floods, and frequent breaches of their dikes result in a rare amphibious brand of vegetation. All are part of the **Schleswig-Holstein Wattenmeer National Park** and all wildlife is vigorously protected.

Pellworm, which has an area of 37 square km, lies 1m below sea level and is protected from daily flooding by an 8m-high dike. The island has the largest European **solar energy plant,** which is now open to the public; ask at the Husum regional tourist office for information. The other Halligens, **Hooge, Amrun, Föhr, Langeneß** and **Gröde** are renowned for their unique flora and fauna as well as the sea-lion banks which lie close by. Adler-Schiffe (tel. (04842) 268) runs day excursions to the Halligens from **Hörnum** on Sylt (DM16-25; call for schedules and reservations). Contact **Schiffsmakler WEF Schmid** (04841) 20 14 for ferry schedules from the whistle-stop town of **Nordstrand-Strucklahnungshörn,** accessible from Husum (DM15-25). **Jugendherberge Wyk-Föhr (HI),** Fehrstieg 41 (tel. (04681) 23 55), on the largest of the Islands, is near the ferry landing (DM16.90, over 26 DM20.40).

Greater Berlin and Environs

Berlin-Brandenburg

After decades as a city divided between East and West, Berlin has become the center of a metropolitan region which belongs to neither half. The new capital, Berlin constitutes its own *Land* (Federal State). The city has also renewed its links with Brandenburg, the state which surrounds it on all sides. But nothing could really contain Berlin; it is Berlin's energy that penetrates and clings to Brandenburg. Complicit in so many historical dramas, Berlin's indefinable, unique identity nevertheless places it in a category of its own

GREATER BERLIN

BERLIN

Berlin is one of the most fascinating cities on earth. For half a century, the divided city personified the undeclared Cold War. Raised in the shadow of open conflict, Berliners responded with a storm of cultural activity and the sort of nightlife you might expect from a population that has its back against the wall. When communist governments fell across Eastern Europe, Berlin suddenly found itself on the border of two distinct but no longer separate worlds. Almost overnight, it became a gateway—*the* gateway, in fact—between East and West. Recent refugees, transient expatriates and first- and second-generation immigrants have made both halves of Berlin truly international.

The result has been a period of dizzying change, and Berlin is both better and worse off as a result. Suddenly, Berlin is once again the capital of Germany; although the bureaucrats stay in Bonn, Berlin has the symbolic power without the tedium (or restraining influence) of governing. The fusion of East and West Berlin's museums, artists, authors, and other cultural prizes has led to an explosion of creative energy that promises to yield untold riches in the coming years. A flourishing squatters' scene has emerged in abandoned buildings in the eastern boroughs of Mitte and Prenzlauer Berg, many left unrestored since World War II; in spite of the city government's best efforts to the contrary, starving artists from around the world have taken up residence, attracted by the sense of community and the sense that Eastern Berlin has not yet been used up by western commercialism. They have been met in turn by carpetbagging western businesspeople, Reconstruction *Wessies,* and a lot of people who just wanted to witness history in the making. Vigorous student protests over the plethora of contemporary social problems—and there's no lack these days—flare up frequently. Eastern Berlin currently suffers from massive unemployment, as the transition from communism to capitalism proves more painful than the Kohl government predicted in the heady days before Germany's first united elections. In those same elections, a surprising thirty percent of East Berlin voted for the PDS, the successor to the East German Communist Party. In stark contrast to Berlin's burgeoning art scene, economic hopelessness and social alienation have encouraged many young Berliners in their fascination with xenophobic neo-Nazi movements. The still-disorganized integrated police force has been largely ineffective against these groups, and against their often brutal attacks on immigrants and nonconformists.

The city is not honestly picturesque; the sudden change in its borders has left Berlin without a single center. Today the Wall's legacy still crops up occasionally in wide, empty spaces of cracked concrete and overgrown weeds. This may not be the case in a decade, when the outward scars of reunification begin to heal. There's something about Berlin that doesn't make sense; it sneaks up on you and hides things. But Berlin's dark side pales in comparison to the exhilaration of being on the cutting edge. As Weimar decadent Karl Zuckmayer wrote, "Berlin tasted of future, and for that one happily accepted the dirt and coldness as part of the bargain."

HISTORY

Prussian Kingdom to World War I

Berlin took its time attaining international importance. The first mention of a town called "Berlin" was in 1237, but it was not until 1710 that the five towns by the river Spree united into the city of Berlin, capital of the Prussian kingdom. In the 18th century, Berlin flourished under the progressive rule of Friedrich II (the Great), and the likes of writer Gotthold Ephraim Lessing and philosopher Moses Mendelssohn turned the growing city into a center of the Enlightenment. Voltaire, who fled the stifling atmosphere of French absolutism to enjoy Friedrich's patronage, marveled at the transformation of Berlin, "things have changed visibly: Sparta has become Athens." In 1871, Berlin became the capital of the German empire established after Bismarck's wars with Austria and France. Its new position as national capital ushered in the period of prosperity, stability, and hypocrisy documented in the novels of Theodor Fontane. However, hundreds of years of political fragmentation left its mark on Germany, and imperial Berlin never became the center of the new nation in the same way that Paris dominated France, or London captained England. Munich and Frankfurt remained cultural and commercial rivals, and many Germans felt little affection for the Prussian capital. It was not until the end of the First World War and the establishment of the first German Republic that Berlin became the undisputed center of national life.

Revolution and Weimar Culture

The First World War and the Allied blockade brought about near-starvation conditions in Berlin. A popular uprising led to the Kaiser's abdication and the declaration of a republic, with Berlin as capital. Locally the revolt, led by Karl Liebknecht and Rosa Luxemburg, turned into a full-fledged workers' revolution which wrested control of the city for several days. The Social Democratic government enlisted the aid of radical right-wing mercenaries, the *Freikorps*, who brutally supressed the rebellion and murdered Liebknecht and Luxemburg. When the *Freikorps* chose the new government as its next target, the workers demonstrated their commitment to democracy and staged a massive strike to defeat the coup. Political and economic instability continued until 1923, when Chancellor Gustav Stresemann's economic plan and generous loans from the United States improved the situation. Meanwhile Berlin had become one of the major cultural centers of Europe. The Expressionists flourished, Bertolt Brecht and Piscator developed revolutionary new theater techniques, Alfred Döblin applied Joycean method in his novels of Berlin, and artists and writers from all over the world flocked to the city. It was an era of decadence and tolerance. Christopher Isherwood (author of *Berlin Stories)* and W.H. Auden were among the prominent, openly gay men who found acceptance in Berlin along with other refugees from rigid heterosexual mores elsewhere in Europe, as did Ernst Röhm, head of Hitler's *Sturmabteilung*. The city's "Golden Twenties" ended abruptly with the 1929 economic collapse. Mass unemployment preceded bloody riots, radicalization, political chaos, and eventually, the ascent of the Nazis.

Capital of the Third Reich

When Hitler took power on January 30, 1933, traditionally left-wing "Red Berlin" was not one of his strongholds. He consolidated his control over the city through economic improvement and totalitarian measures, and found plenty of supporters for the savage anti-Semitic pogrom of November 9, 1938, the Night of Shattered Glass *(Kristallnacht)*. Berliners were unenthusiastic about the start of World War II, but their city was not spared destruction: Allied bombing and the Battle of Berlin leveled a fifth of the city and damaged the rest. With almost all of the healthy men dead or gone, it was Berlin's women, known as the *Trümmerfrauen* (rubble women) who picked up the broken pieces of the city. The pre-war population of 4.3 million sank to 2.8 million. Only 7000 members of Berlin's once-thriving Jewish community of 160,000 survived the Nazi genocide.

After the war ended, the Allies took over control of the city, dividing it into French, English, American, and Soviet sectors under a joint Allied Command. On June 16, 1948 the Soviets withdrew from the joint Command and demanded full control of the city. On June 26 they began an 11-month blockade of most land and water routes into the western half of the city. The city would have starved were it not for a massive Allied airlift of supplies into the city—the *Luftbrücke* (air bridge). On May 5, 1949 the Soviets ceded control of the western half of the city to the western allies.

Divided City

In October 1949 the Soviet-controlled German Democratic Republic was proclaimed, with East Berlin as its capital. The city was then officially divided. Dissatisfaction was great in East Berlin, and it manifested itself in the workers' uprising of June 17, 1953, when widespread popular demonstrations were crushed bloodily under Soviet tanks. One result of the repression was an increase in the number of refugees who fled from East to West Berlin—200,000 in 1960 alone. On the morning of August 13, 1961, the government of the East responded to this exodus of many of its most talented citizens with the almost instantaneous construction of the Berlin Wall, which stopped virtually all interaction between the two halves of the city. The historic city-center was occupied by the Soviets after the war and passed into GDR control. The western sector created its commercial center around Breitscheid Platz and the renowned Kurfürstendamm.

West Berlin remained under joint French, English, and American control. Although there was an elected mayor, the final say rested with the Allied commander-in-chief. The city was not officially a part of the Federal Republic of Germany, but had a "special status." Although Berlin adopted the resolutions of the Federal Parliament, the municipal Senate still had to approve them, and the Allies retained ultimate authority over the city right up until German reunification. Another manifestation of this special status was the exemption of West Berliners from military conscription. Thousands of German artists, punks, and left-wing activists moved to Berlin to escape the draft, and formed an alternative political and artistic scene without parallel anywhere in the world. The West German government, determined to make a showcase of the city, poured subsidies into its economic and cultural life, further increasing its vitality.

The Wall Opens

On November 9, 1989—the 71st anniversary of the proclamation of the Weimar Republic, the 66th anniversary of Hitler's Beer Hall *Putsch,* and the 51st anniversary of *Kristallnacht*—a series of popular demonstrations throughout East Germany culminated in the opening of the Berlin Wall. The image of jubilant Berliners embracing and celebrating atop the Brandenburg Gate that night provided one of the most memorable images of the 20th century. Berlin was officially reunited along with the rest of Germany on October 3, 1990, to widespread celebration. Since then, the euphoria has vanished. Eastern and Western Berliners have discovered that they don't really like each other as much as they once envisioned. Resignation to reconstruction has taken the place of biting criticism and poor-taste jokes. Eastern Berlin remains politically volatile, and Western Berliners are not always so innocent either voters in the western Wedding district recently voted a handful of far-right nationalists onto the town council. The city is slowly synthesizing but it will take a long time before its residents consider themselves neighbors. Most visitors will recognize instantly when they have stepped over the officially nonexistent demarcation of the city.

Although the first united, freely elected Bundestag symbolically convened in Berlin on December of 1990, the June 1991 vote to move the parliament back here bodes no immediate action; Bonn remains the seat of government, and the process is expected to take a decade or more.

ORIENTATION AND PRACTICAL INFORMATION

Berlin surveys the Prussian plain in the northeastern corner of the reunited Germany and is again becoming the hub of the national rail network. It is about four railhours southeast of Hamburg and double that time north of Munich, with a web of rail and air connections to numerous European capitals. Four hours from Prague and six from Warsaw by train, Berlin is well connected to Eastern European countries. Former communist-country airlines have frequent services to Berlin. **Bahnhof Zoo** remains Berlin's major train station and the central point of Berlin's subway and surface rail systems, although the rehabilitation of the eastern stations of Alexanderplatz, Friedrichstr., and Hauptbahnhof is rapidly displacing the space-constricted Zoo station.

Berlin is *immense*—the agglomeration of a national capital and what for decades functioned as a small, isolated democratic state. The eastern and western halves of unified Berlin are two worn puzzle pieces that no longer fit together smoothly. The new Berlin has two hearts, the eastern historic and the western commercial, connected by the grand tree-lined boulevard, **Straße des 17 Juni,** which runs through Berlin's massive **Tiergarten** park.

The commercial district of West Berlin is at one end of Tiergarten, around Bahnhof Zoo and **Breitscheidplatz,** site of the bombed-out Kaiser-Wilhelm-Gedächtnikirche, the boxy tower of Europa Center, and the main tourist office. A star of streets radiates from Breitscheidplatz. Toward the west run **Hardenburgstraße, Kantstraße,** and the great commercial boulevard of modern Berlin, the renowned **Kurfürstendamm,** or **Ku'damm.** 800m down Hardenburgstr. is Steinplatz and the enormous Berlin Technical University. 800m down Kantstr. is **Savignyplatz,** home to cafés, restaurants, and *Pensionen.*

The newly asphalted **Ebert Straße** runs uncomfortably along the path of the deconstructed Berlin Wall from the Reichstag to **Potsdamer Platz.** The landmark **Brandenburg Gate** and surrounding Pariser Platz, reconstructed with the aid of European Community funds, open onto **Unter den Linden,** which leads to the historic heart of Berlin around **Lustgarten,** and the neighboring commercial district of **Alexanderplatz.** Although the region near the Brandenburg Gate now represents the geographic center of a tremendous metropolis, it still shows the scars of what Berliners called "wall sickness." The alternative **Kreuzberg** and **Mitte,** for 40 years fringe back-against-the wall neighborhoods of the West and East respectively, are once again at the crossroads. Distinctions between east and west are being slowly overcome as communication networks—transportation, telecommunication, and utilities—are synthesized and developed from scratch to serve the sprawling metropolis that was created with unification.

The windswept waters of the Wannsee, Tegelersee, Niederneuendorfer See, and Heiligensee lap the city from all sides, connected to one another by narrow canals.

If you're planning to stay more than a few days in Berlin, the blue-and-yellow **Falk Plan** (DM8.80; available at most kiosks) is an immensely useful and convenient city map which folds out like a book; it's indispensable. Dozens of streets and transit stations in Eastern Berlin once took their names from communist heroes and heroines. Most have been renamed, in a piecemeal process completed only recently; be sure that your map is up-to-date (1992 or later). In newly united Berlin, many **municipal services** are gradually being joined and coordinated. Novelist Peter Schneider called the East and West Siamese-twin cities, with, for instance, two matching television towers as navels. When services are duplicated in both parts of the city, *Let's Go* lists those in Western Berlin first, then their Eastern counterparts.

Safety Warning! Although neo-Nazis represent a tiny minority of Berliners, Africans, Asians, and other conspicuously non-German individuals should be on guard in the less-touristed areas of Eastern Berlin. These extreme right groups have also been known to target gay and lesbian couples.

Tourist Offices:
   Main Office: Berlin-Touristen-Information, Europa Center, Budapesterstr. 45 (tel. 262 60 31). From Bahnhof Zoo, walk along Budapesterstr. past the Kaiser-Wilhelm-Gedächtnikirche (5min.); the office is on the right. Fluent English spoken and helpful staff. Open Mon.-Sat. 8am-10:30pm, Sun. 9am-9pm.
   Branch offices: Bahnhof Zoo (tel. 313 90 63), open daily 8am-11pm; the main hall of **Tegel Airport** (tel. 410 131 45), open daily 8am-11pm; and the **Hauptbahnhof** in the east (tel. 279 52 09), open daily 8am-8pm.
   Services: All offices provide a simple city map, *Berlin Tut Gut* (a glossy pamphlet about the city), and a very useful and up-to-date pamphlet, *Unterkünfte für Junge Besucher,* which lists Berlin's budget accommodations with directions and prices. All offices will also book rooms for a DM5 fee. A handy book, *Berlin for Young People,* with suggested walks and information about the city, is also available at no cost.
Budget Travel:
   ARTU Reisebüro, Hardenbergstr. 9 (tel. 31 04 66), down the street from Bahnhof Zoo. Sells Transalpino passes and books flights; last minute specials. Open Mon.-Tues. and Thurs.-Fri. 10am-6pm, Wed. 11am-6pm, Sat. 10am-1pm. **Branch offices** at **Takustr. 47** (tel. 831 50 94), U-Bahn: Dahlem-Dorf; **Nollendorfplatz**

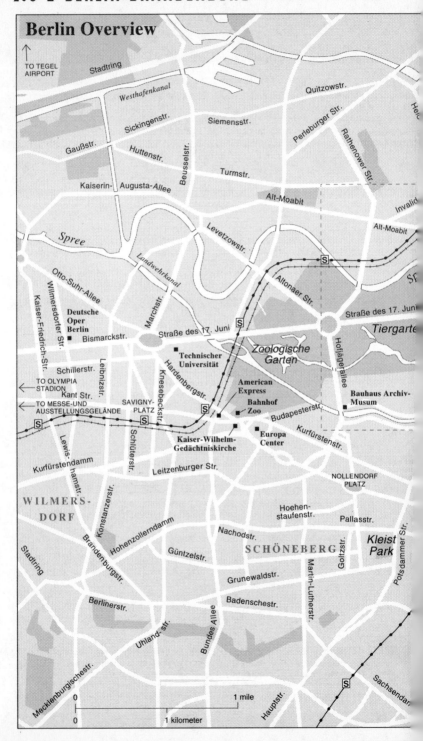

Berlin Overview

Danzigerstr.

Bernauerstr.

Chausseestr.

Kastanen Allee

Schönhauser Allee

Käthe-Kollwitzstr.

Immanuelkirchstr.

Greifswalderstr.

S Invalidenstr.

(former)
Berlin Wall

Elsässerstr.

Chorinerstr.

Lothringerstr.

Prenzlauer Allee

Luisenstr.

S

Rosenthalerstr.

ROSA-
LUXEMBURG
PLATZ

H.-Beimler-Str.

Mollstr.

S Alte
Synagogue

ALEXANDER
PLATZ

Enthält...

Reichstag

MITTE

S

MUSEUMS-
INSEL

S

S

FRIEDRICHS-
HAIN

...enburger
Tor

Toleranzstr.

Unter den Linden

Friedrichstr.

S

...ER
...TEN

Leipziger Str.

Brücken-
str.

Spree

Köpenicker Str.

Kochstr.

TO
TREPTOWER
PARK

S

Stresemannstr.

Wilhelmstr.

Oranienstr.

Mariannenstr.

...ort and
...nology
...useum

KREUZBERG

Heinrich-Heine-Str.

Skalitzer Str.

Kott-

Landwehrkanal

Möckernstr.

Urbanstr.

busser Damm

Sonnenallee

Yorckstr.

Mehringdamm

Gneisenaustr.

Bergmannstr.

Hasenheide

*Victoria
Park*

Dudenstr.

Columbiadamm

Tempelhofer Damm

Hermannstr.

TEMPELHOF

N

**Zentralflughafen
Tempelhof**

7 (tel. 216 30 91; U-Bahn: Nollendorfplatz), and in Kreuzberg at **Mariannenstr. 7** (tel. 614 68 22; U-Bahn: Kotbusser Tor). Open same hours as main branch, but closed an hour for lunch.

SRS, Marienstr. 25 (tel. 281 67 61, fax 28151 33). U-Bahn 6: Friedrichstr. Books student flights and has a useful binder of last minute specials. Open Mon.-Fri. 9am-6pm, Sat. 9am-2pm.

Embassies and Consulates: U.S. Consulate, Clayalle 170 (tel. 832 40 87). Consulate Section (tel. 819 74 54). Open Mon.-Fri. 2:30-4pm. **Canadian Consulate,** Friedrichstr. 95 (tel. 261 11 61). Open 8:30am-noon and 2-4pm. **U.K. Embassy Berlin Office,** Unter den Linden 32-34 (tel. 220 24 31). Open Mon.-Fri. 8:30am-12:30pm and 1:15-4pm. **Australian Consulate,** Uhlandstr. 181-3 (tel. 880 08 80). Open Mon.-Fri. 9am-noon and 2-4pm. **South African Consulate,** Douglasstr. 9 (tel. 82 50 11). Open Mon.-Fri. 8am-4:15pm. **Bulgaria,** Leipzigerstr. 20 (tel. 200 09 22). Open Mon.-Fri. 10am-12:30pm and 1:30-5pm. **Hungary,** Unter den Linden 76 (tel. 220 25 61). Visa section open Mon., Wed., and Fri. 9am-1pm, Tues. and Thurs. 2-5pm. **Russian Federation,** Under den Linden 63-65 (tel. 229 11 10). Visa section open Mon.-Fri. 9am-noon. **Czech Republic,** Toleranzstr. 21 (tel. 220 04 81). Visa section open 8:30-11am. **Poland,** Under den Linden 72-74 (tel. 220 25 51). Visa section open Mon. and Wed.-Fri. 9am-1pm.

American Express: Uhlandstr. 173 (tel. 882 75 75). Mail held, all banking services. Charges no commission for cashing its own traveler's cheques. Open Mon.-Fri. 9am-5:30pm, Sat. 9am-noon.

Currency Exchange: Deutsche Verkehrs-Kredit Bank (tel. 881 71 17), at Bahnhof Zoo on Hardenbergstr. Open Mon.-Sat.7:30am-10pm, Sun. 8am-7pm. Decent rates for exchange; 1% commission on traveler's checks (DM7.50 min.). Branch also at **Hauptbahnhof** (tel. 426 70 29), open Mon.-Fri. 7am-7:30pm, Sat.-Sun 8am-4pm. **Berliner Bank** in Tegel Airport is open daily 8am-10pm. Branches of commercial banks are sprouting up in Eastern Berlin. You can also change money at most **post offices**, which cash traveler's checks for DM3 per check.

Post Offices: In the **Bahnhof Zoo** (tel. 313 97 99). Open 24hrs. **Poste Restante** (held at window 9) should be addressed: Poste Restante/Hauptpostlagernd, Post amt Bahnhof Zoo, 10612 Berlin. Branch office at **Tegel Airport** (tel. 430 85 23) open daily 6:30am-9pm. In Eastern Berlin, in the **Hauptbahnhof,** Postamt Berlin 17, Str. der Pariser Kommune 8-10, 10243 Berlin. Open Mon.-Fri. 7am-9pm, Sat 8am-8pm.

Telephones: At Bahnhof Zoo. Open 24hrs. Note that public phones are rarer in the eastern part of the city. **City code**: 030.When calling Eastern Berlin from overseas, if dialing (30) doesn't work, you'll probably need operator assistance. You may occasionally see a (9) in front of an Eastern Berlin number; this old prefix has almost entirely been phased out; the number itself may be out of date. Give it a try both ways, or call directory assistance to check the number. *Let's Go* list Eastern numbers without the (9) before them. With the shortage of new phone lines, many homes and businesses in East Berlin use mobile phones.

Flights: Flughafen Tegel (tel. 410 11), Bus #109 (from Bahnhof Zoo or Jakob-Kaiser-Platz U-Bahn station): Tegel. Western Berlin's main airport. **Flughafen Tempelhof** (tel. 690 91). Bus #119: Kurfürstendamm. The under-used airport is making a post-reunification comeback, especially for flights within Europe **Flughafen Schönefeld** (tel. 678 70), in Eastern Berlin, is connected by S-Bahn t the city center.

Trains:

Stations: Bahnhof Zoo is Berlin's principal station for locations to the west while **Hauptbahnhof** is the focus of eastern and southern-bound trains. St tions are connected by S-Bahn. Trains from the east also arrive at **Bahnhof Lichtenberg.**

Connections: Dresden (2hr.), Leipzig (2½hr.), Hamburg (3-4hr.), Hanover (4hr. Frankfurt am Main (9hr.), Prague (5hr.), Warsaw (8hr.), Vienna (11hr.).

Information: Bundesbahn and Reichsbahn Information (tel. 194 19). Be pr pared for a long wait. Similarly long lines at information offices in **Bahnhof Zo** and **Hauptbahnhof.** For **recorded** information in German about departure and arrivals there are several lines depending on destinations: Hamburg, Kie

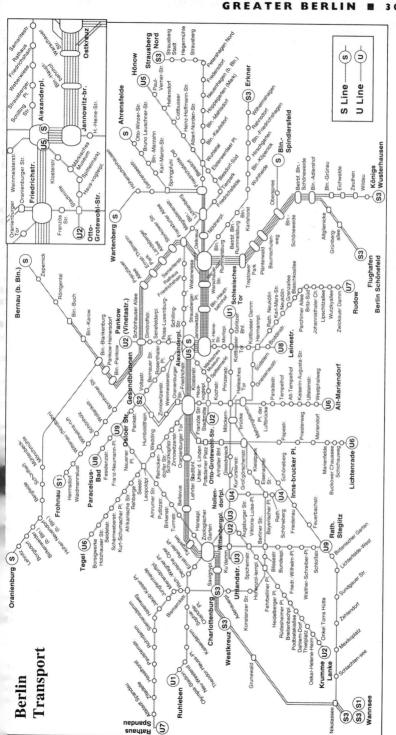

Berlin Transport

BERLIN: PRACTICAL INFORMATION

Rostock (tel. 01 15 31); Hanover, Cologne, Netherlands, France (tel. 01 15 32); Erfurt, Frankfurt, Switzerland (tel. 01 15 33); Leipzig, Munich, Austria, Italy (tel. 01 15 34); Dresden, Czech Republic, Hungary, Romania, Bulgaria (tel. 01 15 35); Poland, Lithuania, Latvia, Comm. of Independent States (tel. 01 15 36).

Buses: ZOB, the central bus station (tel. 301 80 28), is by the Funkturm near Kaiserdamm. U-Bahn 1: Kaiserdamm. Check *Zitty* and *Tip* for deals on long-distance buses; often buses are only slightly cheaper than train or plane.

Luggage Storage: In the Bahnhof Zoo train station; lockers DM2, larger DM3, 72hr. max. At **Hauptbahnhof;** lockers DM2, larger DM4, 72hr. max. At Bahnhof **Lichtenberg** and S-Bahnhof **Alexanderplatz,** Lockers DM2. 24hr. max.

Public Transportation:

Orientation and Basic Fares: It is impossible to tour Berlin on foot, so the public transit system is as indispensable as it is efficient and expensive. The extensive **bus, U-bahn** (subway), and **S-Bahn** (surface rail) systems of Eastern and Western Berlin now operate as one network, the **BVG.** A single ticket for the combined network *(Einzelfahrschein Normaltarif)* costs DM3.20 and is good for 2hr. after validation. An *Einzelfahrschein Kurzstreckentarif* (short-trip fare, DM2.10) allows travel up to 6 bus stops (with no transfers; not valid on airport bus lines) or 3 U- or S-Bahn stations (with one transfer). 4-ride *Sammelkarte* (Multiple Ticket), DM11; short-trip 4-ride *Sammelkarte* DM6.40. You can buy tickets from machines, bus drivers, or ticket windows in the U-Bahn and S-Bahn stations. The fine for cheating is steep (DM60), and inspections are frequent. Children under 6 accompanied by an adult travel free. *All tickets must be canceled in the red validation box before boarding to be valid.*

Special Passes and Maps: Information and tickets are available at the **BVG Pavillon,** Bahnhof Zoo (tel. 256 24 62). Open daily 8am-8pm. The **Berlin Ticket** (DM12, ages 6-14 DM6) is a 24hr. pass on the bus, U- or S-Bahn. A **6-Day Berlin Ticket** (Mon.-Sat.) costs DM30. A monthly **Umweltkarte** costs DM74, a good value for longer stays. The **Kombi-Ticket** is valid for 1 day and allows unlimited travel on the ferry services of **Stern und Kreisschiffahrt** as well as all services of BVG (DM25; also see ferries, below). An extensive **Liniennetz** map costs DM3 and can be bought from subway ticket offices. The **Falk Plan** also has all routes indicated.

Night Transport: U- and S-Bahn do not run 1-4am, except for the **U-1** and **U-9,** which run all night Fri.-Sat. There is an extensive system of **night buses** stopping every half-hour; look for the signs with a moon and stars or pick up the free *Nachtliniennetz* map. All night bus numbers are preceded by **N.**

Lost Property: BVG Fündbüro, Lorenzweg 5 (tel. 17 51 80 21). For items lost on the bus or U-Bahn. Open Mon.-Tues. and Thurs. 9am-3pm, Wed. 9am-6pm, Fri. 9am-2pm. **Fundbüro Deutsche Reichsbahn,** in the Hackescher Markt S-Bahn station (tel. 29 72 16 71). For items lost on trains or S-Bahn. Open Mon., Wed.-Thurs. 10am-4pm, Tues. 10am-6pm, Fri. 8am-noon. **Zentrales Fundbüro,** Platz der Luftbrücke 6 (tel. 69 90).

Car Rental: Avis, Budapesterstr. 43 (tel. 793 19 80) is closest to Bahnhof Zoo. Open Mon.-Fri. 7am-6pm, Sat. 8am-1pm. **Hertz** has an office in Tegel Airport (tel. 41 01 33 15). Open Mon.-Fri. 7am-11pm, Sat.-Sun. 8am-11pm.

Automobile Clubs: ADAC (tel. 86 86 86; eastern Berlin 279 37 42).

Mitfahrzentrale: City Netz, Kurfürstendamm 227, in the Ku'damm Eck mall, has a computerized **ride-share** database (tel. 194 44 or 882 76 04). Open daily 8am-9pm. **Branch offices** at Südstern 2 in Kreuzberg (tel. 693 60 95), open daily 9am-8pm; and at Bahnhof Zoo (tel. 31 03 31), open daily 8am-9pm. **Mitzfahrzentrale Alex** (tel. 242 36 42), in the Alexanderplatz U-Bahn station, specializes in the East. Open Mon.-Fri. 8am-9pm, Sat. 8am-6pm, Sun. 10am-6pm. The **Mitfahrtelephon für Schwüle and Lesben,** Yorckstr. 52 (tel. 216 40 20), matches gay and lesbian drivers and passengers. Open daily 8am-9pm. Berlin has other small *Mitzfahrzentralen*; see *Zitty* or *Tip* magazines for addresses and phone numbers.

Hitchhiking: *Let's Go* does not recommend hitchhiking as a safe mode of transportation. No No No. Those who hitch west and south (Hanover, Munich, Weimar, Leipzig) take S-Bahn 1 or 3: Wannsee, then bus #211: *Autobahn* entrance ramp. Those headed north (Hamburg, Rostock) take U-Bahn 6: Tegel, then bus #224 and ask the driver to be let out at the *Trampenplatz.* Both have huge crowds, but someone gets picked up every few minutes.

Bike Rental: Fahrradbüro Berlin, Hauptstr. 146 (tel. 784 55 62). U-Bahn: Kleistpark. DM15 per day, DM60 per week. Tandems DM25 per day. Deposit DM50; bring ID. Open Mon.-Wed. and Fri. 10am-6pm, Thurs. 10am-7pm, Sat. 10am-2pm. In Eastern Berlin, **Velorent,** Str. der Pariser Commune (tel. 787 50 83), S-Bahn: Hauptbahnhof; under the rail bridge. DM10 per day, DM42 per week. Deposit DM100. Bring passport.

Ferries: Stern und Kreisschiffahrt, Sachtlebenstr. 6 (tel. 810 00 40), operates ferry services along Berlin's waterways from April-Oct. Ferries leave from locations throughout the city. Fares depend on distance traveled (DM3.20-22). Pleasure cruises also available. *Berlin Kombi-Tageskarte* is valid on all regularly scheduled services. For further information contact tourist office or BVG Pavilion.

Pharmacies: Europa-Apotheke, Tauentzienstr. 9-12 (tel. 261 41 42), by Europa Center (close to Bahnhof Zoo). Open 9am-9pm. Closed *Apotheken* post signs directing you to the nearest open one. In **Eastern Berlin: Apotheke am Alexanderplatz,** Hans Beimlerstr. 70-72 (tel. 242 5766). Open Mon.-Fri. 8am-6:30pm, Sat. 8am-1pm. For information about late-night pharmacies call 011 41.

Bookstores: Marga Schoeller Bücherstube, Knesebeckstr. 34 (tel. 881 11 12), at Mommsenstr., between Savignyplatz and the Ku'damm. Large selection of books in English. Open Sun.-Fri. 9am-6:30pm, Sat. 9am-2pm. Second-hand English books bought and sold at **The Original Version,** Sesenheimerstr. 17 (tel. 313 76 22). Open Mon.-Fri. noon-9pm, Sat. 11am-2pm. The **British Bookshop,** Mauerstr. 83-84 (tel. 238 46 80), is a new, artfully stocked addition to Berlin's English book club, stocking books of all descriptions and also English newspapers and magazines. Open Mon.-Fri. 9am-6:30pm, Sat. 9am-2pm. The endless selection at the huge **Kiepert's,** on Hardenbergstr. 4, across from the Technical University, includes works in English. Open Mon.-Fri. 9am-6pm, Sat. 9am-1pm. **Literaturhaus Berlin** is in a wonderful old mansion at Fasanenstr. 23 (tel. 882 50 44), complete with garden café and frequent readings.

Cultural Centers: Amerika Haus, Hardenbergstr. 22-24 (tel. 310 00 10). The library includes English-language books and *The New York Times,* and presents readings by visiting American authors. Offices open Mon.-Fri. 8:30am-5:30pm. Library open Mon., Wed., and Fri. 11:30am-5:30pm, Tues. and Thurs. 11:30am-8pm. **British Council,** Hardenbergstr. 20, next door. Enter through the Informationszentrum Berlin, 2nd floor. Office open Mon.-Fri. 9am-12:30pm and 2-5pm. Library open Mon., Wed., and Fri. 2-6pm, Tues. and Thurs. 2-7pm.

Laundromat: Wasch Centers (tel. 852 37 96) at Leibnizstr. 72, Wexstr. 34, Rheinstr. 62, Markstr. 4, Behmstr. 12 Bergmannstr. 109, and (in Eastern Berlin's Prenzlauer Berg) Jablonskistr. 21. All open daily 6am-midnight. Wash DM8 per 6kg, dry DM2 for 30min. Soap included.

Crisis Lines: Sexual Assault Hotline (tel. 251 28 28). Open Tues. and Thurs. noon-9pm, Sun. noon-2pm. **Schwüles Überfall** (gay bashing) hotline and legal help (tel. 216 33 36), open Sun.-Fri. 6-9pm, Sat. 6pm-4am. English speakers at both. **Drug Crisis,** tel. 218 70 33.

Medical Assistance: The tourist office has a list of English-speaking doctors. **Emergency Doctor:** tel. 31 00 31 (Western), tel. 12 59 (Eastern). If stranded in Eastern Berlin try the emergency room of **Rettungsamt Berlin,** Marienburgerstr. 41-46 (tel. 282 05 61). **Emergency Dentist:** tel. 11 41.

Emergencies: Police: tel. 110. Headquarters at Platz der Luftbrücke 6 (tel. 69 90). **Ambulance and Fire:** tel. 112.

ACCOMMODATIONS AND CAMPING

The immediate euphoria and tourist influx after the fall of the Wall has leveled out and the prices and quality of Berlin accommodations have stabilized. Nonetheless, Berlin is a major tourist center and it is advisable to book ahead.

For a DM5 fee, **tourist offices** will find you a hotel room. Count on spending at least DM60 for a single, DM100 for a double. They also have private accommodations, from DM40 per person with breakfast (2-night min.). The office prefers to fill up the *Pensionen* first, so you may have to ask for private rooms. Although most accommodations are in Western Berlin, the office does have some listings for private rooms in the eastern part of the city. Reserve a room by writing directly to a *Pension* or to the **Verkehrsamt Berlin,** Martin-Luther-Str. 105, 10825 Berlin (tel. (030) 212 34; fax (030) 21 23 25 20). (Note that this is a *different* address from the main tourist office.) The *Verkehrsamt* requires that you state precisely how much you want to spend (minimum DM60 for a single, DM95 for a double). Write at least 4 weeks in advance. The tourist offices also have a pamphlet *Unterkünfte für Junge Besucher in Berlin und Brandenburg* which lists hostels and inexpensive guest houses and hotels. See the introductions to Hostels and Hotels (below) for specifics on each option.

For longer visits (more than 4 days) the various **Mitwohnzentralen** can arrange for you to housesit or sublet someone's apartment. Prices start at DM35 per night, plus a percentage fee, and go down the longer you stay. The **Mitwohnzentrale,** Kurfürstendamm 227/228, in the Ku'damm Eck mall, 2nd (tel. 88 30 51, fax 882 66 94) is the biggest (open Mon.-Fri. 10am-6:30pm, Sat.-Sun. 11am-2pm). **Erste,** Sybelstr. 53 (tel. 324 30 31; U-Bahn 7: Adenauer Platz) tends to exact a smaller commission (open Mon.-Fri. 9am-8pm, Sat. 10am-6pm). **Mitwohnagentur Streicher,** Immanuel-Kirschstr. 8 (tel. 427 41 72), specializes in apartments in Eastern Berlin, often cheaper than in the West (open Mon.-Fri. noon-7pm). Usually the **Mitwohnzentralen** require you to pay your fee up front unless you have, or can find a friend who has, a German bank account. Keep their fees in mind–for short (less than a month) stays the standard commission is 10% of the final sum while for longer stays the rate is usually 1-2% per month of the annual room/apartment rent. This can add up. Unlike the US, leases here start at any time—you don't need to wait for the beginning of a calendar month. Women tend to have an easier time than men finding long-term accommodations.

Hostels and Dormitory-Style Accommodations

Hostels fill quickly with German school groups (especially in summer and on weekends); call ahead. All HI-affiliated hostels are for members only, tend to attract school groups and are liable to be overbooked. For an extra DM4, some hostels will give nonmembers a stamp and let you spend the night. To buy an **HI card,** head to Tempelhofer Ufer 32, 10963 Berlin (tel. 262 30 24, fax 262 95 29). (Open Mon., Wed., and Fri. 10am-3pm, Tues.-Thurs. 2-5:30pm.) For non-Germans, membership cards cost DM36. HI-hostels also have curfews which hinder night-ragers and tend to be stricter in their regulations. Many hostels accept written reservations.

Schöneberg—Wilmersdorf

Jugendgästehaus (HI), Kluckstr. 3, 10785 Berlin (tel. 261 10 97, fax 265 03 83). Bus #129 (from Kurfürstendamm, direction "Hermannplatz"): Jugendgästehaus, or U-Bahn 1: Kurfürstenstr., then walk up Potsdamerstr., left on Pohlstr., right on Kluckstr. You can't miss it: an 8m conceptual "DJH" archway stands in front. Central location, many school groups. Reception open 1-1:45pm, 2:35-9:45pm, and 10:15pm-midnight. Lockout 9am-noon. Curfew midnight; stragglers admitted at 12:30am and 1am. DM27, over 26 DM33. Sheets and breakfast included. Key deposit DM10. Lockers, laundry facilities. Reservations strongly recommended.

Studentenhotel Berlin, Meiningerstr. 10, 10823 Berlin (tel. 784 67 20, fax 788 15 23). U-Bahn 4: Rathaus Schöneberg or U-Bahn 7: Eisenacherstr., or by bus #146 (from Zoo): Rathaus Schöneberg, walk across Martin-Luther-Str. Acceptable dorm accommodations in a green, quiet neighborhood, but within walking distance of Schönberg action. Reception open 24hrs. Doubles DM38 per person. Quads DM34 per person. Breakfast included. Reservations recommended.

Jugendgästehaus Feurigstraße, Feurigstr. 63, 10827 Berlin 62 (tel. 781 52 11, fax 788 30 51). U-Bahn 7: Kleistpark, or bus #146, 148. Good location for the bars and clubs of Schöneberg. Reception 24hrs. Dorms DM34. Singles DM54. Doubles DM44 per person. Sheets and breakfast included. Reservations advisable; at least call ahead.

Jugendgästehaus Central, Nikolsburgerstr. 2-4, 10717 Berlin (tel. 87 01 88, fax 861 3485). U-Bahn 9: Güntzelstr. or U-Bahn 2: Hohenzollernplatz. Looks like a high school, with drab green walls, but worth it if you can get a double. Curfew 1am. 2- to 6-person rooms DM32 per person, many with own shower and toilet. Breakfast included. Full board DM4 extra. Sheets DM7.

CVJM-Haus, Einemstr. 10, 10787 Berlin (tel. 264 91 00). U-Bahn 1, 4: Nollendorf-platz. German YMCA. Grey, institutional setting, but it'll make you feel young again. Reception open 8-11am and 4-9pm. Singles DM40. Doubles DM80. Breakfast included.

Steinplatz

Jugendgästehaus am Zoo, Hardenbergstr. 9a, 10623 Berlin (tel. 312 94 10), directly opposite the Technical University Mensa. Bus #145, or a short walk from Bahnhof Zoo out the back exit and straight down Hardenbergstr. The central location almost makes up for crowded rooms. Mingle at the built-in café. Reception on the 4th floor; best to arrive between 10 and 11am. No curfew. Singles DM47. Doubles DM85. Small dorms (4-12 beds) DM35. No breakfast. No reservations accepted.

Tegel

Jugendherberge Ernst Reuter (HI), Hermsdorfer Damm 48, 13467 Berlin (tel. 404 16 10). U-Bahn 6: Tegel, then bus #125 (direction "Frohnau/Invalidensied-lung"): Jugendherberge. Distant from the center, on the edge of the forest. Likely to have space in July and Aug. when school groups disappear. Curfew midnight. DM22, over 26 DM27. Sheets and breakfast included. Key deposit DM10.

Jugendgästehaus Tegel, Ziekowstr. 161, 13509 Berlin (tel. 433 30 46, fax 434 50 63). U-Bahn 6: Tegel, then bus #222 or night bus N22: Titusweg. Old brick outside, new and bright inside, on the north end of town by the Tegel parks. Often has room. For a more communal experience, check out the neighboring **Internationales Jugendcamp Tegel** (see Camping, below). Under 27 only. No curfew. DM31.50. Breakfast included. Written reservations only.

Elsewhere in Berlin

Jugendgästehaus Nordufer, Nordufer 28, 13351 Berlin (tel. 451 70 30, fax 452 41 00). U-Bahn 9: Westhafen, left over the bridge and left onto Nordufer. Away from the center, but on the pretty, blue, swimmable Plötzersee Lake. Some singles, but more 4-bed rooms. Free use of next-door *Freibad.* Reception open 7am-midnight. No curfew. DM35. Buffet breakfast and sheets included.

Jugendgästehaus am Wannsee (HI), Kronprinzessinnenweg 27, 14129 Berlin (tel. 803 20 34, fax 803 59 08). S-Bahn 1, 3: Nikolassee, walk 10min. toward the Strand Bad Wannsee beach. Far from the center and a bit institutional, but likely to have space, and Wannsee has its own charm. Curfew 1am. DM27, over 26 DM33. Sheets and breakfast included. Key deposit DM20.

Hotels and Pensionen

Prices have finally stabilized as small pension and hotel owners once more cater to small budgets. Most *Pensionen* and small hotels listed in *Let's Go* are amenable to *Mehrbettzimmer,* where extra beds are moved into a large double or triple. Increasing rents and crippling taxes are jeopardizing business for the small hotel owner. If they aren't fully booked they will be very accommodating; ask for these deals. If traveling in a small group (usually up to 5), *Mehrbettzimmer* rates can work out to little more than the price of a bed in a hostel. Most budget hotels are in Western Berlin; the hotels in Mitte are ridiculously expensive, and other areas still do not have the facilities to support many visitors. The best place to find cheap hotel rooms is around Savignyplatz and down along Wilmersdorfstr. and its side-streets.

Steinplatz

Hotelpension Bialas, Carmerstr. 16 (tel. 312 50 25, fax 3124396). Bus #149: Stein-platz, or a walk down Harderbergstr. from the Zoo (10min.). Unusually convenient for Berlin, and the rooms have sculptured ceilings. Reception open 24hrs. Singles DM65, with shower and toilet DM95. Doubles DM65-95, with shower and toilet DM150. Breakfast included.

Savignyplatz

Hotelpension Cortina, Kantstr. 140 (tel. 313 90 59, fax 317 39 6). S-Bahn 3, 5, 6, 9 or bus #149: Savignyplatz. High-ceilings, bright, convenient and hospitable. Reception open 24hrs. Extra beds in rooms upon agreement. Singles DM65. Doubles DM95, with shower DM120. Breakfast included.

Pension Knesebeck, Knesebeckstr. 86, 10623 Berlin (tel. 31 72 55). S-Bahn 3, 5, 6, 9: Savignyplatz. Just north of the park. Friendly, large *alt-berliner* rooms, all with sinks. Reception open 24hrs. Singles DM75. Doubles DM120, with shower DM140. Extra beds in room DM140, with shower DM150. Breakfast included.

Hotel Pension Majesty, Mommsenstr. 55, 10629 Berlin (tel. 323 20 61, fax 323 20 63). S-Bahn 3, 5, 6, 9: Savignyplatz. Very simple, centrally located. Rooms vary widely; avoid those on the ground floor. Reception open 6am-midnight. Singles DM70, with shower DM80. Doubles DM120, with shower DM130. Breakfast included.

Centrum Pension Berlin, Kanstr. 31 (tel. 316 153). Bus #149: Savignyplatz. Big pink building just a block past the Cortina, but slightly scaled down. Singles DM50. Doubles DM75. Triples DM90. Quads DM120. Breakfast DM7.50.

Wilmersdorf —Schöneberg

Pension Münchener, Güntzelstr. 62 (tel. 854 22 26, fax 853 27 44). U-Bahn 9: Güntzelstr. Small, art-filled *pension*. White-walled, clean rooms with colorful comforters. Reception open mornings. Singles DM56. Doubles DM78. Breakfast DM9.

Hotelpension Pariser Eck, Pariserstr. 19, 10707 Berlin (tel. 881 21 45), near Ludwigplatz. U-Bahn 2, 9: Spichernstr. Bright clean rooms on a café-lined corner. If no one answers the doorbell, go to the café next door for assistance. Singles DM50. Doubles DM85, with showers DM95. Showers DM1.50, bath DM2.

Hotelpension Gloria, Wielandstr. 27, 10707 Berlin (tel. 881 80 60). Bus #119: Bleibtreustr. Basic accommodation. Just off a quiet stretch of the Ku'damm. Reception open 7am-8pm. Singles DM60, with shower DM80. Doubles with shower DM130. Breakfast included.

Frauenhotel Artemesia, Brandenburgischestr. 18 (tel. 87 89 05, fax 861 86 53). Pricey, but a rare bird—an immaculate, elegant hotel for women only. The Artemesia Cafe is also open for breakfast (Mon.-Fri. 8am-11am, Sat.-Sun. 8am-3pm) and evenings as a bar for an all-woman, often lesbian crowd. Singles DM99. Doubles DM159, with shower and bath DM195. Breakfast, on the terrace, included.

Kreuzberg

Hotel Transit, Hagelbergerstr. 53-54 (tel. 785 50 51; fax 785 96 19). U-Bahn 6,7: Mehringdamm, bus #119, or night bus N19 (every 10-15min.). Trendy loft accommodation in a reconverted factory. Reception area has a chrome and monochrome bar and a 24hr. (M)TV lounge. Laundry facilities. Reception open 24hrs. Singles with showers DM70. Doubles with showers DM95. Triples with showers DM120. Small dorms DM30 per person. Breakfast included.

Pension Kreuzberg, Grossbeerenstr. 64, 10963 Berlin (tel. 251 13 62). U-Bahn 6, 7: Mehringdamm or bus #119. Clean, high-ceilinged rooms, a little smaller than most, in a grand old building close to the bars and clubs of Kreuzberg. Reception open 9am-8pm. Singles DM60. Doubles DM90. *Mehrbettzimmer* DM40 per person. Breakfast included.

Charlottenburg

Charlottenburger Hof, Stuttgarterpl. 14, 10627 Berlin (tel. 324 48 19; fax 323 37 23). S-Bahn 3, 5, 6, 9: Charlottenburg or U-Bahn 7: Wilmersdorferstr. Sparkling rooms with modern art, cable TV, phones and safes. Open 24hrs. Singles DM65, with shower DM90-110. Doubles DM80-100, with shower DM120-140. Triples DM160. Quads DM180. Breakfast DM5-8.

Elsewhere in Berlin

Hotel-Pension Hansablick, Flotowstr. 6 (tel. 391 40 48, fax 392 69 37). Near Tiergarten. A bit pricey, but for the money it's a Berliner *Jugendstil* pearl, from the decorative ceilings to the marble entranceway and antique-looking streetlamps in front. Few places like this survived World War II bombing, so call, write, or fax ahead for reservations. Reception open 7am-9pm. Singles DM85. Doubles DM115, with shower DM125, with shower, bath, and color TV DM165.

Hamburger Hof, Kinkelstr. 6 (tel. 333 46 02), in the old quarter of Spandau. U-Bahn 7: Altstadt Spandau. Easily accessible. A tiny, comfortable hotel with only 15 beds, but it's so far from the action that they usually have room. Singles DM45. Doubles DM90. Showers and breakfast included.

Camping

Deutscher Camping-Club, runs three of the major campgrounds in Berlin; all are adjacent to the imaginary line tracing the site of the Berlin Wall. Written reservations for any Berlin campsite can be made by writing the Deutscher Camping-Club e.v. (D.C.C.), Mandlstr. 28, 80802 München. Otherwise, call in advance. All sites charge DM6.90 per person, DM5.50 for a small tent, and DM7.50 for larger size tents. All are open year-round.

Dreilinden (tel. 805 12 01). Take U-Bahn 2 to Oskar-Helene-Heim; then bus #118: Kätchenweg; follow Kremnitzufer to Albrechts-Teergfen (about 20min.). Perhaps the most unusual of the camps, surrounded on three sides by the vestiges of the Berlin Wall. The remains of a stretch of the *Autobahn* which fell into disuse after 1949 can be seen through the trees. The site is well-equipped; its bar is an old border checkpoint.

Kladow, Krampnitzer Weg 111/117 (tel. 365 27 97). U-Bahn: Rathaus Spandau, then take bus #135 to the last stop. Follow Krampnitzer Weg another 500m.

Haselhorst, Pulvermühlenweg (tel. 334 59 55). U-Bahn: Haselhorst, then north on Daumster to Pulvermühlenweg. Also in Spandau, but closer to the center.

Internationales Jugendcamp, Ziekowstr. 161 (tel. 433 86 40). U-Bahn 6: Tegel, then bus #222 or night bus N22: Titusweg. Next to Jugendgästehaus Tegel (see Hostels, above). Only open June 21-Aug. 31. Far away, but gets you a mat under a giant tent with shower facilities. Under 27 only. Lockout 9am-5pm. DM9. No written reservations accepted.

FOOD

Berlin's restaurant scene is as international as its population; German cuisine should not be a priority here. One exception is *Berliner Weiße mit Schuß,* a concoction of local beer with a shot of syrup. Specify *rotes* (red) for *crème de cassis* or *grünes* (green) for *Jägermeister.* Much typical Berlin food is Turkish: almost every street has its own Turkish *Imbiß* or restaurant. The *Döner Kepab,* a sandwich of lamb and salad, has cornered the fast food market, with *Falafel* running a close second. For DM4-5, either makes a small meal, but other Turkish dishes are also worth a shot. **Meyhane,** Bleibtreustr. 50, is an inexpensive restaurant with an authentic menu. The second wave of immigration has brought quality Indian restaurants to Berlin, and Italian is always a safe choice.

There is no clear distinction between *Kneipen,* cafés, and restaurants; indeed cafés often have better food than restaurants for much more reasonable prices. A great Berlin tradition in cafés is *Frühstück,* breakfast served well into the afternoon. Leisurely natives enjoy their fruit- and cheese-laden breakfasts; join them and relax with a *Milchkaffee.* Although budget eateries are scarce in Eastern Berlin, new cafés in Mitte and Prenzlauer Berg are rapidly providing stiff competition for their western counterparts; prices tend to be somewhat lower and portions larger. In addition, street vendors with all shapes, sizes, and flavors of cheap eats fill **Alexanderplatz** every day, and the sprawling grocery department on the first floor of the **Kaufhof am Alex** comes complete with salad bar.

Aldi, Bolle, and **Penny Markt** are the cheapest supermarket chains. Markets open Mon.-Fri. 9am-6pm, Sat. 9am-1pm. The best **open-air market** fires up Saturday mornings in Winterfeldplatz, though almost every neighborhood has one; in Eastern Berlin, markets often set up under S-Bahn platforms.

Western Berlin

Mensen (University Cafeterias)

Mensa der Freie Universität, in the huge complex at Habelschwerdter Allee 45. U-Bahn 2: Thielplatz. Meals from DM2, ISIC required. Open Mon.-Fri. 11:15am-2:30pm. The **cafeteria** on the first floor (less hot food, more sandwiches, somewhat more expensive) is open Mon.-Fri. 8:15am-4pm.

Mensa TU, Hardenbergstr. 34. Bus #145: Steinplatz. Hard to miss: says "MENSA" in big letters on the building. More conveniently located, with slightly worse food than the above. Meals from DM2. Open Mon.-Fri. 11:15am-2:30pm.

Bahnhof Zoo-Ku'Damm area

Café Hardenberg, Hardenbergstr. 10. Big Belle Epoque spot, opposite the TU *Mensa*. Cheap food, lots of students. Also good for a few drinks. Open daily 7am-midnight.

Restaurant Marché, Kudamm 14-15 (tel. 882 75 78), down the street from Zoo and the Gedächtniskirche. With an elegant Ku'damm view, and economical but well-prepared buffets. Vegetarians as well as ice cream fans will be pleased. Open daily 8am-midnight.

KaDeWe, Tauentzienstr. 21 (tel. 212 10). U-Bahn 1, 3, or 4: Wittenbergplatz. A department store with a huge food emporium on the 6th floor, is cluttered with stands serving everything from sandwiches to caviar (open Mon.-Wed. and Fri. 9am-6:30pm, Thurs. 9am-8:30pm, Sat. 9am-2pm).

Savignyplatz

Schwarzes Café, Kantstr. 148 (tel. 313 80 38), near Savignyplatz. Hopping with loads of young people and hip music. Dapper waiters in denim vests. Breakfast at all hours (omelettes DM7), and great tortellini (DM10). For a real jolt of caffeine try the café's namesake (DM7). Open 24hrs., except for Tues. 3am-Wed. 11am.

Café Savigny, Grolmanstr. 51 (tel. 312 81 95). Near Savignyplatz. All marble and wood, with classy old music and international papers. Showy but reasonably priced breakfasts or—to treat yourself—meals from DM15. Open daily 10am-2am.

Schöneberg-Wilmersdorf

Rogacki, Wilmerdorferstr. 145. A gargantuan delicatessen, with every sort of hot and cold food imaginable. Something good in every price range (lobster only DM50). Take out, or stand up and eat at the counters in the back. Open Mon.-Fri. 9am-6pm, Sat. 9am-1pm.

Baharat Falafel, Winterfeldtstr. 37. U-Bahn 1 or 4: Nollendorfplatz. Falafel from heaven with a choice of mango or sesame sauce (DM5). Open Mon.-Sat. noon-2am, Sun. 1pm-2am.

Café Belmundo, Winterfeldtstr. 36 (tel. 215 20 70). U-Bahn 1 or 4: Nollendorfplatz. A young crowd, with outdoor tables and breakfast until 3pm. Fresh salads DM4.50-10. Open Mon.-Sat. 9am-1am, Sun. 10am-1am.

Begine, Potsdamerstr. Classy all-women's café, more of a bar by night. Changing art exhibits hang on the 20-foot walls. Cool women's magazines and delish soup, salad and pastries. Open Mon.-Sat. 6pm-1am.

Mediencafé Strada, Potsdamerstr. 131 (tel. 215 93 81). U-Bahn 1: Kurfürstenstr. Elegant café with imaginative well-presented meals. Lots of magazines and newspapers, many in English, to peruse whilst you sit. Meals run DM6-12. Open Mon.-Thurs. 8:30am-2am, Fri. 8:30am-3am, Sat.-Sun. 10am-2am.

Charlottenburg-Tiergarten

Café Voltaire, Stuttgarterplatz 14 (tel. 324 50 28). S-Bahn 3, 5, 7, or 9: Charlottenburg, or U-Bahn 7: Wilmersdorferstr. Café-bistro-gallery with a colorful and talkative crowd. Close to a whole array of cafés, farther down the street at its

intersection with Winterscheidstr. Extensive menu: great breakfasts 5am-3pm (DM6-8), warm meals noon-5am.Open 24hrs., except for a hiatus Mon. 1-7am.
Tiergartenquelle, Stadtbahnbogen 482 (tel. 392 76 15), under the S-Bahn bridge at S-Bahn: Tiergarten. Huge portions in a friendly, student-filled atmosphere. One of Berlin's best bargains. Most entrees under DM12. Open 6pm-midnight.

Kreuzberg

Atlantik-Küche, Bergmannstr. 112, in Kreuzberg. U-Bahn 6 or 7: Mehringdamm. Second-hand shops and street hawkers surround this scene-café. Amid the noise, inventive dishes with a large vegetarian selection (DM8-14) and breakfast until 5pm. Open daily 10am-2am.
Die Rote Harfe, Oranienstr. 13 (tel. 618 44 46), in Heinrichplatz, the center of Kreuzberg. U-Bahn 1: Görlitzer Bahnhof. Young leftists eating solid German food. The *Schweizer Schnitzel* (DM15.90) and the *Algäuer Käsespatzle* (DM9.90) are something else. Open Tues.-Sun. 10am-3am.
Gropius, Stresemenstr. 110 (tel. 262 76 20), S-Bahn 1 or 2: Anhalter Bahnhof. In the Martin-Gropius-Bau (see Museums, below). You probably won't be able to afford the food, but it's a nice place to sit with a coffee and think about art. A relief from the *Topographie des Terrors* exhibit next door. Open Tues.-Sun. 10am-8pm.
Dicke Wirtin, Carmerstr. 9 (tel. 312 49 52), around the corner from Savignyplatz. Huge bowls of stew and thick soup to keep you going, and somehow get you home (DM4-6). Open daily noon-4am.
Max und Moritz, Oranienstr. 163 (tel. 614 10 45), Kreuzberg. U-Bahn 8: Mortizplatz. Old German style taken to the height of campiness. Big hot plates of traditional food. The faded painted-wood faces of Max and Moritz themselves—local Katzenjammer kids—grin down. Open daily 6pm-1am.
Restaurant V, Lausitzer Platz 12 (tel. 612 45 05). U-Bahn 1: Görlitzer Bahnhof. Reasonably priced vegetarian restaurant that also serves great breakfasts until 3pm. Open Wed.-Mon. 11am-midnight.
Graeffitti, Graefestr. 92 (tel. 692 74 02). U-Bahn 1: Kottbusser Tor. Tagged-up café in Kreuzberg with a signature buffet breakfast (served daily 9am-4pm, DM12). Open daily 9am-10pm.
PowWow, Dieffenbachstr. 11. U-Bahn 8: Schönleinstr. Large, satisfying helpings of "American Indian" food. Yes, many Germans *are* obsessed with the American West. Ours not to question why. Note the teutonic cowboys lighting those Marlboros. "Indian" burgers (DM7-11), salads (DM7-16), and vegetarian dishes (DM15-19). Open Sun.-Thurs. 10am-3am, Fri.-Sat. 10am-4am. Kitchen open until 1am.
Sieben-Leben Vollkornbäckerei, Manfred von Richthoferstr. 13 (tel. 784 14 47). U-Bahn 6: Platz der Luftbrücke. An alternative breadbasket, this whole-grain bakery grinds every seed imaginable into 30 different *Brot* and 20 *Brötchen* varieties. Makes bread and cheese much more interesting. Very granola. Salads at lunch; stand and eat them or take 'em out. Open Mon.-Fri. 10am-6pm, Sat. 7am-1pm.

Eastern Berlin

Oranienburger Straße—Mitte

Café Orange, Oranienburgerstr. 32 (tel. 282 00 28). Down the street from the Old Synagogue. U-Bahn 6: Oranienburger Tor or S-Bahn 1, 2: Oranienburgerstr. Uplifting café with big salads and breakfast until 3pm. Classy clientele against a peach-colored decor. Open Mon.-Fri. 9am-1am, Sat.-Sun. 10am-2am.
Keller-Restaurant, Chausseestr. 125 (tel. 282 38 43). U-Bahn 6: Oranienburger Tor. In the basement and back-courtyard of the Brecht Haus; waiters point out the poet-playwright's window. The kitchen follows the recipes of Helene Wegel, Brecht's wife and co-worker. She was a good cook. Reasonable dinner (DM11-17), snacks from around DM6 or sample Helene's *Apfelkrapferln* (DM8). Open Mon.-Sun. from 5pm.
Beth Cafe, Tucholskystr. 40 (tel. 281 31 35). S-Bahn 1 or 2: Oranienburger Str. Berlin's only Kosher restaurant serves inexpensive Israeli specialties as well as a gen-

erous selection of Kosher wines. Bagel with lox and cream cheese DM2.50. Other dishes DM4-12. Open Sun. and Tues.-Thurs. 1-10pm, Mon. 1-8pm

Valentino, Auguststr. 84. U-Bahn 6: Oranienburger Tor or S-Bahn 1, 2: Oranienburgerstr. Crumbling pre-war buildings are the backdrop for this active art deco café, with food until late and changing exhibits by young Berliner artists. Brunch Sundays at the *Frühstücksbuffet* (DM10). Open Mon.-Fri. 4pm-3am, Sat. 2pm-3am, Sun. 10am-3am.

Nikolaiviertel

Zur Rippe, Poststr. 17 (tel. 243 132 34). U-Bahn 2: Klosterstr. Bustling café around the corner from the Nikolaikirche, near the Mühlendamm bridge. Satisfying meals DM10-14, and the *Berlin Weiße mit Rippenshosse* (DM3.80), a bizarre red cocktail, tickles your tongue. Open daily 11am-midnight.

Zur Letzten Instanz, Waisenstr. 14 (tel. 242 55 48), is an historic old-Berlin restaurant, dating back to the 16th century. Located near the Supreme Court, its name means "the last appeal." Brims with atmosphere. Meals run DM12-18, drinks DM2-6. Open Mon.-Sat. noon-1am, Sun. noon-midnight.

Prenzlauer Berg

Café Restauration 1900, Husemannstr. 1 (tel. 44 940 52), at Kollwitzplatz. U-Bahn 2: Eberswalderstr. Alternative interior on a street decorated in Potemkin-village-esque 19th-century style. Decent food at reasonable prices. Open daily noon-2am.

Die Krähe, Kollwitzstr. 84, off Kollwitzplatz. Called "the crow," but with ochre walls, old wooden tables, and a bright crowd. Order from the daily menu on the blackboard. Their breakfasts are superb: the *Großes Frühstück* (DM9.50) comes with 3 cheeses, 3 meats, smoked salmon, and fruit. Basement bar opens at 9pm. Open Tues.-Sun. 9am-2am, Mon. 5pm-2am.

Village Voice, Ackerstr. 1a (tel. 2824550). U-Bahn 8: Rosenthaler Platz. Café *cum* bookstore trying hard for NYC hipness. Multi-lingual literature and inexpensive fare. Café open Mon.-Sat. 10am-2am, Sun. 11am-2am. Bookstore open Mon.-Wed. and Fri. 10am-6:30pm, Thurs. 10am-8:30pm, Sat. 10am-2pm.

Café CC, Rosenthalerstr. 39. U-Bahn 8: Weinmeisterstr. Studio lights illuminate black-clad intellectuals and film-buffs on worn, Victorian-parlor furniture. Inexpensive food and a good place to relax with a book. Occasional film series in back. Open daily from noon.

SIGHTS

Overview: Between Eastern and Western Berlin

For decades a gateway to nowhere, the **Brandenburger Tor** (Brandenburg Gate) is the structure that most marks the future for Berlin and a unified Germany. It is now the center point of the city, opening east onto Unter den Linden (S-Bahn 1, 2: Unter den Linden, or bus #100). Built during the reign of Friedrich Wilhelm II as a symbol of peace, the gate became a symbol of East-West division as a locked door embedded in the Berlin Wall. The gate was not actually opened until December 22, 1989, more than a month after the wall opening. The Western and Eastern Berlin Sights sections, below, both use the Brandenburg Gate as a point of entry and orientation. At night the difference between Eastern and Western Berlin becomes apparent; the decadence and occasional tawdriness of Western Berlin juts against the glassy Stalinist and pompous Prussian architecture of the East. Former East Berlin is easily distinguished by the construction sites visible everywhere.

The **Berlin Wall** itself is a dead dinosaur, with only fossil remains still visible. Fenced off overnight on August 13, 1961, the 160km-long wall arbitrarily separated family and friends, sometimes even running through people's homes. Finally, though, the wave of liberalization in other Communist countries and the mass demonstration of East Germans demanding to cross the border drove the government to open its borders and demolish the wall. The wall no longer exists; portions of the reinforced concrete structure are preserved near the *Hauptbahnhof* and the Reich-

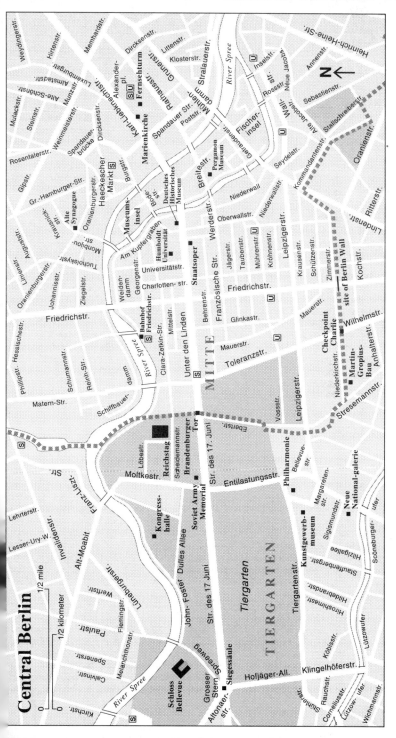

Central Berlin

1/2 mile

1/2 kilometer

stag, but the operational structure is now a memory. The longest remaining bit is the brightly painted **East Side Gallery** (S-Bahn: Hauptbahnhof), the world's largest open-air gallery. The murals on this 1.3km stretch of cement slabs are not the remnants of Cold War graffiti, but rather the efforts of an international group of artists who gathered here in 1989 to celebrate the city's openness, with mementos from later graphic tourists.

The demolished Wall has left an incompletely healed scar across the city center. From the western side, trees have been planted extending the Tiergarten a few meters more. On the eastern side, a grassy wasteland awaits construction workers to drag East to West. **Potsdamer Platz,** cut off by the Wall, was once a major transportation hub of Berlin designed under Friedrich Wilhelm I to approximate Parisian boulevards with the same primary purpose of moving troops quickly. The land surrounding the *Platz* was recently purchased by Sony and Daimler-Benz; don't expect any grassy knolls in the area. At the edge lies the site of the **Führerbunker,** where Hitler married Eva Braun and then ended his life. Plans to restore the bunker have been shelved amid real fears that the site would become a shrine for the radical right. As with the re-opening of *Geisterbahnhöfe* ("haunted stations" under East Berlin, once guarded by troops and bypassed by the U-Bahn), reunification has let all sorts of ghosts loose in Berlin.

Haus am Checkpoint Charlie, Friedrichstr. 44 (tel. 251 10 31; U-Bahn: Kochstr., or bus #129), is a museum on the site of the famous border crossing point. Through film and photo, the museum tells the story of the Wall, including harrowing escape attempts. Just inside stands the car in which Johannes Ehret smuggled his girlfriend across the border in 1988. The museum's staff smiles smugly as visitors tear the car apart to find the life-sized doll. Upstairs there are exhibits on human rights, as well as artistic renderings of the Wall. Documentaries in German are shown daily 9am-5:30pm. (Open daily 9am-10pm. Admission DM7.50, students DM4.50.)

Berlin can be stunning; Berlin can also be disconcerting in its complexity; see Orientation, above, for a guide to the city's major neighborhoods. Below, we have organized sights into four major sections: central Western and Eastern Berlin, followed by the **outer boroughs** to the west and east. **Museums** are listed in a separate section, below. Most of central Berlin's major sights lie along the route of **bus #100,** which travels from Bahnhof Zoo to Alexanderplatz.

Western Berlin

The Reichstag

Just to the north of the Brandenburg Gate sits the **Reichstag** building, former seat of the parliament of the German empire, and future home of the Federal Republic's *Bundestag*. In 1918 Philip Scheidemann proclaimed a German Republic from one of its balconies with the words *"es lebe die deutsche Republik"* ("the German republic lives"). His move turned out to be wise, since two hours later Karl Liebknecht announced a German Socialist Republic in the Imperial Palace down the street, on the site that later supported the parliament of the former GDR, the **Palast der Republik.** Civil war conditions resulted in Berlin, and in much of the rest of Germany. With a constitution drawn up in the safety of Weimar, the Reichstag became the fractured center of the economically troubled Republic. Nazi delegates showed up to sessions in uniform, and on February 28, 1933, a month after Hitler became Chancellor, fire mysteriously broke out in the building. The Reichstag fire provided a pretext for Hitler to declare a state of emergency, giving the Nazis broad powers to arrest and intimidate opponents before the upcoming elections. A conceptual monument outside recalls the 96 members of the Reichstag executed by the Nazis.

At the moment, the Reichstag is not a government building, although the major political parties have opened offices here. It holds an excellent exhibit on German history (see Museums, below).

Tiergarten and Kurfürstendamm

The lush **Tiergarten** in the center of old Berlin is a relief from the sordid burden of history. Spreading over the northeast corner of western Berlin, the vast landscaped park was formerly used by Prussian monarchs as a hunting ground. As you walk along its canals, notice the old streetlamps; each Prussian city sent one to the capital. In the heart of the Tiergarten, the **Siegessäule** (victory column), topped by a gilded winged victory, celebrates Prussia's defeat of France in 1870. In 1938, the Nazis moved the monument from its spot in front of the Reichstag to increase its height and make it more impressive. Despite the bad taste their militarism leaves in the mouth, they did improve the view. Climb the 285 steps to the top for a panorama of the city. (Open April-Nov. Mon. 1-5:30pm, Tues.-Sun. 9am-5:30pm. Admission DM1.50, students DM1.) Radiating out from the column, the **Soviet Army Memorial** (yes, you're still in Western Berlin) stands at the end of **Straße des 17 Juni,** flanked by a pair of giant toy tanks.

After the city's division, West Berlin centered around Bahnhof Zoo. In the middle of the nearby Breitscheidplatz stands a sobering reminder of the devastation caused by World War II. The shattered **Kaiser-Wilhelm-Gedächtniskirche** now houses an exhibit dedicated to peace. The exhibit, however, has lost some of its didactic force amidst the giddy neon of **Kurfürstendamm** (the Ku'damm) and the Europa Center (exhibit open Tues.-Sat. 10am-4pm). The ruins have also been submitted to the eternal torture of juxtaposition with a hideous "modern" church, built in 1960s concrete-and-stained-glass chic (church open daily 9am-7pm). In summertime some of Berlin's many leftists, foreign population, young people and others often gather in front of the church to speak out, converse, play music and act up. The wrecked tower is visible from Bahnhof Zoo. The renowned **Zoo** itself, entrance at Budapesterstr. 34 (the Elephant Gate), across from the tourist office in the Europa Center, houses an exotic collection of fauna as well as the spectacular **Aquarium,** Budapesterstr. 32. (Zoo open daily 9am-6pm; Oct. 16-Feb. 9am-5pm; March-April 9am-5:30pm. Aquarium open daily 9am-6pm. Admission to zoo DM9, students DM7.50, ages 3-15 DM4.50. Admission to aquarium DM8, students and children DM4. Combined admission DM13.50, students DM11.50, ages 3-15 DM6.50.)

Schöneberg and Potsdamer Straße

Further south in the district of Schöneberg stands the **Rathaus Schöneberg** (U-Bahn 4: Rathaus Schöneberg), where West Berlin's city government used to convene. On June 26, 1963, 1.5 million Berliners swarmed the streets outside the *Rathaus* to hear John F. Kennedy reassure them of the Allies' continued commitment to the city. Kennedy's speech ended with the now-famous words, "All free men, wherever they may live, are citizens of Berlin. And therefore, as a free man, I take pride in the words *Ich bin ein Berliner*" (open Tues.-Sun. 10am-6pm). Not too far away is **Fehrbelliner Platz** (U-Bahn 2 or 7: Fehrbelliner Platz), a quintessential example of Nazi architecture. These huge, prison-like blocks were meant to be model apartment houses; try to imagine a city full of them.

Just south of Potsdamer Platz, between the center of Schöneberg and the former no-man's-land at the sight of the Wall stands the **Martin-Gropius-Bau,** Stresemanstr. 110, designed by Martin Gropius, a pupil of Schinkel, and uncle of Walter Gropius. The building today holds a museum of applied and fine arts as well as an extensive **Jewish Musuem** (see Museums, below). Nearby at Potsdamerstr. 33, stands the **Staatsbibliothek Preußischer Kulturbesitz** (tel. 26 61), the library which starred in Wim Wenders's *Wings of Desire*—angels flew around the main reading room. It contains over 3.5 million books and lots of English-language newspapers (open Mon.-Fri. 9am-9pm, Sat. 9am-5pm).

Charlottenburg

The borough of Charlottenburg includes the area between the Ku'Damm and the Spree river; like many of Berlin's neighborhoods, it was once a separate town.

Schloß Charlottenburg (U-Bahn 2: Sophie-Charlotte-Platz, or Bus #145 from Bahnhof Zoo), the vast Baroque palace built by Friedrich I for his second wife Sophie-Charlotte, stands on the western edge of town amid a field of Baroque landscaping. Vaguely Roman marble statues guard the façade (see Museums, below, for the holdings inside). Royal rooms are also open to the commoners, topped by the ornate **Knobelsdorff Wing,** the most decadent of the palace suites. (Open Tues.-Sun. 9am-5pm. Admission to the entire palace complex *(Sammelkarte)* DM6, students DM3, under 14 free. Admission to the Knobelsdorff Wing alone DM2.50, students DM1.50, under 14 free.) Seek out the **Palace Gardens** behind the main buildings, with their small lakes, footbridges, fountains, and carefully planted rows of trees (open Tues.-Sun. 6am-9pm; free). The Gardens surround the **Royal Mausoleum** (open Tues.-Sun. 9am-5pm); **Belvedere,** an 18th-century residence housing a porcelain exhibit; and the **Schinkel Pavilion,** with furniture designed by Prussian architectural master Friedrich Schinkel (open Tues.-Sun. 9am-5pm).

At the western edge of Charlottenburg is the **Olympia Stadion** (Olympic Stadium), one of the more restrained (but still grandiose) examples of Nazi architecture. It was erected for the 1936 Olympic Games, in which Jesse Owens, an African-American, triumphed against Hitler and his racial theories by winning four gold medals. Hitler refused to congratulate Owens because of his skin color, but there's now a Jesse-Owens-Allee to the south of the stadium (U-Bahn 1: Olympia Stadion).

Kreuzberg

Indispensable for a sense of Berlin's famous *alternative Szene,* or counter-culture, is a visit to **Kreuzberg,** an area loaded with cafés and bars. During President Reagan's 1985 visit to Berlin, authorities so feared protests from this quarter that they cordoned the whole Kreuzberg district off without warning—an utterly unconstitutional move. Much of the area was occupied by Hausbesetzer (squatters) during the 60s and 70s. A conservative city government decided to forcibly evict the illegal residents in the early 1980s, provoking riots and throwing the city into total consternation. For a look at its more respectable face, take U-Bahn 6 or 7 to Mehringdamm and wander around anywhere. Particularly interesting is the area around Chamissoplatz, bordered by Bergmannstr. and Fidicinstr. Bergmannstr. features an especially large number of old buildings and secondhand shops. At night many bohemian and punk clubs overflow onto **Yorckstraße,** which heads west from the intersection with Mehringdamm. The cafés and bars on Oranienstr. (U-Bahn: Kottbusser Tor) boast a more radical element; the May Day parades always start on Oranienplatz.

The **Landwehrkanal,** a channel which runs from Tiergarten into Kreuzberg, is where Rosa Luxemburg's body was thrown after her murder in 1919; it was found only recently. The strip of the canal near Hallesches Tor, **Paul-Linke Ufer,** may be the most beautiful street in Berlin. The east end of Kreuzberg, near the old Wall (Tor), is home to Turkish (half of Western Berlin's foreign population is Turkish) and Balkan neighborhoods, and has a correspondingly large number of ethnic cafés and restaurants, popular also with the radicals and students who live in the area. From the Schlesisches Tor U-Bahn station, a three-minute walk takes you to the recently reopened **Oberbaumbrücke,** through a fragment of the wall and into the Friedrichshain district of the former East.

Spandau

Spandau is one of the oldest parts of Berlin (U-Bahn 7: Altstadt Spandau). Many of the old buildings have been restored, including the nearby 13th-century **Zitadelle** (citadel). In 1945, the fort was pressed into service as a prison to hold accused war criminals in preparation for the Nuremberg Trials. Despite its grim name and past, the citadel is a delicate, fairy-tale sort of place, complete with a medieval history museum. (U-Bahn 7: Zitadelle. Open Tues.-Fri. 9am-5pm, Sat.-Sun. 10am-5pm. Admission DM1.50, students DM1, complete tour Sat.-Sun. DM3.) You can catch a boat from near the fort, or take Bus #145: Johannestift (the last stop) into the **Spandau Forest.** Also notable is the exceptionally fine **Rathaus,** which Spandauers defiantly constructed in 1911 (at a cost of 3.5 million marks) in a futile effort to stave off absorption into Berlin (U-Bahn 7: Rathaus Spandau). **Spandau Prison,** where Hitler's deputy Rudolf Hess was the lone surviving inmate, was demolished after Hess allegedly hanged himself in 1987 at the age of 93. Hess, a devoted party member from the beginning (he participated in the Beer Hall *Putsch* and took dictation for Hitler's *Mein Kampf)* and was an unrepentant Nazi until his death. Lately this unsavory character has made a controversial comeback as a latter-day idol for neo-fascist groups; but to Berlin's credit, the local anti-Hess response has been even stronger. In the southern suburbs of Dahlem, Berlin's Botanischer Garten, Königin-Luise-Str., is a delight, especially in the tropical greenhouses. Nearby, a sprawling cultural complex holds a number of important museums (see Museums, below, for information).

To the South: Dahlem, Zehlendorf and the Grunewald

West of Dahlem lies **Zehlendorf,** Berlin's ritziest residential district. At the southwestern corner of the district, the **Glienecker Bridge** crosses the Havel into what was once the GDR. Closed to traffic in Cold War days, it is famed as the spot where East and West once exchanged captured spies. The most famous such incident traded American U-2 pilot Gary Powers for Soviet spy Ivanovich Abel. (Bus #116 from the Wannsee bus station to the end of the line.)

In summer, clear your head in the nearby **Grunewald,** a 745-acre birch forest. While there, visit the **Jagdschloß** (tel. 813 35 47), a restored royal hunting lodge now housing a worthwhile collection of European paintings, including works by Rubens, van Dyck, and Cranach (open Tues.-Sun. 10am-6pm; admission DM2.50, students DM1.50). On summer evenings open-air concerts sound out in the **Schloßgarten,** usually around 8pm (call for schedule information). To reach the Jagdschloß and Grunewald, take Bus #115 to the Brücke Museum and follow Pücklerstr. into the forest.

Eastern Berlin

As Berlin attempts to resynthesize its halves, Eastern Berlin has become, essentially, a major construction site. Socialist-era aluminum-and-green-plastic façades are torn off buildings to be replaced with Western mirror glaze; streets are torn up in order to rejuvenate and create an underground communication network between the two Berlins. The districts of primary aesthetic and cultural interest are **Mitte** (around Unter den Linden, Alexanderplatz, and the Sheuenviertel), **Friedrichshain** and **Prenzlauer Berg.**

Unter den Linden

The Brandenburg Gate opens eastward onto **Unter den Linden,** once one of Europe's best-known boulevards and the spine of old Berlin. All but a few venerable buildings have been destroyed, but farther down, under the infamous statue of Friedrich the Great atop his horse, many 18th-century structures have been restored to their original Prussian splendor. The pompous architecture can only hint at old Prussian dreams of a capital, and kingdom, with Unter den Linden as its axis. Past Friedrichstr., the first massive building on your left is the **Deutsche Staatsbibliothek** (library), with a pleasant café inside. Beyond the library is the **Humboldt Universität,** with its imposing history as one of the finest universities in the world. Its past faculty includes Hegel, Fichte, Einstein, and the Brothers Grimm. Marx and Engels both pursued degrees here, but today the university's fate is up for grabs. In the wake of a recent ideological *Blitzkrieg,* in which "tainted" departments—almost everything outside the natural sciences—were radically revamped or simply shut down, many younger scholars from the west find Humboldt an exciting place to work, a chance to build a truly alternative university from the ground up.

Next door, the old **Neue Wache** (New Guard House), designed by the renowned Prussian architect Friedrich Schinkel, is today the somber **Monument to the Victims of Fascism and Militarism.** Buried inside are urns filled with earth from the Nazi concentration camps of Buchenwald and Mauthausen and from the battlefields of Stalingrad, El Alamein, and Normandy. The honor guard in front changes with full ceremony on Wednesdays at 2:30pm. Across the way is **Bebelplatz**, the site of Nazi book burnings, now named for the old Social Democratic Party leader August Bebel. The building with the curved façade is the **Alte Bibliothek**. On the other side of the square is the handsome **Deutsche Staatsoper**, fully rebuilt from original sketches by Knobelsdorf. The most striking of the monumental buildings is the **Zeughaus**, an old armory which served before the war as the Prussian Army Hall of Fame and military museum; it has calmed down a bit as the **Museum of German History** (see Museums, below). From the museum you can enter the enclosed courtyard and see the tormented faces of Andreas Schlüter's "Dying Warriors."

Gendarmenmarkt

Berlin's most impressive ensemble of 18th-century buildings is a few blocks south of Unter den Linden at **Gendarmenmarkt**, graced by the twin cathedral towers, the **Deutscher Dom** and **Französischer Dom**. Enclosing the far end of the square, the Neoclassical **Schauspielhaus**, designed by Schinkel, is Berlin's most elegant concert space and hosts many international orchestras and classical performers. When it was first built, the hall was described as "music made solid." Destroyed by an air attack in 1945, it was painstakingly reconstructed and reopened in 1984.

Lustgarten and the Museumsinsel

Unter den Linden, as it crosses the bridge over a bend in the Spree, opens out onto the **Museumsinsel** (Museum Island). To the left of the bridge is the **Altes Museum** (formerly the Neues Museum), with a big polished granite bowl in front, and the multiple-domed **Berliner Dom** (Berlin Cathedral). Severely damaged by an air raid in 1944, the cathedral has just emerged from 20 years of restoration. Built during the reign of Kaiser Wilhelm II between 1894 and 1905, the aesthetic sensibility of the ornate interior decoration is questionable (open daily 9am-7:30pm; free). Behind the Altes Museum lie three other enormous museums and the ruins (now being restored) of a fourth (see Museums, below). At the center of this spectacular ensemble, a jungle of pediments, porticoes, and colonnades is the **Lustgarten** park (S-Bahn: Hackescher Markt or bus #100). Formerly called Marx-Engels Platz, the plaza was a vast parade ground for the communist regime, under the glaring amber-colored **Palast der Republik**, where the GDR's *Volkskammer* met. Both the square and the modern assembly hall were constructed on the site of the Kaiser's palace, which was damaged in World War II and then finished off in 1950 for that purpose.

Across the Liebknecht Brücke, in the middle of a park stands a "conceptual memorial" consisting of steel tablets engraved with images of worker struggle and protest surrounding a twin statue of Marx and Engels. In 1990, a graffito appeared on the base of the statue: *"Wir sind unschuldig!"* ("We're innocent!"). The park and the street behind it used to be collectively known as the Marx-Engels Forum; the park has yet to be renamed, while the street is now called Rathausstr.

Alexanderplatz

On the other side of the Museumsinsel, Unter den Linden becomes Karl-Liebknecht-str., and leads into the teeming, concrete **Alexanderplatz** square. Formerly the frantic heart of Weimar Berlin, the plaza was the setting for Alexander Döblin's montage-novel of the modern metropolis, *Berlin-Alexanderplatz*. "Alex," as it is known in the city, is now rather GDR-ugly; construction has begun to remove the edge from the buildings, but it's very unclear whether the revamped version will be any more satisfying. In the 1970s, the East German government made a concession to the people's implacable craving for bright lights and neon by erecting some enormous, brightly lit signs—thus giving the area around Alexanderplatz the superficial trappings of a Western metropolis: "Chemical Products from Bitterfeld!" and "Medical Instruments of the GDR—Distributed in All the World!" Few remain as giant capitalist advertisements are erected to make the skyline almost as garish as the Ku'damm in the west. In the first post-socialist months, Alexanderplatz was a rough place, the natural meeting ground for antagonistic gangs; but the pedestrians, working Berliners and tourists have won out. During the day the square hums with con artists and peddling vendors selling everything from *Fladenbrot* to black market cigarettes smuggled from Russia. Around the U- and S-Bahn stations, the picture becomes seedier—crowds congregate after dusk; watch your bags and pockets.

Friends from all over Berlin often meet at the plaza's **Weltzeituhr,** the international clock, but the undisputed landmark of the district is the **Fernsehturm** (television tower). The tower, the tallest structure in Berlin, bears a vague resemblance to the Death Star. *Fernsehturm* is the German word for television tower, but the literal translation of "see far tower" is just as appropriate in this case—the view from the top is magnificent. In contrast, the most depressing sight in Berlin is that of the tower itself, seen not from Alexanderplatz but from one of Eastern Berlin's more run-down districts, miles away; across low-lying buildings, it is hard to miss the tower blinking away at night. (Open daily 9am-midnight, 2nd and 4th Tues. of each month 1pm-midnight only. Last entrance 11pm. Expect a 1hr. wait. Tower admission DM5, students, seniors, and children DM3.) Bus #100, an excellent and easy way to get a quick overview of most of the above sights, travels the scenic route between Bahnhof Zoo and Alexanderplatz, going down Unter den Linden.

Nikolaiviertel

The **Marienkirche,** a graceful 15th-century church, stands on the wide open plaza behind the *Fersehturm.* Nearby is the gabled **Rotes Rathaus,** Old Berlin's famous red-brick town hall. Behind the *Rathaus,* the twin spires of the **Nikolaikirche** mark Berlin's oldest building. Inside the 13th-century structure, a small museum documents the early history of the city (open Tues.-Fri. 9am-5pm, Sat. 9am-6pm, Sun. 10am-5pm). The church gives the surrounding **Nikolaiviertel,** a carefully reconstructed *Altstadt,* its name. The Nikolaiviertel's narrow winding streets are popular and crowded; among the two dozen historic buildings are the **Knoblauchhaus** and the Rococo **Ephraim-Palais.**

Scheuenviertel—Oranienburger Straße

Northwest of Alexanderplatz is the **Scheuenviertel,** the former ghetto of Berlin, later home to the Jews who fled the Eastern European pogroms only to end up in Hitler's concentration camps. It contains many reminders of Berlin's former Jewish community, once one of the most emancipated and cultured in the world. Cross Monbijoustr. from the upper tip of the Museumsinsel (behind the Bodemuseum), or walk from the Haeckescher Markt S-Bahn station onto **Oranienburger Straße.** At Oranienburger Str. 30 stands the burnt-out shell of Berlin's grand **Synagogue.** This huge temple of worship, once the center of West European Judaism, was torched by the Nazis on *Kristallnacht* (the Night of Shattered Glass, November 9, 1938) as fire fighters stood by to protect neighboring buildings. The building was finished off by an Allied bomb in 1943. Supported by funds from all over the world, restoration work began in 1988. The temple's distinctive gold domes are up and the façade has been largely completed, but the interior will not be finished until 1995. The façade is nonetheless stunning. A simple sign on the side of the building reads "Never forget this." At the end of Große Hamburgerstr., before it intersects with Monbijoustr., are the remains of the **Alter Jüdische Friedhof** (Old Jewish Cemetery). Destroyed by the Nazis, the site now contains only the restored gravestone of the philosopher Moses Mendelssohn; the rest is a quiet park. In front, a plaque marks the site of the **Jüdische Altersheim,** the Jewish old-age home which after 1942 served as a holding place for Jews before their transportation to concentration camps. Nearby is **Sophienstraße,** a beautiful street that runs by the Baroque **Sophienkirche.**

The area around the Berlin Synagogue served as a showpiece for the East German government; many of the old buildings have been restored, and many of the new constructions have a flair unusual for Berlin, Eastern or Western. The area has become a center of a community of artists and squatters, including many from the west, with a corresponding rich quality of cultural and café life.

BERLIN: MUSEUMS

Elsewhere in Mitte

If any single man personifies the maelstrom of contradictions that is Berlin, it is Bertolt Brecht, who called the city home. "There is a reason to prefer Berlin to other cities," the playwright once declared, "because it is constantly changing. What is bad today can be improved tomorrow." To reach the **Brecht-Haus Berlin,** Chausseestr. 125, where Brecht lived and worked from 1953 to 1956, take Oranienburger Str. all the way to Friedrichstr., and bear left. If you understand German, you should take the guided tour, given in a flamboyant Brechtian style. The **Brechtforum** on the second floor sponsors exhibits and lectures on artistic and metropolitan subjects; pick up a schedule. (Tours every ½hr. Open Tues.-Wed. and Fri. 10-11:30am, Thurs. 10-11:30am and 5-6:30pm, Sat. 9:30am-1:30pm.) Just before Brecht's house, the **Dorotheenstädtischer Friedhof** contains the graves of a host of German luminaries, including Brecht, Fichte, and Hegel (open daily 9am-6pm). Also in Mitte, students and other malcontents gather around **Rosa-Luxemburg-Platz,** or in the open galleries on Auguststr. and other sidestreets.

Prenzlauer Berg

East of Oranienburger Str. is **Prenzlauer Berg,** a former working-class district largely neglected by East Germany's reconstruction efforts. Many of its old buildings are falling apart; others still have shell holes and embedded bullets from the World War II. The result is the charm of age and graceful decay, slightly less charming for phoneless local residents with bad plumbing. Restored **Husemannstraße** is especially worthy of a stroll, home to cafés, restaurants, and the **Museum Berliner Arbeiterleben um 1900,** with exhibits on Berlin's working class at the turn of the century. (Open Tues.-Thurs. and Sat. 10am-6pm, Fri. 10am-3pm. Admission DM2, students DM1.) The street also contains the **Friseurmuseum** (see museum listings). The area's population belies the aging architecture: the large number of students, artists, communes, clubs, and cafés have given it a reputation as the "Kreuzberg of the East." The city government's anti-commune policy, heavily supported by the mainstream press, is in danger of destroying this counter-cultural renaissance. Meanwhile, the scene around green **Kollwitzplatz** is especially vibrant. The statue of artist Käthe Kollwitz has been painted over a number of times in the past few years—in acts of playful rather than angry vandalism—most notably when the lady was covered with big pink polka-dots.

The nearby **Volkspark Friedrichshain** is a pretty little park. In the middle of Prenzlauer Berg, the urban renewal project of **Ernst Thälmann Park** used to contain a 19m statue of Lenin; a grand monument to Ernst Thälmann still remains. Until recently, there were probably more East German streets named after Thälmann than anyone but Karl Marx. A staunch opponent of fascism and the leader of the Communist Party of Germany (KPD) during the Weimar era, Thälmann was arrested after the Reichstag fire, imprisoned in a concentration camp, and murdered by the Nazis near the end of the war. His status as a GDR national hero has recently turned against him and his name is gradually disappearing from street signs.

MUSEUMS

With no less than 85 museums, Berlin is one of the world's great museum cities, with collections of art and artifacts encompassing all subjects and eras. Four major complexes—Charlottenburg, Dahlem, Museuminsel, and Tiergarten—form the hub of the city's museum culture with smaller museums dealing with every subject imaginable from transport to sugar. Note that the Charlottenburg complex is closed Friday, the Museuminsel Monday and Tuesday, and the Dahlem and Tiergarten Monday. While permanent collections are generally free, special exhibits can be expensive (DM6-10); bring student ID.

Museum Complexes

Museumsinsel

Museum Island (tel. 20 35 50; S-Bahn 3,5,6,9: Haeckescher Markt) holds the astoundingly broad treasure hoard of the former GDR in four museums. Admission to each of the museums is DM4, students and seniors DM2. *Tageskarte* to all 4, and as a bonus, to the Otto-Nagel-Haus (see below), is DM8, students and seniors DM6.

Pergamonmuseum, Kupfergraben. One of the world's great ancient history museums. The scale of its exhibits is mind-boggling: the Babylonian Ishtar Gate (575 BC), the Roman Market Gate of Miletus, and one of the Seven Wonders of the ancient world, the majestic Pergamon Altar of Zeus (180 BC). The altar's great frieze (125m long and 2.5m high) depicting the victory of the gods over the giants symbolizes the triumphs of Attalus I. The museum also houses extensive collections of Greek, Assyrian, Islamic, and Far Eastern art. Architecture halls (including the altar) only open Mon.-Tues. Last entry 30min. before closing. Tours of Pergamon Altar at 11am and 3pm. Open Wed.-Sun. 9am-5pm. Islamic art section open Wed.-Sun. 10am-6pm.

Alte Nationalgalerie, Bodestr. Solid collection of Expressionist work, including that of Lyonel Feininger, Oskar Kokoschka, and *die Brücke* (the Bridge), the igniters of German Expressionism. Also has a fair share of works by the German Impressionist Max Liebermann and other European masters such as Goya, Cezanne, and Degas. Recently the showcase for penetrating exhibits on art in 20th-century Germany. Open Wed.-Sun. 10am-6pm.

Bodemuseum, Monbijoubrücke. A world-class exhibit of Egyptian art, as well as late Gothic wood sculptures, early Christian art, 15th- to 18th-century paintings, and an exhibit on ancient history. Open Wed.-Sun. 9am-5pm, Egyptian and papyrus collections open Wed.-Sun. 10am-6pm.

Altes Museum, Lustgarten. Belies its name with an exhibit of 20th-century paintings, largely of the socialist-realist school. On its eastern side, accessible by a smaller, difficult-to-find door, is the **Kupferstichkabinett,** a stellar collection of lithographs and drawings by various Renaissance masters, including many Dürers and the sublime illustrations Botticelli drew for the *Divine Comedy.* The building, like many Berlin oddities, was dreamt up by Schinkel. Open Wed.-Sun. 10am-6pm. Lithograph and drawing section open Mon., Wed., and Fri. 9am-noon and 1-4pm.

Deutsches Historisches Museum (Museum of German History), Unter den Linden 2, Zeughaus (tel. 21 50 20). Across from the Museumsinsel. Once a paean to the advent of socialism, now the site of provocative multi-media exhibitions on recent German history. Open Thurs.-Tues. 10am-6pm. Admission DM4, students DM2.

Dahlem

Dahlem Museum, Arnimallee 23-27 and Lansstr. 8 (tel. 830 11). U-Bahn 2: Dahlem-Dorf. A huge complex of seven museums, each one worth a half-day visit. Those listed below are particularly superb. (All are open Tues.-Fri. 9am-5pm, Sat.-Sun. 10am-5pm and all are absolutely free.)

Gemäldegalerie (Painting Gallery), a stunning collection of Italian, German, Dutch, and Flemish Masters (including 26 Rembrandts and *The Man with the Golden Helmet,* once incorrectly attributed to Rembrandt). The Italian Renaissance section includes Titian, Giotto, and some of Botticelli's best works.

Skulpturen-Galerie (Sculpture Gallery), adjacent to the Painting Gallery. Mostly German statuary, with many gnarled, distraught-looking Gothic pieces, and others intended for churches.

Museum für Ostasiatische Kunst (East Asian Art), which houses Japanese, Korean, and Chinese art, including some exquisite lacquerware.

Museum für Islamische Kunst (Islamic Art). Probably the most international of the museums, it follows the culture of Islam in its sojourn around the world. Good visual essays on themes in Islamic design and architecture.

Museum für Indische Kunst (Indian Art). One of the most extensive collections around, with art and artifacts from all of Southeast Asia, including a compelling set of Indian miniature paintings.

Charlottenburg

Schloß Charlottenburg, Spandauer Damm (tel. 32 09 11). U-Bahn 2: Sophie-Charlotte-Platz or Bus #145. The castle's wings hold several museums, set against the romantic *Schloßgarten*. The **Kleiner Orangerie** sports special exhibitions. All are open Sat.-Thurs. 9am-5pm and are free, although admission to the historic rooms of the Schloß costs DM2.50, students DM1.50 (see Sights, above, for more on the *Schloß* and its grounds).

Ägyptisches Museum (Egyptian Museum), across Spandauer Damm from the castle. Houses a fascinating collection of ancient Egyptian art. The most popular item on display is the stunning 3300-year-old bust of Queen **Nefertiti** (1350 BC), thought by some to be the most beautiful woman in the world.

Antikensammlung, across the street from the Egyptian Museum, contains a fabulous collection of Greek, Roman, and Etruscan jewelry and ceramics.

Galerie der Romantik, in the Palace's Neuer Flügel, has works by Kaspar David Friedrich and other passionate Prussians, and more restrained exhibits on Biedermeir design work.

Tiergarten

Tiergarten-Kulturforum, a complex of museums at the eastern end of the Tiergarten park, near the Staatsbibliothek (see Sights, above) and Potsdamer Platz. Bus #129 from the Ku'damm or S-Bahn 1 or 2 or U-Bahn 2: Potsdamer Platz. All are open Tues.-Fri. 9am-5pm, Sat.-Sun. 10am-5pm, and all are free.

Neue Nationalgalerie, Potsdamerstr. 50 (tel. 266 26 62). This handsome building, designed by Mies van der Rohe, houses a remarkable collection of Expressionist works, as well as exhibits of contemporary art.

Kunstgewerbemuseum (Museum of Applied Arts), Matthäikirchstr. 10 (tel. 26 66). Displays ceramics, porcelain, and various handicrafts in wood, silver, and gold from the Middle Ages to the present.

Musikinstrumenten Museum (Museum of Musical Instruments), Tiergartenstr. 1 (tel. 25 48 10). Fittingly next door to the Philharmonic, the museum displays the history of musical instruments.

Elsewhere in Berlin

Western Berlin

Reichstag Museum, Platz der Republik, near Brandenburg Gate. Bus #100 (from Bahnhof Zoo or Alexanderplatz). Emblazoned *Dem Deutschen Volke* (For the German People), the huge Wilhelmine building is half the spectacle; its too-large plaza, where angry crowds of Weimar Germans threatened the Republic, was perfect for the Reunification Day celebrations. Contains an absorbing exhibit on German history from 1800 to 1949. Pick up a free copy of the *Grundgesetz,* Germany's Basic Law. Open Tues.-Sun. 10am-5pm. Free.

Martin-Gropius Bau, Stresemannstr. 110 (tel. 25 48 60). S-Bahn or U-Bahn: Anhalter Bahnhof. Gropius himself designed this neo-Renaissance wedding cake as a museum for and tribute to the industrial arts. Dizzying works from the Dadaists and other early 20th-century types. It now houses smaller museums and special exhibits that have focused on such figures as Walter Benjamin and Bismarck. **Juden in Berlin**, another permanent exhibit, includes documents, pictures, and paintings by and about the Jewish community in Berlin. Most exhibits open Tues.-Sun. 10am-8pm. Admission DM10, students DM5.

Topographie des Terrors, over a Gestapo annex built by inmates over the Sachserhauser concentration camp, details the use of various local buildings by the Nazis, and describes the development of fascism in Germany. Open Tues.-Sun. 10am-6pm. Free.

Prinz-Albrecht-Gelände, a deserted wasteland adjacent to the Topographie des Terrors. Once an area of elegant buildings, it was converted into a concentrated clump of Nazi ministries including the Gestapo, SS, and Reich Security. Rubble and signs mark the sites of the headquarters. Open Tues.-Sun. 10am-6pm. Free.

Bauhaus Archiv-Museum für Gestaltung, Klingenhöferstr. 13-14 (tel. 254 00 20). Bus #129 (from Ku'damm): Lützowplatz. The shimmering modern building designed by Bauhaus founder Walter Gropius displays exemplary works by members of the school (among them, Kandinsky and Klee). Open Wed.-Mon. 10am-5pm. Admission DM3, students DM1.

Käthe-Kollwitz-Museum, Fasanenstr. 24 (tel. 882 52 10). U-Bahn 3: Uhlandstr. A collection of works by one of Germany's most prominent artists, much of it focusing on the themes of war and poverty. Open Wed.-Mon. 11am-6pm. Admission DM6, students DM3.

Brücke Museum, Bussardsteig 9 (tel. 831 20 29). From Bahnhof Zoo, take Bus #115 to Pücklerstr. at Clayallee. The Expressionist museum in Berlin, with wildly colorful works by the German Expressionist school *die Brücke,* which struck the art scene in Dresden and Berlin from 1909 to 1913. Open Wed.-Mon.11am-5pm. Admission DM4, students DM2.

Museum für Verkehr und Technik (Transport and Technology), Trebbinerstr. 9 (tel. 25 48 40). U-Bahn 1: Gleisdreieck or Möckernbrücke. Souvenirs from *Autobahn* speed-devils, medieval printing presses, and trains that run on time. World War I fighting planes hang from the ceiling. Combined admission to a yard of antique locomotives down the street. Open Tues.-Fri. 9am-5:30pm, Sat.-Sun. 10am-6pm. Admission DM4, students DM2.

Postmuseum Berlin, An der Urania 15 (tel. 21 71 17 17). Bus #109 or 219 from Bahnhof Zoo or a short walk from U-Bahn 1 or 4: Nollendorfplatz. Exposes the Post's growth with lots of historic video and techno-fun—play with the toy mail train, light up a historic mail-route map. Also check out the competing Postal Museum in Eastern Berlin. Open Mon.-Thurs. 9am-5pm, Sat.-Sun. 10am-5pm. Free.

Zucker-Museum, Amrumerstr. 32 (tel. 81 42 75 74), U-Bahn 9: Amrumerstr. A cultural history of sugar and the political implications of the development of the sugar industry. Yum. Open Mon.-Wed. 9am-5pm, Sun. 11am-6pm. Admission DM4, students DM2.

Eastern Berlin

Otto Nagel Haus, Märkisches Ufer 16-18 (tel. 279 14 02). U-Bahn: Märkisches Museum. A collection of art exploring social themes, taken from the Nationalgalerie. It includes works by Käthe Kollwitz and an exciting collection of photomontage by the famous anti-Nazi satirist John Heartfield. Open Wed.-Sun. 10am-6pm. Admission DM1.50, students and seniors DM1.

Postmuseum, Leipziger Str. 16 (tel. 22 85 47 22, U-Bahn 2 or 6: Stadtmitte). Like the Western Postmuseum (see above) looks backward in mail history, though with less glitz. A fascinating look at how the GDR and other regimes have stamped their image into a corner of everyday life. Open Tues.-Sat. 10am-6pm. Admission DM1, students DM0.50.

Friseurmuseum, Husemannstr. 8 (tel. 449 53 80). U-Bahn 2: Eberswalder Str. One of the city's strangest and most appealing museums. Contains exhibits on the history of shaving, wigs, and hairstyles. This is the dawning of the age.... Open Tues. 10am-noon and 1-5pm, Wed. 10am-noon and 1-6pm. Free.

ENTERTAINMENT

Berlin has one of the most vibrant cultural scenes in the world. There is always a festival of some description in progress. Exhibitions, concerts, plays, and dance abound (although there is some doubt in this area due to the cutbacks in government subsidies). The listings below have been organized into three categories: Concerts, Opera, and Dance; Theater; and Film.

You can reserve tickets by calling the box office directly. Always ask about student discounts; most theaters and concert halls have student discounts of up to 50%, but only if you buy at the *Abendkasse* (night box office) which generally opens one hour before the performance begins. There are also numerous box offices, which will charge you a commission and cannot get you student discounts. The main box offices are **Theaterkasse Centrum,** Meinekestr. 25 (tel. 882 76 11), with branches in all Karstadt department stores, and in KaDeWe, Tauentzienstr. 21 (tel. 218 10 28). (All charge a small commission and are open Mon.-Fri. 9am-3pm; Sept.-June Mon.-Fri. 9am-noon and 3-5:30pm, Sat. 9am-3:30pm.) **Theaterkasse Zehlendorf,** Teltower Damm 22 (tel. 801 16 52 or 801 30 56), also sells Berlin tickets. (Open Mon.-Fri. 7:30am-6pm, Sat. 8am-1pm.) For last-minute cut-price tickets contact **Hekticket,** Rathausstr. 1 (tel. 242 67 09), near Alexanderplatz (open Mon.-Sat. 4-8pm). Unfortunately, most theaters close from mid-July to late August.

Concerts, Opera, and Dance

Berlin reaches its musical zenith during the fabulous **Berliner Festwochen,** lasting almost the entire month of September and drawing the world's best orchestras and soloists, and the **Berliner Jazztage** in November. For more information on these events (and tickets, which sell out far in advance), write to Berliner Festspiele, Budapesterstr. 48-50, 10787 Berlin (tel. 25 48 92 50; open daily noon-6pm). In mid-July, **Bachtage** (Bach Days) offer an intense week of classical music; every Saturday night in August **Sommer Festspiele** turns the Ku'damm into a multi-faceted concert hall with punk, steel-drum and folk groups competing for attention.

In the monthly pamphlets *Kultur in Berlin* and *Berliner Programm,* as well as in the biweekly magazines *Tip* and *Zitty,* you'll find notice of concerts in the courtyard of the old Arsenal, on the **Schloßinsel Köpenick** (castle island), or in the parks. Tickets for the *Philharmonie* and the *Oper* are often impossible to acquire through conventional channels. Try standing out in front before performances with a small sign saying, *"Suche Karte"* (I seek a ticket); invariably a few people will try to unload tickets at the last moment.

Philharmonie, Matthäikirchstr. 1 (tel. 25 48 80). Bus #129 from Ku'damm: Potsdamer Str. and walk 3 blocks north. The big yellow building is as acoustically perfect within as it is unconventional without, and the *Berliner Philharmoniker,* led for decades by the late Herbert von Karajan, is perhaps the finest orchestra in the world. It is well-nigh impossible to get a seat; check an hour before concert time or write far in advance. The *Philharmonie* is often closed during the summer months. Box office open Mon.-Fri. 3:30-6pm, Sat.-Sun. and holidays 11am-2pm.

Das Schauspielhaus, Gendarmenmarkt (tel. 20 90 20). *Grosser Konzertsaal* and *Kammermusiksaal.* U-Bahn 2 or 6: Stadtmitte. The opulent home of the Berlin Symphony Orchestra, *if* it survives recent cuts in government subsidies. Call for performance information. Box office open Mon.-Fri. 10am-6pm.

Deutsche Oper Berlin, Bismarckstr. 35 (tel. 341 02 49). U-Bahn 1: Deutsche Oper. Berlin's best opera. Box office open Mon.-Sat. 11:30am-5:30pm, Sun. 10am-2pm and 1hr. before performances. Student discounts of up to 50% off, depending on the price of the ticket, 10 min. before performances. Tickets DM10-125.

Deutsche Staatsoper, Unter den Linden 7 (tel. 200 47 62). U-Bahn 6: Friedrichstr., or bus #157. East Berlin's leading opera company. Ballet and classical music, too. Box office open Mon.-Sat. noon-6pm, Sun. 2-6pm. Tickets DM18-35.

Komische Oper, Behrenstr. 55-57 (tel. 229 25 55). U-Bahn 6: Französischestr. Its reputation was developed by its famous post-war director, Felsenstein, but has declined since. The repertoire isn't all comic, and the music isn't all operatic, but it is all in German. Box office open Tues.-Sat. noon-5:30pm, Sun. 1hr. before performances. Tickets DM10-20; 50% student discounts almost always available.

Tanzfabrik, Möckernstr. 68 (tel. 786 58 61). U-Bahn 1 or 7: Möckernbrücke. Down the alley to your left, up 3 flights of stairs. Modern dance performances and a general center for dance workshops. Ticket office open Mon.-Thurs. 10am-1pm and 5-8pm. Tickets DM15. Occasional weekend performances starting at either 8 or 8:30pm.

Theater

Theater listings are available in the monthly pamphlet *Kultur in Berlin, Berlin Programm, Tip,* and *Zitty.* They are also posted in most U-Bahn stations; look for the yellow posters. Berlin has a lively English-language theater scene. **Das Schiller Theater,** the most respected theater company in the country, closed recently because of state cutbacks. In addition to its occasionally inspired works, the more experimental smaller theater *(Werkstatt)* is also closed. Look for theater listings in *Tip* or *Zitty* that say *"in englischer Sprache"* ("in English") next to them. As with concert halls, look out for summer closings *(Theaterferien);* see the introduction to Entertainment, above, for box office information. There is an international **Theater Festival** in May.

Deutsches Theater, Schumannstr. 13a (tel. 28 44 10). U-Bahn 6 or S-Bahn 1-3, 5, 6, 9: Friedrichstr. The word is finally spreading to Western Berlin: this is the best theater in the country. Max Reinhardt made it great a hundred years ago, and it now has innovative productions of the classics and newer works (especially strong on Heiner Müller). The **Kammerspiel des Deutschen Theaters** (tel. 284 42 26) has smaller and often controversial productions. Box office open Mon.-Sat. noon-6:30pm, Sun. 3-6:30pm.Tickets DM15-40; 50% student discount often available.

Freie Volksbühne, Schaperstr. 24 (tel. 881 37 42). U-Bahn 2 or 9: Spichernstr. Smaller repertory theater, with some excellent productions. Box office open daily 10am-2pm and from 6:30pm; tickets DM10.20-31.20.

Renaissance Theater, Hardenbergstr. 6 (tel. 312 42 02). U-Bahn 1: Ernst-Reuter-Platz. As with the Freie Volksbühne, somewhat more modest than the larger theaters, less expensive, with a well-respected company. Box office open Mon.-Sat. noon-6:30pm, Sun. and holidays 11am-6:30pm. Tickets DM18-36.

Stükke, Hasenheide 54 (tel. 692 32 39). U-Bahn 7: Südstern. Controversial, experimental theater in Kreuzberg. A breath of fresh air in experimental theater. Box office open one hr. before shows, or call ahead.

Berliner Ensemble, Bertolt-Brecht-Platz (tel. 282 31 60). U-Bahn 6 or S-Bahn 2, 3, 5, 6 or 9: Friedrichstr. The famous theater established by Brecht has rather listless performances, mostly of the great man's plays. Also some premieres. Box office open Mon.-Sat. 11am-6:30pm, Sun. 3-6:30pm. Tickets DM12-40.

Maxim Gorki Theater, Am Festungsgraben 2 (tel. 208 27 83). U-Bahn 6 or S-Bahn 2,3,5,6 or 9: Friedrichstr.; just off Unter den Linden. Excellent contemporary theater. Has produced some of the biggest hits in Berlin, East or West. Box office open Mon.-Sat. 1-6:30pm, Sun. 3-6:30pm. Tickets DM5-25.

Die Distel, Friedrichstr. 101 (tel. 200 47 04). U-Bahn 6 or S-Bahn 2, 3, 5, 6 or 9: Friedrichstr. A cabaret for political satire. Box office open Mon.-Fri. noon-6pm, Sat.-Sun. 2hr. before performance.

Volksbühne, Rosa-Luxemburg-Platz (tel. 30 87 45). U-Bahn 2: Rosa-Luxemburg-Platz. The famous theater founded in 1912 often has excellent productions hidden in a mass of mediocrity. Box office open Mon.-Sat. noon-6:30pm, Sun. 11am-6:30pm. Usually has good advance-purchase student discount deals.

Film

On any night in Berlin you can choose from 100 different films, many in the original languages. ("O.F." next to a movie listing means original version. "O.m.U." means original version with German subtitles. Everything else is dubbed.) Check *Tip, Zitty,* or subway posters. There is an international **Film Festival** (late Feb.-March).

Filmtheater Babylon-Mitte, Rosa-Luxemburgstr. 30 (tel. 242 50 76). U-Bahn 2: Rosa-Luxemburg Platz. Classics and art films often in original language. Admission DM8, students DM7.

Kino-Arsenal, Welserstr. 25 (tel. 218 68 48). U-Bahn 1: Wittenbergplatz. Berlin's best repertory film house, with in-depth retrospectives and lectures. Admission DM9. 6-month membership for DM12, students DM6, brings the ticket price down to DM7.

NIGHTLIFE

Berlin is wild; every desire is catered to, and few places in the world shake and shout at night like this city. The action never stops; events begun in the early morning continue until late evening, and the Berliners mob bars, clubs, and cafés which stay open until around 3am, later on weekends, or sometimes don't close at all. Take advantage of the night buses from the U-Bahn stations and **U-Bahn 1** and **9,** which run all night on Fridays and Saturdays. There is often a fine line between a café open to the early hours and a *Kneipe* (bar). The best sources of information about what's happening are the bi-weekly magazines *Zitty* (DM3.30) and *Tip* (DM3.70), available at all kiosks and newsagents.

In Western Berlin, the best places to look are the **Savignyplatz, Schöneberg, Wilmersdorf, Kreuzberg,** and **Scheunenviertel** districts. The Ku'damm is best avoided at night, unless you especially enjoy fraternizing with drunken businessmen and middle-aged unenlightened tourists. The north is a bit more inviting to the youthful: the middle point is Savignyplatz and it includes Grolmanstr., Knesebeckstr., Bleibtreustr., and Schlütterstr., as well as Steinplatz, along Carmerstr. to the north. Café Hardenberg and the Schwarzes Café, listed under Food, are also excellent for a drink at night. South of the Ku'damm, the area between Uhlandstr. and Olivaer Platz is littered with crowded late-night cafés. The main focus of Schöneberg nightlife is around **Nollendorfplatz,** encompassing café-*Kneipen* on Winterfeldplatz and Goltzstr., and more bars on Kleiststr. Pushing up against the remains of the wall in the western section of the city is the center of the **Kreuzberg** *Szene*. On the more trafficked West End of Kreuzberg, offbeat bars and clubs line Yorckstr., near Mehringdamm. The scene in East Kreuzberg is more intense, with radically alternative bars along Oranienstr. between U-Bahn 1: Kottbusser Tor and U-Bahn1: Görlitzer Bahnhof. The area is not well lit at night and can be unsafe for those traveling alone.

The clubs which have been sprouting in Eastern Berlin are giving their counterparts a run for their money. Some of the more interesting bars abound in the **Scheunenviertel,** especially along Oranienburger Str. (not to be confused with Oranienstr.) near the old Synagogue. The **Prenzlauer Berg** area also boasts some fun, interesting places along Prenzlauer Allee, Schönhauser Allee, Kastanienallee, and especially the area around Kollwitzplatz. The cafés and bars of the east tend to have a grittier, more vital feel to them and attract an exciting mixture of people.

Bars and Clubs

For more nightclub listings, see Lesbian and Gay Berlin, below.

Savigny- and Steinplatz Area

Quasimodo, Kantstr. 12a (tel. 312 80 86). S-Bahn 3, 5, 6, 9: Savignyplatz. A basement pub, with live jazz and rock and a lively crowd. Open daily from 8pm; concerts usually begin at 10pm. Cover depends on performance, ranging from free to DM30. Often has big names. Concert tickets available from 5pm or at Kant Kasse ticket service (tel. 313 45 54).

Café am Steinplatz, Hardenbergstr. 12 (tel. 312 90 12). S-Bahn 3, 5, 6, 9 or U-Bahn 1 or 9: Zoologischer Garten. Popular café which attracts artsy crowd from cinema next door. Open daily 10am-2am.

Schöneberg

Metropol, Nollendorfplatz 5 (tel. 216 41 22). U-Bahn 1 or 4: Nollendorfplatz or night buses N19, N29, or N85. Still *the* place to go. Nude male and female statues fraternize on the gray façade. Live band or disco music. Cover about DM10. Music usually lasts until 4am. Concerts, usually by indie-label artists, upstairs in the *Loft* tickets DM15-20 (for info. tel. 216 10 20). Open Fri.-Sat. 10pm; Loft days and times vary.

Orpheou, Marburgerstr. 2 (tel. 211 64 45). U-Bahn 1 or 2: Wittenbergplatz. The chic-est disco in Berlin. Selective admission—try to look cool with your some-what limited backpacker's wardrobe. Open daily from 11pm. Cover DM10.

M, Goltzstr. 33 (tel. 216 70 92). U-Bahn 7: Eisenacherstr. One of the more interest-ing Schöneberg bars, slightly wild late at night. Black is eternally "in." Open Sun.-Thurs. 8:30am-midnight, Fri.-Sat. 8:30am-3am.

The New York, Olivaer Platz 15 (tel. 883 62 58). U-Bahn 8: Adenauer Platz. Full of what some call the *schicki-micki* crowd—young and all-too-fashionable. Open Sun.-Thurs. 10am-4am, Fri.-Sat. 10am-6am.

Kreuzberg

Yorck-Schlösschen, Yorckstr. 15 (tel. 215 80 70). U-Bahn 7 or S-Bahn 1or 2: Yorckstr. Enjoyable pub sometimes with live music late in the evening. Now and then draws a punkish crowd. In an old Kreuzberg tenement. Pleasant garden in front. Live jazz Sun. from 2pm. Open Mon.-Thurs. 9am-3am, Fri.-Sun. 9am-4am.

Alibi, Oranienstr. 166. U-Bahn 1 or 8: Kottbusser Tor. Crowded bar with offbeat regulars, up to something at all hours. Open Sun.-Thurs. 10pm-2am, later Fri.-Sat.

Café Wirtschaftswunder, Yorckstr. 81 (tel. 786 99 99). U-Bahn 7 or S-Bahn 1 or 2: Yorckstr. Colorful Kreuzberg café with tiny tables virtually overlapping. A great way to meet the folks on either side. Name ironically refers to Germany's Eco-nomic Miracle. Serves drinks daily 4pm-4am.

Golgota, Dudenstr. 48-64. U-Bahn 6: Platz der Luftbrücke, or night bus N19. In Kreuzberg's Viktoria Park. Beer garden for the alternative crowd and other urban types. Sprawling, full at all hours, with a dance floor inside. Open daily 4pm-6am.

Ex, Mehringhof, Gneisenaustr. 2a (tel. 693 58 00). U-Bahn 6 or 7: Mehringdamm or night bus N19. A *Kneipe* in a courtyard run by a famed collective and hangout for the people from the independent scene. Blackboard often has information on political and cultural events. Piped-in music and punk rock. Occasional concerts. Open Mon.-Thurs. 11am-1am, Fri.-Sun. 8pm-1am.

SO 36, Oranienstr. 190 (tel. 615 26 01). U-Bahn 1: Görlitzer Bahnhof. Famous con-cert hall with Friday night heavy metal discos. Name refers to the pre-war postal code for what is now the wildest part of Kreuzberg. Open daily 10pm.

Oranienburger Straße—Mitte

Silberstein, Oranienburger Str. 27. U-Bahn 6: Oranienburger Tor or S-Bahn 1 or 2: Oranienburger Str. Next door to the synagogue. The theme is wrought-iron and rust, with vaguely human bronze statues that seem to creep around you. So do the art-loving patrons. Drink beer (DM4) and don't look surprised. Open daily noon-4am.

Tacheles, Oranienburgerstr. 53-56 (tel. 282 61 85). U-Bahn 6: Oranienburger Tor. Huge alternative art commune with a busy bar. The squatters here have kept the party going through some tumultuous incidents over the past four years. Has live music and a dance club which plays lots of house on Saturdays. Complex open daily around 4pm-late.

Tresor, Leipziger Str. 8 (tel. 229 23 46). U-Bahn 2: Mohrenstr. More dancing in an old string of bank vaults that survived socialism, now holding up against techno. Young crowd. Cover DM10. Open Fri.-Sat. midnight-9am.

Exit, Fischerinsel 12 (tel. 240 92 86). U-Bahn 2: Spittlemarkt or Märkisches Museum. One of the most exciting rave/house clubs in Berlin. On Saturday morn-ings the music starts again at 6am. Open Fri.-Sat. from 11pm.

Prenzlauer Berg

Knaack-Klub, Greifswalderstr. 224 (tel. 426 23 51). S-Bahn 8 or 10: Ernst-Thäl-mann Park. Probably the most "normal" place in Berlin. Different types of music each night; Saturday is disco night. Still popular among local Prenzlauer Berg crowd. Cover DM2, DM4 on weekends.

Franz-Klub, Schönhauser Allee 36-39 (tel. 448 55 67). U-Bahn 2: Eberswalder Str. Another favorite among Prenzlauer Bergers and *Wessies* in the know. Live music or performances; cover varies.

Café-Kunstfabrik Schlot, Kastanienallee 29 (tel. 208 20 67). Amiable alternative crowd enjoys free jazz at 9pm. Open daily from 5pm.

LESBIAN AND GAY BERLIN

Berlin's gay and lesbian population is surprisingly above ground and active in political and cultural arenas. Traditionally, the social nexus of gay and lesbian life has centered around the Nollendorfplatz—Christopher Isherwood lived at Nollendorfstr. 17 while writing his collection of stories *Goodbye to Berlin*, later adapted as the Broadway musical *Cabaret*. A marble pink triangle plaque outside the Nollendorfplatz U-Bahn station reads: "Beaten to death; abandoned to death," and remembers the thousands of gays and lesbians deported to concentration camps from the station. The demure and wild history of homosexuality comes out at the **Schwules Museum,** Mehringdamm 61, 3rd floor (tel. 693 11 72; open Wed.-Sun. 2-6pm; free). Lesbians can also look at the past and get information for the present at the **Lesben-Archiv Spinnboden,** Burgdorfstr. 1 (tel. 465 20 21; open Mon.-Thurs. 2-6pm, Fri. 5-9pm; admission DM5). The gay info center **Mann-o-Meter,** Motzstr. 5 (tel 216 80 08), off Nollendorfplatz, dispenses everything from K-Y jelly to posters for political activities. They have pamphlets and a notice board with listings of apartments and other accommodations (open Mon.-Sat. 3-11pm, Sun. 3-9pm).

The **Prinz Eisenherz** bookstore, Bleibtreustr. 52 (tel. 313 99 36) has lots of information and books, many in English (open Mon.-Wed. and Fri. 10am-6:30pm, Thurs. 10am-8:30pm, Sat. 10am-2pm). The travel guide *Berlin von Hinten* ("Berlin from Behind") costs DM16.80, but details gay life in Berlin extensively in English and German. The free magazine *Siegessaüle* details gay events for the month and is available in gay bars and bookstores. **Labrys,** Hohenstaufenstr. 64 (tel. 215 25 00), and **Lilith-Frauenbuchladen,** Knesebeckstr. 86 (tel. 312 31 02; open Mon.-Fri. 10am-6:30pm, Sat. 10am-2pm), are women's bookstores with a focus on lesbian issues. Both take their "women only" signs quite seriously. *Blatt Gold* (DM5 from women's bookstores and some natural food stores) has information and dates for women on a monthly basis. Many of the *Frauencafés* listed below are not exclusively lesbian, but offer an all-woman setting. Some do have "mixed" nights or days.

Travelers should also take note of the safety warning on **gay bashing** in the Practical Information section. Otherwise, have fun. Berlin is an open city.

Lipstick, Richard-Wagner-Platz 5 (tel. 342 81 26). U-Bahn 7: Richard-Wagner-Platz. A teeming lesbian dance hall, the hottest in the city. Men (many gay) can creep in Tues., Thurs. or Sun. nights only; the first Fri. of the month is also mixed. Open daily from 10pm.

Café Anal, Muskauerstr. 15 (tel. 618 70 64). U-Bahn 1: Görlitzer Bahnhof. Alternative gay and lesbian bar in Kreuzberg. The bar has a seashell-shaped canopy. Mon women only, Tues. men only. Open Mon.-Sat. from 5pm, Sun. from 3pm.

Pool, Motzstr. 19 (tel. 213 45 70). U-Bahn 1 or 4: Nollendorfplatz. Hottest gay dance club in the city. The place to find Berlin's young beauties. Cool down in **Tom's,** the leather bar up the street. Open daily 10pm-6am.

Wu Wu, Kleiststr. 4 (tel. 213 63 92). U-Bahn 1or 4: Nollendorfplatz. A gay bar and disco; men only. Fri.-Sat. cover DM3. Sun. night is showtime from 11:30. Open daily 10pm-7am.

Oranienbar, Oranienstr. 168 (tel. 615 68 17). U-Bahn 1 or 8: Kotbusser Tor. Red lighting and techno music attract gays and lesbians to this experimental Kreuzberg bar. Open daily from 6pm.

Zufall, Pfalzburger Str. 10 (tel. 883 24 37). U-Bahn 2: Hohenzollern Platz. Stylish chic, lesbian bar and disco. Mon., Thurs., and Fri. mixed. Open Wed.-Mon. from 10pm.

Zum Burgfrieden, Wichertstr. 69 (tel. 449 98 01). U-Bahn 2: Schönhauser Allee. In Prenzlauer Berg; the most popular gay bar in Eastern Berlin. Open daily 7pm-3am.

Pour Elle, Kalckreuthstr. 10 (tel. 218 75 33). U-Bahn 1 or 4: Nollendorfplatz. Lesbians dance the night away in this women's disco. Some men show up on Tues. Open daily from 9pm.

Anderes Ufer, Hauptstr. 157 (tel. 784 15 78). U-Bahn 7: Kleistpark. German for "the other shore." Stylish gay/lesbian mixed café with rotating art exhibits. Open daily 11am-2am.

Die Busche, Muhlenstr. 11-12. U-Bahn 1: Schlesisches Tor, then cross footbridge and through the wall. Popular and sweaty disco—this place is Stayin' Alive playing 70s and early 80s hits. Open Fri.-Sat. 9pm-5am, Sun.9pm-4am. Cover DM5-6.

Schocko-Café, Mariannenstr. 6. U-Bahn 1 or 8: Kottbusser Tor. Lesbian women's central; a café with a cultural center upstairs and dancing from 8pm on.

SHOPPING

When Berlin was a lonely outpost in the Eastern Bloc consumer wilderness, Berliners had no choice but to buy native. Thanks to the captive market, the city accrued a mind-boggling array of things for sale: if you can put a price tag on it, you can buy it in Berlin. The high temple of the consumerist religion is the seven-story **KaDeWe** department store on Wittenbergplatz, the largest department store on the European continent. The name comes from the German acronym for "Department Store of the West" *(Kaufhaus des Westens),* and for the tens of thousands of product-starved Easterners who flooded Berlin in the days following the Wall-opening, KaDeWe *was* the West—a gleaming cornucopia of high quality and higher fashion. Even for Westerners who are used to this sort of thing, the materialism on display can be awe-inspiring or sickening, depending on your personality. (No photograpy allowed!) In particular, the store's food department, sixth floor, has to be seen to be believed (see Food, above, for open hours).

The entire **Kurfürstendamm** is one big shopping district, but the **Ku'damm Eck** (the corner of Joachimstalerstr.) and **Ku'damm Block** (around Uhlandstr.) are the most notable parts. Bleibtreustr. has stores closer to the budget traveler's reach, while the boutiques on Nürnbergerstr. (especially around Tauentzienstr.) are suitable primarily for idle drooling. Wilmersdorfer Str. in Charlottenburg is home to a number of reasonably priced stores with some very good deals on shoes. Pick up a copy of *Shopping in Berlin* from the tourist office for all the gory details.

Theodore Sturgeon astutely observed that "Ninety percent of everything is shit," and the **fleamarkets** that regularly sprout up in Berlin are no exception. Nevertheless, you can occasionally find that fantastic bargain that makes all the sorting and sifting worthwhile. The market on **Straße des 17 Juni** is the best, with antiques, art, earrings, and lots of junk stacked up on sturdy stands (open Sat.-Sun. 8am-4pm). **Winterfeldmarkt** overflows with food, flowers, and people crooning Dylan tunes over their acoustic guitars (open Wed. and Sat. mornings). *Krempel* means "junk" in German, and the **Kreuzberger Krempelmarkt** is the place to get it. Turks and Yugoslavs display everything from crates of oranges to marmalade to homemade whiskey on sheets spread out on the ground (open Sat.-Sun. 8am-afternoon). Berlin's **Türkenmarkt** is almost indistinguishable from a Turkish bazaar: the wares are the same (cheese, bread, rugs, fabrics) and you may have to communicate with gestures (open Tues. and Fri. noon-6pm).

Zweite Hand (second-hand), an aptly named newspaper appearing Tuesday, Thursday and Saturday (DM3), consists of ads for anything anyone wants to resell, from apartment shares and plane tickets to silk dresses and cats; it also has good deals on **bikes. Bergmannstraße,** in Kreuzberg, is one used clothes and cheap antique shop strip. **Garage,** Ahornstr. 2, near Nollendorfplatz, sells second-hand clothes in everything from old-fashion to height-of-fashion for DM25 per kg. (Open Mon.-Sat. noon-9pm.) **Made in Berlin,** Potsdamerstr. 63 (U-Bahn #1: Kurfürstenstr.), generally has funkier second-hand stuff, all reasonably cheap. Get your leather jacket here.

■■■ THE OUTER BOROUGHS

These suburbs of Berlin lie within the *Berliner Außenring*, a massive roundabout of highways and train lines which circles the greater metropolitan area. The towns and city districts listed below are generally reachable by public transportation, and make for good afternoon or daytrips away from the rush of the city. See Brandenburg, below, for other excursions.

OUTER BOROUGHS: WESTERN

Wannsee

The reputation of the charming village of Wannsee is indelibly tarnished by the memory of the notorious Wannsee Conference of January 20, 1942. It was here that Hitler and leading officials of the SS completed the details of their "Final Solution" to exterminate all of European Jewry. The conference took place in the **Wannsee Villa,** Großer Wannsee 56, formerly a Gestapo Intelligence Center. In January 1992, the 50th anniversary of the Nazi death-pact, the villa reopened as the **Haus der Wannsee-Konferenz** (tel. 805 00 10), a documentary museum with permanent Holocaust exhibits and historic film series (open Tues.-Fri. 10am-6pm, Sat.-Sun. 2-6pm; free). Along the shores of the **Kleiner Wannsee,** the troubled young author Heinrich von Kleist and his mistress Henriette Vogel committed suicide in 1811. Kleist's sometimes puzzling works gained acclamation only after his death.

From Wannsee, ferries (DM6.50) also run to the **Pfaueninsel** (Peacock Island) where Friedrich the Great's successor Friedrich Wilhelm II built a *trompe l'oei* "ruined" castle as a private pleasure house in which he and his mistress could play by themselves. A flock of the island's namesake fowl roams about the gardens surrounding the castle. From Wannsee, ferries also sail to Tegel, Charlottenburg': Schloßbrücke, Spandau, Potsdam, Werder, and Kladow. Contact Stern und Kreiss chiffahrt (tel. 803 87 50) or visit them at the Wannsee waterfront near the S-Bahn station. Wannsee also has lengthy stretches of sandy beach along Havelufer Promenade. To reach Wannsee, take the triangle bus from either the Wannsee or Nikolassee S-Bahn stations to "Strandbad Wannsee" (for the beach) or to the end o Nikolskoer Weg (for the boats).

Tegel and Plötzensee

The forest and lake in Tegel (U-Bahn 6: Tegel) are among the most serene in Berlin You can swim, water-ski, or go boating on the lake (head down Alt Tegelstr.). Th forest has been left mostly untouched, and you can follow *Wanderwege* (walkin paths) to deserted parts of the woods. From the U-Bahn, walk up Karolinenstr. c take buses #133 or 222 two stops to get into the heart of the forest.

A chilling monument to the victims of Nazism, the **Gedenkstätte Plötzense** (Plötzensee Memorial; tel. 344 32 26; Bus #123 from S-Bahn, direction "Tiergarten to Goerdelerdamm, and follow Hüttingpfad 200m away from the Kanal, along a ta brick wall), housed in the former execution chambers of the Third Reich, exhibi documents recording death sentences of "enemies of the people," including th officers who attempted to assassinate Hitler in 1944. More than 2500 people wen murdered within these walls. The building survived World War II bombing and ha been preserved. Still visible are the hooks from which victims were hanged. Th stone urn in front of the memorial contains soil from Nazi concentration camps. L erature on the monument is available in English at the office. (Open daily 8am-6pr Feb. and Oct. 8:30am-5:30pm; Nov. and Jan. 8:30am-4:30pm; Dec. 8:30am-4pr Free.)

OUTER BOROUGHS: EASTERN

Treptow

The powerful **Sowjetische Ehrenmal** (Soviet War Memorial; S-Bahn: Treptower Park), is a mammoth promenade built with marble taken from Hitler's Chancellery. The Soviets dedicated the site in 1948, honoring the millions of soldiers of the Red Army who fell in what Soviets know as the "Great Patriotic War." Massive granite slabs along the walk are festooned with quotations from Stalin, leading up to colossal bronze figures in the socialist realist style, symbolically crushing Nazism underfoot. Despite the pomp, it's rather moving. Buried beneath the trees surrounding the monument are the bodies of 5000 unknown Soviet soldiers who were killed during the Battle of Berlin in 1945. The memorial sits in the middle of **Treptower Park,** a spacious wood ideal for morbid picnics. Its fate has been uncertain since the fall of the GDR but so far it has resisted change. The neighborhood adjoining the park is known for its pleasant waterside cafés and handsome suburban mansions.

Lichtenberg

In the suburb of Lichtenberg on Normannenstr. stands perhaps the most hated and feared building of the GDR regime—the **Staatsicherheit** or **Stasi headquarters.** On January 15, 1990, a crowd of 100,000 Berliners stormed and vandalized the building to protest the continued existence of the police state. The building once contained six million individual dossiers on citizens of the GDR—a country of only 16 million inhabitants. Since a 1991 law returned the records to their subjects, contents of the "Horror-Files" have rocked Germany, exposing informants—and wrecking careers, marriages, and friendships—at all levels of the political and cultural world. Last year the building opened to the public as the **Forschungs und Gedenkstälte Normanneustraße,** Ruschestr. 59, Haus 1 (tel. 23 72 46 10). S-Bahn 8 or 10: Frankfurter Allee. The archive contains exhibits about the GDR, especially Stasi operations, as well as photographs and accounts of victims of barbarous Stasi persecution.

Friedrichshagen and the Müggelsee

Friedrichshagen (S-Bahn 3) features pre-war houses—some from the 18th century—and cobblestone streets. It's right next to the **Berliner Stadtforst** (city forest) and the pleasant lake of **Müggelsee,** where you can catch a *Weiße Flotte* boat or sit in crowded lakefront cafés.

Marzahn and Wartenburg

For an idea of how bleak residential life in Eastern Berlin can be, take the S-Bahn to **Marzahn** (S-Bahn 7: Ahrensfelde) or **Wartenburg** (S-Bahn 75: Wartenburg). Here are the housing projects that make Alexanderplatz seem exquisite in comparison. Marzahn was created in 1979. On 31 sq. km., 170,000 people live in apartments described by many as "worker-lockers." They presently shelter unemployed, disillusioned youth, many of whom are nostalgic for the old East Germany, and some of whom have drifted into neo-Nazi parties. (The area is unsafe for Africans, Asians, and other conspicuous non-Germans; *all* tourists should probably avoid the area at night.) The area is in transition, with splashes of quickly and cheaply bought brightness blending in with the colorless landscape.

BRANDENBURG

Bordering Berlin on three sides, the province of Brandenburg is overshadowed by the sprawling metropolis. The Hohenzollern family, which eventually ruled the German Empire, came out of the forest here and onto the political stage. The stunning palaces in Potsdam are what remains of that moment in Brandenburg's past. Many believe that Brandenburg, now an agrarian hinterland, will unite with Berlin in the future, to form a single federal state. Potsdam, essentially a suburb of Berlin, has served as the seat of the state government since 1990. Brandenburg's lakes and forests are all easily accessible from Berlin, and provide a soul-saving break from the overloaded existence of the capital.

■■■ POTSDAM

Potsdam, city of Friedrich II (the Great) and get-away spot for the Kaisers, is an easy and essential foray from Berlin. The castles in Sans Souci Park are the key to Potsdam's aesthetic and historic importance; this was the home Kaiser Wilhelm fled in 1918, going into exile with no fewer than 60 carriages full of its furnishings. Far from missing out on the frenetic culture of Weimar Berlin, Potsdam was Germany's own Hollywood from 1921 until World War II, as the suburb of Babelsberg became one of the capitals of the European film industry. Site of the 1945 Potsdam conference that divied up Germany among the Allies, the 1000-year-old town gained new respectability in 1991, when Brandenburg voters chose it as their new state capital.

Orientation and Practical Information The **tourist office,** Friedrich-Ebert-Str. 5 (tel. (0331) 211 00), is near the streetcar stations "Alter Markt" and "Platz der Einheit." All streetcars from the bus or train station go to one of the two stops. From the S-Bahnhof Potsdam Stadt it's a 10-minute walk across Lange Brücke and straight onto Friedrich-Ebert-Str. The office provides information on local events, a modest map, and private accommodations, generally the cheapest way to spend the night in Potsdam. Dial a separate number for accommodations (tel. (0331) 233 85). Rooms run DM15-25 per person, per night, DM20-35 with private bath. Private bungalows are also available for DM35-50 per person. The fee for booking is DM5 for the first five nights and DM1 for each additional night (office open Mon.-Fri. 9am-8pm, Sat.-Sun. 9am-6pm). S-Bahn 3 and 7 run directly from Berlin-Zoo to Potsdam-Stadt, the center of town. Berlin rapid transit tickets are valid on the S-Bahn, for regular public transportation, and for reduced fares on the bus lines to tourist areas.

Accommodations Potsdam has no hostel—the closest are those in Wannsee (see Berlin listings) which are close to the Nikolassee S-Bahn station. Hotels are scarce and quite expensive; see Practical Information, above, for information on private rooms. The main **campground** is **Intercamping-platz Riegelspitze am Glindower See** (tel. (03327) 23 97), 13km away, on the other side of Lake Havel from Potsdam. (Bus #631 runs from the main bus station on Bassinplatz and *Hauptbahnhof* to the campground. DM5 per person, DM4 per tent. Reception open 8am-1pm and 3-10pm.)

Food and Entertainment Brandenburger Str. is filled with restaurants—including two bakeries open Sundays—and *Döner Kepab* stands and Mexican fast food. In contrast to many of the gaudy cafés on Brandenburger Str., **Artur,** Wilhelmischestr. 16, is a tastefully decorated and relaxed café serving light meals and breakfast (DM3-6; open daily from 11am). Many of the night spots in Potsdam cater to the West Germans who are rediscovering the town, rather than to young people. One notable exception is **Lindenpark,** Stahnsdorferstr. 76-78 (S-Bahn 3: Babelsberg; tel. (0331) 789 80), with a wild range of live music performances nightly; call for a schedule. For other pickings and a selection of second-hand sales, buy direct from farmers at the **Floh- und Bauernmarkt,** on Weberplatz in Babelsberg (S-Bahn 3: Babelsberg, then walk) on Saturdays from 9am to 4pm. The alternative market is the **Potsdamer Kunstmarkt,** Lindenstr. 53-56, with *Imbiß* stands to feed gawkers at the craft and street artists' exhibits (streetcar #91 or 96 from Potsdam Stadt: Wilhelmischestr.; open Sat. 10am-5pm, 2nd and 4th Sun. in the month noon-5pm).

Sights The 600-acre **Sanssouci Park** houses four Baroque palaces and countless exotic pavilions. The largest of the royal quartet, the **Neues Palais** (tel. (0331) 97 31 43) was originally built by Friedrich the Great while he was pouting after several unsuccessful wars. Inside is the 19th-century *Grottensaal,* a reception room whose ribbed walls glitter with seashells and semi-precious stones. The palace also houses a luxurious café (café open daily 11am-7pm, closed 2nd and 4th Sat. of the month) and a theater (open most of the summer), with occasional afternoon and evening performances. At the opposite end of the park stands **Schloß Sanssouci** (tel. (0331) 239 31) where Fred used to go to escape his wife and other troubles *(sans souci* is French for "without a care"). Unfortunately, visits are not always carefree; reunification has made this truly beautiful Baroque work accessible, and lines can run up to 45 minutes long. Come early. Next door, the fabulous **Bildergalerie** houses works by Caravaggio, van Dyck and Rubens beneath its gilded ceiling. In a macabre reunification gesture, Friedrich's remains, which had been spirited away in 1945 to a Hohenzollern estate near Tübingen to save them from the Red Army, were brought back to rest in the cemetery on the grounds of Sanssouci in 1991. Romantic **Schloß Charlottenhof** melts into landscaped gardens and grape arbors at the south of the park. Nearby lie the **Römische Bäder** (Roman baths). Overlooking the park from the north, the pseudo-Italian **Orangerie-Schloß** is famous for its 67 dubious Raphael imitations and for the **Neue Kammern** (royal guest chambers) alongside it. The most bizarre of the park's pavilions are its "oriental" houses: the **Chinesisches Teehaus** is a gold-plated opium fantasy, complete with a rooftop Buddha (a.k.a. Neptune with a parasol). (Park open 9am-sundown; free. Palaces open 9am-5pm, Oct. and Feb.-March 9am-4pm, Nov.-Jan. 9am-3pm. Neue Kammern closed Fridays. All palaces closed 1st and 3rd Mon. of each month. Admission to each palace DM6, students DM3. Compulsory German tours of Sanssouci, Neue Kammern, Schloß Charlottenhof; in others you can wander on your own.)

The **Brandenburger Tor,** a less famous cousin of Berlin's Brandenburg Gate, sits amidst traffic flowing through Luisenplatz. From here, Brandenburgerstr. leads down to the 19th-century **Peter-Pauls-Kirche.** One block before the church, Friedrich-Ebertstr. heads left to the red-brick **Dutch Quarter.** The sumptuous if somewhat decrepit mansions along Hegelallee hint at Potsdam's bygone Court grandeur. The yellow turrets of the **Nauener Tor** are visible at the end of the street. Towards the waterfront on Friedrick-Ebert-Str. the impressive dome of the **Nikolaikirche** rises above its neighbors. On closer inspection, the church looks a little awkward—the dome and the granite cube it sits on don't seem to match. The interior was renovated *à la* GDR with glass and sound-tiles detracting from the form of the architecture (open Mon. 2-5pm, Tues.-Sat. 10am-5pm, Sun. 11am-5pm).

Potsdam's second park, the **Neuer Garten,** nuzzling the Heiligersee, contains several royal residences (R3 or 4 to Potsdam *Hauptbahnhof,* then Bus #695 to Cecilienhof, or from S-Bahn station, Tram 96 to Platz der Einheit and change to Tram 95: Alleestr.). The most worthwhile is **Schloß Cecilienhof** (tel. (0331) 239 31), built to look like an English country manor. Exhibits document the **Potsdam Treaty,** signed at the Palace in 1945. The odd-looking pyramid in the landscaped garden, a 19th-century ice-shed, is more light-hearted. (Open daily 9am-5:15pm; Nov.-April 9am-4:15pm; closed 4th Mon. of each month. Admission DM3, students and seniors DM2, under 6 free.) **Kolonie-Alexanderowka,** the "Russian colony" just south of the Neuer Garten (Tram 95 to Am Neuer Garten), is not as Cold War-like as the name implies. In 1826, Friedrich Wilhelm III brought a gang of Russian prisoners singled out for their singing talents here and put them to work in his choir. Some never left, and built their own ornate half-timbered houses, many of which are still standing, and the Russian-style **Alexander Nevsky church,** complete with onion-bulb domes.

Fritz Lang made *Metropolis* and Marlene Dietrich got her first break in what today is know as **Filmstadt Babelsberg,** August-Bebelstr. 26-52 (tel. (0331) 72 27 55; S-Bahn 3: Greiebnitzsee, then Bus #693: Bahnhof Rehbrücke). In the studios, you can see old film sets and tour costume, make-up and cutting rooms. (Open daily 9am-

6pm. Last entry 4:30pm. Admission DM11, students DM8.) Back in town, the **Film-museum,** Schloßstr. 1 (tel. (0331) 236 75), features historical exhibits and daily flicks. (Museum open Tues.-Sun. 10am-5pm. Admission DM6, students and seniors DM4, under 6 free. Tourist office has film times.)

■ Near Potsdam: Werder

On the other side of Lake Havel lies Werder, a town with almost more orchards and vineyards than people. To get there, take Bus #631 from Bassinplatz or R3 from Potsdam Stadt or Cecilenhof tram stations. Besides the green view, stop here for a look at the Obstbau Museum (fruit cultivation museum), Karl-Marx-Platz 2 (tel. (03327) 446 88), with comparative histories of apples, cherries and grapes. (Open Wed. 11am-5pm, Sun. 1-5pm. Admission DM2.50, students DM1.)

■■■ BRANDENBURG

Brandenburg, over a thousand years old, gave Berlin its civic freedom when it was capital of the province. The town may have fallen from the political limelight, but it remains one of the best-preserved cities in the region to which it gave its name. Only parts of the city were leveled to make way for GDR architecture; the rest was left to decay. Behind the die-cut apartment blocks opposite the railway station, old houses and calm parks are connected by narrow, winding cobbled streets. Brandenburg's proud citizens have set about restoring their beautiful *Altstadt* and signs saying *Brand neu* are scattered throughout the city.

Brandenburg is surrounded by lush greenery and water. The River Havel flows gently by the **Dom St. Peter und Paul,** begun in Romanesque style and completed in Gothic. The renowned 19th-century architect Friedrich Schinkel added a few touches: the "Schinkel-Rosette" and the window over the entrance. The **Dommuseum** inside has an array of relics and local-history treasures. (Open Mon.-Tues. and Thurs.-Sat. 10am-noon and 2-4pm, Wed. 10am-noon, Sun. 11am-noon. Museum tours Tues., Wed., and Sun. 10:30am, Thurs. and Sat. 10:30am and 2:30pm.) The **St. Katharinen Church,** built at the end of the 14th century, is a beautiful example of *Backstein* (glazed brick) Gothic. The carved altar dates back to 1474 (open daily 10am-5:30pm). Both churches are the focus of cultural events: both regularly schedule organ concerts and the Dom hosts theater in the *Petrikloster* during the summer months. For 500 years a 6m statue of the legendary hero Roland has stood in front of the **Rathaus**—the socialist GDR-era was just a ripple in time to this medieval symbol of free commerce. Several remaining towers from the 12th-century city walls add historic flavor to the *Altstadt* and the streets around **Neustadter Markt.** Incidentally, *Neustadt* (new town) is a relative term—it was founded in 1196.

Two routes run to Brandenburg from Berlin: either hop on trains towards Magdeburg and Hanover, or take S-Bahn 3 or 7 from Bahnhof Zoo to Potsdam-Stadt and change for the R-3. The **tourist office,** Hauptstr. 21 (tel. (03381) 237 43), is just off Neustadter Markt. From the train station walk along Große Gartenstr. and turn right on Jacobstr. and left at the end of Steinstr. Alternatively, take Tram 1,2, or 9 from the train station to Neustadter Markt. The immensely helpful staff will answer your every question and will book rooms free of charge. Brandenburg does not yet have a strong hotel culture; the best value is private accommodations running at about DM30 for singles, DM40 for doubles. The tourist office will also supply information on cultural events and history and will give free maps and brochures in English to those who visit them.

The **Jugendherberge (HI),** Hevellastr. 7 (tel. and fax (03381) 52 10 40), lies across the Mühlendamm from the cathedral and right beside the lake. (Members only. DM15.50, over 26 DM19.) **Campingplatz Malge** is in the middle of the woods but only 20 minutes away from the city center. Take bus B from Neustadter Markt. It's right by a lake, and you can rent boats to fish or just play with the ducks. (DM per person, DM3 per tent. Showers included. Fishing permits from campground reception or tourist office. Open April-Oct.) The campground also has two-person bungalows for DM30 per night. To make reservations call **Amt für Tourismus** (tel. (03381) 51 21 34) or the tourist office. Inexpensive **restaurants** and fast-food joints line the pedestrian area of Hauptstr., which also features a **supermarket** and an open-air **farmers' market** behind the St. Katharinen Church. **Zum Kaffeekannchen,** Hauptstr. 16, serves coffee and ice cream (with or without alcohol) on a balcony overlooking the shoppers (open Mon.-Fri. 10am-7pm, Sat.-Sun. 1:30-6:30pm).

■■■ NEAR BERLIN

BERNAU AND WANDLITZ

The eastern satellite town of Berlin, **Bernau** offers a well-preserved, 600-year-old city wall and precious little else. Its saving grace is the nearby forest, accessible by bike or bus. Besides the city wall, the 16th-century **St. Marien's Church** has a splendid altar with Lucas Cranach-style artwork. Due to its fragility, it can only be viewed Sunday afternoons and through prior arrangement with the tourist office. The **Heimatmuseum** (tel. (03338) 56 14) at Steintor gives local history a nervous edge with an excessive display of weapons (open Tues.-Fri. 9am-noon and 2-5pm, Sat.-Sun. 10am-1pm and 2-5pm; admission DM3, students DM1). If **biking** is your thing, rent one in Berlin and bring it with you on the S-Bahn. Beautiful rides through the woods end at stunning lakes, including **Wandlitz,** the former retreat of East German government bigwigs (6km by bike trail, or bus #94 from Bernau). When the GDR regime fell, Wandlitz became one of the more notorious symbols of its corruption. Few things angered ordinary East Germans more than the sight of the aristocratic **hunting lodges,** formerly off-limits, complete with stables and stocked with game. The feeling was that grim, garden-variety socialists were bad enough, but hypocritical ideologues were just a bit too much to bear. If the fishing and sailing at Wandlitz win you over, **Zur Kahlheide,** Bernauer Chaussee 28 (tel. (033397) 214 93), has hotel rooms, but at decadent hunting-lodge prices (singles DM110, doubles DM140). The Bernau tourist office can make reservations.

To get to Bernau from Berlin, take S-Bahn 8 from Ostkreuz (45min., Berlin rapid transit ticket valid). From the train station, go straight until the first corner, turn left, then zigzag right and left until you reach the Marktplatz (market square). The **tourist office** (Fremdenverkehrsamt), Am Marktplatz 2, 16321 Bernau (tel. (03338) 59 71, fax 87 36), books private rooms (DM20-35 per person, with breakfast) and provides brochures (open Mon.-Fri. 9am-4pm, Sat. 10am-3pm).

ORANIENBURG AND SACHSENHAUSEN

The small town of Oranienburg, just north of Berlin, is indelibly tarnished with the memory of **KZ Sachsenhausen,** a Nazi concentration camp in which over 100,000 Jews, communists, gypsies, and homosexuals were killed between 1936 and 1945. In 1961, the GDR opened the site as a **Memorial Center** (tel. (03301) 80 37 15) to the victims of Nazi terror. Much of the camp has been preserved in its original form including its cell block, where "special" prisoners were kept in solitary confinement and tortured daily, and a pathology department where Nazis performed medical experiments on inmates both alive and dead. Only the foundations of Station Z remain, but the windswept grounds convey the horrors which were committed here. The center has several museums detailing the history of many concentration camps, including Sachsenhausen. Some exhibits which date from the early GDR years are being redone. To get to Sachsenhausen, take S-Bahn 3 (direction "Oranienburg") to the end of the line. From the train station walk along Straslunder Str. and turn right on Bernauer Str., left on Str. der Einheit and right on Str. der Nationen. The walk takes about 30 minutes. (Memorial Center open Tues.-Sun. 8am-6pm, Oct.-March 8am-4:30pm. Free.)

■■■ THE SPREE FOREST (Spreewald)

About 100km southeast of Berlin, the Spree River splits apart and branches out over the countryside in a maze of streams and canals more than 1000km long. This is the home of the legendary *Irrlichter,* a sort of Saxon leprechaun who lights the waterways (for a price) for travelers who lose their way and leads astray those who refuse to pay. Here folklore, tradition, and wildlife have survived in remarkable harmony and unparalleled beauty. Hire a barge, rent a paddle boat, or take to the trails by foot and you'll soon see why locals insist that the Spreewald—not Amsterdam, Stockholm, or St. Petersburg—is the true "Venice of the North."

But this is an agrarian Venice, where farmers row to their fields and noisy children paddle home from school. It's a green Venice as well, where the fields and forests teem with owls, storks, kingfishers, otters, and foxes, animals known to most Europeans only through textbooks and television documentaries. In a country infamous for its pollution and *kaputt* environment, the Spreewald is mysteriously idyllic.

Until the 17th century, these waterways meandered through one of Europe's densest forests. The Prussian kings cleared out many of the trees for furniture and shipped in settlers to fill the resulting fields with pumpkins, cucumbers, and fruit trees. Though heavily bombed at the end of World War II, the forest recovered quickly. Socialist industry was not kind; a decade ago coal-power stations towering outside of Lübbenau drew their cooling water from these streams as their smoke choked the sky. Through it all, native flora and fauna adapted and took refuge in the sheltering wetlands and the unscarred **Oberspreewald** (southern Spree forest).

One of reunification's economically mixed blessings is the planned close of the power plants in 1996. The Spreewald is now a *Biosphätenreservat* (biological preserve) recognized by the U.N. Some inner parts of Spreewald are closed to everyone all the time; some other sections are closed during mating and breeding season but not during tourist season. Guided tours are offered by reservation; the local tourist offices have information. Already though, the traditional way of life is straining under the weight of increased tourism. Obey the signs, stick to the pathways, and do your part to ensure that capitalist tourism does not make worse the destruction begun by socialist industrialization.

The Sorbs, Germany's Slavic minority, settled the Spreewald's villages; see the Introduction to Upper Lusatia (Oberlausitz) for more on the Sorbs. Although Sorbian culture exists in many Lusatian towns, in this region it is—with scattered exceptions—encountered mostly in museums, and in the occasional use of Sorbian place names alongside the German versions.

If your German is shaky, the **Spreewaldbüro** (U-Bahn: Turmstr.), Zwinglistr. 5a, 1 Berlin 21 (tel. (030) 392 30 22) in Berlin is your best source of information on the region. They speak English well and make reservations for private rooms in the Spreewald (appointments by phone only). It is best to make reservations in advance because of a distinct lack of tourist accommodations in the forest; many towns lack hostels and hotels, and the beds that *do* exist usually don't come cheap.

LÜBBEN

Lübben is a good starting point for a tour of the forests of the **Unter-Spreewald** (Lower Spreewald) stretching northward toward Leibisch. The **harbor** is watched by an ancient **Schloßturm** (castle tower); its waterways join the Spree River. Lübben is about an hour southeast of Berlin by train or on the Berlin-Cottbus *Autobahn.* In Lübben's *Altstadt* the architectural prize is the newly restored **Paul Gerhardt Kirche,** named for the most famous German hymnwriter after Luther. Gerhardt is buried inside, where no visitors are allowed except with a guided tour organized by the tourist office. To get to the church and the main market square from the station, take a right on Bahnhofstr., then a left on Logenstr., right on Friedenstr., then a left on Spreeuferstr. At the light take a right on Hauptstr. Crossing back to **Hauptstraße**, note the difference in elevation; during the Thirty Years War this area was destroyed and rebuilt so often that its height rose above the market.

Lübben's **tourist office** *(Fremdenverkehrsverein)*, Lindenstr. 14 (tel. (03546) 30 90, fax 25 43), directly on the harbor, provides trail maps and a room-finding service (primarily doubles, DM25 per person) for a DM5 fee. They also **rent bikes** for DM10 (open Mon.-Wed. 1-6pm, Tues., Thurs.-Fri. 9am-6pm). You can also rent a bike at the train station for DM10 (open daily 7am-9pm). The **Fahrmannsverein Lübben/ Spreewald**, Ernst von Houwald Damm 16 (tel. 71 22 or 80 05) offers **boat trips** (1½ to 8hr., DM6-22). Trips depart from Strandcafé-Kahnan Legestelle after 10am; the boats leave when full. Go straight from the tourist office, cross the bridge, then go right. You can also rent a **row boat or paddle boat** at **Bootsverleih Gebouer** on Lindenstr. (tel. 71 94). From the tourist office, go straight and take a right before you reach the bridge. Rentals start at DM21 per day for a one-seat paddle boat.

The **Jugendherberge Lübben (HI)**, Zum Wendenfürst 8 (tel. (03546) 30 46), is a 30 minute hike from the train station: turn right down Bahnhofstr. until you hit the end of Luckauer Str., turn right and take the first left onto Eisenbahnstr., cross Pushkinstr. and continue down Dorfstr. until it curves back toward three gray buildings on the water. The hostel is as rustic as the landscape surrounding it, but the staff is friendly. (Reception after 3pm. Curfew 10pm. DM15.50, over 26 DM19. Breakfast included.) **Camp** at **Am Burglehn** (tel. (03546) 70 53), also a hike. From the train station, turn right on Bahnhofstr., left on Luckauerstr., right onto Burgtehnstr., and continue along the footpath to the campground. One of the cheaper restaurants in Lübben is **Gaststätte "Kinoklause,"** across from the church on Poststr. Their *schnitzel* with mushrooms and fries (DM6) is good (open Mon.-Fri. 8am-midnight, Sat. 2pm-midnight, Sun. 10am-midnight). **Waegner's Fruchtoase** is on Bahnhofstr. is a good place to stop for groceries, including the famous *Spreewaldgurken* (odd pickled cucumber; open Mon.-Fri. 8am-5pm, Sat. 8-11am). There is also an open market in front of the church Tuesday to Friday.

Near Lübben stands **Straupitz**, an otherwise forgotten spot where, for reasons unknown, master architect Karl Friedrich Shinkel erected an unusual, striking church. Saved from obscurity, Straupitz is accessible by barge or by bus (from Logenstr.; bus #665, direction "Vetschar"; also bus #700, direction "Cottbus," or #708, direction "Straupitz"; all to Straupitz Dorf). Look into guided tours, the only way to actually enter the church, at Lübben's tourist office.

LÜBBENAU AND LEHDE

Though the crowded streets of Lübbenau verge on the urban, they open immediately onto the wooded paths and villages of the **Oberspreewald** (Upper Spree). The forest here is more dense than that above Lübben, crossed with a spider's web of canals. The *Altstadt* (old center of the town) with its 18th-century houses is a 10-minute hike from the station. Go straight on Poststr. until you come to the marketplace, dominated by the baroque **Church of St. Nikolai**. The phallic pillar in front served as an 18th-century crossroads post, marking distance in terms of *Stunden,* an antique measurement equalling an hour's walk (approximately 4.5km). The church interior can only be visited as part of a guided tour through town on Tuesdays (DM4, children DM3). The town was without aristocracy from 1944, when the local duke was executed after being implicated in an attempt on Hitler's life. After the *Wende,* the duke's three sons returned from the West to restore the local castle. The **castle park** is not half bad, and **Spreewaldmuseum Lübbenau** in the park offers an overview of the development of the Spreewald. Traditional Spreewald costumes, including the ornate headresses women wore as late as the 1930s, are on display (open April-Sept. Tues.-Sun. 10am-6pm; Oct. 10am-5pm; admission DM3).

Lübbenau is nine minutes by train from Lübben on the Berlin-Cottbus route. The **tourist office**, just left of the church on Ehm-Welk-Str. 15 (tel. (03542) 36 68), provides maps, information in English, information on bike trails, and a room-finding service (DM30; open Mon.-Fri. 9am-6pm, Sat. and holidays 10am-6pm). **Kowalski,** on Poststr. 6 (tel. 28 35) near the tourist office, rents **bikes** (DM10 per day; open Mon.-Sat. 9am-6pm). **Gondola tours** are available from the harbors on Dammstr. (tel. 22 25, fax 36 04). Take a right on Ehm-Welk-Str., then a right on Dammstr. The boats take on customers (starting 9-10am) until they are full and then leave, with no set departure time. Tours last from two to seven hours (DM8-14). No English tours yet, but hilarious commentary if you speak German and understand Saxish. To strike out on your own, rent a **paddle boat** at **Manfred Franke**, Dammstr. 72 (tel. (03542) 27 22); from the station, turn right down Bahnhofstr. and then left at the next intersection (open 8am-7pm). **Am Schloßpark Lübbenau** (tel. 35 33) is a beautiful **campground** in the park across from the castle. Follow Ehm-Welk-Str. away from the market toward the castle, cross the canal, and turn onto Clara-Zetkin-Str., which leads right to the campground (might close after 1993—be sure to call or check with tourist office). For cheap food, check out the assorted snack bars at the harbor.

From Lübbenau it's only a hop and a paddle to **Lehde,** the most romantic village in the Spreewald and only accessible on foot or by barge. By foot, follow the trail signs from the **Schloßpark** in Lübbenau. If you prefer waterways, take a boat trip from the harbor. Most round-trips include a stay in Lehde, where most homes are still dependent on the canals for access to the rest of the world. Check out the **Freilandmuseum,** where things are still as they were in the old days. The museum displays three restored farm houses and craft works. Local artists also show their work (open April-Sept. daily 10am-6pm; Oct. daily 10am-5pm; admission DM3).

BURG

Burg, farther east and harder to reach, is probably the most expansive village in Europe, with 600 farms and 200 private homes spread over 52 square km. The village is accessible by bus from Lübben (#700 to Cottbus); get off at "Burg Bleske." By bus from Cottbus, take #47 (direction "Schmolzen") or bus #46 (direction "Burg") and get off at "Burg Bleske." You really need to get off at "Burg Bleske"; otherwise, you'll spend a long time walking. The most impressive view of Burg is from the **Bismarckturm** (Bismarck tower), overlooking the surrounding forests and the 300 streams and bridges that thread through it. Go towards the harbor on Spreestr., cross the bridge and follow trail signs straight ahead for 1km (open Tues.-Fri. 10am-5pm, Sat. 10am-7pm, Sun. 10am-6pm; DM2, children DM1). The **tourist office**, Am Hafen 1 (tel. (035603) 417) is to the right, before the bridge. They offer a listing of available rooms. For **gondola tours**, go to the harbor (right before the bridge) at Str. Zum Kahnhafen 51 (tel. 278). Boat trips start after 10am and cost around DM4 per hour. **Zweiradhaus Schmidt** at Bahnhofstr. 17 (tel. 376) rents **bikes** for DM8 a day. The local **Youth Hostel** is on Jugendherbergsweg 8 (tel. 225). From the bus stop walk towards the harbor and take a left before you get to the "OK" supermarket. Then turn right at the "Jugendherberge" sign. This rustic, pleasant hostel offers cabins and rooms; bathrooms are mostly in a separate area. (Reception 7pm. Curfew 10pm. DM16; over 26 DM19.50. Breakfast included.) The **OK supermarket** on Spreestr. offers basic groceries (open Mon.-Fri. 8am-6pm, Sat. 7:30-11am.)

COTTBUS (Chosebuz)

Most of Cottbus (Sorbian Chosebuz) looks like the old textile mill town it is; only the old market squares around Berlinerstr. keep the look of the Spreewald villages to the west. The riverside extends past the urban center to **Schloß Branitz**, an old yellow castle with a notable park. The landscaping includes, strange to tell, medium-sized **pyramids** dating from the tenure of the Egyptophile Hermann von Pückler-Muskau in the mid-19th-century. Now covered with vines, one pyramid seems to float in the center of the castle lake.

Built on the Spree, with a direct rail link to Berlin and bus lines to Burg and other hamlets, Cottbus offers an opening for Spreewald tours. The bus station is a 15-minute walk from the train station. Walk across the bridge on Bahnhofstr. and take a right on Marienstr. The **tourist office** is located at Berlinerstr. 1a (tel. (0355) 242

55) and offers a room service for a DM5 fee (rooms DM30-50; open Mon.-Fri. 10am-6pm, Sat. 10am-noon). Take a tram (#1, 2, or 4) towards the city center and get off at Stadthalle. Walk up Berliner Str. towards the marketplace. The modern, clean **Youth Hostel** at Klosterplatz 2-3 (tel. 225 58) is three minutes away from the tourist office. Take a left on Wendestr. and go around the church. (Reception 8am-1pm and 7-9pm. Curfew 10pm. DM16.50, over 26 DM19.50. Breakfast included.)

HALBE

Trains between Berlin and Lübben stop briefly in this unobtrusive village; a five-minute walk due south of the train station will bring you to the grim **Gedenkstätte Waldfriedhof** (memorial forest cemetery). On April 19 and 20, 1945, these forests witnessed the last great European battle of the Second World War. Two hundred thousand war-weary German soldiers met the advancing Soviet front. Some 40,000 of them perished. Today they lie under gray stones stretching as far into the forest as the eye can see. Victims of the Soviet occupation's forced-labor camps are also buried here. If you do visit these haunted woods, note well the words carved on the park's marble obelisk: *Die Toten mahnen für den Frieden zu Leben*—the dead remind us to live for peace.

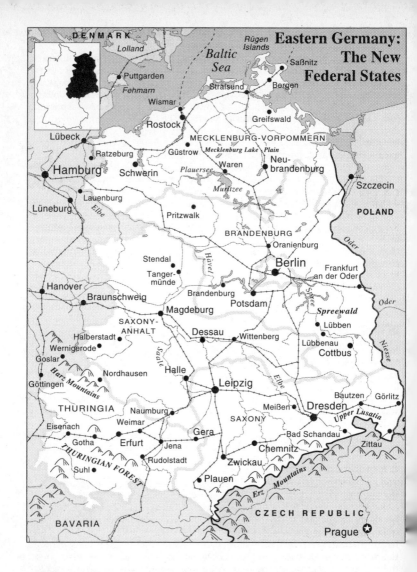

Eastern Germany: The New Federal States

▪ Eastern Germany

While it may be difficult to find traces of the former border between the two Germanys, it is not quite so difficult to tell that you have crossed into the former GDR. Don't expect to enter the *neue Bundeslander* (the new Federal States, how Germans refer to the former GDR) and actually find exactly what you thought you'd find. Those visiting the former GDR for the first time will be surprised to find that the lion's share of Germany's cultural and historic monuments belong to the Eastern states. The streets of Potsdam, Weimar, Eisenach and Wittenberg offer travelers a satisfying sense of discovery. Here one can walk in the footsteps of Luther, Goethe,

Schiller, Nietzsche, Bach, Mozart, Handel, Brecht, and so many others. However, much of the former GDR is in rough shape. Careless industrialization has decimated the environment, the economy is a shambles and millions have lost their jobs; the disparity in living standards between Eastern and Western Germany is still striking. The unpredictability of life in the new Federal States has translated into anger and fear: radical right gangs loiter in many eastern cities. Caught somewhere between division and unity, many Germans are having second thoughts. The people who live here have enthusiastically embraced new freedoms, but if you have come expecting to dance on the Wall, you're late.

SAXONY (SACHSEN)

Known to foreigners primarily for Leipzig and Dresden, the two largest and most fabled cities in Eastern Germany after Berlin, Saxony's beauty really lies in its less trumpeted cities and regions. A daunting cathedral and a thriving porcelain industry attract visitors to Meißen, and Saxon Switzerland, with its dazzling views and challenging hiking trails, retains the grace of past centuries in a way that war-ravaged Dresden may have lost forever. Saxony is also the gateway to the East, with Bautzen and the Zittauer Gebirge on the border of what used to be Czechoslovakia.

■■■ DRESDEN

No matter where you go in Dresden, you will not be able to forget the fact that the "Florence on the Elbe," a city of minimal military importance but incredible cultural value, was incinerated by Allied bombers during World War II, claiming over 50,000 lives. For 40 years, Dresden lived in the shadow of its former glory and great destruction. Unlike Munich or Hamburg, where reconstruction obscured the wounds of war, Dresden remained scarred. But in the Dresden of the 1990s, the phoenix-from-the-ashes metaphor fits. With a skyline dominated by construction cranes and long-term renovation plans stretching well past the year 2000, Dresden is poised to regain its prewar elegance. If you've come to see the ruins, you'd better hurry.

ORIENTATION

The capital of the *Land* (federal state) of Saxony, Dresden stands magnificently on the Elbe River about 80km northwest of the Czech border and about 180km south of Berlin. This city of 500,000 people is fast becoming a major transportation hub between Eastern and Western Europe. From the **Dresden Hauptbahnhof** (main train station) travelers shoot off to Warsaw, Paris, Kraków, Berlin, Budapest, Copenhagen, Munich, and Frankfurt. Another station, **Bahnhof Dresden Neustadt,** sits on the other side of the Elbe and bears a striking physical resemblance to its mate; trains leave from here to Leipzig and other Eastern German cities. Don't be fooled. If you are (and you won't be the first), trains run between the stations approximately every 20 minutes; streetcars #3, 11, and 26 connect them as well.

Dresden is divided into two halves by the Elbe. The *Altstadt* is on the same side as the *Hauptbahnhof;* the *Neustadt,* to the north, is now paradoxically the oldest part of the city, having escaped most of the bombing. South of the *Altstadt* are the contrasting suburbs of Plauen and Strehlen. Dresden has just about completed the process of removing socialist-era names from streets and squares. Pick up a map at the tourist office, or any postcard stand—if you pay less than DM5, ask how old it is.

Safety warning! Despite the external beautification, Dresden is becoming uglier in other respects; violence and petty crime have increased, though Dresden is still no worse than many major European cities. Economic chaos has also fueled an Aryan-supremacist skinhead movement; Dresdener neo-Nazis aim their hatred specifically at Polish, African, Middle Eastern, and Vietnamese guest workers, and nearly all violence occurs in the economically depressed residential areas these groups share. Non-white travelers and all conspicuous non-Germans should stick to the well-traveled *Altstadt,* and be careful at night in the area north of Louisenstr. in Dresden-Neustadt, in the industrial suburbs of Strehlen and farther south.

PRACTICAL INFORMATION

Tourist Office: Dresden Information, Pragerstr. 10 (tel. 495 50 25, fax 495 12 76). Turn left out of the front door of the *Hauptbahnhof,* cross Wiener Platz, and walk straight down Pragerstr. for about 5min. The office is on the right hand side behind Breuniger and McDonald's. Decent English. They'll help with rooms in hotels or private homes (DM20-50 plus a DM5 fee), maps, theater tickets, and guided tours. Open Mon.-Sat. 9am-8pm, Sun. 9am-noon; Nov.-Feb. Mon.-Sat. 9am-6pm, Sun. 9am-noon. For friendly, less hectic service, check the **Tourist Information Neustädter Markt** in the tunnel north of the Augustusbrücke (tel. 535 39); same services as the main branch. Open Mon.-Fri. 9am-6pm, Sat.-Sun. 11am-4pm; Oct.-March Mon.-Fri. 9am-6pm, Sat. 9am-4pm, Sun. 11am-4pm.

Currency Exchange: Deutsche Verkehrs Bank AG Hauptbahnhof, in the main hall of the train station. Open Mon.-Fri. 7:30am-7:30pm, Sat. 8am-4pm. There are also a number of banks on Pragerstr. After hours, the self-service exchange machine in the *Hauptbahnhof* will do, but rates are poor.

American Express: Köpckestr. 15 (tel. 566 28 65), in the Bellevue Hotel across the Elbe from the Opera. Streetcar #5 (from the *Hauptbahnhof,* direction "Weinböhla"): Neustädter Markt. Friendly English-speaking representatives change traveler's checks for no fee and recommend nightclubs in the area. Money sent, mail held. Open Mon.-Fri. 10am-noon and 1-5:30pm, Sat. 9am-noon.

Post Office: The once and future **Hauptpostamt** now fills several trailers on Hertha-Lindner-Str.; during renovation, the actual office is in Dresden-Neustadt, Königbrückerstr. 21/29, 01099 Dresden (tel. 594 40). Open Mon.-Fri. 8am-6pm, Sat. 8am-noon. **Postamt 72,** Pragerstr., 01069 Dresden, is near the tourist office.

Telephones: At the post offices. **City Code:** 0351.

Flights: Dresden's airport (tel. 589 30 80) is about 15km from town. Buses (DM6-8 one-way) leave both stations hourly; call (tel. 43 43 59) for schedules.

Trains: For information, call (tel. 471 06 00) or use the computerized schedule center in the main hall of the *Hauptbahnhof.*

Public Transportation: Extensive but noisy, the bus and streetcar system takes you where you want to be. As you board, punch your ticket (DM1, package of 6 DM6, day pass DM5, week pass DM12). Tickets and maps are available at major stops and the **Verkehrs-Info** stand outside the *Hauptbahnhof.* Open Mon.-Fri. 5:30am-7:30pm, Sat. 7am-6pm, Sun. 9am-6pm. Most major lines run once an hour after midnight. Dresden's **S-Bahn** network reaches from Meißen (DM3) to the Czech border (DM4); buy tickets from automats in the *Hauptbahnhof.* Validate them in the red contraptions; insert the ticket and press hard. No, harder.

Ferries: Weiße Flotte Dresden (tel. 502 26 11) offers trips to the Sächsische Schweiz and the vineyards near Meißen (DM10-22, under 16, 50% off). For information head to the Elbe docks just below the Brühlsche Terrasse.

Taxis: tel. 459 81 12.

Car Rental: Available at all of the major hotels on Pragerstr.

Bike Rental: Pacher und Partner, Wallstr., just 2 blocks left of the intersection of Pragerstr. and the Altmarkt. DM10 per day. Open Mon.-Wed. and Fri. 9:30am-6:30pm, Thurs. 9:30am-8:30pm, Sat. 9am-1pm.

Hitchhiking: *Let's Go* does not recommend hitchhiking as a safe mode of transportation. Those headed to Berlin take streetcar #3 or 6: Liststr., then bus #81: Olter and walk back to the *Autobahn* interchange. Those headed to Prague take bus #76: Südhöhe, then hitch southbound on Innsbruckerstr. Those headed to Eisenach and Frankfurt am Main take streetcar #1: Zschonergrundstr. (4 stops past "Dresden Cotta"—telling the driver they want to get off at the *Autobahn* to make sure the bus stops), then walk left (away from the river) to the interchange.

Mitfahrzentrale, Nürnbergerstr. 57 (tel. 463 60 60), rideshare office. Rides to Prague easy to come by weekends. Open Mon.-Fri. 10am-7pm, Sat. noon-2pm.

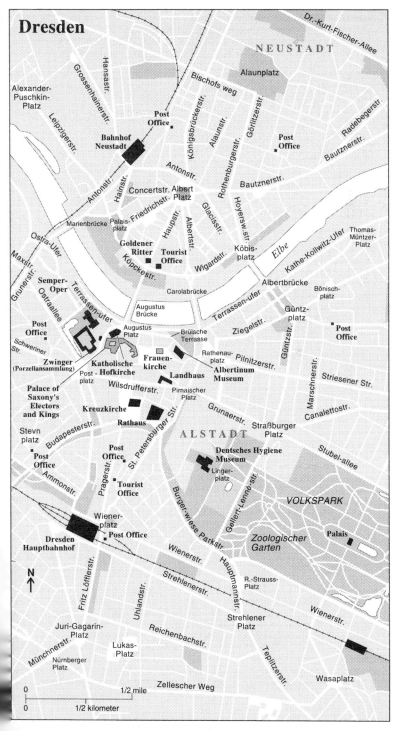

Dresden

NEUSTADT

Dr.-Kurt-Fischer-Allee

Alaunplatz

Alexander-
Puschkin-
Platz

Hansastr.

Grossenhainerstr.

Bischofs weg

Königsbrückerstr.

Alaunstr.

Görlitzerstr.

Leipzigerstr.

Post
Office

Post
Office

Radebegerstr.

Bautznerstr.

Bahnhof
Neustadt

Antonstr.

Antonstr.

Rothenburgerstr.

Bautznerstr.

Hainstr.

Concertstr. Albert
Platz

Friedrichstr.

Hauptstr.

Albertstr.

Glacisstr.

Hoyersw.str.

Elbe

Marienbrücke

Palais-
platz

Köbis-
platz

Kathe-Kollwitz-Ufer

Thomas-
Müntzer-
Platz

Ostra-Ufer

Goldener
Ritter

Tourist
Office

Köpckestr.

Wigardstr.

Maxstr.

Semper-
Oper

Ostraallee

Terrassen-ufer

Carolabrücke

Albertbrücke

Bönisch-
platz

Grunerstr.

Augustus
Brücke

Terrassen-ufer

Güntz-
platz

Post
Office

Gruner str.

Post
Office

Augustus
Platz

Brülsche
Terrasse

Ziegelstr.

Güntzstr.

Schweriner
Str.

Zwinger
(Porzellansammlung)

Katholische
Hofkirche

Frauen-
kirche

Post
platz

Rathenau-
platz

Pilnitzerstr.

Marschnerstr.

Striesener Str.

Albertinum
Museum

Palace of
Saxony's
Electors
and Kings

Wilsdrufferstr.

Landhaus

Pirnaischer
Platz

Canalettostr.

Kreuzkirche

Rathaus

Budapesterstr.

St. Petersburger Str.

Grunaerstr.

Straßburger
Platz

Stevn
platz

ALSTADT

Stubel-allee

Post
Office

Post
Office

Pragerstr.

Tourist
Office

Deutsches Hygiene
Museum

Linger-
platz

VOLKSPARK

Ammonstr.

Burger-wiese Parkstr.

Gellert-Lenne-str.

Zoologischer
Garten

Palais

Dresden
Hauptbahnhof

Wiener-
platz

Post Office

Wienerstr.

Wienerstr.

Hauptmannstr.

R.-Strauss-
Platz

Wienerstr.

N
↑

Fritz Löfflerstr.

Uhlandstr.

Strehlenerstr.

Strehlener
Platz

Teplizerstr.

Juri-Gagarin-
Platz

Münchnerstr.

Nürnberger
Platz

Lukas-
Platz

Reichenbachstr.

Wasaplatz

0   1/2 mile

Zellescher Weg

0   1/2 kilometer

Luggage Storage and Lockers: At both train stations. Lockers DM2-3. Storage DM4 per piece, DM6 per checked bicycle. Open daily 6am-9pm.

Bookstore: Das Internationale Buch, Kreuzstr., directly behind the Kreuzkirche, has English books on the 2nd floor. Open Mon.-Wed. and Fri. 9am-6pm, Thurs. 9am-8:30pm, Sat. 9am-1pm, first Sat. in the month 9am-4pm.

Laundromat: Bärensteiner Waschsalon, Bärensteinerstr. 10 (tel. 302 50). At the far end of the Großer Garten. Wash, dry, and iron for DM13. Open Mon.-Fri. 8am-9pm, Sat.-Sun. 8am-4pm. The laundromat at **Louisenstraße.** 48 (tel. 502 35 33) is closer to the action. Washers at **Jugendherberge Dresden** are DM2 per load.

Pharmacy: Call (tel. 01 15 00) to find out which pharmacy is on 24-hr. duty. Closed pharmacies lead you to open ones.

Crisis Lines: Frauen in Not (tel. 33 22 33) is for women in emergency situations. **Ausländer in Bedrängis** (tel. 484 55 08) is for victims of racial violence.

Women's Center: SOWIESO Frauenzentrum (tel. 514 70) is at Angelikastr. 1, north of the Elbe.

Gay and Lesbian Center: Gerede-Dresdner Lesben, Schwule und alle Anderen, in **Haus der Jugend,** Wienerstr. 41 (tel. 464 02 20), near the station.

Emergencies: Ambulance: tel. 115. **Fire:** tel. 112. **Police:** tel. 110.

ACCOMMODATIONS

Dresden sorely lacks budget accommodations, so arrive early and expect a struggle. With the influx of Western German development aid, most hotels are full most of the time. With the exception of the hostels and the campground, private rooms are really the only option for budget travelers. The tourist office will find you one; expect to pay DM20-50 for singles, DM40-100 for doubles with a DM5 fee tacked on. The castle perched above the Elbe that once housed a superb youth hostel has been converted to a luxury hotel. Ah, capitalism.

Jugendherberge Dresden (HI), Hübnerstr. 11 (tel. 471 06 67, fax 472 89 59). Streetcar #5 (direction "Südvorstadt") or #11 (direction "Plauen"): Nürnberger Platz, continue down Nürmbergerstr. and turn right onto Hübnerstr.; the hostel is at the first corner on your right. To hoof it from the *Hauptbahnhof,* walk down 2 blocks on Fritz-Löffler-Str., turn right on Reichenbach, which becomes Altenzellerstr., for about 4 blocks, and turn left onto Hübnerstr. A 73-bed hostel in a mansion built by the sewing machine magnate Isaac Singer. International clientele packed into small 8-bed rooms. Endearingly modern (and hot) showers. DM19.50, over 26 DM23, including breakfast and required sheet rental.

Jugendherberge Oberloschwitz (HI), Sierksstr. 33 (tel. and fax 366 72). Streetcar #10 (direction "Laubegast") or #26 (direction "Johannstadt"): Fetscherplatz (6 stops); switch to streetcar #1 (direction "Tolkewitz"): Schillerplatz (7 stops); cool off at the **Biergarten** (en route), then walk across the Elbe on the Loschwitzer bridge to Körnerplatz. At Körnerplatz ride the *Schwebebahn* (hill train—*not* the *Standseilbahn*) up to Sierkstr. (DM2.50). The whole process takes about an hour (not including the beer), but the beautiful location is worth it. Reception open 4-8pm. No lockout or curfew. DM16, over 26 DM19. Breakfast included.

Jugendherberge Radebeul, Weintraubenstr. 12 (tel. and fax 747 86). S-Bahn (from either train station, direction "Meißen"): Radebeul-Weintraube. Turn right as you leave the station, and follow the street which curves left; the hostel is at the first gate. A sprawling complex, not all of which has been renovated. Not as nice as Oberloschwitz or as central as Dresden, but lots of beds. DM14, over 26 DM17.

Campingplatz Mockritz, Boderitzerstr. 30 (tel. 471 82 26). One hour away by bus (from the *Hauptbahnhof,* direction "Moritzburg" or "Moritzburg/Radeburg"): Sonnenland. Reception open until 10pm. DM10 per person, DM6 per tent. Bungalows with kitchens, DM20 per person.

FOOD

Every time a new restaurant opens in Dresden, an old one closes. Unfortunately, a rise in tourism also means a rise in prices, especially in the *Altstadt.* The cheapest eats are at supermarkets or *Imbiß* stands on Pragerstr.; the **Karstadt** here looks like a giant fishbowl, but it does have groceries (open Mon.-Wed. 9am-6:30pm, Thurs. 9am-8:30pm, Fri. 9am-6:30pm, Sat. 9am-2pm, first Sat. in the month 9am-4pm).

Neue Mensa, Bergstr. 47 (tel. 463 64 95). From Nürnbergerplatz, go down Nürnbergstr., away from the city center, right on Bergstr., and walk uphill a few min. More a restaurant than a *Mensa*. Meals DM5-10. Open mid-Oct. to Feb. and April-June. Hours vary, depending on school sessions and nighttime music offerings.

Café Toscana, Loschwitzbrücke, in Schillerplatz, right near the Blaues Wunder Bridge. Creative and experimental ice-cream dishes served in sumptuous glass patio overlooking the Elbe. Salads and *Abendrot* (bread-and-cheese spread) as well. Open Mon.-Sat. 7am-10pm, Sun. 1-10pm.

Tagesbar "Der Löwe," Hauptstr. 48, also across from the Albertplatz. Once the trendiest bar in communist Germany, now privately owned with rain-or-shine patio seating. A bit expensive. Try their specials (DM7-20) or green salads (DM6-10), a rarity in this town. Open daily 10am-midnight.

Raskolnikoff, Böhmische Str. 34, in a run-down pre-war brownstone. Late-night joint, but more a café than a bar. Tues.-Sun. 8pm-1am.

Dynamo Gaststätte, Lennéstr., near the Rudolf-Harbig soccer stadion. Big portions for big Germans. Free-flowing beer. When the Dresden Dynamo European Football (soccer) team is in town, watch out for rowdy crowds. Meals DM10. Open Mon.-Sat. 11am-1am.

Mandarin, Gewandhausstr. 5 (tel. 496 31 93), just around the corner from the Kreuzkirche, off Wilsdrufferstr. Heaping plates of spicy Chinese food in a green and red environment. A bit expensive for dinner (DM15-20), but lunch specials with soup hover at DM10. Open daily 11:30am-2:30pm and 5:30-11:30pm.

SIGHTS

From the banks of the Elbe, the **Electors of Saxony** once ruled nearly the whole of central Europe. The extravagant collection of Emperor Augustus the Strong and the magnificent palace he built to house it, the **Zwinger,** once rivalled the Louvre in Paris. Inside the palace courtyard, the sky-blue porcelain bells of the *Glockenspiel* gate chime the hour. The northern wing of the palace, a later addition, was designed by Gottfried Semper, revolutionary activist and master architect. Semper's famed Opera House, the **Semper-Oper,** echoes the robust style of the palace wing. Its painstaking restoration, both inside and out, has made it Dresden's major attraction. The interior is open for tours between shows every few weeks. Ask at the tourist office or call 484 23 33. Not far from the entrance to the Porzellansammlung depart Dresden's most affordable tours by streetcar (Mon.-Fri. 10:30am and 1:30pm, Sat.-Sun. noon and 3:30pm; DM10, students and seniors DM5).

Near the Zwinger lie the ruins of the **Palace of Saxony's Electors and Kings,** levelled by the firebombing on February 13, 1945. Note the lighter stone work and cleaner fronting—this is all brand spanking new. Since the fall of 1990, restoration has been proceeding at light speed. Part of the **Residenzschloß** is now open to the public, featuring a display on the Renaissance and Baroque eras of the palace. (Open Fri.-Wed. 10am-6pm. Admission DM3, students and seniors DM1.50. *Tageskarte* valid.) A private walkway connects the palace to the **Katholische Hofkirche** (Catholic Cathedral). Originally the royal family's private chapel, the church was built to hide the family's Catholic pageantry from their Protestant subjects. In 1980 the church was reopened and ordained a public cathedral by the Vatican. (Open for tours Mon.-Thurs. 11am and 2pm, Fri.-Sat. 1pm and 2pm, Sun. 1pm, but usually open other times as well.) Adorning the alley leading to the main entrance of the Catholic cathedral, the **Fürstenzug** (Procession of Kings) is a 150-meter pictorial in Meißner porcelain tiles tracing the history of Saxony since the Middle Ages, so if you're getting Friedrich the Earnest confused with Friedrich the Pugnacious you may want to double back here for a quick history lesson.

From the Catholic Cathedral, the 16th-century **Brühlsche Terrasse** offers a prime photo opportunity of the Elbe River (best at sunset). Turn right at the end of the terrace to reach the **Albertinum,** another of Dresden's fabulous museum complexes (see Museums, below), created out of a former arsenal, with a courtyard sculpture collection of Greek and Roman works.

From the Albertinum, a walk to the Neumarkt will take you to the shell of the **Frauenkirche,** once Germany's most splendid Protestant church. Plans are now underway to reconstruct practically from scratch, with the completion date estimated to be around 2006. The first Protestant celebration of communion took place at the **Protestant Kreuzkirche** on the *Altmarkt.* Some tourists are fortunate enough to catch a performance by the **Kreuzchor,** one of the world's most famous boys' choirs. Others amuse themselves by checking out the smoke damage caused not by the fires of 1945, as many believe, but by pollution. Climb to the top for a bird's-eye view of that giant reconstruction site known as downtown Dresden. (Church open Mon.-Sat. 10am-6pm. Sun. services at 9:30am. Tower open Mon.-Tues. and Thurs.-Fri. 10am-6pm, Wed. 10am-5pm, Sat. 10am-4:30pm. Admission to tower DM2, students and seniors DM1.)

Paradoxically, Dresden's **Neustadt** (new town) is now the oldest part of the city, as it escaped the worst of the bombing. These streets were the haunting grounds of the author Friedrich Schiller; his fans can check out the **Schillerhaus,** Schillerstr. 19 (tel. 495 23 02; open Sat.-Sun. 10am-5pm or by appointment. Admission DM2, students and seniors DM1). In front of the Catholic church, the picturesque **Augustus Brücke** spans the Elbe to the **Goldener Reiter,** a gold-plated statue of Friedrich August II with a very healthy glow. The former emperor's nickname, Augustus the Strong, was an homage to his remarkable (some would say unseemly) virility—he supposedly fathered over 354 children. The pedestrian **Hauptstraße,** a cobblestone, tree-lined avenue of shops and restaurants, promenades from the river bank to **Albertplatz** (formerly Platz der Einheit), still surrounded by handsome 19th-century mansions. Also see the **Dreikönigskirche** (Church of the Three Kings), farther down Hauptstr., one of the oldest original structures in the city. (Open daily 9am-6pm. Free organ concerts Mon.-Fri. 5:30-6pm.) For a taste of Dresden's pre-war atmosphere, venture farther out to Blasewitz and Loschwitz, connected by **Blaues Wunder,** Dresden's favorite bridge and the only one not destroyed by the SS when the Soviets invaded—rumor has it that someone cut the explosives cable.

In a less savory part of town, the **Schlachthofringe** (Slaughterhouse Circle) is little-changed since the buildings were commandeered as a camp for prisoners of war. The American novelist Kurt Vonnegut was imprisoned here during the bombing of Dresden, moving him to write *Slaughterhouse Five.* The sight of the box-like buildings is chilling without any exhibits; take streetcar #9 (direction "Friedrichstadt") to the last stop and walk up.

MUSEUMS

If you're going to visit either the Albertinum or the Alte Meister collections and any other museum, a worthwhile investment is the *Tageskarte* (DM10, students and seniors DM5), allowing free entrance to the Zwinger museums, the museums of the Albertinum, the Residenzschloß, and a host of other sights.

Zwinger

Gemäldegalerie der Alten Meister, Zwinger Palace; remains one of the world's premiere collections of painting from 1500 to 1800. The first floor of the gallery begins with local works; Canaletto's series of 18th-century cityscapes show Dresden's landmarks at their finest, and have, in fact, been used to guide current restoration. Also on the first floor hang the sprawling Flemish and Dutch collections: Rembrandt, Vermeer, Dürer, and Lucas Cranach. On the mezzanine level is the outstanding Italian Renaissance collection, centered around Raphael's *Sistine Madonna*, accompanied by Bellini, Tintoretto, and Titian. The third floor is a hodge-podge, with Velazquez and El Greco and a collection of portraits of the densely inter-married European royalty; portraits by such women as Rosalba Carriera and Theresa Maron are on display. Open Tues.-Sun. 10am-6pm. Free tours Sun. 4pm. Admission DM7, students and seniors DM3.50.

Porzellansammlung (Porcelain collection), out the back gate of the Zwinger courtyard and around to the left. Dresden's premier tourist trap, the museum traces the history of Saxony's famous porcelain industry through a never-ending procession of outlandishly delicate yet lifeless tureens, vases, and knick-knacks. Open Fri.-Wed. 10am-6pm. Admission DM3, students and seniors DM1.50.

Rüstkammer, just across from the *Alte Meister,* a collection of royal personal effects, including an impressive collection of armor and jousting materials Open Tues.-Sun. 10am-6pm. Admission DM3, students and seniors DM1.50.

Albertinum

Gemäldegalerie der Neuen Meister. Here the small but representative collection of Gauguins and Monets pale beside the power and intensity of pre-war paintings by local Jewish and anti-fascist artists. Open Fri.-Wed. 10am-6pm. Admission DM7, students and seniors DM3.50.

Grünes Gewölbe, the highlight of the Albertinum and the treasure chest of the House of Saxony, which literally dazzles with priceless coins and gem-studded treasures, and the *pièce de résistance,* a carved cherry pit with over 180 miniature heads. Same hours as *Neuen Meister.*

Elsewhere in Dresden

Museum zur Dresdner Frühromantik, Hauptstr. 13, where you can get teary-eyed over people like playwright Heinrich von Kleist or painter Caspar David Friedrich getting teary-eyed over 18th-century Germany. Open Wed.-Sun. 10am-6pm. Admission DM2, students and seniors DM1.

Verkehrsmuseum (Transport Museum), Neumarkt, traces the history of German transport, from carriages to bullet trains and BMWs. Open Tues.-Sun. 10am-5pm, last entry 4:30pm. Admission DM4, students and seniors DM2; Fri. half-price.

Museum für Geschichte der Stadt Dresden, Wilsdrufferstr., in the 18th-century Neoclassical **Landhaus**. The exhibit contains some numbing photos of the city from 1945, as well as a chronicle of events in Dresden in the fall of 1989. Open Sat.-Thurs. 10am-6pm, Wed. to 8pm. Admission DM2, students and seniors DM1.

ENTERTAINMENT AND NIGHTLIFE

For those convinced the East German nightlife consists of standing around white plastic tables getting drunk at an *Imbiß,* Dresden may be a bit of a surprise. The *Altstadt* (especially the area near Brühlscher Terrasse) and **Hauptstraße** are home to Dresden's burgeoning café culture. But Dresden's most exciting offering is its rock scene. With ground zero at the intersection of Alaunstr. and Louisenstr. in Neustadt, this is Dresden's version of Kreuzberg, Berlin's wildly alternative district. Heavy metal, speed metal, and rap dominate, and the atmosphere is decidedly hardcore (and rabidly anti-neo-Nazi). Don't miss it, but don't head out alone too late—Neustadt is not Dresden's most attractive neighborhood. The local magazine *Blitz,* free at the tourist office, runs down the city's cultural calendar, but *SAX* (DM2.50 at any newsstand), is more complete and is the best source for the Neustadt *Szene.*

For centuries Dresden has been a focal point for theater, opera, and music. The incredible **Semper-Oper** has premiered many of Strauss and Wagner's greatest, and for German-speakers, Dresden offers all kinds of drama. With the availability of American movies and the disappearance of state-sponsored 25pf tickets, many locals have sworn off the arts for a while, making tickets a bit easier to come by.

Bars and Clubs

Die Tonne, Tzschirnerplatz 3 (tel. 495 13 54), hops to great jazz in the basement of one of Dresden's last remaining ruins across from the Albertinum. Performances most nights at 9pm. Cover DM5-12.

Studentenklub Bärenzwinger, Brühlscher Garten (tel. 495 14 09), in a hard-to-find bunker under the Brühlsche Terrasse not far from the Albertinum. An old favorite. Raucous beer hall atmosphere and MTV-Europe soundtrack. No cover.

Klub Neue Mensa, Bergstr. 47 (tel. 463 64 95), not far from the youth hostel. Musical fare varies from techno-pop disco to live guitar rock and heavy metal. Call ahead. No cover.

Scheune, Alaunstr. 36/40 (tel. 555 32). The heart of the Neustadt scene, in a former youth center. Pub grub for between sets; reasonably priced drinks. Open daily 8pm-4am.

Star Club, Altbriesnitz 2a (tel. 43 66 93), in the suburb of Cotta, attracts larger-name groups; check SAX or call for the program.

Theater and Cabaret

projekttheater dresden, Louisenstr. 47 (tel. 530 41). Experimental theater in the heart of the Dresden Neustadt. So cool they don't use capital letters. Have a drink in the café and observe the customers: most think they've just walked off the stage. Tickets DM6-12.

Dresdner BREttL, Maternistr. 17 (tel. 495 41 23); take Annenstr. from Postplatz behind the Zwinger. Famous for its satirical cabaret. Tickets DM10-15; students DM5-7.50.

Podium, Hauptstr. 11 (tel. 532 66) offers good mime a few times each week. Other times they play old movies and more intimate productions. Tickets DM10.

Concerts, Opera, and Dance

Sächsische Staatsoper-Semper Oper, Theaterplatz 2 (tel. 484 2491 or 484 2323). Opera's finest in glorious surroundings. The box office unloads unsold tickets 1hr. before the performance for DM5-10. Book ahead at the tourist office if you like, but expect to pay at least DM60. Box office at the Schinkelwache near the opera open Mon.-Wed. and Fri. noon-5pm, Thurs. noon-6pm, Sat.10am-1pm, and 1hr. before performances.

Kulturpalast, am Altmarkt (tel. 486 63 06). Home to the **Dresdner Philharmonie;** other music groups and several small dance ensembles also perform here. During intermission, check out the embarrassing socialist mural under the tarp on the outside wall. Box office (tel. 486 66 66) open Mon.-Fri. 9am-6pm, Sat. 10am-2pm. Leftovers go on sale 1hr. before curtain time.

Schauspielhaus, Ostra-Allee 3 (tel. 484 25 67; box office 484 24 29), produces classics from Goethe's *Faust* to Brecht's *Three Penny Opera*. Tickets DM10-20. Box office open Mon. and Wed.-Fri. 10am-6pm, Tues. 10am-6:30pm, Sat.10am-3pm. The Schauspielhaus also runs the **Kleines Haus,** located at Glacisstr. 28 near Albertplatz, with lighter fare and some musicals.

Kleine Szene, Bautzner Str. 107 (tel. 484 23 33), in Neustadt. Under the direction of the Semper Oper, the Kleine Szene performs simple ballet, modern dance, and light opera in a former dance school. Tickets DM10, students and seniors DM5. No last-minute discounts. Get tickets at the Schinkelwache near the Semper Oper or at the door.

■ Near Dresden: Meißen

Meißen has something of an advantage over Dresden, in that it was barely touched by World War II bombs—but then again the town has not grown much since it was trashed by the Swedes in the Thirty Years' War. This town on the Elbe was the center of the porcelain craft from the 18th century on, when career soldier Augustus the Strong was struck by what his more philistine advisors called his *Porzellankrankheit* (porcelain sickness), his mania for controlling the porcelain industry, and collecting its finest products. German classical scholar Winckelmann derided the art of Meißen dollmakers, especially, as pandering to the emperor's crude tastes, but many others—like the eccentric Czech nobleman in Bruce Chatwin's novel *UTZ*—have been obsessed with the eerie beauty of Meißen dolls. Restoration efforts and half-hearted modernization under the GDR have yielded mixed results, but

Meißen did outpace Dresden until the Renaissance, and is still crowded with teetering 16th- and 17th-century homes. Daytrip it from Dresden.

Wander the narrow, romantic, run-down alleyways of the *Altstadt*, and climb up to the **Albrechtsburg,** a castle-cathedral-fortress overlooking the city. From Bahnhof Meißen, turn left and cross over to the Elbe footbridge; across the river, take the path to the end, turn right onto Hahnemannplatz, and walk up. The exquisite complex was built between 1471 and 1498, and a whole procession of Saxon princes have inhabited the castle since. It was here in 1710 that Augustus the Strong, Elector of Saxony and renowned egoist (see Dresden, above), built Europe's first top-secret **porcelain factory.** (Open Feb.-Dec. daily 10am-6pm; last entry 5pm. Admission DM5, students DM3.) Next door inside the fortress complex is the **Meißener Dom,** a textbook early Gothic cathedral. Four priceless 13th-century **statues** behind the altar—among them Otto I, who founded the city in 968, the Virgin Mary, and John the Baptist—are thought to be the work of the Naumburg Master. (Open daily 9am-6pm; Nov. March 9am-4pm. Last entry 40min. before closing. Admission DM2.50, students DM1.20. Organ music daily at noon; concerts Sat. 6pm.)

Meißen's porcelain factory was once as tightly guarded as KGB headquarters for fear that competitors would uncover its intricate techniques; today, however, anyone can tour the **Staatliche Porzellanmanufactur** at Talstr. 9. The **Schauhalle** serves as a museum where you can see finished products (open Tues.-Sun. 8:30am-4:30pm; admission DM5, students DM4). The **Schauwerkstadt** shows the process from clay to painted porcelain (English tapes available; open Tues.-Sun. 8:30am-12:30pm and 1-4:30pm; admission DM4, students DM3). Meißen's gothic **Rathaus** and the **Frauenkirche,** whose porcelain bells chatter every 15 minutes, are right on the main market square (open May-Oct. daily 10am-noon and 1-4pm).

The **tourist office,** An der Frauenkirche 3 (tel. (03521) 45 44 70) is tucked neatly behind the church. Pick up maps or find a room in a private home (DM30 per bed) for a DM4 fee. (Open Mon.-Fri. 10am-6pm, Sat.-Sun. 11am-3pm; Nov.-Easter, closed weekends.) Meißen's best accommodation deal is at the **Jugendherberge (HI),** Wilsdrufferstr. 28 (tel. (03521) 45 30 65), a small house overlooking the city, but it's often booked solid. To get there from the station, cross the footbridge and take the path to the end. Turn left over the tracks and all the way up the hill until you see a store on your left; the hostel is across the street. (Reception open 7-10am and 5-8pm. No lockout, no curfew. DM12.50, over 26 DM15. Breakfast included.)

Meißener Fummel is a very puffed, almost hollow pastry that served as a sort of canary-in-the-mineshaft for traditional porcelain carters; they were required to carry fresh-baked cakes, and drive smoothly enough to keep the air in the *Fummel*. Many *Altstadt* bakeries vend this puffery. At **Spargelzeit,** Hahnemannplatz 17 at the Sächsischer Hof, choose from asparagus, asparagus, or asparagus. (Open daily 11:30am-2:30pm and 5:30-11pm.). Buy your own at the farmers' **market** (Tues.-Fri.). The cityalso has more than its share of **Weinstube**n and **Weinkellers,** including several lining the otherwise taxing route up to the Albrechtsburg.

■■■ SAXON SWITZERLAND (Sächsische Schweiz)

Saxon Switzerland has long been one of Eastern Germany's most beloved holiday destinations; since reunification it has become Germany's newest national park. The region is "Swiss" because of the stunning landscape—Switzerland is used as a catchword. Sandstone cliffs emerge from dense vegetation, offering dramatic views of the surrounding areas from the summit, and excellent hiking on the way up. Less than an hour from Dresden on the Dresden-Prague rail line, the region is a must-see for those convinced that Eastern Germany comes only in shades of gray.

KONIGSTEIN

From Dresden, take the S-Bahn (round-trip DM4) or a *Weiße Flotte* boat (round-trip DM17.50, children DM8) south toward **Schöna** and alight at **Königstein.** The spectacular medieval **fortress** on the cliff has a long and colorful history. Once a retreat for the kings of Saxony during times of civil unrest and marital discord, it was later converted into the most feared state prison around; Nikolai Bakunin and August Bebel were imprisoned here. During the Third Reich, it was used by the Nazis to stash stolen art, and between 1949 and 1955 it served as a juvenile correction center. Recently, skeletons were found in the fortress's torture chamber; no one yet knows which of its incarnations produced them. The complex now houses museums on everything from weapons to porcelain. The view from the fortress is worth every drop of sweat expended to get there—from the city it's a half-hour struggle straight up unless you catch the **Festungs Express,** a tacky train-like vehicle imported for limping Western tourists (DM4; round-trip DM6). From the train station, turn right down Bahnhofstr. Trains for the fortress leave the square regularly (8am-8pm, Oct.-April 9am-5pm), and tour Königstein on their way. (Fortress open mid-April to Sept. 9am-8pm; Oct. 9am-6pm; Nov. to mid-April 9am-5pm. Admission DM5, students DM3. Tours in English available.)

The **tourist office,** on the Marktplatz across from the Festungs Express stop (tel. (035021) 261) books rooms for DM20-30, but in summer it's wise to call ahead. (Open Mon.-Tues. and Thurs.-Fri. 9am-5:30pm, Wed. 1-5:30pm, Sat. 9am-noon; Nov.-March may be open shorter hours.) The nearest **Jugendherberge (HI)** is across the river by ferry (under the train station), and upstream five to 10 minutes by foot at Halberstadt 13 (reception open 7-10am and 3-5:30pm and 7-8pm; DM14, over 26 DM17; breakfast included). The **campground** (tel. (035021) 224) is on the banks of the Elbe about five minutes upstream from the Königstein train station (DM7.50 per person with tent; open April-Oct.).

RATHEN, WEHLEN, AND HOHNSTEIN

Just across the Elbe from Königstein lies a string of villages and the trail heads for a number of hikes varying in difficulty. Climb the challenging **Lilienstein,** or take the S-Bahn downstream from Königstein to **Rathen** and explore the sandstone curiosity **Die Bastei,** a group of towering cliffs in enchanting shapes connected by a constructed sandstone bridge that teeters between the cliffs over the Elbe.

Decent weather facilitates a 5km hike from Rathen to **Wehlen.** Lockers (DM2) for backpacks are available in both towns. The small, cabin-like **Jugendherberge Rathen,** Auf den Halden 33 (tel. (035024) 425) sits in the nature park above Rathen, near the Bastei stones. (Reception open 7-10am and 3-7pm. DM14, over 26 DM16. Breakfast included.) For those with enough time to explore the area, there are great hostels in the small villages nearby. 20km from Königstein or by rail to Pirna and then a half-hour bus ride (direction "Hohnstein") lies **Hohnstein Jugendherberge (HI)** (tel. (035975) 202), housed in a castle with 200 beds, TV, VCR, campfires, and a barbecue. This is as good as hostel life gets. (Reception open 7-10am and 3-10pm. DM13-14, over 26 DM15.50-17. Breakfast included.)

BAD SCHANDAU

One stop farther upstream from Königstein lies Bad Schandau, a miniature village between the Elbe and the mountains. From the train station, take the **ferry** (DM0.80 one-way) to the town of Bad Schandau and follow the signs to the **tourist office,** Markt. 8 (tel. (035022) 24 12), which provides hiking maps and a list of accommodations (open Mon.-Fri. 9am-noon and 1-6pm, Sat. 9am-noon). One wall of the office is plastered with transport schedules; take the Kirnitzschtalbahn to the **Lichtenhainer Waterfall,** a favorite starting point for full-day hikes on the **Schrammsteine.** The tourist office can provide suggestions for shorter or longer hikes, but daytrippers beware; the last ferry back to the Bad Schandau train station leaves at 5:15pm. Overnighters should head on up to the **youth hostel,** Dorfstr. 14 (tel. (035022) 24

08; fax (035022) 24 09), on a plateau above the town (reception open 7-10am and 3-8pm; DM18, over 26 DM21; breakfast included).

■■■ UPPER LUSATIA (Oberlausitz)

Between Dresden and the Polish border stretch the rolling hills of Upper Lusatia (Oberlausitz). Flanked by two former Warsaw Pact neighbors, Upper Lusatia was seldom visited by Westerners. Consequently, the Politburo left much of the region's medieval, Renaissance, and Baroque architecture to rot almost beyond repair. But as the homeland of Germany's only national minority, the **Sorbs** (also called *Wenden*), the area around Bautzen is rich in traditions and customs long abandoned elsewhere. Yes, the Sorbs.

Through historical chance and a tenacious adherence to tradition, small Sorbian-speaking communities totaling about 75,000 members have held on to the region. Sorbian, a Slavic language with similarities to Czech and Polish, was suppressed in Hitler's Reich. While the East German regime made at least a show of tolerating the Sorbian culture, Sorbs were encouraged to leave villages, channeled to the coal mines, and special Sorbian schools were kept under particularly harsh state supervision. The Sorb saga is picking up steam again; a Sorbian National Assembly convened just two days after the fall of the Berlin Wall. The last five years have seen increased attention and protection for the Sorbs, but the pressure to Westernize that affects all of the former GDR is just as strong here, and fewer young people are continuing those old Sorbian ways.

Farther east, the city of Görlitz reveals some of the most ignored, and therefore best-preserved examples of Saxon architecture. Görlitz is also a fine base for hiking, camping, and skiing in the Zittauer Gebirge, a small cranny of Germany between Poland and the Czech Republic. With poor, overbooked hotels and dilapidated cities, this region does not spoon-feed its tourists, and *Ausländer* (foreigners) are still a rare commodity here. But with a dense web of bus connections and steadily improving rail lines, the region's infrastructure is no longer quite so lacking.

BAUTZEN (Budysin)

About 50km northeast of Dresden (1hr. by train), just outside of **Bautzen,** the *Autobahn* ends suddenly. Construction of this famous Nazi work project stopped permanently when Hitler led his people to war in 1939. The highway leaves you in an important cultural capital more than a millennium old, with ancient towers on a hill high above the Spree River. The sight of the old city walls was, in recent decades, a threatening one for the many political prisoners the GDR assigned here. The bilingual street signs (in German and Sorbian) are a dead giveaway that Bautzen (Budysin) is the capital of the **Sorbs**. The **Sorbisches Museum** in the Orlenburg complex in the *Altstadt* (tel. (03591) 424 03), explains the history and culture of the Sorbs, including samples of their writing, life-sized costumes, and the specialty of the area: painted Sorbian Easter eggs. (Open daily 10am-12:30pm and 1-5pm; Nov.-March 10am-12:30pm and 1-4pm. Admission DM2, students DM1.)

To reach the **Altstadt** from the station, walk straight through Rathenauplatz, bear left onto Bahnhofstr., turn left at the post office onto Goschwitzstr., and finally right onto Lavenstr. **Dom St. Petri** (St. Peter's Cathedral) is Eastern Germany's only *Simultankirche,* that is, both Catholic and Protestant at the same time. The division of the church seems a remarkably peaceful 16th-century compromise despite the 4-meter fence that separated the two denominations. The **Domschatz** (cathedral treasure), a phenomenal collection of jewel-studded gowns, icons, and neat gold stuff, is open to tourists only by prior arrangement. Send inquiries to Dom St. Petri zu Bautzen, 02625 Bautzen. (Cathedral open June-Sep. 10am-noon and 1-5pm; May and Oct. 10am-noon and 1-3pm.) Follow the narrow street An der Petrikirche downhill from the cathedral until you see the **Nikolaiturm** to your right. Crossing through the gate, note the face carved above the entrance. Locals claim that this is a likeness of one of their former mayors, the one who was bricked alive into the tower as retribution for opening the city gates to Hussite attackers in the 16th century. Behind the wall lie the ruins of the **Nikolaikirche,** long since used as a local cemetery (open daily dawn-dusk).

From the Nikolaiturm or the Sorbisches Museum, follow the **Osterweg** path around the city walls and along the Spree, taking in the towers of the **Muhlbastei** (milltower), **Alte Wasserkunst** (old water tower), and **Michaeliskirche** along the way. Inside the old water tower is a small museum of crafts and tools (open May-Oct. daily 10am-5pm; admission DM1, students and seniors DM0.50). On the way back up the hill on the other side of the fortress lies the **Hexenhäusrl** (witches' cottage). The small wooden structure was the only home in the area to survive two devastating fires, which led the villagers to shun the inhabitants as witches, though the fire was actually averted by a well inside the house. The cottage is still inhabited.

The **tourist office** (tel. (03591) 420 16) is next to the cathedral on the Fleischmarkt. (Open Mon.-Fri. 9am-6pm, Sat.-Sun. 10am-noon, Oct.-April Mon.-Fri. 9am-6pm, Sat. 10am-noon.) They proffer listings of accommodations in hotels, pensions, or private homes, which may be your best bet as there are few vacancies at the ancient defense tower-*cum*-**Jugendherberge (HI)** in the city center, Am Zwinger 1 (tel. (03591) 440 45), just to your right as you walk through Nikolaiturm. (Reception open daily 7am-10pm. No lockout. Curfew 10pm. DM12.50, over 26 DM15. Breakfast included.) For a taste of local cuisine, the **Sorbisches Café,** just across from the post office, has hearty homemade soups for DM4 (open Mon.-Fri. 8am-11pm, Sat. 11am-midnight, Sun. 11am-11pm). Or, try dining at **Wjelbik,** Kornstr. 7, a period building with an old-style Sorbian spread (open daily 11am-midnight).

NEAR BAUTZEN

Today the Sorbian language is seldom heard in the city, but buses leave regularly for villages such as **Panschwitz-Kuckau** and **Neuschwitz,** where both the mother tongue and the colorful, traditional costumes are alive and well. If your timing is right, you can take in one of the raucous celebrations held on Catholic holidays. Easter, when the people of Bautzen and neighboring towns gather to ride around on horses "proclaiming the good news," is the highlight of the year. Another favorite is January 25, the **Marriage of the Birds** (Vogelhochzeit), when Sorbian children dressed in awkward bird costumes run screeching through the village to represent local birds' gratefulness for the birdseed left by their human friends.

To learn more before you go, or for transport information, head to the **Sorbische Kultur-Information,** Kurt-Pchalek-Str. 26 (tel. (03591) 421 05) in Bautzen, around the corner from the post office (open Mon.-Fri. 9am-4:30pm). For regional bus information, go to the terminal at August-Bebel-Platz in Bautzen where the **Überlandlinien** (long-distance) boats depart, and take time to decipher the schedules.

GÖRLITZ

The easternmost town in Germany, Görlitz offers an untouristed *Altstadt* that has changed little since Napoleon came back and forth in his unsuccessful invasion of Russia. The pastel Baroque elegance of the homes of local *Burgermeisters* are a real surprise. With relatively direct rail connections to Bautzen, Zittau, and Dresden (as well as Wroctaw and Breslau in neighboring Poland), and access to a number of major bus routes, Görlitz is a good base for exploring Upper Lusatia.

The **Dreifaltigkeitskirche,** on the Obermarkt, is open only on weekdays from 3 to 5pm and for Sunday services. Originally a 13th-century Franciscan monastery, the church shows signs of frequent expansion, but its 1428 choir benches are still in use today. Pick up information on other local sights including the best astronomical clock this side of Prague and the nearby **Marienthal cloister** at the **tourist office,** Obermarkt 29 (tel. (03581) 40 69 99) which also sells maps and finds rooms (DM25-35) in private homes for a DM5 fee (open Mon.-Fri. 9am-5pm, Sat. 9am-noon). Görlitz has one of the largest **youth hostels** in the area, Goethestr. 17 (tel. (03581) 40 65 10). You'll likely find a bed here. To reach the hostel, take the south exit (*Südausgang*) of the train station, bear left up the hill, turn right onto Zittauerstr., and take it all the way around until you meet Goethestr. Turn left; the hostel is ahead on the right. (Reception open 5-10pm. No lockout. Curfew 10pm. DM17.50, seniors DM20. Breakfast included.) For food, shun the overpriced cafés on Berlinerstr. and head for the *Altstadt*, where many small restaurants serve up hearty fare, often with a slightly Slavic feel. Try *Ujlbanka* soup, a clear broth with *Wurst*.

■■■ ZITTAUER GEBIRGE

In a sliver of Germany that borders on both Bohemia and Poland rise the rocky cliffs of the Zittauer Gebirge. In 1491, this was the scene of the vicious **Bierkrieg** (beer war). The citizens of Görlitz protested Zittau's success as a beer-brewing town by destroying several barrels of the beverage. The Zittauers stole animals from surrounding farms in retaliation and the spat wasn't resolved until nearby towns agreed to chip in on reparations payments. More recently, the local forests have suffered from a heavy concentration of textile industry, though these days it is the people of the region who are hurting as their inefficient factories close. If you're cutting through Czechoslovakia to get from the mountains to Dresden or Königstein, **trains** leave daily from Zittau for **Decín** (DM15). Buy a ticket that isn't restricted to Reichsbahn trains. Decín is also a good hub for traffic bound to Prague and Budapest. Direct connections to Zittau from Dresden take two hours.

ZITTAU

Zittau is itself an attractive, though neglected, town of about 4000. Its major attractions are the **Rathaus,** designed by Prussian architect Frederick Schinkel, and the **Stadtmuseum,** housed in a former Franciscan monastery. Don't miss the spellbinding collection of medieval torture devices in the cellar. (Open Wed. 10am-noon and 1-6pm, Thurs. 10am-noon and 1-4pm, Fri. 10am-1pm, Sun. 9am-noon and 2-5pm. Admission DM2.50, students DM1.50) The **tourist office,** Rathausplatz 6 (tel. (03583) 51 26 31) right behind the city hall, helps with rooms and provides hiking maps (open Mon.-Wed. and Fri. 9am-5pm, Tues. and Thurs. 9am-6pm). The four hotels in town run about DM50 per person; getting a private room or vacation cabin through the tourist office is more economical. Near the tourist office is the historic, hearty fare of the **Kloster Stüb'l,** between Klosterplatz and Marktplatz (open Mon.-Sat. 11am-10pm). The restaurant, founded in 1050, claims to be the oldest cloister brewery in the world. Try the *Mauke mit Gewiegtebrutl und Sauerkraut* (DM8).

OYBIN

From the train station, hop on the **Schmalspurbahn** (steam train) and steam into Oybin on the 100-year-old coach. **Oybin,** with its half-timbered houses and monumental cliffs, is a nice half-day trip for sightseers, and will keep hikers and skiers amused for longer. At the top of the cliffs are the ruins of a High Gothic **fortress.** In the summer, concerts are held in the halls of the old **monastery.** From here one can see far into Czech Bohemia. The **tourist office,** Feiligrathstr. 8 (tel. (035844) 346) will outfit you with hiking maps, town maps, bus schedules, and rooms in private homes or pensions. Although list prices hover at DM10-15, beware of the *Kurtax*. As a *Kurort* (curing place), accommodations here cost a few marks more, a relic of the *Magic Mountain*-era attempt to tax tuberculosis patients as they came to the hills to breathe the clean air and rest (office open Mon.-Fri. 9am-5:30pm, Sat. 10am-3pm). Accessible by **Schmalspurbahn** (steam train), the **Jugendherberge Jonsdorf (HI)** consists of two houses about 1km apart. The office is at Hainstr. 14; call in advance (tel. (035844) 220; DM14, over 26 DM17). Take a bus or hike the 5km to Jonsdorf's twin hostel in **Waltersdorf** (tel. (035841) 26 50), accessible only by foot from the village (DM15, over 26 DM18).

CHEMNITZ

■■■ CHEMNITZ

For forty years, the old city of Chemnitz went by the name "Karl-Marx-Stadt." In 1953, the city was renamed in an unsubtle tribute to the philosopher, who never even called it home. Marx might not have objected, however, as Chemnitz was full of the factory workers whose social position was the focus of his life's work. Reunification has brought back the name Chemnitz, but has not done much about the scars of decades of haphazard industrial growth; the city has been largely ignored by redevelopers. The Chemnitzers' decision to leave all their socialist-era statues, plaques, and paraphernalia intact give the city a kind of twisted-nostalgia value. You've come to the right place to see Karl-Marx-Str. or signs reading "*Es lebt die mächtige Sowietische Union!*" (Long live the mighty Soviet Union!). Tourist information will tell you to hurry before it's gone, but the city government is more honest, promising only long-term changes.

The most interesting attractions in Chemnitz are the city's remaining socialist-inspired public artwork. Every streetcorner has a statue or two, but nothing can outshine the distressingly pompous **head of Karl Marx** at the corner of Str. der Nationen and Brückenstr. **Straße der Nationen** is itself quite a period piece; the aggressively broad avenue is lined with boxy socialist-era towers designed to evoke certain post-Stalinist districts in Moscow. They're all too successful, in spite of the Siemens and Mercedes billboards that have been added in the last few years.

Continuing down Str. der Nationen will take you to the minuscule remnants of the city's once-sprawling **Altstadt.** Chemnitz's strategic industrial importance guaranteed heavy Allied bombing in the last war. Practically all that remains is the **Roter Turm,** a 12th-century relic of the city walls (open Tues.-Sun. 9am-6pm; admission DM2, students and seniors DM1), and the old **Rathaus** and the *Jugendstil* structures surrounding it. Closer to the train station is the **Museum am Theaterplatz,** with painting, local history, and natural history on display in a wide hall behind a grove of petrified trees. (Open Tues. and Thurs.-Sun. 10am-6pm, Wed. 10am-9pm. Admission DM3, students and seniors DM2.) The **Hotel Chemnitzer Hof,** also on Theaterplatz, is one of the Bauhaus architectural school's last original constructions.

Tourist Information Chemnitz, Str. der Nationen 3 (tel. (0371) 620 51), fax 615 83), sings the praises of the city a little too fervently, but the staff is helpful and they're very good natured about the whole Karl Marx thing. Buy your postcard of the bust here or sign up for a tour. (90min. Tues. and Thurs. at 10am, Sat. at 1:30pm. DM9, students and seniors DM6.)

Chemnitz charges big-city prices for elusive hotel rooms. Even private rooms are overpriced. Expect to pay DM50-70 per person (plus a DM2 fee) if you book through the tourist office. **AIGNER** (tel. and fax (0371) 451 91), a private agency in the main hall of the train station, runs DM35-50 per person (fee included; open Mon.-Fri. 8am-8pm, Sat.-Sun. 8am-2pm). A stunningly renovated **Jugendherberge (HI)** awaits at Augustusburger Str. 369 (tel. (0371) 713 31). Take streetcar #1 or 6 (direction "Gablenz") to the end, or regional bus #T245 and ask the driver to let you off. Don't even think of walking. From May to September, some renovated bungalows add to the capacity. (Reception open 3-7pm with reservations, 5-7pm without. DM17.50, over 26 DM21. Bungalows DM12.50, over 26 DM15. Breakfast included.) Check the program at the **Schauspielhaus,** Str. der Nationen 33 (tel. (0371) 614 15), on the Theaterplatz (ticket office open Mon.-Fri. 10am-5pm and before shows).

■ Near Chemnitz: Augustusburg

After the dubious architecture and choking air-quality in Chemnitz, get a bus (from the *Busbahnhof*, down Georgstr. from the train station; 20min.) for Augustusburg, a mountaintop hamlet. The Renaissance **hunting lodge** of the Saxon Electors is perched above town. A guided tour (required) of the royal playhouse will lead you through the **Brunnenhaus** (well house), a **carriage museum,** and the intimate **Schloßkapelle,** whose walls are festooned with Cranach-School paintings depicting royals dining with Jesus and assisting John the Baptist (tours every 20-30min.; admission DM2.50, students and seniors DM1.50). On your own time, explore the **Motorcycle Museum** (admission DM5, students and seniors DM3), the **Hunting and Game Museum** (admission DM3, students and seniors DM2), or climb the tower (admission DM1) for an excellent view of the nearby Erz Mountains. (*Schloß* open Mon.-Fri. 9am-6pm, Sat.-Sun. 9am-6:30pm; Nov.-March Mon.-Fri. 9am-5pm, Sat.-Sun. 10am-5:30pm). The **Jugendherberge (HI)**, in the castle (tel. (037291) 250), may soon be in the hands of luxury hotel builders; call ahead.

■■■ LEIPZIG

Leipzig is remembered, along with Frankfurt, as one of the cradles of German liberty. The "Wars of Liberation" that kicked Napoleon out of Germany in 1815 began here two years earlier, and the city enthusiastically joined the wave of rebellions that broke out in Europe in 1830 and 1848-49. More recently, Leipzig has become Germany's *Heldenstadt* (city of heroes) for its role as the crucible of *die Wende*, the sudden toppling of the GDR, in 1989. What began as weekly "Monday Meetings" at the Nikolaikirche exploded into a series of massive popular protests until the communist government finally called on the military to quash the demonstrations. On October 9, 1989, 70,000 people marched in Leipzig, called the government's bluff, and stood their ground. For reasons that may never be entirely clear, the government backed down. The next Monday the crowds grew to over 120,000 demonstrators, and two days later Party chief Erich Honecker resigned.

Badly scarred in World War II, Leipzig compensates for its lack of beauty with one of Europe's more brilliant cultural pedigrees. Originally, the city gained its fame through music and letters; Goethe loved Leipzig for its well-educated populace. His alma mater, Leipzig University, founded in 1409, upholds an illustrious tradition that embraces the names of Leibniz, Lessing, and Nietzsche, among others. The dozens of bookstores in the *Altstadt* recall Leipzig's pre-war position as capital of the European publishing industry, and several major international book fairs take place here annually. Leipzig's musical heritage began in 1723 when Johann Sebastian Bach settled here, entrancing local churchgoers with his early works. A century later, Felix Mendelssohn founded the *Leipzig Gewandhaus Orchester*, still a superb ensemble. Conductor Kurt Masur, who led the city's orchestra to international prominence in the 1980s, was one of many figures in the arts who helped the 1989 demonstrations to remain peaceful and move forward in 1989; their experience typifies the sometimes chaotic convergence of culture, politics, and urban life which is still deeply felt in Leipzig.

ORIENTATION AND PRACTICAL INFORMATION

Leipzig is a fairly compact city, with most sights and the entertainment center in the **Innenstadt,** a circular area lying just south of the main train station. The **Leipziger Hauptbahnhof** is one of Europe's largest train stations; its cavernous halls recall the grander days of rail travel. Fast inter-city trains now make Dresden and Berlin less than two hours away. Few trains run out of the **Bayerischer Bahnhof,** but as the oldest station in Europe still taking traffic, it is worth seeing for its looming, Neoclassical facade. By the summer of 1993, the project of changing socialist-era political street names (Ho-Chi-Minh-Str., etc.) was virtually complete, and all maps and street signs bear the new names.

Tourist Office: Leipzig Information, Sachsenplatz 1 (tel. 795 90). From the train station, walk through the Platz der Republik in front of the main station and bear right past the Park Hotel, about a 5-min. walk. Grab a copy of their city brochure and the magazines *Leipzig Live* and *Blitz*. Book rooms here for a DM5 fee. Reception open Mon.-Fri. 9am-7pm, Sat.-Sun. 9:30am-2pm. *Zimmervermittlung* (room-finding service) open Mon.-Fri. 9am-8pm, Sat. 9:30am-2pm. These services may merge by 1994. Another information office is located at the **Hauptbahnhof.** It has the same services but less information (open Mon.-Fri. 9am-6pm, Sat. 9am-noon). Another location is at **Flughafen Leipzig-Halle,** with the same services (open Mon.-Fri. 7am-9pm, Sat.-Sun. 9am-6pm).

Tours: The tourist office leads 2-hr. bus tours daily at 1:30pm for DM20, students and seniors DM12. Walking tours (1½ hrs.) daily in the summer at 4pm for DM10. Some English-speaking guides.

Budget Travel: Bavaria Geschäfts und Studentenreisebüro, Augustusplatz 9, in a courtyard just off Universitätstr. (tel. 211 42 40). Affiliated with STA and Kilroy travel (open Mon.-Fri. 10am-6pm).

Consulates: U.S., Wilhelm-Seyferth-Str. 4 (tel. 211 78 66). Entrance on Wächstr. behind the Museum der bildenen Kunst (open Mon.-Fri. 9am-noon or by appointment). Also home to the **Amerika Haus Bibliothek** (tel. 211 78 70; open Tues. and Thurs. 11am-5pm, Wed. 11am-7:30pm).

Currency Exchange: Deutsche Verkehrsbank in the *Hauptbahnhof* (tel. 29 48 89). DM1 fee per transaction. Decent rates. (Open Mon.-Fri. 7am-7:30pm, Sat. 8am-6pm.) There is no place that will change money in Leipzig on Sundays, so plan accordingly.

American Express, Maritim Hotel Astoria, across from the Rudolf-Breitscheid-Str. exit of the *Hauptbahnhof.* Currency exchange, money wired, mail held. Rates similar to banks and train station (open Mon.-Fri. 9am-5:30pm, Sat. 9am-noon).

Post Office: Hauptpostamt 1, across from Augustusplatz on Grimmaischestr., 04109 Leipzig. A 5-min. walk from train station: bear left past the opera to Augustus Platz and cross to the 50s-style structure. **Poste Restante** in phone section. Open Mon.-Fri. 8am-7pm, Sat. 9am-2pm, Sun. 10am-1pm. Not all services are available from 6-7pm or on weekends. **Postamt 17,** in the *Hauptbahnhof* across from platforms 7-10, has been closed since 1991, but may reopen by 1994.

Telephones: At the post office, or use the flashy new telephone card booths all over the city center. City code: 0341.

Flights: Flughafen Leipzig-Halle in Schkeudingasse about 20km from Leipzig. International service throughout central Europe. Buses leave from the *Hauptbahnhof* Mon.-Fri. and Sun. every half-hour from 5am-9pm, Sat. every 45min. 5am-8:45pm.

Trains: (tel. 702 11). Leipzig lies on the Berlin-Munich line with regular InterCity service to Frankfurt am Main. Information counter on the platform near track 15.

Public Transportation: Streetcars cover the city (DM0.50, day-card from 9am-midnight DM3, 24-hr. card DM4.20, 72-hr. card DM8). Unless you are staying in an outlying area, the cards won't pay off. An efficient S-Bahn service covers outlying suburbs. Both S-Bahn and streetcars run from 5:30am until about 1am, with infrequent night service on some streetcar lines. Free maps are available from the tourist office.

Taxis: tel. 74 11 or 795 55.

Car Rental: Avis, Richard-Wagner-Str. 1-5 (tel. 214 58 44). **Europcar InterRent** in the west Hall of the Hauptbahnhof (tel. 211 38 34; open Mon.-Fri. 7am-6pm). **Sixt Budget,** Augustusplatz 5-6, in the Hotel Deutschland (tel. 214 66). All also have offices at the airport. Names of smaller, cheaper agencies are available through the tourist office.

Hitchhiking: *Let's Go* does not recommend hitchhiking as a safe mode of transportation. Those headed to Dresden and Prague may take S-Bahn #2 or bus #65 to "Engelsdorf Ost," turn left onto Bahnhofstr., then right onto Leipzigerstr., then walk to the *Autobahn* interchange. Those headed to Berlin might consider taking streetcar #16 to "Essener Str.," switching to bus F, get out at Sachsenpark and walking to the *Autobahn.* For ride shares, the **Mitfahrzentrale** is at Rudol Breitscheidstr. 39 (tel. 211 42 22, fax 20 06 71). Open daily 9am-8pm. Another Mitfahrzentrale is located at Universität Leipzig (tel. 719 20 97), near the student travel office.

Luggage Storage: Lockers at the station are located by tracks 3 and 24 and between the east and west halls of the station (DM2). Luggage storage down the stairs from platform 1 charges DM4 per piece per day, DM 6 per bike. Open daily 6am-9:45pm

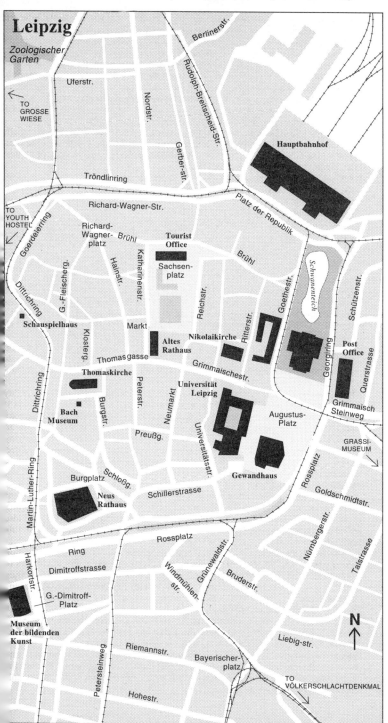

Leipzig

Zoologischer Garten

TO GROSSE WIESE

TO YOUTH HOSTEL

Uferstr.

Nordstr.

Gerber-str.

Berlinerstr.

Rudolph-Breitscheid-Str.

Trödlinring

Richard-Wagner-Str.

Platz der Republik

Hauptbahnhof

Goerdelerring

Richard-Wagner-platz

Brühl

Brühl

Tourist Office

Sachsenplatz

Schwanenteich

Dittrichring

G.-Fleischerg.

Hainstr.

Katharinenstr.

Reichstr.

Goethestr.

Schützenstr.

Schauspielhaus

Markt

Klosterg.

Ritterstr.

Georgiring

Post Office

Querstrasse

Thomasgasse

Altes Rathaus

Nikolaikirche

Grimmaischestr.

Grimmaisch Steinweg

Thomaskirche

Burgstr.

Peterstr.

Neumarkt

Universität Leipzig

Augustus-Platz

GRASSI-MUSEUM

Bach Museum

Preußg.

Universitätsstr.

Gewandhaus

Rossplatz

Goldschmidtstr.

Martin-Luther-Ring

Dittrichring

Schloßg.

Burgplatz

Neus Rathaus

Schillerstrasse

Nürnbergerstr.

Talstrasse

Harkortstr.

Ring

Dimitroffstrasse

Rossplatz

Windmühlen-str.

Grünewaldstr.

Bruderstr.

G.-Dimitroff-Platz

Museum der bildenden Kunst

Riemannstr.

Bayerischer-platz

Liebig-str.

N

Petersteinweg

Hohestr.

TO VÖLKERSCHLACHTDENKMAL

Lost Property: Fundbüro, on the eastern side of the train station (tel. 724 32 65). Open Mon. and Wed.-Fri. 7am-noon and 12:30-3:15pm, Tues. 9:45am-noon and 12:30-6pm.

Bookstores: Internationale Buchhandlung, Peterstr. 13 (tel. 20 95 20). A small assortment of English. **Buch und Medium International,** Salzgäßchen 21/Handelshof (tel. 29 17 94), specializes in foreign novels and travel guides. **Buchhandlung Franz-Mehring-Haus,** Goethestr. 3-5, near the opera house (tel. 29 26 45) will have a wide selection of English books by 1994. Open Mon.-Wed. and Fri. 9am-6pm, Thurs. 9am-7pm, and Sat. 9am-1pm.

Laundromat: Waschsalon, Georg Schwartzstr. 124 or Diekaustr. 53.

Pharmacies: Löwen Apotheke, Grimmaischestr. 19 (tel. 29 20 14), is open Mon.-Tues. and Fri. 8am-6pm, Wed. 9am-6pm, Thurs. 8am-7pm, and Sat. 9am-2pm. Whenever the shop is closed, push the button by the door for emergency service.

Information Lines: Frauenberatungsstelle (Women's Aid Hotline) tel. 237 42 29. **Gay and Lesbian Information:** tel. 882 11 94.

Ambulance: tel. 115. **Police:** tel. 110

ACCOMMODATIONS AND CAMPING

Leipzig's hotels have always catered to Western business people. Budget travelers are still a novelty here, though they are not, unfortunately, as rare as budget rooms to house them. The tourist office books rooms in private homes, but even these range upwards from DM40 for a single with breakfast. Although there's no danger of not finding a room, the youth hostels and camping grounds are without a doubt your best bet. For longer stays the **Mitwohnzentrale,** Rudolph-Breitscheidstr. 39 (tel. 211 42 22) can be of service. According to the tourist office, plans are underway to open at least one more youth hostel in central Leipzig. Of the numerous nearby hostels, only **Jugendherberge Grethen (HI)** in Grethen (tel. (03437) 34 49) is a tolerable distance from Leipzig by rail (DM15, over 26 DM18; breakfast included).

Jugendherberge Leipzig Centrum (HI), Käthe-Kollwitz-Str. 64 (tel. 47 05 30, fax 47 58 88). Streetcar #2 (from the main station, direction "Plagwitz") or streetcar #1 (direction "Lausen"): Marchnerstr. (4 stops). Continue down the street; the hostel is on the right. A large institutional hostel with plenty of beds. Also conveniently close to the city center, with plenty of urban sounds to lull you to sleep. Reception open 7-9am and 2:30-10pm. Curfew 1am. DM17.50, over 26 DM21. Breakfast included.

Jugendherberge Leipzig Am Auensee (HI), Gustav-Esche-Str. 4, 04159 Leipzig (tel. 571 89), in the nearby suburb of Wahren. Streetcar #10 or #28 (from the main station, direction "Wahren"): Rathaus Wahren, turn left at the city hall and follow the signs. A restful abode in a leafy area overlooking a relatively pristine lake. Tidy rooms and gracious owners. This place soothes the soul. Reception open 7am-8pm. No curfew. DM14, over 26 DM17. Half- or full-pension may be a good idea, as the hostel is far from the city center, and there are few food options in Wahren. Management recommends booking 2 months in advance, but call from the station.

Hotel Grünau, Gärtnerstr. 177, 04209 Leipzig (tel. 412 61 50, fax 412 61 58). S Bahn 1 (direction "Militzer Allee"): Grünauer Allee (8 stops). Come up the stairs from the station and the hotel is in sight. Large hotel in a harmless suburb 20min from city center. Newly renovated rooms, some with TV. Dinner in the restaurant downstairs under DM10. Reception open until 11pm, but call ahead. Singles DM52-69. Doubles DM82-109. Breakfast included.

Pension Hilleman, Rosa-Luxemburg-Str. 2 (tel. 28 24 82). From the east hall of the *Hauptbahnhof,* cross over to Wintergartenstr., following this for two blocks, after which you will see the pension on the other side of the intersection with Rosa-Luxemburg-Str. A handful of spacious and well-kept rooms will bed down the wandering traveler for the night, and a hall shower will wash away the grime. No curfew. Singles with TV DM35. Doubles with TV DM70. Breakfast included.

Campingplatz am Auensee, Gustav-Esche-Str. 5 (tel. 212 30 31), down the road past the youth hostel. Tents DM5. Caravans DM10.

Campingplatz am Kulkwitzer See, Seestr. in Markrandstadt (tel. 478 21 68). Streetcar #8 (direction "Lausen") to the last stop and bear right. Open April 15-Oct. 15.

FOOD

The **Innenstadt** offers a whole range of *Imbiß* (snack joints), bistros, and restaurants, many of which have gone very upmarket in the last few years. Local farmers and Greek and Turkish merchants offer their fresh produce Tuesdays and Fridays in **Sachsenplatz,** in front of the tourist office. **Tengelmann Supermarket** is on Brühl, also near the tourist office (open Mon.-Wed. and Fri. 7am-6:30pm, Thurs. 7am-8:30pm, Sat. 7am-2pm).

Bistro am Brühl, on the Brühl, just across from the supermarket and down the street from the tourist office. This sidewalk café (not to be confused with the pricey restaurant upstairs) feeds for DM6-10. The view isn't lovely, but at least you can sit outside. Open daily 11am-10pm.

Universität Leipzig Mensa, streetcar #17 (direction "Böhlitz-Ehrenberg") to the 4th stop. Student cafeteria has plain fare for pretty prices. Meals DM3-8. ID technically required, but look like a German student and they'll take your money. Go to the last register to pay in cash. Open mid-Oct. to Feb. and April to mid-July.

Antiquitäten Café Galerie "Kleinod", Käthe-Kollwitz-Str. 71. From the hostel, turn left and walk about two blocks; the restaurant is across the street. Elegant mismatched chairs at antique tables among beautiful boudoirs, faulty accordions, and dusty hand-puppets. Eleven different clocks show eleven different times—an excuse to linger. Arty clientele enjoys soups and small salads (chicory salad with honey and nuts, DM8). Open daily 2-10pm; kitchen closes at 9:30pm.

Auerbachs Keller, Mädlerpassage (tel. 20 91 93), behind the *Altes Rathaus*. Rumor has it that Goethe stayed here late into the night writing the classic *Faust*. In any case, the restaurant appears in the play and frescoes inside the building depict some of the more famous scenes. Mephisto brought forth free wine here, and that may well have been the last bargain the place ever saw. Very touristy, with prices to match. Entrees around DM30; the Goethe thrill might not be worth it. Open Mon. 10:30am-6pm, Tues.-Sat. 10:30am-noon and 3-6pm, Sun. 11am-noon and 4-8pm.

Restaurant Nudelmacher, Peterstr., just off the Markt and across from Thomaskirche. Locals pack in for pasta and meat dishes. (Open Mon.-Wed. and Fri.-Sat. 9am-8pm, Thurs. 9am-9pm, Sun. 11am-8pm. DM8-12.)

SIGHTS

Leipzig's historic *Innenstadt* suffered less from the bombing of World War II than from the frenzied and poorly planned building of the socialist era. But in **Sachsenplatz,** the sooty façades of early 18th-century **Bürgerhäuser** (Burgers' Houses) can be seen clearly if you look past the tired cement of the Platz itself. The heart of the city beats on the **Marktplatz,** a colorful, cobblestone square, guarded by the somewhat crooked, 16th-century **Altes Rathaus.** Inside, a grand festival hall runs above the **Museum für Geschichte der Stadt Leipzig,** offering a straightforward look at Leipzig's history. (Open Tues.-Fri. 10am-6pm, Sat.-Sun. 10am-4pm. Admission DM3, students DM1.50, children DM0.50.) Behind the *Altes Rathaus,* on Nikolaistr., the 300-year-old **Nikolaikirche** saw the birth of Bach's *Johannes Passion* and Germany's peaceful revolution. (Open Mon.-Fri. 10am-6pm, Sun. services 9:30am, 11am, and 5pm.)

Continuing away from the Marktplatz, take Universitätsstr. to the former Karl Marx University, now rechristened **Universität Leipzig.** Its "Sharp Tooth" tower, a steel and concrete behemoth, displaced the centuries-old Universitätskirche and other popular buildings following a wave of student protests in 1968. A massive outdoor frieze of Lenin leading the students now overlooks Augustusplatz, but the dated icon may fall soon. The university also has an **Ägyptisches Museum** (Egyptian Museum), Schillerstr. 6 (tel. 28 21 66), created out of archaeology department finds. (Open Tues.-Fri. 2-6pm, Sun. 10am-1pm. Admission DM1, students DM0.50.)

Past the University and down Grimmaischer Steinweg is the **Grassimuseum,** Johannisplatz, an Art Deco building home to three small museums. The university's **Musikinstrumenten-Museum** contains more than 3500 musical instruments, some dating back to the 16th century. (Open Tues.-Fri. 9am-5pm, Sat. 10am-5pm, Sun. 10am-1pm. Admission DM3, students DM1.50.) Enter the courtyard to find the **Museum des Kunsthandwerk.** (Open Tues. and Thurs.-Fri. 10am-6pm, Wed. 10am-8pm, Sat.-Sun. 10am-5pm. Admission DM3, students DM1.50.) The **Austellungsraum Grassimuseum,** on the far side of the Grassimuseum on Pragerstr., is an increasingly well-noted magnet for international art exhibitions. Recent temporary exhibits in this bright, bare, quasi-industrial space have mostly consisted of modern and postmodern artists from all over Europe.

The striking but not-entirely-pretty **Neues Rathaus** lies at the end of Schillerstr.; behind it cross over Martin-Luther-Ring to the **Museum der Bildenden Kunst,** Georg-Dimitroff-Platz 1, a ponderously impressive collection of more than 2500 paintings and sculptures, including works by van Eyck, Dürer, Rubens, Kolbe, Rembrandt, and Rodin. (Open Tues. and Thurs.-Sun. 9am-5pm, Wed. 1-9:30pm. Admission DM5, students DM2.50, free on Sun.) Just north of the *Neues Rathaus* and close to the Marktplatz is the **Thomaskirche** where J.S. Bach served as cantor. When Bach's original burial site was destroyed in World War II, his remains were interred here in front of the altar; the memorial statue, showing Bach with empty pockets, says a lot about the genius's impoverished success. A stained-glass window commemorates Martin Luther's trip here in the early Reformation. Mozart and Mendelssohn also performed in this church, and Wagner was baptized here in 1813 (open daily 8am-6pm; in winter 9am-5pm; services Sun. 9:30am and 6pm). Across the street, the **Johann-Sebastian-Bach-Museum,** Thomaskirchehof 16, chronicles Bach's work and years in Leipzig, 1723-1750. (Open daily 9am-5pm; last entry 4:30pm. Admission DM2, students and seniors DM1. Tours daily at 11am and 3pm.)

Not far north of the Thomaskirche is Leipzig's newest and most moving museum. The **Museum der "Runden Ecke,"** Dittrichring 24, the former headquarters of the East German Ministry for State Security, or **Stasi,** is now home to a permanent exhibition "Stasi-Macht und Banalität" (Power and Banality, an echo of Hannah Arendt's line on the "banality of evil"). The small collection fills just a few rooms of the giant building from which Leipzig residents were constantly surveyed. On exhibit are the excesses of paranoia and power that allowed Stasi to monitor nearly every phone call, car trip, and letter sent in the area.

The museum also chronicles the process by which Leipzig's citizens overthrew the Stasi terror. As the Monday Demonstrations in the Nikolaikirche grew progressively larger, Stasi nerves began to jitter; video cameras over the Innenstadt recorded the faces of thousands of protestors. The weekly marches often ended at the Stasi headquarters; the wax from candlelight vigils on the front steps can still be seen. On the night of December 4-5, 1989, the people of Leipzig took over the Stasi building. Inside they found some 50,000 letters seized over the last 40 years, and entire floors devoted to documentation of the actions and whereabouts of suspected resistors. The simple sight of 10,000 names of Stasi-suspects on one wall (reminiscent of the Vietnam War memorial in Washington, D.C.) sums up the experience with eloquent force.

Outside of the city lies a memorial to Leipzig's first self-liberation. The **Völkerschlachtdenkmal** (tel. 861 19 62) on the *Süd-Friedhof* remembers the 400,000 soldiers engaged in the 1813 Battle of Nations—a struggle that turned the tide against Napoleon and determined many of Europe's present national boundaries. The monument itself is an interesting remnant of Prussian nationalistic pomposity. Climb the 500 steps to the platform for a view all the way to the Harz Mountains. To reach the monument, take streetcar #15 or 20 (direction "Meusdorf" or "Probstheida,

20min.) from the *Hauptbahnhof* to the Völkerschlachtdenkmal stop. (Open daily 9am-5pm. Admission DM2, students and seniors DM1.)

ENTERTAINMENT

Leipzig's streets echo with the very best in classical music. Try to hear the **Gewandhaus Orchestra,** a major international orchestra since 1843. Kurt Masur still leads the Gewandhaus, even as he shuttles to conduct the New York Philharmonic. Some concerts are free; otherwise buy tickets (DM7 and up; 30% student discount) at the Gewandhaus box office, Augustusplatz 8 (tel. 713 22 80; open Mon. 1-6pm, Tues.-Fri. 10am-6pm, Sat. 10am-2pm; no concerts in August). Leipzig's **Opera** (tel. 29 10 36) is also widely praised, and gives Dresden's Semper company a run for its money. Tickets run from DM8-50, with a 50% student discount (except premieres). Head to the ticket counter, Augustusplatz 12, for more information (open Mon.-Fri. 10am-6pm, Sat.-Sun. 10am-1pm, and 90 minutes before a show).

The opera house is also the entry point to Leipzig's diverse **theater** scene. Leipzig's opera company heads up the **Kellertheater** (tel 29 10 36), in the basement of the opera house, a home for experimental theater. Soon to reopen is the opera's **Musikalische Komödie Theater,** Dreilindenstr. 30 (tel. 29 10 36), which belts out Broadway-type musicals and show-tune medleys, many in English. Always recognized for its theater, Leipzig has experienced a wave of experimental plays in the wake of the revolution. Check local magazines for other theater possibilities or play it safe with the gallant old favorite, the **Schauspielhaus,** Bosestr. 1, just off Dittrichring (tel. 792 21 66; open Mon.-Fri. 10am-6pm, Sat. 10am-1pm).

In 1994, Leipzig will celebrate a musical and political triumph as the 69th **Bach-Fest** runs from March 30 to April 5, 1994. The first since the fall of the GDR, the Bach Festival can now proceed without socialist restrictions, and most importantly, is timed to coincide with Holy Week, allowing Bach's Saint Matthew and St. John *Passions* and Easter cantatas to be performed on exactly the days and in exactly the churches for which Bach himself envisaged them. For tickets, write the **Bach-Archiv,** Thomaskirchhof 16, 04109 Leipzig, or call (0341) 78 66, or fax at (0341) 27 53 08. Also stop by the **Thomaskirche** for a performance of the world-class **Thomanerchor** (Thomas Choir) or an organ recital. (Dates vary; tel. 47 56 12 or 47 03 34 for specifics.) The Bach Museum also has information on its weekly concerts in the **Bach-Saal** (tickets DM12, students and seniors DM7).

Cult movies, usually in the original language, are shown three times a day at the **Kino im Grassi,** Täubchenweg 2d in Johannisplatz (tel. 28 71 39). Ask at the tourist office for a schedule. Movies run about DM5. Take in a film and discuss it at the **film inter café,** Burgstr. 7 (tel. 20 08 30), near Thomaskirche (open daily 11am-1am).

NIGHTLIFE

Locals complain that the nightlife isn't what it used to be in the days before the Wall fell, since those most willing to walk on the wild side went west after the borders opened. Common among those who stayed is a belief that West is Best. All the same, remaining students keep things hopping.

Bars, Clubs, and Discos

Moritzbastei, just off Augustusplatz (tel. 29 29 32) is a fascinating student nightclub amid the ruins of the old town wall. Sometimes you'll think that the entire student population is here to take in live jazz, rock, and folk concerts, or to dance away the late-night hours in the disco. Diverse alternative crowd; gay and lesbian couples barely get a second look. Café/bar open daily 2pm-midnight. Disco or concerts from 9 or 10pm. Admission DM4-10. Ticket counter open Mon. noon-6pm, Tues.-Fri. noon-2pm and before shows.)

Schauspielhaus (tel. 28 10 23). A disco, not to be confused with the theater hall. A trendy multi-story affair on Dittrichring (open daily 9pm-5am).

Haus Leipzig, Elsterstr. 22-24 (tel. 269 99 99), might be hosting a local folk dancing troupe or a ranting rave; try your luck.

Esplanade, Richard-Wagner-Str. 10 (tel. 28 23 30), plays disco and dance music for a thirty-something gay crowd. Open nightly 9pm-5am.

Cabarets

Kabarett "Academixer," just off Universitätstr. on Kupfergasse 6 (tel. 20 08 49). The Leipzig student community deploys wry satire and recreates a 1920s Cabaret atmosphere—very Joel Grey, very last days of the Weimar Republic.

The Leipziger Pfeffermühle, Thomaskirchhof 16 (tel. 29 58 77), offers even more political jabs; Chancellor Helmut Kohl is an ample source. (Ticket office open Mon.-Fri. 2-8pm, and before shows.)

■ Near Leipzig: Naumburg

Between Leipzig and Weimar towers the stupendous **Naumburger Dom,** a phenomenal cathedral begun in 1042 but glamorized two centuries later when one of Germany's greatest sculptors stopped by and chiseled 12 lifelike figures out of the cathedral walls. Because he was too humble to carve his name on the base, the artist is remembered today simply as the *Naumburger Meister* (the Master of Naumburg). The cathedral's structure is intricate and immense; the gothic apse is fitted between two sets of towers—one Romanesque, one Gothic. Inside, carved into an emotional frieze of Christ's Passion by the Master, a dozen medieval town leaders look down on the bus loads of tourists shuffling by. Not by the Master's hand, but equally fascinating, are the wrought-iron carvings of St. Francis of Assisi and his animal friends, which line the bannisters up to the east choir. To reach the cathedral from the station, bear right on Markgrafenweg to the end of the street, turn left, climb the cobblestone path, and follow the signs. (Open Mon.-Sat. 9am-5:30pm, Sun. noon-5:30pm. Admission DM3.50, students and seniors DM2.)

The rest of the town has recovered surprisingly well from the 45 years it spent as a backwater Red Army post. Follow Steinweg past the cathedral through the cheerfully restored Marktplatz to reach the **Wenzelkirche,** with a couple of Cranachs and a **tower** that should reopen by 1994. (Open Mon.-Sat. 10am-4pm; winter hours vary according to the whims of the church volunteers.) Still, Naumburg is best as an impressive daytrip; well-situated on the rail network, it's easy to reach from Leipzig, Halle, Weimar, or Erfurt. Back on Lindenring between the Dom and the Wenzelkirche is the proto–**tourist office** (tel. (03445) 25 14) in the **Nur Touristic** travel bureau. Get a superfluous map here, or book a room in a private home (open Mon.-Fri. 9am-6pm, Sat. 9am-noon). Look for places to eat in the sidestreets of the market square, but don't expect bargains. If you're just going for the day, bring a picnic.

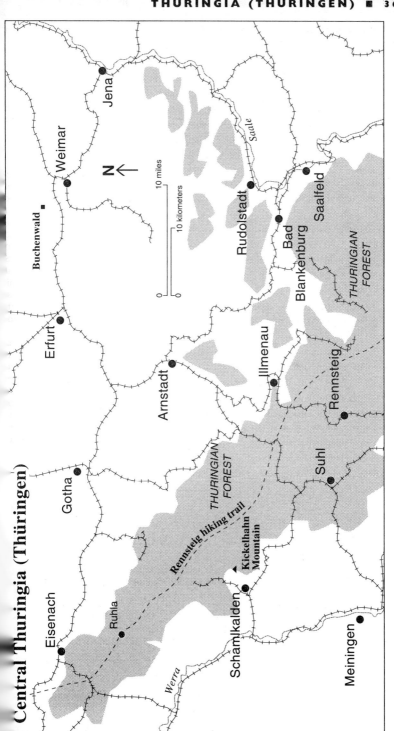

Central Thuringia (Thüringen)

THURINGIA (THÜRINGEN)

Not only the most beautiful of the new Federal States, Thuringia may be the most impressive region, culturally as well as aesthetically, anywhere in Germany. Bach, Goethe, Schiller, Luther and Wagner all left their mark on this landscape; what is more, it left its mark on their work. Echoes of Thuringia are heard in any rendition of Europe's cultural canon. The Thuringia forest (Thüringer Wald) is the deep green center of gravity at the heart of the *Land*. Thuringia itself is the midpoint of Germany: it is the hub of a wheel formed by Bavaria, Saxony, Sachsen-Anhalt, Lower Saxony, and Hesse. There are two routes through Thuringia, which mesh neatly with each other. One is to follow the necklace of historic cities—among them Jena, Weimar, Erfurt, Eisenach—joined by a direct east-west rail line. Extending downward from the cities is the forest itself, run through by the historic Rennsteig hiking trail. The best way to the forest is through the state capital, Erfurt.

■■■ WEIMAR

> My estate is so diverse, so important, not only for my descendants but also for the whole of intellectual Weimar, yea indeed for all of Germany....
>
> Johann Wolfgang von Goethe, last will and testament, 1831

In 1919, after Germany's defeat in World War I, the writers of its new constitution gathered in Weimar, which gave its name to the new Republic. They chose to meet in this old university town because it was "safer" than the capital, Berlin, which had just been rocked by a failed revolution. Weimar was safer for ideological as well as practical reasons; as the home of Goethe and Schiller, the city was considered a monument to German humanism and all that was "best" in the German cultural tradition. Nietzsche, Bach, Herder, Liszt, Wieland, and Cranach all unleashed their genius upon the city. The name Weimar still evokes many contradictory pictures—that of Goethe as well as of the roaring creativity of 1920s Weimar Culture, which resolved itself in economic crisis and the defeat of democracy. And behind this cultural capital, with its old city, shrines to poets, and palaces, are the darkest shadows of the past; Himmler built the Buchenwald Concentration Camp 20km north of the city on the site of one of Goethe's favorite mountain retreats.

ORIENTATION AND PRACTICAL INFORMATION

Practically in the center of Germany, Weimar is well-situated on the Dresden-Frankfurt and Berlin-Frankfurt lines. Bus #4 links Weimar's train station with **Goetheplatz** in the center of town. To walk it, head straight down Carl-August-Allee for about 10 minutes. From Goetheplatz, the pedestrian **Schillerstraße** winds its way to the Markt and major sights.

Tourist Office: Weimar Information, Marktstr. 4 (tel. 21 73, fax 612 40). Just off the Markt down a sidestreet near the **Rathaus.** Maps, brochures, and all that Ticket agent for Deutsches Nationaltheater. Books rooms in private homes or calls ahead to hotels, pensions, or hostels for no fee. Walking tours depart from the tourist office daily at 11am and 2pm (DM5). Or go it on your own with the DM0.50 German-language walking tour brochure. Open Mon.-Fri. 9am-7pm, Sat. 9am-4pm; Nov.-Feb. Mon.-Fri. 9am-6pm, Sat. 9am-1pm.

Currency Exchange: A number of banks line Schillerstr., but beware: none are open between Sat. afternoon and Mon. morning.

Post Office: *Hauptpostamt*, Goetheplatz, 99423 Weimar (tel. 76 00). Open Mon.-Fri. 7am-6pm, Sat. 7am-1pm, Sun. 10-11am.

Telephones: City Code: 03643

Trains: Call for information (tel. 33 30).

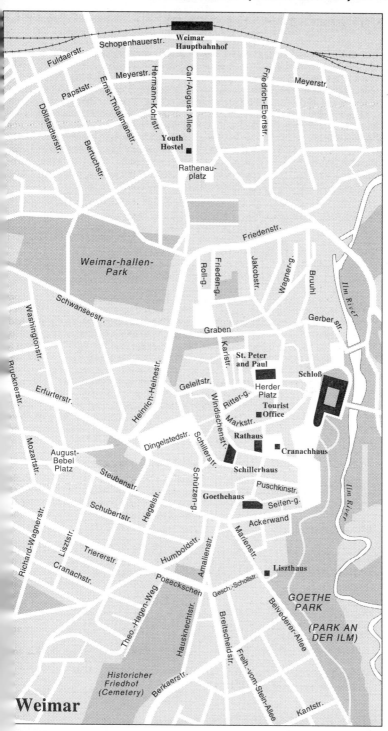

Weimar

Weimar Hauptbahnhof

Schopenhauerstr.

Fuldaerstr.

Papststr.

Meyerstr.

Ernst-Thälmannstr.

Hermann-Kohstr.

Carl-August Allee

Friedrich-Ebertstr.

Meyerstr.

Döllstädterstr.

Bertuchstr.

Youth Hostel

Rathenau-platz

Friedenstr.

Weimar-hallen-Park

Roll-g.

Frieden-g.

Jakobstr.

Wagner-g.

Bruhl

Ilm River

Schwanseestr.

Washingtonstr.

Brucknerstr.

Schwanseestr.

Graben

Gerber str.

Karlstr.

St. Peter and Paul

Schloß

Erfurterstr.

Heinrich-Heinestr.

Geleitstr.

Ritter-g.

Herder Platz

Tourist Office

Mozartstr.

August-Bebel Platz

Dingelstedstr.

Windischenstr.

Markstr.

Rathaus

Cranachhaus

Richard-Wagnerstr.

Steubenstr.

Hegelstr.

Schillerstr.

Schützen-g.

Schillerhaus

Puschkinstr.

Goethehaus

Seifen-g.

Schubertstr.

Ackerwand

Ilm River

Lisztstr.

Triererstr.

Cranachstr.

Humboldtstr.

Poseckschen

Theo.-Hagen-Weg

Amalienstr.

Marienstr.

Gesch.-Schollstr.

Liszthaus

GOETHE PARK

(PARK AN DER ILM)

Hausknechtstr.

Berkaerstr.

Breitscheidstr.

Freih.-vom-Stein-Allee

Belvederer-Allee

Historicher Friedhof (Cemetery)

Kantstr.

Public Transportation: Weimar's lack of streetcars is more than compensated for by an extensive **bus** network. All lines run past the *Hauptbahnhof* and through Goetheplatz; buy your tickets (DM1) from the driver. Get maps at the info booth outside the main train station. Open Mon.-Fri. 5:45am-6pm, Sat. 8am-2pm. Buses stop around midnight.

Taxis: tel. 36 00.

Bicycle rental: Head to the unmarked bicycle shop at the corner of Jakobstr. and Graben. DM10 per day. Open Mon.-Fri. 9am-1pm and 2-6pm, Sat.9am-noon.

Luggage Storage: At the train station. Lockers DM2 or 3 depending on size.

Laundromat: Wascherei, Humboldtstr. up the hill from the Jugendherberge Am Poseckschen Garten. Open Mon.-Fri. 8:30am-6pm, Sat. 8:30-11:30am.

Pharmacy: Theater Apotheke, Steubenstr. 30 (tel. 50 22 50), behind the Frauen-plan, has night service more often than not.

Police: tel. 110. **Fire:** tel. 112. **Ambulance:** tel. 115.

ACCOMMODATIONS

Thanks to Weimar's three youth hostels, finding a place to stay is easier in Weimar than in some other Eastern cities. But if you're out of luck, despair not; although the city's hostels are outrageous and pensions start at DM100, there's an ample supply of private rooms within walking distance of the city center. Expect to pay DM20-30 per person; up to DM40 if you arrive late or on weekends. Weimar's "finest," **Hotel Elephant,** Am Markt 19 (tel. 614 71), has catered to such discerning travelers as Napoleon, J.S. Bach, Richard Wagner, Leo Tolstoy, and Thomas Mann (who set his novel *Lotte in Weimar* in the hotel). But in case you don't have the requisite DM200 per person, console yourself: Hitler stayed there too.

Jugendherberge Germania (HI), Carl-August-Allee 13 (tel./fax 20 76). Super friendly. Super-convenient. From the station, head straight down the hill for 2min.; the hostel in on your right, a sea-foam green vision in cinder block. Reception open 3-11pm. Lockout 10am-1pm. Curfew 11pm. DM16.50, over 26 DM20.50. Breakfast included.

Jugendherberge Am Poseckschen Garten, Humboldtstr. 17 (tel. 640 21). Even closer to town (though not to the train station). Bus #6 (direction "Ober grunstedt"): Poseckschen Garten, and continue to the corner of Humboldtstr. where you'll see the hostel. A turn-of-the-century brownstone with a doggedly GDR-era feel; the rooms are well-furnished, but the hostel has just 1 shower room. Reception open 2:30-10pm. No lockout, no curfew. DM15, over 26 DM18.50. Breakfast included.

Jugendgästehaus Weimar (HI), Zum Wilden Graben 12 (tel. and fax 34 71). Bus #8 (from the station, direction "Merketal"): Wilder Graben. Pleasantly located amidst old villas. Very modern facilities. Reception open 4-8pm. Curfew 11pm. DM18.50, over 26 DM22.50. Breakfast included.

FOOD

Weimar serves up very rich cooking for rich tourists; console yourself at the daily **produce market** in the Marktplatz, or at the **Ladenmarkt grocery store** at the corner of Marktstr. and Windischenstr.; facing the tourist office, turn left and walk block (open Mon.-Fri. 8am-6pm, Sat. 8am-noon).

Scenario, Carl-August-Allee 15 (tel. 41 96 40), at the corner of Meyerstr. next the youth hostel. Pizzas and salads in a jazzy venue, with abstract paintings staring from the walls. Re-materializes as a bar at night. Live music on weekends. DM 10. Open daily 11am-1am; kitchen closes at 11pm.

Hochschule für Architektur und Bauwesen, Marienstr., just across the footpa in front of the Bauhaus building. Also accessible from the Park an der Ilm. The local architecture school runs a **Mensa, cafeteria,** and **restaurant** in this complex with meals starting at DM6 in the *Mensa* and peaking at DM15 in the restaurant. Open daily 11am-11pm.

Theatergastätte Pierrot, on the corner of Hummelstr. and Gropiusstr. just behind the national theater. This dark, smoky restaurant is designed for theater performers and their poverty-stricken friends, not the fur-clad theater-goers. Delicious spring rolls DM5. Open daily 11am-10pm.

Gastmahl des Meeres, Herderplatz 16, near the Herderkirche. No one seems to mind that the ocean is 1000km away from this seafood restaurant, as you get a lot of atmosphere in the 1554 *Burgerhaus* for only about DM10-15 at dinner, less at lunch. Open Mon.-Fri. 11am-10pm, Sat.-Sun. 11am-3pm.

SIGHTS AND ENTERTAINMENT

Goethe and Schiller

One hundred and fifty years after his death, botanist, geologist, government officer, doctor, artist, and poet Johann Wolfgang von Goethe still presides over these streets. Such immortality would likely not surprise the egotistical poet; nor would the numerous sights which dwell upon him and his friend, collaborator, and rival, Friedrich Schiller. Especially impressive are his flawless manuscripts and private chambers in the **Goethehaus,** Frauenplan 1, where the poet lived for 50 years. A stalwart English guide, *Goethe's House on the Frauenplan at Weimar,* is a necessary companion for the otherwise-unlabeled collection of many trinkets that fill the rooms where Goethe entertained, wrote, studied, and ultimately died. (Open Tues.-Sun. 9am-5pm; Nov.-Feb. Tues.-Sun. 9am-4pm. Admission DM5, students DM3.)

The **Schillerhaus,** Schillerstr. 12, former residence of the playwright, displays original drafts, early editions of plays, and a biographical chronicle of his life. (Open Wed.-Mon. 9am-5pm; Nov.-Feb. Wed.-Mon. 9am-4pm. Admission DM5, students DM3.) Around the corner, Schiller and Goethe are reconciled in stone before the **Deutsches Nationaltheater,** which first breathed life into their stage works. The contemporary repertoire varies, but still includes works by the city's favorite sons. Tickets are fairly expensive (DM20-60), but there are 50% discounts for students, as well as great deals one hour before the show on unsold seats (as low as DM7 for students). The box office (tel. 75 53 34) is all the way around at the back of the theater. (Open Mon.-2-6pm, Tues.-Fri. 10am-1pm and 4-6pm, Sat. 10am-noon and 3-6pm. Tours of the interior Sat. 3-5pm.)

At the **Wittumpalais** and **Wieland Museum** across the square at Palais 3, Goethe, Schiller, and Herder sat at the round table of their patron, Duchess Anna Amalia (open Tues.-Sun. 9am-noon and 1-5pm; Nov.-Feb. Tues.-Sun. 9am-noon and 1-4pm; admission DM3, students DM2).

On the river, the **Park an der Ilm,** landscaped by Goethe, sprouts numerous 18th-century pavilions and shelters grazing sheep and goats. Of particular note are the fake ruins built by the Weimar shooting club and a statue of Shakespeare (Schiller was his finest translator) still bearing scars from when the Nazis painted him black after the war with England began in 1939. Perched on the park's far slopes is Goethe's **Gartenhaus,** Corona-Schöfer-Str., the poet's first home in Weimar and later his retreat from the city. (Open Tues.-Sun. 9am-noon and 1-5pm. Admission DM3, students DM1.) South of the town center, Goethe and Schiller lie in rest at the **Historischer Friedhof** (cemetery). (Open Mon.-Sun. 9am-1pm and 2-5pm.) The two poets lie side by side in the local ducal sarcophagus. Goethe arranged to be sealed in an airtight steel case. Schiller, who died in an epidemic, was originally buried in a mass grave, but Goethe later combed through the remains until he identified Schiller and had him interred in the tomb. Skeptics argued for a long time that Goethe was mistaken, so until the 1960s, a couple of "Schillers" lay here side by side. In the 1960s, a team of Russian scientists finally determined that Goethe had been right after all. (Tomb open daily 9am-12:45pm and 1-5pm; Nov.-Feb. 9am-1pm and 2-4pm. Free.)

Elsewhere in Weimar

Straight down Frauenstr., the cobblestone **Marktplatz** spreads out beneath the neo-Gothic **Rathaus** and the colorful Renaissance façade of the **Lucas Cranach Haus** (both closed to the public). Between the Frauenplan and the marktplatz is the beginning of Weimar's central artery, **Schillerstraße,** a vivacious shop-lined pedestrian zone crammed with antiques and bookstores.

From the Marktplatz wind your way left to the **Schloßmuseum,** Burgplatz 4. The first floor is a **Lucas Cranach**-fest; the second floor is a minor-league collection of 19th-century German works, as well as a Rodin sculpture and one of Monet's Rouen cathedrals. (Open Tues.-Sun. 10am-6pm; Sept. -May 9am-5pm. Admission DM4, students DM2.) Cranach himself rests in the church yard of the **Jakobskirche** on Am Graben (open Mon.-fri. 10am-noon). Cross back over Am Graben and down Jakobstr. to reach the handsome **Stadtkirche St. Peter und Paul,** with Cranach's last triptych altarpiece. The church is also called the **Herderkirche,** for philosopher Johann Gottfried von Herder who once preached here regularly (open Mon.Sat. 10am-noon and 2-4pm, Sun. 2-3pm). The **Kirms-Krackow Haus,** Jakobstr. 10, documents the life and times of Herder, but was closed for restoration in the summer of 1993.

The **Bauhaus school,** now at the **Hochschule für Architektur und Bauwesen** (College for Architecture and Construction), offers no exhibits related to the iconoclastic design movement, and is in fact a 1911 creation of Henry van de Velde, himself a pioneer of the *Jugendstil* movement. Bauhaus work is better represented by the **Denkmal der Märzgefallenen,** designed by Gropius to honor those killed in the 1919 revolution (between WWI and the Weimar Republic, when Germany almost became independently socialist), past the Goethe and Schiller graves in the historic cemetery (see above). Completed in 1923, the monument was considered deeply scandalous and led to the Bauhaus's expulsion from Weimar and their flight to Dessau. (If the Bauhaus is really your cup of tea, see Dessau, below.)

Steps away is the **Franz Liszt Haus** where the composer spent his last years. The instruments and furnishings are supposedly original, but given Liszt's torrid love life, the single bed seems improbable. (Open Tues.-Sun. 9am-1pm and 2-5pm; Nov.-Feb. 9am-1pm and 2-4pm. Admission DM2, students and seniors DM1.)

■ Near Weimar: Buchenwald

Everywhere you turn at Buchenwald, there are reminders of those who died in the concentration camp here. Even the streets were paved with prisoners' ashes. It is a sight not easily forgotten.

The camp is difficult to reach by public transportation. Take regional bus #31 from right near the Weimar train station (7, 8:15am, noon, 2, and 3pm; additional less regular departures; Mon. service is particularly erratic). You can also take bus #6 from downtown Weimar (direction "Etterburg"): Buchenwald, but even if you ask the driver to let you off at the nearest stop, you face a 5km walk to the site.

From 1937 to 1945, the concentration camp held over 250,000 Jews, political prisoners, gypsies, and gays; most did not survive the Holocaust. What remains is the **Nationale Mahn-und Gedenkstätte Buchenwald** (National Buchenwald Memorial). At the memorial, signs will point to the **KZ Lager** or the **Gedenkstätte.** The former refers to the remains of the camp, while the latter is a solemn monument overlooking the valley. Ask at the office marked *"Anmeldung"* for English-language viewings of a documentary, "O Buchenwald," about the camp. The film is shown regularly in German, but certainly no language barrier will keep you from being moved by the film's images. Expect apologies from the monument staff for the pre 1989 ideological content of the film, which emphasizes the stories of the communist detainees over the experience of the many Jews who were murdered here.

Since reunification, the focus of the camp exhibits has shifted from the internment of German communists under the Third Reich to the Soviet use of the camp site from 1945 to 1950, when some 32,000 Germans, most former Nazi war crimi nals, some opponents of the Communist regime, were interned here by the Soviet Army; 10,000 died of hunger and disease. It may be painful for those who come here to mourn that a complete look at the more extensive Nazi history of the death camp and the victims of the Holocaust is still lacking. Along with the stillness of the old buildings at Buchenwald, one is struck by the continuation of a long and dangerous silence about the other victims of the camp: Jews, gypsies, homosexuals, and other groups towards which neither regime holds a spotless record. This silence permeates many of the camp's told and untold stories. (For a discussion of some of the issues currently surrounding interpretation of the Holocaust, see Life and Times section, above.)

Downhill from the reception are the remains of the camp, including a historical museum and a display of anti-fascist resistance art, both of which have been updated to address the Soviet use of the camp. A **memorial stone** on the site of a former Jewish children's barracks will be laid on November 9, 1993—the 55th anniversary of *Kristallnacht* (Night of Shattered Glass), when the Nazis' violent campaign against European Jewry began. The path on the right when facing the main gate leads to an austere memorial to those who died under the Communist control of the camp.

The museum and film buildings are open Tuesday to Sunday 9:30am-5:45pm (Oct.-March 8:45am-4:45pm). The camp **archives** are open Tuesday to Friday to anyone searching for records of family and friends between 1938 to 1945; expansion of the archives is being planned. The memorial grounds can be visited until nightfall.

■■■ JENA

At the turn of the 19th century, the Romantic movement sank its first roots into German soil at Jena, home to Germany's premier university under the stewardship of Hölderin, Schlegel, Novalis, and Tieck. Philosophers Hegel, Fichte, and Schelling argued for a new conception of intellectual and political freedom within the walls of the already centuries-old *Collegium Jenense*, and in 1789, Friedrich Schiller gave his first lecture on the ideals of the French Revolution. Today, Jena's university here bears his name. Even more than its full memories, architectural relics, street conversations and protest banners for causes such as *Asylrechte* (immigration rights) mark Jena as an active, collegiate town.

Practical Information Jena was built in the Saale Valley about 50km east of Weimar. Trains between Dresden and Erfurt stop at **Bahnhof Jena West,** while trains on the Berlin-Munich line stop at **Jena Saalbahnhof,** about 10 minutes north of the more interesting bits. The main transfer point for Jena's bus and streetcar system is the **Zentrum** stop, near Eichplatz and the Markt, midway between the two stations. From Bahnhof Jena West, head to Bahnhofstr. until it becomes Schillerstr. A left turn will take you to the present-day university building. **Jena-Information,** Löbderstr. 9 (tel. (03641) 246 71, fax 233 82), just south of the market, hands out maps and schedules of special events. (Open Mon.-Fri. 9am-7pm, Sat. 9am-4pm; Nov.-April Mon.-Fri. 9am-6pm, Sat. 9am-2pm.) Rent **bicycles** at **Fahrradhaus Kamter,** at the corner of Löbdergraben and Unterrm Markt near the Romantikerhaus. (DM10 per day; mountain bikes DM15 per day. Open Mon.-Fri. 9am-1pm and 2-6pm, Sat. 9am-noon.)

Accommodations and Food There is no youth hostel in Jena, so you might want to push on to Weimar, but why pay DM19 for a Jugengästehaus filled with screaming kids?—the tourist office (see Practical Information, above) books rooms in private homes for a DM3 fee (about DM20-40). **Café Daneben** bustles with student activity on Eichplatz and doubles as a bar at night (open Mon.-Sat. 10am-4am, Sun. 3pm-4am), while a more alternative crowd puts down vegetarian specialties in the nuclear-free zone of **Café Immergrün,** Fürstengraben 30 (open Mon.-Sat. 11am-11pm).

Sights The **Romantikerhaus,** Unterm Markt 12a, just off of Jena's **Markt** (the old market square), was once home to the Romantics' poetry parties; the house now contains the **Fine Arts Museum of Jena** (open Tues.-Sat. 10am-1pm and 2-5pm; Admission DM1.50, students and seniors DM1). Similar soul-searching presumably went on at Schiller's summer home on Schillergässchen, the **Schiller Gedenkstätte** (tel. (03641) 822 23 53) on Schillergäßen, just off (you guessed it) Schillerstr. (Open Tues.-Fri. 10am-noon and 1-4pm, Sat. 11am-4pm. Admission DM1, students and seniors DM0.50.) The original university building, just up the street from the Romantikerhaus, dates back to the 13th century; it housed a Dominican monastery until the Wittenberg university moved here to escape the plague. The 1755 Baroque tower of the **Rathaus** in the market catches attention on the hour, when its Gothic **Glockenspiel** begins to *spiel* and *Schnapphans* doll figures pop out to dance.

But despite all of that, Jena's real center is on **Eichplatz,** a student meeting point in the shadows of the late GDR-era university building. The **Stadtkirche St. Michael,** just off Eichplatz, presides proudly over **Luther's tombstone.** He is not here himself, though the stone was intended for him. The church claims that it was shipped here by mistake, while back at the gravesite in Wittenberg tour guides mutter indictments about 17th-century plundering. (Open Mon.-Fri. 10am-5pm, Sat. 10am-2pm. Sunday services at 9:30am and 6pm.) Follow the main street up and turn left onto Fürstengraben, where you can observe the **Botanischer Garten** (open dawn-dusk), or the row of statues of prestigious university faculty; notice that teachers and students of **Marx** received particularly large statues. Up ahead are the Pulverturm and the Johannistor, remnants of the medieval university walls.

■ Near Jena: Dornburg

By far the best reason to come to Jena is its proximity to the village of **Dornburg,** 18km to the north, home of the **Dornburger Schlößer,** a series of three palaces perched above the Saale River valley. Dornburg is also known for rose cultivation; during the last weekend in June, the **Dornburg Rose Festival** marks the anniversary of King Karl August's lavish birthday parties here a century ago. The townspeople elect a sort of German homecoming queen who hands out candy and food to the spectators. The locals don their party hats again during the last week in August, to celebrate **Goethe's birthday** (as though the man didn't get enough attention already).

The **Altes Schloß,** the eldest castle, was built in 937, when the Kaisers still visited Dornburg. The first German *Reichstag* met here, and the building was used as a prison by both the Nazi and Communist regimes. Look but don't touch—the interior is closed to the public. The summer residences of the Grand Duke of Sachsen–Weimar-Eisenach, the **Barockschloß** and the **Rokokoschloß,** preside majestically and frivolously (respectively) over the magnificent rose gardens where Goethe practiced his horticultural skills while amusing his lover, Charlotte von Stein (see Thuringian Forest section for the steamy details). The Baroque castle is a relatively plain collection of royal belongings in comparison to the 1740 Rococo pleasure palace. Visitors are given loose slippers to protect the floor of the main hall, and can partake in the voluptuous pleasure of gliding from *objet* to *objet* along the slick surface. (Admission DM4, students DM2 for students. Open daily 9am-noon and 1-5pm; Oct. and March open daily 10am-noon and 1-4pm; Nov.-Feb. closed. Gardens open daily dawn-dusk or 8pm, whichever comes first.)

During festival times, all 20 guest beds in Dornburg are filled, but at other times you have a good chance of finding a room through the **Stadtverwaltung** (tel. (036427) 209), the closest thing to a tourist office, in the *Rathaus* just up the steps from the castles (open Mon., Wed., and Fri. 9am-noon, Tues. 9am-noon and 1-4pm,

Thurs. 9am-noon and 1-6pm). The **Schloßcafé** in the Baroque Schloß offers cakes, coffee, and a river-view terrace, with a fresh bouquet of roses on every table.

To get to Dornburg from **Jena**, grab the train from Bahnhof Jena-Paradies on Kahl-aische-Str., about a five-minute walk from Bahnhof Jena-West (the main train station). Dornburg is also an easy and attractive **bike ride** from Jena, though you may want to save your strength for the 194 steps up to the castles, visible from below.

■■■ ERFURT

A visit to the new capital of Thuringia is without question one of the high points of a trip to Eastern Germany. While Erfurt was never a cultural powerhouse like Dresden, or even Gotha or Eisenach, it seems to have attracted its fair share of politicos. Napoleon based his field camp here for over a year, Konrad Adenauer lived here before World War II, and more recently Willy Brandt met with Erich Honecker here in 1970 in the early stages of German-German reconciliation. For the budget traveler, Erfurt offers a stunning cathedral, a handful of museums, and a cultural life fueled by its three colleges. Because of its political importance and its 1250th birthday celebration last year, most of the inner city has been beautifully restored, giving Erfurt a look of style all too rare in the cities of the East. The city is also a logical departure point for the green hills of the Thüringer Wald (see below).

ORIENTATION AND PRACTICAL INFORMATION

Erfurt lies in the heart of Thuringia, only 15 minutes from Weimar, 90 minutes from Leipzig, and three hours from Frankfurt. The train station lies south of the city center. Head straight down Bahnhofstr. to reach the **Anger**—the main drag—and then the *Altstadt*, which is cut though by the **Gera River**. From the river, **Marktstraße** leads to the **Domhügel** hill, one of the oldest districts and site of the cathedral.

Tourist Office: Erfurt Fremdenverkehrsamt, Bahnhofstr. 37 (tel. 262 67, fax 233 55). From the station, head straight down Bahnhofstr. to the intersection with Juri-Gagarin-Ring; the office is on the left. Pick up the monthly *Erfurt Magazin*, with a worthy map in the center. Maps of the Thüringian Forest are available as well. Reserves tickets and books rooms in costly hotels and more affordable private rooms (singles DM30-40, doubles DM40-60, plus DM5 fee). Open Mon.-Fri. 10am-6pm, Sat. 10am-1pm). The **branch office** in the middle of the Anger (tel. 269 53) does all the same stuff, but doesn't book rooms. 2-hr. tours leave here daily at 1pm; Nov.-March Sat. 1pm (DM6). Open Mon.-Fri. 10am-6pm, Sat.-Sun. 10am-4pm. A third branch in a cottage on the **Krämerbrücke** (tel. 234 36) has weekend hours and is particularly eager, though they don't book rooms either. Open Mon.-Fri. 10am-6pm, Sat.-Sun. 10am-4pm.

Currency Exchange: Deutsche Verkehrs Bank, in the station, has average rates and late-ish hours. Open Mon.-Fri. 8am-7pm.

Post Office: The *Hauptpostamt*, 99084 Erfurt, occupies an imposing *fin-de-siècle* beast overlooking the Anger. **Post Restante** available in the small room before the main hall. Open Mon.-Fri. 8am-6pm, Sat. 9am-noon, Sun. 10-11am.

Telephones: City Code: 0361

Trains: From the *Hauptbahnhof*, trains shoot off to Dresden (every 2hrs.), Leipzig (every 2hrs.), Würzburg (every 3hrs.), and Frankfurt (every 3hrs.).

Public Transportation: Typical Eastern streetcars, blue with clanging bells. DM1.20 for 15 min., DM5 for 5 tickets, day pass DM4. Seniors get 50% discount. As always, validate your tickets on board. For info, call 642 13 22 or stop by the office on the Anger. Open Mon.-Sat. 6am-8pm, Sun. 8am-8pm. Streetcars and buses don't run past midnight.

Taxis: tel. 511 11.

Bicycle rental: ATW, on Juri-Gagarin-Ring. From the tourist office, turn left. DM8-10 per day; leave a passport or a deposit. Open Mon.-Fri. 9am-6pm, Sat. 9am-noon.

Luggage storage: No luggage-checking office, but small (DM2) and large (DM3) lockers ought to do the trick.

Pharmacy: Schwan-Apotheke, on Bahnhofstr. near the Anger, has a wider selection than most and a listing of the all-night pharmacy of the week. Open Mon.-Fri. 8am-6pm, Sat. 9am-noon.

Women's Center: Frauenzentrum, Espechstr. 3 (tel. 260 68) in the southwest part of the city, has information, counseling, and a café, all open Mon. 2-9:30pm, Tues.-Thurs. 9:30am-9:30pm, Fri. 9:30am-2pm, Sat.-Sun. 2-6pm.

Emergency: Police: tel.110. **Fire:** tel 112. **Ambulance:** tel. 115.

ACCOMMODATIONS

Housing options are limited. Try your luck with the **Jugendherberge (HI),** Hochheimerstr. 12 (tel. 267 05), in an old mansion a fair distance from the center. The newly renovated interior is much more accommodating than the overgrown exterior. From the station, take streetcar #5 (direction "Steigerstr."): Steigerstr. (last stop), backtrack a little, turn left onto Hochheimerstr., and the hostel is on the left corner at the first intersection. (Reception open 6-9am and 3-7pm. Lockout 10am-3pm. Curfew 10pm. DM17, over 26 DM20-50. Breakfast included.) The **Zimmervermittlung** at the tourist office (see above) will do nicely; if they're out of rooms, head to the private agency at **Tourismus Agentur Otto,** Schmidstedter-Str. 28 (tel. and fax 643 09 71), down the road across from the tourist office, which has rooms in private homes for DM36-50 (fee included; open Mon.-Fri. 9am-8pm, Sat. 10am-2pm). In a pinch, Weimar's hostels are a 15-minute train ride away.

FOOD

What it lacks in accommodations, Erfurt makes up for with food. If you're traveling on the cheap, you can head to the **Topmarkt** on the Anger behind the post office (open Mon.-Fri. 8am-6pm, Sat. 8am-noon) or fill up at the **market** on Domplatz (open Mon.-Sat. 6am-2pm). But Erfurt does offer some of the better restaurants in the *neue Bundesländer*; replenish necessary spices at some of the more exotic (if less authentic) Chinese, Italian, or Argentine restaurants, or try the succulent and toothsome local specialty, *Thüringer Bratwurst*. This ain't no wiener; this is an experience.

La Cave, in the Galerie am Fischmarkt, across from the *Rathaus*. All the usuals, plus felafel and kosher dishes inside or on the marketplace terrace. Amusingly flamboyant service. Open daily noon-midnight.

Tomate, Schmidtstedterstr. 10, down the street across from the tourist office. Brick, tile, mirrors, and Italian dishes DM3.50-9. Open Mon.-Sat. 11am-midnight, Sun. 6-10pm.

Das Café Restaurant, Bahnhofstr. 45, between Juri-Gagarin-Ring and the Anger. Local specialties in a glass and marble duplex. Meals under DM10. Open Mon.-Fri. 7:30am-8pm, Sat. 10am-6pm.

SIGHTS

Towering above the city skyline on the Domhügel hill is one of Eastern Germany's most impressive **cathedrals.** The effect is heightened by the broad case of stone steps set into the hill, by its sheer magnitude, and by the stained-glass elegance of the choir. Luther was invested as a priest here, and interrupted his first mass by throwing the Bible across the altar. He claimed that his target was the devil himself, standing there in living color as he prepared the eucharist. The Bishop was not charmed. The complex also includes the **Church of St. Severi,** whose simple sandstone interior is dominated by the Saint's sarcophagus. (Cathedral and church open Mon.-Fri. 9-11:30am and 12:30-5pm, Sat. 9-11:30am and 12:30-4:30pm, Sun. 2-4pm.)

From the sprawling Domplatz, a broad Marktstr. leads down to the **Fischmarkt,** bordered by former guild houses with rather wild façades, and the 1869 **Rathaus** (open daily 9am-4pm). Markstr. runs to the **Gera River,** spanned by the **Krämer-**

brücke, a covered medieval bridge teeming with small shops dating from the 12th century. In the 1400s this bridge was part of a direct trade route between Kiev and Paris. Walking on this unique "bridge with buildings," one is cut off from any sight but that of its archaic walls, but it is even more fascinating from underneath: glance up from the water's edge. On the far end is the **Brückenmuseum,** a small house that chronicles the bridge's history as well as local customs and medieval period costumes. (Open Tues.-Sun. 10am-6pm. Admission DM2, children DM1.)

From the far side of the bridge, follow Gotthardtstr., and cut left through Kirchengasse to reach the **Augutinerkloster,** where Martin Luther spent 10 years as a Catholic priest and Augustine monk. He got his way; the cloister now functions as a Protestant college. (Tours Tues.-Sat. hourly 10am-noon and 2-4pm; Nov.-March Tues.-Sat. at 10am, noon, and 2pm, as well as after the 9:30am Sun. services.) The **library** here has one of Germany's most priceless collections, including a number of early Bibles with personal notations by Luther himself. During World War II, the books were moved to make room for a bomb shelter. When U.S. bombers destroyed the library in February 1945, 267 people lost their lives but the books remained unscathed.

From the Krämerbrücke, head down Futterstr. and turn right on Johannesstr. to reach the **Kaufmännerkirche,** where Bach's parents tied the knot (open Mon.-Fri. 10am-noon and 2-4pm, service Sat. 6pm and Sun. 10am). In front of the church, feet planted firmly on a pedestal decorated with scenes from his university days here, a somewhat squat **Martin Luther** casts a holier-than-thou glance at the **Anger,** a wide promenade with statues and fountains that is one of the most attractive shopping streets in Eastern Germany. While it's not Milan (or even Dortmund, for that matter) the two Benettons, fast food, and a multiplex cinema have brought Erfurt firmly into the realm of commodity fetishism. The architecture lining the street—most of it 19th-century Neoclassical or *Jugendstil*—is for the most part fascinating, though some GDR-era behemoths mar the effect. Across from the post office lies **house #6,** where Russian Tsar Alexander I stayed when he came here to meet with Napoleon in 1808. Check out the **Angermuseum,** Anger 18, with its collection of very exciting medieval things (open Tues. and Thurs.-Sun. 10am-5pm, Wed. 10am-8pm; admission DM2, students and seniors DM1).

Bear right at the end of the Anger and follow Regierungstr. to the **Staathalterei,** the massive Baroque building from which the communists ruled the city. Here, in a small salon on the second floor, Napoleon had breakfast with Goethe in 1808. Goethe later wrote that Napoleon spent the entire time chastising him for his gloomy tragedies, which the French dictator seemed to know inside and out. In the version of this tale related by Czech novelist Milan Kundera in *Immortality,* Napoleon gets Goethe confused with Schiller.

ENTERTAINMENT AND NIGHTLIFE

With 220,000 inhabitants, Erfurt can't lack a nightlife, though what there is rather low-key. Take in opera or drama at the **Opernhaus** (Opera House) or **Schaupielhaus** whose combined ticket agency (tel. 243 14) is in the Opera House at Dalbergsweg 2. (Open Tues.-Fri. 10am-1pm and 2-5:30pm, Sat. 10am-1pm, Sun. 10am-noon, and 1hr. before performances, when prices drop 60% on unsold seats.) Just off the Domplatz is the **Theater Waidspeicher** (tel. 238 28) with intricate wooden marionette and puppet theater (DM10, children DM2.50) and a cabaret on weekend nights. (Tickets DM10. Box office open Tues.-Fri. 10am-2pm and 3-5:30pm, Sat. 10am-1pm, Sun. 10am-noon.)

Student nightlife centers on the **Studentclub Engelsburg,** Allerheilgenstr. 20/21 (tel. 290 36), just off Marktstr., where local and imported folk, rock, and jazz bands play. (Open Tues. 8pm-midnight, Wed. and Fri. 8pm-1am, Thurs. 10pm-12:30am, Sat. 9pm-1am. Café open Wed. and Sat. 4-10pm. Cover DM4-10, free entry for students on Tues. and Thurs.) Strangely, there's a lot of life in Erfurt's museums at night: **La Cave** (see Food listings, above) runs a lively café bar until midnight, and blues and classic rock rule at the **Museumskeller** (tel. 249 94) in the basement of the otherwise dull **Museum für Thüringer Volskunde,** Juri-Gagarin-Ring 140a (open daily from 10pm on).

■■■ THURINGIAN FOREST (Thüringer Wald)

"The area is magnificent, quite magnificent...I am basking in God's world," wrote Goethe from the **Thuringian Forest** in a letter more than 200 years ago. Today, Goethe's exclamation has lost nothing of its validity. The time-worn mountains—a perfect skiing area during the winter—and the peaceful pine woods of the Thuringian Forest have attracted Germans for generations. The small towns in the hills, with a rich cultural life from the Classic Period on, fostered and inspired many of Germany's composers, philosophers, and poets. Most famous among them were Goethe and Schiller, who scribbled some of their most brilliant poetry on these slopes. The forests stretch south of Eisenach, Weimar, and Erfurt to the border with Bavaria. Trains and buses trek regularly from any of these larger cities to the smaller, wood-framed villages.

The **Rennsteig,** a famous 168km-long scenic hiking trail, snakes through this forest. Before the war, the Rennsteig was one of Germany's favorite wilderness trails. History books date the trail at 1330, but locals claim that it was first worn down by prehistoric hunter-gatherers. During the years of division, much of the route was closed because of its potential as an escape route. But now hikers can wander all 170km from Hörschel near Eisenach right into Bavaria. Veterans of the five-day hike won't shut up about the route's delights. **Erfurt,** the new state capital, is without question the door to the Thuringian Forest. The **tourist office** there (see Erfurt listings, above) will equip you with guides and maps if you're planning an extended jaunt. Keep in mind that foreign tourists and the conveniences they expect are rare here. English is only understood in larger tourist offices, although increasing numbers offer brochures and other literature in English.

ARNSTADT

30km beyond Erfurt at the fringe of the Forest lies Arnstadt, the oldest town in Thuringia. Johann Sebastian Bach began his career as an organist in what is now the **Bachkirche** (open March-Sept. 10:30am-12:30pm and 2-4pm). The local authorities, however, found Bach's behavior with certain women and musical experimentation unfavorable, and politely but firmly asked him to leave the town for good. Nevertheless, a statue on the Marktplatz—the young Bach, slumped on a stool, looking irate—commemorates the life of the famous composer, and the Renaissance-era building **Haus Zum Palmbaum,** Markt 3 (tel. 29 78) serves as both a **town museum** and a **Bachmuseum.** (Open Mon.-Fri. 8:30am-noon and 1-4:30pm; admission DM2.50, students DM1.)

The **Neues Schloß** (new palace), Schloßplatz 1 (tel. 29 32) houses the **doll museum "Mon Plaisier."** In the mid-18th century, the local princess made court employees and craftsmen fashion a miniature panorama of the local community. More than 400 *unheimlich* (uncanny) dolls are displayed in 24 dollhouses, with a total of 84 furnished rooms. (Open May-Oct. Tues.-Sun. 8:30am-noon, 1-4:30pm. Nov.-April Tues.-Sun. 9:30am-4pm. Admission DM2.50, students DM2.) Although it has less of an anecdote-worthy history than the nearby Bachkirche, the **Liebfrauenkirche** is one of the most beautiful churches of the Romanesque Gothic period (Open March-Sept. 10:30am-12:30pm and 2-4pm. Otherwise call the *Pfarramt* for opening hours, tel. 74 09 60; admission DM1.)

The **tourist office, Arnstadt Information,** Markt 3 (tel. (03628) 20 49) operates a room-finding service (fee DM3, rooms from DM25); turn left from the station and then right on Bahnhofstr., and walk up Ledermarkt to the Markt (open Mon.-Fri. 9:30-noon, 12:30-6pm, Sat. 9am-noon). They also organize bus tours (DM5-10) to the **Drei Gleichen** (three matching castles) near Arnstadt, and have information on hiking trails. Mail letters at the **post office**, Ritterstr., 99310 Arnstadt (open Mon.-Fri. 8:30am-6pm, Sat. 8:30am-noon). **Zobel's Zweiradshop,** Zimmerstr. 17 (tel. 24 32) rents **bikes** for DM10 per day (open Mon.-Fri. 9am-6pm, Sat. 9am-noon). **Feinbäck-erei und Café am Jakobsturm,** Ried 18, bakes the essentials: cakes, pastries, savory pizza (DM5; open Mon.-Fri. 6:30am-6pm, Sat. 6:30-11am, 2-5pm, Sun. 2-5pm). For typical (i.e., hot sausages sold here) Thuringian meals (DM10), try the **Ratsklouse,** Ledermarkt 3 (open Mon.-Thurs. 7am-3pm, Fri. 8am-3pm, Sat. 8am-2pm).

Near Arnstadt, the ruined monastery of **Paulinzella,** on the line to Saalfeld and Rudolstadt, remains one of the most striking monuments of the Romanesque period in all of Thurnigia. The **Zinnsboden museum** nearby has a model of the monastery and information about its history (open May-Sept. daily 9am-noon and 2-5pm).

ILMENAU TO THE GOETHE TRAIL (GOETHEWANDERUNG)

Goethe first worked in Ilmenau reorganizing the Thuringian mining industry while he was a government minister under the Duke of Weimar, and came back to the area as a poet looking for a place of his own. "Ilmenau cost me much time, effort, and money," he wrote, "but I learned something as well, and developed a way of looking at nature which I would not give up at any price." In fact, the main attrac-tions on the way to the market square are the stunning scenery and a number of his old haunts. (From the train station, walk to the pedestrian zone and turn right on Marktstr.) South of the city center, parallel to Waldstr., stretches the 18km **Goethe Trail (Goethewanderung),** a route marked by Goethe's own over-flourished **"G"** monogram, which leads through the forest to **Stützerbach.**

About 4km into the trail (much of which is uphill), in his hut on the **Kickelhahn,** you can read the poetry he scratched on the walls as a young man. A year before his death at age 83, Goethe himself returned to the hut on a tour of his past, to trace his own handwriting and remember. Farther along, stop at the **Jagdhaus Gabelbach** (tel. (03677) 26 26), often visited by Goethe in summer and now dedicated to his scientific experiments. (Open May-Oct. Tues.-Sun. 9am-noon and 1-5pm; Nov.-March Wed.-Sun. 9am-noon and 1-4pm. Closed Nov. 15-Dec. 15. Admission DM2, students DM1.) The hike ends in **Stützerbach,** where the local glass-works magnate often hosted the poet. The house is now a **Goethe memorial,** but as a nod to the patron, there are live demonstrations of traditional **glass-blowing** on the first floor (open Tues.-Sun. 9am-noon and 1-5pm; admission DM3, students DM2). In Ilmenau, you can visit another glass-blowing studio where you can try the craft for yourself and buy hand-blown vases; ask the tourist office for more information.

Ilmenau, 45 minutes by train or bus south of Arnstadt, is a good springboard for the more dense woods. The **tourist office** is at Lindenstr. 12 (tel. (03677) 23 58, fax 25 02); walk down Bahnhofstr. across Wetzlarer Platz and follow the pedestrian zone until it becomes Lindenstr. (15min.). They provide maps and hiking brochures (DM5) and book private rooms (from DM15) for DM2 per person (open Mon.-Fri 9am-6pm, Sat. 9am-noon). You can obtain a **map** of the Goethe Trail from the tour-ist office, or just head for the **Amtshaus** (tel. (03677) 26 67; open May-Oct. daily 9am-noon and 1-4:30pm; Nov.-March daily 10am-noon and 1-4pm) and follow the "G" signs. The **post office** on Poststr., 98693 Ilmenau, is located at the beginning of the pedestrian zone (open Mon.-Fri. 8am-5pm, Sat. 9am-noon). The train station rents **bikes** for DM10-12 per day.

The **youth hostel** in Ilmenau, Waldstr. 22 (tel. 24 13), located in a beautiful build-ing in the town, lies at the beginning of the trail. From **Bahnhof Ilmenau-Bad,** walk straight ahead and uphill. (Reception open 7am-8pm. Curfew 10pm. DM14.50, over 26 DM18.50. Breakfast included.) The campus of the **Technische Hochschule** Technical College) and its **Mensa** are a hike from the train station; go left on Langewiesenstr., cross the railroad track, take the second street to your left and walk uphill. The *Mensa* is on your right (open 11:30am-1pm for lunch, 5-8pm for dinner). **Die Arche,** Str. des Friedens 28, a café (*paella* DM8) and shop, is popular with students (open Tues.-Thurs. 11am-9pm, Fri. 11am-midnight, Sun. noon-8pm); many of them post ride-share notices at the **Mitfahrzentrale** in the same building (tel. 47 11; open Mon.-Thurs. 3-7pm, Fri. 8am-7pm, Sat.-Sun. 9am-noon). Behind the Raiffeisenbank on the right side of Bahnhofstr., the **market** offers fresh fruits and vegetables (open Mon.-Fri. 8am-5pm, Sat. 8am-11am). **Zur Post,** Mühltor 6 (tel. 20 48) offers Thuringian specialties (DM10). (Open Mon.-Fri. 8:30am-midnight, Sat.-Sun. 11am-midnight.)

Ilmenau also makes a good starting point for a hike along the **Rennsteig** (take the train to Schmiedefeld). Other worthwhile destinations, easily accessible by train from Ilmenau, include **Lauscha** with its glass-blowing museum, **Sonnenberg** and its toy and doll museum, the weapon museum in **Suhl, Schmalkalden** and the late-Renaissance castle complex, **Oberhof** with its *Rennsteiggarten* (botanical garden) and the theater-town of **Meiningen.**

RUDOLSTADT AND BAD BLANKENBURG

Underneath Weimar the Saale River Valley winds down to **Rudolstadt.** This small city of 40,000 gave Richard Wagner his first big break; he lived at Zetkinstr. 47 while working as a local choir director. **Schillerstraße 25** marks the spot where Goethe and Schiller met for the first time, thus beginning one of literature's greatest symbiotic relationships. For decades the two authors worked in close consultation, checking and editing each other's work. Rudolstadt is also a route to the scene of one of Goethe's torrid affairs, Groß Kochberg (see below).

During the 18th century, social life centered on the princes of Schwarzburg-Rudolstadt and the Baroque-towered **Heidecksburg palace,** accessible through Vorwerkgasse, an uphill path behind the *Rathaus.* The **museum** in Heidecksburg (tel. 221 45 or 41 22) displays furnishings, paintings, and a light-wood sunlit library for guests to visit and use. There are also rare pieces of the porcelain which was Rudolstadt's stock-in-trade through the 19th century; local craftworkers still deal in hand-painted china dolls. (Open May-Oct. Tues.-Sun. 10am-6pm, Nov.-April Tues.-Sun. 9am-4pm; admission DM5, children DM2.50.) The **Volskundemuseum Thüringer Banernhäuser** (Thuringian Farmhouse museum; tel. 224 65), an open-air display of several regional farmhouses, completely restored and furnished. Go right from the station and cross the bridge into the park. (Open Wed.-Sun. 9am-noon and 1-5pm Sept.-April Wed.–Sun. 9am-noon and 1-4pm. Admission DM2, children DM1.)

Trains and buses from Weimar (bus #14) and Erfurt (bus #13) take about an hour To reach the **tourist office,** Marktstr. 57 (tel./fax (03672) 245 43), walk down Bahnhofstr. to Marktstr. and turn left (open Mon.-Fri. 9am-5pm, Sat. 9am-1pm). They will help you find a room for a DM3 fee (rooms DM20-25). To explore the town you can rent a **bike** at the train station for DM10-12 per day. (Open Mon.-Fri. 5am-10pm, Sat.-Sun. 6am-8:30pm.) On Wednesdays (6am-6pm) and Saturdays (6am-noon), buy fresh vegetables and fruits at the **farmer's market** on the *Marktplatz* **Café Bröniel,** Bahnhofgasse 1 (tel. 220 76) serves pastries, pies, and other—by German standards— light fare (stuffed chicken DM9; open Mon.-Sat. 8am-6pm, Sun. 1-6pm).

The nearest **hostel** is in **Bad Blankenburg,** Am Kesselberg 1 (tel. (03674) 25 28) a 20-minute bus ride away. From Anton-Sommer-Str. (just cross the square from the Rudolstadt station) take bus A, B, or C (direction "Bad Blankenburg"; buses run every 20min. during the day) to the Bad Blankenburg *Bahnhof.* Walk straight on Bahnhofstr., then right on Zeigerheimer Weg, up the stairs, and keep slightly to the right. (Reception open 2-7pm, curfew 10pm, 5-day max. stay. DM15.50, over 2 DM18.50. Breakfast included.) From the hostel it's only a 10-minute hike uphill to the ruins of the **Castle Greifenstein.** Bad Blankenburg's **tourist office,** Magdeburger Gasse 1 (tel. 26 67) is straight ahead from the station. From Bad Blankenburg you can wander through the idyllic **Schwarzatal Valley** to Schwarzburg.

G
O
T
H
A

Near Rudolstadt: Groß Kochberg

From Rudolstadt, bus #21 (40min., 10 per day) and foot trails run the eight km north to **Groß Kochberg.** Here lies the beautiful moated palace **Schloß Kochberg.** This was once the summer home of **Charlotte von Stein,** the inspiration for many of Goethe's powerful love poems. Goethe and Frau von Stein frolicked here in the beautiful English gardens while her husband stayed in Weimar with the kids. For 10 years, the two carried on their charged existence until Goethe fled to Italy to sort things out. When he returned two years later, he took up with a simple factory girl 20 years his junior. Frau von Stein, a tad bitter (understandably) about the whole affair, promptly returned everything Goethe had ever given her. When Goethe reciprocated, she publicly burnt her letters to him and composed a nasty tragedy, *Dido,* as a thinly veiled attack on the poet. (Castle open Tues.-Sun. 9am-noon and 1-5pm; Sept.-April Wed.-Sun. 9am-noon and 1-5pm. Admission DM3, students DM2.)

If you plan on a day trip by **bus,** be sure to leave early; the last bus from Groß Kochberg to Rudolstadt leaves around 6pm. (Call tel. 226 12 for updated schedule information. Buses leave from the terminal to the left of the Rudolstadt station.) Signs in front of the castle direct you to **Rosas Bauernstübel,** one of the few restaurants in the area. Try the *Bauernfrühstück* at dinnertime, DM5.50 (open Tues.-Sun. 11am-9pm).

SAALFELD

25 minutes by train from Rudolstadt lies Saalfeld, most famous for its underground **Feengrotten** (fairy grottoes). The Feengrotten, Feengrottenweg 2 (tel. 23 51), were discovered in 1910 near an old aluminum shale mine, which had been worked since the 16th century but abandoned in 1736. Draped with stalactites, the phosphorescent caverns are intensely colorful; the main orange and amber **Märchedom** (fairy cathedral) chamber branches off into the **Blaugrüne Grotte** (blue-green grotto) which glows with teal light. From the marketplace go straight on Brudergasse and then on to Pfortenstr., take a left on Melanchthonstr. and follow the signs. (Feb. to mid-Nov. daily 9am-5pm, guided tours every 45min. DM5, students DM4, children DM3, not open to children under 4, also not wheelchair accessible.)

The town's other bits of color are the **Joahnneskirche** (entrance on Blankenburger Str.) with its stained-glass windows (open Mon.-Sun. 10am-4pm), and the Renaissance **Rathaus** (town hall). The **Thuringer Heimatmuseum,** Münzplatz 5 (tel. 350 10), in the former Franciscan monastery, exhibits medieval artifacts and woodcarvings. (From the market, go straight down Brudergasse. Open Tues.-Fri. 8am-noon, 1-4pm, Sat.-Sun. 9:30am-noon, 1-4pm. DM1.50.)

Saalfeld's **tourist office,** Blankenburger-Str. 4 (tel. and fax (03671) 339 50) has a room-finding service for a DM1 fee (rooms from DM25). From the station walk left on Bahnhofstr. and across the bridge; at the Saaltor gate, take Saalstr., turn right at Markt onto Blankenburger Str. (open Mon.-Fri. 9am-6pm, Sat. 9am-1pm). The train station **rents bikes** for DM10-12 (Mon.-Sun. 7am-6pm). Saalfeld's **youth hostel,** Schieferhof 4 (tel. 28 02 or 51 03 94) is a 25-minute hike from the station. At the Saaltor gate go right on Am Bleichanger and follow the street until Schieferhof. (Reception open 3-7pm. Curfew 10pm. DM14, over 26 DM17. Breakfast included.)

Café Flair, Blankenburgerstr. 8-10 (tel. 21 03) serves mostly coffee-house edibles; a cheese plate will cost you DM6 (open Mon.-Sun. 6am-6pm). **Roter Hirsch,** Markt 6 (tel. 22 85) offers Thuringian wild game (venison "stag plate" DM10; open Mon.-Sun. 9am-10pm). Buy fresh vegetables and fruits at the local **farmer's market** on the market square (Tues. and Thurs. 9am-5pm, Sat. 9am-noon).

◀■■ GOTHA

There are two things to know about the history of Gotha (pronounced GO-ta, not like the poet Goethe): the Social Democratic Party was founded here in 1875, and the Dukes of Saxony-Coburg-Gotha, including Price Albert, who married Queen Vic-

EISENACH

toria of England, lived here. Queen Elizabeth and Prince Charles are direct descendants of this house; the royal family's House of Windsor title is the product of a World War I-era name change, when suddenly no one liked being German.

Schloß Friedenstein, a relatively simple, though immense palace dominating the entire city, was the residence of Prince Albert and other Dukes. The first stop on a tour of the palace is the **Schloßmuseum,** which includes the royal family's art collection—a respectable lot of 16th- and 17th-century works highlighted by a series of Cranachs and the serene *Gothaer Liebespaar* (Lovers of Gotha), a late 15th-century work by a German artist known only as The Master of the Housebook. The royal classical collection is outstanding, especially the quasi-sepulchre with five Egyptian mummies. Upstairs are the royal apartments, well-preserved and empty (open Tues.-Sun. 9am-5pm; admission DM3, students and seniors DM1.50). Also in the palace buildings are the **Museum für Regionalgeschichte,** a small *Waffensammlung* (arms collection) of guns and knives, and the world's first museum of maps, the **Kartografisches Museum.** The medieval and early Mercator (named after the Flemish cartographer) maps are especially gratifying: you know more geography than they did. Clever architectural tricks and optical illusions broaden the tiny stage of the 1683 **Eckhof Theater,** one of the oldest indoor theaters still in use. (Museums and theater open Tues.-Sun. 9am-5pm. Admission DM2.50, students and seniors DM1.25. *Sammelkarte*, DM5, students and seniors DM2.50, allows entry to the *Schloß* and surrounding museums.) Gotha's Baroque **palace garden** is the largest in Europe. Much of it is densely grown like a city park; the area around the *Orangerie* is still painstakingly symmetrical and orderly.

The **Haus am Tivoli,** at the intersection of Cosmartstr., was where August Bebel and others got the Social Democratic Party (SPD) act together. The modern SPD, less radical than its 19th-century incarnation, is still one of the largest political parties in Germany. A GDR-era plaque outside the house commemorates the founding as a "glorious moment in the history of the German working class," even though Marx himself had accused the Social Democrats of selling the proletariat short in his scathing *Critique of the Gotha Programme*. Now that Gotha's residents are sorting out their history, they don't know exactly what to do with the Social Democratic past of the place, and Am Tivoli, is closed indefinitely.

From the far side of the palace, you'll see the *Hauptmarkt,* a collection of 17th-century homes and businesses set on a 45-degree incline. A wave of renovation is currently lapping the hill, but don't hold your breath. Since reconstruction of the *Altstadt* started, the **tourist office,** Blumenbachstr. 1-3 (tel. (03621) 540 36, fax 210 31 34), has temporarily left the Marktplatz for the low-rent district. Facing the *Rathaus* entrance, go left down the narrow Hützelsgasse past the socialist-era apartment block until you see it. Get information on the *Schloß* and the nearby Thuringian Forest, or book a room in private quarters (DM25-35 per bed) for a DM3 fee. Beware: on days when Motörhead tickets go on sale, this place is mobbed.

Gotha's **Jugendherberge (HI),** Mozartstr. 1 (tel. (03621) 540 08, fax 269 23) claims to be located in a building of the Schloß, but it's clear the royals never slept here. From the train station, walk an easy two blocks straight ahead; the hostel is on the right. (Reception open 3-10pm. Loose 10pm curfew, but there's not much to do at night anyway. DM15, over 26 DM18. Breakfast included.) The number of sit down restaurants in Gotha can be counted on the fingers of one hand, and none astounds; load up at the *Markt* and picnic under the elms at the palace gardens Gotha is connected by frequent **trains** to Erfurt and Eisenach, both 20min. away.

■■■ EISENACH

Birthplace of Johann Sebastian Bach and home-in-exile of Martin Luther, Eisenach boasts impressive humanist credentials. Yet inside the walls of the town's Wartburg castle, student fraternities convened in 1817 to promote their bizarre admixture of democracy and xenophobic nationalism; they celebrated their dedication to liberal tolerance by burning conservative books. The writings of Karl Marx and Friedrich Engels were so well received in Eisenach that the duo called the local communist faction "our party." Adolf Hitler called Wartburg "the most German of German castles," and fought a pitched battle with the local church to replace its cross with a swastika. More recently, the East German Communist regime dubbed its "luxury" automobile the *Wartburg*. It is oddly fitting that Eisenach—this humanist, romantic, rationalist, conservative, radical, democratic, despotic bundle of contradictions—should be one of the new Germany's most treasured national symbols.

Practical Information Eisenach's **tourist office,** a short walk from the station at Bahnhofstr. 3-5 (tel.761 62, fax 761 61), has plenty of information on the Wartburg and books rooms in private homes (plus or minus DM25) for no fee (open Mon. 10am-6pm, Tues.-Fri. 9am-6pm, Sat. 10am-2pm). Send your Wartburg postcard from the **post office** on the *Markt*, 99817 Erfurt (open Mon.-Fri. 8am-6pm, Sat. 8am-noon). The **city telephone code** is 03691. The **Ost-Apotheke,** Bahnhofstr. 29 (tel. 32 42), has a list of **pharmacies** open in the evening, but be warned: "evening" means until 8pm on weekdays (open Mon.-Fri. 8am-6pm, Sat. 8am-noon). The best **train** connections to Eisenach are from Erfurt or Weimar in the east, and through Bebra on the IC or IR from the west.

Accommodations and Food Jugendherberge Artur Becker (HI), Marientalstr. 24 (tel. 36 13), fills a comfortable old villa located beyond the castle. From the station, take Bahnhofstr. to Wartburger Allee, which runs into Marientalstr.; the hostel is a long walk down and to the right just past the pond (35min.). Alternately, take the infrequent Mariental bus #3 from the station, get off at Lilienstr., and the path to the hostel will be a few meters in front of you. (Reception open 9am-8pm. Curfew 10pm. DM16, over 26 DM19.50. Fresh breakfast with *müsli* and fruit included.) **Jugendherberge Erich Hornstein,** Bornstr. 7 (tel. 73 20 12), is currently a little rustic, but the next year should bring new beds, hot showers, and likely a name change. Call ahead, as renovations will close the hostel on and off over the next year (DM15, over 26 DM18.50). The nearest **camping** option is at **Am Altenberger See** (tel. (03691) 741 37), offering showers and a view of the lake in the hamlet of Eckardshausen. From the Eisenach station, take the bus toward Bad Liebenstein (4 departures daily 7:35am-5:35pm) and tell the driver your destination as you board. (Reception open until 8pm. DM10 per person.)

Take in the well-priced local food specialties at the **Gestätte Zum Schwan,** Bahnhofstr. 12, with lunch deals under DM8 (open Mon.-Fri. 8am-6pm). Head into the airy **Konditorei-Café Günter Brüheim,** Marienstr. 1 near the Bachhaus, and pout over lemon macaroons and a DM3 cappuccino (open Mon.-Sat. 10am-6pm, Sun. 2-6pm).

Sights Eisenach's medieval half-timbered houses ornament the northwestern slope of the Thüringian Forest. High above them, the Romanesque **Wartburg Schloß** sheltered Martin Luther after his excommunication. The reformer translated the Bible into German here, and after working it bit too late one night, was visited by the devil. By Luther's account, it only took a toss of an ink pot to dispel the beast. Later visitors took him literally and mistook a smudge of stove grease for the damned ink spot, gutting the wall (now one big hole) in their scrabble for a black fleck of souvenir. Otherwise, the simple study has been perfectly preserved. The castle's *Festsaal* preserves the memory of the 1817 meeting of 500 representatives of university fraternities who threw a party, got inspired, and formed Germany's first bourgeois opposition—which was ruthlessly crushed two years later. The flag they toasted still hangs there. Down the hall a wall-sized copy of lyrics from Wagner's *Tannhäuser* is illustrated with ornate Romantic murals of the 12th-century contest of musicians that inspired the opera. This cartoonish bit of decor is itself an artifact of a mid-19th-century renovation. From the top of Wartburg's courtyard

tower, trace the line of your path through the countryside below. The view is amazing—if you turn to the side opposite Eisenach, you can see the Thuringian Forest and all the way to Hesse. The first floor of the tower is a deep, dark former dungeon.

Wartburg sits on the south side of Eisenach, a short stroll down **Wartburger Allee** from the train station. City bus W from the station (DM1) is so infrequent that there are really only two ways up—take the toy-train **Wartburg Express** (one-way DM3, DM2 for those with disabilities) and feel like a tourist, or hike 30 wooded minutes through rich-smelling pines and lilacs and feel like a pilgrim. If you weigh 60kg (132 lbs.) or less, you can opt for a donkey ride for the last stretch (DM1.50). When Eastern Germany was East Germany, Western Germans were issued special visas that allowed them to visit the castle and nothing else, and even these visas were hard to come by. Now, legions of sightseers are making up for lost time. On weekday mornings, expect crowds of schoolchildren; on weekday afternoons, expect crowds of pensioners; on weekends just expect crowds. The interior of the castle can be visited only with a tour, and you may have to wait an hour to enter. (Open daily 8:30am-5pm; Nov.-March 9am-3:30pm. Admission to the whole complex DM10, students and children DM6, seniors and people with disabilities DM7. Admission to museum and Luther study only DM5, DM4, and DM3.)

Back at the base of the mountain, the **Bachhaus,** Frauenplan 21 (tel. (03691) 37 14), where Johann Sebastian stormed into the world in 1685, recreates the family's living quarters. Downstairs are period instruments, on which some guides perform. If you understand German, the guide's anecdotes about Bach's progressively more physically tortuous pedagogical techniques are hilarious. Turn off Wartburger Allee down Grimmelgasse to reach the house (open Mon. noon-5:45pm, Tues.-Sun. 9am-5:45pm; admission DM5, students and seniors DM4). The **Reuter-Wagner Museum,** Reuterweg 2, below the Wartburg, is dedicated to the joint memory of writer Fritz and composer Richard (open Tues.-Sun. 10am-5pm; admission DM2, students and seniors DM1). Town life centers on the pastel **Markt,** bounded by the tilting dollhouse of a **Rathaus** and the latticed **Lutherhaus,** Lutherplatz 8, home to young Martin from 1458 to 1501 (Lutherhaus open daily 9am-1pm and 2-5pm; Oct.-April Mon.-Sat. 9am-1pm and 2-5pm; admission DM3, students DM1.50).

■■■ NORDHAUSEN

Poor Nordhausen. After three major fires, two devastating wars, and one bubonic plague, this 1000-year-old town is getting tired of rebuilding. Though currently dominated by nondescript apartment buildings and shops, Nordhausen has one huge scenic asset: it's a terminus of the **Harzer Querbahn,** the best route through the Harz. (See Wernigerode for more on this narrow-gauge steam train through pristine mountain terrain.) Once you're in town, though, there is precious little to occupy your time. Flattened in 1945, the **Rathaus** has been rebuilt on the *Markt* in all its 18th-century splendor. The interior is closed, but a nervous-looking vibrantly colored statue of **Roland** guards the entrance. Roland is the town's tourism catchword; swill some of the locally brewed *Roland Bräu,* or catch Nordhausen's **Rolandfest** on the second weekend in June. In the Roland off-season, Nordhausen's accomplished theater company performs in the Neoclassical **Stadttheater** on Töpferst.

The **tourist office, Nordhausen Information,** Markt 15 (tel. (03631) 575 86 or 575 40, fax 575 25), across from the *Rathaus,* books rooms in private homes for a DM5 fee (rooms from DM20). From the station, head up Bahnhofstr., which turns into Rautenstr. and take a left on Markt (open Mon.-Fri. 9am-5:30pm). The **postal code** for all of Nordhausen is 99734. Cut off from other Eastern Harz towns only by the state border between Thuringia and Sachsen-Anhalt, Nordhausen is nonetheless essential to any mountain itinerary and a route into the hills from the larger cities to the east (be sure to see the Eastern Harz section in Sachsen-Anhalt, below). Frequent trains run to Erfurt (2hr.), and to Halle (1hr. 45min.) with connections to Leipzig. The station for the Querbahn, **Nordhausen Nord,** is left of the main train station

Nordhausen Bahnhof. The **Nordhausen-Altentor** station is farther from the town center, but near the hostel.

To reach the **Jugendherberge (HI),** Johann-Kleinspehnstr. 1 (tel. (03631) 85 87), get off the Querbahn at Nordhausen-Altentor, turn left onto Bochumerstr., bear left on Hauptstr., and then right onto Johann-Kleinpehnstr. From the main station, catch the bus (direction "Nordhausen-Salza") around the corner (to the right of the entrance, past the wall map, and across the street to the left) to Hauptstr., continue in the same direction, then turn right at Johann-Kleinspehnstr. (Reception open 5pm-8pm. Curfew 10pm. DM14, over 26 DM17.50. Breakfast included.) Fresh vegetables and fruits can be purchased at the local **farmers' market** on Blassiikirchplatz, behind the *Rathaus* and to your left (open Tues.-Fri. 9am-5pm). Just off the Blassiikirchplatz, the **Café Altstadt,** Kranichstr. 19 (tel. 34 82) serves up savory meals (steak DM11) as well as cakes and other sugar items (open Tues.-Sat. 11am-7pm, Sun. noon-7pm).

SACHSEN-ANHALT

Eastern Germany's most polluted province, the cities in this region used to belch enough toxic filth into the atmosphere to make the air in Los Angeles look healthy by comparison. But Sachsen-Anhalt is rapidly cleaning up its act, and in the meantime it contains a number of worthwhile destinations: Wittenberg, city of Luther and home of the Protestant Reformation; and Tangermunde, a medieval town the world seems to have been forgotten since the 14th century.

■■■ WITTENBERG

Martin Luther claimed that Wittenberg was the source and font of his life's work. He preached, taught, married, raised children, and led the Protestant Reformation from this picturesque city, and when he died in Eisleben in 1546, his body was returned here and buried directly beneath the pulpit of the **Schloßkirche** (castle church). In 1938, after taking note of the steady stream of Luther pilgrims, the town returned the compliment and officially renamed itself "Lutherstadt Wittenberg."

Luther managed to hang onto his celebrity status in the officially atheistic DDR (he was a harsh critic of Catholic wealth, inciting early bourgeois revolutions here and there). He also had a presence in the civil sphere; for many East Germans the image of Luther risking life and limb to nail his 95 complaints to the door of the *Schloßkirche* became an emblem of courageous resistance. A successor of Luther in the *Schloßkirche* (as Mark Twain wrote, if history doesn't repeat itself, it certainly does rhyme), Pastor Friedrich Schorlemmer was a key player in the peaceful upheaval of 1989. Since that year, the pilgrims have returned, and the slow shuffle of Scandinavian church groups has pushed up the prices in local *gastätte* (restaurants) and put a new coat on the town's architectural remnants.

Practical Information Wittenberg Information is at Collegienstr. 29 (tel. (03491) 22 39), between the Lutherhalle and the market. (Open Mon.-Fri. 9am-6pm, Sat. 10am-2pm, Sun. 11am-3pm.) The **pharmacy** on the Marktplatz where Lucas Cranach pushed drugs to support his art habit still meets your medicinal needs. (Open Mon.-Tues. and Thurs.-Fri. 8am-12:30pm and 2-6pm. A sign guides you to an open pharmacy when this one is closed.) The **post office** is at the corner of Fleischerstr. and Lutherstr. near the Lutherhalle (open Mon.-Fri. 8am-6pm, Sat. 9am-noon). **Rent a bike** from the regional tourist office, Mittelstr. 33 (tel. (03491) 26 10), across Collegienstr. from the Lutherhalle. (DM1 per hr., DM5 per day. Open daily 9:30am-5:30pm; Nov.-March Mon.-Sat. 9:30am-5:30pm)

Wittenberg is a mere hour and a half from Berlin by train (DM14.40), Halle (DM9.80), or Leipzig (DM9.80), making it an excellent daytrip from any of the aforementioned hubs. Store your pack at the station (DM4; open Mon.-Fri. 6am-6pm, Sat.-Sun. 8am-6pm).

Accommodations and Food Hotels in the *Altstadt* are overpriced, but the tourist office (see above) can help locate private rooms (singles DM40-60) for a DM3 fee; rooms in nearby towns can be as little as DM15 for a single with breakfast, but check transport schedules carefully. The **Jugendherberge (HI)** in the castle has a unique atmosphere and reasonable prices (tel. (03491) 32 55). The hostel is a 20-minute walk from the station, capped by 69 steps to the reception desk. (Reception open 7-10am and 5-10pm. Lockout 10am-4pm. Curfew 10pm. DM15, over 26 DM18.)

Even the most stubborn papist will enjoy the *suppe* (soup, DM4) at **Zur Schloßfreiheit,** Coswigstr. 24 (tel. (03491) 29 80; open Sun.-Fri. noon-2pm and 6pm-midnight). Or pick and choose from the overpriced restaurants in town. Pub grub and Guinness on tap are Wittenberg's latest: the **Irish Harp Pub,** Collegienstr. 71, across from the tourist office, offers Irish hospitality in the heart of Sachsen-Anhalt. Open daily from 10am to 1am, with live music on weekends. Women can get away from it all at the **Frauencafé** in the rather worn municipal entertainment complex, Lutherstr. 41/42 (tel. (03491) 2844).

Sights This town is home to a handful of major sights, three of them connected to the life of the uppity minister. As you exit the train station, head straight and swing under the tracks onto Collegienstr.; the street is only 1.2km long and encompasses all major sights. On your right stands the sickly **elm tree** under which Luther defiantly burned the papal bull (a decree of excommunication, not a Catholic horned beast). At Collegienstr. 54 lies Luther's home, the **Lutherhalle,** to which he moved in 1508. Pick up an English-language brochure (DM1) from the desk. The **museum** inside follows the course of the Reformation and Luther's ground-breaking German translation of the Bible. Bibliophiles will enjoy the antique printing press and the pristine copy of the first book printed in the West, the **Gutenberg Bible.** The family's living room on the second floor has been preserved intact along with one obnoxious tourist's graffito: Russian Tsar Peter the Great scribbled his name above the door when he stopped by in 1702. (Open Tues.-Sun. 9am-6pm. Last entry 5:30pm. Admission DM4, students and seniors DM2.)

St. **Marienkirche** (St. Mary's Church), known for its distinctive altar painted by pharmacist-*cum*-artistic genius **Cranach the Elder,** is farther down Collegienstr. near the market square. This artist anachronistically incorporated Luther himself, as well as several other town notables, in the biblical scene (open Mon.-Sat. 9am-noon and 2-5pm, Nov.-April Mon.-Sat. 10am-noon and 2-4pm). Nearby towers Wittenberg's **Rathaus,** with its imposing façade, and late-Renaissance portal frame. Matching statues of Luther and Melanchthon share the square with the **Jungfernröhrwasser** (fountain of youth), a 16th-century well whose refreshing (and potable) waters still flow through original wooden pipes. The tourist office sells small pots of this "water of youth," actually filled with good German schnapps.

Continue down Collegienstr. to the **Schloßkirche,** crowned with a sumptuous Baroque cupola. Inside you'll find a copy of the complaints which Luther nailed to these doors. At the front of the church, the man who fought to translate the scriptures into the common man's tongue is interred, ironically, under a Latin plaque. Historical hanger-on Phillip Melanchton isn't far from Luther, even in death. Credit for the exemplary condition of the local church rests with Kaiser Karl V, who paid for the restoration in the 1840s. At the same time he arranged for 15 people to check and make sure that old Luther really was buried here. The crypt opening was conducted in secret for fear that failure to find Luther would discredit the church. They found the remains—or so they said (open Mon. 2-5pm, Tues.-Sat. 9am-noon and 2-5pm, Sun. 10:30am-noon and 2-5pm; Nov.-April Tues.-Sat.10am-noon and 2-4pm, Sun. 2-4pm, Sun. services 9am).

To enjoy nature for a few hours, take a bus (5 per day) from Mauerstr. to the **Wörlitzer Park,** built by a local prince who wanted his quaint palace and Gothic house to be surrounded by exotic flora and fauna. (Open dawn to dusk.)

■ ■ ■ DESSAU

Dessau, about 30km west of Wittenberg, is home to one of the greatest architectural monuments of this century, the sleek Gropius-designed **Bauhaus art school.** For a brief period from 1925 to 1932, Bauhaus instructors Walter Gropius, Hannes Meyer, Lazlo Maholy-Nagy, and their students struggled with the aesthetic implications of modernity and attempted to reconcile human living spaces with 20th-century industrialization. Ironically, Dessau is also home to some of the less successful building projects in recent memory—row upon row of DDR-era apartment blocks. Innocent travelers can easily bypass the city center for the leafier neighborhoods northwest of the train station.

HALLE

The Bauhaus began in Weimar in 1919, but was pressured into leaving by the conservative local oligarchy. The school brought its theory of constructive and artistic unity to Dessau in 1925; in 1932 the school fled again to permissive Berlin before being driven from the country entirely by the Nazis in 1933. Despite this unfortunate need to either keep moving or die, the masters of Bauhaus inspired an architectural renaissance that reached its logical conclusion in the sleek skyscrapers of America's larger cities. After the war, as Dessau rebuilt, the shapely Bauhaus legacy was ignored in favor of great, gray, bestial buildings. Since 1977 the **Bauhaus,** Gropiusallee 38 (tel. (0340) 70 51), has been open again as a design school. The Bauhaus currently decorates its sparse and linear walls with the works of *Bauhausmeisters* Gropius, Klee, Kandinsky, Feinger, and Marianne Brandt. Moving through the exhibit, examine the building's details from window panes to door handles–the Bauhaus was designed to be looked at. To get to the school from the station, turn left, go up the steps, and go left over the railroad tracks. Turn left at the first street onto Kleiststr., and then right onto Bauhausstr. (open Tues.-Sun. 10am-5pm, last entry 4:30pm; admission DM4, students and seniors DM2).

On the other side of the intersection of Puschkinallee and Kleiststr. is the **Schloß Georgium,** home to the **Anhaltische Gemäldegalerie** (tel. (0340) 21 38 74). Set in the midst of painstakingly tended formal gardens, this 17th-century country estate displays a range of lesser-known paintings from the 16th to the 19th century, several Lucas Cranach works, and a painting by Brueghel. (Open daily 10am-6pm. Admission DM3, students and seniors DM1.50. Gardens always open to the public.)

For daytippers, Dessau is a brief 40 minutes from Wittenberg by train (8 per day), an hour from Leipzig (12 per day), and two hours from Berlin-Lichtenberg station (3 per day). To get to the local **tourist office,** Friedrich-Neumann-Str. 12 (tel. (0340) 21 46 61), take the streetcar from in front of the station's main exit or head down Antoinettenstr. through the park (open Mon.-Fri. 10am-6pm, Sat. 9am-noon). They will find you a room (about DM30) for no fee, or guide you to the clean but slightly impersonal **Jugendherberge (HI),** Waldkaterweg 11 (tel. (0340) 21 33 12). To go it on your own, follow the directions to the Bauhaus, walk through Bauhausplatz and bear right down Fischereistr. After two blocks, turn left on Zebigkerstr.; Waldkaterweg is on your left. (Reception open 6:30am-10am and 5-11pm. No lockout. Curfew 11pm. DM14, over 26 DM18. Breakfast included.)

The chic artistic **Klub am Bauhaus** in the Bauhaus school basement seems as out of place in this city as the school itself, but they have good, light fare at good, light prices such as pizzas and *Abendbrötchen* sandwiches under DM10 (open Mon.-Fri. 8am-midnight, Sat. 10am-1am, Sun. 10am-10pm).

■■■ HALLE

Halle an der Salle, the fortunate town saved by Katrin's drumming in the climactic scene of Brecht's *Mother Courage,* was also lucky enough to emerge from World War II more or less unscathed. While other cities dug themselves out of the rubble, the people of Halle thanked the heavens for their good fortune. Three months after war's end, the occupying Americans swapped Halle for a piece of Berlin under the terms of the Yalta agreement; in the post-war decades it drew tens of thousands of new residents as Sachsen-Anhalt's political and industrial capital. Halle is marked by its Neustadt, a pre-fab district of housing projects for chemical plant workers, and the highest level of air pollution in the former DDR. Since reunification, at least 15,000 workers have lost their jobs, adding a sharp edge to the urban outlook. Yet despite the uncertainty, Halle's unchanged cobblestone streets, historic Moritzburg Fortress, gabled apartment blocks, and screeching streetcars still provide a unique glimpse of what the historic German city must have been.

PRACTICAL INFORMATION

Most of Halle is walkable, but the rattling streetcar system covers the margins (DM1.70 per ticket, day pass DM4). The S-Bahn system serves the gritty and economically depressed suburbs, including Halle-Neustadt.

Tourist Office: (tel. (0345) 233 40 for information, tel.(0345) 283 71 for room-finding service). In the *Roter Turm* on the Marktplatz. From the main station, cross beneath the underpass to the left as you exit the building, follow the pedestrian tunnel and follow Leipzigerstr. past the *Leipziger Turm* to the Marktplatz (15min.) Or, streetcar #4 (direction "Heide/Hubertusplatz") or #7 (direction "Kröllwitz"): Markt (4 stops). They hand out a skimpy city map and book rooms (singles DM35-40, doubles DM45-90). Open Mon.-Tues. and Thurs.-Fri. 9am-6pm, Wed. 10am-6pm, Sat. 9am-1pm.

Currency Exchange: Decent rates at most major banks, including the one at the main train station. Open Mon.-Fri. 8am-12:30pm and 1:30-3pm.

Post Office: The office is at the corner of Hansening and Großessteinstr., across from the opera and about 10min. from the Marktplatz. Open Mon.-Fri. 7am-6pm, Sat. 8am-noon.

Telephone Code: 0345

Mitfahrzentrale, Weingärter 28 (tel. (0345) 244 26).

ACCOMMODATIONS

Hotels and pensions are far above the budgetary means of simple folk, though the tourist office lists some reasonable rooms in private homes. The best bet is to head for the **Jugendherberge (HI),** August-Bebel-Str. 48a (tel. (0345) 247 16), in a newly restored mansion north of the market. Thin mattresses are more than compensated for by the quiet residential street, balconies, new bathroom fixtures, and the hardwood elegance of the common areas. Take streetcar #7(direction "Kröllwitz") six stops from the train station or two stops from the market, then follow Große Ulrichstr. one block, turn right onto Puschkinstr., turn right onto August-Bebel-Str. at the Hong Kong restaurant, walk two blocks, and the hostel is on your left. (Reception open 7-10am and 5-11pm, lockout 10am-5pm, curfew 11pm; DM16, over 26 DM20; breakfast included.)

FOOD AND NIGHTLIFE

Affordable sit-down restaurants are a rare find in this town, but Halle is a city of cafés. Coffeehouses, ice cream parlors, and cafés line Leipzigstr. and the Marktplatz. Between the Marktplatz and Moritzburg are cafés geared toward the younger student crowd. Nightlife is centered on the Moritzburg Fortress.

Turm, (tel. (0345) 292 26), in the north tower of the Moritzburg Fortress. Hosts the city's Studentenclub. Foreign students with ID are heartily welcomed; join the Germans for a cheap drink, live jazz, and a dance. Open Mon.-Sat. 7pm-midnight, closed during university vacations.

Café Die Insel, Kleine Klausstr. A pleasant café whose sidewalk tables overlook a 15th-century Fachwerk building. You could do a lot worse in this world.

neues theater café, Große Ulrichstr. 51, is an especially inviting spot on a café-lined street. One good neighbor, **Casablanca,** Große Ulrichstr. 80, serves up drinks and light food to a noisy student crowd daily from 10am till the wee hours.

Kabarett "Die Kleibitzensteiner" (tel. (0345) 249 62). Visit this political satire cabaret in the south tower of the Moritzburg fortress.

Galeriecafé, in the **Staatliche Galerie Moritzburg Halle** museum (see Sights). You can mix water and wine among the displays of medieval chalices or drink tea surrounded by four centuries of teapots. Open Tues. 11am-8pm, Wed.-Fri. 10am-5pm, Sat.-Sun. 10am-5:30pm.

SIGHTS

Halle revolves around the **Marktplatz** which buzzes with streetcar traffic, vegetable stands, three-card monte con artists, and international vendors. At its center stands the **Roter Turm**, a bell tower built 400 years ago. Various rumors exist to explain the origin of the tower's name; some credit the copper roof, others say the architect was a Herr Rote. The most gruesome version tells that after it was built (1418-1506), the blood of the people executed at the adjoining gallows splattered onto the tower, giving it a grisly tinge. (The interior of the tower is closed to the public.) Across from the tower lies the **Marktkirche unsere lieben Frauen,** whose altar is adorned with a triptych painted by students under the direction of Lucas Cranach. Protestants finished the half-built church in 1554, but traces of its Catholic past can be seen in the style of the altar, the 14th-century baptistry, and the 15th-century wooden crucifix at the back of the church. Above the altar is the organ on which Händel began his studies, silent for over 100 years until recent renovations. (Open Mon.-Wed. and Fri. 10am-noon and 3-6pm, Thurs. 4-5pm, Sat. 9am-noon and 3-5pm, Sun. services at 10am. Free 30-min. organ concerts Tues. at 5:30pm and Fri. at 11:30pm.) The 16th-century **Marktschlößchen,** a rather small castle, overlooks the Marktplatz with its simple, clean architectural detail and unassuming presence.

An 1859 centennial memorial to the composer Georg Friedrich Händel also decorates the Marktplatz, but the most important Händel shrine is his family home. The outstanding **Händelhaus,** Große Nikolaistr. 5-6 (tel. (0345) 246 06), a short walk from the market down Kleine Klausstr., offers high-quality stereo soundtracks in 19 languages to guide pilgrims through Händel's career in Germany, Italy, and England. More recent echoes are heard in the museum's recordings of workers' choirs, and the low key with which it sounds out the composer's emphasis on religion. (Museum open Mon.-Wed. and Fri.-Sun. 9:30am-5:30pm, Thurs. 9:30am-7pm. Admission DM2, students DM0.50, seniors DM1, Thurs. free.) June 3-7, 1994 witnesses the annual **Händel-Festspiele,** a four-day celebration of the Baroque and its master. Tickets are available from the tourist office, but the festival does not generally sell out. From Händel's home to the **Dom** (cathedral) is a five-minute walk down Nikolaistr. The ancient complex, begun in 1250, was once a major repository of religious relics. Today the church's most treasured artifacts are 17 life-size figures by Peter Schroh from the 16th century (cathedral closed for renovations in 1993, possibly continuing in 1994).

To reach Halle's most impressive sight, the **Moritzburg Fortress,** go around the far side of the Dom, down the hill, turn right, and walk up the hill. Most of this 15th-century giant is reserved for the **Staatliche Galerie Moritzburg Halle** (tel. (0345) 370 31), a mid-size art museum focusing mostly on 19th- and 20th-century German painters. Halle's extensive Expressionist collection—including works by Max Beckmann, Paul Klee, Edvard Munch and Oskar Kokoschka—was particularly offensive to Hitler, who drew heavily from this museum to create the infamous exhibit of "degenerate" art that toured throughout Nazi Germany. Although much of the collection was burnt or sold off by the Nazis, the salvaged works remain an impressive monument to artistic freedom. The museum also houses the **Galeriecafé** (see Food). (Museum open Tues. 11am-8:30pm, Wed.-Fri. 10am-5:30pm, Sat.-Sun. 10am-6pm. Last admission 30min. before closing. Admission DM3, students DM1, free on Tues.) Between the Moritzburg and the Marktplatz are a host of sidestreets lined with unkempt architectural treasures from Baroque to *Jugendstil.*

■■■ EASTERN HARZ (Ostharz)

Heinrich Heine wrote that even Mephistopheles stopped and trembled when he approached the Harz, the devil's dearest mountains. It's easy to see why Heine—as well as Goethe, Bismarck, and a host of others—fell in love with the mist-shrouded woodlands. Harz towns have a common element in the ubiquitous statues of **Roland,** the mustached, sword-wielding nephew of Charlemagne immortalized in

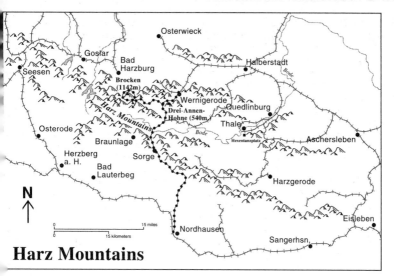

Harz Mountains

N ↑

the "Song of Roland" and co-opted for obscure reasons by local communities as a folk hero. Stubborn, half-abandoned castles stand over Wernigerode, Quedlinburg, and Halberstadt. Pragmatic transportation becomes an exhilarating attraction with the **Harzquerbahn**, a stylishly antique, narrow-gauge railway that steams through the Harz from Nordhausen to Wernigerode, passing through the unfortunately named towns of **Sorge** and **Elend** (Sorrow and Misery) and reaching a 540m peak on **Drei-Annen-Hohne**. The removal of Germany's internal border has opened the mountains to ever more vacationers seeking historic villages, good skiing and better hiking; the Eastern Harz is learning to court tourism again.

Some of the smaller towns in the area include **Ilsenburg,** with its open-air theater (DM2.20) and mining museum, and **Elbingerode,** home to the **Shaubergwerk "Buchenberg"** mining caverns and museum (tel. (039454) 22 06). The famed **Hermannshöhle** and **Baumannshöhle** of **Rübeland** are also just a bus ride away; learn again, and forget again, the difference between stalactites and stalagmites in these two monstrous caves. Hermannshöhle (tel. (039454) 91 10; open Mon.-Sun. 9:15-4:15pm, DM7, students DM3.50); Baumannshöhle (tel. (039454) 92 08; same hours and prices). The main Wernigerode *Bahnhof* is also next door to the regional **bus station,** which has tentacles extending throughout the Eastern Harz. The state borders between the *Länder* Lower Saxony, Sachsen-Anhalt, and Thuringia all run through the region. New bus lines connecting the Eastern and **Western Harz** are restoring the area's common identity. As of summer 1993, buses left from Bad Harzburg at 8:15, 8:50, 9:50am, 12:45, 1:50, 5, and 6:15pm; and leave Wernigerode for Bad Harzburg at 6:40, 7:50, 9:50, 10:45am, 2:20, 3:45, and 7:15pm. (For information on the Western Harz Mountains see Lower Saxony.) In June, *Harzkirschen,* cherries grown in the mountains, are in season and sold from stands in every town.

WERNIGERODE

Wernigerode was one of Goethe's secret spots in the hills, and in some ways it is still the same small town he visited on his trips through the Harz, replete with half-timber and topped by a castle. The sky around Wernigerode is partly filled by the **Brocken,** the Harz's highest and supposedly most haunted mountain. This *Bergstadt* (mountain city) is a well-preserved and well-worth-it destination for riders of the Querbahn, the narrow gauge rail that cuts through the Harz. Wernigerode is the crossing-over point from the Western to Eastern Harz, but more than that, it is the region's most touristy town, and with good reason.

Practical Information Wernigerode's busy **tourist office,** Breitestr. around the corner from the *Rathaus* (tel. (03943) 330 35), books rooms in private homes or hotels for 10% of the first-night price (open Mon.-Fri. 9am-6pm, Sat.-Sun. 10am-3pm). The privately owned souvenir-stand-*cum*-**Harz-Touristen** office, Burgberg 9a, (tel. 232 34), at the foot of the *Schloß*, also finds rooms, but only in private homes (open Mon-Fri. 11am-5pm, Sat.-Sun. 11am-3pm; room service open Mon.-Fri. 11am-7pm). **Change money** and mail cards at the **post office,** Marktstr., 38855 Wernigerode (open Mon.-Fri. 8am-7pm, Sat. 9am-noon). The **telephone** city code is **03943.** Women can find tips on the Harz or other assistance at the **Frauenförderzentrum,** Kochstr. 19 (tel. 29 81 26; open Mon.-Thurs. 3-4pm). **Hans-Joachim Hallerman,** Breite Str. 27 (tel. 325 08) will rent you a **bicycle** to explore the forest (DM15 per day). To reach Wernigerode from Halle or Magdeburg, change trains at Halberstadt; a bus runs directly to Bad Harzburg. The town has two central **train stations** to serve its 37,000 citizens. **Wernigerode-Westentor** is the next-to-last stop on the *Harzquerbahn,* and close to the city center—just head up Mittelstr., then right on Bahnhofstr., and you're at the *Markt.* The antique steamer also stops at the main **Bahnhof Wernigerode,** next to the regional **bus terminal.**

Accommodations and Food To reach Wernigerode's **Jugendgästehaus,** Friedrichstr. 53 (tel. 320 61), take bus A or D to Kirchstr., or walk from the Westentor station right on Unter den Zindeln (25min.), and then turn right on Friedrichstr. Guests sleep in motel-style rooms, but the central building is attractive. (Reception open 5-7pm. DM14.50, over 26 DM18.50. Breakfast included.) **Hotel zur Post,** Marktstr. 17 (tel. 324 36), is right around the corner from the *Rathaus*. The rooms are small but newly-renovated, with wall-to-wall carpeting. (Reception open 7am-midnight. Singles DM45. Doubles DM85. Breakfast included.) **Hotel zur Tanne,** Breite Str. 57 (tel. 325 54), is closer to the *Bahnhof,* less expensive, and fills up quickly; call ahead. (Reception open 9am-2pm and 5pm-midnight. Singles DM35. Doubles DM55. Breakfast included.) Meals at **China Restaurant,** Schöne Ecke (tel. 431 13), are still more Chinese than German (under DM10). **Fruchthaus Lucke** on Westerstr. has a good stock of fresh fruits (open Mon.-Fri. 9am-6pm, Sat. 8am-noon). There is a farmers' **market** in the pedestrian zone (Tues. and Thurs. 10am-5pm).

Sights Wernigerode's magnificent **Schloß,** perched in the mountains above the town, was maintained by the GDR as a museum of feudalism, and it's just grand. Graf Otto zu Stolberg-Wernigerode, one of Bismarck's main flunkies, once hosted Kaiser Wilhelm here for wildly extravagant, aristocratic hunting expeditions. The **Königszimmer** guest room has been perfectly preserved, down to the red-and-green brocaded wallpaper. Outside on the terrace, cannons are still poised in defense, and a fountain is angled to catch the sun; from here, you can see straight to Brocken. (Open daily 10am-6pm; Oct.-April Tues.-Sun. 9am-4pm. Admission DM5, students DM4, under 14 DM3; add DM1 for a tour.) Ride up to the *Schloß* on the **Bimmelbahn,** a truck-train that leaves every 20 minutes from the clock with flowers marking the hours, at the intersection of Teichdamm and Klintgasse, behind the *Rathaus.* (Departures every 30min. daily 9:30am-5:30pm, Nov.-April every 45min. daily 10:30am-4:30pm. One-way DM2.50, under 10 DM1.) If you'd rather walk, take either the gravel *Christiantalweg* path or follow the white brick road marked "Burgberg," and branch off for a hike in the wooded park around the castle.

Wernigerode relishes its *Fachwerk* (half-timbered) streets and squares. The **Krummelsches Haus,** Breitestr. 72, is so completely covered with ornate wood carvings that the original *Fachwerk* is hardly visible. The **Ältestes Haus,** Hinterstr 48, is the oldest house in the city, and has survived several fires, two bomb runs, and various acts of God since its construction in the early 15th century. The **Kleinste**

Haus, Kochstr. 43, is 2.95m wide, 4.2m to the eaves, and, for the less than tall, the door is only 1.7m high. Wernigerode has two museums. The **Krellsche Museum Schmiede,** Breite Str., is a smithy (open Wed.-Thurs. and Sat.-Sun. 1-5pm, Fri. 10am-3pm; admission DM1, students DM0.50). The **Harz Museum,** Am Klint, is an all-Harz gathering of, well, mountain stuff (open Mon.-Sat. 10am-4pm).

The *Harzquerbahn* steam train stops at Drei-Annen-Hohne for a few minutes after it leaves Wernigerode, enough time to either look around the highest point of the route or to jump on the **Brockenbahn,** which spirals up and around the mountain. (DM30. For more on the bewitching beauty of Brocken's peak, see the Western Harz information.)

HALBERSTADT

If you plan to travel any farther east than Wernigerode, chances are good you'll have to make a connection in Halberstadt, the one town in the region with a legitimate claim to the title "gateway to the Eastern Harz." Halberstadt, known up to World War II as a producer of cigars, gloves, and sausages (everything a gentleman needed), appears to be a grimy town from the moment you enter the train station. Reserve your final judgment until you gaze upon the *Altstadt.* Follow Bahnhofstr. and turn left on Magdeburgerstr. to reach the multi-colored bricks of **Breiter Weg**; this pedestrian lane ends at the **Fischmarkt,** where citizens gather every Tuesday, Friday, and Saturday to sell their wares in front of the **Martinikirche** (market open Tues., Fri. 8am-5pm, Sat. 8am-noon). The opposite façade boasts the oldest **Roland statue** in former East Germany, built in 1433, now scarred by time and bombs.

The unquestioned focus of the *Altstadt,* though, is the **Domplatz,** framed by the **Liebfrauenkirche** and the **Dom St. Stephanus,** a Gothic cathedral *par excellence.* The only way to see the **Dommuseum** and its **treasury,** complete with gilded everything and the oldest known tapestries (dating from 1150), is to take a combined tour of it and the *Dom.* (Open Tues.-Fri. 10:30-11:30am, noon-2pm, 2:30-3:30pm, and 4-5pm; Sat. 10:30-11:30am, noon-2pm, and 2:30-4:30pm; Sun. noon-2pm and 3-4:30pm. Tours Mon.-Fri. at 10am, 11:30am, 2pm, and 3:30pm, Sat. 10am and 2pm, Sun. 11:30am and 2:30pm; Nov.-April Mon.-Sat. 10am and 2pm, Sun. 11:30am.) In front of the *Dom,* a group of quartz-like stones pay tribute to Halberstadt's once-thriving Jewish community, completely wiped out by the Holocaust. On the night of the dedication in 1992, the memorial was plastered with fascist and neo-Nazi symbols; the *Denkmal* was fully cleaned the following morning.

Follow the *Dom's* **rose garden** out and around to the **Städtisches Museum** (tel. 242 16), a scrapbook of Halberstadt history, and the **Museum Heineanum** (tel. 230 10), a gallery of our feathered friends. (Both open Tues.-Fri. 9am-5pm, Sat.-Sun. 10am-5pm. Museum admission DM2, students DM1. Ornithological hall admission DM1.50, students DM0.75.) At the city's southern limits, the **Jagdschloß** holds dominion over not much more than Germany's oldest **wine keg,** storing 132,760 liters of rotten grape juice. The **Belvedere tower** and **mausoleum,** both in the same park, are also worth lifting a glass to.

The newly renovated **tourist office,** Düsterngraben 3 (tel. (03941) 583 15), down an alley just in front of the *Dom,* will have information on these sights and more and will find you a room (from DM30) in one of the three hotels or myriad guest houses for a DM5 fee (open Mon.-Fri. 9am-1pm and 2-6pm, Sat. 10am-1pm). From April-Sept. you can **rent a bike** at the train station (DM10-12; open daily 6:30am-7:30pm). There's no *Jugendherberge* here, but the romantically-named **Campingplatz SH 200** (tel. (03941) 245 96) is right on the *Halberstädter See* in the northeast part of town. From the station follow Bahnhofstr., then right on Magdeburger-Str. and left on Warmholzberg (30min. hike). (Reception open daily 7-9:30am and 3-7pm. DM 4.50 per person, DM5.50 per tent.) The **Galerie/Café 1580** at Düsterngraben, just around the corner from the tourist office, backs its meals with changing exhibits of work by local artists; the art is more ambitious than the food. (Open Mon.-Sat. 11am-midnight, Sun. 11am-10pm, except for the first Fri., Sat., Sun. of each month.)

QUEDLINBURG

It is hard to capture the sight of Quedlinburg's streets on paper. No other destination in the Harz can match this town. Almost every corner is packed with half-timbered houses that look as though they've been around since 919, when Heinrich I waited in the market square for the news that he'd been chosen as emperor. Quedlinburg was a bit run down over the past forty years, but locals are busy painting and patching. Recently, Quedlinburg has gained some notoriety as party to an international art-theft scandal. In 1945, medieval manuscripts and other ecclesiastical gems from the church were hidden in a basement to protect them from the bombing. An American G.I. came across them, threw the lot in his pack, and took it all home to Texas. The story came out only after his recent death, when his heirs tried to dispose of the goods. The German government mounted a knock-out legal battle, and this small town got the prize, now on display in the church in the **Burgberg castle** above town.

Heinrich I died within the original walls of the Burgberg, an old Saxon stronghold in 936. The current 13th-century structure has been a favorite residence-in-exile for the ruling family's widows and inconvenient relatives. The castle complex (tel. (03946) 27 30) consists of three parts: the **Schloßmuseum,** the **Schloßgarten,** and the **Stiftskirche.** The museum primarily depicts city history from way back when until the present (open Tues.-Sun. 10am-6pm; Oct.-April Tues.-Sun. 9am-5pm). The Stiftskirche is the castle church, where the purloined art treasures, now back from Texas, are on permanent display. The church is only accessible by guided tour, although it hours may be extended in 1994. (Tours every half-hour May-Oct. Tues.-Sat. 11am-4:30pm; Nov.-April Tues.-Sat. 11am and 2pm, Sun. 2pm.) The **Schloßkrug** is a terraced restaurant on top of the mountain that only the resident royalty can afford. Instead, loiter in the gardens around the *Schloß*, or walk down the castle path past an impressive row of old houses, cramped together on the hillside.

Underneath the castle the **Feininger museum,** Finkenherd 5a (tel. (03946) 22 38) displays the torrid work of the Expressionist painters who belonged to the *Brücke* artist circle (open Apr.-Sept. Tues.-Sun. 10am-noon, 1-6pm; Oct.-Mar. Tues.-Sun. 9am-noon and 1-5pm). The unavoidable stone statue of **Roland** guards the ivy-covered **Rathaus,** while the neighboring **Ecktürmchen** has the distinction of being the smallest Gothic tower in the new Federal States. The **Benediktikirche** graces the *Markt* with its 13th-century base; the twisting Solomonic columns of the altar are truly exceptional (closed for renovation through 1994). The **Lipertikirche,** a prime example of Romanesque architecture, can only be visited with a guided tour organized by the tourist office (tours Apr.-Sept. daily at 11am; meet at the tourist office). It's natural that the Quedlinburg **Fachwerkmuseum,** Wordgasse 3 (tel. (03946) 38 28), should itself be a prime example of early crossed-wooden-beams-and-brick architecture (open May-Sept. Mon.-Wed. and Fri.-Sun. 10am-5pm; admission DM2).

From Wernigerode, change trains at Halberstadt for Quedlinburg. If you're looking for a hostel, or even a hotel under DM60 per person per night, you're in the wrong town; however, Quedlinburg's **tourist office,** Markt 12 (tel. (03946) 26 33) will find you a private room (from DM25; no fee), sell you museum tickets, take you on tours, and generally provide everything else short of a massage. From the train station walk across the bridge then straight on Bahnhofstr., then take a left or Heiligegleiststr., then a right on Steinbrücke (open Mon.-Fri. 9am-6pm, Sat.-Sun 10am-3pm; Oct.-April Mon.-Fri. 10am-3pm). **Rent bikes** at the train station from DM10-12 per day (open Mon.-Fri. 5am-8pm, Sat. 8am-4pm, Sun. 8am-6pm).

On the way to the castle, the **Brauerei Lüdde,** Blassiistr. 14 (tel. (03946) 32 52 offers beer with the obscene name *Pubarschknall* (a name which hardly merit translation; something about bad digestion) and hearty meals (DM9); they also offe sweet brewing demonstrations (open Mon.-Sun. 11am-1am). Just across from th Feininger Museum, the **Café "Am Finkenherd,"** Schloßberg 15 (tel. (03946) 38 41 serves pastries and light entrees (DM4.50) in a reconstructed half-timber house Local **farmers** sell their products at the Marktplatz (Wed. 9am-5pm, Sat. 9am-noon

THALE

A short train ride from Quedlinburg lands you in Thale (pronounced TAHL-uh, not "Thail"), a small town with notoriety more for the wonders outside its walls than from within. The **Hexentanzplatz,** the plateau where witches gather to dance *Walpurgisnacht* away, is just outside of the town center (see the Western Harz introduction for specifics on this April 30 display of hedonism). In 1901, someone decided to capitalize on the tourist potential, and the **Walpurgishalle** was built. This barn-like structure, graced with the helmed head of a Viking deity, is now a museum dedicated to witches and other Harz pagans (open May-Aug. daily 9am-4pm; admission DM1). The **Schwebebahn** (tel. (03947) 22 54), a gondola ski lift, runs from the town to the plateau. (Every 15min. May-Sept. daily 9:30am-6pm; Oct.-Apr. daily 10am-4:30pm. DM5, children DM3.50, roundtrip DM8, children DM5.)

Another cable car, the **Sessellift,** stretches up to the **Roßtrappe** (lift runs Sat.-Sun. DM4, children DM3; roundtrip DM6, children DM4). This overlook over the greater Harz gorge area is right on the 10km Thale-Treseburg **hiking path,** one of the many routes wandering among small streams and gigantic waterfalls, hills and precipitous cliffs. The Roßtrappe itself is a "hoofprint" in the rock, supposedly immortalized in the *Nibelungenlied*. The beautiful Brünnhilde on her tremendous war-house (hence the print) was being pursued (again) by a savage named Bodo. Brunhilde's horse managed to cross the gorge; Bodo jumped off the horse to tackle his quarry, but misjudged the wind velocity and ended up several hundred meters farther down than he'd expected. A legend also envelops the nearby **Teufelsmauer,** a collection of strangely stacked stones. Local elders claim the devil erected a wall to enclose his chosen dominion, but Christianity broke through.

Thale information is located just outside the train station at Rathausstr. 1 (tel. (03947) 25 97, fax 22 77), will help you find a room (from DM20) for no fee. They also have cable car schedules and hiking maps (open May-Aug. Mon.-Fri. 9am-6pm, Sat.-Sun. 10am-3pm; Nov.-Dec. Mon.-Fri. 9am-4pm; Jan.-Apr. and Sept.-Oct. Mon.-Fri. 9am-5pm). The Thale **Jugendherberge (HI),** in Bodetal-Waldkater (tel. (03947) 28 31), will be closed for renovation until spring of 1995, but call anyway—in summer 1993 they were trying to organize an alternative rooming service. For food, try the **Grüne Tanne,** Roßtrappenstr. 10 (tel. 24 40). Cross the train tracks and the bridge, then take the third street to the right (entrees DM7-10; open Wed.-Sat. noon-9pm, Sun. 10am-2pm and 5-8pm). While you're in the mountains, take in some of humanity's creations as well, at the **Bergtheater Thale.** This massive open-air theater has a view of the forest that may almost distract you from the show at hand. (Tickets DM10-20. Call (03947) 23 24 for more information).

■■■ MAGDEBURG

Magdeburg has been hard hit by war and ideology for three and a half centuries, but continues to pull through. On May 10, 1631, the city was decimated in one of the most gruesome battles of the Thirty Years War, after Protestant town leaders refused to cut a deal with the Catholic troops outside the gates. The industrial output of this city made it a prime target for the Allied forces in World War II. When the air-raid sirens malfunctioned, the bombing took a particularly high toll on the civilian population. After the war, Magdeburg was rebuilt with the broad boulevards and boring apartment blocks of the East—a sort of socialist version of nearby Hanover. For years, thousands of travelers en route to West Berlin whizzed through here on the special transit strip that transected the industrial outskirts of the city. Meanwhile, the government ensured that those who did stop to look around encountered a city of exemplary stature; consequently, the city is in better shape than most of its neighbors. In the months before reunification, Magdeburg had the good luck to triumph over Halle to become the new capital of Sachsen-Anhalt, and its new status has already brought in more money to renovate and revitalize the city's cultural life.

ORIENTATION AND PRACTICAL INFORMATION

Travelers en route to Berlin from other Eastern cities can often save time by taking a detour through Magdeburg, one of the few Eastern cities with direct connections to Berlin's centrally located Bahnhof Zoo. (Otherwise, you'll probably arrive at Berlin's Bahnhof Lichtenberg, a 45min. S-Bahn ride to the city center.) Magdeburg is also connected to the bullet trains (ICE) in Hanover. Most museums, churches, and sights are located at Otto-von-Guericke-Str. and on Breitzer Weg, within 15 minutes of the train station.

Tourist Office, Alter Markt 9 (tel. (0391) 316 67), is on the main market square. From the train station, turn left and head down Ernst-Reuter-Allee, then left at the second intersection onto Breiter Weg, and turn right onto the market. The **Zimmervermittlung** (tel. (0391) 35 35 21), in the same building, will help you find a room (from DM20) for no fee. Open Mon.-Fri. 10am-6pm, Sat. 10am-1pm. Tours Mon.-Fri. at 11am, DM5. Inquire about tours in English.

Currency Exchange: Vereins-und-Westbank, Otto-von-Guericke-Str. 28 (tel 329 22) to your right from Ernst-Reuter-Str. Open Mon. and Wed. 8:30am-12:30pm and 2-5pm, Fri. 8:30am-12:30pm.

Post Office: Breiter Weg, 39104 Magdeburg, in the direction of the Dom. Open Mon.-Fri. 8am-6pm, Sat. 8am-noon.

Telephones: city code 0391.

Bus Terminal: For towns near Magdeburg; to the right of the train station.

Bicycle Rental: Herr Koch, Simonstr. 2 (tel. 572 09), DM19 per day; limited stock. Open Mon.-Fri. 9am-noon and 2-6pm.

Mitfahrzentrale: Lessingstr. 64 (tel. 36 43 62 or 34 32 38), open Mon.-Fri. 10am-6pm, Sat. 10am-noon.

Women's Information Center: Courage, Porsestr. 14 (tel. 489 80).

ACCOMMODATIONS

As in many Eastern German cities, hotels are not the best budget option; do ask about rooms in **private homes** at the tourist office (see Practical Information above). Otherwise, there is a **Jugendgästehaus** (tel. 429 09) in the Ottersleber suburb, Luttgen-Ottersleber 19a, 39119 Magdeburg; from the town center take streetcar #10 to Sudenburg, then the bus (direction "Ottersleber"): Ottersleber Teich, and follow the "Jugendherberge" signs. (Reception open 3-8pm, curfew 10pm. DM15.50, over 26 DM17.50. Breakfast included.) Camp at **Campingplatz Am Barliber See** (tel. 50 32 44); streetcar #10 (direction "Barliber See") to the last stop, continue on the main street and cross underneath the highway bridge. **Rental bikes** available for DM6 per day. (Reception open daily 8am-4pm. DM4 per person, DM per tent.

FOOD

Many of the cheaper restaurants are crowded into the street around the intersection of Breiter Weg and Einsteinstr. in Hasselbachplatz, the only section of downtown to survive bombing during the war. Buy vegetables and fruits at the market at the **Alte Markt,** Tues.-Fri. 9am-6pm, Sat. 9am-1pm. In addition to groceries, the **Karstadt Cafeteria** offers basic meals, including a large salad bar. (Open Mon.-Fri. 9am-6:30pm, Sat. 9am-2pm.)

Mensa, Am Universitätsplatz at the Technische Universität can be found by taking a left on Breitestr. Extremely institutional: go for the contact with students, not the subsidized food.

Ratskeller, Alte Markt. One of those historic set-ups, in the basement of the Baroque Rathaus. Dinner, especially with wine, is a little steep, but lunch specials go for just DM7.50. Open Mon.-Sun. 11am-midnight.

Magdeburger Kartoffelhaus, Otto-von-Guerike Str. 57 (tel. (0391) 34 34 20) serves potatoes in all forms: salads, soups, and yes, even international potato dishes for DM10. Open Mon.-Sat. 11:30am-midnight.

Mansefalle, Breiter Weg 224 (tel. 301 35) attracts a young crowd, including many students. They serve up spaghetti dishes for DM10. Open Mon.-Fri. 8:30am-2am, Sat.-Sun. 8:30am-3am. Hot food served until 2am.

SIGHTS

Magdeburg itself is grey, a setting which offers no challenge to its few very striking sights. The city's prime landmark and symbol is the **Magdeburger Dom** (cathedral) on Breite-Str. At the front of the cathedral lies an inconspicuous tomb, grave site of the first Holy Roman Emperor Otto, buried here in 973. Local ghost-stories credit the former Kaiser's guardianship with preservation of the cathedral during the fires of 1631 and 1945. Once proudly dubbed the nation's largest cathedral, reunification has forced the Magdeburger Dom to yield that honor to its cousin in Cologne (the *Dom* still retains its less dynamic distinction as the first Gothic dome begun in Germany). Take some time to wander through the attached **courtyard** just off the altar. (Open daily 10am-6pm; tours at 10am and 2pm. Admission free, tours DM4, students DM2.)

Near the *Dom,* between all the faceless apartments, lies the **Kloster Unser Lieben Frauen,** Regierungstr. 4/6 (tel. (0391) 337 41), a 12th-century nunnery now employed as a museum for visiting exhibitions and a concert hall (open Tues.-Sun. 10am-6pm; DM2). Head through the parking lot in front of the *Dom* onto Breiter Weg and go down Danzastr. On your left will be the **Kulturhistorisches Museum,** Otto-von-Guerike-Str. 68-73 (tel. (0391) 326 45), where you can see everything from creations by Magdeburg's own junior-varsity Einstein, Otto von Guerike, to the history of the city (open Tues.-Sun. 10am-6pm; admission DM1, students DM0.50). Back down Danzestr., a left on Breiter Weg will take you back to the **Alter Markt.** The ruins of the **Johanniskirche** are now a museum and memorial dedicated to the bombing of 1945, but the city recently announced plans to rebuild the city landmark. The only snag is that the Protestant Church has already said that it wants nothing to do with the plan—they already have too many churches and too few churchgoers. Climb the **tower** and survey the city (open Wed.-Sun. 10am-6pm; admission DM1, students DM0.50).

Across from the church rise the spires of the 17th-century **Rathaus.** Directly on the marketplace in front of the *Rathaus* is the **Magdeburger Reiter** (built 1240), the oldest free-standing equestrian figure in Germany. Behind the cathedral lies the Elbe River; follow the Remtergang just off the Domplatz and look out over the river from **Auf dem Wall,** the ramparts of the old city fortifications. Along the Elbe to the North, see massive and somehow elegant cranes at work; the **Schiffshebewerk** actually lift ships 16m in the air, to and from the Elbe to the waterways of the Mittelland Kanal.

ENTERTAINMENT

The Magdeburger *Kabarett* (cabaret) **Die Klingelblitze,** Breiter Weg 200, was already well-known during the GDR era, and the last four years have just given rein to its sardonic sensibility. (Performances every evening, starting at around 8pm. Call tel. 339 59 for ticket information.) There's straight-out drama at the **Freie Kammerspiele Theater,** Otto-von-Guericke-Str. 64. **Club ExLibris,** Weitling Str. (tel. 55 10 44) sets the scene for concerts, with a regular late-night dance club (open Tues.-Sun. 8:30pm-2am).

■■ TANGERMÜNDE

In 1373, Kaiser Karl IV gave up the spires of Prague to lay out a new capital on the banks of the Elbe. For five years Tangermünde became the place to see and be seen, as people flocked from throughout the Holy Roman Empire to the new capital. But when the emperor died, Tangermünde slipped back into provincial status. Filled with glazed brickwork and crowded with wood frame houses,

Tangermünde's magnificent *Altstadt* sits as if forgotten. In fact, Tangermünde has been out of the picture for so long that any mention of it in the West is likely to bring blank stares. The dearth of tourists is one of the major attractions of this place but be aware of the flip side: strangers are not always greeted with open arms.

Practical Information The **tourist office**, Marktstr. 13 (tel. (039322) 37 10) in the **Buhneukopf** building, will help you find a room for no fee (rooms from DM35). Walk down Marktstr., behind the *Rathaus*. They have small guides in German (open Mon.-Fri. 9am-noon and 1-5pm). **Bergarde** at Langestr. 38 (tel. 23 43) rents bikes for DM15 per day (open Mon.-Fri. 9am-6pm, Sat. 9am-noon).

Nicknamed "Rothenburg des Nordens" (Rothenburg of the North) by locals, Tangermünde lies on the Elbe River about 30km downstream from Magdeburg. Getting here can be a real hassle; trains or buses leave three or four times daily from Stendal *Hauptbahnhof,* less frequently on weekends; plan to leave early in the morning.

Accommodations and Food To reach **Hotel Villa Altmarkt,** Arneburger-str. 37 (tel. (039322) 23 44), go down Bahnhofstr., make a right on Pritschschu-lenberg and a left on Arneburgerstr. (Singles DM38.50. Doubles DM68.50. Breakfast DM10.50. Call ahead.) **Zur Post,** Lange-Str. 4 (tel. (039322) 25 34) is a quirky small-town restaurant. There is a **green market** at the *Markt* on Thursdays 9am-6pm.

Sights As a member of the Hanseatic League and the second-largest harbor on the Elbe after Hamburg, this was a wealthy town in the 15th century, and it shows. From the train station, turn right down Bahnhofstr. and then left down Karlstr.; continue through the **old city walls** to the town's main square. The houses in the square date mostly from the 17th century, replacing the 500 residences that fell victim to a large fire in 1617. At the time irate villagers found a scapegoat in the young Margaret Minde, who was tried, found guilty, and burnt for **witchcraft** on this square in 1619. The innocent young "witch" and the nasty villagers of Tangermünde later provided the inspiration for Theodor Fontane's classic *Grete Minde,* though locals are quick to point out that the novel is, of course, largely fictional.

The stupendous **Rathaus (**town hall) on the square is one of the most impressive Gothic glazed-brick structures in Germany. The *Rathaus* houses a museum of the town's history. (Open Tues.-Sun. 10am-7pm. Admission DM2, student and children DM1.) Down Lange-Str., behind the *Rathaus,* towers the **Neustädter Tor,** until 1925 the main entrance through the city walls. Note the tile work outside—there are frescoes of Medusa and of the banners of everyone entitled to collect taxes in the town. (Interior closed except by prior arrangement. Ask at the tourist office.)

Outside the old city, on the other side of the Neustädter Tor, are the ruins of the **Dominiker Kloster** (Dominican Monastery, 1438), abandoned by the monks during the Thirty Years War. Entering back through the city gate, wind your way to the church towers in the background. The imposing **St. Stephanskirche** was begun in the 14th century. The organ and the Renaissance tombs inside are further evidence of the town's former prosperity (open Sat. 3-4pm, Sun. 11am-noon; free). Near the church is the **Hühnerdorfer Tor**; cross through here and continue down Hühnerdorfer Str. to reach the remains of the fortress. Inside its walls, Tangermünde came closer than Bonn to becoming the capital of great Germany. At the side of the fortress the **Kanzlei** (Imperial dance hall) is the only remnant of those heady days, but the stroll around the memorial and down to the harbor is highly scenic. Wander back up near the harbor and the *Hohlweg.*

MECKLENBURG-VORPOMMERN

More than 1700 lakes, the Baltic Sea coast its old Hanseatic towns unmistakably mark the landscape of Mecklenburg-Vorpommern. Once a favorite vacation spot of East Germans—largely by default—this sparsely populated, northernmost province of the former GDR still possesses a fair amount of natural beauty. Unfortunately, it doesn't possess much of a tourist industry, especially if you're living cheap; the available hotels have long since been overrun by Western German executives, and prices have risen accordingly. The frequently chilly but still lovely beaches of the Baltic coast are worth a visit as long as you're not obsessed with creature comforts like hot water. On the extreme northwest, Rügen remains a rugged solace, and the Hanseatic architecture in the coastal cities of Rostock and Stralsund testifies to a unique cultural heritage. These towns constantly see visitors pass through on their way to the islands or to ferries, but are themselves are economically troubled. Recent years have seen increased violence against foreigners; see Rostock, below.

■■■ SCHWERIN

A keepsake of Henry the Lion's 12th-century march through the East, Schwerin (pronounced shvayr-EEN) makes a restorative stop on the way to the swarming Baltic seacoast. With reunification, the city regained the status it lost in the former GDR as capital of Mecklenburg-Lower Pomerania—a *Land* of fallen *Junkers*, rye bread, tall brick churches, and seagulls. The Swedes burned much of Schwerin to the ground in 1616, but the Allies spared the place in World War II; thus the *Altstadt* is particularly well-preserved, with an old-fashioned look of shabby gentility.

Practical Information Schwerin **Information** is at Am Markt 11(tel. (0385) 81 23 14, fax 86 45 09). From the station head up Zum Bahnhof, go right on Wismarchestr., left on Arsenal, and finally right on Bischofstr. They sell maps and, for a DM5 fee, book private rooms (DM25-40), frequently booked solid (open Mon.-Fri. 9am-6pm, Sat. 10am-5pm, Sun. 10am-3pm). The main **post office** is on Mecklenburgstr., 19053 Schwerin; from the *Markt*, go up Schmiedestr. and turn right. The **telephone city code** is **0385.** The **Apotheke am Markt,** Am Markt 8 (tel. (0385) 86 40 24), posts the addresses of other open pharmacies. From the train station, **rent bikes** for DM10-12 (open Mon.-Fri. 8:30am-6pm, Sat.-Sun. 8:30-7pm). Schwerin lies on the Magdeburg-Rostock **rail line,** and is also easily accessible by train from Hamburg.

Sights The **Alter Garten** square was the site of mass demonstrations that preceded the downfall of the Eastern regime in 1989, and anchors the **Altstadt.** The main structure of the **Gothic cathedral** at the center of the old district dates from the 13th century; the impressive 110m tower was tacked on at the end of the last century (open Mon.-Fri. 10am-noon and 2-4pm, Sat. 10am-1pm, 2-5pm, Sun. 1-4pm; free). The most fanciful structure is the **Märchenschloß** (fairy-tale castle), a white-turreted old arsenal on Wismarschestr.

Schwerin's serious **Schloß** presides over its own island fiefdom just south of the center over the bridge at the end of Schloßstr. This grandiose residence was the seat of the Dukes of Mecklenburg, who ruled the area until the upheaval of 1918; its intricately decorated Baroque cupolas reek of power. Inside, the throne room and banquet hall have been lavishly restored. An unearthly **Archeological Museum** (tel. 51 28 65) takes up the first floor gallery (open Tues.-Sun. 10am-5pm; admission DM4, students DM2). Besides ruling, 18th-century Duke Christian Ludwig II had a wild passion for the Dutch Renaissance, and his bushels of 17th-century Old Masters are housed in the *Gemäldegalerie* of the **Staatliches Museum,** along with collections of German decorative art. The museum faces the castle on Alter Gartenplatz (open Tues.-Sun. 10am-5pm; admission DM2, students DM1). The striking building next door is the **Mecklenburgisches Staatstheater Schwerin** (tel. 88 21 26), which is in the midst of a dramatic revival (box office open Tues.-Fri. 10am-1pm and 2-6pm, Sun. 10am-1pm; tickets DM 15-25, students DM10).

The **Mahn- und Gedenkstätte der Jüdischen Landesgemeinde Mecklenburg,** Schlacterstr. 3, was intended as a tribute to the memory of the province's Jewish community. It closed recently after an interior looting by area skinheads and because, as the tourist office chose to phrase it, no local audience could be found for its exhibits. The town keeps its own historical house with permanent exhibits on Schwerin's checkered past in the **Heimatmuseum** (tel. 86 43 81) on the *Markt* (open Tues.-Sun. 9am-6pm).

Accommodations, Zoo, and Food The **Jugendherberge (HI),** Waldschulenweg 3 (tel. (0385) 21 30 05), lies south of town in a woodsy setting overlooking the lake. With Schwerin's popularity ever-increasing, the hostel often fills up; call ahead. From the train station, go right on Wismarchestr., left on Schloßstr., turn right on Mecklenburgstr., and catch bus #15 at the terminal up ahead. Get off at the last stop, walk towards the Zoo and take a left at the "Jugendherberge" sign. (Reception open 4-9pm. Curfew 10pm. DM14.50, over 26 DM19.50. Breakfast included.) The Jugendherberge borders the **Schweriner Zoo** (tel. (0385) 21 30 00), a modest menagerie. (Open Tues.-Fri. 9am-6pm; Sat.-Sun. 9am-5pm; Oct.-Apr. Sat.-Sun. 9-4pm. Admission DM3.) **Kaiser's,** on Schmiedestr., is the most convenient area supermarket (open Mon.-Fri. 8am-6pm, Sat. 8am-1pm). **Restaurant Zum Mecklenburger,** Puschkinstr. 81 (tel. 86 40 67) serves local cuisine; full meals run about DM10 (open Mon.-Fri. 11am-10pm, Sat.-Sun. 11am-4pm).

■■■ MECKLENBURG LAKE PLAIN (Mecklenburgische Seenplatte)

Otto von Bismarck marveled that this land of rolling hills and pristine lakes plodded along centuries behind the rest of Europe. He claimed that when things got hectic in Berlin, refuge could always be found among the reserved but sincere folk of the Mecklenburg Lake Plain (Mecklenburgische Seenplatte). Long derided by their Sachsen neighbors as country bumpkins, the locals are not noted for opening their hearts to strangers. They will, however, give you the opportunity to be alone in the most sparsely populated region of the country, along its necklace of lakes. A popular vacation area for over a century, the Lake Plain towns do become crowded during summer; make reservations in advance.

Little industry plus few people equals lousy transportation. Though infrastructure is improving, plan carefully and leave yourself extra time. Pick one stop and stay there; moving from place to place is likely to be a nerve-shattering hassle.

WAREN

Waren makes a good base camp for exploring the surrounding regions. Conveniently located within two hours of both Rostock and Berlin, the town draws mostly German tourists to the northern edge of **die Müritz**, Germany's second-largest freshwater lake. Smaller streams weave from the lake into the Muritz National Park, unique preserve of rare birds and marshland. Ask the Waren tourist office about guided tours in this paradise for hikers or bikers on their way north.

Two 13th-century red-brick churches, **Pfarrkirche St. Georg** and **Pfarrkirche St. Marien**, dominate the town. St. Marien lay in ruins for a century after the Thirty Years War, and was only rebuilt in its present form in 1739 (open 9:30-11:30am and 2-4pm April-Sept.). But don't waste time on shore; the waterways are the main attraction here. The best way to see the area is on a ferry through the harbor. **Wa**

ener Schiffahrts und Handelsgesellschaft, GmbH., Kietzstr. 14a (tel. and fax (03991) 47 57), and **Müritzwind Personerschiffahrt,** Strandstr. (tel. and fax (03991) 23 53) both offer tours varying in length from one to four hours (DM7.50-22). The **Müritzmuseum Waren,** Friedenstr. 8 (tel. 37 42 or 43 68) keeps samples of the woodlands in its aquarium and birdpark (open Tues.-Fri. 9am-6pm, Sat.-Sun. 9am-noon and 2-5pm; admission DM4, students DM2).

Waren Information is in the town square at Neuer Markt 19 (tel./fax (03991) 41 72); they deal in maps, brochures, and rooms in the DM20 to 25 range. From the train station, cross under the tracks to Schweriner Damm and walk left, then right on Friedenstr. and left on Langestr. (open Mon.-Fri. 10am-noon and 2-5pm, Sat. 10am-3pm). **Bike rental** can be found at the train station (open Mon.-Fri. 6am-10pm; Sat.-Sun. 8am-8pm. DM8.) Waren's **postal code** is 17192.

The **Jugendherberge (HI),** Auf dem Nesselberg (tel. (03991) 22 61), is in the woods south of town. Take bus #3 (direction "Ecktannen") from the Schweriner Damm (about 100m to the left as you leave the train station) to Wasserwerk, or enjoy the 25-minute walk from the station. Cross under the tracks to Schweriner Damm, bear right at the fork in the road, and walk along the harbor for about 15 minutes down Zur Steinmole, Strandstr., Müritzstr. and Am Seeufer. When you reach the wooded hill on the left, head straight up the path. Space is limited, but the management will set up tents if you call in advance. They will also help you plan a tour of the area and fix you up with something to eat. (Reception open at 9am, 1, 6, and 9pm. Curfew 10pm. DM13.50, over 26 DM16.50. Breakfast included. Open March-Nov.) In addition, there is camping at **Azur-Camping Waren-Ecktannen** on Fontanestr. (tel. (03991) 26 07). The **City Ristorante,** Friedenstr. 8, offers pizza for DM6 (open Mon.-Thurs. 10am-10pm, Fri.-Sun. 10am-11pm). For groceries, shop at the Spar **supermarket** on Langestr.

NEUBRANDENBURG

Poet Fritz Reufer called Neubrandenburg "the pearl of the Mecklenburg realm." Set on Lake Tollensee, an hour from both Waren by bus or Berlin by train, the town of Neubrandenburg is another pleasant day-trip and recreation resort. The medieval fortifications (*Wehranlage*) with four arched gates (*Tore*) are the prestigious landmarks of the town. Ranked high on Unesco's list of international cultural treasures, the fortifications stretch 2.3km around the old city. From the station, take Stargarderstr. and then right on Treptowerstr. to **Treptower Tor,** a left on Friedländerstr. for **Friedländer Tor,** a left on Neutorstr. for **Neues Tor,** or keep straight on Stargarderstr. for **Stargarder Tor.** The two gothic churches **Marienkirche** on Stargarderstr. and **Johanniskirche** on Ringstr. are both closed for visitors as they are undergoing renovations for Neubrandenburg's 750th anniversary in 1998. For a round-trip ride on the Tollensee, make reservations at **Naherholung Neubrandenburg**, Parkstr. 3 (tel. (0395) 64 82 or 663 42). Tours range from 1½ to 2½ hours. (Departures June-Aug. Tues.-Sun. 10:30am, 1pm, 3pm; May and Sept. Tues.-Sun. twice a day; DM7-10.)

The **tourist office**, Turmstr. 11, 17033 Neubrandenburg (tel./fax (0395) 22 67), provides maps and a room-finding service (rooms DM 25-40; fee DM5). From Stargarderstr. take a left on Turmstr. before the Kaufhof department store (tourist office open Mon. 11am-6pm, Tues.-Fri. 9am-6pm, Sat. 9am-noon). The town **post office** is located at Stargarderstr. 6 (open Mon.-Fri. 8am-6pm, Sat. 8am-noon). Margaret Klimst, Hufelandstr. 31 (tel. 737 32) runs a **Mitfahrzentrale** ride-share office. The train station rigs up **bike rentals** (DM12).

The **Youth Hostel** is at Ihlenfelderstr. 73, 17034 Neubrandenburg (tel. and fax (0395) 422 58 01). From the adjacent bus and train stations, take bus #7 (direction "Trollenhagen Süd") to Ravensburgstr.; on weekends, bus #5 to Ihlenfelder Str. By foot (a 25-min. hike), take a left on Friedrich-Engels-Str., at intersection cross the bridge onto Demminerstr. and then right on Ihlenfelderstr. (Reception open 3-8pm. Curfew 10pm. DM9.50, over 26 DM14.50. Breakfast DM5.) The **Mitropa** (self-service cafeteria) in the station offers *schnitzel* for DM6 (open Mon.-Fri. 6am-10pm, Sat. 8am-9pm). The open stands of the **farmer's market** in front of the station vend great vegetables and fruits (open Mon.-Sat. 9am-6pm), rivaling the **supermarket** on the first floor of the Kaufhof department store.

GUSTROW

Between Rostock and Waren lies Gustrow, the former residence of the Duke of Mecklenburg. Though the Duke has been gone for almost 200 years, the town has maintained a polished appearance that should be the envy of surrounding cities. Begin at the Renaissance **Schloß** (tel. (03843) 50 21); after the royalty left town in 1811, the palace was used as a home for the elderly. Recently renovated, the show-piece *Schloß* is huge, and more than impressive. Head down Domstr. from the *Markt* (open Tues.-Sun. 9am-5pm). Most of the *Altstadt* is off-limits to automobiles; wander around the market and the sidestreets to absorb the atmosphere. From the castle, turn left on Ph.-Brandin-Str. to reach the cathedral—the Gothic **Dom** is filled with ancient artifacts, but is famous for the modern bronze statue to the left of the pews. *Der schwebende Engel* (The Hovering Angel) by Ernst Barlach dangles from the ceiling as a testament to the horrors of war. Originally cast in 1926, the statue was publicly melted down and cast into bullets in 1941. The purpose of the Nazis' little display was to demonstrate the futility of pacifism while defaming Barlach, a popular modern artist. After World War II, a plaster cast of the statue was found bur-ied in Western Germany, and in 1952, the angel was returned here and rededicated to the memory of war's victims (open Mon.-Sat. 10am-noon and 1-5pm, Sun. 1-5pm; tours Sat. 2pm; free). Further evidence of Barlach's work is on display at the artist's moving memorial in the **Gertrudenkapelle,** Gertrudenplatz 1 (tel. (03843) 630 01). From the station walk down Eisenbahnstr., then take a right on Gertrudenstr. (open Tues.-Sun. 10am-5pm; admission DM3, students DM1.50).

Gustrow Information is just off the Marktplatz at Gleviner Str. 33 (tel. (03843) 610 23, fax 630 75). From the train station, go down Eisenbahnstr., then left on Pfer-demarkt to the *Markt.* They operate a room-finding service (from DM20-25), asking a DM4 fee (open Mon.-Fri. 9am-6pm, Sat. 9:30am-1pm, Sun. 9:30-1pm). Eighty small lakes lie within 20km of Güstrow; you can **rent a bike** at the train station (DM10-12). Fresh **fruit** and **vegetables** are sold on the Marktplatz (Tues. and Thurs. 10am-6pm, Sat. 10am-noon). Near the tourist office **Wiener Café,** Gleviner Str., serves Renaissance cakes (open Mon.-Fri. 8am-7pm, Sat. 2-7pm, Sun. 2-7pm). The **Stadtk-rug,** Eisenbahnstr. 8 (tel. (03843) 631 15) offers average, but very German food for reasonable prices (DM8-12; open Tues.-Sun. 10am-2pm and 5-10pm).

■ ■ ■ ROSTOCK

"The chanting was filmed and syndicated abroad....There were no distractions this time, not Kabul, not Sarajevo. ROSTOCK it said in big letters wherever you look," wrote Günter Grass. On August 24, 1992, a hostel for foreigners seeking political asylum in Germany was attacked by local right-wing and neo-Nazi youths, and set on fire. While skinheads assaulted hostel residents, ordinary citizens stood by and cheered. The police were not very effective. East German schoolchildren were taught to think of Rostock, the largest and most active port in Eastern Germany, as socialist Germany's "gateway to the world." Since unification, Rostock's booming business has all but disappeared, as ships take their business to Hamburg. After the events of August 1992, any picture of Rostock is like a reflection in a broken mirror. Some fragments still catch the red brick of the old Hanseatic trading town. Others show a fading modern harbor. Still other shards show a face of Germany that most would prefer not to see. You might come to see the old church towers, or use the city as a route to the Scandanavian countries whose proximity influenced Rostock for centuries. Whatever the case may be, keep Grass's conclusion in mind: "Since Rostock, Germany has changed."

ORIENTATION

Think very carefully about where you are in Rostock. The arson attacks and riots were not all that long ago, and even in the historic areas where tourists face no physical threat, the sight of the swastikas painted on the walls in certain districts can be an assault on the imagination. Be wary of the newer districts outside of the *Altstadt*. These newly built quarters contain extremely grey apartment blocks; the residents have been known to be angry and aggressive. The riots themselves were in the Liechtenhagen neighborhood, one of the newer developments. This is not to absolutely discourage a visit to Rostock; stay in the *Altstadt*, and you may never touch Rostock's worse side. Warnemünde, a fishing village and ferry port recently incorporated into Rostock proper, is more pleasant. And again, this is the regional transport hub, with frequent trains to Berlin, and ferry connections to Scandanavia.

PRACTICAL INFORMATION

Tourist Office: Schnickmannstr. 13/14, 18055 Rostock (tel. 459 08 60 or -61, fax 346 02). Streetcar #11 or 12 (from the main station): Langestr. The office just off of Langestr. Room service finds rooms from DM30 for a DM5 fee. They also lead tours through the town (1½hrs. May-June and Sept. Wed. and Fri.-Sun. 2pm). Open Mon.-Fri. 9am-6pm, Sat.-Sun. 10am-4pm, Oct.-Apr. Mon.-Fri. 9am-6pm, Sat. 10am-4pm. The office has another branch at the **Hauptbahnhof,** with similar services. Open Mon.-Sat. 9am-8pm. There is also an office in **Warnemünde,** Heinrich-Heine-Str. 11 (tel. 511 42); take any streetcar from the main station except #4 3 stops west. Open Mon.-Fri. 9am-6pm, Sat.-Sun. 10am-4pm; Oct.-April Mon.-Fri 9am-6pm, Sat. 10am-4pm.

Currency Exchange: Sparkasse (tel. 456 20), Lange-Str. 7/8, just across from the Kaufhof. Open Mon. and Fri. 8:30am-3pm, Tues. and Thurs. 8:30am-6pm, Wed. 8:30am-12:30pm. The **Deutsche Bank,** Kröpelinerstr. 84 (tel. 456 50) has an ATM (automatic teller machine).

Post Office: *Hauptpostamt*, Neuer Markt, 18055 Rostock. Open Mon.-Fri. 9am-6pm, Sat. 9am-11pm.

Telephone: city code 0381.

Trains: frequent connections to all major towns on the Baltic Coast, and also to Hamburg and Berlin.

Public Transportation: streetcars #11 and 12 shuttle from the main station to the *Altstadt.* Single ticket DM1.50. Combined 1-day ticket for strectcar, bus, and S-Bahn DM5.50. The **S-Bahn** leaves from the main station to Warnemünde and the newly-built quarters of the suburbs every 30min. To get to bus station for lines to smaller towns, exit the *Hauptbahnhof* through the Südstadt exit.

Ferries: Boats for **Scandanavia** leave from the **Überseehafen** docks. **TR-Linie,** Hansakai (tel. 36 63 22 02, fax 42 21 35) runs to Trelleborg, Sweden (3 per day, 5hr.; one way DM44, students DM33, children DM22), and Bornholm, Denmark (departures Sat. 9pm; DM94, students DM70, children DM47); **Europa-Linie GT link** (tel. 36 63 10 30, fax 36 62 17 89) to Gedser, Denmark (5 per day, 2hr., one way DM7.50). Ferries also leave from the **Warnemünde** docks; the Deutsche Bahn's **Fährverkehrsgesellschaft Ostsee,** (tel. 514 06, fax 514 09) sails to Gedser, Denmark, with special trips to other Scandanavian ports (7 per day; DM10-16, children DM5-8; round-trip DM 20-32, children DM10-16).

Bike rental: Fahrradausleihe Koch, Friedrich-Franz-Str. 12 (tel. 541 44), in Warnemünde. Open Mon.-Fri. 8-10am and 1-7pm, Sat. 8-10am.

Mitfahrzentrale: Platz der Freuudschaft 1 (tel. 72 52 16), matches riders with drivers. Take the Südstadt exit from the main station. Open Mon.-Fri. 9am-7pm, Sat.-Sun. 10am-2pm.

Women's Center: Beginenhaus-Frauenzentrum am Rosengarten (tel. 235 91).

Emergency: Ambulance tel. 115. **Police:** tel. 110. **Fire:** tel. 112.

ACCOMMODATIONS

Jugendherberge Rostock-Warnemünde (tel. 523 03), on Parkstr. 31. From the Warnemünde S-Bahn station, head left, cross the bridge, and go past the church;

the hostel is a bit farther on the left. In the suburbs but near the water, and you won't have to walk through the less savory new districts. DM14.50, over 26 DM19.50. Breakfast included. Closed Dec. 20-Jan. 10.

Jugendgästeschiff Rostock-Schmarl (tel. 71 62 24, fax 71 40 14) S-Bahn (from the main station, direction "Warnemünde"): Lütten Klein, then follow Warnow-allee down toward the harbor and around to the left; the hostel is docked at the end of the road. Be aware that this is not necessarily the best area for a foreigner to be alone, especially at night. The floating hostel has taken over a great old ship in the harbor. DM25, over 26 DM31. Breakfast included.

FOOD AND NIGHTLIFE

It's difficult to find reasonable prices for good food in Rostock. As a rule, the closer you get to the water, the more expensive eateries become. There is a **supermarket** in the train station (open Mon.-Sun. 6am-9pm). **Supermarket Spar** at Kröpeliner Str. offers a sizeable selection (open Mon.-Wed., Fri. 8am-6pm, Thurs. 8am-8pm, Sat. 8am-1pm). There is a **farmers' market** on Auf dem glatten Aal, the square behind the town hall (open Mon.-Fri. 8am-4pm, Sat. 8-11pm). **Breitestraße** is filled with various *Imbiß* vendors.

Mensa, Südring, Albert-Einstein-Str. From train station, leave through the Südstadt exit; take bus #39 towards Lütten Klein: Mensa. A typical university cafeteria; the food isn't spectacular, but it is one cheap eatery in which you're sure to meet students. Check the bulletin boards here for special local events.

Pizzeria Taverne, Kröpeliner Str. 54/55 (tel. 45 34 19), serves standard pizza for DM9. Open Mon.-Sat. 11:30am-midnight, Sun. 5-11pm.

Wicking Burger, Breite-Str. (tel. 459 10 10), offers typical fast-food fare for DM3-5 Open daily 8:30am-1am.

Studentenkeller, Universitätsplatz (tel. 45 59 28). The backyard café attracts a student crowd. Open daily 8:45am-5:30pm. After dark, rock away in the Keller bar, often to live music. Open daily 9pm-1 or 2am. Cover DM2, Sat.-Sun. DM5, students DM3. No cover Thurs.-Tues. before 10pm.

SIGHTS

In the 14th century, Rostock's Baltic harbor made it a proud member of the Hanseatic League of city-states. Whatever its recent history, strikingly beautiful relics of Rostock's past still stand. Leaving the train station, take the streetcar down to the *Altstadt.* Although half the city was destroyed in World War II, many of the half-timbered and glazed brick houses and Gothic churches here have been restored. The **Kröpeliner Straße,** the main pedestrian mall lined with 16th-century *Bürger* houses, runs east to the former town gate. Parallel lies **Langestraße,** the city's central artery, lined with modern brick buildings that fit in well with the traditional architecture. The main buildings of the **Universität Rostock,** the oldest university in Northern Europe, are farther down Kröpeliner Str. Next to the university, along the remains of the city wall, sits the **Kloster zum Heiligen Kreuz,** an expertly restored cloister originally built by a Danish queen in 1217. Check out the museum or grab a piece of cake in the relaxed café (open Tues.-Sun. 10am-6pm; admission DM2).

Rostock's main architectural landmark is the 13th-century **Marienkirche,** a monster of a brick church near the main square at the end of Kröpliner Str. (open Tues.-Sat. 10am-noon and 3-5pm, Sun. 11am-noon). In the final weeks of the revolution of 1989 the services here overflowed with political protesters who had come to hear the inspiring sermons of Pastor Joachim Gauck. Among them were many members of the Stasi, the feared secret police, determined to report their disruptive comrades. In one of the more heroic gestures of the revolution, Pastor Gauck began to publicly chastise the secret police, calling out the names of those Stasi members whom he could identify from the pulpit. After reunification, Gauck was the only man trusted enough to guard the files kept by the Stasi. The church features a towering organ, a finely-sculpted Renaissance pulpit, and a massive bronze baptismal font. The 11m **astronomical clock** behind the altar dates from 1472; it has a calendar set to run until Easter 2017. At noon and midnight, mechanical figures of the apostles strut out in circular procession. Near the church is the Renaissance **Rathaus**, topped by seven Gothic towers.

The **Schiffahrtmuseum der Hansestadt,** August-Bebel-Str. 1 (tel. 226 97) gives an overview of the history of seafaring along the Baltic coast (open Sat.-Thurs. 9am-5pm; admission DM2). The city's main port and beach are at **Warnemünde** on the Baltic (25min. by S-Bahn). As you emerge from the station, amble across the wooden bridge and survey the **Alter Strom** (old harbor), adorned with cottages and fishing boats. Follow the crowded promenade to the lighthouse. Warnemünde's most famous restaurant, the circular **Teepot,** stands just behind the beach on the boardwalk, which leads to a high-rise hotel. Fishing vessels anchored in the harbor sometimes fry their catch and sell it on the docks.

■ ■ ■ STRALSUND

Albrecht von Wallenstein, commander of the Catholic army that besieged Stralsund during the Thirty Years War, lusted after the prize: "Even if it was chained to heaven, I want to have it." He never got it—Stralsund was the only town to successfully resist his attacks—and much of the beauty that appealed to Wallenstein is still here. Stralsund's location between the Strelasund (the sound that separates the mainland from the island of Rügen) and two inland ponds gives the *Altstadt* the appearance of an island. Buildings grown dignified with age and the three enormous red-brick churches stand as witness to the former glory and wealth of Stralsund, a free city after 1234. Stralsund helped to found the powerful Hanseatic League in 1293, and soon become a major trading hub and shipbuilding center. For almost two centuries after the Thirty Years War, Stralsund was ruled by Sweden, and the long occupation left indelible Scandinavian marks on the city. World War II exacted a heavy toll, and though much has been rebuilt, forty years of neglect have left some sights looking as if they might collapse again. The city has pledged a massive renovation effort, and many buildings bear signs indicating that they will soon be restored. When the dust settles, Stralsund should be an attraction to match any in Germany, but it may take a while.

ORIENTATION AND PRACTICAL INFORMATION

All the major sights and attractions are concentrated in the *Altstadt.* The three distinctive church spires make excellent navigational points. **Ossenreyerstraße,** the main pedestrian zone, runs north to south and encompasses a department store, several supermarkets, and several bakeries. The most direct rail connection to Stralsund is from Rostock, and then Berlin. Trains to the island of Rügen leave almost every hour.

Tourist Office: Alter Markt (tel. 25 22 51, fax 25 44 27), in the *Rathaus.* Bus #4 or 5: Kütertor, take a right on Heilgeiststr., and turn left on Ossenreyerstr. Distributes free maps in English and a brochure with accommodations listings. A more detailed city map, depending on the quality, can cost from DM1-7.50. The office sells tickets for tours through the *Altstadt* (DM6), departing from the *Rathaus* daily at 2pm. Open Mon. 10am-5pm, Tues.-Thurs. 9am-5pm, Fri. 9am-7pm, Sat. 9am-noon; Oct.-May open Mon. 10am-5pm, Tues.-Thurs. 9am-5pm, Fri. 9am-7pm.

Post Office: Neuer Markt, 18439 Stralsund, in the red-brick building opposite the Marienkirche. Open Mon.-Fri. 8am-6pm, Sat. 9-11am.

Telephones: city code: 03831

Currency Exchange: Sparkasse, Neuer Markt 7 (tel. 220).

Public Transportation: Bus lines #1-6 circle the *Altstadt,* serving the outskirts of town. Single fare DM0.50. The central **bus station** at Frankenwall is the departure point for **intercity buses** to Rügen and other surrounding areas; check the **information desk** at the train station.

Ferries: water tours of the harbor and the *Strelasund* depart daily at 10am from the Seestr. dock (1hr., DM6, children DM5). Ferry trips to Rügen or the island Hiddensee via **Weiße Flotte** leave 3 times daily from Fährstr. 16 (tel. 69 23 71); for tickets call (tel. 69 24 73) or stop at the ticket booth on the harbor. From the Alter Markt, walk down Fährstr. and turn left at Seestr. to the departure point. Stralsund-Hiddensee roundtrip DM18, children DM12, one way DM10, children DM7.

Bike Rental: in train station. DM10-12 per day. Open Mon.-Fri. 6am-9pm, Sat. 7am-2:30pm, Sun. 9am-4:30pm.

Pharmacy: Bahnhofsapotheke, Tribseer Damm 6 (tel. 29 23 28).

Emergency: Ambulance: tel. 115. **Police:** tel. 110. **Fire:** tel. 112.

ACCOMMODATIONS

With the tourism industry just cranking up and masses of people pouring into Stralsund, the chances of finding a cheap room in the summer are slim. Private rooms and hotels are normally booked up by noon; try to make reservations in advance, or get over to the room-finding service desk of the **Zimmerbörse** in the **Ostsee-Reiseservice,** Ossenreyerstr. 23 (tel. 29 38 94; open Mon.-Fri. 9am-6pm, Sat. 10am-noon).

Jugendherberge Stralsund (HI), Am Küter Tor 1 (tel. 29 21 60, fax 29 76 76). Bus #4 or 5 (from the station, turn right onto Iribseer Damm and go straight to the "Hauptbahnhof." bus stop): Küter Tor (second stop), turn right and take the first left; the hotel is just before the big gate on the left. Enter through the wooden gate. An old hostel located in the town hall with a courtyard and a convenient location. Brace yourself for the onslaught of tourists in summer; call ahead. Reception open 7-9am and 3-10pm. Lockout 9am-3pm. Curfew 10pm. DM14.50, over 26 DM19.50. Choice of breakfast included. Closed Dec. 15-Jan. 15.

Jugendherberge Stralsund-Devin (HI), Strandstr. 21 (tel. 27 03 58). Bus #3 (from the *Hauptbahnhof*): Devin (25min.; DM2.50). Located in the nearby village of Devin, it's a lot bigger than the Stralsund hostel, but harder to reach. Reception open 1-3pm and 7-8pm, curfew 10pm. DM14.50, over 26 DM19.50. Breakfast included. Open Feb. 1-Dec. 21.

FOOD

Most of the restaurants and cafés are located in the inner city. The cheapest offerings are the numerous snack bars operating out of little trailers all over town; try **"Teddybär,"** in the pedestrian zone, for fast German food (open daily 7am-9pm).

Ristorante Romantica, Alter Markt (tel. 29 36 07). Ethnically confused Italian-German restaurant. Stylish and modern furnishings, including monumental china vases in the windows. Pizza from DM9, *Schnitzel* DM12. Open daily 11am-midnight.

Gastmahl des Meeres, Ossenreyerstr. 49 (tel. 29 41 55), in the pedestrian zone. Serves every imaginable make of fish. Full meals from DM7.50. Open Mon.-Fri. 11am-9pm, Sat.-Sun. 11am-3pm.

Zur Kogge, Tribseerstr. 26 (29 38 46). More fish, and a maritime interior-decorating theme (DM10). Open daily. 10am-1am, kitchen open until 11pm.

Café Lütt, Alter Markt 12 (29 23 48), serves small, brightly-iced cakes (DM3-5), including some Northern German raritites. Open Mon.-Sun. 8am-7pm.

Stadtbäckerei, Ossenreyerstr. 43 (29 40 82), is a bakery combined with a café. Open Mon., Wed. and Fri. 7am-6pm, Thurs. 7am-6pm, Sat. 8am-5pm, Sun. 1-5pm.

SIGHTS

All the major sights are concentrated on the quasi-island of the *Altstadt* and are easily seen on foot. Atrocious socialist-era architecture pollutes the less savory outskirts of the city; focus on the more eye-catching elements of old Stralsund. The **Alter Markt** in the center is surrounded by several of Stralsund's oldest buildings. The spectacular 14th-century red façade of the Gothic **Rathaus** is embossed with the coats-of-arms of cities like Rostock and Hamburg, a testament to Stralsund's supremacy in the Hanseatic League. The courtyard was designed in 1680, after a devastating fire precipitated the decision to transform this former warehouse into the town hall (interior closed to visitors).

Just behind the *Rathaus* is the impressive red-brick Gothic **St. Nikolaikirche,** also constructed in the 13th century. The two sturdy towers are out of joint with each other; after a fire, an ornate dome was placed on one while the other just got a plain, makeshift roof. (Open Tues.-Fri. 10am-noon, 2-4pm, Sat. 10am-noon, Sun. 11am-noon. Tours Fri. 3pm. Free.) From the *Markt,* stroll through the Fährstr., with its Gothic and Baroque houses, including the **Scheele-Haus.** On the other side of the *Markt,* the "newer" **Mönchstraße, Ravensburgerstraße,** and **Badenstraße** all feature Renaissance buildings, most of them beautifully restored.

From the *Alter Markt,* **Ossenreyerstraße** (turn right at the end) takes you to the lovely **Neuer Markt** (new market) and the **Marienkirche,** with its 104m tower. The interior could use a fresh coat of paint, but the Baroque organ built in 1659 by the organmaster Stellwagen of Hamburg still shows the richness of its carving. Climb all 345 narrow, steep steps to the lookout in the tower for a magnificent view of Stralsund and the Baltic Sea, with Rügen in the distance. (Open Mon.-Sat. 10am-5pm, Sun. 11am-5pm. Church admission free, tower DM2.) Just in front of the church is a remnant of the 40-year communist era: an exaggeratedly kitschy monument singing the praises of the Soviet Army. The third of Stralsund's monumental churches, the **St. Jakobi** on Böttcherstr., was heavily damaged in an air raid in 1944; it can only be visited from the outside, as the interior has not yet been restored.

Located between the *Alter* and *Neuer Markt* are Stralsund's two major museums, both housed in the **St. Katharinen Monastery** (tel. 29 51 35), filling the void left when the monks were driven out after the Reformation hit town. The renowned **Oceanographic Museum,** Katharinenberg 15 (tel. 51 35), tells all about marine biology and the underwater world. Aquariums display domestic and exotic fish, turtles, corals, and more more more (open Mon.-Thurs. 9am-6pm, Fri.-Sun. 10am-5pm; Sept.-Apr. daily 10am-5pm; admission DM4, students DM1.50). Just around the corner, the **Museum of Cultural History,** Mönchstr. 26 (tel. 29 21 80), documents the history of the city (open Tues.-Sun. 10am-6pm; admission DM4, students and children DM1.50).

Take your time walking along the **Sundpromenade,** where you can catch a glimpse of Rügen across the bay, glowing a spectacular red and gold in the sunset. Another beautiful walk runs along **Knieperwall,** alongside the **Knieperteich** (pond) and the remains of the **town wall.** Note the old gates **Kniepertor** and **Kütertor,** both of which date back to the 13th century. An alternate route from the *Alter Markt* runs through the Külpstr. to the Schillstr., ending at the **Johannniskloster,** a Franciscan monastery founded in 1254, 45 years after Francis of Assisi founded the order. Today the building houses the city's Baroque archives, several thousand books in all.

Stralsund isn't exactly full of thrills at night, though information about evening entertainment is available from the tourist office.

■■■ RÜGEN ISLAND

Chilling in the Baltic Sea north of Stralsund, Rügen's 597km of coastline make it Germany's largest island. It encompasses a dazzling array of natural wonders: white beaches and the rugged chalk cliffs of the *Stubbenkammer,* farmland and beech forests, heaths and swamps. But Rügen is not all unsettled wilds; the island does have a long, and at times tumultuous, history. Ruins dating back to the Stone Age and megalithic graves (easily identifiable piles of giant stones) are scattered all over the island. Teutonic tribes were pushed out by Slavs during the migration of nations in the 5th century; 500 years later, the pagan Slavic rule was ended by Danes who

Christianized the island, destroying the Slavic sanctuary at **Kap Arkona,** on the northern tip of Rügen. In the 19th century, the island was discovered by the nobility and transformed into a resort center stuffed with expensive Neoclassical buildings. This prosperity waned under communist rule, but tourists are quickly rediscovering the island's natural and cultural charms. The tourism industry on Rügen is currently booming, with *Ossis* and *Wessis* alike pouring onto the island. Finding a room is difficult—the only hostel is in **Binz** (see below). Take your camping gear and you'll be safe, for there are campgrounds scattered all over Rügen; or call the ever-expanding room-finding services well in advance. A good helper is the tourist map *Wander und Freizeitkarte von Rügen und Hiddensee* (DM8.90) which includes hiking trails, campgrounds, and sights. Rügen can be approached by train, bus, or ferry from Stralsund, Sweden, or Denmark. The major cities are **Bergen** in the center, **Putbus** in the south, and **Saßnitz** in the north. The *Rasender Roland*, an narrow-gauge rail line, connects the towns at the southern end of the island.

BERGEN

Bergen is Rügen's capital, with buses and trains connecting frequently to Stralsund (where it may be easier to find accommodations). On the hillside is a memorial for **Ernst Moritz Arndt,** a 19th-century writer and member of the 1848 Pauls-Kirche-Parliament, who was born on Rügen; from its tower, there's a fantastic view of the island. (Open May-Oct. daily 10am-6pm, Nov.-Apr. Mon.-Fri. 10am-4pm, Sat.-Sun. 10am-5pm; DM 1.50, students DM1.) Bergen's **Marienkirche,** a Romanesque basilica built around 1200, is Rügen's oldest building (open Mon.-Fri. 9am-noon and 1-5pm; free).

Bergen's **tourist information,** Markt 27 (tel. (03838) 231 12, fax 231 56), has information on the entire island. Take a left from station and head uphill on Bahnhofstr., then take a left onto Markt. Their room-finding service charges a DM5 fee (open May-Sept. Mon.-Fri. 9am-8pm, Sat. 9am-2pm; Oct.-Apr. Mon.-Fri. 9am-6pm). The **post office,** 18528 Bergen, is just to the right of the tourist office (open Mon.-Fri. 9am-6pm, Sat. 9-11am). **Bike rental** at the station is DM10-12 per day (open daily 5am-8:30pm). **Rügenscher Hof,** Bahnhofstr. 5 (tel. (03838) 228 34) serves reasonably priced meals; steak will cost you DM12 (open Mon.-Sat. 8am-11pm). From Bergen, trains run frequently to Putbus.

PUTBUS, LAUTERBACH, AND VILM

Putbus, colloquially known as *"Weißerdorf,"* or "White Town," was founded by Prince Malter von Putbus as a private residence and resort in 1810. This highly organized town is built in the Neoclassical style fashionable in the early 19th century. From the train station, walk down Bahnhofstr. to the **Circus,** a round plaza encircled by gleaming white villas and mansions. Alleestr. will lead you to the English-style **Schloßpark** (Palace Park), a more pastoral manifestation of the Prince's personal aesthetic. Sit back, relax, and enjoy fully the natural surroundings. The statue of the prince remains standing, though it's stood alone since the run-down palace was torn down as a "decadent stigma" in 1962. Only the remains of the terrace can be seen.

The privately operated **tourist office,** Bahnhofstr. 2 (tel. (038301) 605 13) has a room-finding service for a grand fee of DM10 (rooms from DM20; open Mon.-Fri. 9am-6pm, Sat. 10am-2pm). The train station **rents bikes** for DM10-12 per day. Stroll a bit farther past the remarkable theater to the **market,** with yet more early 19th-century constructions surrounding a minor park.In Putbus, hop on the **Rasender Roland** ("Racing Roland"), a narrow-gauge steam train, and relive the good old days. The Roland crawls through sleepy farming areas and shadowy beech forests at the whirlwind speed of 30kph (single fare DM7, Tramper-Monats Ticket valid, interruptions possible on the same day).

East of Putbus lies **Lauterbach,** with a beach and a beautiful neo-classical spa house also built by the Prince of Putbus. The island of **Vilm,** south of Putbus and Lauterbach, was once a heavily guarded vacation resort for the GDR's party bosses.

It was strictly off-limits to the *hoi polloi*—a prohibition that fanned the flames of gossip and intrigue. Today, it's an utterly guileless **nature reserve. Ferry trips** around Vilm are available from Lauterbach. (Departures Wed., Thurs. and Sat.-Mon. 10am, 1pm, and 3pm; Tues. and Fri. 10am, 1pm, 3pm and 7pm; DM12, children DM6. The ferries only circumnavigate the island; to actually disembark, you must obtain special permission—call (tel. 605 13) for details.)

BINZ

Binz, the biggest of Rügen's spas, is a seaside town with a pristine, 4km-long beach. Once a fashionable and luxurious resort for aristocrats and foreigners, the town has declined a bit over the years, and fairly reeks of faded glory. The **Kurhaus,** a promenade along the beach, is lined with beautiful wood mansions gone a bit shabby, mere echoes of those glamorous years. But this is bound to change, for with the lifting of Eastern travel restrictions, Binz has gained thousands of visitors.

Finding a room can be murderous; hotels are completely booked in the summer months. Try the room-finding service of the **tourist office,** Schillerstr. 15 (tel. (038393) 27 82); rooms start at DM25, and they don't charge a fee (open Mon.-Fri. 9am-7pm, Sat.-Sun. 9am-5pm). The scarcity of rooms is also evident at Rügen's only **Jugendherberge (HI),** Strandpromenade 35 (tel. (038393) 24 23), directly on the beach. (Reception open 8am-noon, 5:30-7pm. Curfew 10pm. DM15.50, over 26 DM20.50; resort tax DM2.50, students DM1.25. Breakfast included.) There is a **campground** on Poststr., (tel. (038393) 20 20) in **Prora,** north of Binz along the beach. (Reception open 7am-10pm. DM10 per person, DM10 per tent. Resort tax DM1.25.) To ride along the dunes, stop at the **bike** rental shop situated by the train station (DM10-12 per day, open daily 8am-4pm); they also sell maps. The *Rasender Roland* narrow-gauge train stops in Binz.

GRANITZ AND GÖHREN

The panorama across the island from the **Jagdschloß Granitz** (tel. (038393) 22 63), a castle-like hunting lodge built in 1836, is breathtaking. Walk up the *Tempelberg* (follow the signs and the crowd from the station) to the lookout tower with its cast-iron staircase, designed by the Prussian architect Schinkel. (Open daily 9am-9pm; Nov.-March Tues.-Sun. 9am-4:30pm. Admission DM4.50 students DM3.) The *Roland* narrow-gauge train also stops at the *Jagdschloß*; after passing the similar resort stops of Seilin and Baabe, the train's final destination is **Göhren,** on the Mönchgut peninsula.

The town itself has not held up to 40 years of neglect very well, but the promenade and the glorious white beach bordered by a beech forest are a worthy endpoint to a tour of Rügen. While in Göhren, don't miss the **Mönchgut Museum,** with its trio of exhibits: the **Museumshof** on Wilhelm-Pieck-Str., an old-fashioned farm with thatched roofs (open May-Sept. Tues.-Sun. 9am-5pm; admission DM2.50, children DM1.50), the **Heimatsmuseum** on Thiessowerstr., a museum of local history (look for the convention of anchors in the front yard; open May-Sept. Tues.-Sun. 9am-5pm; admission DM2.50, children DM1.50), and the **Rokhus,** a lovely thatched-roof house (open May-Sept. Wed.-Mon. 9am-5pm; admission DM2.50, children DM1.50).

For information go to the **tourist office** *(Kurverwaltung),* Schulstr. 8 (tel. (038308) 21 50; open Mon.-Fri. 7am-6pm, Sat.-Sun. 10am-noon). You can rent a **bike** at the campground (distribution 8am-noon, return 8-9pm). The **campground** (tel. (038308) 21 22) is close to the beach—from the train station, turn right and follow the signs; the camp is on the right-hand side. (Reception open 7am-10pm. DM4.50 per person, DM2.50per tent.) For the less athletically inclined, **buses** leave Göhren for Bergen, Binz, and Saßnitz.

SAßNITZ

Saßnitz, the primary focus of the northern part of the island, was a 19th-century sea-side resort so popular it prompted Theodor Fontane to write in his novel *Effi Briest,* "To travel to Rügen means to travel to Saßnitz." In the socialist era, Saßnitz had a highly subsidized fishing industry, which is now floundering. It's an ordinary indus-trial town, but an excellent base for exploration of the **Jasmund National Park.** The peninsula of Jasmund is surrounded by the *Große und Kleine Jasmunder Bodden* and the Baltic Sea; *Bodden* are shallow salt-water lakes scattered over the island, dividing it into numerous peninsulas. The National Park covers one-third of Jasmund peninsula, and incorporates two *Bodden* and the accompanying wildlife. Several marked hiking trails run through the **Stubnitz beech forest.** From the far side of the town, an 8km trail takes you along the shore past the **Wissower Klinken,** jagged chalk cliffs only slightly less spectacular (but much less crowded) than their big brother up north, the Stubbenkammer—*the* attraction of Rügen (see below).

The **tourist office,** Hauptstr. 70 (tel. and fax (03892) 230 37), is down Bahnhofstr. from the station; turn left on Hauptstr. They provide a room-finding service (DM20-40, DM5 fee); call in advance (open Mon.-Fri. 7:30am-7pm, Sat.-Sun. 3-7pm; Nov.-Mar. Mon.-Fri. 7:30am-5pm). The train station **rents bikes** for DM10-12 per day (open daily 7:30am-4pm). Hauptstr. is the main street with the **post office, banks,** and shops.

Ferries leave Saßnitz for **Trelleborg,** Sweden and the Danish island of **Bornholm.** The ships of the **Reederei Arkona,** Bahnhofstr. 19 (tel. (03892) 224 55) leave from Saßnitz at 9am, reach Bornholm after four hours, and leaves Bornholm again at 4:30pm. (May-Sept. Round-trip DM45, children DM24, bus round-trip in Bornholm DM18.) **TS-Line,** Trelleborger-Str. (tel. (03892) 222 67 or 33 071, fax 222 66 or 330 55) offers trips to Trelleborg. (5 per day. 4hrs. DM40, students DM30, ages under 11 DM20. Roundtrip DM60, students DM45, ages under 11 DM30.) Other companies send boats out for **water tours** around the Stubbenkammer and Kap Arkona from Saßnitz harbor. (Boats run daily 9am-5pm. DM10-15, children DM8.)

Rügen Tourist, Hauptstr. 50 (tel. 223 77), offers day trips through Rügen. The curiously-named **Café-Restaurant New York,** Stralsunder Str. 46, offers pizza and other vaguely Italian dishes (pizza DM10; open daily 11am-1am). **Am Kai** fries fish directly on the harbor (entrees DM8-12; open daily 10am-midnight).

GROßE STUBBENKAMMER

A visit to Rügen is just not complete without a glimpse of the spectacular chalk cliffs of the Große Stubbenkammer, easily accessible from Saßnitz. Caspar David Friedrich, the great Romantic painter, fell in love with the cliffs and made them a pri-mary subject of his work. A scenic marked hiking trail (4km) takes you to the Stubbenkammer past the Herthasee lake and two megalithic graves. The formations of the Große Stubbenkammer include the **Königsstuhl** (king's chair), a 110m chalk cliff; legend has it that the kings of Rügen of ages past had to climb up to the top in order to be crowned upon the stone chair. A **lookout** (admission DM2, students DM1) offers another fabulous view across the cliffs and the Baltic Sea. Unfortu-nately, you'll also get a great view of swarms of picture-taking tourists, especially on Sundays. To find a little solitude, walk down the steep and windy paths to the flint-covered beach—the last part of the path consists of ladders set into the stone. The **Victoriasicht** overlook, a five-minute hike to the south of the Königsstuhl, furnishes a great view of the cliffs.

Buses to the Stubbenkammer leave from the Saßnitz train station. (Mon.-Fri. 8:15 9:30, 10:30am, and 2:30pm; Sat.-Sun. 9:30, 10:30am, and 2:30pm. Call tel. (03892) 321 55 for updated bus information.) The closest campground is **Campground Nip-merow** (tel. (038302) 92 44), underneath ancient beech trees next to the National Park. Catch the bus from Saßnitz and ask the driver to let you out at the camp-ground. (Reception open daily 6am-10pm, DM5 per person, DM5 per tent. Open mid-April to Oct.)

KAP ARKONA AND VITT

The northernmost attraction on Rügen is **Kap Arkona,** Germany's one and only cape. Take the bus tours from Saßnitz that also include the Stubbenkammer, or if you're of a more independent bent, hop on the bus to Putgarten (change in Altenkirchen). From Putgarten, walk a little less than 1km to the tiny village of **Vitt** (pronounced "fit"). As you approach, only the white octagonal church can be seen, but trust us, there's a village there. Walk down into the folds of the cliff to find the cache of houses with reed-thatched roofs. This tiny port was once one of the most important fish-trading spots on Rügen. Beleaguered fishers now offer boat trips around Kap Arkona to supplement their income (departures daily 10am-6pm). From Vitt, walk along the cliffs another 1km to Kap Arkona itself and enjoy the windy view from the top across the Baltic Sea—it's only 77km to Sweden. Look west of Rügen for the sinuous island of **Hiddensee** (see near Rügen, below). Before reunification, the two **lighthouses** on Kap Arkona were in a restricted area belonging to the GDR's National People's Army. Since the *Bundeswehr* (West German Army) took over, the quadrangular beacon, designed by Schinkel in classicist style, is open to view-seeking climbers.

The **tourist office** (Informationsamt) in Putgarten, Dorfstr. 15 (tel. (038391) 316), has detailed maps of hiking trails around the cape (open Mon.-Thurs. 8am-4pm, Fri. 8am-noon). The tourist office in **Altenkirche,** Karl-Marx-Str. 6 (tel. 038391) 293 or 294, runs a room-finding service (open Mon.-Fri. 8am-5pm). The **Drewoldke campground** (tel. 484) is just east of Altenkirche. (Reception open 8am-9pm. DM5 per person, DM2 per tent. Open April-Oct.)

■ Near Rügen: Hiddensee

West of Rügen lies the small island of Hiddensee, which the residents call *dat söte Länneken* (the sweet island). Its beauty and natural seclusion have always attracted artists and scientists—among them Sigmund Freud, Albert Einstein, Thomas Mann, and Käthe Kollwitz. The great naturalist author Gerhardt Hauptmann lived most of his life on Hiddensee and is buried in the *Kloster* (monastery), where there is a memorial to the man and his work (open daily 10am-5pm; DM3, children DM1.50). More than a millennium ago, Slavic tribes built a temple fortress here to honor their highest god, Svantevit. Remains of the wall can still be seen. From the northern tip of Hiddensee, called the **Dornbusch** (thorn-bush), one can enjoy a view across the whole island to Rügen. South of the *Kloster,* the Hiddensee flatlands follow covered partly by heath, including the villages **Vitte** and **Neuendorf.** The south consists solely of sand dunes filled with hiking trails and sandy beaches.

The **tourist office**, Kurverwaldtung Hiddensee, Norderende 55, 18565 Vitte, (tel. 038300) 242) operates a **room-finding service** (DM30, fee 7%). The office is open Mon.-Thurs. 7am-noon, m12:30-4pm; Fri. 7am-noon, 12;30-5pm, Sat. 1-3pm). You can **rent bikes** in every harbor on Hiddensee. **Ferry** connections are available to Hiddensee from Stralsund on the mainland and Schaprode on Rügen. Ferries leave Schaprode approximately 6 times per day (45min.) Prices run DM8, children DM6, roundtrip DM12, children DM8. No cars are allowed on the island.

SWITZERLAND (Suisse, die Schweiz, Svizzera, Confederatio Helvetica)

US$1 = 1.47 franc (SFr)
CDN$1 = 1.11SFr
UK£ = 2.22SFr
IR£1 = 2.06SFr
AUS$1 = 0.99SFr
NZ$1 = 0.81SFr

1SFr = US$0.68
1SFr = CDN$0.90
1SFr = UK£0.45
1SFr = IR£0.48
1SFr = AUS$1.01
1SFr = NZ$1.23

Divided by impassable Alpine giants and united by neither language nor religion, it is curious that Switzerland is a nation at all. What is now a confederation of 23 cantons was first conceived in 1291, and jelled into its present form at a slothful pace all the way through the 19th century. Swiss politics have an old fashioned feel; approximately 3000 local communes retain a great deal of power, and major policy disputes are routinely settled by national referenda.

Official neutrality since 1815 has kept the ravages of war away from this postcard-perfect haven. Placidity has also nurtured the growth of Big Money in the staid banking centers of Geneva and Zürich. You might find some personalities in Switzerland to exemplify staidness as well—for many big-city locals, an accepted idea of a good time is sitting in a bank watching gold prices change (dial 166 from any place in Switzerland to reach the stock market bulletins hotline). Walter Abisch refers to the "Idea of Switzerland": "Switzerland is simply a catchword....I am, of course, thinking of the image Switzerland evokes.... A kind of controlled neutrality, a certain antiseptic tranquility that even I find soothing." Spurred by its love of prosperity, Switzerland now seems on the verge of change. Though Switzerland remains neutral in relationship to its European neighbors, Swiss citizens have recently shown interest in the affairs of the country; voters are turning out in droves to cast their ballots for or against integration into the European Economic Community.

One aspect of Switzerland will likely always overshadow whatever internal divisions exist: the majestic Alps. John Keats glorified them in his Romantic poetry, while others have fallen silent against a landscape that defies words. Snow-capped peaks lord over half the country's area, enticing hikers, skiers, bikers, and paragliders from around the globe. Switzerland has developed one of the most finely-tuned tourist industries in the world. Victorian scholar John Ruskin called the Swiss Alps "the great cathedrals of the earth;" you're welcome to worship here if you can spare the cash.

ONCE THERE

■■■ TOURIST INFORMATION

Swiss tourist offices, called *Verkehrsbüro*, *Kurverein*, or *Syndicat d'Initiative*, are marked by a blue **"i"** and can usually be found in the vicinity of the train station or town center. Swiss tourist officials tend to respond much more efficiently to specific questions, like "Where are your campgrounds?" than to vague imperatives, like

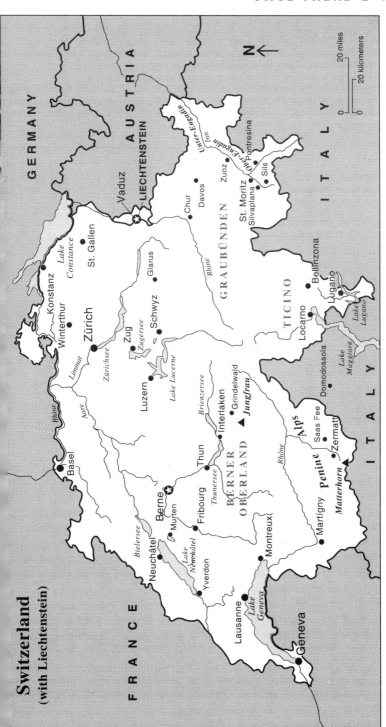

Switzerland
(with Liechtenstein)

SWITZERLAND: INTRODUCTION

"Tell me about the town." Ask for a hotel or room list, insist on a good map, and collect any hiking or biking information available. Banks usually distribute free maps as well. See Alpine Hiking and Skiing below for more publications with maps and trails helpful for visitors to Switzerland.

■■■ EMBASSIES AND CONSULATES

If you're seriously ill or in trouble, your embassy can provide a list of doctors or lawyers, and can also contact your relatives. In *extreme* cases, they can offer emergency financial assistance.

U.S.: Embassy: Bern, Jubiläumsstr. 93 (tel. (031) 43 70 11). Open Mon.-Fri. 9:30am-noon and 2:30-4pm. **Consulates: Zürich,** Zollikerstr. 141 (tel. (01) 422 25 66); **Geneva,** 1-3, av. de la Paix (tel. (022) 738 50 95).

Canada: Embassy: Bern, Kirchenfeldstr. 88 (tel. (031) 44 63 81). Open Mon.-Fri. 8am-noon and 1-4:30pm. **Consulates: Bern,** Belpstr. 11 (tel. (031) 25 22 61). Open Mon.-Fri. 8am-12:30pm and 1-4pm; **Geneva,** 1, ch. du Pré-de-la-Bichette (tel. (022) 733 90 00).

U.K.: Embassy: Bern, Thunstr. 50 (tel. (031) 44 50 21). Open Mon.-Fri. 9am-12:30pm and 2-5pm. **Consulates: Zürich,** Dufourstr. 56 (tel. (01) 261 15 20); **Geneva,** 37-39, rue de Vermont (tel. (022) 733 23 85).

Ireland: Embassy: Bern, Kirchenfeldstr. 68 (tel. (031) 44 14 42). Open Mon.-Fri. 10am-noon and 3-4:30pm.

Australia: Embassy: Bern, Alpenstr. 29 (tel. (031) 43 01 43). Open Mon.-Thurs. 10am-12:30pm and 1:30-3pm, Fri. 10am-12:30pm. **Consulate: Geneva,** 56-58, rue de Moillebeau (tel. (022) 734 62 00).

New Zealand: Consulate: Geneva, 28a, chemin du Petit-Saconnex (tel. (022) 734 95 30).

■■■ GETTING AROUND

■ By Train

Getting around Switzerland is gleefully easy. Federal and private railways connect most towns and villages, with trains running in each direction on an hourly basis. **Schnellzüge** (express trains) speed from metropolis to metropolis while **Regionalzüge** chug into each cowtown on the route. Yellow signs announce departure times (*Ausfahrt*) and tracks (*Gleis*). White signs are for arrivals (*Ankunft*). Although Eurailpasses are valid for the state-run railways that connect major cities and comprise 60% of train service, private owners monopolize mountain routes, raising prices to Alpine heights. Each city has small booklets listing train schedules; you can also ask for a free white booklet listing all prices of major fares within the country.

To beat ruinous transportation costs, those planning to spend much time in the country should seriously consider the myriad rail options. The most extensive of these is the **Swisspass,** which entitles you to unlimited free travel on government operated trains, ferries, buses in 30 Swiss cities, and private railways, but only a 25-50% discount on many mountain railways and cable cars. The pass is sold abroad through Rail Europe or any major U.S. travel agency. Most travel agencies add a handling fee which, though small, can make a difference. Depending on current exchange rates, it may be cheaper to buy the pass in one of the train stations in Switzerland. The pass also has a very strict no-replacement policy. The **Swiss Flexipass** is priced at US$148, valid for any three days of second-class travel within 15 days. The regular **Swisspass** costs US$186 for eight consecutive days of unlimited travel, US$214 for 15 days, and US$296 for one month (ages 6-16 ½-price). Unless you're on a speed tour, the pass may not pay for itself. Instead, opt for the **Half-Fare Travel Card** (75SFr for 1 month), which entitles you to a 50% discount on all trips on federal and private railroads, postal buses, and steamers. Show your passport or ISIC receive a one-month card. After one or two trips, the card pays for itself. This card is only available in Switzerland; it *cannot* be purchased abroad. Those without Eurail can cash in on one of the 8 **Regional Passes** (50-175SFr), available in major tourist offices (see Berner Oberland: Getting Around). The **Swiss Card,** sold *only* abroad, works as a one-month Half-Fare Card but also gives one free round-trip from an airport.

■ By Bus

PTT **postal-buses,** a barrage of banana-colored-three-brake-system-coaches delivered to you expressly by the Swiss government, connect rural villages and towns, picking up the slack where trains fail to go. Swiss Passes are valid on many buses; Eurailpasses are not. Even with the Swiss Pass, you might have to pay a bit extra (5-10SFr) if you're riding one of the direct, faster buses. In cities, public buses transport commuters and shoppers alike to outlying areas; tickets must be bought in advance at automatic machines, found at most bus stops. The system works on an honor code and inspections are infrequent, but expect to be hit for 30-50SFr if caught riding without a valid ticket. *Tageskarte,* valid for 24 hours of free travel, run 3-5SFr, but Swiss cities are so small that you might as well travel by foot.

■ By Car

Car travel, whether by taxi or rental car, is extremely expensive. It's also a bit risky if you're accustomed to large flat expanses or slow-paced drivers—the Swiss don't fool around when it comes to speed, yet they're not quite as quick-reflexed as their German neighbors. Prepare yourself. **Taxi** dispatchers (expensive) can generally be reached at tel. 141. Rates for all cars rented in Switzerland include a 30SFr (approx. US$21) annual **road toll** called a *Vignette;* rent in another country unless you have the money to burn. Roads are easy to follow and use international signs. **Gasoline stations** are self-service and open around the clock. To use them, insert money (in increments of 10 or 20SFr bills) into the pump before filling. U.S. gasoline credit cards are not accepted at Swiss gas stations. The **minimum driving age** in Switzerland is 18. Seatbelts *must* be worn by all passengers. **Speed limits** are 120kph on expressways, 80kph on highways, and 50kph in cities, unless otherwise marked. Cars must carry a red triangular warning flag, available from the **Swiss Touring Club,** 9, rue Pierre-Fatio, CH-1200 Geneva (tel. (022) 234 36 60) and at post offices, customs posts and gas stations. The club operates road patrols that assist motorists-in-need; call 140 for help. Dial 162 for **road conditions** in English, 140 for **emergency automobile assistance**.

■ Hitchhiking

Let's Go does not recommend hitchhiking as a safe means of travel. Short distances and Swiss reserve make hitchhiking difficult. Those who hitchhike head to the town outskirts near, but not on, the highway. To signal, they point at the ground or use a flat hand. More successful hitchers make a sign with their destination in big, bold letters, followed by the local word for "please" *("bitte"* in German, *"s.v.p."* in French, *"per favore"* in Italian). Holding up a small flag of the hitcher's home country reportedly triggers that famous Swiss hospitality. It is illegal to hitchhike on main thoroughfares; standing in front of the on-ramp is not.

■ Alpine Hiking and Skiing

A pocket knife with a corkscrew, a leathern drinking cup, a spirit-flask, stout gloves, and a piece of green crepe or coloured spectacles to protect the eyes from the glare of the snow, should not be forgotten," wrote Karl Baedeker in his 1907 travel guide to Switzerland. The Swiss National Tourist Office still suggests ski glasses to prevent **snow blindness,** but the spirit flask has dropped out of the picture.

For those with a sense of adventure and the stamina to match, hiking offers most rewarding views of Switzerland. Thirty thousand miles of **hiking trails** lace the entire country; yellow signs give directions and traveling times (*Std.* or *Stunden*= hours) to nearby destinations. Trails are marked by bands of white-red-white; if you don't see any markings, you're on an "unofficial" trail—which is not always a problem, for most trails are well-maintained. Lowland **meandering** at its best can be found in the Engadin valley near St. Moritz; for steeper climbs, head to Zermatt or the Interlaken area. Local tourist offices can provide invaluable advice regarding the most scenic paths.

Swiss Alpine Club (SAC) **huts** are modest and extremely practical for those interested in trekking in higher, more remote areas of the Alps. Bunk rooms sleep 10 to 20 weary hikers side by side, with blankets (no electricity or running water) provided. SAC huts are open to all, but SAC **members** get discounted rates. The average rate for one night's stay without food is 30SFr for non-members, and 20-25SFr for members. Those serious about conquering the summits and becoming SAC members must pay 111SFr (approx. US$80) to join; as a bonus you'll receive the titillating publication *Die Alpen*. Contact the SAC, Sektion Zermatt, Haus Granit, 3920 Zermatt, Switzerland.

Contrary to popular belief, **skiing** in Switzerland is often less expensive than in the U.S., if you avoid the pricey resorts. Ski passes (valid for transportation to, from, and on lifts) runs 30-50SFr per day and 100-300SFr per week, depending on the size of the region covered by the pass. A week of lift tickets, equipment rental, lessons, lodging, and *demi-pension* (breakfast plus one other meal, usually dinner) averages 475SFr. Summer skiing is a possibility from June through October on the Jungfraujoch in Interlaken, the foothills of the Matterhorn in Zermatt, and Diavolezza in Pontresina. Lifts generally operate from 7am to 2pm at the latest.

Kummerly & Frey, Hallerstr. 6-10, 3001 Bern (tel. (031) 23 51 11, fax 24 59 03), has an extensive selection of maps and books. **Bundesamt fur Landestopographie,** Seftigenstr. 264, 3084 Wabern (tel. (031) 963 21 11, fax 963 23 25) can provide the avid hiker or skier with detailed topographical maps of Switzerland's vast ranges.

■ Other Options

Despite the hills, **cycling** is a splendid way to see the country. Bicycles can be **rented** from approximately 200 train stations and returned to any station. A standard seven-gear city-bike goes for 10SFr per half day, 15SFr per day, and 76SFr per week. Rock-conquering **mountain bikes** cost a bit more; children's bikes less. Trains charge 5SFr for bike transport. May, June, and September are prime biking months; remember you can send your belongings ahead by train if you don't want to be burdened on your trans-Switzerland biking venture. Ask any tourist office for maps. **Bike routes** are marked with red signs with route letter and destination. The **Touring Club Suisse,** Div. cyclo-loisers & Jeunesse, 11-13, Chemin Riantbosson, Case postale 176, 1217 Meyrin 1 (tel. (022) 785 1222, fax 785 1262), will send you including cycling routes and descriptions, maps, and mileage charts.

Ferries ply many of the larger lakes. Fares are no bargain, but a Eurailpass often gets you free passage, and a Swisspass almost always earns a free ride. Major **airlines** fly into Zürich and Geneva; connecting flights serve Basel, Bern, and Lugano.

■■■ LANGUAGE

Switzerland is quatrilingual. *Schwyzerdütsch* (Swiss German), a dialect nearly incomprehensible to other German speakers, is spoken by the majority of the population (65%). Many Swiss are perfectly capable of speaking in standard (official) Ge man, but choose not to because of its historical affiliations. French is spoken in the west by 18% of the population, Italian in the southern canton of Ticino (10%), and Romansch (a relative of Latin and Etruscan; 1%) in parts of the canton of Graubünden (Grisons). Whatever language people speak first, they often know at least two others, including English. Nearly all train ticket-sellers (not conductors), officials, hotel proprietors, and tourist shop employees speak English.

■■■ MONEY

The primary unit of Swiss currency is the **Swiss franc** (SFr). A franc is divided into 100 centimes (called *Rappen* in German Switzerland). Bills are issued in 10, 20, 50, 100, and 1000SFr denominations; coins in 10, 20, and 50 centimes, and 1, 2, and 5SFr. **Currency exchange** *(Geldwechsel)* is easiest (and open latest) at train stations, where rates are the same as or very close to bank rates. American Express services are usually tied to a travel agency. There are AmEx offices in Basel, Bern, Geneva, Lausanne, Lucerne, and Zürich. Most banks are open Monday through Friday from 8:30am to 4:30pm with a break from noon to 2pm, and Saturday mornings until noon. Many **ATM** machines take Swiss bank cards only; don't rely on them. A few banks offer credit-card cash advances (min. usually US$200).

■■■ ACCOMMODATIONS AND CAMPING

For more general information on accommodations in Switzerland, see Essentials: Accommodations. If you are planning to approach Switzerland via the outdoors (we suggest it), take special note of the Essentials: Camping subsection; that's where we put the good advice we have distilled from our time in the wilderness.

■ Hostels

All things Swiss are meticulous, orderly, and expensive. Excluding occasionally draconian curfews, the uniformly cheery youth **hostels** *(Jugendherbergen)* provide a refreshing break from their counterparts in less orderly nations (now *there's* a sweeping generalization). Members can expect to pay 14-22SFr; if you're not a member, become one. A one-year membership costs 30SFr in most hostels. Otherwise, you'll be charged a 7SFr surcharge for 6 nights, at the end of which you get a free membership card. Prices almost always include sleepsacks and a breakfast of bread and hot chocolate or tea; convenient and generally tasty dinners add 9-10SFr to the bill. Hostels give preference to members under 26; unfortunately, they also give preference to groups, making it tougher to find a bed in July and August. Use the excellent voucher system. If you're traveling from one Swiss hostel to another, pay 10SFr at the hostel you're leaving; they'll reserve a spot for you at another hostel, and give you a 9SFr voucher for that hostel. You must arrive by 7pm to keep your reservation.

■ Hotels

Inexpensive hotels are few and far between, but expensive ones often have a few bathless rooms they'll rent cheaply. The Swiss Hotel Association grades hotels with one to five stars. Most hotels listed in this book are one-star establishments, which are still pretty nice by global standards. Expect to pay 50-65SFr for a single without bath, 80-100SFr for a double. In rural and vacation areas, cheaper rooms in private homes *(Privatzimmer)* abound. Look for the *"Zimmerfrei"* signs, or inquire at local tourist offices, which have comprehensive lists of rooms and can often make a reservation for little or no charge.

STAYING IN TOUCH

■ Camping

As befits a country so blessed by Mother Nature, Switzerland teems with more than 1200 **campgrounds**. Some are so beautiful that they take on spiritual value; others are glorified backyards. This land of property and order forbids freelance camping along roads and in public areas. Campers will find a range of pitching areas—some cater to European caravans, others to those seeking out-of-the-way idylls. Most tourist offices distribute exhaustive lists of regional sites. Prices average 3-6SFr per person, 4-9SFr per tent; with exceptions, most campgrounds are open in summer only.

■■■ STAYING IN TOUCH

Local calls cost 40 centimes. Phones take 10, 20, and 50 centime and 1 and 5SFr coins. Change is not returned; press the red button to make additional calls before the money runs out. City codes are three digits long, numbers themselves six or seven. In all areas, dial 111 for **information** (including directory assistance, train schedules, and other minutiae), and 191 or 114 for an **English-speaking international operator.** Switzerland maintains a rapid and efficient postal system. **Letters** take between one and three days for delivery in the country, 10 to 14 to North America. Within Europe, a second-class letter or postcard of up to 20g costs 1.40SFr, a second-class postcard 0.80SFr. To the U.S. or Canada, the first-class rates are 2.70SFr and 1.80SFr respectively, second-class 1.60SFr and 0.90SFr. Post offices provide services Monday through Friday from 8:30am to noon and from 1:30 to 6:30pm, Saturday from 7:30 to 11am. In French Switzerland, **general delivery,** address mail to Janis JOPLIN, *Poste Restante,* 1 (city name) Hauptpost, Suisse. In German Switzerland, send mail to Mike VAZQUEZ, *Postlagernde Briefe,* 1 (city name) Hauptpost, die Schweiz. For Ticino, address letters: Zoe SARNAT, *fermo Posta,* 1 (city name) Hauptpost, Svizzera.

■■■ FOOD

Dining in Switzerland would be an ultimately forgettable experience were it not for the remarkably high prices. Although the Swiss are hardly culinary daredevils, restaurant meals are as a rule well-prepared and satisfying. Dining *à la carte* will ruin your budget, but most establishments offer a daily *menu* (10-15SFr) that includes soup or salad, entree, and a vegetable. Swiss restaurant and hotel prices include a service charge, so tipping is neither necessary nor expected.

Gastronomically colorless when compared to its western and southern neighbors, Switzerland does offer a few real treats. In **French Switzerland,** try the cheese specialties: **fondue** is always excellent, as is *raclette* (melted cheese served with pickled onions and boiled new potatoes). In the **German-speaking** parts, food is heartier. Try *Züricher Geschnetzeltes* (veal strips in a delicious cream sauce) and *Rösti* (almost-hashbrowned potatoes with onion and other add-ons). Swiss **chocolate** and **cheese** are, in general, the best in the world.

Daily or weekly **markets** sell fresh fruits and vegetables, and the bread, cheese and ultra-creamy milk is straight out of Dairy Heaven. Those cooking for themselves need look no further than the local supermarkets, many of which sell whole roast chickens for just 8SFr. A loaf of bread runs 1-2.20SFr, milk costs about 2SFr. Common chains are **Migros** (announced by garish neon orange M's), **Coop** (pronounced kope), or **EPA.** Many of these also run cafeteria-style restaurants, as do the ubiquitous **Manora** eateries, with decent prices and a wide variety of yummies, including gargantuan salad bars.

Travelers who maintain **vegetarian** diets will rarely find veggie-only restaurants but when they do, they can gorge on generally gigantic salads. Fruit and vegetable stands offer the freshest and tastiest produce, but charge equally high prices. With less than .05% of the population professing Judaism as its religion, **kosher** cuisine i at best difficult to find. Cosmopolitan urban centers may have a few establishments catering to this need.

■■■ SPECIAL CONCERNS

Women travelers who have visited other countries in Western Europe are likely to be relieved upon reaching Switzerland. The country's conservative social attitudes create a fairly hassle-free environment for females, but traditional precautions should still be taken. **Seniors** can take advantage of discounts on transportation systems and at many museums. A passport meets proof-of-age requirements. **Gay and lesbian** travelers should know that Switzerland is—at this particular historical moment—less tolerant of homosexuality than is Germany.

Travelers with disabilities can use the frequent wheelchair ramps cut into sidewalks and leading up into stores and restrooms. Few buildings have staircase entrances. The Swiss Federal Railways are in the process of adapting most of their coaches for improved wheelchair access. Intercity and long-distance express trains have wheelchair compartments. Travelers with disabilities can contact **Mobility International Schweiz,** Hard 4, 8408 Winterthur (tel. (052) 25 68 25, fax 25 68 38).

■■■ CLIMATE

Like its terrain, Switzerland's weather varies crazily from area to area. As one might expect, the rain falls mainly on the temperate swath of plain that extends across from Lake Constance in the northeast through Zurich and Berne down to Geneva. In the Alps, snow is the norm; much of Alpine Switzerland cuddles up under snow cover for half the year. Sense does not always dictate weather patterns; freaky instances of a weather pattern called Fohn (temperature inversion) occasionally keeps the mountains warmer than the plain. The Italian-speaking canton of Ticino lies in a lowish plateau, and boasts a pseudo-tropical clime. Figures below are degrees Farenheit.

	July	October	January	April
Basel	56-79	43-59	27-40	40-61
Berne	56-74	41-56	25-36	40-58
Geneva	59-77	45-58	29-40	41-59
Interlaken	54-74	41-59	23-36	38-59
Locarno	63-79	40-58	38-49	45-61
Lucerne	58-76	41-52	34-43	40-58
Zurich	58-77	43-58	27-36	40-59

LIFE AND TIMES

■■■ HISTORY

Although modern-day Switzerland has an unshakeable reputation as a peaceful, egalitarian society, the country has not always been aloof from international conflict. From ancient times until the not-so-distant past, Switzerland was a crossroads for marauding armies and a hotbed of political intrigue. During an unsuccessful campaign against Rome in the 2nd century BC, the Carthaginian general Hannibal led his troops from northern Africa through the Alps and down into Italy. Julius Caesar defeated the **Helvetti tribes** living in Switzerland in 58 BC, thereby securing control of the **Great St. Bernard Pass** and enabling future northward Roman expansion. **Romansch,** a language more closely related to Latin than any other Romance language, is still spoken by denizens of the Roman-occupied territories.

After the fall of Rome, the cantons that comprise modern-day Switzerland were absorbed into the Holy Roman Empire. The **Houses of Savoy, Habsburg,** and **Zähringen** fought over the individual territories after the dissolution of Carolingian rule and the divisions wrought by the **Investiture Conflict.** In 1291, the three forest cantons of **Uri, Schwyz,** and **Unterwald** signed a secret agreement forming the **Ewige Bund** (Everlasting League); Switzerland celebrated the 700th anniversary of the confederation in 1991. After the **Battle of Morgarten** in 1315, Habsburg leaders agreed to a long truce and granted the alliance official recognition.

Over the next several centuries, the three-canton core of Switzerland gradually expanded through merger and conquest. The confederation's power peaked in the 15th century, but after the Burgundian Wars, Switzerland's power rapidly waned. The leadership of **Niklaus von Flüe** (a.k.a. Brüder Klaus), a mystical hermit-farmer, prevented conflict from breaking out over the issue of expansion; the crisis averted, Swiss soldiers became mercenaries for anyone that would hire them, especially the Pope and the northern Italian city-states. A **Swiss Guard** still defends the Vatican.

The **Protestant Reformation** rocked the confederation to its foundation. Radical theologian **Ulrich Zwingli** of Zürich (see Religion, below) used his great influence over the local government in ugly ways; the differently-minded **Anabaptists** were banned. **John Calvin** dominated Genevan affairs to an even greater extent; his opponents were summarily executed. In 1527, brawls broke out between Roman Catholic and Protestant cantons. Eventually Protestants were given the freedom to remain Protestant, but they were prohibited from imposing their faith on others.

Despite religious differences, the confederation remained neutral during the Thirty Years War, escaping the devastation wrought on the rest of Central Europe. The **Peace of Westphalia** in 1648 recognized the independence and neutrality of the 13 cantons. The next century was characterized by a long-standing alliance with France and chronic rumblings caused by internal divisions. French troops invaded Switzerland in 1798 and established the **Helvetic Republic.** The relationships between the individual cantons and the federal government were restructured, and citizens were granted freedom of religion and equality before the law. Napoleon later added six cantons and redesigned the confederation: church and state were separated, free trade was established among the cantons, and the peasantry was emancipated. After Napoleon's defeat, the Congress of Vienna recognized **Swiss neutrality** and created a new conservative constitution. It also added two cantons and returned Geneva from France to Switzerland, bringing the total to 26.

In the second half of the 19th century, Bern became the capital of the confederation. The central government established a unified postal, currency, and railway system, and ushered in a free-trade zone among all the cantons. During this time, Switzerland cultivated its reputation as leader in efforts to resolve international conflicts. The **Geneva Convention of 1864** established international laws for the conduct of war and the treatment of prisoners of war. At the same time, the **International Red Cross** set up its headquarters in Geneva. Because it was not embroiled in the tangle of alliances that characterized the turn-of-the-century European balance of power, Switzerland avoided involvement in **World War I.** In 1920, Geneva welcomed the headquarters of the **League of Nations,** establishing itself as a neutral host state for international diplomacy. Switzerland's **World War II** record, however, was a bit spotty. While some Jews and other refugees from Nazi Germany found refuge in Switzerland, the Swiss government in general impeded passage through its territory, not eager to incur the wrath of the monster that surrounded on all sides.

Switzerland's policy of **armed neutrality** persists to the present: there is no standing army, but every adult male faces compulsory military service. With the threat of an east-west conflict fading, a 1989 referendum proposing to **disband the army** garnered a surprisingly large number of votes. Although Switzerland is home of the **United Nations** and a participant in many U.N. international agencies, it is not a member of the organization. Apparently, though, Swiss citizens feel strongly about the EC issue; a recent vote which resulted in the rejection of the treaty on a **European Economic Area** (EEA) boasted a voter turnout of almost 80%. So while Austria, Sweden, Norway, and Finland await negotiations on EC membership applications, the "No" vote on the EEA indicates that Switzerland will sit another round out. The division between those who opt to resist change in order to retain *Sonderfall Schweig* (the Swiss Way) and those who envision growth and involvement with the EEC reveals a brutal split along linguistic lines; all six Francophone cantons lean towards approval of integration, while the German-speaking cantons of Central Switzerland and Italian-speaking Ticino fear being swallowed by their neighbors. Still in the memories of German- and Italian-speaking Swiss are the fascist dictatorships that developed just across the borders just a half-century ago. Nonetheless, with the easing of Cold-War tensions, many Swiss now believe that their country should progress with the rest of the EEC.

■ Exiles and Emigrés

Voltaire arrived in Geneva in 1755; since then, the stream of intellectuals, artists, and other soon-to-be-famous personalities to call Switzerland home has reached a steady continuum. The notion of Switzerland as a refuge of neutrality among more quarrelsome nations has held appeal for many since November 20th, 1815 when the Treaty of Paris recognized Switzerland as the eternally impartial next-door neighbor.

George Gordon, otherwise known as the opium-smoking Romantic **Lord Byron,** quit England in 1816 and fled to Switzerland where he met **Percy Shelley,** there "on tour." The two composed some of their greatest works while observing the Swiss landscape. Byron wrote his *Sonnet on Chillon* while brooding on Lake Geneva, while Shelley crafted his *Hymn to Beauty* and *Mont Blanc* in the vale of Chamonix. Byron's revelation that "High mountains are a feeling, but the hum of human cities torture" reveals an Emersonian encounter with Switzerland's natural beauty. During an especially wet summer in Switzerland, some ghost stories fell into **Mary Wollstonecraft Shelley's** hands; the atmosphere of Swiss mountains rearing through the rain, in addition to the supernatural themes of her nightly conversations, was enough to inspire her to infuse Gothic elements into her latest conception, *Frankenstein*.

From a closer neighbor, just across the border in Germany, flocked more great minds. **Johann Wolfgang von Goethe** caught his first distant view of Italy from the top of St. Gotthard Pass in the Swiss Alps, the clouded path that would serve as an allegory for the rest of his life. **Friedrich Schiller** came forth with the play *Wilhelm Tell*, later to be made into an opera for which Felix Mendelssohn would compose the William Tell Overture (a.k.a. the Lone Ranger theme song). **Friedrich Nietzsche,** while on holiday in the Engadine Valley, conjured up some crazy stuff about Superman and Eternal Return in his *Thus Spoke Zarathustra*. His very complex personal relationship with **Richard Wagner** also began here, while Nietzsche held a professor's chair at Basel University. Zürich served as a wellspring for intellectual revolution in respect to the sciences; **Albert Einstein** studied there and by 1901 he was a Swiss citizen. His move to Bern was a pivotal moment in his life, for it was in that city that he conceived the foundation for his Theory of Relativity.

Switzerland's broad tolerance and neutral status brought it hordes of talented refugees from the World Wars. **James Joyce** fled to Zurich where he wrote the greater part of his modernist work *Ulysses*, and World War II drove him to Zürich once again where he died in 1941. **Herman Hesse** moved to the town of Montagnola in southern Switzerland after being branded an enemy of his fatherland during World War I; in Montagnola he produced his revered works *Steppenwolf* and *Siddhartha*. Such a congregation of artistic personalities, combined with the breakdown of pre-war decadence, culminated to produce the **Dada** explosion in Zürich in 1916 led by **Hans Arp** and **Tristan Tzara.**

■■■ CULTURE

Switzerland's location at the convergence of three cultural spheres—German, French, and Italian—has allowed it to participate intimately in the arts of all its neighbors. This multiplicity of influence has often distracted the Swiss from a unified and independent art of their own; nevertheless, there has been a long line of determinedly, unmistakably Swiss cultural heroes.

■ Visual Arts

The history of the arts in Switzerland is less one of a Swiss tradition, than of a pageant of distinctive Swiss artists. The Renaissance years brought **Urs Graf** to the fore as a swashbuckling soldier-artist-poet excellently suited to court portraiture. **John Henry Füssli** was the most significant Swiss painter of the 19th century, echoing the advent of Romanticism with his emotionally powerful works, often filled with horrifying images of demons and goblins, doing much to further the popularity of Romanticism in Switzerland. **Ferdinand Hodler,** an early Symbolist painter, worked with powerful images of Swiss landscapes and characters to convey metaphysical messages.

Twentieth century artist **Paul Klee** was born near Bern, but spent his childhood and early career in Germany, producing highly unique, personal works as a member of *der blaue Reiter*, and was also a member of the Bauhaus faculty. He returned to Switzerland near the start of World War II. The **Zürich School of Concrete Art** between the wars united the Surrealists with the Constructivist ethos that filtered in from Russia and from architectural theory. **Max Bill's** Mondrian-derived canvases, focusing on color relationships and the texture and form of the surface itself, were the essence of Concrete painting. The school also included Paul Klee and **Meret Oppenheim,** famous for her *Fur Cup* and other objects; object art and environment as art were two of the interactions of human and space explored by the group. Sculptor **Alberto Giacometti's** celebrated works in the 1930s were guided by this philosophy of creating a completely new spatial reality within each work. Later, Giacometti rejected the premise of Surrealism in order to concentrate upon representation; his ideas of representation were invariably small, exaggeratedly slender figures, like his *Man Pointing.* **Jean Tinguely** worked in kinetic sculpture, creating mechanized Dada fantasies in celebration of motion as beauty.

■ Architecture

The prolific German architect **Gottfried Semper** was born in Switzerland; his works can be seen in most large German cities, particularly Dresden. **Robert Maillart** developed the slab technique for bridge design in 1900, and for the first years of the century produced elegant ferro-concrete bridges that were much more efficient and light in feeling than any that had preceded it. The ferro-concrete building technique was applied to domestic and commercial building by the world-acclaimed architect **Le Corbusier.** Some of the architect's earliest conceptions were formed by his impressions of the Swiss Jura where he grew up; his walks through the Alpine landscape were lessons in seeing. Using rugged materials and geometric shapes, Le Corbusier brought a new and animated spirit to contemporary architecture in Paris, Moscow, Stuttgart, Zürich, and Cambridge, Massachusetts.

■ Religion and Philosophy

Switzerland contributed largely to the **Protestant Reformation** and adopted its conclusions on a broad scale. Native son **Ulrich Zwingli** was a contemporary of Luther's, and his *Theses,* published at Zürich in 1523, were nearly as influential. These *Theses* expounded a less literal reinterpretation of the symbols and gestures of Catholicism. The two men later quarreled bitterly over fine points of Reform theo ogy. **John Calvin,** Geneva's contribution to Protestantism, took a more philosophical approach, attributing salvation to the knowledge of God's sovereignty through Scripture, and decrying all humanity as corrupt since Adam's fall. For a short time, Geneva was completely under Calvin's control as a theocratic city, and the man's influence spread widely, taking particular hold in England. **Jean Jacques Rousseau,** born in Geneva and best known for his *Social Contract* which provided inspiration for the French Revolution, always proudly recognized his Swiss background despite the fact that he spent most of his time outside the country.

J.J. Bodmer and **J.J. Breitinger** were among the pioneers of modern literary thought in Switzerland, advocating the supremacy of feeling and imaginative vision that was central to Romanticism. **Madame de Stael** (Germaine Necker) was the primary force behind the spread of Romanticism from Germany to France, transmitting the information through her correspondence with Friedrich Schlegel, a major writer of the early Romantic period, and with her family in France and French Switzerland.

Switzerland became a center of psychological study in the early years of the 20th century by virtue of **Carl Gustav Jung's** residence in Basel and Zürich. Jung began his psychological career as an acolyte of Freud, but split with him by 1915 over Jung's publication of *Symbols of Transformation,* a work in direct contradiction of Freud's system. Jung's systems remain interesting to students of spirituality and its role in social structures.

■ Literature

Gottfried Keller was a popular Swiss novelist and poet who was integral to the rising influence of Poetic Realism in late German Romanticism. But it is **Conrad Ferdinand Meyer** who is acknowledged by most authorities as the greatest Swiss poet. His works feature strongly individualistic heroes, and were some of the only German works to effectively unite Romanticism and Realism.

Twentieth century Switzerland has produced two widely respected modern playwrights. **Max Frisch** has been lauded for his Brechtian style and thoughtful treatment of Nazi Germany; his most widely known work is the play *Andorra*. **Friedrich Dürrenmatt** has written a number of excellent plays dealing with individual responsibility and morality, most notably *The Visit of the Old Lady* and *The Physicists*. **Robert Walser** has been celebrated for his diffuse, existential novels written before his death in 1956; they were largely ignored during the author's lifetime by an audience expecting clearly defined morals and themes.

Switzerland also has a life in the literature of other nations. Henry James's Daisy Miller toured here; Mark Twain incorporated cuckoo clocks into his revenge fantasies, and followed well-touristed paths with his own rough grace. It was only when struck by the majesty of the Swiss Alps that David Copperfield, one of Charles Dickens's greatest characters, was able to cry over the death of his wife Dora, "as I had not wept yet."

Switzerland

CENTRAL SWITZERLAND

The ellipse of lakes at the center of Northern Switzerland includes both Inner Switzerland, the area around Zurich which oversaw the birth of the Swiss Confederation centuries ago, and Lake Lucerne. The Inner Swiss are their own people, jealously laying claim to William Tell and other all-too popularized historic legends, and have traditionally distanced themselves from their near-neighbors in Lucerne. But the slouch in the mountains around these central cities draws them together. Like any two cities of the world, Lucerne and Zurich speak the same cosmopolitan language. While Switzerland as a whole is defined by its harsh landscape, this mostly German-speaking region is, topographically, pretty tame compared to its close neighbors.

■■■ ZÜRICH

Rich and aloof, Zürich is the quintessential banker's town. Battalions of briefcase-toting, loafer-clad executives charge daily to the fourth-largest stock market in the world, and the world's biggest gold exchange pumps enough money into the economy to keep the hoity-toity boutiques and expense-account restaurants quite well-fed. The city was the seat of the Reformation in German Switzerland, led by the 16th-century anti-Catholic firebrand Ulrich Zwingli. Since then, Protestant asceticism has gradually been overwhelmed by the indecent tide of money that floods the city. But there is more to Zürich than money. Its mien today retains something of the avant-garde spirit of 1916, a year in which artistic and philosophical radicalism shook the calm institutions of Zürich. Living at Universitätstr. 38, James Joyce toiled away on what was to become *Ulysses,* The Quintessential Modernist Novel. Not far away at Spiegelgasse 14, Russian exile V.I. Lenin bided his time, read Marx and Engels, and dreamed of revolution. At the same time, raucous young artists calling themselves Dadaists—some, legend has it, living next door to Lenin and irritating him immensely—were founding the seminal proto-performance-art collective known as the *Cabaret Voltaire.*

ORIENTATION AND PRACTICAL INFORMATION

Zürich sits on the northern tip of the *Zürichsee* (Lake Zürich), in the center of Northern Switzerland. The **Limmat River** flows into the Zürichsee and splits the city down the middle. Grand bridges, each offering a lovely view of the elegant and stately old buildings which line the river, connect the *Altstadt* to the other side of town, where visitors can find the shopping mecca of **Bahnhofstraße,** as well as a host of smaller churches, museums, and squares. Zürich's industrial district is centered in **Wipkingen** on the river, the university on a hill above. Water is ubiquitous in Zürich, be it the lake or one of the three rivers flowing into it.

Tourist Offices: Main office in the train station at Bahnhofplatz 15 (tel. 211 40 00). Exit the station to Bahnhofplatz, and walk to the left alongside the building. Crowded and capitalistic. You can sign up for expensive excursions here or pay for maps (1SFr) available for free at local banks (try the Union Bank of Switzerland at Bahnhofstr. 45). Wade through the line for a copy of *Zürich News* and answers to any specific questions you have. Finds rooms for a fee of 5SFr. Open Mon.-Fri. 8:30am-9:30pm, Sat.-Sun. 8:30am-8:30pm; Nov.-March Mon.-Fri. 8:30am-7:30pm, Sat.-Sun. 8:30am-6:30pm. Also at **airport terminal B** (tel. 816 40 81), same ser-

ZÜRICH

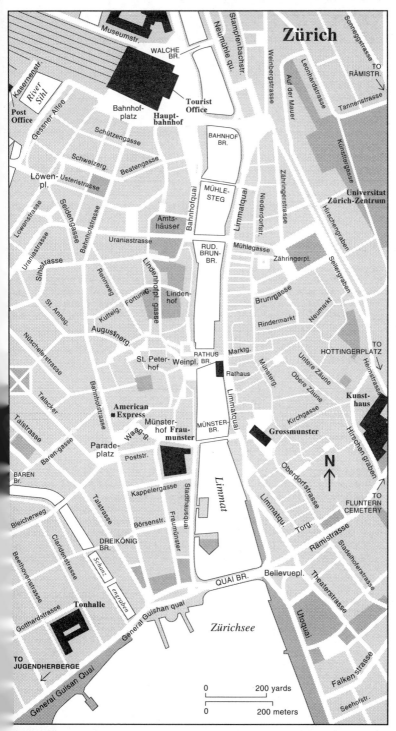

Zürich

vices as Zürich station office, as well as hotel reservations in all of Switzerland for 10SFr. Open daily 10am-7pm.

Budget Travel: SSR, Leonhardstr. 10 (tel. 242 30 00), across the river from the station and up the hill to the left. Offers reduced airfares, beach holiday packages, and guided trips throughout the world. Sick of Swiss prices? SSR will tell you the quickest, cheapest route to Thailand. For more detailed coverage of Thailand, see *Let's Go: Thailand 1994.* Open Mon.-Fri. 10am-6pm.

Consulates: U.S., Zollikerstr. 141 (tel. 422 25 66). Open Mon.-Fri. 9-11:30am and 1:30-4pm. **U.K.,** Dufourstr. 56 (tel. 261 15 20). Open Mon.-Fri. 9am-noon and 2-4pm; visas must be procured at embassy in Bern. **Canadians, Australians,** and citizens of **Ireland** should contact their embassies in Bern. **New Zealand's** consulate is in Geneva.

Currency Exchange: Train station rates are comparable to most banks. Open daily 6:15am-10:45pm. Also try **Swiss Credit,** Bahnhofstr. 89. Open Mon.-Wed. and Fri. 7am-6:30pm, Thurs. 7am-9pm, Sat. 9am-4pm. **Swiss Bank,** Bahnhofstr. 70, is also an option. Open Mon.-Fri. 9am-6:30pm, Sat. 9am-4pm. These banks have other branches all over town.

American Express: Bahnhofstr. 20, near Paradeplatz (tel. 211 83 70). Mail held. All banking services. Open Mon.-Fri. 8:30am-5:30pm, Sat. 9am-noon. Traveler's checks **emergency line** toll-free (tel. 046 050 100).

Post Office: Main office at Kasernenstr. 95/97. Open Mon.-Fri. 6:30am-10:30pm, Sat. 6:30am-8pm, Sun. 11am-10:30pm. 1SFr charge for *Poste Restante* after 6:30pm. Address **Poste Restante:** Sihlpost, Kasernenstr., Postlagernde Briefe, CH-8021 Zürich. Another branch is at the **Hauptbahnhof** next to the tourist office. Open Mon.-Fri. 6:30am-10:30pm, Sat. 7:30am-11am. A third office at **Fraumünster,** on Kappelergasse, has the same hours as the train station office.

Telephones: PTT phones at the train station and at Fraumünster post office. Open Mon.-Fri. 7am-10:30pm, Sat.-Sun. 9am-9pm. **City code:** 01.

Public Transportation: Swissly efficient streetcars crisscross the city, originating at the *Hauptbahnhof.* Long rides 2.80SFr (press the blue button on automatic ticket machines), short rides 1.70SFr (yellow button). Go with the 24-hr. *Tageskarte* if you plan to ride more than twice; it's a steal at 6.40SFr. Tickets must be purchased before boarding. Validate the ticket by inserting it into the little slot on the ticket machine. *Tageskarte* valid for ferry rides down the Limmat River. All public buses, trams, and trolleys run 5:30am-midnight.

Flights: Reach the airport with one of 100 daily trains from the *Hauptbahnhof* (10min., 4.50SFr, railpasses valid). Trains run every 10-20min. 5am-11pm.

Trains: For train information, call 211 50 10. To: Bern (42SFr), Geneva (73SFr), Lugano (58SFr), Basel (29SFr), Lucerne (18.60SFr).

Ferries: Boat trips on the **Zürichsee** range from 1½hr. jaunts between isolated villages (8.40SFr) to a "grand tour" (4hr., 25.20SFr, free with Eurailpass; boats leave from Bürgkliplatz). Ferries carry passengers on short (9.40SFr), medium (15.80Sfr), and long (25.20SFr) tours of the lake. Lunch ferries leave from the top of the Bahnhofstr. harbor daily at 1:15pm (7SFr not including lunch). Ferries down the **Limmat River** run April to mid-Sept. For more information, contact **Zürichsee-Schiffahrtsgesellschaft** (tel. 482 10 33, fax 482 84 00).

Bike Rental: At the baggage counter *(Gepäckexpedition Fly-Gepäck)* in the station. Rent from any train station, return to any train station (19SFr per day). Open daily 6am-7:40pm.

Hitchhiking: Though hitchhiking is not unheard of in Switzerland, *Let's Go* does not recommend it as a safe mode of transportation. Those who hitch to Basel, Geneva, Paris, or Bonn, take streetcar #4 from the station: Werdhölzli. Those bound for Lucerne, Italy, and Austria, take streetcar #5 or 14: Bahnhof Wiedikon, and walk 1 block down Schimmelstr. to Silhölzli. Hitchers headed to Munich take streetcar #14: Milchbuck, and walk to Schaffhauserstr., toward St. Gallen and St. Margarethen. Hitchhiking is illegal on the freeway.

Mitfahrzentrale: (tel. 261 68 93) matches drivers with riders.

Luggage Storage: Lockers all over the train station, 2-5SFr. 24hr. access.

Bookstore: Daeniker's Bookshop, In Gassen 11, between Paradeplatz and the river. English books, including *Let's Go.* Open Mon.-Fri. 8:15am-6:30pm, Sat. 9am-

4pm. Also **Stäheli Buchhandlung,** Rennweg and Bahnhofstr. Open Mon.-Fri. 9am-6:30pm, Sat. 9am-4pm.
Libraries: Payot and Naville, Bahnhofstr.9, sells a wide selection of French and English books. Open Mon.-Fri. 9am-6:30pm, Sat. 9am-noon.
Laundromat: Speed-Wash, at Müllerstr. 55, Mattengasse 29, and Friesstr. 4. Open Mon.-Sat. 7am-10pm, Sun. 10:30am-10pm. **Laundry Mühlegasse,** Mühlegasse 11. 17SFr per 5kg. Open Mon.-Fri. 7:30am-noon and 1-6:30pm.
Emergencies: Police: tel. 117. **Ambulance:** tel. 144. **Medical Emergency:** tcl. 47 47 00.
Rape Crisis Line: tel. 291 46 46.

ACCOMMODATIONS AND CAMPING

Expensive as Zürich can be, there are some budget options, mainly hostels. These accommodations are usually somewhat distant from the town center, but easily accessible with Zürich's extensive public transportation system.

Jugendherberge Zürich (HI), Mutschellenstr. 114 (tel. 482 35 44). Streetcar #7 (from the *Hauptbahnhof*, direction "Wollishofen"): Morgental. From there, head right and follow signs (5min.). Impeccably clean, this busy hostel caters to a motley crew of travelers. If you're feeling out of touch, you can tune in CNN. During high season, arrive early. Reception open 2pm-1am. Checkout 6-9am. Members 26SFr, nonmembers 33SFr. Showers, sheets, and a huge breakfast included. Decent dinner 9SFr. Lockers available. Laundry 8SFr. Reserve a few days in advance.

Martahaus, Zähringerstr. 36 (tel. 251 45 50, fax 251 45 40). Left out of the station, cross the Balinkof Brücke, and take the second right after Limmat Quai (it will be a sharp right at the Seilgraben sign). Simple but comfortable, with a pleasant dining room and lounge. Prime location, but busy to the point of madness. Reception open 24hrs. Dorms 30SFr. Singles 60SFr. Doubles 90SFr. Triples 105SFr. Showers and breakfast included.

Foyer Hottingen, Hottingerstr. 31 (tel. 261 93 15). Take streetcar #3 (direction "Albisrieden"): Hoffingerplatz. Sparkling white, filled with plants and the occasional screaming child. Guardian nuns admit *women, married couples, and families only*. Curfew midnight. Dorms 20SFr. Singles 50SFr. Doubles 80SFr. Showers 1SFr; bath 2SFr per hr. Breakfast included.

Glockenhof, Sihlstr. 33 (tel. 221 36 73), next to the more expensive Hotel Glockenhof (10min. from the station). Clean but spartan. *Men only*. Reception open Mon.-Fri. 8:15am-7:45pm, Sat. 9:45am-3:45pm, Sun. 8:30am-1pm. Curfew 11pm. Singles 40SFr. Shower included. Open summer only as a rule.

Hotel Regina, Hohlstr. 18 (tel. 242 65 50). Take streetcar #3 (direction "Albisrieden") or 14 (direction "Triemli"): Kaserne, walk straight to Zeughausstr., turn right, follow to Hohlstr. Reception open 24hrs. Hotel divided into an old section and a renovated section. In old section, singles from 50SFr, doubles from 70SFr; showers and toilets on each floor. In renovated section, singles 85SFr, doubles 110SFr. All include shower and toilet. Rooms for 3-4 available at 40SFr per person. No breakfast, but a popular café a few steps down Hohlstr. attracts guests from the hotel. Reservations recommended. AmEx, Visa, MC.

Hotel du Théâtre, Seilergraben 69 (tel. 252 60 62, fax 252 01 54). Follow directions to Martahaus, but don't turn left on Zühringerstr. The hotel stands between Zühringerstr. and Seilograben. A bargain, in the heart of the *Altstadt*. Reception open 24hrs. Singles 70-80SFr, with shower 110-145SFr. Doubles with shower 170SFr. Triples 210SFr. Breakfast included.

Camping Seebucht: Seestr. 559 (tel. 482 16 12), somewhat far away, but in a scenic lakeside location. Train 7: Wollishofen, and walk the remaining 15min. along the shore to the right; or bus #161 or 165 (from Bürgkliplatz, at the lake-end of Bahnhofstr.): Grenzsteig. 5SFr per person, 8SFr per tent. Open early May to late Sept.

FOOD

The cheapest meals in Zürich can be found at *Wurstli* stands, which sell sausage and bread for 3-4SFr, or at fruit and vegetable stands. Supermarkets are also a good idea. For hearty appetites, Zürich prides itself on *Geschnetzeltes mit Rösti,* slivered veal in cream sauce with country-fried potatoes, which is found almost everywhere. Pick up the free brochure *Preiswert Essen in Zürich* (Budget Food in Zürich) from the tourist office for other options.

Epicureans will have a field day perusing Zürich's beverage and chocolate industries. The **Hürlimann Brewery,** Brandschenkestr. 150, offers tours by appointment and darn good samples (free). Call Herr Gyger (tel. 228 26 26) a couple of weeks in advance. Down the road at Brandschenkestr. 60, **Landolt & Co.** has a wine warehouse with good prices, a super staff, and free wine-tasting for the buyers (open Tues.-Fri. 9am-12:30pm and 1:30-6pm, Sat. 9am-1pm). For an experience in utter decadence, tour the **Lindt & Sprüngli** chocolate factory; call (tel. 716 22 33) a week or two in advance. (English tours Thurs. 1:15pm; German tours Thurs. 2pm.) Wash it all down with a cup of coffee from the **Johann Jacobs Museum,** Seefeldquai 17 (corner of Feldeggstr.), which will tell you everything you always wanted to know about the beverage (open Fri.-Sat. 2-5pm, Sun. 10am-5pm; free). Every Saturday morning from 7-11am, visit the **farmer's market** at the square near the Central streetcar stop for fresh fruits and vegetables.

Mensa der Universität Zürich, Rämistr. 71. Streetcar #6 (from Bahnhofplatz; to return from Tannenstr.): ETH Zentrum, or walk. Stunningly edible—even students who feed here every day approve. Take a look at the bulletin boards in the university buildings for informations on rides, apartments, and rooms for rent, as well as cultural events. Hot dishes 5.50-6.50SFr with ISIC, salads 6.90SFr. Open Mon.-Sat. 11am-1:30pm and 5-7:30pm. **Mensa Polyterrasse** is just down the street at #101 with the same food and prices. Open Mon.-Thurs. 11:15am-1:30pm and 5:30-7pm, Fri. 11:15am-1:30pm and 5:30-7:15pm, Sat. 11:30am-1pm; mid-July to mid-Sept. lunch only.

Vier Linden, Gemeindestr. 48, near the Foyer Hottingen Hotel, just above Hottingerplatz. Imaginative vegetarian food; crunch all the greens you've been missing. Not so easy on the budget: meal-sized salads 8-13.50SFr. *Menus* 17-19SFr. Open Mon.-Fri. 6am-9pm. **Vier Linden Reform Produkte** health food store and bakery across the street. Open Mon.-Fri. 7am-12:30pm and 2-6:30pm, Sat. 7am-

Cafeteria Freischütz, Freischützgasse 1, at Militärstr., on the other side of the Sihl ("the other river"), near the main post office. Just like Mom's—if Mom cooks Swiss. Jumbo dishes for 10-14SFr. Open daily 9am-7pm.

Restaurant 1001, Niederdorfstr. 4. Just a bar and some stools. Turkish specialties here are good and greasy, 5.50-15.50SFr. Open daily 11am-midnight.

Zeughauskeller, Bahnhofstr. 28a (tel. 211 26 90), near Paradeplatz, serves Swiss specialties (many sausage varieties) ranging from 11-28SFr. Outdoor dining offers prime people watching; however, sitting indoors will give you good Swiss vibes as well (dark, heavy wood roof-beams and coats of arms). Kitchen open 11:30am-9:30pm.

Migros market and restaurant, at the double orange "M;" Streetcar #7: Morgental. Market open Mon.-Fri. 8am-6:30pm, Sat. 8am-4pm. **Café** next door has sandwiches (1-4SFr), hot *Tagesmenu* (5-9SFr). Open Mon.-Fri. 7am-6:30pm, Sat. 7am-4pm.

SIGHTS

Stately and colorful **Bahnhofstraße** runs from the station to the Zürichsee. Though budget travelers probably can't afford to buy anything from the shops that line the promenade, window shopping is a perverse delight. **Bürgkliplatz,** at the Zürichsee end, hosts a colorful Saturday market (May-Oct. 7:30am-3:30pm); vendors sell everything from old records to giant cowbells.

Two towering cathedrals stare each other down from opposite sides of the river in the *Altstadt.* To the east loom the rather brutal twin towers of the **Grossmünster**

ZÜRICH

a Romanesque cathedral with riotous modern stained-glass windows by **Alberto Giacometti.** Zwingli spearheaded the Reformation in Switzerland with fiery tirades from the pulpit here. Across the river on the west bank rises the steeple of the dreamier 13th-century **Fraumünster,** which boasts an even more stunning set of stained-glass windows by Chagall. (Grossmünster open Mon.-Fri. 9am-6pm, Sat. 9am-5pm, Sun. after services until 6pm; Oct.-March Mon.-Sat. 10am-4pm, Sun. after services until 6pm. Fraumünster open Mon.-Sat. 9am-noon and 2-6pm; March-April and Oct. daily 10am-noon and 2-5pm; Nov.-Feb. daily 10am-noon and 2-4pm.) Walk around the Fraumünster to Fraumünster-Str. to admire the ethereal wall paintings in the Gothic archways of the courtyard.

The **Schweizerische Landesmuseum** (Swiss National Museum), behind the train station, runs a broad gamut from exhibits on Swiss life through the centuries to an impressive archaeological collection to reconstructions of rooms from grandiose Swiss buildings of all periods. (Open Tues.-Sun. 10am-5pm. Free.) Zürich's **Kunsthaus,** on Rämistr. at Heimplatz, is a national treasure; your eyes and brain will be bowled over by its glorious holdings. Impressionists are well-represented, as are 20th-century painters like Klee, Kandinsky, and Chagall. Constantly changing special exhibitions bring art from museums all around the world to Zürich (open Tues.-Thurs. 10am-9pm, Fri.-Sun. 10am-5pm; admission 4SFr, students 3SFr). The **Tin Figures Museum,** near the Grossmünster at Obere Zäune 19, displays a vast collection of tin and lead toy figures (open Tues.-Fri. 2-4pm, Sat. 2-5pm, Sun. 10am-noon and 1-4pm; admission 4SFr, children 2SFr). The **Beyer Musuem of Time Measurement**, Bahnhofstr. 31, invites watch lovers in to admire antique watches and time-pieces from 1400 BC to the 20th century (open Mon.-Fri. 10am-noon and 2-4pm; free). The **University of Zürich** opens its specialized museums to tourists, and boasts all sorts of architectural wonders. Take streetcar #3 from the train station: EHF-Center. **Kulturama Schulanlage Letzi School,** Espenhofweg 60 (tel. 493 25 25), a rare Swiss museum, is neither quaint nor charming but indeed a bit weird and slightly psychotic; a collection of preserved body parts, skeletons, and pieces of the anatomy of animals from the mouse to the mammoth. Includes casts from prehistoric skulls (open Mon.-Fri. 10am-5pm).

To feed your head, make the pilgrimage to the **Thomas-Mann-Archiv,** Schönberggasse 15, where the study and library of the author are preserved (open Wed. and Sat. 2-4pm; free). **James Joyce** is buried in the **Fluntern cemetery,** and **Johanna Spyri** (author of *Heidi*) lies in the Sihlfeld cemetery. Experience the elusive Swiss beach culture at the grassy and frequently topless **Strandbad Mythenquai** (open Mon.-Fri. 9am-10pm, Sat.-Sun. 9am-7:30pm; 3SFr).

ENTERTAINMENT AND NIGHTLIFE

Zürich's **nightlife** revolves around Niederdorfstr., Münstergasse, and Limmatquai. These streets are lined with cafés and bars and are all teeming with activity after hours. Many establishments charge double drink prices or a 2SFr tax after midnight, so plan your night accordingly. Avoid the clubs entirely and enjoy the numerous street performers and boisterous revelers, or duck into one of countless cabarets and bars. Many movie theaters offer English **films** (marked "E/d,f,") with German and French subtitles; check at Bellevueplatz and Hirschenplatz.

Casa Bar, Münstergasse 30, a teeny, crowded pub with first-rate live jazz. No cover, but drink prices could bankrupt you. Open daily 7pm-2am.

Bar Pigalle, just uphill from Hirschenplatz, attracts a young, environmentally concerned crowd with food and drink. Open Mon.-Sat. until 2am.

Bar Odeon, Limmatquai 2, near the Quaibrücke. Thornton Wilder and Lenin used to get sloshed in this atmospheric joint. Now an artsy, mostly gay coterie hangs out here. Great street-side seating, but make sure to go in and look at the interior if even you choose the outdoors.

Mr. Pickwick's Pub, Niederdorfstr. 52, usually teems with tourists, especially those of the English-speaking variety.

Oepfelchammer, near Rindermarkt 12, a favorite among the locals, with authentic old Swiss atmosphere inside. If you can climb to a high balcony inside, you can immortalize yourself by carving your name into one of the ancient tables.

■ Near Zürich: Zug

The capital of Switzerland's wealthiest canton, Zug has enough tax havens to make Liechtenstein look socialist in comparison. The captivating view of the Alps from the lake stands in marked contrast to the eastern half of the city, dominated by the grime and steel. The labyrinthine streets of the Altstadt form the social and cultural center of Zug. The 16th-century **Capuchin Monastery St. Anna** on Aegerstr., with dark wood altars trimmed in gold, and the Gothic **St. Oswaldskirche,** housing a stunning gold altar and magnificent stained glass, are the two main churches in Zug. Scale the 13th-century **Zytturm** (clock tower) for an excellent view of the old city at **Burg Zug,** Kirchenstr. 11, Zug's original fortification (key available from the police station next door, accessible weekdays 10am-4pm).

Zug's official **tourist office** is at Bahnhofstr. 23 (tel. (042) 21 00 78); maps and free hotel reservations available (open Mon.-Fri. 8:30am-noon and 1-6pm, Sat. 8:30am-noon). The train station offers **currency exchange;** the **post office** is downtown at Poststr. 2 (open Mon.-Fri. 7:30am-noon and 1:30-6pm, Sat. 8-11am). Zug is easily accessible by train from Zürich's Hauptbahnhof.

To reach the new **Jugendherberge Zug (HI),** Allmendstr. (tel. (042) 21 53 54), take bus #11: Stadion. Or, to walk, take Gotthardstr., walk through the underpass, and continue left on the main street which becomes General-Guisen-Str.; a staircase on the left and sign point to the hostel. With a garden, barbecue pit(!), and kitchen. (Reception open 7-8:30am and 5-10pm. Lockout 10am-5pm. Curfew 11:30pm. Members 25SFr, nonmembers 32SFr. Kitchen 2SFr. Laundry 6SFr. Dinner 9SFr. Breakfast, showers, sheets included. Fully wheelchair accessible.) The nearest **campground, Innere Lorzenallmen** (tel. (041) 31 50 34), is a 10-minute walk from Landsgemeindeplatz along the Chalmer footpath. (5SFr per person, 5SFr per tent. Campground open April 8-Oct. 3.)

For affordable and fresh produce, stop by the **farmer's market** on the Landsgemeindeplatz (Sat. 7am-noon). During the month of July cherry vendors can be found there (Mon.-Fri. 3-7pm). Zug claims to be the cherry capital of the world (note the cherry markets), and *Kirschwasser* and cherry confections can be found at every corner. Sample the *Kirschtorte* at **Meier,** Alpenstr. 14, around the corner from the train station (3.50SFr). (Open Tues.-Fri. 7am-noon and 1-6:30pm, Sat. 8am-5pm. Another branch store at Baarerstr. 47, open Mon.-Fri. 6am-6:30pm, Sat. 6am-2pm.)

■■■ WINTERTHUR

Overshadowed in all things commercial by its omnipotent neighbor Zürich, Winterthur fights anonymity with cultural hauteur; private and city-run museums rule the town. If you've only got time for one, choose the **Oskar Reinhart "Am Römerholz" Collection,** set in the late industrialist's private villa and lush garden at the edge of the forest (bus #3: Spital, backtrack to Haldenstr., turn left and hike it for 10min.). A passel of Renoirs, Manet's *Au café,* and Vincent van Gogh's *L'hôpital à Arles* headline the collection, which also includes some of proliferate Picasso's early drawings and a few works by El Greco, Goya, Monet, and Rembrandt (open Tues.-Sun. 10am-4pm; admission 3SFr, students 1SFr).

Winterthur's **Kunstmuseum,** Museumstr. 52, holds an extensive collection of 16th- to 18th-century Swiss and French works, as well as German works from the 19th and 20th centuries including a few token Impressionist pieces. Walk up the Marktgasse from the station, turn left on Oberer Graben which turns into Lind-St Museumstr. is the second intersection (open Tues.-Sun. 10am-noon and 2-5pm; admission 5SFr, students 3SFr). The *Kunstmuseum* building also holds the cit

library. Closer to the town proper, down Stadthausstr. to the right of the train station, the **Oskar Reinhart Foundation,** Stadthausstr. 6, balances broad international holdings with exhibitions of 18th- to 20th-century Swiss, Austrian, and German works (closed for renovations April 1993-Feb. 1995). The miniatures of the Dutch "little masters" and timepieces from every corner of the globe await perusal in the early town hall at the **Uhrenmuseum Kellenberger und Museum Jakob Briner,** Marktgasse 20 (open Tues.-Sat. 2-5pm, Sun. 10am-noon and 2-5pm; admission 1SFr, students 0.50SFr). Out-of-the-ordinary: **Technorama der Schweiz,** Technoramastr. 1, much farther down Marktgasse (turns into Obertor, then Römerstr.). They display a collection-o-rama of the hist-o-rama of techno-rama. Hands-on exhibits (open daily 10am-5pm; admission 8SFr, students 6SFr).

The **Stadtkirche St. Laurentius** (take Unt. Kirchgasse off Marktgasse) was first built in 1180, and then renovated in the late Gothic style between 1501 and 1515. The Baroque organ dating back to 1766 was acquired from the Salem Cloister in 1809. It includes stained glass windows by **Alberto Giacometti** (1923) and a vivid wall painting by Paul Zehnder (1924-1930; church open daily 10am-4pm). The **Stadthaus,** Stadthausstr. 4a, is a monumental sandstone structure built between 1866-1868 by Gottfried Semper, the man behind the legendary Dresden Opera House; today it holds a concert hall.

Winterthur's culturally up-to-date **tourist office** is at Bahnhofplatz 12 (tel. (052) 212 00 88), across the streets from the left end of the train station. (Hotel reservation 3SFr. Open Mon.-Fri. 8am-noon and 2-6pm, Sat. 8am-noon and 2-4pm.) **Currency exchange** (daily 6:10am-9:30pm), as well as **bicycle rental** (19SFr per day, open Mon.-Sat 6am-9pm). Stop by the **Vogel Bookstore,** Marktgasse 41, and admire both the selection of English books and the architecture; the place looks like a modern art museum. By sheer coincidence, there is a modern art gallery upstairs. (Open Mon. 1:30-6:30pm, Tues.-Fri. 8:30am-6:30pm.) The **rape crisis** line is tel. 213 61 61.

Spend the night in the 15th-century castle that is **Jugendherberge Hegi (HI),** Hegifeldstr. 125 (tel. (052) 242 38 40). To reach the castle, take the train or bus # 1 to Oberwinterthur; backtrack a few steps along Frauenfeldstr., turn left on Hegistr., and left again on Hegifeldstr. after going through the underpass, and then walk on (10min.) from there. Set in a large garden filled with peacocks, turkeys, and ducks, the hostel itself is extremely simple: just two large dorm rooms, no lockers. But what you give up in convenience you get back tenfold in ambience. (Reception open 5-10pm. Lockout Mon. and Fri. 10am-5pm, Tues.-Thurs. and Sat.-Sun. 10am-2pm. Curfew 10pm. Members only. 15SFr. No breakfast, but guests are welcome to use the kitchen.) The **castle** is itself also open for viewing (March-Oct. Tues., Thurs. and Sat. 2-5 pm, Sun. 10am-noon and 2-5pm; free).

Moving **markets** engulf the city center on Tuesdays and Fridays. The **Co-op City** across from the tourist office also has a café. **Jazz** pours out from the portals of the **Albani Bar,** Steinberggasse 16 (tel. 22 69 96) until 2am on Fridays and Saturdays.

■ ■ ■ LUCERNE (Luzern)

While tourism is peripheral to Zürich, Bern, and Geneva, for Lucerne it stands front and center. Moreover, the area has historically attracted some pretty classy tourists. In 1868, Queen Victoria scampered up Mount Pilatus. At about the same time just across the glistening Vierwaldstättersee, Mark Twain fell asleep repeatedly in his desperate attempt to see the sun rise on the Rigi Kulm. Wagner composed his masterful *Meistersinger* and *Siegfried* here, and even Goethe was swept away by the beauty of the mountain scenery. A steady stream of modern visitors continues to gaze at the city in appreciation: medieval turrets, 16th-century wall paintings, and myriad museums resting under the watchful gaze of the Lion of Lucerne.

PRACTICAL INFORMATION

Tourist Office: Frankenstr. 1 (tel. 51 71 71). Look for signs in the train station; the office is one block from the river on Zentralstr. Large selection of city maps as well as maps and excursions for central Swiss region. Hotel reservations from 11am on (4SFr fee). **Guided walking tours** of the city swing past the major monuments for 1SFr, Mon.-Sat. 10am and 4pm. Office open Mon.-Fri. 8:30am-6pm, Sat. 9am-1pm; Nov.-March Mon.-Fri. 8:30am-noon and 2-6pm, Sat. 9am-noon and 2-5pm.

Budget Travel: SSR, Mariahilfgasse 3 (tel. 51 13 02). Student travel and discount flights. Open Mon. 1:30-6pm, Tues.-Wed. and Fri. 10am-6pm, Thurs. 10am-9pm.

Currency Exchange: At the station. Open Mon.-Fri. 7am-8:45pm, Sat.-Sun. 7:30am-7:30pm; Nov.-April Mon.-Sat. 7:30am-7:30pm, Sun. 8am-6pm. The best rates in town, however, are at **Migros Bank,** Seidenhofstr. 6, off Bahnhofstr. Open Mon.-Fri. 8:30am-6:30pm, Sat. 9am-4pm.

American Express: Schweizerhofquai 4 (tel. 50 11 77). All services, ATM machines. Open Mon.-Fri. 8am-5pm, Sat. 8am-noon.

Post Office: Main branch is across the street from the station at Bahnhofstr., 6000 Luzern 1. Open Mon.-Fri. 7:30am-6:30pm, Sat. 9:30-11am.

Telephones: Available at post office and downstairs in the train station. Open Mon.-Fri. 7:30am-8pm, Sat. 8am-4pm. **City code:** 041.

Trains: tel. 21 33 11. To: Basel (29SFr), Bern (29SFr), Locarno (52SFr).

Buses: Single-ride tickets 1.50-3SFr. Visitors can get a 2-day pass at most hotels and hostels, 5SFr. Otherwise, a 1-day *Tageskarte* is also 5SFr.

Luggage: At the station. Lockers 2-5SFr.

Bike Rental: At the train station. 19SFr per day. Open daily 7am-7:45pm.

Bookstore: Buchhandlung Josef Stocker, Wernmarkt 8. Some English-language books. Open Mon. 1:30-6:30pm, Tues.-Wed. and Fri. 9am-6:30pm, Thurs. 9am-9pm, Sat. 8am-4pm. **Paperback Bookstore,** Schweizerhofquai 2. Large selection of English books. Open Mon.-Fri. 8:30am-noon and 1:30-6:30pm, Sat. 8:30am-4pm.

Emergency: Police: tel. 117.

ACCOMMODATIONS AND CAMPING

Unless you stay at the hostel, lodging prices are sky-high. A few *Pension*-style establishments do exist; the tourist office will find rooms (see above).

Jugendherberge Am Rotsee (HI), Sedelstr. 12 (tel. 36 88 00). Bus #18: Goplismoos. After 7:30pm you must take bus #1: Schlossberg, and walk 15min. down Friedentalstr. Reception open 4-10pm; bring a book or a newspaper for the queue. Lockout 9:30am-4pm. Curfew 11:30pm. Members 21SFr, nonmember 28SFr. Showers and breakfast included. Laundry 9SFr. Dinner 10SFr. Crowded in the summer months; reserve a few days in advance.

Touristen Hotel Luzern, St. Karliquai 12 (tel. 51 24 74, fax 52 84 14). From th station walk left on Bahnhofstr., continue left on Reuss-steg and cross the secon covered bridge, Spreuerbrücke. Turn left on St. Karliquai. Well-located, with great view across the river and a good breakfast and shower included. Double 44-50SFr, with shower 62SFr. Triples 129SFr. Quads 164SFr. 8-bed room 33SF per person. 10% discount with ISIC. Baggage storage and currency exchange ε usurious rates.

Pension Pro Filia, Zähringerstr. 24 (tel. 22 42 80). Walk up Pilatusstr. from the st. tion, or bus #2, 9, or 18: Pilatusplatz. Friendly management and all the comforts ε home. Reception open until 8pm. No curfew. Singles 60SFr. Doubles 95-105SF Triples 125SFr. Quads 145SFr. Showers and breakfast included.

Hotel Schlussel, Franziskanerplatz 12, near the Franciscan Church (tel. 23 10 61 Bus #2, 9, or 18: Pilatusplatz, turn right on Hirschengraben to Rütlig, then left the hotel. Newly renovated, this clean and comfortable hotel looks out onto th *Altstadt.* Restaurant and outdoor café downstairs. Reception open 8am-6pm. Do bles 86-100SFr, with shower 130-140SFr. Breakfast included.

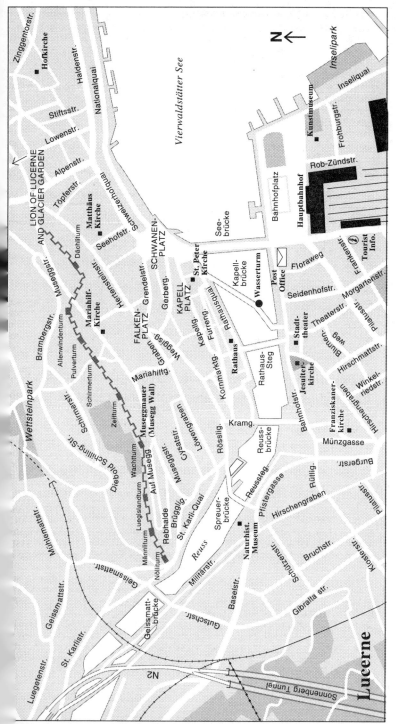

LUCERNE (LUZERN)

LUCERNE (LUZERN)

Camping: Camping Lido, Lido-Str. 8 (tel. 31 21 46), is a ½hr. hike from the station on the Lido beach. Cross the Seebrücke and turn right along the quay, or bus #2: Verkehrshaus. Mini-golf, tennis, and swimming nearby. Reception open 8am-6pm. 6SFr per person, 3SFr per tent. Dorms 12SFr. Open April-Oct.

FOOD

Saturday morning markets along the river purvey fresh fruit, vegetables, and meat for an inexpensive picnic. For sit-down meals, budget *menus* cost 12-15SFr just about everywhere. Tearooms and cafés are cheapest and quickest for lighter fare. **Migros Market,** Hertensteinstr. 44 (open Mon.-Wed. and Fri.-Sat 8am-6:30pm, Thurs. 8am-9pm) and **Nordmann's Market** (in basement of department store), Weggisgasse 11 (open Mon.-Fri. 8:30am-6:30pm and Sat. 8:30am-4pm), offer the best prices in town for groceries from A to Z.

Waldstätter Hof, Zentralstr. 4 (tel. 23 54 93), 5min. from the river, next to the tourist office. Ideal for a meal before hopping the rail. Veg served. *Menu* 15SFr. Open daily 6:30am-8:30pm.

Restaurant Karibia, Pilatusplatz (tel. 23 61 10). Serves the best vegetarian meals around. Spring roll (9.50SFr), samosas (8.50SFr), and spinach *Strußel* (11.50SFr). Large seafood buffet 5.50-12.50SFr. Takeout available. Open Tues.-Sat. 7am-midnight, Sun.-Mon. 10am-midnight.

Reussfähre, along the river on Sentimattstr. Serves sausage and beer (4-6SFr) among Native American headdresses and Confederate flags. Apparently, they know something about the Old West which has escaped us thus far. Open daily 11am-12:30am.

EPA, corner of Rössligasse and Mühleplatz, has a decent supermarket downstairs. Restaurant upstairs battles Migros prices with tempting 6-8SFr *menus.* Open Mon.-Wed., Fri. 8am-6:30pm, Thurs. 8am-9pm, Sat. 8am-4pm.

Reformhaus Müller, on the Kornmarkt near Hirschenplatz. Tofu, lentils, and whole-grain everything. Open Mon.-Fri. 7:45am-12:15pm and 1-6:30pm, Sat. 7:45am-12:15pm and 1-4pm.

Restaurant Walliser Spycher Le Mazot, Eisegasse 15, in the heart of the *Altstadt.* Swiss atmosphere and Swiss specialties. Entrees 10-23SFr. Large wine selection. Outdoor seating available. Open Mon.-Fri. 4pm-12:30am, Sat. 11:15am-12:30am.

SIGHTS AND ENTERTAINMENT

The cobblestone streets of Lucerne's *Altstadt* spread out across both sides of the sparkling Reuss River. The 660 year-old **Kapellbrücke,** a wooden-roofed bridge running from the station to the *Altstadt* decorated with graphic scenes from Swiss history, has been the leading light on the Lucerne landscape since the Middle Ages. On August 17th, 1993, a barge hit the bridge and set off a spectacular fire which burnt into the night. It is unclear whether repair work will be completed by 1994, but damaged or no, the medieval structure retains its power. The bridge is the best vantage point for the **Water Tower,** an ancient torture chamber that has become the rather perverse symbol of the city. Down the river, grapple with your mortality as you cross the covered **Spreuerbrücke,** adorned with Kaspar Meglinger's eerie *Totentanz* (Dance of Death) paintings. The *Altstadt* is famous for its decorated squares; check out the colorful scenes of the **Hirschenplatz.** Lucerne's famous **towers** are located off Museggstr. north of the river; climb the ancient **city rampart** from tower to tower to view Lucerne from dizzying heights (open daily 8am-7pm). The **Franzimer Kirche St. Maria,** on the Franziskanerplatz, holds magnificent red and grey marble altars, the central one flanked by slender, colorful stained glass windows. The walls are decorated with paintings of the old flags of the region. The **Hofkirche St. Leodegar und Mauritius,** at the end of the Schweizerhofquai, was erected in the 8th century as a Romanesque basilica, and then refurbished in the 14th in the Gothic style. The church was re-erected between 1634 and 1639 after fire destroyed it, but the two towers, dating back to 1504-1525, survived. The church houses stunning gold Baroque altars and intricate iron-work in front of the central, black marble altar.

The city mascot, the great **Lion of Lucerne,** is carved out of the base of a cliff on Denkmalstr. The 9m monument honors the Swiss Guard who died defending Marie Antoinette in Revolutionary Paris. Right next door is the **Glacier Garden,** preserving the giant potholes made by glaciers 20 million years ago. The 6.50SFr ticket (students 4.50SFr) also includes admission to the **Glacier Garden Museum** and the narcissistic **Spiegellabyrinth** (Labyrinth of Mirrors. Open May-Oct. 8am-6pm daily; March-April and Oct. to mid-Nov. 9am-5pm daily; late Nov.-Feb. Tues.-Sun. 10:30am-4:30pm.) Get a combined ticket (students 6SFr) to include admission to the **Bourbaki-Panorama** on the other side of the Lion Memorial, a spectacular panoramic painting of a Franco-Prussian battle. You can see the first active service of the Swiss Red Cross depicted here. (Open May-Sept. 9am-6pm; March-April and Oct. 9am-5pm. Entry to panorama alone 3SFr, students 1.50SFr.)

Hordes of photogenic but foul-tempered swans roam the waters of the Vierwaldstättersee lake. A fabulous and free beach sits at the **Seepark** between the *Bahnhof* and the Wagner museum.

MUSEUMS

Verkehrshaus der Schweiz (Transport Museum), Lidostr. 5, features a planetarium, a history of transportation over land, sea, and air, and the **Swissorama,** a mind-boggling 360-degree panorama. It's a long strange trip, folks. Open daily 9am-6pm. Admission 15SFr, students 11SFr.

Kunstmuseum, Robert-Zünd-Str. 1, next to the train station, houses a collection of paintings from the 16th century to the present, particularly Swiss landscape paintings of the 19th century and Lucerne's master painters. Also visiting exhibits of modern Swiss and international artists. Open Tues. and Thurs.-Sat. 10am-noon and 2-5pm, Wed. 10am-9pm, Sun. 10am-5pm. Admission 7SFr, students 5SFr.

Picasso Museum, Am Rhyn Haus, Furrengasse 21, shelters a collection of Picasso's last works, most of them lithographs. Open daily 10am-6pm; Nov.-March Fri.-Sun. 11am-noon and 2-5pm. Admission 5SFr, students 3SFr.

Richard Wagner Museum, Wagnerweg 27. Bus #6 or 8: Wartegg, or walk along the lake from the train station. Provides Wagner lovers with displays of original scores, letters, and instruments of the late composer. Wagner wrote *Siegfried* and *Die Meistersänger* here. Open Tues.-Sun. 10am-noon and 2-5pm; Oct-April Tues., Thurs. and Sat.-Sun. 10am-noon and 2-5pm. Admission 4SFr, students 2SFr.

NIGHTLIFE

Lucerne's nightlife centers around the crowded corridors of the *Altstadt.* The **Red Rose** nightclub and cabaret and **Babylonia** buzz from 9pm to 2am every night, or stop by **Cacadou,** Hirschenplatz 2, a nightclub-bar in Hirschen (open daily 9:30pm-2:30am). Fish and chips for 7SFr renders the riverfront **Mr. Pickwick's** a popular pub (open Mon.-Sat. 11am-12:30am, Sun. 4pm-12:30am). **Tony's Bar zur Gerben,** Sternplatz 7, is where the Lucerne locals meet each night from 7pm until 2am. Dance, eat, and thrill to Swiss folklore on the **Night Boat** (departures May-Sept. at 10:45pm; 34-80SFr, with Eurail 28-74SFr), or enjoy late-night coffee and ice cream at any of the perpetually open tearooms.

■ Near Lucerne: Engelburg and the Vierwaldstättersee

Lucerne's position in the heart of Switzerland makes it a daytrip departure point *par excellence.* Boat trips from the train station cruise the Vierwaldstättersee; get a list of good destinations from the tourist office (13-34SFr, Eurail and Swisspass free). Cable cars to **Mount Titlis** at 3020m bring you to the highest outlook in Central Switzerland in just 45 minutes, through green valleys into the high Alpine glaciers. The rotating gondola gives magnificent views of the crevasses below. Ice grotto and glacier walks at the summit, as well as a restaurant and observation deck. (69SFr, with Swisspass 49SFr, with Eurailpass 52.80SFr.) Or visit the glorious glacier **Trübsee** (29SFr, with Swisspass 22SFr, with Eurailpass 24.60SFr); both excursions start from **Engelberg,** accessible by train from Lucerne (15SFr) or by taking a boat from Lucerne to **Stansstad** and a train from there (39.40SFr total). Engelberg opens up the alpine world to its guests, both winter and summer, with excellent hiking as well as skiing. Daily ski passes here cost 45SFr, and they get cheaper if you buy them later. A 4-in-7-day pass costs 148SFr. Engelberg is also a good launchpad for hikes around nearby **Brunni;** most take two to five hours.

Engelberg's **tourist office,** Dorfstr. 34 (tel. (041) 94 11 61, fax 94 41 56; exit the train station, turn left on Bahnhofstr. and right onto Dorfstr.), leads **guided hikes** on Tuesday (10am-4pm) and Thursday (8:30am-4pm) for 10SFr, and **river rafting** on Wednesday (10am and 1pm, 45SFr). (Office open Mon.-Fri. 8am-noon and 2-5:45pm, Sat. 9am-noon, high season also Sat. 3-7pm.) The highest **bungee jump** in Europe falls 120m from a cable car here; rates are best if you sign up at **Balmer's Herberge** in Interlaken (see Berner Oberland section). (Bungee reservations: tel. (036) 23 43 63. 169SFr, 119SFr for "wimpy" 70m jump. Balmer's is cheaper, same jumps.) To reach the Swiss-chalet style **Jugendherberge Berghaus (HI),** Dorfstr. 80 (tel. (041) 94 12 92), turn left from the station on Bahnhofstr., then left on Dorfstr. (Reception open 9-11am and 5-10pm. Curfew 10:30pm. Members 20SFr, with *halb-pension* 28SFr. Otherwise dinner 10SFr.)

■ Mount Pilatus and the Rigi Kulm

We could not speak. We could hardly breathe. We could only gaze in drunken ecstasy and drink it in.

—Mark Twain

Mount Pilatus is the landmark of Lucerne. Rising 2154m into the skies, the view from the peak stretches into Italy on clear days. Legend has it the devil threw Saint Pilatus up here during the Ascension, but *Let's Go* does not recommend the Evil One as a safe mode of transportation. The cable cars are much more reliable. Join a daily escorted excursion, meeting at 12:30pm at the Luzernerhof on the Nationalquai (tel. (041) 51 20 55) and catch a boat to Alpenachstad and ascend by the **steepest cogwheel train in the world** (75SFr); return by cable car to Kriens and bus to Lucerne by 4:30pm. (Details at tourist office in Lucerne.) For those unable to tear themselves from the magnificence of the mountaintop, **Hotel Bellevue** (tel. (041) 96 12 55) cling to Pilatus's crags with three-star ratings at one-star prices (singles 55SFr, with bath 110SFr). Though banned until the 17th century for fear of angry ghosts, it is now legal to climb Pilatus by foot. The hiking trails take about 4½ hours from Pilatus down to Kriens, and a bit longer to get up.

Sunrise on the summit of the **Rigi Kulm** is one of Lucerne's many musts. Sunsets get pretty good reviews too. See Mark Twain's 1879 travelogue, *A Tramp Abroad,* for the best account of this Alpine ritual in all of its absurd sublimity. From Lucerne take a ferry to Vitznau, then a train to the mountain top. Return the same way, or hike downhill an hour to reach **Rigi Kaltbad,** where a cable car floats down to Weggis, where you can catch the boat back to Lucerne (76SFr, discount with passes).

SWISS JURA AND FRIBOURG

The long, narrow sprawl of Lake Neuchâtel divides French Switzerland from the rest of the country; however, the entire Jura, from Basel all the way south to Fribourg, cannot be divided easily along linguistic lines. In canton Fribourg alone, two thirds of the people speak French, while the other one-third are native German speakers; most all locals can switch back and forth between the two. From the